MARKETING MANAGEMENT

MARKETING

Philip Kotler
Northwestern University

MANAGEMENT

analysis,
planning,
and
control

PRENTICE-HALL, INC., Englewood Cliffs, New Jersey

Marketing Management: Analysis, Planning, and Control
Philip Kotler

Quotations from *Applied Imagination,* 3rd rev. ed., by
Alex F. Osborn, are reprinted with the permission of
Charles Scribner's Sons. Copyright 1953, © 1957,
© 1963 by Charles Scribner's Sons.

Library of Congress Catalog Card Number: 67-10170

Printed in the United States of America
C-55735

Current printing (last number):

10   9   8   7   6   5   4   3   2

Prentice-Hall International, Inc., London
Prentice-Hall of Australia, Pty. Ltd., Sydney
Prentice-Hall of Canada, Ltd., Toronto
Prentice-Hall of India (Private) Ltd., New Delhi
Prentice-Hall of Japan, Inc., Tokyo

To Nancy

Preface

Surely among the most difficult business decisions are those that have to do with marketing. The variables in a marketing problem do not generally exhibit the neat quantitative properties of many of the problems in production, accounting, or finance. Attitudinal variables play a larger role in marketing; marketing expenditures affect demand and costs simultaneously; marketing plans intimately affect planning in the other business areas. Marketing decisions must be made in the context of insufficient information about processes that are dynamic, nonlinear, lagged, stochastic, interactive, and downright difficult.

These characteristics could serve as an argument for intuitive marketing decision making. Yet to this author and to many colleagues and marketing executives they suggest quite the opposite: they suggest the need for *more* theory and analysis in marketing, not less.

In fact, the past decade has witnessed a rapid growth of quantitative and behavioral tools, concepts, and models that hold great promise in improving marketing decision making. Some of these developments have been published in journals; others have been confined to corporate executive suites. Although they are becoming the prototype for new thinking in marketing, they have not generally made their way into the typical textbook.

This book attempts to synthesize the new marketing thought into a framework that will be helpful to today's and tomorrow's marketing executives. The reader will find three distinct emphases as he studies this text.

A Decision Orientation

This book recognizes that the major function of the business executive is decision making. It focuses, therefore, on the major types of decisions facing the marketing executive in his attempt to harmonize the objectives and resources of the firm with the opportunities found in the market place.

An Analytical Approach

This book does not provide answers so much as ways of thinking about and analyzing recurrent marketing problems. Descriptive material is held to a minimum in order to permit the greatest freedom for developing the analytical content of marketing.

A Reliance on Basic Disciplines

This book relies heavily upon the basic disciplines of *economics, behavioral science,* and *mathematics.* Economics provides the fundamental tools and concepts for seeking optimal results in the use of scarce resources. Behavioral science provides fundamental concepts and findings for the interpretation of buyer and executive behavior. Mathematics provides the means of developing explicit statements about the relationships among variables in a problem.

*　　*　　*　　*　　*

The twenty-three chapters in this book are organized into four parts, corresponding to the administrative processes of analysis, organization, planning, and control. Part 1 deals with the analysis of marketing opportunities and begins with an examination of the powerful marketing concept —its meaning, elements, and relevance to the contemporary business scene. The marketing concept emphasizes that company planning must take its start from a consideration of opportunities in the market place. Chapter 2 discusses the major markets and forces that define a company's opportunities, while Chapter 3 shows these markets to be made up of distinguishable segments that present different opportunities to the firm. The ultimate unit in the market place—the buyer—is the subject of Chapter 4, which attempts to conceptualize the behavioral processes by which each buyer translates his needs into buying decisions. Chapter 5 examines how markets and market segments can be measured quantitatively so that their attractiveness can be appraised and an appropriate allocation of marketing effort can be determined.

Part 2 considers the activities that marketing managers perform in the pursuit of marketing opportunity. How business defines its goals and sets up an organization for their accomplishment is the subject of Chapter 6. Chapter 7 examines marketing planning as the firm's means of adapting its long-run resources to its opportunities. The ultimate unit of marketing planning—the decision—is discussed in Chapter 8, which explores how modern decision theory can be used to improve marketing performance. Chapters 9 and 10 spell out the important roles of marketing information and marketing model-building in the development of marketing strategy. And Chapter 11 emphasizes for contrast the importance of the non-analytical process known as creativity in heightening the marketing executive's sensitivity to new opportunities and novel strategies.

Part 3 turns to the major marketing decisions facing the firm. Chapter 12 sets the stage by developing the normative principles for making decisions on the level, mix, allocation, and strategy of marketing effort. The next seven chapters consider specific marketing decision areas: product policy (Chapters 13 and 14), price (Chapter 15), channels (Chapter 16), physical distribution (Chapter 17), advertising (Chapter 18), and sales force (Chapter 19). Chapter 20 discusses how various marketing decisions must be tempered by legal and political factors that have evolved for the protection of business and consumers.

Part 4 deals with the firm's need for continual control measures to insure the achievement of its objectives. Chapter 21 develops the theory of marketing control and the importance of continuous marketing intelligence for adapting to change. Chapter 22 describes sales and cost analysis as two specific management tools for appraising the effectiveness of current marketing effort. And Chapter 23 considers the marketing audit as a more sweeping tool for the periodic assessment of the company's marketing effectiveness in the light of its marketing objectives, resources, and opportunities.

PHILIP KOTLER
Northwestern University

Acknowledgments

This book bears the imprint of many persons who in a formal review or in informal conversation made a significant contribution to its development. My first debt is owed to my present and former colleagues in the marketing department of Northwestern University for their zest in blending marketing theory with administrative practice: Ira D. Anderson, Harper W. Boyd, Jr., Steuart H. Britt, Richard M. Clewett, Vernon Fryburger, James R. Hawkinson, Sidney J. Levy, Robert M. Olsen, Stanley F. Stasch, Lynn H. Stockman, Eugene Webb and Ralph Westfall. In addition, my work has benefited from the constant encouragement of former Dean Richard Donham and present Dean John A. Barr.

My second debt is owed to Professor Ronald E. Frank of the University of Pennsylvania, who acted as academic consultant throughout the development of the manuscript. He was a constant source of excellent ideas on manuscript organization and content, and the final form of this book owes much to his perceptive reviewing.

My third debt is owed to three academic colleagues who reviewed the manuscript at later stages of its development: to Professor Joseph W. Newman of the University of Michigan, who made valuable suggestions regarding several chapters in Part 3; to Professor Ralph Westfall of Northwestern University, whose critical appraisal of the over-all manuscript sent me back to work in pursuit of more precision; and to Professor Fred W. Kniffin of Pennsylvania State University, whose constructive suggestions in a final review led to several improvements.

I am also appreciative of the expert typing and secretarial services of Mrs. Marion B. Bernhardt, Miss Mary Ann Norton, and Miss Lillian Mattson Bozé.

My original and overriding gratitude is to my wife, Nancy, to whom this book is dedicated.

Contents

1

Analyzing Marketing Opportunities

Marketing management is the study of how business firms can best adapt resources and objectives to outside opportunities. These opportunities provide the proper starting point for marketing planning, and they form the subject matter of Part 1.

Chapter 1, "Marketing Management and the Marketing Concept," examines the contemporary rationale for orienting company planning and effort around the needs of target markets. Chapter 2, "Markets and the Marketing Environment," examines how broad market characteristics and trends provide the initial definition of the firm's opportunities. Chapter 3, "Marketing Segmentation," shows that most markets are made up of distinguishable submarkets with enough differences among them to lead a firm to consider differentiating or concentrating its marketing effort. Chapter 4, "Buyer Behavior," carries the analysis of markets to its ultimate unit, the individual buyer, and examines how and why he buys as he does. Finally, Chapter 5, "Market Measurement and Forecasting," examines the problem of quantifying the size and importance of different markets and submarkets as a prelude to the selection of target markets and the allocation of company resources.

chapter 1

Marketing Management and the Marketing Concept

American industry pours out each year over $600 billion worth of goods and services. Out of the factories, offices, and shops rolls an incredible avalanche of automobiles, insurance services, shoes, bread, radios, homes, missiles, machinery, and a million other goods and services that somehow find their way into homes and businesses in every part of the world.

Most of these goods and services are made available before being ordered by specific customers. They find their way into homes and businesses through the workings of a gigantic and complex marketing apparatus manned by specialists in the art of finding customers for goods. Marketing is traditionally viewed as the business function entrusted with the task of finding customers.

At the same time, marketing is increasingly recognizing another, somewhat converse responsibility. Marketing's short-run task may be to adjust customers' wants to existing goods, but its long-run task is to adjust the goods to the customers' wants.

This last point, that production must start with customer needs, is embodied in the *new marketing concept* that is revolutionizing the approach of businessmen to the problems of achieving viable business growth. It enlarges the role of marketers from one of selling what has been produced to one of influencing what is being produced. Marketing may stand officially at the end of the assembly line, but unofficially its influence must be felt on the drawing boards.

THE CONTEMPORARY MARKETING TASK VIEWED HISTORICALLY

The new view of marketing's task arises out of a consideration of the evolution of the American economy. The first stage was characterized by a scarcity of goods and services, and the central problem was to increase output. To this end, the major emphasis was placed on increasing productive efficiency. The business leaders of this era were engineers and innovators like Whitney and Carnegie, and the firms were heavily oriented toward production.

In the second stage, the scarcity of goods was less pronounced and the real opportunities for profit lay in the rationalization of the industrial structure through mergers and financial consolidations. In this era, lawyers and financiers, men like Mellon and Morgan, gained ascendancy in business enterprises through skillful financial consolidation.

The third and present stage of the economy is marked not by a scarcity of goods, but by a scarcity of markets. The major problem of most firms is to find sufficient customers for their output. While it is not true, at least for the time being, that American customers are satiated and physically unable to digest more goods and services, many are unwilling and others are unable to buy more of the present types of goods. As a result, each firm must examine customers' needs more closely to learn how it can improve the appeal of its present products and to discover which new products deserve to be born.

The Old Concept of Marketing

THE CASE OF THE ELGIN WATCH COMPANY [1]

The marketing problems of many American companies in this stage of our economic history are dramatized by the experience of the Elgin National Watch Company. Since its founding in 1864, Elgin Watch enjoyed a reputation as one of America's finest watchmakers. Management placed its major emphasis on maintaining a superior product and merchandising it through a large network of leading jewelry and department stores. By 1957, it employed a sales force of over fifty men and spent almost a million dollars each year on advertising. In that year, its sales approached $42 million. From then on, however, its sales and market share began to slip. In 1958 it lost over $2 million. What happened to challenge this firm's dominant position?

The available evidence suggests that the firm's management did not pay enough attention to significant changes occurring in the market place. Much had happened to products, customers, channels, and competition that should have caused Elgin's management to review the basic assumptions of its marketing program.

With regard to *products,* low-priced imported and pin-lever watches were growing rapidly in popularity. Many of them were styled in new and attractive ways in comparison with the more traditional character of the Elgin watches. With regard to *customers,* many were losing interest in the idea that a watch should have superior time-keeping accuracy, carry a prestigious name, and last a lifetime. They expected a watch to tell time, look attractive, and not cost too much. With regard to *channels,* an increasing number of watches was being sold through mass distribution outlets and discount stores. This suggested that Americans wanted to avoid the higher markups of the local jeweler; and also that buying watches had impulse characteristics that could be exploited by increased store exposure with resulting increased sales. With regard to *competitors,* many had added lower-priced watches to their line and had begun to sell them (and some of the higher-priced ones, too) through mass distribution channels.

Elgin's management noticed these changes but ignored them until it was almost too late. It continued to sell its traditionally styled watches through traditional channels. It thought that it was doing a good job of marketing because it backed its products with generous expenditures on advertising and personal selling.

[1] Adapted from Ralph Westfall and Harper W. Boyd, Jr., *Cases in Marketing Management* (Homewood, Ill.: Richard D. Irwin, Inc., 1961), pp. 16-24.

Elgin's problem was that it held on to an obsolete concept of marketing. This concept is rooted in the notion that firms perform three separate tasks in the pursuit of profit: they raise money, produce (or acquire) products, and sell them. The first task is called finance; the second, production; and the third, marketing.

In many companies, this sequence represents the order of tasks not only in time but also in importance. According to a top executive at Pillsbury, ". . . not too many years ago the ordering of functions in our business placed finance first, production second, and sales last." [2] Marketing's responsibilities began after the products spilled off the production lines; they ended when the products were sold.

According to this view, marketing is selling. The selling job itself consists of a number of activities. The company has to determine its potential buyers (marketing research). The company's products have to be favorably impressed upon the minds of buyers (advertising). The company may have to call and persuade buyers personally (personal selling). Agreements have to be drawn up and arrangements made for shipping the goods (pricing, negotiation, and physical distribution).

For a long time, these activities were carried on in different company departments. There was an advertising department, a sales department, a marketing research department, and so on. The managers of these departments usually recognized their common purpose and coordinated their activities to some degree on a formal or informal basis. Some companies moved in the direction of more formal coordination and established a single head over these activities, typically the sales manager, to whom the advertising manager and marketing research manager reported.

But the movement toward coordinating marketing activities did not necessarily expand the view of the marketing task. There are many companies today that possess all the trappings of a modern marketing operation but none of the substance. In these companies, marketing still is considered the department whose responsibilities begin and end with selling the existing products. Management treats its factories, resources, and product line as more or less fixed and holds marketing responsible for ringing up sufficient sales to keep production going.

This view lingers even in the latest official definition of marketing prepared by the American Marketing Association:

> MARKETING—The performance of business activities that direct the flow of goods and services from producer to consumer or user.[3]

Again we see the suggestion that the activities known as marketing begin with a set of goods and end with their sale.[4]

[2] Robert J. Keith, "The Marketing Revolution," *Journal of Marketing,* XXIV (January 1960), 35-38. The *Journal of Marketing* is the national quarterly publication of the American Marketing Association.

[3] *Marketing Definitions: A Glossary of Marketing Terms,* compiled by the Committee on Definitions of the American Marketing Association, Ralph S. Alexander, Chairman (Chicago: American Marketing Association, 1960), p. 15.

[4] Other definitions of marketing are summarized in the following statement: "It has been described by one person or another as a business activity; as a group of related business activities; as a trade phenomenon; as a frame of mind; as a coordinative,

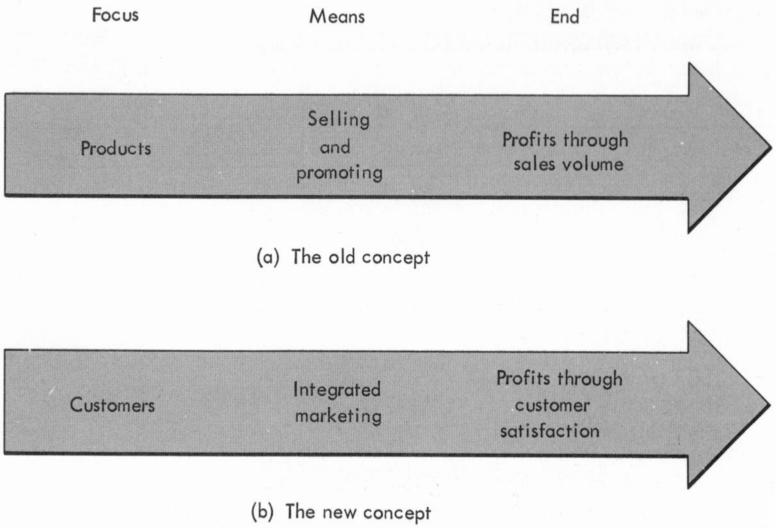

Focus	Means	End

Products → Selling and promoting → Profits through sales volume

(a) The old concept

Customers → Integrated marketing → Profits through customer satisfaction

(b) The new concept

FIGURE 1-1
The old and new concepts of marketing

The New Concept of Marketing

As already noted, the new marketing concept replaces and to some extent reverses the logic of the old one. The two views are contrasted in Figure 1-1. The old concept starts with the firm's existing products and considers marketing to be the use of selling and promotion to attain sales at a profit. The new concept starts with the firm's existing and potential customers; it seeks profits through the creation of customer satisfaction; and it seeks to achieve this through an integrated, corporate-wide marketing program. These are the three pillars of the new marketing concept.[5]

CUSTOMER-ORIENTED FOCUS

The new marketing concept holds that firms can gain more by being oriented outward toward the market instead of inward toward the products. We hear:

Under the marketing concept, the customer is at the top of the organization chart.

A company should prefer a franchise over a market to a franchise over a plant.

Look at the company through the customer's eyes.

"Instead of trying to market what is easiest for us to make, we must find

integrative function in policy making; as a sense of business purpose; as an economic process; as a structure of institutions; as the process of exchanging or transferring ownership of products; as a process of concentration, equalization, and dispersion; as the creation of time, place, and possession utilities; as a process of demand and supply adjustment; and as many other things." (Marketing Staff of the Ohio State University, "A Statement of Marketing Philosophy," *Journal of Marketing,* XXIX [January 1965], 43.)

[5] The newer marketing concept has been described in many ways. See *The Marketing Concept: Its Meaning to Management,* Marketing Series No. 99 (New York: American Management Association, 1957).

out much more about what the consumer is willing to buy. In other words, we must apply our creativeness more intelligently to *people,* and their wants and needs, rather than to *products."* [6]

Does a marketing orientation really make better business sense, or does it just represent, as many critics have charged, a pious utterance to conceal the ambitions of marketers to enhance their own importance in the company? In other words, what benefits flow when management keeps its eyes on the market rather than on the product? At least four can be cited.

The first benefit is that *management realizes that customer needs are more basic than particular products.* Many prosperous horse-and-carriage companies disappeared in the 1900's because they failed to see that customers required transportation in general and not carriages in particular. Many hotel chains fell into financial difficulties because they continued to build hotels in the face of the growing popularity of motels. On the other hand, companies that recognize the difference between basic customer needs and transient products are led to redefine and expand the definition of their business to provide a more durable base of operations.

> American Telephone and Telegraph's recent investments reflect a view of itself not as operating a telephone system but as satisfying communication needs.
> International Business Machines views itself not as a computer manufacturer so much as a business meeting "problem-solving" needs.
> The Radio Corporation of America views a basic part of its business to be devoted to meeting mass entertainment needs.

The second benefit is that *attention to customer needs helps management spot new product opportunities more quickly.* In this age companies have lost the privilege of standing still. Existing products and brands are under constant attack by competition. The firm can defend itself only by developing or acquiring new products with some regularity. The ideas for these new products can come from a number of sources, such as technological breakthroughs and competitors' new products. But one of the best sources of new ideas is the unsatisfied needs of the company's customers. Many examples can be cited:

> Ford developed its Mustang because it recognized that a large number of people had a keen interest in sports cars but could not afford the ones currently on the market.
> Bell and Howell developed its electric-eye movie camera after recognizing that many people felt incapable of making good manual adjustments.
> Seat-belt companies developed the retractable seat belt because customers complained about always having to search for their seat belts.
> Various innovations of the airlines, such as "fly now, pay later," "fly-drive plans," "holiday travel packages," and "air shuttle services," came out of close studies of what customers want when they fly.

The third benefit is that *merchandising becomes more effective.* The

[6] Charles G. Mortimer, "The Creative Factor in Marketing," Fifteenth Annual Parlin Memorial Lecture, Philadelphia Chapter, American Marketing Association, May 13, 1959.

firm which starts with its products sees its job as *creating demand,* interesting many groups of people in its products. The firm which starts with the needs of a definite group of people in mind sees its job as *supplying want satisfaction* to this group.[7] One trouble with taking the route of creating demand is that the product can rarely represent the best value for all users, because their desires, susceptibilities, and purchasing habits vary widely. The company can often be more effective by adapting and adjusting its offerings to the needs of clearly defined buyers. The physical product may be a small part of the satisfactions the buyer seeks, for he wants convenience, service, and certain aesthetic and symbolic values, too. Merchandising is more effective when these values are recognized.

The fourth benefit is that *management brings its own interests into greater harmony with society's interests.* Management's interests lie in the achievement of profit and providing steady employment for its resources. Society's interest lies in the steady enhancement of human welfare. A market orientation means that management builds its future profits on seeking better ways to satisfy human needs.

Had the Elgin National Watch Company been conscious of this, it would have recognized that its generic business was helping people meet their time measurement needs. It would have recognized buyers' desires for convenience (self-winding watches), durability (water- and shock-proof watches), economy (pin-lever watches), and so forth. The buyers' desires would have led Elgin to adjust its product line, merchandising, and channels. Elgin would have studied its customers after the sale to see whether basic satisfactions were achieved and what further satisfactions were sought. Lacking this market orientation, Elgin kept its eyes on the wrong variables.

INTEGRATED MARKETING

An orientation outward toward buyers on the part of top management is not enough. The orientation must be backed by organizational changes within the company. Integrated marketing management is the second pillar of the marketing concept.

In a product-oriented company, each department develops its own logic of operations. Research and development thinks in terms of exploiting the existing technology; engineering thinks in terms of creating the product cheaply; procurement thinks in terms of keeping down the cost of materials; production thinks in terms of utilizing present facilities; marketing thinks in terms of maximizing sales volume; traffic thinks in terms of keeping down traffic costs; and collections thinks in terms of reducing credit losses. But all these logics will affect the buyer, as shown in Figure 1-2a.

The new marketing concept insists on the substitution of a single logic for these many logics. It requires that departments be guided by the logic of customer-need satisfaction at a profit.

Under this concept, the marketing department has an expanded responsibility. Its responsibility is to seek a coordination of company actions impinging on the buyers. These forces make up the "marketing mix" as

[7] See Wendell R. Smith, "Product Differentiation and Market Segmentation as Alternative Marketing Strategies," *Journal of Marketing,* XXI (July 1956), 3-8.

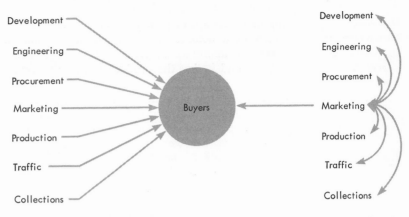

FIGURE 1-2
Contrast between nonintegrated and integrated marketing

(a) How buyers are affected when the marketing task is not integrated

(b) How buyers are affected when the marketing task is integrated

seen through the buyers' eyes. This conception is illustrated in Figure 1-2b.

There is less unanimity on how much authority marketing should have to carry out its expanded responsibility. At least three different positions are taken. The most popular position is that the chief marketing officer should have formal authority only over the sales force, advertising, and marketing research; that is, the traditional marketing functions. Yet he should have close relationships with the other departments and should be backed by a president who has embraced the marketing concept. This position is illustrated in Figure 1-3a.

An advanced position holds that the chief marketing officer should have authority over certain additional departments whose efforts affect customers closely. The areas usually mentioned in this connection are research and development, physical distribution, purchasing, credit, and public relations. This view of integrated marketing is shown in Figure 1-3b.

The most radical position is that the chief marketing officer should direct the entire company operation. Marketing would be the only line function, and all the others would be staff functions. Dominance by marketing would insure the use of a customer logic in the operation of all departments.

The last two positions have become a reality in some large consumer-goods companies. Yet, these extreme positions go beyond the essential spirit of the marketing concept, and would not be appropriate in many companies. They involve a conception of marketing's authority which has engendered much antagonism to the new marketing concept. What is essential in the marketing concept is that customer logic should permeate the various parts of the company and that marketing should seek an integration of various customer-impinging company activities into a well-coordinated program. How this is to be secured is not part of the concept.

PROFIT THROUGH CREATING CUSTOMER SATISFACTION

When it is proposed that all company functions operate on a customer logic, the question immediately arises whether profits are to be sacrificed to sales. A substantial increase in sales is no cause for management satisfaction if it is accompanied by a decline in profits.

How far should a company go in trying to meet customer needs and

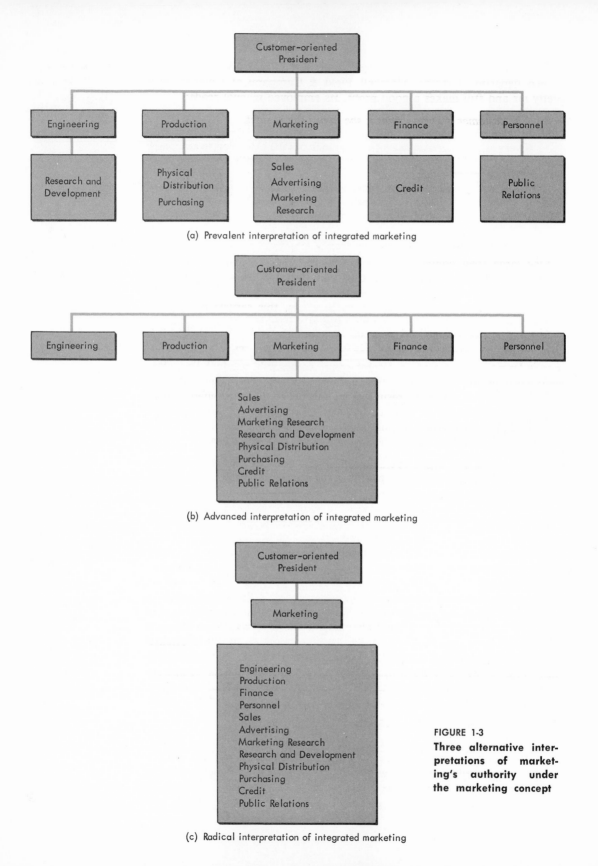

(a) Prevalent interpretation of integrated marketing

(b) Advanced interpretation of integrated marketing

(c) Radical interpretation of integrated marketing

FIGURE 1-3
Three alternative interpretations of marketing's authority under the marketing concept

desires? This is not an easy question to answer. One of the world's best-known department stores, Marshall Field & Company of Chicago, goes pretty far and still makes a good profit. Its employee manual reads:

> The customer is always right if she thinks she is right.
> We are more interested in pleasing a customer than in making a sale.
> Every sale of merchandise or services includes the obligation to accept the article for credit, refund, exchange or adjustment promptly and courteously to the customer's satisfaction.
> We sell only merchandise of the best quality obtainable at the price.
> We offer merchandise in a broad assortment from lowest to the highest price at which the quality, fashion and value measure up to our store's standards.
> We strive to give completely satisfactory service to every customer.

One large steel company makes a special point of meeting customer needs. It will incur extra production and delivery costs in order that customers or potential customers get a needed delivery on time. Although the company often loses money on such orders, this service is expected to lead in the long run to a profitable sales relationship with its customers.

Yet the desire to please customers can be carried too far. Each company must determine the breakeven point for itself. The slow-moving, money-losing items found in almost every company's product line often were born in the desire to cater to every possible customer taste. An overabundance of salesmen results from the belief that customers should have salesmen almost on call. The executive vice-president of Pillsbury's consumer-product division, in his description of Pillsbury's evolution from a production- to a marketing-oriented company, had this to say:

> When we first began operating under this new marketing concept, we encountered the problems which always accompany any major reorientation. . . . The idea was almost too powerful. The marketing concept proved its worth in sales, but it upset many of the internal balances of the corporation. Marketing-oriented decisions resulted in peaks and valleys in production, schedules, labor, and inventories.[8]

He then described how Pillsbury has been moving toward a new stage where marketing policies are tied closer to profit goals through long-run profit planning.

Thus, the third pillar of the marketing concept is the achievement of good profits by giving the customer what he wants. In an economy marked by intense competition and rapid changes in customer wants, profits must be founded on producing customer want-satisfaction. A customer orientation is the logical basis for profit planning in a consumer-sovereign economy. This is the basis on which many of the most successful companies in America, such as General Electric, International Business Machines, Procter and Gamble, Scott Paper, and Du Pont, have operated at a profit.

What Is Marketing?

We have examined the new marketing concept in this detail in order to define the point of view of this book. Marketing is more than the set of

8 Keith, *op. cit.*

activities undertaken by a company to sell its products. Our definition is:

> Marketing is the analyzing, organizing, planning, and controlling of the firm's customer-impinging resources, policies, and activities with a view to satisfying the needs and wants of chosen customer groups at a profit.

This definition is used for three reasons.

It suggests the three main elements of the modern marketing concept; that is, integrated marketing . . . to create customer satisfaction . . . at a profit.

It suggests the "marketing-mix" idea [9] through its reference to the management of customer-impinging resources, policies, and activities, and the "market-segmentation" idea [10] through its reference to chosen customer groups.

It specifies that marketing comprises the administrative activities of analysis, organization, planning, and control. The four parts of this book correspond with these four activities.

Questions and Problems

1. Do you think the marketing concept should provide the major orientation for every company? Could you cite companies which do not particularly need this orientation? Which companies need it most?

2. What will the marketing challenge be if the American economy continues to move from abundance to affluence? Will the marketing job be harder, easier, or nonexistent?

3. Offer a definition of the basic business of each of the following large companies: (a) General Motors; (b) Bayer's (maker of aspirins); (c) Massachusetts Investors Trust (a mutual fund); (d) Sears; and (e) *Time* magazine.

4. Do you think the railroad passenger business is doomed? Why or why not? Could the passenger business be made profitable through adoption by management of the marketing concept? Give illustrations.

5. What do you think are the major alternative approaches to the study of marketing?

[9] See Chapter 12.
[10] See Chapter 3.

chapter 2

Markets and the Marketing Environment

Chapter 1 dealt with the tasks and responsibilities of marketing management under the new marketing concept. Now it is time to move outside of the firm and examine the nature of markets and the marketing environment. The first section of this chapter summarizes the major features and trends in domestic consumer markets, domestic business markets, and international markets. The second section examines major forces in the marketing environment, such as technology, marketing channels, and culture, with the main focus of attention on the opportunities and challenges they pose for marketing management.

Markets

The term "market" has many different usages. To a stock broker, the market is the place where stocks are traded. To a produce merchant, the market is a location in the city where produce is received, sorted, and sold. To a sales manager, the market is a geographical unit, such as a city or region, for which decisions are made with respect to distributors, advertising effort, salesmen, and possibly prices. To an economist, the market is all the buyers and sellers interested or potentially interested in a product group. Finally, to a marketer, the market is *all persons or business units who buy or may be induced to buy a product or service*. It is in this last sense that we shall use the term "market" in examining domestic consumer markets, domestic business markets, and international markets.

DOMESTIC CONSUMER MARKETS

One of the most popular exhibits at the New York World's Fair of 1964-65 was a huge "demograph" which changed every twelve seconds to record the latest gains in United States population. When the fair opened in April, 1964, the demograph read 191,510,364; by October, 1964, it read 192,974,586, and by April, 1965, it passed the 194,000,000 mark. Almost 3,000,000 people were added to the population in the course of a year. At this rate, by 1980 there will be 45,000,000 more people, or a United States population approaching 240,000,000.

Each new person consumes a fantastic amount of goods and services during his lifetime. And consumption is likely to increase over time, as incomes rise. Indeed, the future demand for goods and services is staggering to contemplate—but American firms will still not be able to sell all they produce. Their resources and technology appear to be keeping pace with, and possibly growing faster than, the growth in demand. Companies will continue to be pitted against each other in a fierce battle for customers. They will continue to need new markets for their productive capabilities. They will have to keep a closer tab than ever on the direction and evolution of consumer needs and wants.

What are the major characteristics and trends that describe the American consuming population?

CHANGING AGE STRUCTURE.   The two major trends in the age structure of the American population are the relative growth of the school-age group (5-19) and the elderly (65+). Between 1950-60, the first group went from 23.2 per cent of the population to 27.2 per cent, and the second group, from 8.1 per cent to 9.2 per cent.[1]

The substantial growth in the school-age group has spurred the sales of such items as teen-age clothing, records, books, and sporting equipment.[2] The attainment of young adulthood will soon be reflected in an increased rate of new family formation, carrying with it a growing demand for housing, appliances, automobiles, and baby goods.

The steady increase in the relative number of persons over 65 (almost 10 per cent of the population) is the result of improved medical knowledge, better sanitation, and increased incomes. Our "senior citizens" have specific tastes and needs in the way of food, housing, clothing, recreation, and medical attention; they constitute a major market for cruises, health foods, and hearing aids.[3] Marketing for this group must take into consideration their special needs and values. Older persons tend to be conservative and to value the quiet life. This should be considered in developing the marketing mix, especially with regard to the advertising message, packaging, and even price.

VIABLE NATIONAL, RELIGIOUS, AND RACIAL GROUPS.   America is the original "melting pot." In this country are represented more diverse cultural groups in sizable numbers than in any other country. Where a product or service is directly oriented toward a cultural group or where brand loyalty or product interest varies culturally, firms will want to pay close attention to major trends in group size and attitudes.

One important cultural group in the United States is the 18,872,000 Negroes who constituted 10.5 per cent of the total population as of 1960. In the past, large manufacturers rarely distinguished their products or methods of marketing for the Negro community. The feeling in some cases was that the Negro market was too small (because of low purchasing power) and in other cases that it was insufficiently different to warrant market segmentation policies. Nevertheless, the growth in Negro incomes

---

[1] Much of the data in this chapter is drawn from U.S. Bureau of the Census, *Statistical Abstract of the United States, 1964* (85th edition) Washington, D.C., 1964. It will not always be specifically referenced.

[2] "Catering to Kids," *The Wall Street Journal,* September 17, 1962, p. 1.

[3] "How the Old Age Market Looks," *Business Week,* February 13, 1960, pp. 72-78.

and "class consciousness" suggests to some the desirability of applying more differentiated marketing effort.[4]

HIGH MOBILITY. Profitable marketing requires not only observing who the people are but also where they live. The 190 million Americans are scattered unevenly over an area of 3.6 million square miles. Their concentration is heaviest in the North Atlantic States, along the Great Lakes, and along the California seaboard, where the largest American cities are found.

There is nothing static about the geographical distribution of the American population. Americans are a mobile people and seem to be increasingly so; it is estimated that currently one out of every five Americans moves each year.[5] Nor are their movements random. States like Florida, Nevada, Arizona, and California have attracted decennial population increases in the order of 50 to 80 per cent, while states like Arkansas and West Virginia have suffered decennial population decreases in the order of 6 to 10 per cent. These regional shifts in population are of special interest to marketers because of marked differences in regional expenditure patterns and customer behavior. Customers in the West, for example, spend relatively less on food and relatively more on automobiles than their counterparts in the Northeast.[6]

Another geographical movement of considerable marketing significance is the continuous migration from rural to urban areas. This movement has been going on for over a century. From a nation where approximately 70 per cent of the population lived in rural areas in 1880, the situation has now reversed to where approximately 70 per cent live in urban areas.

The rural population includes all persons living in places having a population of less than 2,500 and a population density of less than 1,500 per square mile, including farmers, mechanics, local factory workers, retailers, service repairmen, and so forth. However, almost all the decline in rural population has been a decline in the number of farm families rather than rural nonfarm families. Only 9 per cent of the United States labor force still work on farms, and it is estimated that by 1975 the figure will be only 6 per cent.[7] The decline in the number of farmers is primarily due to technological advances in agriculture, especially in machinery and fertilizers, which have enabled the individual farmer to cultivate increasing amounts of acreage. Agricultural productivity has expanded at a much faster pace than the demand for agricultural output, eliminating the need for many farms and farmers, depressing the incomes of marginal farms, and stimulating urban migration.

[4] See Henry Allen Bullock, "Consumer Motivations in Black and White," *Harvard Business Review,* May-June 1961, pp. 89-104, and July-August 1961, pp. 110-124; also Jules J. Paglen, "Letter of Comment—From the Thoughtful Businessman," November-December 1961. Also see Arnold M. Barban and Edward W. Cundiff, "Negro and White Response to Advertising Stimuli," *Journal of Marketing Research,* November 1964, pp. 53-56.

[5] *Sales Management,* April 6, 1962, p. 44.

[6] See Life Magazine, *Study of Consumer Expenditures,* Vol. I (New York: Time, Inc., 1957).

[7] "Big Farms, Little Farms, in 1970," *Looking Ahead,* National Planning Association, May 1962, p. 1.

Firms that have invested heavily in rural markets really have two tasks: they must keep up with, if not ahead of, changes in the kinds of goods needed by the modern farmer, and they must diversify into product and service lines that appeal to the urban population. Any diversification should, however, recognize the marketing differences in urban and rural areas. The rural-oriented firm that moves into urban marketing must expect to confront a greater diversity of channels, more impersonal buying, and better financed competition.

Urban areas themselves are far from homogeneous. Larger cities are characterized by a faster pace of living, more commuting, typically higher incomes, and a greater variety of goods and services than the small towns that dot America. The largest cities, such as New York, Chicago, and San Francisco, account for most of the sales of expensive furs, perfumes, luggage, and works of art, and they still boast most of what there is of opera, theater, and other forms of "high culture" in the United States, although some dispersion of the arts is taking place. Each major metropolitan area constitutes a complex market in its own right, and profitable marketing often requires expert knowledge of the metropolitan area's unique characteristics.

Also significant is the movement from the city to the suburbs. Over the years, many city workers have moved further away from their places of work, owing largely to the development of automobiles, major highways, and rapid rail and bus transit for commuters. Cities have become surrounded by suburbs and these suburbs in turn by "exurbs." [8] The U.S. Census Bureau has created a separate population classification for sprawling urban concentrations, called Standard Metropolitan Statistical Areas (SMSA).[9] Over 63 per cent of the nation's entire population (and 95 per cent of the nation's urban population) are estimated to live in the 212 recognized Standard Metropolitan Statistical Areas, and it is the SMSA's rather than the cities proper that constitute the primary market focus of firms.

Nevertheless, firms have to distinguish between the city and the suburban segments of the metropolitan areas. About 50 per cent of the total metropolitan population now live in suburbs, and it is estimated that this may reach 60 per cent by 1980. The distinction is important because suburban areas are frequently marked by a style of living different from that in the cities. Suburbs tend to be characterized by casual, outdoor living, greater neighbor interaction, higher incomes, and younger families.[10] Suburban dwellers are the source of much of the demand for station wagons, home workshop equipment, garden furniture, lawn and gardening tools and supplies, and outdoor cooking equipment. Furthermore, they are becoming less interested in traveling great distances into the cities to buy these products or even to buy clothing and household goods. Retailers have

[8] Highly populated areas which are within five miles of a city limit or urban fringe boundary are called suburbs; areas still considered metropolitan but lying beyond the five-mile designation are called exurbs.

[9] An SMSA consists of the counties of an integrated economic area with a large volume of daily travel and communication between a central city of 50,000 inhabitants or more and the outlying parts of the area.

[10] See "The New Suburbia," pp. 267-391, in William H. Whyte, Jr., *The Organization Man* (New York: Simon and Schuster, 1956). For a different view, see Bennett M. Berger, "The Myth of Suburbia," *Journal of Social Issues,* January 1961, pp. 38-49.

recognized the importance of convenience and have brought their goods out to the suburbs through the development of branch department stores and suburban shopping centers.

At the same time, manufacturers must not overlook a more recent counter movement back to the central city into new high-rise apartment buildings. In many cases the older and wealthier families are returning. The children have grown up, and the parents now wish to be closer to the cultural, recreational, and business facilities of the central city. In some cases, younger families who want these advantages and have grown tired of commuting, gardening, and household chores also move back. The major marketing implication of this counter movement is obvious. Manufacturers and retailers would be shortsighted if they concentrated only on the visibly burgeoning suburban and exurban areas and neglected the less dramatic revitalization of the central city as a market for goods and services. The trend back to the city is being aided by urban housing renewal programs, improved traffic arteries, and renewed investments by large retailers and other firms in downtown areas, and it holds out the hope that central cities will retain their marketing primacy in the sale of many goods and services.

RISING INCOMES, EXPENDITURES, AND ASSETS. The vast majority of America's 57 million households have enjoyed rising incomes. Between 1950 and 1962, per capita income rose by almost 60 per cent in money terms and by 26 per cent in real terms (base: 1947-49 dollars). Per capita income stood in 1962 at $2,366, and average household income (with 3.4 persons in the average household) stood at $8,044.

As income grows, there are pronounced shifts in the relative demand for different categories of goods and services. The particular types of shifts were stated as early as 1857 by the German statistician Ernst Engel, who compared the budgets of individual working-class families. Engel observed that while rising family income tended to be accompanied by increased spending in all categories, *the percentage spent on food tended to decline, the percentage spent on housing and household operations tended to remain constant, and the percentage spent on other categories (clothing, transportation, recreation, health, and education) and savings tended to increase.* These "laws" have been generally validated in subsequent budget studies.[11]

A knowledge of income trends must be supplemented by a close watch on trends in consumer credit and in household financial assets. What a consumer can spend is a matter not only of what he earns (income), but also what he can borrow (credit) and what he owns (physical and financial assets). Over the years, more and more consumers have overcome their fear of using credit, as the memory of the Great Depression has dimmed and as social security has spread. By 1961, outstanding consumer credit (exclusive of home mortgages) stood at close to $57 billion, or over $1,000 for every household. About three-fourths of that amount represented installment credit arising largely from the purchase of major consumer durables, and the other fourth represented noninstallment credit (debts to be fully paid in a month or two) arising from charge accounts

11 See Life Magazine, *op. cit.*

and single-payment loans. The increased use of credit has been a boon to both the credit users and the business community. Any developments affecting the ease or difficulty of obtaining consumer credit or the amount obtainable or the cost of credit figure significantly in the marketing policies of all consumer-goods manufacturers and sellers.

Consumer asset holding has also been rising. In 1963, 76 per cent of all spending units [12] held some liquid assets,[13] the median amount being $900; 17 per cent owned corporate stock, the median amount being $3,500.[14] As these percentages and amounts rise, household units will feel freer to make major purchases of durable goods, vacations, and housing. At the same time, the current ownership of different physical assets is an important indicator of which goods will be wanted. The sales of goods which already command widespread ownership, such as television sets (91 per cent of all households as of 1963) and vacuum cleaners (73 per cent), can be expected to grow less rapidly than the sales of freezers (20 per cent), dishwashers (7 per cent), air conditioners (14 per cent), and so forth.[15] Much can be learned by studying the age distribution of these goods, the geographical areas of greater and lesser ownership, and owner characteristics, as well as the percentage of homes that own them.

RISING EDUCATIONAL LEVELS. American families are attaining higher levels of education. The portion of the adult population which has completed high school rose from 20.2 per cent to 28.3 per cent between 1950 and 1962. The corresponding figures for college graduates are 6.0 per cent and 9.0 per cent.[16]

The trend toward higher education is likely to accelerate and will have considerable marketing significance. Strides in education point to a substantial growth in the demand for books, art, travel, and cultural activities. They imply greater buyer discrimination and deliberation in the choice of products and brands and an interest in higher quality. They suggest that promotional copy may have to be upgraded in both factual content and in taste. They imply something about the kinds of stores people will want to shop in and the kinds of salesmen who will be effective.

RISING LEISURE. Along with increases in income and education, the typical American family is enjoying more leisure time. From about fifty-eight hours of work per week at the turn of the century, the average worker is now down to forty hours and in some cases less. Automation, or if not, the unions, will probably bring about a further shortening of the workweek. Although many Americans are unaccustomed to this leisure and some are positively afraid of it, it is not too difficult to predict how the extra time will be used. Certainly total spending will rise as leisure time increases. The family man with more time to spend around the house will

---

[12] *Spending units* are households as well as any members of a household who earn fifteen dollars a week or more and keep more than half of it for personal use.

[13] *Liquid assets* consist of U.S. savings bonds, checking accounts, savings accounts in banks, and shares in savings and loan associations and credit unions, but not currency.

[14] *Statistical Abstract of the United States, 1964,* p. 345.

[15] *Statistical Abstract of the United States, 1965,* p. 761.

[16] *Statistical Abstract of the United States, 1964,* p. 113.

attack various home-improvement projects involving purchases of lumber, tools, and paint. He and his family will also participate in more sport and cultural functions. Extra vacation time will lead to an increased demand for camping, skiing, hunting, and boating clothing and equipment, for automobile and public transportation services, for restaurant meals, hotels, and motels. The family will spend more time shopping together for food, clothing, and appliances. More time for family shopping may mean more impulse purchasing of smaller items but also may mean reduced need to buy large-ticket items from the first outlet visited. Last but not least, individual family members will have more time for self-development, spurring the markets for books, hobby materials, phonograph records, and educational courses.[17]

The leading trends in American population composition, geographical distribution, and family characteristics tell a great deal about the future shape of consumer markets. These trends are beyond the control of individual firms, but they constitute the environment in which alert firms will seek their opportunity and try to adapt their marketing policies.

DOMESTIC BUSINESS MARKETS

Although all firms will want to keep abreast of major trends in consumer markets, not all of them will be selling in these markets. In fact, most firms do not sell to final households. Instead, their output is marketed to a great number and variety of business firms who use and/or resell this output.

A classification of the major business buyers of goods and services is given in Table 2-1. Nine different business divisions are shown. Altogether,

TABLE 2-1
Major business divisions by number of establishments, employees, and national income *

	Number of establishments (thousands)	Number of employees (thousands)	National income ($ billions)
Farms	3,711	5,178 ⎱	23.9
Extractive industries	83	1,999 ⎰	
Manufacturing	313	17,035	137.5
Contract construction	470	3,029	25.1
Finance, insurance, and real estate	1,010	2,866	48.4
Transportation, communication, and public utilities	36	3,913	38.7
Service industries	942	8,297	59.1
Distribution			
Wholesalers	332	3,143 ⎱	77.8
Retailers	2,032	8,722 ⎰	
Government	105	9,535	64.6
Total	9,034	62,917	475.1

* 1963 or latest available figure. The only important group left out is institutions (hospitals, churches, and educational facilities).
Source: *Statistical Abstract of the United States,* 1964, various sections.

[17] One of the best studies of leisure-spending patterns is George Fisk, *Leisure-Spending Behavior* (Philadelphia: University of Pennsylvania Press, 1963).

there are approximately 9 million different business buying units, and each one is a market for specific types of goods and services. They employ over 63 million workers, generate an annual national income of $475 billion, and constitute the selling environment for most firms.

More dollars are involved in sales to business buyers than to final households. To bring a simple pair of shoes into existence, hide dealers (mainly meat packers) must sell the hides to tanners, who sell the leather to shoe manufacturers, who sell the shoes to wholesalers, who in turn sell the shoes to retailers. Each party in the chain of production and distribution pays more than the previous party. The transactions based on one pair of finished shoes selling for $15 may have been $7 (tanner to hide dealer), $9 (shoe manufacturer to tanner), $11 (wholesaler to shoe manufacturer), and $13 (retailer to wholesaler), making a total of $40, whereas the transaction to the consumer involved but $15. More business marketing goes on than consumer marketing, although many people have the opposite impression.

The tremendous variety of business buyers makes it difficult to generalize about over-all characteristics. Yet certain things can be observed in a qualified way.

BUYING ORIENTED TOWARD PROFITS. A major reason for treating all business buyers in one large category is that their purchasing is undertaken for motives different from those of households. Households buy goods and services mostly for the satisfactions they will get in personal consumption. ("Satisfaction" is used here in the broadest sense of meeting their personal and family needs.) Business buyers buy transformers, cash registers, insecticides, repair services, and pig iron as ingredients or adjuncts of a business operation where the motive is profits or, in the case of government and some institutions, public welfare. These buyers are sometimes called "intermediate buyers" because their purchases are directed toward a further purpose. Their demand for all these goods is a *derived* demand.

BUYING PROCESS MORE RATIONAL. A second major reason for treating these diverse buyers in one large category is that they typically buy with more knowledge, skill, and calculation than household buyers. Because their livelihood depends on their skill in purchasing, business buyers are generally better informed than the average housewife, however efficient and shrewd she may be about the sources of supply, prices, product differences, and general values. Business buyers develop considerable expertise in reading catalogs, dealing with salesmen, and judging values, and they tend to adhere more strictly to benefit criteria (reliability, service, quality, cost, reputation, and so forth).

RELATIVELY SMALL NUMBERS OF ACTUAL BUYERS FOR SPECIFIC PRODUCTS OR SERVICES. Typically, there are fewer buyers of specific business goods than of specific consumer goods. A cookie manufacturer has a potential market of 194 million individual customers. A television set manufacturer has a potential market of 57 million households. Most business-goods manufacturers have far fewer actual customers. They usually produce products of interest to a limited number of business divisions, such as manufacturers in the case of motors; sometimes only one buyer is involved, as in the case of defense weapons for government. The business-goods firm may further specialize by customer size, customer type, or region. A great number of business-goods manufacturers have fewer than 100 firms that can be considered as potential customers.

RELATIVE GEOGRAPHIC CONCENTRATION OF BUYERS. Compared to ultimate customers, business buyers tend to be concentrated geographically, both nationally and regionally. The seven states of New York, California, Pennsylvania, Illinois, Ohio, New Jersey, and Michigan contain within their borders over half of the nation's manufacturing firms. Particular manufacturing industries, such as petroleum, rubber, and steel, show even greater geographic concentration. Most agricultural output comes from a relatively small number of states, and specific commodities, such as tobacco and citrus fruit, are grown in even fewer states. Wholesalers are found in all large cities, but even wholesaling establishments, or at least certain types, tend to cluster within a city. Retailers are found everywhere, but they, too, cluster in neighborhoods, and often stores selling the same goods locate near each other. All of this geographical concentration of business buyers helps to reduce the costs of selling to them. For this reason, business goods sellers will want to watch any pronounced tendencies toward or away from further geographic concentration.

PRONOUNCED SIZE DIFFERENCES AMONG BUYERS. Whereas households tend to need or buy roughly comparable amounts of consumer products, the opposite tends to be true of business buyers. Many manufacturing industries are characterized by high concentration ratios. For example, the top four companies in tin cans account for 80 per cent of total output, in cigarettes, 79 per cent, and in motor vehicles, 75 per cent.[18] These ratios indicate that various business buyers will want considerably different quantities of inputs. In addition to manufacturing, there is increasing concentration in agriculture, distribution, commerce, and some service industries like motels and restaurants. This has continued in spite of the government's stepped-up antitrust and antimerger activity.[19]

TOTAL MARKET DEMAND LESS SENSITIVE TO MARKETING EFFORT. The demand of business buyers for goods and services is largely a *derived* demand. The amount of steel, machinery, and supplies ordered depends largely on the economic outlook for the business buyer's products.[20] Business buyers cannot be convinced to buy more than they need unless perhaps special price concessions are offered to encourage inventory buildup or input substitutions. The fact that total demand of business buyers is derived not only makes demand more inelastic but also makes business demand typically subject to larger fluctuations than consumer demand.

[18] *Statistical Abstract of the United States, 1964,* pp. 784-86.
[19] See Chapter 20.
[20] A good way to estimate how inputs are affected when an industry's output increases is to look at interindustry tables. See Robert E. Johnson, "The Application of Input/Output Analysis in Industrial Marketing Management," in Peter D. Bennett, *Marketing and Economic Development* (Chicago, Ill.: American Marketing Association, 1965), pp. 309-20.

This has been called the *acceleration effect,* and the historical record confirms the greater relative volatility of total business investment compared to total personal consumption expenditure.[21] The firm selling to business buyers, to the extent that it has less control over the factors which influence total demand, must be more careful in developing good forecasts and adopting marketing policies which reduce the risks of this greater volatility.

HIGHER TOTAL DOLLAR TRANSACTIONS.   The average business purchase involves substantially more dollars than the average consumer purchase. The average consumer's income is small, and he is geared to making small and frequent purchases. The average business buyer finds it more economical to place large orders less frequently and carry large inventories. For this reason, business goods firms put out substantial effort to get each order. Much more money is involved in each business transaction than in each consumer transaction. Business-goods sellers will want to watch trends in the purchasing and inventory policies of their business buyers and to ferret out their significance for frequency of sales call, credit terms, and other policy variables. The seller's task is to develop marketing policies which take into account the distinct characteristics of business buyers' behavior.

INTERNATIONAL MARKETS

The United States represents the largest single national market in the world for goods and services. Yet it would be a mistake to overlook the varied marketing opportunities found in other parts of the world. The United States contains only 6 per cent of the world's customers. The earth's population, now at 3.1 billion people, is expected to grow to 4.0 billion by 1975. Consumer incomes are rising rapidly in many parts of the world. Consumer wants are rising even faster. Most of the world's governments are carrying out long-range programs to accelerate their nation's rate of economic growth. Whether their plans emphasize industrial or agricultural development, these countries have a growing need for goods of all kinds. Private as well as public capital is flowing at unprecedented rates from the rich nations to the poor nations. International markets are providing some of the most attractive contemporary marketing opportunities.

The hundred-odd nations of the world differ greatly in the kinds of goods and services, both industrial and consumer, they are ready to use. It would be as much a mistake for an American manufacturer of electric rotisseries to seek a market in Nigeria as for Nigerians to seek a market for native loincloths here. On the other hand, American bicycles fetch a premium in Nigeria, and Nigerian palm oil is imported in large quantities into the United States. A nation's readiness for different products and services and the size of the markets for them depend upon a host of factors, the most important of which are the country's population, its industrial structure, its level and distribution of income, and its cultural traditions and characteristics.

[21] The acceleration effect is described in economic textbooks. See Paul Samuelson, *Economics: An Introductory Analysis,* 5th ed. (New York: McGraw-Hill Book Company, 1961), pp. 295-99.

POPULATION. Markets are made up of people. If everything else were distributed equally, the world's largest markets would be China (647 million persons), India (449 million persons), and the U.S.S.R. (221 million persons).[22] This is not the case, however, because of great differences in national output and income. In fact, the United States, with only 6 per cent of the world's people, enjoys about 38 per cent of the world income, and Europe, with 22 per cent of the people, enjoys another 36 per cent.[23] Yet population is still an important correlate of total demand, especially for basic items like food, clothing, and shelter, and for more advanced goods over time as nations advance economically.

INDUSTRIAL STRUCTURE. The types of goods and services needed by a society clearly depend upon its industrial structure. In this connection, the following fourfold classification is useful:

Subsistence economies. A subsistence economy is one in which the vast majority of people are engaged in simple agriculture. They consume most of their output and barter the rest for simple goods and services. Such an economy usually lacks a money medium and also lacks much in the way of natural resources. Subsistence economies can be found in parts of South America, Africa, and Australia. For obvious reasons, they offer few opportunities for exporters.

Raw-material exporting economies. These are economies which are rich in one or more natural resources but poor in other respects. Much of their revenue comes from exporting these resources. Examples are Chile (tin and copper), Congo (rubber), and Saudi Arabia (oil). The extractive industries are usually dominated by foreign firms which ship out most of the output and profits, after providing varying amounts of amenities for local education, sanitation, and housing. The era of absolute foreign domination is ending as independent governments demand a larger share from the foreign operators or, in some cases, expropriate them. These countries are good markets for extractive equipment, tools and supplies, materials-handling equipment, and trucks. Depending on the number of foreign managers, engineers, and bureaucrats, and also the number of wealthy native rulers and landholders, they are also a market for Western-style commodities and luxury goods.

Industrializing economies. An industrializing economy is one in which manufacturing is beginning to play a role of some importance, probably accounting for somewhere between 10 and 20 per cent of the country's gross national product. Among the countries in this category are Egypt, the Philippines, India, and Brazil. Industrializing economies are seeking, through private or government enterprise or a combination, to increase the amount of domestic manufacturing. There may be a variety of motives for industrializing, such as creating more employment, reducing dependence on imported manufactures, trying to earn the profits of processing raw materials, or seeking to develop into a military power. Regardless of the motive or the economic justification, these economies are not able to achieve mass manufacturing overnight. Their capital is limited by what they can earn through exporting raw materials, attracting tourists, and scaring up

[22] *Statistical Abstract of the United States, 1964,* pp. 906-907.
[23] Samuelson, *op. cit.,* pp. 777-78.

foreign aid. Mass manufacturing is further inhibited by the lack of skilled and educated manpower, power, communication and transportation facilities, and urban housing and amenities. Part of the developing nation's income, therefore, must be put into building social capital, which slows down the rate of manufacturing expansion. As manufacturing increases, the country relies more on imports of textile raw materials, steel, and heavy machinery, and less on imports of finished textiles, paper products, and automobiles. The industrialization tends to create a new rich class and a small but growing middle class, both demanding new types of goods, some of which can be satisfied only by imports.

Industrial economies. Industrial economies are those which have built up their industrial base to the extent that they become exporters of manufactured goods and investment funds. They trade manufactured goods among themselves and also export them to other types of economies in exchange for raw materials and semifinished goods. Some of them develop manufacturing specializations, and their goods in these specializations are known the world over: for example, Japan for cameras, toys, and electronic equipment; Switzerland for watches and candies; France for perfumes, linens, and wines; and so forth. The industrial economies also tend to build up sufficient capital reserves and skilled manpower to become promoters and partners in the efforts of other nations to industrialize. The large and varied manufacturing activities of these industrial nations and their sizeable middle class make them rich markets for all sorts of goods.

INCOME LEVEL AND DISTRIBUTION. A third factor of considerable influence is the level and distribution of national income. People must not only want goods but must have the ability to buy them. The industrial structure usually indicates something about the level and distribution of incomes, for higher incomes are usually associated with more advanced industrial structures. But there is sufficient variation even here to merit separate examination. Five different national income profiles can be distinguished:

Very low family incomes. Subsistence economies tend to be characterized by very low family incomes. The families spend long hours at hard work eking out a bare living from the soil. Starvation is an ever present threat. Home-grown food and home-made clothing and simple services, like blacksmithing and medicine, constitute the bulk of consumer goods and services.

Mostly low family incomes. Economies which are seeking industrialization along Marxist lines, such as Cuba and those in Eastern Europe, are typically characterized by low family incomes as the government bureaucrats force as much surplus from the working class as possible for capital formation. In the early stages, the bureaucrats themselves tend to live austerely and the whole consumer scene is characterized by drabness and uniformity in the available products. Most consumer goods are produced domestically by state-owned enterprises. These nations present some opportunities for trade, depending upon Cold War factors.

Very low, very high family incomes. Several countries of the world are characterized by extremes of income, where most of the population is very poor and a small minority is very rich. This income situation is often found in raw-material exporting economies (particularly in the

Middle East, Latin America, and colonial Africa) and in some of the industrializing nations. This makes the market for consumer goods very bizarre. The masses live on subsistence farming, supplemented by the import of needed foodstuffs and textiles, and the rich live on the import of expensive cars, appliances, and Western amenities.

Low, medium, high family incomes. Industrialization tends to be accompanied by the rise of a middle class, consisting of factory officials, office workers, commercial employees, and government bureaucrats. The very low- and very high-income classes tend to persist along with their distinct consumption patterns. The middle class is able to afford basic necessities and have some left over for such amenities as radios and small appliances for the lower-paid middle class and automobiles and expensive furniture for the higher-paid middle class. This national income profile characterizes many of the industrializing nations of the world and many of the advanced nations.

Mostly medium family incomes. The advanced industrial nations tend to develop institutions which reduce the extremes of incomes. Low incomes tend to decline as jobs and skills are upgraded, as workers organize into unions, and as governments adopt social security measures for old age and unemployment. High incomes and estates tend to diminish relatively through progressive income and estate taxes. The result is a very large and comfortable middle class confronted with a wide array of branded products, able to own automobiles and major appliances, as well as to enjoy leisure and take vacations. A distinction can be drawn between what Ernest Dichter calls "the almost classless society, contented countries," primarily Scandinavia, where there is much equalization of consumer goods and possessions and where utilitarian consumer values predominate, and "the affluent countries," primarily the United States, West Germany, Switzerland, Holland, and Canada, where there is greater individuality in product choice and where taste and status operate as important values.[24] Both types of economies offer the greatest opportunities for imported, mass-produced, consumer shopping and specialty goods, and these imports usually figure significantly in these markets.

CULTURAL CHARACTERISTICS AND TRADITIONS. Marketing opportunities in various countries are also shaped by the cultural characteristics and traditions of the people. It would be the height of folly to try to merchandise cosmetics on a mass scale in the Middle East or hamburgers in India. Such products are either taboo or would appeal only to a very small Westernized segment of the population. Even where taboos do not apply, some cultural habits may be difficult to break. According to Dichter, only one Frenchman out of three brushes his teeth, and only one German out of five changes his shirt more often than once a week.[25] Clearly, the markets for dental products and laundry detergents, respectively, are not as good as the size and incomes of the respective populations in these countries would indicate. Habits can be changed slowly over time by sustained industry-wide promotion, but in the meantime

[24] Ernest Dichter, "The World Customer," *Harvard Business Review,* July-August 1962, pp. 113-22.
[25] *Ibid.,* p. 113.

no one manufacturer can expect to change total demand significantly.

Culture affects not only the absolute size of the market but also relative preferences for competitive products. Too often the foreign operator fails to adapt his product's qualities and his marketing methods to the cultural tastes and patterns of the purchasing country. A director of the Nestlé Company recently said:

> It is evident that worldwide operations . . . cannot be successful if there is a tendency to exercise the individual characteristics, policies, and attitudes of one country and its nationals on all the others.[26]

American canned soups do not go over well (unless more spices are added) in Mexico, sex-appeal advertising does not work in Pakistan, and American-style back-slapping salesmanship gets a chilly reception in Great Britain. It is not just a matter of American culture versus European culture versus Latin American culture versus Eastern culture. Each country (and often groups within each country) has its own cultural dispositions, preferences, and bugaboos, and overlooking or ignoring them may be marketing suicide.[27]

The Marketing Environment

In trying to meet the needs of markets, a firm has to consider many factors affecting sales. Those which are under the firm's control can be called company *decision variables*. Those outside of the firm's control can be called *environmental variables*. The marketing environment is defined as the set of forces and institutions which affect the company but which are not affected by it.

Although the marketing environment cannot be controlled, no management can afford to ignore it. The environment defines the firm's opportunities and constraints. The firm must continuously adapt its policies to environmental trends if the policies are to be effective.

There are many ways to classify the complex outside forces and institutions affecting markets and marketing decisions. The environment is frequently factored into its demographic, economic, sociological, legal, and technological dimensions. We have already reviewed demographic and economic factors, and we will review legal factors in a later chapter.[28] Here we will explore three other important environmental forces—technology, trade channels, and American culture—and examine how they challenge marketing management.

TECHNOLOGY

Perhaps the most dramatic and cogent of all environmental forces facing the marketer, the one laden with the greatest opportunities and the greatest

---

[26] Eberhard Schmidt, in an address at the 13th International Management Congress, September 1963.

[27] Portraits of the cultural characteristics of different European nations as they affect marketing are found in Henry Deschampsneufs, *Selling in Europe* (London: Business Publications, Ltd., 1963). Cultural aspects of advertising in foreign countries are discussed in S. Watson Dunn, *The Handbook of International Advertising* (New York: McGraw-Hill Book Company, 1964).

[28] See Chapter 20.

threats, is the unprecedented pace of technological change. A top executive of the Chrysler Corporation put it this way:

> . . . the opportunities open to business management are more numerous than at any time in the past. And under these conditions there is always the possibility that a genius or a group of geniuses in somebody's planning staff, or tucked away in a laboratory, will come up with a new product idea or a new process that will put a company, even an entire industry, in jeopardy. . . . the manager, who has to relate his business strategy to all these changes, sometimes finds it pretty hard to play his cards . . . because every day he is dealt a new hand, every week he gets a new deck, and every month he finds himself sitting in on a new kind of game entirely.[29]

In the same vein, *Business Week*'s research department estimated as much as 20 per cent of the products in 1969 will not have been around in 1960.[30] This will mean the rise and fall of thousands of businesses, the lot falling to those whose managements were sensitive and imaginative enough to cope with technological change as a major environmental force.

MAJOR FEATURES OF THE TECHNOLOGICAL REVOLUTION. Technology is changing at such a rapid rate that it is difficult for scientists and engineers, let alone laymen and businessmen, to comprehend what various scientific breakthroughs mean and where they will lead. Three things, however, do stand out about this revolution:

All industries affected. No longer are there any industries which can safely assume that their products and technology will be the same twenty years from now. Today, innovations of major significance are occurring in every field of endeavor: electronics, chemistry, biology, architecture, mechanical engineering, hypersonics, meteorology, transportation, space science, military science, and so forth. What is more, these innovations feed upon each other. Every research discovery breeds new questions and leads to a chain reaction of still new discoveries. "The thing that seems to be happening in our time is that all the once widely separated avenues of scientific and technological knowledge are converging." [31]

Skyrocketing R&D budgets. One of the fastest growing budgets in this generation has been the research and development budget. In 1928, R&D expenditures totaled less than $100 million. By 1953, it had grown fifty times larger, to $5 billion, and by 1962, R&D stood at over $16 billion, or at 3 per cent of gross national product (GNP).[32] This rate of growth has been much faster than the growth of GNP.

The federal government is by far the largest supplier of R&D funds, and industry is by far the largest user. Almost 90 per cent of the funds go to applied R&D. The remainder is spent on basic research, almost half of which takes place in colleges and universities. Basic and applied research expenditures have tended to grow at roughly the same rate during the last decade.

---

[29] Robert Anderson, "Planning Profitable Products in a Changing Environment," a speech given at the Northwestern University Fall Management Conference, 1962.

[30] From *The Research Revolution,* by Leonard Silk, p. 230. Copyright 1960 by McGraw-Hill Book Company. Used by permission.

[31] *Ibid.,* p. 163.

[32] *Statistical Abstract of the United States, 1964,* p. 541.

The five industries spending the most on R&D (in billions of dollars) are aircraft and missiles ($4.2), electrical equipment and communication ($2.5), chemicals and allied products ($1.1), machinery ($0.9), and motor vehicles and other transportation ($0.9).[33] These five industries account for almost 60 per cent of total R&D expenditures and boast such research-minded firms as Aerojet-General, Du Pont, General Dynamics, General Electric, Minnesota Mining & Manufacturing, Pfizer, Searle, Texas Instruments, and so forth. The least R&D spending is found in such industries as lumber, wood products, furniture, textiles, apparel, and paper and allied products. Industries at the top range spend between 5 and 10 per cent of their sales dollars for R&D expenditures, and those in the lowest range spend less than 1 per cent of their sales dollar.[34]

Scientific team research. Today's research scene is marked by huge and expensive company research laboratories manned by dozens of company scientists. These laboratories are a comparatively new development on the industrial scene.

As late as the second half of the nineteenth century, new industrial discoveries were typically the accomplishment of isolated inventors—men like Samuel F. B. Morse, Alexander Graham Bell, and Thomas A. Edison. Then there began to appear in the United States, Great Britain, and particularly Germany, small industrial institutes and laboratories. The research in these laboratories was primarily of an applied nature, the goal being to develop better processes of manufacture. With the advent of World War II, research became marked by the drawing together of specialty scientists to develop nuclear reactors, synthetic rubber, and so forth. This continued in the postwar period in the form of larger research organizations, team research, and the inclusion of basic research aims.

MARKETING OPPORTUNITIES CREATED BY TECHNOLOGICAL ADVANCES. Some marketing men are undoubtedly unmoved by the picture of endless technological progress. They feel like the farmer who was invited to take courses in an agricultural college and declined, saying "I can't use half of the knowledge I have now." Yet this attitude may be fatal. One cannot afford to stand still while competitors search for new and better ways to do things. Marketing executives bear a special responsibility to keep abreast of the major opportunities being opened up by technological change.

One can distinguish between those innovations which have already appeared and those which are yet to come. Jet transports, earth satellites, atomic reactors, and electronic computers are all now part of the scene. Examine the following list of other major innovations and their rate of annual sales growth during the decade 1948-58: [35]

10 to 15 per cent per year	*15 to 20 per cent per year*
Automatic dishwashers	Food disposal units
Transparent film for packaging	Frozen foods
Home freezers	Automatic transmissions for
Sulfa drugs	automobiles

[33] *Ibid.,* p. 543.
[34] *Management of New Products* (New York: Booz, Allen & Hamilton, 1960), p. 5.
[35] Based on Silk, *op. cit.,* pp. 56-58.

20 to 30 per cent per year

    Polyvinyl resins
    Electric blankets
    Rayon and nylon cord
    DDT

30 to 40 per cent per year

    Synthetic fibers (except rayon)
    Electric dryers
    Automatic coffee makers
    Room air conditioners
    Tape recorders

40 or more per cent per year

    Transistors
    Titanium sponge
    Power steering
    Power brakes
    Antibiotics
    Television sets
    Polyethylene
    Styrene plastics and resins
    Vitamins
    Helicopters (nonmilitary)
    Synthetic rubber
    Synthetic detergents

As one scans the list, it becomes apparent that each innovation has created new businesses and weakened or destroyed old ones. This is why it is essential that management watch and correctly appraise technological change.

Many technological developments are still in the blueprint or testing stage, but they promise to become realities tomorrow. Long shots like small flying cars, lightweight one-man rocket belts, turbine-power automobiles, practical desalinization systems, counter-air-pollution systems, electronic refrigeration, nuclear-powered aircraft, food pills, and family computers await development by companies willing and able to gamble on them.[36] An astute student of the technological scene, James R. Bright, stated that the strongest technological trends were occurring in transportation, energy, organic- and inorganic-life research, new materials, instrumentation, mechanization of physical activities, and mechanization of intellectual activities. His detailed description of the specific types and means of advance, as well as the results, constitutes an excellent guide to new opportunities.[37]

Many innovations first occur in the course of research connected with national defense. The recent work on earth satellites and rockets has led to further miniaturization of computer systems, improved propellants and lubricants, new plastics, food pills, and improved materials for space suits.[38] The astute firm considers these items as "product fallout" and is quick to recognize their commercial applications.

The choice before most companies is to what extent they should pioneer innovations and to what extent they should follow the lead of others. Pioneering means making all the mistakes before the right combination is found. The costs of innovation are high, but the rewards are also high, for the innovator typically gains and holds the major share of the market (consider Du Pont and Texas Instruments, for example). For the most part, pioneering research is a gamble for the small firm and a sound investment for the large company. The small firm gambles a high proportion of its resources on one project, which may or may not make

---

[36] See Milton Greenberg, "As Technology Shapes Tomorrow," *Printers' Ink,* May 29, 1964, pp. 278-80.

[37] James R. Bright, "Opportunity and Threat in Technological Change," *Harvard Business Review,* November-December 1963, pp. 76-86.

[38] "Space Magic in the Marketplace," *Time,* September 24, 1965, p. 95.

it. The large firm sponsors hundreds of such projects and trusts to the "law of large numbers" to achieve results. Therefore, the amount of desirable pioneering research depends largely on the size of the company.

MARKETING CHANNELS

The marketer has to contend with continuous shifts and innovations in the area of marketing channels as well as the quickening pace of technological change. Contemporary distribution is marked by institutions and methods in retailing, wholesaling, and physical distribution which were not around a generation ago. In the past, many firms could chose their marketing channels and correctly assume they would remain suitable for years. Even today, many firms show a tendency to remain loyal to existing channels and to play down the importance of change, for it is very difficult in the midst of change to appraise the significance of new institutions. The typical firm prefers to follow Alexander Pope's advice: "Be not the first by whom the new are tried, Nor yet the last to lay the old aside." Although the firm cannot change its channels frequently, it should note whatever changes are taking place at every level of retailing, wholesaling, and physical distribution.

CHANGES IN RETAILING. Of all the changes in distribution during the last century, those taking place in retailing have been the most dramatic. Totally new institutions have appeared in an industry which a hundred years ago consisted only of small general and specialty stores.

Department stores first came on the American scene in the 1860's, about a decade after they started in Europe. They were made possible by the growing size of cities and improvements in street transportation.

Shortly thereafter, *mail-order houses,* such as Montgomery Ward (1872) and Sears Roebuck (1886), began. Their main success was in rural areas and small towns, because they were able to offer more extensive merchandise and better prices than the rural population could obtain from general stores. Their appearance around this date was made possible by the completion of the railroads and improvements in rural postal service.

During the 1920's, another important retailing trend began in the form of rapidly expanding *chain-store organizations*. During this decade, chain-store organizations increased their share of total retail sales from about 5 per cent to around 30 per cent. Their rapid growth during and since this period has been due to a number of factors. The nation was growing increasingly urbanized, and large urban areas made it possible for chain organizations to achieve many economies in warehousing, delivery, and advertising. These economies enabled them to charge lower prices, which stimulated their sales further. The growth of chain organizations has showed no signs of abating. According to one estimate, in 1940 about 400 giant retailers controlled about 50 per cent of the nation's total retail volume in their major merchandise categories; by 1962 growth of chains had further reduced the number to 100 giant retailers; and by 1970 this figure may well apply to only 40 giant retailers.[39] This endless growth of chain organizations, whether they represent consolidated ownership,

[39] E. B. Weiss, "The Shrinking Headquarters Target," *Sales Management,* July 6, 1962, pp. 44-48.

franchised operations, or chains of independents, has profound implications for the manufacturer, his customers, and his selling methods.

The principal retailing innovation in the 1930's was the *supermarket*. The supermarket introduced a number of principles of mass merchandising which cut costs and increased volume at a time when family incomes were strained. The original supermarkets, in fact, were physically unattractive, offering low prices and operating on a cash-and-carry basis. The supermarkets introduced the principle of self-service whereby the customer did the leg work, thus reducing personnel costs and increasing the volume of business which could be handled. Self-service undoubtedly increased the volume of impulse purchases and also made clear to manufacturers the need for more attractive packaging. Another principle was broader assortments of merchandise to attract a large number of customers. Supermarkets gradually discovered that they could sell profitably many things in addition to food, and the age of "scrambled merchandising" began. To support the larger stores and broader assortments, supermarkets adopted mass merchandise display and promotion techniques. The success of supermarkets was tremendous. One estimate holds that in 1922 a food producer's sales organization had to cover 300,000 food stores (run by about 250,000 "buying offices") to achieve 80 per cent distribution; today, the same producer only has to cover about 50,000 food stores (run by about 1,500 buying offices) to achieve 80 per cent distribution.[40] The growing concentration in supermarkets of the sale of food and other commodities has required radical changes in the sellers' sales organization.

The late 1940's were marked by the appearance of *planned suburban shopping centers*. These centers grew in response to the great migration to the suburbs, the increased ownership of automobiles, and the growing traffic congestion of downtown areas. Consumers like the idea of being able to park easily and satisfy all their shopping needs in one center. For the manufacturer, these centers meant new opportunities and new restrictions in selling their products. Located in middle-income markets, shopping centers became a great channel for many types of goods. At the same time, centers operated as integrated retail units, and it was not always easy to get goods into what might otherwise appear to be logical outlets. The manufacturer also became concerned with the implication of shopping centers for the future of downtown areas.

The growth of *discount houses* marked the major retailing development of the 1950's. Some appeared in the Thirties and again after World War II, but major expansion took place when discount houses began to merchandise nationally advertised hardgoods (appliances and other consumer durables) at considerable markdowns compared to conventional outlets. Their lower prices were made possible through higher volume, often direct buying, and a policy of minimum service. Customers, having by this time gained sufficient confidence in manufacturers' national brands to dispense with retailer services, enjoyed the price savings. Manufacturers, in turn, had excess capacity after the first postwar rush of buying subsided, and embraced these outlets as promising ways to dispose of surplus output. The mass merchandising tactics of the discounters (self-service, low prices, heavy promotion) caused the conventional outlets to lower

[40] *Ibid.*

their traditional markups and increase their promotion, all of which helped tremendously to stimulate demand. Eventually, an increasing number of the discount houses began to up-grade their services and decor, causing the distinction between them and department stores to narrow considerably.

The 1950's also marked a rapid expansion of *automatic merchandising.* Although vending machines had appeared as early as the 1880's, vending-machine sales grew at a faster rate than ever before during the 1950's. By 1964 their total sales reached $3.5 billion.[41] Their greatest volume is still in soft drinks, cigarettes, and candy. For these products, vending is an important channel, accounting for 28 per cent of all cigarette sales, 18 per cent of hot-drink sales, and 12 per cent of candy-bar sales.[42] Manufacturers need to watch for further innovations in vending equipment which might make them important channels for a whole slew of new products. Two companies recently licked the problem of how to make these machines change dollar bills, thus overcoming a long-time obstacle. Vending machines now merchandise fresh fruit, bread, eggs, hot soups, hot food, frozen foods, pastries, corsages, shoe shines, record albums, paperback books, stockings, and flight insurance. They are appearing with increasing frequency in industrial cafeterias (General Electric's main cafeteria at its Lynn, Massachusetts, plant relies mainly on vending machines to serve its 13,500 employees), hotel commissaries, railway dining cars, and gasoline stations. They offer the advantages of twenty-four-hour selling, lower prices, self-service, and less pilferage and damaged merchandise. Robot retailing has already been successfully applied to laundry and dry-cleaning establishments, and the next decade may mark the appearance of food outlets which are completely mechanized.[43] At least these are trends to which the manufacturers of convenience goods must pay close attention.

Other major developments in retailing have also challenged management's conventional methods of selling. *Trading stamps* have grown into a multimillion-dollar industry and moved from their original use in food outlets to instruments in the competition of gasoline stations, department stores, clothing stores, and, in one case, funeral parlors. An increasing number of stores are facing decisions on *night and Sunday openings* as the trend toward family shopping continues. *House-to-house selling* may be making a comeback through its successful use by such companies as Avon Products, Inc., and the principle is being extended by some firms to sell major and minor appliances. More people in the cities as well as urban areas are attempting to save shopping time by buying through the catalogs of giant mail-order houses; Sears alone sent out eleven million catalogs in one mailing in 1965. People are also attempting to conserve capital by renting instead of buying many types of durables through "rent-all" stores.

The retailing revolution is thus a many-faceted thing. It is a process of "creative destruction." Some of the changes in retail institutions, but not

---

[41] *Vending in 1964,* National Automatic Merchandising Association, Chicago, Illinois, 1965.

[42] *Ibid.*

[43] For some interesting prophecies in the area, see "The Robot Retailing Revolution" in E. B. Weiss, *Management and the Marketing Revolution* (New York: McGraw-Hill Book Company, 1964), chap. 5.

all of them, can be explained by the *wheel of retailing* hypothesis.[44] According to this hypothesis, many new types of retailing institutions first begin as low-status, low-margin, low-price operations. They become effective competitors of more conventional outlets, which have grown "fat" over the years. Their success gradually leads them to upgrade their facilities and proffer additional services. This increases their costs and forces price increases until they finally resemble the conventional outlets which they displaced. They, in turn, become vulnerable to still newer types of low-cost, low-margin operations. This wheel pattern appears to explain plausibly the original success and later troubles of department stores, supermarkets, and, more recently, discount houses. On the other hand, it does not explain the growth of suburban shopping centers and automatic retailing, both of which started out as high-margin and high-cost operations.

When new institutions first appear, the typical pattern is one of institutional *conflict* followed later by *accommodation*. The established institutions band together and use all their power to thwart the new institution. One thing they do is threaten to break off business relations with those who supply the new institution. This was the position in which national-brand appliance manufacturers found themselves when they started dealing with discount houses, milk producers when they allowed their brands to appear in vending machines, and drug manufacturers when they started to sell some of their products through food outlets. Another weapon of the established retailers is to lobby for restrictive legislation against the new retailing outlets. They try to pass laws placing special taxes on these organizations, or restricting their hours of operation, or preventing them from selling certain goods. These tactics, plus a great amount of scare propaganda, are used by vested retailing interests to destroy or slow down the growth of newer retailing institutions.

But the newer firms, where they represent a real advantage, generally survive this onslaught, and in the next phase the more progressive established firms begin to accommodate their selling methods to the new ones. They reduce their margins, cut down some of their frills, form chains, expand their parking space, and in general reduce the competitive advantage of the newer firms. In time, the differences between them grow very blurred.

One of the greatest evidences of this process of institutional accommodation in retailing is the increasing phenomenon of *scrambled merchandising,* which occurs when specific retailing institutions take on unconventional lines. They do this to improve their competitive appeal and to raise their profit margins. Many drugstores faced with the loss of much of their sales volume in beauty aids and health remedies have added such items as costume jewelry, toys, lounge furniture, electric shavers, and even movie cameras. Supermarkets have crossed over into records, hardware, drugs, and, in some cases, appliances. Some discount houses and department stores have been moving into supermarket operations.

Scrambled merchandising presents a major opportunity and a major

[44] Malcolm P. McNair, "Significant Trends and Developments in the Postwar Period," in *Competitive Distribution in a Free, High-Level Economy and Its Implications for the University,* ed. A. B. Smith (Pittsburgh: University of Pittsburgh Press, 1958), pp. 1-25. Also see the critical discussion by Stanley C. Hollander, "The Wheel of Retailing," *Journal of Marketing,* XXV (July 1960), 37-42.

headache for manufacturers. On the positive side, it means more product exposure than ever before. It also means lower retailer margins as the battle to sell these goods grows fiercer. Both factors stimulate sales. On the negative side, the manufacturer must deal with more channels, many of which are totally unfamiliar with how to merchandise the specific products. Where manufacturers of household tools formerly sold mainly through hardware wholesalers to hardware retailers, now they must also sell to department stores, variety stores, discount houses, automobile accessory stores, and even supermarkets and drugstores. This has considerably increased the size of the sales organization they need. Furthermore, they face opposition to every new channel from their established customers. They have to proceed cautiously in the terms they offer, lest the older channel members complain of favoritism. The total effect of scrambled merchandising has been to increase the need for multichannel management, with all its political and economic headaches.

Probably the most profound challenge of the changing retail scene for manufacturing firms stems from the trend toward *giant retailing*. An indication of the growing power of giant retailers was given earlier in the discussion of chain organizations. What this means is that the manufacturer has to sell to fewer and fewer accounts to achieve a substantial level of retail distribution. A positive benefit is that the manufacturer can reduce the size of his sales force and hence cut his selling costs.[45] But for this he pays a considerable price. In the first place, his future now rests on the treatment he receives from a small number of retailing organizations. Each account he gains or loses has a major impact in his revenue. In the second place, the manufacturer's salesman finds it harder to do effective selling; he deals with one buyer, but the chain's decisions are typically made by *buying committees*. The buyer, in fact, often has only a small influence over the final decision. Furthermore, the larger retailers will rely increasingly on *computer programs* to make the more routine buying decisions.[46] In the third place, many chains are turning increasingly to *private branding;* that is, selling products made by owned or controlled firms under its own brand name. Today, 90 per cent of Sears' total volume is in its own brands, and 25 per cent of A&P's volume is sold in this way. With fewer major retailers selling more and more output under their own brand names, the manufacturers of national brands face a real threat involving the very survival of manufacturers' brands.

CHANGES IN WHOLESALING. Changes in wholesaling have been less dramatic than changes in retailing, but no less important for the formulation of marketing channel policy. At one time wholesalers occupied the dominant position in the channels of most manufacturers. Most small manufacturers and small retailers could not operate without their services. As manufacturers and retailers grew in size, however, the larger ones were able to find ways to avoid or reduce the charges of wholesaling middlemen. During the 1920's, many thought that the majority of wholesalers were doomed

[45] Some manufacturers, such as Campbell's and Procter & Gamble, have decided to retain a large sales force or independent brokers to deal directly with the chains' individual stores for the purpose of achieving special merchandising cooperation and stimulation.

[46] "Now Retailers Put it All on Tape," *Business Week,* January 16, 1965, p. 31.

by the growth of chain operations. Wholesalers declined in relative importance from 1929 on, and did not regain their former relative position until as late as 1954.[47] Absolute wholesale sales volume has continued to grow, but in relative terms wholesalers have just been holding their own.

The wholesalers who passed out of existence or fell into deep trouble were typically those who failed to recognize and adapt to the continual and dramatic changes taking place in retailing, materials-handling technology, and manufacturers' new marketing policies. Many wholesalers had enjoyed a protected position in their areas and had grown "fat and lazy." Their main activities were to break bulk and fill customer orders, most of which did not result from any aggressive selling program. They tended to render similar services with similar charges to all customers, even though some customers wanted more services and others wanted less. It is understandable why both manufacturers and retailers continually sought ways to circumvent the wholesaler.

The progressive wholesalers were those who were willing to change their ways to meet the challenges of chain organizations, discount houses, and rising labor costs. This meant (1) seeking to adapt their services more to the wishes and needs of their customers and (2) seeking cost-reducing methods of transacting business. Wholesalers became much more selective in choosing their customers, preferring to drop those who appeared to be unprofitable according to an analysis of sales and service costs. They placed more emphasis on increasing order size and promoting the higher-turnover merchandise. They concentrated on customers with potentially good sales and increased the range of their management advisory services to help their customers do a better job. They offered assistance to customers in locating, leasing, designing, opening, and modernizing stores and in doing a better job of selling, advertising, promoting, and displaying their wares.[48] Progressive wholesalers selected their salesmen more carefully and gave them better training. Many wholesalers met the threat of chain organizations by organizing the smaller retailers into voluntary chains. Others met the challenge by becoming specialty wholesalers and taking on functions which neither manufacturers nor customers were performing.

An example of the challenge to independent wholesalers is found in the drug industry. The fortune of independent drug wholesalers is intimately bound with the fortune of independent retail druggists, who are meeting the roughest competition in years from discount houses, prescription mail-order companies, supermarkets, union stores, and membership clubs. According to E. B. Weiss:

> The drug wholesaler is just now beginning to comprehend that the old order in drug retailing is changing, and that he had better step up his own scope and pace of change. In the spring of 1962, less than five per cent of all drug wholesalers had started voluntary chains. A year later, that figure had doubled. . . . Some drug wholesalers are now arranging to finance new locations for independent druggists, especially in shopping center locations.

[47] Paul D. Converse, "Twenty-Five Years in Wholesaling: A Revolution in Food Wholesaling," *Journal of Marketing*, XXII (July 1957), 40-41.

[48] See Herman C. Nolan, "The Modern Wholesaler and His Adjustment to a Changing Economy," in *Successful Marketing: At Home and Abroad*, ed. W. David Robbins (Chicago: American Marketing Association, 1958).

A few drug wholesalers are opening jointly owned stores with independent druggists. Cash-and-carry drug wholesaling is being tested . . . private-brand development is being stepped up by some drug wholesalers . . . the cost-plus wholesaler has also made his appearance in drug wholesaling.[49]

To meet the challenge of rising costs, alert wholesalers have been making time and motion studies of materials-handling procedures. An executive at McKesson & Robbins, Inc., a large drug wholesaler, reported that work-simplification studies alone enabled his company to handle one-third more tonnage with 9 per cent fewer persons on the payroll.[50] In addition, wholesalers are adopting new materials-handling equipment. The ultimate development is the automated warehouse, where the orders are key punched on tabulating cards which are then fed into a computer. The items are picked up by mechanical devices and conveyed on a belt to the shipping platform where they are assembled.[51] This type of mechanization is progressing rapidly, and so is the mechanization of many office activities. Many wholesalers are turning to electronic data processing to carry out such functions as accounting, billing, inventory control, and forecasting, and they are alert to other technological developments which save office costs.

CHANGES IN PHYSICAL DISTRIBUTION.   In addition to changes in the structure of retailing and wholesaling, the marketing policies of manufacturers are affected by a host of developments and trends in the area of physical distribution. These developments, especially in transportation, communication, materials handling, and information processing, continue to spell new opportunities for marketing management, and in some cases new problems.

Developments in the area of *transportation* have always presented marketing management with new chances for profit. At one time, producers had to depend mainly on the railroads, and to a lesser extent on the waterways, to serve distant markets. Train schedules were slow, necessitating larger inventories at distant points from the plants. The advent of trucks and the steady improvement of highways changed all this. The manufacturer could penetrate new sales areas formerly not accessible by railway and in many cases could ship his goods with more speed. The advent of airfreight opened still further opportunities for speed and profit. In the face of these developments, the railroads lost a lot of potential revenue and began to recognize the need to innovate. New cars were designed to facilitate the transportation of particular products, such as automobiles, oil, grains, perishable goods, and so forth. Train schedules were improved, and often freight charges were cut to meet competition. Today, most modes of transportation are highly competitive and in-

---

[49] From *Management and the Marketing Revolution,* by E. B. Weiss, pp. 75-76. Copyright 1964 by McGraw-Hill Book Company. Used by permission.

[50] Nolan, *op. cit.*

[51] See Stuart Shryer, "Automated Order Picking," *Food Business,* November 1960; "Mail Order House Spends $3-Million to Save Money," *Business Week,* January 27, 1962; and "Bulk Picking, Electronic Sorting Spell Fast Service for Catalog Customers," *Modern Materials Handling,* January 1960. All are reprinted in Section V of *Contemporary American Marketing,* eds. Harper W. Boyd and Richard M. Clewett (Homewood, Ill.: Richard D. Irwin, Inc., 1962).

novative and constitute an area which marketing management will want to watch carefully.

Advances in *communication* must also be studied for the opportunities they present to increase sales and cut costs. A large company may have factories, warehouses, and branch sales offices scattered throughout the country. The speed of communication can be an important factor in apprising branch offices of new sales opportunities and in keeping down inventory costs. On routine matters company officers keep in touch through the mail and on more urgent matters through the telephone or tele-type machine. Advances in communication are also making it possible to conduct closed-circuit conferences among company executives in different locations and to exchange large amounts of data speedily through hookups of company computers in different locations.

Materials handling is also undergoing many changes which make it possible for companies to fill more orders faster at a substantially lower cost. Earlier we referred to the automated warehouse as an example. In the same connection, the automation of accounting, billing, and inventory control through electronic data processing is a powerful factor in cutting physical distribution costs and improving management control.

CULTURE

More than ninety years ago the English anthropologist Edward B. Tylor defined culture as "that complex whole which includes knowledge, belief, art, morals, law, custom, and any other capabilities and habits acquired by man as a member of society." [52] Tylor's definition is classic in defining some of the major facets of culture and emphasizing that culture is something learned.

Most Americans know how to speak English, handle money, turn on a television set, tie a shoelace, shake hands, write letters, dance a waltz, hold a fork, pay income tax, shop in a supermarket, and read a newspaper. These seem easy and natural. Yet people from quite a different society would be confused by these customs just as we would be confused if we saw them rub noses, pierce lips, fast regularly, eat insects, and speak incomprehensibly. Culture comprises the way in which we do things, see things, use things, and judge things, and this varies from society to society.

Culture used to change slowly, for it expressed the people's long-term response to their physical environment and experiences. A man who awoke in his society after twenty years of sleep would find it much the same. This is not true of modern societies whose culture, especially material culture, changes at such a rapid rate that a modern Rip Van Winkle would be utterly confused when he awoke.

Even some of the basic values and ideas of a people—the nonmaterial aspects of culture—undergo observable transformations through time. Consider some of the major shifts which seem to be taking place in American values:

self-reliance ⟶ government reliance
"hard work" as a
good in itself ⟶ the "easy life"

[52] Edward B. Tylor, *Primitive Culture* (London: John Murray, Ltd., 1871), p. 1.

religious convictions ⟶ secular convictions
husband-dominated home ⟶ wife-dominated home
parent-centered household ⟶ child-centered household
respect for individual ⟶ dislike of individual
               differences
postponed gratification ⟶ immediate gratification
saving ⟶ spending
sexual chastity ⟶ sexual freedom
parental values ⟶ peer group values
independence ⟶ security

This is not the place to judge these changes, if indeed they are actually taking place to a significant degree. The major point is that the ideas and values of a people, especially in a modern society, can undergo change even within a generation. These changes can have profound significance for the marketing of goods and services. To see this, we shall examine more closely four evolving values in American culture: leisure preference, hedonism, other-direction, and security.

LEISURE PREFERENCE—THE SOFT LIFE. Americans no longer have to spend all their hours at work in order to buy basic necessities. They are enjoying a growing surplus of discretionary time. As the amount of discretionary time increases, however, the number of tempting ways to use this time seems to increase even faster. People want more time for reading, traveling, listening to music, golfing, and pursuing hobbies. Hence, we find the paradox of a growing feeling of time scarcity in the midst of increased leisure.

Some marketing experts believe that Americans will increasingly place more value on time than on goods.[53] Doctors and other professionals often take month-long vacations, although this means giving up a large income. New job applicants often turn down jobs with higher pay for ones which will keep them in the office only until 5 P.M. Housewives generally want to purchase appliances that reduce household chores, because they no longer feel the value of their time is zero.

The marketing significance of this cultural shift to leisure preference is at once apparent. Anything the seller can do to increase convenience, to simplify a chore, to save the customer time may give the company an important competitive edge. Manufacturers and retailers in the food industry have responded with frozen and convenience foods, night hours, checking services, larger parking areas, and faster check-out service. Retailers in other lines have increased their mail-order and home-shopping services. Industrial marketers have turned to selling systems rather than individual items to save the buyer time and simplify his decision making.

Saving the customer time is only one of the marketing opportunities posed by this trend. Another one is to create goods and services for filling his time. Nelson Foote pointed out that General Electric has its foot in both doors. "Time gained from a dishwasher allows more hours at the TV set." [54] The consumer's growing wish to use his time for relaxation, edification, and sociability will spell a bright future for the sale of such

[53] See the remarks of Ferdinand F. Mauser and Nelson N. Foote, quoted in "The New Strategy: Try to Beat the Clock," *Business Week*, February 14, 1964, pp. 50-51.
[54] *Ibid.*, p. 51.

goods as sports equipment, television and tape recorders, vacation-related goods and services, and books and records.

HEDONISM—THE SWEET LIFE.   What does the modern American want out of life? There is a distinct movement away from ascetic and puritanical life values toward a pure-and-simple hedonism. Americans want to have fun, to have a good time, and to have it now. They hate the idea of postponing their gratification, of saving when the future is so uncertain. They will take vacations on a "fly now-pay later" basis, incur large debts in order to drive a sports car or own a boat. The accent of American culture is on being young and enjoying life. Adult Americans would like to live like their children, carefree, with a plenitude of amusements and lots of activity and sociability. They want to keep slim, dine out, take exotic vacations, spend freely, live high, and keep their hair from turning gray.

All this will mean a boom for the producers of the accoutrements of hedonistic living—swimming suits and sports wear, fine evening wear, personal-care items, sport cars, hi-fi sets, and color television. It also suggests the themes which are likely to be effective in merchandising and advertising: youth, good grooming, romance, virility. The great success of the "Playboy" theme attests to an age of increasing interest in high living.

OTHER-DIRECTION—THE SOCIABLE LIFE.   Where do Americans get their sense of values, the sense of what is important in life? The answer of course is complex, but over a decade ago the sociologist David Riesman and his collaborators claimed that the major source of personal values was changing.[55] In the past, Riesman argued, Americans largely adopted the values and goals of their parents. People were inner-directed in that they absorbed the strongest formative influence from the home. The values of their parents were internalized and acted like a "psychological gyroscope" to guide the inner-directed persons through difficult decisions and social relationships. Inner-direction was most clearly exemplified by "the banker, the tradesman, the small entrepreneur, . . . the technically oriented engineer . . ." [56]

Now this is changing. Urbanization, suburbanization, and high mobility mean that Americans are living in closer quarters, and are exposed to more new people than ever before. Affluence means a decline in the motifs of hard work, self-discipline, and thrift. Leisure means more time to be with other people. In this environment, people are becoming "other-directed." They increasingly assimilate the values of their contemporaries —neighbors, friends and associates. They find it more important to come to terms—harmonious terms—with other people than to maintain or defend any rigid ethos or prejudices inherited from their parents.

Of particular interest is the fact that inner- and other-directed types show different patterns of consumer behavior. Says Riesman:

> . . . the inner-directed person's energy was channeled relentlessly into production. Inner-directed patterns often discouraged consumption for

[55] David Riesman, Nathan Glazer, and Reuel Denney, *The Lonely Crowd,* abridged ed. (Garden City, N.Y.: Doubleday & Company, Inc., 1956). Quoted by permission of Yale University Press.
[56] *Ibid.,* p. 36.

adults as well as children. But at other times, and especially in the higher social strata less affected by Puritan asceticism, the inner-directed person consumed—with time out, so to speak, for saving and for good behavior— as relentlessly as he (or his progenitors) produced. Most clearly in the case of upper-class conspicuous consumption, he lusted for possessions and display, once the old tradition-directed restraints had worn away. He pursued clear acquisition and consumption goals with a fierce individualism. . . . These relatively stable and individualistic pursuits are today being replaced by the fluctuating tastes which the other-directed person accepts from his peer-group. . . . He is kept within his consumption limits not by goal-directed but by other-directed guidance, kept from splurging too much by fear of others' envy, and from consuming too little by his own envy of the others.[57]

Other-direction suggests a number of things to marketers. It suggests the possible greater effectiveness of using social appeals instead of individualistic appeals to advertise company products.[58] It suggests the desirability of concentrating advertising on taste and opinion leaders rather than diffusing it to everyone. It suggests the possible greater effectiveness of personal over impersonal selling methods.

All of these of course have to be qualified because a culture is never homogeneous—it contains its own contradictions and deviants. Marketers should not forget the significant minority who are indifferent to or who react against the prevailing trends. Although a great many people use goods to obtain social acceptance, others see goods as ways to achieve personal differentiation. The urge to differentiate oneself is always present, in spite of a strong desire to be accepted.

SECURITY—THE SAFE LIFE.   Although the average American enjoys more security than ever in the past, security remains one of his greatest concerns. He is haunted by the spectre of the Bomb, by aggressive communism, by racial tension. On a more personal level, he worries about the effect of illness or inflation on his savings, the cost of educating his children, the possibility of an economic recession, the burdens of old age. The effects of these uncertainties are not uniform. Some people are driven into more conservative politics and would like to turn the clock back to a mythical past. Others react to insecurity by favoring stronger programs of government welfare. Some react by enjoying life now, while others count their pennies and put them carefully into insurance and mutual funds. Some turn to escapist entertainment, small talk, and "commoditism"—a heightened, almost fetishistic interest in goods. To reduce the amount of insecurity others turn to positive efforts by joining the Peace Corps, entering politics, giving substantial sums to charity.

In an age of insecurity, people look for symbols to give them confidence and a feeling of continuity. The growth of bigness in government, in business, and in education is helped along by the tendency to equate bigness and security. General Motors, General Electric, and Sears are patronized by increasing numbers of people who want to feel secure about the products they purchase and the organization from which they purchase them.

[57] *Ibid.,* p. 100.
[58] Harold H. Kassarjian, "Social Character and Differential Preference for Mass Communication," *Journal of Marketing Research,* May 1965, pp. 146-53.

The significance of this cultural theme for marketers is clear. In their product planning, advertising, and other marketing efforts, companies should strive for a reputation and image of dependability. People do not want their lives further complicated by uncertainties about product or company performance.

Summary

The firm hoping to make a successful adaptation to marketing opportunities must understand the characteristics of different major markets and environmental forces. Several trends characterize American consumers, particularly the growing population, changing age structure, high mobility, and rising income, educational, and leisure levels. Business buyers tend to differ from household buyers in being oriented toward profit rather than satisfaction, showing more skill in buying, being both larger and more concentrated geographically, and being more influenced by the level of economic activity. Marketing opportunities in foreign countries are influenced by population, industrial structure, income levels, and cultural traits. Many foreign markets present extremely attractive opportunities, but they must be approached judiciously in view of their varying political, social, and marketing practices.

The marketing environment includes such basic factors as technology, marketing channels, and culture. The current technological revolution affects all industries; it is resulting in skyrocketing research and development budgets and spurring new forms of team research. Each company must define how market-oriented its research should be, what research areas are most promising, and whether it wants to lead or follow in technological development. A distribution revolution is also taking place—in retailing, wholesaling, and physical distribution. Although each firm can change its marketing channels only slowly, it must constantly be alert to changes. Finally, trends in American culture toward the soft, sweet, sociable, safe life have profound import for marketing opportunity and policy.

Questions and Problems

1. Per capita incomes have steadily risen in America. The per capita figure, however, overlooks the distribution of income. What seems to be happening to the distribution of income in the United States? How does the distribution affect the demand for various types of consumer products?

2. Choose one of the major business divisions listed in Table 2-1. Do some research on the number of buying concerns in this business division, their size distribution, geographical concentration, what and how they buy. List the

major developments which may have implications for those who sell to firms in this business division.

3. Do you believe that business buyers are more "rational" than household buyers?

4. Does American business appear to be taking full advantage of the marketing opportunities in foreign markets? How important is it for American businessmen to participate vigorously in foreign markets?

5. Technological change clearly creates new opportunities for a company. It also creates new threats. In what sense? What are some of the major tensions between company engineer-scientists and company marketing executives?

6. Do you agree that the cultural trends cited in this chapter are taking place? Does it follow that firms should move with majority values?

chapter 3

Market Segmentation

In the previous chapter we described features of markets and the marketing environment which are largely beyond the control of the individual firm. They constitute the raw forces that define the firm's opportunities and constraints. The challenge for the individual firm is to make an intelligent adaptation to these forces, for it does have some latitude in choosing markets and marketing policies. In this chapter we shall examine how the firm may achieve some control over its future through proper analysis and selection of its markets.

The first section discusses the nature of market segmentation. The second describes the major bases available for segmenting a market. The third discusses three major alternative strategies a company can adopt toward market segments. The final section explores how the firm can evaluate the attractiveness of different segments of the market.

Meaning of Market Segmentation

Whenever a market for a product or service consists of two or more buyers, the market is capable of being segmented; that is, divided into meaningful buyer groups. The purpose of segmentation is to determine differences among buyers which may be consequential in choosing among them or marketing to them.

DIFFERENT WAYS TO SEGMENT A MARKET

Figure 3-1a shows a market consisting of six buyers before it is segmented. The maximum number of segments a market can consist of is the total number of buyers constituting the market. Each buyer is a separate market in principle, because his needs and desires are unique. Ideally, a seller might study each buyer in order to tailor the best marketing program to his needs. Where there are only a few customers this is to some extent possible. For example, the major producers of airplanes face only a few buyers and treat them as separate markets. This ultimate degree of market segmentation is illustrated in Figure 3-1b.

Most sellers do not find it worthwhile to study every individual buyer and "customize" the product to satisfy each buyer's individual needs. Instead, the seller generally searches for broad classes of buyers who differ in product interests or marketing susceptibilities. For example, the seller may discover that product interests or marketing susceptibilities vary among different income groups. In Figure 3-1c, a number (1, 2, or 3) is used to

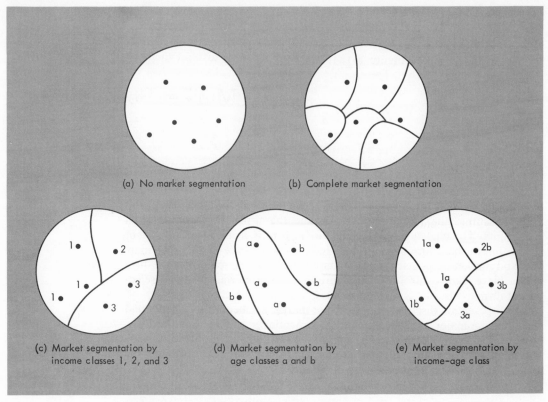

(a) No market segmentation   (b) Complete market segmentation

(c) Market segmentation by income classes 1, 2, and 3

(d) Market segmentation by age classes a and b

(e) Market segmentation by income-age class

FIGURE 3-1
Different approaches to market segmentation

identify each buyer's income class. Lines are drawn around buyers in the same income class. Segmentation by income class results in three segments, the most numerous one being income Class 1 in the illustration.

On the other hand, the seller may find pronounced differences in buyer behavior between younger and older buyers. In Figure 3-1d, the same individuals are shown, except a letter (a or b) is used to indicate the buyer's age class. Segmentation of the market by age class results in two segments, both equally numerous.

It may turn out that income class and age class both count heavily in differentiating the buyer's behavior toward the product. The seller may find it desirable to partition the market according to those joint characteristics. In terms of the illustration, the market can be broken into the following six segments: 1a, 1b, 2a, 2b, 3a, and 3b. Figure 3-1e shows that segment 1a contains two buyers, segment 2a contains no buyers (a null segment), and each of the other segments contains one buyer. In general, as the market is segmented on the basis of a larger set of joint characteristics, the seller achieves finer precision in his segmentation, but this is at the price of multiplying the number of segments. If the seller tried to segment the market using all conceivable characteristics, he would arrive at Figure 3-1b again, where each buyer would be a separate segment.

How can the seller determine which buyers' characteristics produce the best partitioning of a particular market? The seller does not want to treat all the customers alike (Figure 3-1a), nor does he want to treat them all differently (Figure 3-1b). The usefulness of particular characteristics for segmentation purposes increases as certain conditions are approached.

The first condition is *measurability,* the degree to which information exists or is obtainable on various buyers' characteristics. Unfortunately, many suggestive characteristics are not susceptible to easy measurement. Thus it is hard to measure the respective number of automobile buyers who are motivated primarily by considerations of economy versus status versus quality.

The second condition is *accessibility,* the degree to which the firm can effectively focus its marketing efforts on chosen segments. This is not possible with all segmentation variables. It would be nice if advertising could be directed mainly to opinion leaders, but their media habits are not always distinct from those of opinion followers.

The third condition is *substantiality,* the degree to which the segments are large enough to be worth considering for separate marketing cultivation. A segment should be the smallest unit for which it is practical to tailor a separate marketing program. Segmental marketing is expensive, as we shall shortly see. It probably would not pay, for example, for an automobile manufacturer to develop special seats for midgets.

BENEFITS OF SEGMENTATION

The seller who is alert to the needs of different market segments may gain in three ways. First, *he is in a better position to spot and compare marketing opportunities.* He can examine the needs of each segment against the current competitive offerings and determine the extent of current satisfaction. Segments with relatively low levels of satisfaction from current offerings may represent excellent marketing opportunities. Second, *the seller can use his knowledge of the marketing response differences of the various market segments to guide the allocation of his total marketing budget.* The ultimate bases for meaningful segmentation are differences in customer response to different marketing tools.[1] These response differences become the basis for deciding on the allocation of company marketing funds to different customers.[2] Third, *the seller can make finer adjustments of his product and marketing appeals.* Instead of one marketing program aimed to draw in all potential buyers (the "shotgun" approach), the seller can create separate marketing programs aimed to meet the needs of different buyers (the "rifle" approach). More will be said about this later.

Bases for Segmenting Markets

Income class and age class were just cited as two useful segmentation variables. In fact, the most frequently used market segmentation variables are

[1] William F. Massy and Ronald E. Frank, "Short Term Price and Dealing Effects in Selected Market Segments," *Journal of Marketing Research,* May 1965, pp. 171-85, especially pp. 178-79.
[2] See Chapter 12, pp. 274-78.

TABLE 3-1

Some segmentation variables and their typical breakdowns

Variables	Typical breakdowns
Socioeconomic	
Age	1-4; 5-10; 11-18; 19-34; 35-49; 50-64; 65+
Sex	Male; female
Family size	1; 2-3; 4-5; 6+
Income	Under $5,000; $5,000-$7,999; $8,000 and over
Occupation	Professional, executive, and business; clerical and sales; crafts and operatives; all others
Education	Completed less than 5 years; 5-7 years; 8 years; 9-11 years; 12 years; 13-15 years; 16 years +
Family life cycle	Young, single; young, married, no children; young, married, youngest child under six; young, married, youngest child six or over; older, married, with children; older, married, no children under 18; older, single; other
Religion	Catholic; Protestant; Jewish; other
Race	White; Negro; Oriental
Nationality	American; British; French; German; Eastern European; Scandinavian; Italian; Spanish; Latin American; Middle Eastern; etc.
Social Class	Lower-lower; upper-lower; lower-middle; middle-middle; upper-middle; lower-upper; upper-upper
Geographic	
Region	Pacific; Mountain; West North Central; West South Central; East North Central; East South Central; South Atlantic; Middle Atlantic; New England
County size	A; B; C; D
City size	Under 5,000; 5,000-20,000; 20,000-50,000; 50,000-500,000; 500,000+
Density	Urban; suburban; rural
Climate	Northern; southern
Personality	
Compulsiveness	Compulsive; noncompulsive
Gregariousness	Extrovert; introvert
Autonomy	Dependent; independent
Conservatism	Conservative; liberal; radical
Authoritarianism	Authoritarian; democratic
Leadership	Leader; follower
Ambitiousness	High achiever; low achiever
Buyer Behavior	
Usage rate	Nonuser; light user; medium user; heavy user
Buyer class	Unaware; aware; interested; intending to try; trier; regular buyer
Buyer motive	Economy; status; dependability
End use	(Varies with the product)
Brand loyalty	Brand A; Brand B; Brand C
Channel loyalty	Store D; Store E; Store F
Degree of loyalty	None; light; strong
Price sensitivity	Indifferent; low price sensitivity; high price sensitivity
Service sensitivity	Indifferent; low service sensitivity; high service sensitivity
Advertising sensitivity	Indifferent; low advertising sensitivity; high advertising sensitivity

socioeconomic ones, such as age, sex, income level, education, and occupation. In many cases they are used because they have proved to be good predictors of differential buyer response. In some cases, they are used because they are the only variables for which data are available. It would be unfortunate, however, if sellers considered only these variables in breaking down their markets.[3] A large number of other types of variables can also serve as useful bases for segmenting a market. Some of them are listed in Table 3-1.

Not all segmentation variables are appropriate for every market. Industrial markets are usually segmented on such bases as customer size, location, industrial classification, and usage rate. Consumer markets are usually segmented on such bases as income, age, and family size. Additional variables are brought in when they can shed further light. In fact, creative market segmentation involves the search for new ways to segment established markets, in the hope of discovering fresh marketing opportunities.

SOCIOECONOMIC VARIABLES

Socioeconomic variables have long been the most popular bases for distinguishing significant groupings in the market place. One reason is that these variables correlate well with the sales of many products; another reason is that they are easier to recognize and measure than most other types of variables.

The following example shows how a manufacturer of margarine can segment the market in terms of socioeconomic variables. Suppose that the company's market research reveals significant differences in the purchase rate of margarine by age of head of household, size of family, and level of income. Figure 3-2 shows a joint segmentation of the market according to these variables. Each variable is subdivided into the number of levels deemed useful for analysis; the result is 36 ($4 \times 3 \times 3$) distinct segments. Every family using margarine belongs to one of these 36 segments. Having conceptualized the market in this way, management can proceed to determine the varying profit potential of each segment. This involves estimating for each segment the number of families, the average purchase rate, and the extent of competition. These pieces of information can be combined to estimate the value of each segment.

GEOGRAPHIC VARIABLES

Most sellers recognize geographic variations within their market. A small retailer may distinguish between neighborhood customers and more distant customers. A local fertilizer salesman may distinguish between city customers and rural customers. A regional manufacturer in the West may distinguish between northern and southern California customers. A national manufacturer will classify his customers by sales territory. In all these cases, the geographical units become the bases of differentiated marketing effort.

PERSONALITY VARIABLES

For some products and brands, personality variables may lie at the bottom of differences in buyer behavior. For example, it has been argued

---

[3] See Daniel Yankelovich, "New Criteria for Market Segmentation," *Harvard Business Review,* March-April 1964, pp. 83-90.

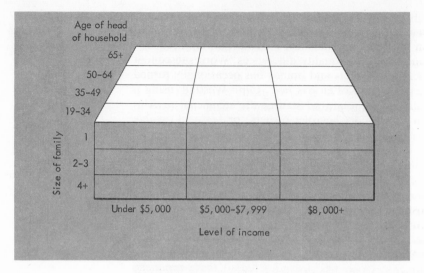

Age of head
of household

Size of family

Level of income

FIGURE 3-2
Segmentation of the margarine market by three socioeconomic variables

that different personalities are attracted to buying Ford versus Chevrolet automobiles. Ford owners have been described in opinion surveys as "independent, impulsive, masculine, alert to change, and self-confident, while Chevrolet owners are conservative, thrifty, prestige-conscious, less masculine, and seeking to avoid extremes." [4]

Franklin B. Evans set out to investigate these alleged personality differences in the late Fifties.[5] He collected psychological test information as well as socioeconomic information on 146 owners of 1955-58 Chevrolets and Fords in Park Forest, Illinois. Each owner took the Edwards Personal Preference test, which attempts to measure one's need for achievement, deference, exhibition, autonomy, affiliation, intraception, dominance, abasement, change, aggression, and heterosexuality. Evans examined the differences between the group means of Ford and Chevrolet owners for each psychological need and found that only one need, dominance, yielded a difference which appeared statistically significant (Ford owners exhibited the greater need). Otherwise he concluded that "the distributions of scores for all needs overlap to such an extent that discrimination is virtually impossible."

Critics have disputed Evans' conclusion because of his small and highly localized sample, his choice of the Edwards psychological test, and his statistical methodology.[6] Advertising agency men especially believe personality factors operate in many brand choices. The theory behind the ad-

[4] Quoted in Franklin B. Evans, "Psychological and Objective Factors in the Prediction of Brand Choice; Ford versus Chevrolet," *Journal of Business,* October 1959, pp. 340-69.

[5] *Ibid.*

[6] See the following articles in the *Journal of Business:* Gary A. Steiner, "Notes on Franklin B. Evans' 'Psychological and Objective Factors in the Prediction of Brand Choice,'" January 1961, pp. 57-60; Charles Wineck, "The Relationship Among Personality Needs, Objective Factors, and Brand Choice: A Re-examination," January 1961, pp. 61-66; Franklin B. Evans, "You Still Can't Tell a Ford Owner from a Chevrolet Owner," January 1961, pp. 67-73; Alfred A. Kuehn, "Demonstration of a Relationship between Psychological Factors and Brand Choice," April 1963, pp. 237-41; and Franklin B. Evans and Harry V. Roberts, "Fords, Chevrolets, and the Problem of Discrimination," April 1963, pp. 242-49.

vertising of such products as Smirnoff vodka and Schweppes tonic water is an appeal to special personality types. Yet the final proof of the extent of personality segmentation must rest on statistical evidence. Sorely needed is a better set of tests for measuring personality differences. Work subsequent to Evans on a wide variety of products and brands has occasionally turned up personality differences but more often has not. Ralph Westfall, using a somewhat amended methodology, found no statistically significant personality differences between Ford and Chevrolet owners, or between owners of standard and compact cars. He did find some evidence of personality differences, however, between the owners of convertibles and nonconvertibles, the former appearing to be more active, impulsive, and sociable.[7] The Advertising Research Foundation was not able to discern significant personality differences among the purchasers of toilet tissue.[8] Tucker and Painter found some statistically significant but weak personality correlations for nine products in their study.[9]

These research studies are not directed at whether products and brands have different images—the evidence suggests that many of them do—but whether different consumer personalities are attracted to these products. Each product must be studied separately for the possible strength of personality factors in purchase behavior. The theoretical connections between product images and personality types remain to be worked out better.

Even where evidence is found of personality differences in purchase behavior, the implications for marketing strategy are far from clear. Suppose Ford really did attract more "independent, impulsive, masculine" owners. Should Ford intensify its efforts to attract this personality type, in which case it would deepen its dominance in this segment, or should Ford make a pitch to the more "conservative, prestige-conscious, less masculine" personality type to attract away Chevrolet owners? These alternatives will have fundamentally different long-range effects on Ford, and warrant a most searching analysis.

BUYER BEHAVIOR VARIABLES

Variables which describe one aspect or another of the buyer's relation to a specific product may be called buyer behavior variables. Variables such as usage rate, buyer motive, brand loyalty, and the like can be quite useful in segmenting a market.

USAGE RATE. A seller often finds it useful to subdivide people into *nonusers, light users,* and *heavy users* of his product. The nonusers in turn comprise two types of people, those who generally do not use this product (nonpotential users) and those who might use the product (potential users).

Caution should be exercised before writing off people as nonpotential users. Some individuals within a group may behave exceptionally. Some women smoke pipes, some indigent people buy Cadillacs, and some middle-aged men ride motor scooters. However, they are often too few to matter.

[7] Ralph Westfall, "Psychological Factors in Predicting Product Choice," *Journal of Marketing,* XXVI (April 1962), 34-40.

[8] *Are There Consumer Types?* (New York: Advertising Research Foundation, 1964).

[9] W. T. Tucker and John J. Painter, "Personality and Product Use," *Journal of Applied Psychology,* October 1961, pp. 325-29.

Second, the group itself may change over time from a nonpotential user status to a potential or actual user status. The classic example of this is when women began to smoke cigarettes. The final caution is that nonpotential users may nevertheless be buyers. This happens in gift giving and also occurs when a user asks a nonuser to make the purchase, sometimes leaving the brand choice up to him.

As for potential users, they can be defined as people who do not now use the product but who are not barred from its use for any functional, cultural, or economic reason. The potential users of cigarettes are adults who do not smoke, and the potential users of expensive sport cars are the financially able who do not have them. People may be in the status of potential users for a number of reasons including ignorance of the product, inertia, or psychological resistance. The possible causes of potential buyer status must be carefully distinguished by the firm interested in converting potential users to actual users. Ignorance of the product calls for extensive information dissemination; inertia calls for repetitive advertising; and psychological resistance calls for subtle thematic advertising designed to overcome resistance.

Actual users themselves can be separated into light users and heavy users, and an effort should be made to determine what, if any, differences exist between the two groups. Some consumer panel data on usage rates for popular consumer products are shown in Figure 3-3.[10] Using lemon-lime as an example, the chart shows that 42 per cent of the panel members did not use this beverage. The 58 per cent who did were ranked from low to high in their usage rates. The lower 29 per cent were classified as light users and accounted for only 9 per cent of the total sales volume. The heavy half accounted for 91 per cent of the sales volume; that is, for ten times as many sales as the light users. Looking at the other products, we see that in virtually all cases heavy product users bought between four and ten times as much as light product users. Clearly, a seller would prefer to attract one heavy user to his brand over a light user, or even a couple of light users. Unfortunately, this segmentation variable is easy to appreciate but difficult to implement. Socioeconomic and personality characteristics have tended to be rather weak in distinguishing light users from heavy users, although the seller who can unlock the key has a great advantage over his competitors.[11]

BUYERS' MOTIVES.   Since a product can satisfy a variety of needs and motives, it is sometimes useful to divide the market for the product according to which motive may predominate. Figure 3-4 shows the (hypothetical) importance of three different motives—economy seeking, status seeking, and quality seeking—in the purchase of automobiles. However, some cautions must be observed. Undoubtedly other motives operate in individuals when they consider the purchase of an automobile. Furthermore, the individual rarely tries to satisfy only one motive; he is more often trying to

[10] See Dik Warren Twedt, "How Important to Marketing Strategy Is the 'Heavy User'?" *Journal of Marketing,* XXVIII (January 1964), 71-72.

[11] A new service called the Brand Rating Index may represent the long-awaited breakthrough in measuring the characteristics of the heavier users of brands. See Norton Garfinkle, "A Marketing Approach to Media Selection," *Journal of Advertising Research,* December 1963, pp. 7-14.

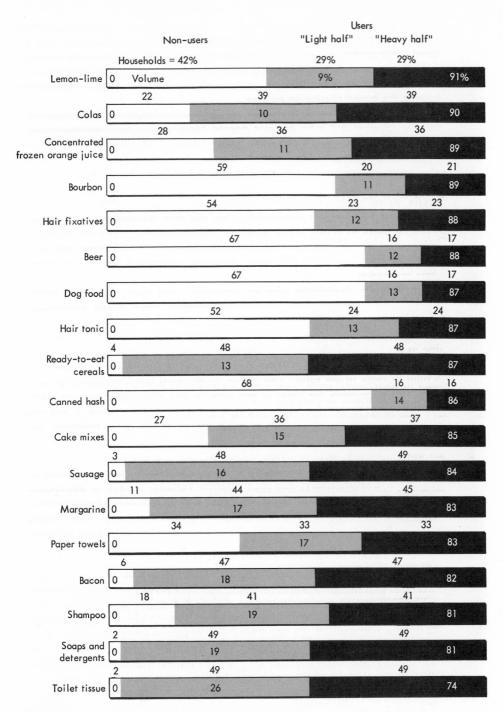

FIGURE 3-3

Percentage of total volume (for 18 product categories) purchased by different user groups

Redrawn from Dik Warren Twedt, "How Important to Marketing Strategy Is the 'Heavy User'?" *Journal of Marketing*, XXVIII (January 1964), 72.

FIGURE 3-4
Segmentation of the automobile market by primary motive

nice possibility for economy-seeking impact w/ status-seeking sublimation [handwritten marginal note]

satisfy a combination of motives, some of which may be in conflict. Yet even when several motives operate in the same individual, one may dominate and shape the purchaser's orientation. This predominant motive may be superficial and cover up something deeper—in foreign-car purchases an economy rationalization may cover up a status motive—yet economy seeking is a datum for the manufacturer who wishes to predict or influence the purchaser.

Although the various motives operating in the market for a particular product can be discovered through research, it is harder to establish the relative number of persons in each of the motive segments, and the problem is further complicated by the fact that the proportions change over time.[12] That this is a difficult estimation problem is dramatically illustrated by the failure of American automobile manufacturers in the late Fifties to guess correctly the importance of the economy-seeking motive. The industry opposed producing compact cars on the grounds that the economy-seeking segment was too small to offer mass production economies. Yet American sales of European cars continued to rise and finally forced American manufacturers to reconsider the size of this segment.

BRAND LOYALTY. An increasing number of sellers are classifying buyers on the basis of brand loyalties. The sellers see their task as holding on to their present customers and selectively drawing new customers away from competitors. The word "selectively" is used because the seller may work harder to attract away the customers of certain competitors than of other competitors. A competitor with a large hard-core group of loyal buyers is less attractive as a target than a competitor whose current customers lack high loyalty.

Unfortunately, the concept of brand loyalty has some ambiguities. What may appear to be brand loyalty may be explainable in other ways. Suppose a housewife purchased brand B on the last seven shopping occasions. The purchase pattern BBBBBBB would seem to reflect intrinsic preference for the product but may really reflect habit, indifference, a lower price, or the nonavailability of substitutes. The pattern BBBBAAA for another housewife would seem to indicate a switch in loyalty but may only reflect the fact that her store dropped brand B, or that she switched stores, or that she

[12] In a study of consumer motives in purchasing watches, the investigator did claim to measure the size of the segments. As of 1962, "approximately 23 per cent of the buyers bought (watches) for lowest price, another 46 per cent bought for durability and general product quality, and 31 per cent bought watches as symbols of some important occasion." See Yankelovich, *op. cit.*, p. 85.

52

switched to brand A because of a price promotion. Marked brand continuity in brand-purchase sequences is not necessarily evidence that individual brand loyalty exists or is strong.

Another ambiguity is that brand loyalty probably increases as a company loses customers, because the less loyal ones leave first. Thus high brand loyalty is not necessarily a favorable sign.

The degree of brand loyalty varies among products as well as brands. One investigator found loyalty to be weakest among products "with many brands available, where number of purchases and dollar expenditures per buyer are high, where prices are relatively active, and where consumers might be expected to simultaneously use a number of brands of the product." [13]

PRODUCT EXAMPLES OF THE APPLICATION OF SEGMENTATION VARIABLES

It was stated earlier that not all segmentation variables are appropriate for every market. The firm's task is to discover which ones make the most sense in each case. Let us now examine several illustrations of how the markets for some specific products (timepieces, aspirins, automobiles, transistors, and air travel) can be broadly conceived in terms of want-satisfying purposes and then segmented into significant parts.

TIMEPIECES.   The basic want-satisfying purpose of a watch or clock is to measure time. Persons and institutions depend upon time measurement as a framework for ordering their activities. Because many different activities are involved, a large variety of different time measurement devices have been developed. A firm which manufactures men's wrist watches should recognize that it is really in the business of manufacturing devices for time measurement and that a wide range of end uses exists. Segmentation of the market for time measurement devices by end use is illustrated in Figure 3-5.

The watch firm interested in broadening its product line will want to evaluate the potential of the various segments and the extent to which competition is adequately serving each segment. Suppose a watch firm decides to examine the market for travel clocks in more detail. It might begin by asking what types of people travel, what role the travel clock may play in travel behavior, and why other time devices might not be an adequate substitute. This analysis will probably bring out the importance of manufacturing a travel clock with such features as dependability, rugged construction, compactness, a luminous face, and an alarm. It may also indicate that attractiveness and price are two other considerations. They are conflicting considerations, and the market can be segmented between those who are willing to pay a high price for an attractive travel clock and those who care less about attractiveness and prefer to pay less.

ASPIRIN.   The basic want-satisfying purpose of aspirin is to relieve headache pain and/or reduce fever. As such, it is one of many competitive pain

[13] John U. Farley, "Why Does 'Brand Loyalty' Vary Over Products?" *Journal of Marketing Research,* November 1964, pp. 9-14. For other views, see George H. Brown, "Brand Loyalty—Fact or Fiction," *Advertising Age,* January 26, 1953, pp. 75-76; and Ross M. Cunningham, "Brand Loyalty—What, Where, How Much?," *Harvard Business Review,* January-February 1956, pp. 116-28.

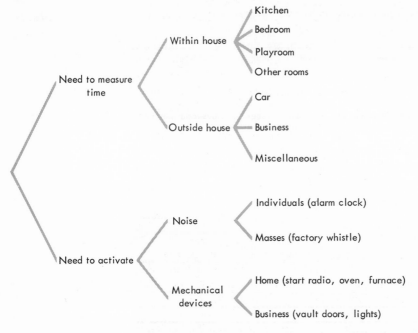

Kitchen
Bedroom
Playroom
Other rooms

Within house

Need to measure time

Car
Business
Miscellaneous

Outside house

Individuals (alarm clock)
Masses (factory whistle)

Noise

Need to activate

Home (start radio, oven, furnace)
Business (vault doors, lights)

Mechanical devices

FIGURE 3-5
Segmentation of the market for time-measurement devices by need and location
Adapted from Ralph Westfall and Harper W. Boyd, Jr., *Cases in Marketing Management* (Homewood, Ill.: Richard D. Irwin, Inc., 1961), p. 37.

relievers whose vague product-class boundaries include tranquilizers and sleeping pills on the one hand and cold remedies on the other. Some individuals use a wide variety of pain relievers and possess a good amount of information about their differences; other people are occasional users who are less precise about their needs and in their knowledge of the differences among various pain relievers.

The marketing strategy of a manufacturer of aspirin can be aided by research designed to discover differences among heavy users, light users, and nonusers of the product. One psychological hypothesis is that compulsive persons are likely to be heavy users of aspirin. Compulsive persons, in trying to achieve a high degree of order in their lives, are likely to be frequently frustrated. In addition, susceptibility to pain may be related to such variables as occupation, income, educational level, race, and social class. Some occupations are highly stress-laden, and it may be hypothesized that persons in these occupations will be heavy users of aspirin. Usage may also be heavier among lower educated groups because they tend to have more self-punitive attitudes.

Given these hypotheses, research strategy consists in designing an appropriate measuring instrument and sampling plan. The psychological characteristics of aspirin users were studied by Maurice Gottlieb, and one portion of his results is reproduced in Table 3-2. The hypothesis that heavy aspirin users tend to be more compulsive seems confirmed by observing the results within age-education groups. On the basis of testing these and other hypotheses, Gottlieb was able to derive useful information on the importance of different market segments for aspirin.

AUTOMOBILES. The basic want-satisfying purpose of the automobile is to provide transportation. It is, therefore, in a class with such products as

TABLE 3-2
Average annual dosage of different segments of the market for aspirin

Age	35 or under		36 to 50		Over 50	
Education	Low	High	Low	High	Low	High
Compulsive	6.5	3.5	14.5	13.9	9.2	8.2
Noncompulsive	4.2	2.3	9.9	12.9	10.0	4.5

Source: Maurice J. Gottlieb, "Segmentation by Personality Types," in *Advancing Marketing Efficiency*, ed. Lynn H. Stockman (Chicago: American Marketing Association, 1959), p. 154.

bicycles, scooters, and private planes; yet its degree of substitutability is very low because of its unique physical attributes. Within the product class of automobiles, most are equally capable of supplying the same essential service of transportation with roughly the same efficiency. Nevertheless, automobiles are available in an incredible variety of styles and prices; and this suggests that other human wants operate in the market.

Historically, the principal dimension for segmenting the automobile market has been income, and the manufacturer designed his car and set his price in terms of the perceived desires of a given income class. More recently it has been observed that automobiles designed for a specific income segment are also bought by other income segments. Thus many lower-income families buy brand-new medium- or high-priced cars, and many upper-middle-income families buy low-priced cars. This suggests that income may no longer be a sufficiently precise guide for segmenting the automobile market.

Richard P. Coleman has suggested that car selection can be better understood in terms of the interplay between income and social status than in terms of either dimension taken alone.[14] Men in the same income class, say, eight to ten thousand dollars, can be vastly different in social background and aspiration. A factory worker in this income class has a great deal of discretionary income in terms of his aspirations, and he may decide to "use up" some of it by purchasing a medium- or high-priced car. A college professor in the same income class sees himself as having very little discretionary income in relation to his aspirations, and he may decide to conserve by buying a lower-priced car. More formally, Coleman suggests that social-class theory becomes useful in explaining durable-goods purchases when a distinction is drawn between the "underprivileged" segments and "overprivileged" segments of each social class. The cheapest, most economic cars are not bought by the really poor, but rather by "those who think of themselves as poor relative to their status aspirations and to their needs for a certain level of clothing, furniture, and housing which they could not afford if they bought a more expensive car." On the other hand, medium-priced and expensive cars tend to be purchased by the overprivileged segments of each social class; the Big Three automobiles tend to be purchased by those whose incomes match their social aspirations.

The implications for marketing strategy of this particular way of concep-

[14] Richard P. Coleman, "The Significance of Social Stratification in Selling," in *Marketing: A Maturing Discipline*, ed. Martin L. Bell (Chicago: American Marketing Association, 1961), pp. 171-84.

tualizing the automobile market are many. Apparently American Motors sensed these distinctions when it first introduced the Rambler as an economy-designed car. Instead of a merchandising and advertising strategy aimed at working-class families, which would be the implication of a simple income analysis, the company appealed to all who wanted a sensible, gadgetless, reliable car. In all social classes there were families who were "underprivileged" in terms of income and who needed a rationale for buying a cheaper car; Rambler provided this in terms of a "sensibility snobbery."

TRANSISTORS.   The market for transistors consists of three submarkets: military, industrial, and commercial. The buyer behavioral differences among these three markets can be analyzed clearly.[15]

The military buyer attaches utmost importance to the producer's quality standards and the adequacy of his plant facilities. Only after these two considerations have been realized does price become a factor.

Quality is also of great importance to industrial customers such as computer manufacturers, for their products are used by industrial manufacturers like themselves. Loyalties can be established in this segment through high quality and good service. Price itself is not a critical matter unless it becomes completely out of line.

Commercial buyers, such as pocket radio manufacturers, are in the most competitive user market and consequently buy their components completely on price and delivery. No loyalty to suppliers exists, and quality requirements are usually minimal.

Because of these differences, marketing strategies have to be varied. In order to sell transistors in the military market, firms must make a considerable investment in R&D, use salesmen who know military buying procedures, and specialize in limited-line products. In order to sell in the industrial market, firms must make a modest investment in R&D, use salesmen who have technical knowledge concerning the product, and offer a broad line. In order to sell to the commercial market, firms need little or no R&D effort, use salesmen who are high pressure and relatively nontechnical, and offer the most common lines producible on a mass production basis.

AIR TRAVEL.   A close look at the market for air travel reveals the two major segments of personal travel and business travel. Each of these can be further subdivided. Personal travel may be motivated by vacations, emergencies, and relocations. Business travel may be classified as regular and occasional. The main reason for distinguishing between personal and business travelers is the difference in response to changes in fares, departure schedules, and so forth.

Alternative Strategies Toward
Market Segments

Every market can be segmented to some extent, since the buyers who compose it are never all alike. They may differ in their location, socioeconomic characteristics, personalities, and/or buying characteristics.

[15] Adapted from R. G. Fisk in an unpublished paper, Northwestern University, 1964.

(a) Undifferentiated marketing   (b) Differentiated marketing   (c) Concentrated marketing

FIGURE 3-6
Three alternative strategies toward market segments

The firm is usually aware of these differences. However, it may or may not shape its marketing policies around them. In fact, three different strategies are available. The firm may put out only one product and try to draw in all buyers with one marketing program. This can be called *undifferentiated marketing*. Or it may design separate products and/or marketing programs for each segment. This can be called *differentiated marketing*. Finally, it may concentrate all its efforts in one or a few lucrative segments of the market. This can be called *concentrated marketing*. These three strategy alternatives are illustrated in Figure 3-6.

UNDIFFERENTIATED MARKETING

Historically, most firms have tended to follow a policy of undifferentiated marketing. Two examples are Coca-Cola and cigarettes:

> For many years, Coca-Cola meant only one thing to consumers. It was a patented drink available in only one flavor and one bottle size. It was advertised with one theme, "The Pause That Refreshes."
>
> The same homogeneity used to characterize cigarettes. Regardless of brand name, they were 2¾ inches long, wrapped in white paper, and packaged in the same soft container. All advertising was based on the theme of smoking pleasure.

In these and other cases, the firm chooses not to recognize the different demand curves that make up the market. Instead, it treats the market as an aggregate, focusing on what is common in the needs of people rather than on what is different. It tries to design a product and a marketing program which appeal to the broadest number of buyers. It relies on mass channels, mass advertising media, and universal themes. It aims to endow the product with a superior image in the minds of people, whether or not this is based on any real difference.[16]

Undifferentiated marketing is primarily defended on the grounds of cost

---

[16] This strategy has also gone under other names, such as "product differentiation" or "market aggregation." See Wendell R. Smith, "Product Differentiation and Market Segmentation as Alternative Marketing Strategies," *Journal of Marketing*, XXI (July 1956), 3-8; and Alan A. Roberts, "Applying the Strategy of Market Segmentation," *Business Horizons*, Fall 1961, pp. 65-72.

economies. It is thought to be "the marketing counterpart to standardization and mass production in manufacturing." [17] The fact that the product line is kept narrow minimizes production, inventory, and transportation costs. The undifferentiated advertising program enables the firm to enjoy media discounts through large usage. The absence of segmental marketing research and planning lowers the costs of marketing research and executive overhead. On the whole, undifferentiated marketing results in keeping down several costs of doing business.

Nevertheless, an increasing number of marketers have expressed strong doubts about the optimality of this strategy. Gardner and Levy, for example, admitted that "some brands have very skillfully built up reputations of being suitable for a wide variety of people" but added:

> in most areas audience groupings will differ, if only because there are deviants who refuse to consume the same way other people do. . . . It is not easy for a brand to appeal to stable lower middle-class people and at the same time to be interesting to sophisticated, intellectual upper middle-class buyers. . . . It is rarely possible for a product or brand to be all things to all people.[18]

The firm practicing undifferentiated marketing typically develops a product and marketing program aimed at the broadest segment of the market. When several firms in the industry do this, the result is hypercompetition for the largest segment(s) and undersatisfaction of the smaller ones. Because the majority of purchasers wanted them, American automobile manufacturers for a long time produced only large automobiles, while foreign firms capitalized on the smaller segments. And because the majority of Americans prefer situation comedies on TV, the networks are saturated with them. The situation comedy viewer is treated with the opportunity to choose among several situation comedies—often to his frustration—while the non-situation comedy viewers, representing a considerable population, are lost to all sponsors.

The "majority fallacy," as this has been called by Kuehn and Day, describes the fact that the larger segments may be less profitable because they attract disproportionately heavy competition.[19] The recognition of this fallacy has led many firms to re-evaluate the opportunities latent in the smaller segments of the market.

DIFFERENTIATED MARKETING

Under differentiated marketing, a firm decides to operate in all segments of the market but designs separate product and/or marketing programs for each. By offering product and marketing variations it hopes to attain higher sales and a deeper position within each market segment. It hopes that a deep position in several segments will strengthen the customers' over-all identification of the company's name with the product field. Furthermore, it hopes for greater loyalty and repeat purchasing because the firm's offer-

---

[17] Smith, *ibid.,* p. 4.

[18] Burleigh Gardner and Sidney Levy, "The Product and the Brand," *Harvard Business Review,* March-April 1955, p. 37.

[19] Alfred A. Kuehn and Ralph L. Day, "Strategy of Product Quality," *Harvard Business Review,* November-December 1962, pp. 101-2.

ings have been bent to the customer's desire rather than the other way around.[20]

In recent years an increasing number of firms have moved toward a strategy of differentiated marketing. This is reflected in trends toward multiple product offerings and multiple trade channels and media:

> Coca-Cola is now sold in different bottle sizes as well as cans.

> Cigarettes are now manufactured in a variety of lengths and filter types. The customer often has the option of buying his favorite brand filtered or unfiltered, or long or short.

> Chevrolet is no longer a single-style, low-priced automobile, but rather the name for several car types which vary in body size, cost, and features. Instead of one car designed to attract everyone, Chevrolet has become a set of cars matched to distinctly different market segments.

> Ivory soap used to be Procter & Gamble's major brand, but now it is only one of several P&G brands to meet the varying needs, real and apparent, of customers.

The same trend is found in industrial marketing. Industrial firms are showing a greater willingness to customize their products to meet buyers' varying needs.

The net effect of differentiated marketing is to create more total sales than undifferentiated marketing. "It is ordinarily demonstrable that total sales may be increased with a more diversified product line sold through more diversified channels." [21] However, it also tends to be true that differentiated marketing increases the costs of doing business. The following costs are likely to be higher:

Production costs. Generally speaking, it is more expensive to produce m units each of n differentiated products than mn units of one product. This is especially true the longer the production setup time for each product and the smaller the sales volume of each product. On the other hand, if each model is sold in sufficiently large volume, the higher costs of setup time may be quite small per unit.

Administrative costs. Under differentiated marketing, the company has to develop separate marketing plans for the separate segments of the market. This requires extra marketing research, forecasting, sales analysis, promotion, planning, and channel management.

Inventory costs. It is generally more costly to manage inventories of differentiated products than an inventory of only one product. The extra costs arise because more records must be kept and more auditing must be done. Furthermore, each product must be carried at a level which reflects basic demand plus a safety factor to cover unexpected variations in demand. The sum of the safety stocks for several products will exceed the safety stock required for one product. Thus carrying differentiated products leads to inflated inventory cost.

[20] Differentiated marketing has also been described as the strategy of "market segmentation." However, market segmentation fails to distinguish between differentiated marketing and concentrated marketing as the terms are used here. Market segmentation in this text will refer to the act of segmenting a market to understand it better, rather than to describe one particular policy out of the three that the company may adopt.

[21] Roberts, *op. cit.,* p. 66.

Promotion costs. Differentiated marketing involves trying to reach different segments of the market through advertising media most appropriate to each case. This leads to lower usage rates of individual media and the consequent forfeiture of quantity discounts. Furthermore, since each segment may require separate creative advertising planning, promotion costs are increased.

To summarize, differentiated marketing is likely to produce more company sales but at the price of creating higher company costs. Therefore, nothing can be said a priori regarding the relative optimality of this strategy. Yet the literature is full of implications that differentiated marketing is more nearly optimal. All that can be said is that differentiated marketing is sales-oriented, and this explains why marketing men like the strategy. But whether it is profit-oriented depends upon whether it can cause sales to rise by more than costs.

CONCENTRATED MARKETING

Both differentiated marketing and undifferentiated marketing imply that the firm goes after the whole market. However, many firms see a third possibility, one that is especially appealing when the company's resources are limited. Instead of going after a small share of a large market, the firm goes after a large share of one or a few submarkets. Put another way, instead of spreading himself thin in many parts of the market, it concentrates its forces to gain a good market position in a few areas.

Many examples of concentrated marketing can be cited:

> Volkswagen has concentrated on the segment of the auto market which wants compactness, good engineering, and economy in its transportation.
>
> Jonathan Logan, Inc. is a successful dress manufacturer whose styles are mainly created for the teen-age market.
>
> Gerber has concentrated its efforts on the baby foods segment of the prepared food market.
>
> Many textbook publishers specialize at the elementary grades, or the high-school level, or the college level. There is often further specialization within these levels. Richard D. Irwin, Inc., has specialized in economics and business college texts, and John Wiley & Sons in mathematics college texts.

Through concentrated marketing the firm achieves a strong market position in the particular segments it serves owing to its greater knowledge of the segments' needs and the special reputation it acquires. Furthermore, it enjoys many operating economies because of specialization in production, distribution, and promotion. If the segment of the market is well chosen, the firm can earn high rates of return on its investment. Maurice Gottlieb provided a good illustration of this in his study of the aspirin market. His research findings indicated that the largest-volume aspirin would be:

> a lower social class product which made extensive claims, advertised regular use, and tasted good. Actually the single dominant product in the field was one used widely by the higher status groups, which advertised very specific use and made fewer broad claims than other products. . . . It didn't taste particularly good. . . . The reason for the unexpected success of this leading product was simple. Instead of competing with other products for the

most profitable segments of the antacid-analgesic market, that contrary product had captured the less prominent—but still highly significant minority segments—where it has no competitor.[22]

Concentrated marketing involves tying the company's future growth to one segment of the market, and this carries obvious risks. A major risk is that other companies will eventually recognize the opportunities in this segment and enter it. Because of the possibility of good and bad segments, one would also expect a higher variance in the rates of return of companies which concentrate their marketing than of companies which diversify over the entire market through differentiated or undifferentiated marketing. Going after the whole market brings a more normal rate of return, because the good and poor segments are averaged.

SELECTING A MARKETING STRATEGY

We have described undifferentiated marketing, differentiated marketing, and concentrated marketing as three alternative strategies facing a firm. In practice, the firm may find the merits of one strategy so overwhelming that there is no decision issue at all. Or the firm may find one strategy completely inappropriate, so that the choice boils down to a decision between the two remaining strategies. In general, particular characteristics of the seller, the product, or the market serve to constrain and narrow the actual choice. The most important characteristics for selecting a strategy are company resources, product homogeneity, product stage in the life cycle, market homogeneity, and competitive marketing strategies.[23]

The first factor, company resources, was mentioned earlier in discussing concentrated marketing. Where the firm's resources are too limited to permit complete coverage of the market, its only realistic choice is concentrated marketing.

The second factor, product homogeneity, refers to the invariance of the product's characteristics. Most consumers do not perceive differences in such basic commodities as salt, grapefruit, steel, or gasoline. An undifferentiated marketing strategy for such products is, therefore, more natural than a differentiated or concentrated marketing strategy. On the other hand, products which are capable of great variation, such as cameras and automobiles, are more naturally suited to differentiation or concentration.

The third factor, product stage in the life cycle, makes a difference, especially at the extreme stages of market introduction and market saturation. When a firm introduces a new product into the market place it usually does not find it practical to introduce more than one or, at the most, a few product versions. The firm's first interest is to develop primary demand, and undifferentiated marketing seems the suitable strategy. The firm may alternatively develop the product for a particular segment of the market and concentrate its efforts there. As the product moves through its life cycle toward the saturation stage, the firm starts to search harder for new and untapped needs in order to maintain or increase sales. Thus in the mature

[22] Maurice J. Gottlieb, "Segmentation by Personality Types," in *Advancing Marketing Efficiency,* ed. Lynn H. Stockman (Chicago: American Marketing Association, 1959), p. 154.

[23] These factors were suggested by R. William Kotrba in an unpublished paper, Northwestern University, 1964.

stage of the product life cycle, firms tend to pursue a strategy of differentiated marketing.

The fourth factor, market homogeneity, refers to the degree to which customers are alike in their needs, preferences, and characteristics. In such markets segmentation would be somewhat forced. Thus, the firm could try to stimulate customers to have more diverse preferences, but, in general, homogeneous markets are best tapped by an undifferentiated marketing strategy. Conversely, heterogeneous markets can be tapped either by differentiated marketing or concentrated marketing.

The fifth factor, competitive marketing strategies, refers to what competitors are doing. When competitors are practicing active segmentation, it is hard for a firm to compete through undifferentiated marketing. It would lose most of the battles. On the other hand, when competitors are practicing undifferentiated marketing, a firm can often gain by practicing active segmentation, especially if some of the previous factors favor it.

Evaluating the Worth of Different Market Segments

The problem facing all firms which segment their market, whether they go after all segments or only a few segments, is how to estimate the value of operating in each of the segments. The firm which pursues differentiated marketing must know this in order to allocate its marketing effort over the various segments. The firm which pursues concentrated marketing must know this in order to decide which segments offer the best opportunities.

A useful analytical approach is illustrated in Figure 3-7.[24] The analysis proceeds in three stages. Stage 1 is a representation of the whole product market. Stages 2 and 3 show how a particular segment, or cell, of the market can be analyzed.

The market in this illustration is the one for the mechanical line of a steel fabricating company. Stage 1 shows a segmentation of this market using as two variables the customer-prospect mix and the product-service mix. The customer-prospect mix consists of contractors in the electrical, general, and plumbing line, respectively. The product-service mix consists of three products sold to these contractors: pipe hangers, concrete inserts, and electrical supports. Nine cells result from this joint segmentation of the market. Each cell represents a distinct submarket, or product-market segment. A (hypothetical) dollar figure is placed in each cell, representing the company's sales in that submarket. For example, the company sold $200,-000 worth of concrete inserts to general contractors. This submarket accounted for one-sixth (200,000/1,200,000) of total company sales.

Relative company sales in the nine submarkets provide no indication of their relative profit potential as segments. The latter depends upon market demand, company costs, and competitive trends in each submarket. To get at relative profit potentials, each of the nine submarkets must be analyzed in depth in order to reveal the relative desirability of cultivating the different submarkets.

[24] The approach was originally developed in William J. Crissy and Robert M. Kaplan, "Matrix Models for Marketing Planning," *Business Horizons,* Summer 1963, pp. 48-66. The particular illustration was developed by Rhett W. Butler in an unpublished paper, Northwestern University, 1964.

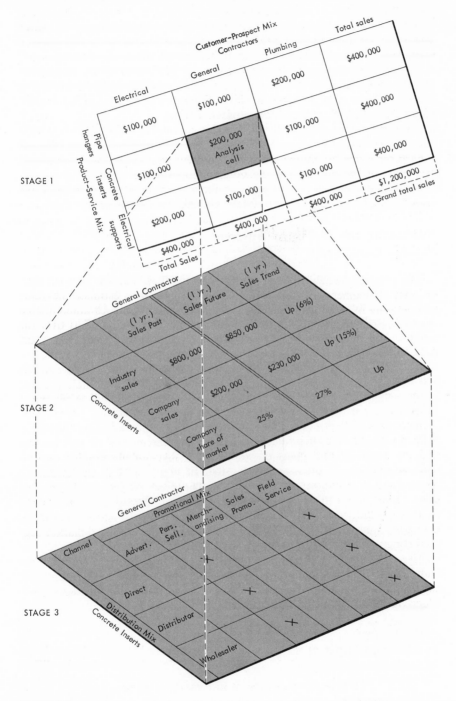

FIGURE 3-7
Analyzing the worth of different market segments for steel fabricated products
From an unpublished paper by Rhett W. Butler, Northwestern University, 1964.

Stages 2 and 3 show how a particular product submarket, the general contractor market for concrete inserts, can be analyzed in depth. The same analysis would be repeated for each of the nine product submarkets. Stage 2 involves an attempt to appraise present and future sales in the selected submarket. The vertical axis accommodates estimates of industry sales, company sales, and company market share. The horizontal axis is used to project future sales in these categories and market share. According to Figure 3-7, the company sold in this submarket last year $200,000 worth of goods, or one-fourth of total estimated industry sales. Looking ahead, the company expects industry sales in this submarket to rise by 6 per cent and its own sales to rise by 15 per cent. These should not be "out-of-the-hat" figures, but rather the result of a careful analysis of past trends and projection of future competitive investments and plans.

Stage 3 is introduced to spell out the marketing thinking behind the sales forecasts of Stage 2. The horizontal axis shows the promotional mix which the company is using or plans to use to stimulate the sales of concrete inserts to general contractors. The promotional mix consists of a blended program of advertising, personal selling, merchandising, sales promotion, and field service. The vertical axis shows the distribution mix which the company is using or plans to use to move concrete inserts into the hands of general contractors. The distribution mix here consists of direct distribution, distributor distribution, and wholesaler distribution. The actual promotion-distribution mix could be detailed by placing budget figures (funds and men) in the relevant cells. In the illustration, however, X's have been used to indicate the main contours of the company's mix. The company will use all three types of distribution and rely mainly on personal selling and field service for stimulating sales to general contractors.

By carrying out this analysis and planning for each submarket the seller gains a number of benefits. He is led to think systematically about each segment as a distinct entity and opportunity. The potential of a segment is defined in relation to such factors as its size, its current level of satisfaction, and the activities and plans of competitors. Some segments will appear underdeveloped and others oversaturated. In reviewing the desirable promotion and distribution mix for each segment, he can judge whether the sales opportunities in the segment justify the involvement costs. If his resources are limited he may decide to pursue a policy of concentrated marketing in a few lucrative segments. Otherwise, he can pursue differentiated marketing, offering a full line and allocating his efforts according to the relative attractiveness of the different segments. His marketing goals and budget are built from the bottom up, according to the needs and attractiveness of different segments, rather than imposed from the top down and allocated arbitrarily over the segments.

Summary

The opportunities present in a market increase when the seller recognizes that it is made up of many parts, not all of which are likely to be receiving complete satisfaction from the current offerings of sellers.

Markets may be segmented on several different bases. While segmentation is most commonly carried out along socioeconomic and geographic lines, some markets can be usefully segmented along personality and/or buyer-behavior dimensions. The important thing about segments is that they represent groupings of customers which tend to respond differently to product features or marketing-mix variables. To be ultimately useful, the segments should be measurable, accessible, and substantial.

Firms have shown different strategies toward the existence of market segments, some ignoring them (undifferentiated marketing), some developing a variety of products and marketing programs to meet different needs (differentiated marketing), and some going after only a few segments (concentrated marketing). No particular strategy is superior to the others in all circumstances. There can be underdifferentiation, overdifferentiation, or overconcentration. Much depends on such characteristics as company resources, product homogeneity, product stage in the life cycle, market homogeneity, and competitive marketing strategies. The firm must analyze the attractiveness of the different market segments as a prelude to setting market target goals and allocations of company resources.

Questions and Problems

1. Define the primary want-satisfying purpose(s) of the following goods: (a) cars; (b) bread; (c) oil; (d) pillows; (e) pens; (f) novels; (g) textbooks; (h) uniforms; (i) watches; (j) detergents.

2. For each of the following products, suggest a group of persons who by and large would be nonusers: (a) cigarettes; (b) pipes; (c) expensive sport cars; (d) steel beams; (e) books; (f) radios.

3. Market segments can be developed by cross-classifying different variables deemed to be important in the market. What are the problems which arise in trying to cross-classify more than a few variables?

4. Suggest a useful way to segment the markets for the following products: (a) household detergents; (b) animal feeds; (c) household coffee; (d) automobile tires.

5. Select a particular product or service, and describe a useful way to segment the market. Then answer the following questions: (a) Why is this a useful way to segment the market? (b) Are data available for estimating the size of the various market segments? (c) How much is known about the behavioral characteristics of the different segments? (d) What marketing strategy is appropriate to each segment?

chapter 4

Buyer Behavior

The previous chapter described how a firm could segment its markets in order to improve its appraisal of marketing opportunities and establish appropriate marketing policies. Market segmentation should lead to a better choice of company market targets. But to be effective with target buyers, the company must demonstrate its understanding of their needs, attitudes, and behavior in its selection of marketing channels, advertising messages, prices, and other instruments of marketing policy.

Customers are neither simple in themselves nor in their behavior toward the world of product objects. As Berelson and Steiner write:

> Human behavior itself is so enormously varied, so delicately complex, so obscurely motivated that many people despair of finding valid generalizations to explain and predict the actions, thoughts, and feelings of human beings—despair, that is, of the very possibility of constructing a science of human behavior.[1]

If human behavior is so varied and complex, can the marketer find anything of value in studying it? Are there any generalizations upon which he can build a better program for satisfying human wants?

The answer lies somewhere between total knowledge and total ignorance of human behavior. Customers are neither so simple that they do not require study nor so complex that there are no rewards from study. In fact, Berelson and Steiner's *Human Behavior* is an attempt to codify the knowledge accumulated by behavioral scientists. It presents a long inventory of empirically founded generalizations about individuals, small groups, institutions, and social processes and demonstrates that *behavioral science* has substantial accomplishments in spite of the fact that it is barely seventy-five years old.[2]

Knowledge about such general human mechanisms as motivation, cognition, and learning are only the starting point for the planning of specific marketing programs. Buyers have layers of behavior which are always specific to particular products or services. A simple product like soap

---

[1] Bernard Berelson and Gary A. Steiner, *Human Behavior: An Inventory of Scientific Findings* (New York: Harcourt, Brace & World, Inc., 1964), p. 3.

[2] There are many generalizations in Berelson and Steiner's book having clear implications for buyer behavior. Several applications are listed in Richard Buskirk, *Principles of Marketing: The Management View,* rev. ed. (New York: Holt, Rinehart and Winston, Inc., 1966), pp. 200-206. For a collection of direct studies, see Perry Bliss, ed., *Marketing and the Behavioral Sciences: Selected Readings* (Boston: Allyn and Bacon, Inc., 1963).

evokes a special constellation of needs, attitudes, and images. It is neither obvious how soap is purchased nor obvious how it is used. Therefore, besides being understood in general behavior terms, buyer behavior must be researched in its product-market context.

The ultimate aim of a firm should be to develop a theory of how its market works. This means knowing who its customers are, what they want, how they buy, and how they use and react to the product. Included is the need to know how various marketing variables, such as price, product features, advertising message, and corporate image, affect the buyer. This aim is never perfectly realized, if for no other reason than because attitudes and behavior change, but it is nevertheless a worthy goal for the marketer.

[handwritten: THE OBJECTIVE IS A MODEL OF THE MARKET]

It is customary to dissect customer behavior into separate compartments marked economic, psychological, and sociological. We cannot avoid doing some of the same later on in this discussion, but we shall start by viewing the buyer in the context of a total action system called *the buying process*. Then we shall note that the buyer never goes through the buying process alone; he is always influenced by others, those present either physically or mentally—people whom we shall call *buying participants*. Finally, we shall want to consider why he makes the buying decisions he does; that is *the theory of buyer choice*.[3]

Stages in the Buying Process

Of the dozens of categories of human action—working, sleeping, voting, eating, breathing, arguing, buying, and so forth—the one of primary interest to the marketer is buying. As an act, buying is typically more complicated than breathing or sleeping but probably less complicated than choosing a job or a wife. But the buyer's decision-making process can be very simple or very elaborate—contrast the purchase of a package of cigarettes with the purchase of a new home. The decision made by United Air Lines in 1965 to order Boeing jets instead of Douglas jets was complicated indeed. William A. Patterson and his executive committee spent months of agonizing appraisal before deciding to commit the bulk of a $750 million investment to Boeing.[4]

The buying decision seems the telling act as far as the seller is concerned, but this is a mistaken view. The buying decision is only one act in a larger process that begins before, and ends after, the decision. Marketers must comprehend the whole process, not just the purchase decision step, in order to do an effective job of meeting customer wants.

The stages of the buying process, in considerably simplified form, are illustrated in Figure 4-1. The customer is seen as going from a *felt need* to *prepurchase activity* to a *purchase decision* to *use behavior* to *postpurchase feelings*. Each step along the way poses a significant challenge to marketing management, both in understanding what is happening and in building an effective marketing program to capitalize on what is happening.

[3] The behavior of buyers toward new products, called the consumer adoption process, is discussed in Chapter 14, pp. 342-48.

[4] "United Air Lines $750-million Decision," *Chicago Sun-Times,* April 11, 1965, pp. 73, 77.

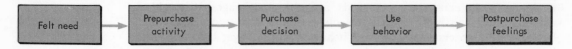

| Felt need | → | Prepurchase activity | → | Purchase decision | → | Use behavior | → | Postpurchase feelings |

FIGURE 4-1
Stages in the buying process

FELT NEED

The starting point of the buying process is a felt need. It may be a specific need for a spring hat or a vague need for excitement or diversion. It may be a basic physiological need for food or a psychological need for security. It may be a need that is intense or casual, highly conscious or only vaguely conscious. It may be a need that arose spontaneously, or was created by social or business processes.

Needs have also been called wants, wishes, motives, urges, drives; distinctions between these terms are not worth making here. What they all have in common is that they represent a state of tension. A need is something that a person seeks to satisfy or reduce, and presumably some object or activity will do this.

Many attempts have been made to pass judgment on the importance of different human needs, with the implication that a great number of them are frivolous or unessential.[5] It is true that most of modern man's needs are not related to survival; he can get along on very little. Buddhists and some other religious groups have tried to establish that happiness is a matter of curbing desires rather than indulging them; however, Western man generally has chosen to expand his desires and his means of gratifying them.

Most of Western production and marketing is based on the premise that human wants are insatiable in their variety:

> Since all stoves cook, washing machines wash, and all foods eliminate hunger, selection today is not based on these characteristics but on the refinements by which they perform their tasks according to socially defined criteria. These desirable characteristics have come to be values in themselves.[6]

Marketers do not pass judgment on wants. Rather, they consider it their responsibility to satisfy them insofar as they are able. Admittedly, they go beyond this and stimulate new, specific wants. Some quarrel with the philosophical implications of wants that business stimulates for the purpose of maintaining employment and profits;[7] but the persuasion powers of business are not absolute, and in a free economy, the consumer, rather than someone else, selects the wants that he will satisfy.

The significance of felt needs for the marketer is to suggest that purchases are born in a set of motivations far more fundamental than the

[5] See, for example, Vance Packard, *The Waste Makers* (New York: David McKay Company, Inc., 1960).

[6] M. E. John, "Classification of Values That Serve as Motivators to Consumer Purchases," *Journal of Farm Economics,* November 1956, p. 957.

[7] John Kenneth Galbraith, *The Affluent Society* (Boston: Houghton Mifflin Company, 1958), chap. XI.

particular product objects. The product is only the means, often one among many, for satisfying the more basic want. The challenge to the marketer is to uncover the latent need structure surrounding his particular product. "What is the customer really seeking through the purchase of this product?" is the question to answer. Charles Revson, President of Revlon, gave one answer: "In the factory we make cosmetics, and in the drugstore we sell hope."

The product's basic want-satisfying purpose is only the start of the answer. If transportation was all one sought from automobiles, there would be no market for the higher-priced models. The intense respect for Cadillacs and Lincolns is based on more than their workmanship. W. I. Thomas's discussion of four basic "wishes"—for security, recognition, response from others, and new experience [8]—goes a long way to explain the motivational context in which many products are bought. Good marketing is very much a matter of recognizing the various needs that operate in a particular product market and being the first to recognize insufficiently developed or insufficiently satisfied needs. This, plus the ability to develop the right product, to project the right symbolic qualities, and to establish the right distribution, is the key to marketing success.

PREPURCHASE ACTIVITY

"The need is father to the deed." The person, as a result of a felt need, becomes sensitive to cues in his environment which might bring him closer to satisfying his need. If the need is compelling, as in the case of hunger or thirst, hardly any time will elapse before the person seizes upon some object that serves his purpose. Most needs, however, are less than compelling. The person is ready to live with many of his needs before they must be satisfied. The housewife accumulates several food needs before she makes a trip to the supermarket. She may want a dress for weeks before she acts. The husband watches automobile ads and talks to friends before he is ready to buy a car. During this time, the person's perception is energized and directed by his need. He learns and accumulates experience. In the case of the husband, weeks may pass before he ventures into an automobile show room, and more weeks before he buys. He nurses his need until one day he arrives at the right time and the right place to buy.

The duration and kind of prepurchase activity vary with the type of product and the personality of the buyer. Convenience goods are purchased with very little deliberation quite soon after the need for them is felt. Purchase of major consumer appliances, on the other hand, is typically delayed after the need is first felt; there is much more prepurchase activity, including shopping, talking to friends, and watching advertisements. Industrial buyers also show varying amounts of prepurchase activity, depending upon whether the product is a standard commodity, a piece of capital equipment, or something else.

The product category explains much but not all of the variability in prepurchase activity and duration. Within each product category buyers differ greatly in how they act on their needs. Some buyers have a great need for closure, for psychological completion. A need absorbs all their attention, and postponement is intolerable. Buyers also vary in the amount

[8] William I. Thomas, *The Unadjusted Girl* (Boston: Little, Brown & Co., 1928).

of deliberateness and rationality they show in prepurchase activity. Some buyers exhibit a rationalistic style; they actively seek information on values and prices, make mental or manual calculations, and generally do not act until they can rationalize their choice to their satisfaction. Others are more casual or impulsive in their purchases.

Prepurchase activity is supposed to create a sequence of state-of-mind changes that bring the buyer closer to the act of purchase. These stages have been described as:

Awareness→Knowledge→Liking→Preference→Conviction→Purchase [9]

The central idea is that as the buyer moves from product awareness to product knowledge, liking, preference, and conviction, each succeeding stage increases the probability that he will move soon, in time, to action to satisfy his need.[10]

The significance of prepurchase activity for the marketer is the awareness that needs incubate for a time before crystallizing in purchasing action. During this time the buyers are ripe for information and stimulation concerning product values. They watch for advertisements, listen to salesmen, and heed the opinions of acquaintances. During this period the firm's communications program represents an investment in trying to guide the receptive person's attention to the values of the firm's product. The communications can inform and persuade, but only infrequently are they sufficient to trigger buying action. This is why advertising is so necessary and yet so difficult to evaluate.

PURCHASE DECISION

Not all felt needs are destined to be satisfied. People grow weary of some, which wither away along with the tension. Other needs linger on indefinitely, unable for various reasons to culminate in a purchase. A need may become a pleasant fantasy satisfying in itself. But most felt needs that have a reasonable relationship to the person's means eventually drive the person to gratify them. His investigations and exposures and dawdling end in the act of making a purchase.

The purchase decision is really a set of decisions. At the very least it may involve a *product,* a *brand,* a *style,* a *quantity,* a *place,* a *dealer,* a *time,* a *price,* and a *way to pay.* Figure 4-2 illustrates some of the components of a buyer's decision to purchase a typewriter. Six different decision issues are shown. Given only these six decision issues and the two or three choices he can make regarding each, he can travel down 48 ($1 \times 2 \times 2 \times 3 \times 2 \times 2$) different decision paths. The one he actually travels down is hardly something he himself plans at the start of his decision trip. As he comes to each new fork in the road he is influenced by a host of factors, some highly personal, some circumstantial, and a few highly economic or social in character.

The manufacturer's problem of operating profitably in an economy replete with choice becomes apparent from this diagram. His sales will

[9] Robert J. Lavidge and Gary A. Steiner, "A Model for Predictive Measurements of Advertising Effectiveness," *Journal of Marketing,* XXV (October 1961), 59-62.

[10] For a critical appraisal, see Kristian S. Palda, "The Hypothesis of a Hierarchy of Effects: A Partial Evaluation," *Journal of Marketing Research,* February 1966, pp. 13-24.

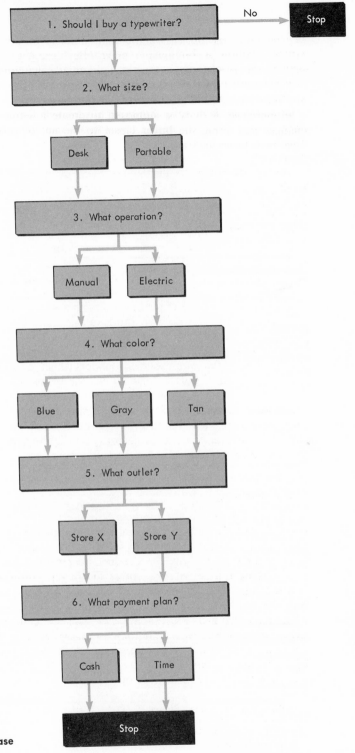

FIGURE 4-2
**Decision to purchase
a typewriter**

71

depend upon his producing the right number of desk and portable type-writers, electric and manual typewriters, blue, gray, and tan typewriters, and having all of them in the right places and available on the right terms. Overproducing each product variant can guarantee against stockouts, but secures sales at the expense of profit. His real problem is to forecast how many of each, say, thousand buyers will travel down each decision path. It is difficult to predict this for the individual buyer, but it may be feasible for the aggregate of buyers, even if the forecast only amounts to projecting the distribution of past decisions.

But let us return to the buyer. Each decision path will strike him as having some risk attached. The amount of risk perceived by a consumer depends on the *amount at stake* and the *degree of subjective certainty* that he will do well.[11] People try to reduce the perceived risk by seeking in-formation.[12] The final selection of a path by the consumer will reflect his balancing of expected rewards, costs, and risks.

For the marketer the significance of the purchase decision is that it is really a composite of decisions. The buyer agonizes over several decisions, not just one. The decision on portability may be just as grueling as the decision to buy a typewriter in the first place.

The marketer can do two things about this. He can create more in-formative communications, written and oral, so that some decisions can be made with more confidence. For example, he can spell out more clearly for the buyer the circumstances under which a desk typewriter makes more sense than a portable, or an electric typewriter than a manual. The marketer can also develop a package offer so that one decision obviates the need for several. A movie-camera manufacturer recognized that many sales were being lost because people were afraid to make separate deci-sions on a movie camera, projector, film, lighting equipment, and screen; he assembled and advertised a complete home movie kit so that only one decision had to be made and had great success.[13]

USE BEHAVIOR

As we said earlier, the marketer's interest in the buying process should not end with the sale of the product. The product was purchased not for its own sake but for its ability to satisfy a felt need. Attention should there-fore be directed to how the product becomes articulated into the larger need system and activity system of the buyer.

Much can be learned by studying how buyers use the product. Who uses the product; how is it used; where is it used; when is it used; with what other products is it used? Consider these questions in connection with the household use of frozen orange-juice concentrate. Someone in the household, usually the wife, prepares the juice when a need for it is felt. The preparation usually take place in the morning but also occurs, though with less frequency, at other times in the day. The preparation is

[11] Donald F. Cox and Stuart U. Rich, "Perceived Risk and Consumer Decision Making—The Case of Telephone Shopping," *Journal of Marketing Research,* November 1964, pp. 32-39.

[12] Raymond A. Bauer, "Consumer Behavior as Risk Taking," in *Dynamic Marketing for a Changing World,* ed. Robert S. Hancock (Chicago: American Marketing Association, 1960), pp. 389-98.

[13] Walter Talley, "Marketing R & D," *Business Horizons,* Fall 1962, pp. 31-40.

typically time-consuming, because the can must be opened, the contents added to a measured amount of water, and the mixture stirred or shaken before use. Because of these processing requirements, children generally do not prepare it, nor does the husband. So its use depends upon the housewife's decision to prepare it. Its greatest use is as a prelude to breakfast. It is also used, though less frequently, with other meals or at snack time. Most of the pouring is done in the kitchen, and the drink is consumed there or in the dining room. Children are apt to consume more than other members of the family. They are expected to drink a minimum of juice for health reasons; yet they are discouraged from overdrinking it because it is expensive.

From this bare outline of how frozen orange-juice concentrate is used, a number of insights can be gained that might improve the marketing process. Any innovation which would help ease the preparation chore might increase consumption and sales. One possibility is to develop a can that opens more easily so that children can make the juice themselves; another is to merchandise plastic juice containers at a very low price or as a premium so that the housewife has a proper receptacle for the juice. Use behavior also suggests that households do not think enough about drinking orange juice at times other than breakfast. This suggests the possible value of an advertising campaign showing people drinking orange juice on the tennis court, on the patio, and in the family room. The point is that orange juice competes with other thirst quenchers like milk, soda, coffee, and tea, and the marketer's job is to associate the use of orange juice in drinking situations other than breakfast time.

Boyd and Levy have suggested that there is value in thinking about the *consumption systems* in which a product is imbedded. The consumption system describes "the way a purchaser of a product performs the total task of whatever it is that he or she is trying to accomplish when using the product." [14] Preparing orange juice is part of the larger consumption system of ministering to the family's food needs. The housewife sees her task as providing nutritious and enjoyable food experiences within the confines of a limited time and money budget for food making. Orange juice is chosen because it delivers nutrition and enjoyment; the concentrate may be used because it does not require much effort. She might be ready to replace it with something that gave comparable values and was easier to use, such as chilled orange juice in cartons. Her interest is not in the particular product but in the contribution it makes to certain tasks which she must perform within larger systems of consumption activity.

The significance of use behavior for the marketer is to broaden his perspective of the opportunities latent in the product and the marketing of it. The product is imbedded both functionally and symbolically in one or more consumption systems. The manufacturer of desks for the home must recognize that the consumer will be interested in articulating the desk with other furnishings and into some pattern of family activity, requirements, and usage. The manufacturer of cigarettes can benefit by viewing the product as part of one system used by the individual to mitigate his tensions and as part of another system he uses to achieve social recognition. View-

[14] Harper W. Boyd, Jr., and Sidney J. Levy, "New Dimensions in Consumer Analysis," *Harvard Business Review*, November-December 1963, pp. 129-40.

ing products in the context of the overlapping systems in which they play a role sensitizes management to latent opportunities and factors useful in designing and marketing the product.

POSTPURCHASE FEELINGS

Most studies of buyer behavior deal with the feelings and behavior of buyers before and during the purchase decision. More recently marketers have recognized the value of observing the customer's feelings after the purchase. Did the buyer experience the satisfaction he expected, or has the product provoked some postpurchase uncertainty?

There are two broad reasons why the purchaser, especially of an expensive product, may be seized afterwards with feelings of doubt or regret. In part the uncertainty may be a carry-over from the prepurchase period when he was having trouble deciding among the different possible choices. If the product was a typewriter, for example, each alternative had attractive and unattractive qualities. Presumably he selected the alternative with the most attractive qualities for him, but this does not resolve his doubts after the purchase about the unattractive qualities of the product he purchased or the attractive qualities of the alternatives he rejected.

Negative postpurchase feelings may not be a carry-over from the predecision period but may arise afterwards. The purchaser may hear information that reflects badly on his choice; a rumor may reach him that the product is being discontinued; he may learn that he could have purchased the product for less elsewhere. Negative feelings may arise through the sheer act of using the product and finding its performance disappointing or encountering unanticipated trouble.

The occurrence of postpurchase anxiety is related to what Leon Festinger calls "cognitive dissonance." [15] There is often a dissonance, or lack of harmony, among the buyer's various cognitions about the product purchased and the foregone alternatives. "The magnitude of post-decision dissonance is an increasing function of the general importance of the decision and of the relative attractiveness of the unchosen alternatives," according to Festinger.[16] For these reasons, dissonance is common among purchasers of homes, automobiles, and major appliances, and among businessmen who have just made a major business investment.

The tension introduced by dissonance leads the buyer to seek its reduction. Festinger postulates a drive in the human organism "to establish internal harmony, consistency, or congruity among his opinions, knowledge, and values." [17] This drive leads the dissonant purchaser to one of two courses of action. He may try to exorcise the dissonant cognition by removing the product, returning it for a credit where this is possible or selling it to someone else; or he may try to alleviate the dissonant cognition by confirming the product, seeking information which might establish its superiority.

The manufacturer's hope is in having the dissonance reduced through the

[15] Leon Festinger, *A Theory of Cognitive Dissonance* (Stanford, Calif.: Stanford University Press, 1957). A brief and lucid account is found in Bruce Straits, "The Pursuit of the Dissonant Consumer," *Journal of Marketing*, XXVIII (July 1964), 62-66.

[16] Festinger, *op. cit.*, p. 262.

[17] *Ibid.*, p. 260.

consumer's finding confirmation for his choice. The buyer's success in finding favorable support for his choice will have a direct bearing on the probability of his repeating the purchase or recommending it to others. Of course, the probability will also be affected by the user's experience with the product, but in this connection the manufacturer's main contribution is to design a good product.

The existence of possible negative postpurchase feelings indicates that the marketer might profit from directing some of his communications to the recent buyer, rather than all of them to the potential buyer. The recent buyer may need assurance that he has made the right choice. If he is in a dissonant state, he will be looking for supportive evidence in the form of advertising and other communications. The appliance manufacturer may take the opportunity of building assurances into the information brochures that accompany his product. Manufacturers also can run advertisements showing recent purchasers showing satisfaction with their choice and why. Unless the seller dispels the dissonance by some positive efforts, he may lose the customer unnecessarily.

THE BUYING PROCESS—TWO EXAMPLES

The previous pages outlined a model of the buying process in which the buyer passed through the five stages of a felt need, prepurchase activity, purchase decision, use behavior, and postpurchase feelings. Any one of these stages can be modeled in much more detail to exhibit factors of specific interest to the investigator. Two examples will be used to show customer behavior models in greater detail.

DU PONT MODEL. The first model was developed at Du Pont to fill in details of the purchase-decision stage of the buying process.[18] The model is reproduced in Figure 4-3. It represents an explicit statement of the steps a hypothetical group of prospective users might go through in making a purchase decision. A prospective user first decides whether or not to purchase the product. If he decides to buy, he may patronize an outlet which does not handle the Du Pont brand, or which handles only Du Pont, or which handles Du Pont as well as other brands. In the last case, the customer may ask for Du Pont or another brand or rely on the salesperson's recommendation. The total market share depends on the proportion of all purchasers who end up in one of the boxes representing Du Pont's brand (the black ones).

This model was developed by Du Pont researchers primarily to help them discover at what points advertising might favorably affect Du Pont's share of the market. The model suggested five possible effects of advertising:

1. It might influence the number of people buying the product in a given year ("primary demand").
2. It might increase the number of outlets handling the Du Pont brand and/or the number of people going to existing Du Pont outlets.
3. It might influence more customers to specify a brand as opposed to letting the salesperson specify it.
4. It might increase the fraction of customers who specify the Du Pont brand.

[18] The model is described in Robert D. Buzzell, *Mathematical Models and Marketing Management* (Boston: Division of Research, Graduate School of Business Administration, Harvard University, 1964), pp. 163-64, 177.

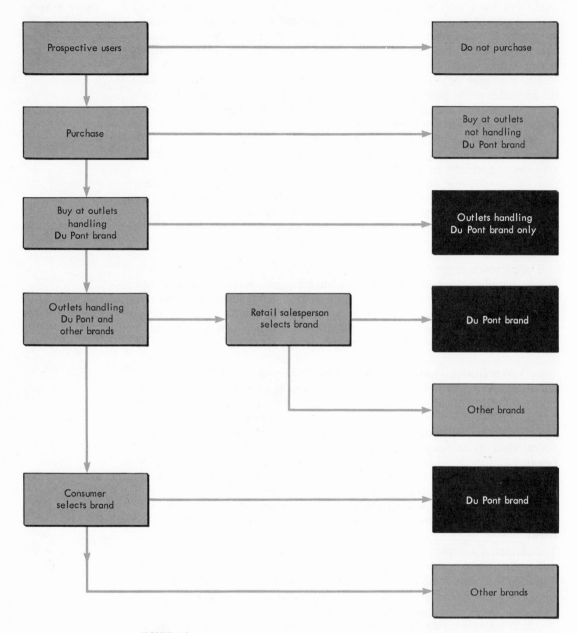

FIGURE 4-3

E. I. du Pont de Nemours & Co. (Inc.) schematic diagram of customer behavior model

Redrawn from Robert D. Buzzell, *Mathematical Models and Marketing Management* (Boston: Division of Research, Graduate School of Business Administration, Harvard University, 1964), p. 177.

The subsequent field experiments carried out by Du Pont were designed in part to measure these separate effects.

ANDREASEN MODEL.   The second example of a customer behavior model is shown in Figure 4-4.[20] It is a richly detailed elaboration chiefly of stages 2 and 3 of the buying process (prepurchase activity and the purchase decision). It can be described in terms of four components: information, filtration, disposition changes, and outcome.

The input stimuli consists of *information* about competing products and their varying attributes, such as price, availability, and so forth. This information is carried to the prospective customer through impersonal sources (principally advertisements), independent impersonal sources (popular articles or television or radio programs), advocate personal sources (principally salesmen), and independent personal sources (family members, friends, associates).

The information is subject to selection and distortion by the individual buyer. He *filters* it in a unique way based on his constellation of attitudes and prior information.

The filtered information, along with other factors, affect the *disposition* of the prospective buyer toward the product. The other factors are the strength and quality of the wants, the degree to which it is expected that the object will satisfy the wants, the personality of the buyer, and so forth. Theoretically, the buyer's disposition toward the object can be measured along a continuum ranging from rejection (minus one) through neutrality (zero) to selection (plus one).

The *outcome* of this information processing by the prospective buyer may take one of three forms: selection, search, or no action. If a selection decision is made, the buyer will probably acquire the object unless he is forced to a holding position by objective constraints, such as insufficient funds, prior needs, or capacity limitations. Or he may delay the purchase pending other decisions on brand choice or outlet choice. When these constraints are overcome, he acquires the product, and his experience with it has a feedback on his disposition toward repeating the purchase. On the other hand, the individual may make a search decision, which amounts to a continuation of active prepurchasing activity such as gathering information. According to Andreasen, the amount of search will be a function "of want-strength, the perceived quantity and quality of information initially received and those aspects of personality related to intelligence and need for cognitive clarity." The third possible outcome may be no action, the individual deciding neither to select the product nor to search for further information. However, in this state he is still likely to have a heightened perception to environmental cues concerning the product.

Andreasen's model ties together several elements of the buying process. It suggests various points at which marketing management can make contact with the prospective buyer through thoughtful communications.

[19] *Ibid.,* p. 164.
[20] Alan R. Andreasen, "Attitudes and Customer Behavior: A Decision Model," in *New Research in Marketing,* ed. Lee E. Preston (Berkeley, Calif.: University of California Institute of Business and Economic Research, 1965), pp. 1-16.

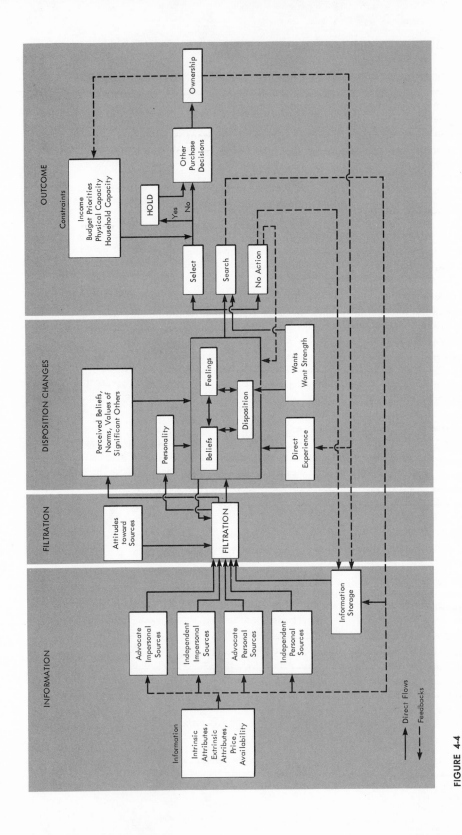

FIGURE 4-4

Customer decision model

Redrawn from Alan R. Andreasen, "Attitudes and Customer Behavior: A Decision Model," in *New Research in Marketing*, ed. Lee E. Preston (Berkeley, Calif.: University of California Institute of Business and Economic Research, 1965), pp. 1-16.

The buying process has been described from felt need through post-purchase feelings. The analysis may be extended to cover the large number of purchasing situations involving more than one active participant. Several participants generally share in family buying and industrial buying. This section will examine more clearly the roles of different participants in the buying process and the nature of the interaction in family and industrial buying situations.

ROLES IN THE BUYING PROCESS

When viewing the buying odyssey of a single person, we saw him seek out information, make the decision, buy the product, and use it. Yet in many purchasing situations these activities are undertaken by different persons. The following four roles can be distinguished: influencers, deciders, buyers, and users.

INFLUENCERS.   Influencers are persons who stimulate, inform, or persuade at any stage of the buying process. Examples of influencers are the movie star who demonstrates a product on TV, the neighbor who describes her experiences and feelings about a particular brand, the husband who expresses his preference but leaves the decision to his wife, and the floor salesman who recommends a particular brand. A number of studies have shown that personal influence can play a large role in product and brand choice.[21] It has been shown to be quite important in the adoption of new drugs by physicians[22] and the adoption of new farming techniques by farmers.[23] This suggests that the firm might find it efficient to direct its communications to those who are likely to be important influencers in the buying situation.

DECIDERS.   Deciders are persons who make the purchase decision, or any component subdecision. Examples of deciders are the woman who sees a dress she likes and buys it, the child who points to the toy he wants for his birthday, the store buying committee which takes a final vote on the brands to carry, or the company president who makes the final decision on the company computer. Whether one person or several, the decision-making agent is the major target for marketing communications. The seller's success depends on how well he can influence those who make the final decision.

BUYERS.   Buyers are persons who make the actual purchase. Examples of buyers are the husband who goes to the supermarket with his wife's shopping list or the purchasing agent who phones in an order requisitioned by the plant manager. Those who are strictly buyers, executing but not influencing the purchase decisions of others, are far less important targets

---

[21] See, for example, Elihu Katz and Paul F. Lazarsfeld, *Personal Influence* (New York: Free Press of Glencoe, Inc., 1955).

[22] James Coleman, Elihu Katz, and Herbert Menzel, "The Diffusion of an Innovation among Physicians," *Sociometry,* December 1957, pp. 253-70.

[23] J. Bohlen and G. Beal, *How Farm People Accept New Ideas,* Special Report No. 15 (Ames, Iowa: Agricultural Extension Service, Iowa State College, 1955).

for marketing communications than the deciders. Often, however, the roles of decider-buyer or influencer-buyer are combined in the same person, in which case marketing communications reaching the buyers can be influential.

USERS. Users are persons who consume or use the product or service. Examples of users are the person who receives a gift and the production worker who operates the machine. Those who are strictly users, who have received a product chosen by someone else, are a meaningful target for marketing communications if they may be deciders or influencers in the future. The user who feels dissonance after the purchase may influence the future repurchase rate directly or indirectly. Where this seems likely, supportive communications may be called for.

INTERACTING ROLES IN FAMILY BUYING

The family is a complicated purchasing organization which buys a tremendous variety of goods and services during the course of a year. To carry out the purchasing operation, there is task specialization backed by certain tacit authority relationships. These arrangements vary greatly from family to family and with respect to different products.

The wife still remains the major purchasing agent for the family's everyday needs, in spite of a distinct trend toward more family shopping. She buys the soaps, the bedsheets, the paper products, the foods, and most of the clothes and makes the decisions on brands. Other members of the family bring some influence to bear where the product or service is destined for their use. The husband is the dominant decider in a few limited areas such as cigarettes, fishing equipment, and tools. The children influence the choice of toys, their own clothing, and sundry foods; in some cases they make the decision and do the buying. All or most members of the family participate in some way in the buying of vacations, television sets, and the automobile. Even here, one can talk about the relative dominance of different members of the family in the decision-making process. In a study of 727 families, the type of car was chosen more by the husband than the wife in 70 per cent of the cases, equally by the husband and the wife in 25 per cent of the cases, and by the wife more than the husband in 5 per cent of the cases.[24] Another study showed that the initial suggestion to buy a car came from the husband, and he exercised the most influence on brand choice; the model was largely chosen by both of them; and the wife had the greatest influence on the color.[25]

INTERACTING ROLES IN INDUSTRIAL BUYING

Industrial buying is another area in which several persons tend to participate in the buying process. Buying arrangements vary greatly according to the type of industry, the size of the firm, and the product classification. In small businesses the owner may make all the buying decisions. As the firm gets larger, the buying function tends to be placed in the hands of purchasing agents, although major buying decisions are still made by top

[24] Harry Sharp and Paul Mott, "Consumer Decisions in a Metropolitan Family," *Journal of Marketing,* XXI (October 1956), 152.

[25] Daniel Starch and Staff, *Male vs. Female: Influence on the Purchase of Selected Products* (Greenwich, Conn.: Fawcett Publications, Inc., 1958).

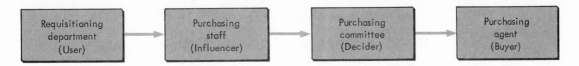

FIGURE 4-5
Participants in an industrial buying situation

management. In large firms, the buying organization is apt to be quite complex with various people making or influencing the buying decision.

A model of one possible arrangement of buying participants in an industrial buying situation is shown in Figure 4-5. The buying process is initiated by a requisition from a prospective user in the company. The requisition is sent to the purchasing department where it is checked by someone on the staff. When the requisition involves an expensive piece of equipment, it may be put on the agenda of a purchasing committee which considers the request in the light of the staff report and renders a decision. If the committee approves the purchase, then a purchasing agent takes over the responsibility of actually placing the order, checking its status, and inspecting the equipment when it arrives. The purchasing agent may make some component decisions, such as choosing the supplier and negotiating the delivery date.

Large retailers show variations from the arrangements shown in Figure 4-5. Most department stores utilize specialized buyers who combine a number of roles. The department-store buyer typically originates and decides on the goods to be bought. He is aided by assistant buyers who carry out preliminary research and the clerical tasks involved in ordering. Supermarkets, on the other hand, are making increasing use of buying committees, which spend most of their time reviewing new product proposals and accepting or rejecting them. It has been estimated that the larger food chains are asked to add about 150 to 250 new items each week, of which store space does not permit more than 10 per cent to be accepted.[26] Proposals are submitted to the store buyer in written form along with samples. He screens out the better proposals, which are reviewed by the store buying committee. The few which are accepted are then turned back to the buyer who orders them.

Thus several persons in the industrial organization typically participate in the buying process. For example, a 1959 study of the buying practices of 106 industrial firms reported that three or more persons influence the buying process in over 75 per cent of the companies examined.[27] Multiple-person influences in industrial buying pose a twofold challenge to the marketer. The first challenge is to map the buying procedures in each customer's organization. The second challenge is to determine the most effective way to influence the buying participants. Distinguishing the buying participants helps the marketer to develop relevant messages and to aim them at the right parties.

[26] E. B. Weiss, *Winning Chain-Store Distributors for New Products* (New York: Doyle-Dane-Bernbach, Inc., 1956), pp. 4-38.

[27] Quoted in Ralph S. Alexander, James S. Cross, and Ross M. Cunningham, *Industrial Marketing,* rev. ed. (Homewood, Ill.: Richard D. Irwin, Inc., 1961), p. 47.

Models of Buyer Choice Processes [28]

Up to now, we have looked at the more overt aspects of buyer behavior, specifically the buying stages and the buying participants. We have yet to examine the underlying processes of buyer decision making. The problem is to figure out what happens in the buyer's mind from the time he first receives impressions about products until he makes his purchasing decisions.

Many influences trace a complex course through the buyer's mind. Unfortunately, no comprehensive model of the workings of the buyer's mind exists.[29] It is largely a "black box." Nevertheless, *the marketing strategist should recognize the potential interpretative contributions of different partial models for explaining buyer behavior.* Depending upon the product, different variables and behavioral mechanisms may assume particular importance. A psychoanalytic behavioral model might throw much light on the factors operating in cigarette demand, while an economic behavioral model may be useful in explaining machine-tool purchasing. Sometimes alternative models shed light on different demand aspects of the same product.

What behavioral models are most useful in interpreting the transformation of buying influences into purchasing responses? Five different models of the buyer's "black box" are presented here, along with their respective marketing applications. They are the Marshallian model, stressing economic motivations; the Pavlovian model, learning; the Freudian model, psychoanalytic motivations; the Veblenian model, social-psychological factors; and the Hobbesian model, organizational factors. These models represent radically different conceptions of the mainsprings of human behavior.

THE MARSHALLIAN ECONOMIC MODEL

Economists were the first professional group to construct a specific theory of buyer behavior. The theory holds that purchasing decisions are the result of largely "rational" and conscious economic calculations. The individual buyer seeks to spend his income on goods that will deliver the most utility (satisfaction) according to his tastes and relative prices.

The antecedents for this view trace back to the writings of Adam Smith and Jeremy Bentham. Smith set the tone by developing a doctrine of economic growth based on the principle that man is motivated by self-interest in all his actions.[30] Bentham refined this view and saw man as finely calculating and weighing the expected pleasures and pains of every contemplated action.[31]

Bentham's "felicific calculus" was not applied to consumer behavior,

[28] The following material is adapted from Philip Kotler, "Behavioral Models for Analyzing Buyers," *Journal of Marketing,* XXIX (October 1965), 37-45.

[29] The lack of a single, generally accepted model of buyer choice processes was highlighted at a conference of behavioral scientists held at Stanford in 1964. See "Where Experts Are Worlds Apart," *Business Week,* November 7, 1964. The papers are published in *On Knowing the Consumer,* ed. Joseph W. Newman (New York: John Wiley & Sons, Inc., 1966).

[30] Adam Smith, *An Inquiry into the Nature and Causes of the Wealth of Nations,* 1776 (New York: The Modern Library, 1937).

[31] Jeremy Bentham, *An Introduction to the Principles of Morals and Legislation,* 1780 (Oxford, England: Clarendon Press, 1907).

as opposed to entrepreneurial behavior, until the late nineteenth century. Then, the "marginal utility" theory of value was formulated independently and almost simultaneously by Jevons [32] and Marshall [33] in England, Menger [34] in Austria, and Walras [35] in Switzerland.

Alfred Marshall was the great consolidator of the classical and neo-classical traditions in economics; his synthesis in the form of demand-supply analysis constitutes the main source of modern microeconomic thought in the English-speaking world. His theoretical work aimed at realism, but his method was to start with simplifying assumptions and to examine the effect of a change in a single variable, say, price, when all other variables were held constant.

He would "reason out" the consequences of the provisional assumptions and in subsequent steps modify his assumptions in the direction of more realism. He employed the "measuring rod of money" as an indicator of the intensity of human psychological desires. Over the years his methods and assumptions have been refined into what is now known as *modern utility theory;* that is, economic man is bent on maximizing his utility and does so by carefully calculating the "felicific" consequences of any purchase.

> Suppose on a particular evening John is considering whether to prepare his own dinner or dine out. He estimates that a restaurant meal would cost two dollars and a home-cooked meal fifty cents. According to the Marshallian model, if John expects less than four times as much satisfaction from the restaurant meal as from the home-cooked meal, he will eat at home. The economist typically is not concerned with how these relative preferences are formed by John or how they may be psychologically modified by new stimuli.
>
> Yet John will not always cook at home. The principle of diminishing marginal utility operates. Within a given time interval, say, a week, the utility of each additional home-cooked meal diminishes. John gets tired of home meals, and other products become relatively more attractive.
>
> John's *efficiency* in maximizing his utility depends on the adequacy of his information and his freedom of choice. If he is not perfectly aware of costs, if his estimate of the relative delectability of the two meals is mistaken, or if he is barred from entering the restaurant, he will not maximize his potential utility. His choice processes are rational, but the results are inefficient.

MARKETING APPLICATIONS OF THE MARSHALLIAN MODEL. Marketers have usually dismissed the Marshallian model as an absurd figment of ivory-tower imagination. In viewing a man as calculating the marginal utility of a restaurant meal over a home-cooked meal, one certainly misses the behavioral essence of the situation.

Eva Mueller has reported a study where only one-fourth of the consumers in her sample bought with any substantial degree of deliberation.[36]

[32] William S. Jevons, *The Theory of Political Economy* (New York: The Macmillan Company, 1871).

[33] Alfred Marshall, *Principles of Economics,* 1890 (London: The Macmillan Company, 1927).

[34] Karl Menger, *Principles of Economics,* 1871 (New York: Free Press of Glencoe, Inc., 1950).

[35] Leon Walras, *Elements of Pure Economics,* 1874 (Homewood, Ill.: Richard D. Irwin, Inc., 1954).

[36] Eva Mueller, "A Study of Purchase Decisions: The Sample Survey," in *Consumer Behavior: The Dynamics of Consumer Reaction,* ed. Lincoln H. Clark (New York: New York University Press, 1954), pp. 36-87.

This was in the purchase of large household appliances; even less deliberation would occur in the case of smaller items. Yet the model may be viewed in a number of ways.

From one point of view the Marshallian model is true by definition. The model holds that the buyer acts in the light of his best interest. But this is not very informative.

A second view is that this is a *normative* rather than a *descriptive* model of behavior. The model provides logical norms for buyers who want to be "rational." Although the consumer is not likely to employ economic analysis to decide between a box of Kleenex and Scotties, he may apply economic analysis in deciding whether to buy a new car. Industrial buyers even more clearly would want an economic calculus for making good decisions.

A third view is that economic factors operate to a greater or lesser extent in all markets and, therefore, must be included in any comprehensive description of buyer behavior.

Furthermore, the model suggests useful behavioral hypotheses, such as: (1) The lower the price of this product, the higher the sales. (2) The lower the price of substitute products, the lower the sales of this product. (3) The lower the price of complementary products, the higher the sales of this product. (4) The higher the real income, the higher the sales of this product, provided that it is not an "inferior" good. (5) The higher the promotional expenditures, the higher the sales.

The validity of these hypotheses does not rest on whether *all* individuals act as economic calculating machines in making their purchasing decisions. Some individuals may buy *less* of a product when its price is reduced. They may think that the quality has gone down or that ownership has less status value. If a majority of buyers view price reductions negatively, then sales may fall, contrary to the first hypothesis.

But for most goods a price reduction increases the relative value of the goods in many buyers' minds and leads to increased sales. This and the other hypotheses are intended to describe average effects.

The impact of economic factors in actual buying situations is studied through experimental design or statistical analyses of past data. Demand equations have been fitted to a wide variety of products, including beer, refrigerators, and chemical fertilizers.[37] More recently, the impact of economic variables on the fortunes of different brands has been pursued with significant results, particularly in the case of coffee, frozen orange juice, and margarine.[38]

But economic factors alone cannot explain all the variations in sales. The Marshallian model ignores the fundamental question of how product and brand preferences are formed. It represents a useful frame of reference for analyzing only one small corner of the "black box."

THE PAVLOVIAN LEARNING MODEL

The Russian physiologist Ivan Pavlov's discovery of conditioned responses is almost too well known to need rehearsal here. In a series of

[37] See Erwin E. Nemmers, *Managerial Economics* (New York: John Wiley & Sons, Inc., 1962), Part II.

[38] See Lester G. Telser, "The Demand for Branded Goods as Estimated from Consumer Panel Data," *Review of Economics and Statistics,* August 1962, pp. 300-324; and William F. Massy and Ronald E. Frank, "Short Term Price and Dealing Effects in Selected Market Segments," *Journal of Marketing Research,* May 1965, pp. 171-85.

experiments in which the feeding of a dog was preceded by the sound of a bell, Pavlov found that much of learning is an associative process and that many of our responses are conditioned by association.

Experimental psychologists have continued this mode of research with rats and other animals, including people. Laboratory experiments have been designed to explore such phenomena as learning, forgetting, and the ability to discriminate. The results have been integrated into a stimulus-response model of human behavior, or, as someone has wisecracked, the substitution of a rat psychology for a rational psychology.

The model has been refined over the years, and today is based on the four central concepts of drive, cue, response, and reinforcement.[39]

Drives, also called "need" or "motive," are an individual's strong internal stimuli impelling action. Psychologists draw a distinction between primary physiological drives—such as hunger, thirst, cold, pain, and sex— and learned drives which are derived socially—such as cooperation, fear, and acquisitiveness.

A drive is general and impels a particular response only in relation to a particular configuration of cues. *Cues* are weaker stimuli in the environment and/or in the individual which determine when, where, and how the subject responds. Thus, a coffee advertisement can serve as a cue which stimulates the thirst drive in a housewife. Her response will depend upon this cue and other cues, such as the time of day, the availability of other thirst-quenchers, and the cue's intensity. Often a relative change in a cue's intensity can be more impelling than its absolute level. The housewife may be more motivated by a two-cents-off sale on a brand of coffee than the fact that the brand's price was low in the first place.

The *response* is the organism's reaction to the configuration of cues. Yet the same configuration of cues will not necessarily produce the same response each time in the individual. This depends on the degree to which the earlier experience had been rewarding; that is, drive-reducing.

If the experience is rewarding, a particular response is *reinforced;* that is, it is strengthened, and there is a tendency for it to be repeated when the same configuration of cues reappears. The housewife will tend to purchase the same brand of coffee each time she goes to her supermarket so long as it is rewarding and the cue configuration does not change. But if a learned response or habit is not reinforced, the strength of the habit diminishes and may eventually be extinguished. Thus, a housewife's preference for a certain coffee may become extinct if she finds the flavor has deteriorated.

Forgetting, in contrast to extinction, is the tendency for learned associations to weaken because of nonuse, not because of the lack of reinforcement.

Cue configurations are constantly changing. The housewife sees a new brand of coffee next to her habitual brand or notes a special price deal on a rival brand. Experimental psychologists have found that the same learned response will be elicited by similar patterns of cues; that is, learned responses are *generalized.* The housewife shifts to a similar brand when her favorite brand is out of stock. This tendency toward generalization over

[39] See John Dollard and Neal E. Miller, *Personality and Psychotherapy* (New York: McGraw-Hill Book Company, 1950), chap. iii.

less similar cue configurations is increased in proportion to the strength of the drive. A housewife may buy an inferior coffee if it is the only brand left and if her drive is sufficiently strong.

A countertendency to generalization is *discrimination*. When a housewife tries two similar brands and finds one more rewarding, her ability to discriminate between similar cue configurations improves. Discrimination increases the specificity of the cue-response connection, while generalization decreases the specificity.

MARKETING APPLICATIONS OF PAVLOVIAN MODEL. The modern version of the Pavlovian model makes no claim to provide a complete theory of behavior—indeed, such important phenomena as perception, the subconscious, and interpersonal influence are inadequately treated. Yet the model does offer a substantial number of insights about some aspects of behavior of considerable interest to marketers.[40]

An example would be the problem of introducing a new brand into a highly competitive market. The company's goal is to extinguish existing brand habits and form new habits among consumers for its brand. But the company must first get customers to try its brand, and it has to decide between using weak and strong cues.

Light introductory advertising is a weak cue compared with distributing free samples. Strong cues, although costing more, may be necessary in markets characterized by strong brand loyalties. For example, the Folger Company usually introduces its brand of coffee in a new market by distributing thousands of pounds of free coffee samples.

To build a brand habit, it helps to provide for an extended period of introductory dealing. Furthermore, sufficient quality must be built into the brand so that the experience is reinforcing. Since buyers are more likely to transfer allegiance to similar brands than to dissimilar brands (generalization), the company should also investigate what cues in the leading brands have been most effective. Although outright imitation would not necessarily effect the most transference, the question of providing enough similarity should be considered.

The Pavlovian model also provides guidelines in the area of advertising strategy. The American behaviorist John B. Watson was a great exponent of repetitive stimuli; his view was that man can be conditioned through repetition and reinforcement to respond in particular ways.[41] He emphasized the desirability of repetition in advertising. A single exposure is likely to be too weak a cue, hardly enough to excite a person's drives above the threshold level.

Repetition in advertising has two desirable effects. It "fights" forgetting, the tendency for learned responses to weaken in the absence of practice. It provides reinforcement, because after the purchase the consumer becomes selectively exposed to advertisements of the product.

The model also provides guidelines for copy strategy. To be effective as a cue, an advertisement must arouse strong drives in the person. The

---

[40] The most consistent application of learning-theory concepts to marketing situations is found in John A. Howard, *Marketing Management: Analysis and Planning*, rev. ed. (Homewood, Ill.: Richard D. Irwin, Inc., 1963).

[41] John B. Watson, *Behaviorism* (New York: The People's Institute Publishing Company, 1925).

strongest product-related drives must be identified. For candy bars, it may be hunger; for safety belts, fear; for hair tonics, sex; for automobiles, status. The advertising practitioner must dip into his cue box of words, colors, and pictures and select the configuration of cues that provides the strongest stimulus to these drives.

THE FREUDIAN PSYCHOANALYTIC MODEL

The Freudian model of man is the latest in a series of philosophical "blows" to which man has been exposed in the last five hundred years. Copernicus destroyed the idea that man stood at the center of the universe; Darwin tried to refute the idea that man was a special creation; and Freud attacked the idea that man even reigned over his own psyche.

According to Freud, the child enters the world driven by instinctual needs which he cannot gratify by himself. Very quickly and painfully he realizes his separateness from the rest of the world and yet his dependence on it.

He tries to get others to gratify his needs through a variety of blatant means, including intimidation and supplication. Continual frustration leads him to perfect more subtle mechanisms for gratifying his needs.

As he grows, his psyche becomes increasingly complex. A part of his psyche, the id, remains the reservoir of his strong drives and urges. Another part, the ego, becomes his conscious planning center for finding outlets for his drives. And a third part, his superego, channels his instinctive drives into socially approved outlets to avoid the pain of guilt or shame.

The guilt or shame which man feels toward some of his urges, especially his sexual urges, causes him to repress them from his consciousness. Through such defense mechanisms as rationalization and sublimation, these urges are denied or become transmuted into socially approved expressions. Yet these urges are never eliminated or under perfect control; they emerge, sometimes with a vengeance, in dreams, in slips of the tongue, in neurotic and obsessional behavior, or ultimately in mental breakdown when the ego can no longer maintain the delicate balance between the impulsive power of the id and the oppressive power of the superego.

The individual's behavior, therefore, is never simple. His motivational wellsprings are not obvious to a casual observer nor deeply understood by himself. If he is asked why he purchased an expensive foreign sports car, he may reply that he likes its maneuverability and its looks. At a deeper level he may have purchased the car to impress others or to feel young again. At a still deeper level, he may have purchased the sports car to achieve substitute gratification for unsatisfied sexual strivings.

Many refinements and changes in emphasis have occurred in this model since the time of Freud. The instinct concept has been replaced by a more careful delineation of basic drives; the three parts of the psyche are regarded now as theoretical concepts rather than actual entities; and the behavioral perspective has been extended to include cultural as well as biological mechanisms.

Instead of the role of the sexual urge in psychic development—Freud's discussion of oral, anal, and genital stages and possible fixations and traumas—Adler [42] emphasized the urge for power and the manifestation of

[42] Alfred Adler, *The Science of Living* (New York: Greenberg, 1929).

its thwarting in superiority and inferiority complexes; Horney [43] emphasized cultural mechanisms; Fromm [44] and Erikson [45] emphasized the role of existential crises in personality development. These philosophical divergencies, rather than debilitating the model, have enriched and extended its interpretative value to a wider range of behavioral phenomena.

MARKETING APPLICATIONS OF FREUDIAN MODEL. Perhaps the most important marketing implication of this model is that buyers are motivated by *symbolic* as well as *economic-functional* product concerns. The change of a bar of soap from a square to a round shape may be more important in its sexual than in its functional connotations. A cake mix that is advertised as involving practically no labor may alienate housewives because the easy life may evoke a sense of guilt.

Motivation research has produced some interesting and occasionally bizarre hypotheses about what may be in the buyer's mind regarding certain purchases. Thus, it has been suggested at one time or another that:

> Many a businessman doesn't fly because of a fear of posthumous guilt—if he crashed, his wife would think of him as stupid for not taking a train.
>
> Men want their cigars to be odoriferous in order to prove that they (the men) are masculine.
>
> A woman is very serious when she bakes a cake because unconsciously she is going through the symbolic act of giving birth.
>
> A man buys a convertible as a substitute mistress.
>
> Consumers prefer vegetable shortening because animal fats stimulate a sense of sin.
>
> Men who wear suspenders are reacting to an unresolved castration complex.

There are admitted difficulties in proving these assertions. Two prominent motivation researchers, Ernest Dichter and James Vicary, were employed independently by two separate groups in the prune industry to determine why so many people dislike prunes. Dichter found, among other things, that the prune aroused feelings of old age and insecurity in people, whereas Vicary's main finding was that Americans had an emotional block about prune's laxative qualities.[46] Which is the more valid interpretation? Or if they are both operative, which motive is found with greater statistical frequency in the population?

Unfortunately, the usual survey techniques of direct observation and interviewing can establish the distribution of such superficial characteristics as age and family size in a population but are not successful in establishing the frequency of mental states presumed to be deeply "buried" within each individual.

Motivation researchers have to employ time-consuming projective tech-

[43] Karen Horney, *The Neurotic Personality of Our Time* (New York: W. W. Norton & Co., 1937).

[44] Erich Fromm, *Man For Himself* (New York: Holt, Rinehart & Winston, Inc., 1947).

[45] Erik H. Erikson, *Childhood and Society* (New York: W. W. Norton & Company, Inc., 1949).

[46] L. Edward Scriven, "Rationality and Irrationality in Motivation Research," in *Motivation and Marketing Behavior,* eds. Robert Ferber and Hugh G. Wales (Homewood, Ill.: Richard D. Irwin, Inc., 1958), pp. 69-70.

niques in the hope of throwing individual "egos" off guard. When carefully administered and interpreted, techniques such as word association, sentence completion, picture interpretation, and role playing can provide some insights into the minds of the small group of examined individuals, but a "leap of faith" is sometimes necessary to generalize these findings to the population.

Nevertheless, motivation research can lead to useful insights and provide inspiration to creative men in the advertising and packaging world. Appeals aimed at the buyer's private world of hopes, dreams, and fears can often be as effective in stimulating purchase as more rationally directed appeals.

THE VEBLENIAN SOCIAL-PSYCHOLOGICAL MODEL

While most economists have been content to interpret buyer behavior in Marshallian terms, Thorstein Veblen struck out in different directions.

Veblen was trained as an orthodox economist, but evolved into a social thinker greatly influenced by the new science of social anthropology. He saw man as primarily a *social animal,* conforming to the general forms and norms of his larger culture and to the more specific standards of the subcultures and face-to-face groupings to which his life is bound. His wants and behavior are largely molded by his present group memberships and the group memberships to which he aspires.

Veblen's best-known example is his description of the leisure class.[47] He dissected the consumption habits of this class to show the many purchases which were motivated not by intrinsic needs or satisfaction so much as by the search for prestige. He held that conspicuous consumption was the goal of this class and that the other classes sought to emulate it.

In today's perspective, some of his points seem overstated. The leisure class does not serve as everyone's reference group; many persons aspire to the social patterns of the class immediately above their own. And important segments of the affluent class practice conspicuous underconsumption rather than overconsumption. Many people in all classes are more anxious to "fit in" than to "stand out." As an example, William H. Whyte found that many families avoided buying air conditioners and other appliances before their neighbors did.[48]

Veblen was not the first nor the only investigator to comment on social influences in behavior, but the incisive quality of his observations did much to stimulate further investigations. Another stimulus came earlier from Karl Marx, who held that each man's world view was determined largely by his relationship to the "means of production." [49] The early field work in primitive societies by men like Boas [50] and Malinowski [51] and the later

[47] Thorstein Veblen, *The Theory of the Leisure Class* (New York: The Macmillan Company, 1899).

[48] William H. Whyte, Jr., "The Web of Word of Mouth," *Fortune,* November 1954, pp. 140 ff.

[49] Karl Marx, *The Communist Manifesto,* 1848 (London: Martin Lawrence, Ltd., 1934).

[50] Franz Boas, *The Mind of Primitive Man* (New York: The Macmillan Company, 1922).

[51] Bronislaw Malinowski, *Sex and Repression in Savage Society* (New York: Meridian Books, 1955).

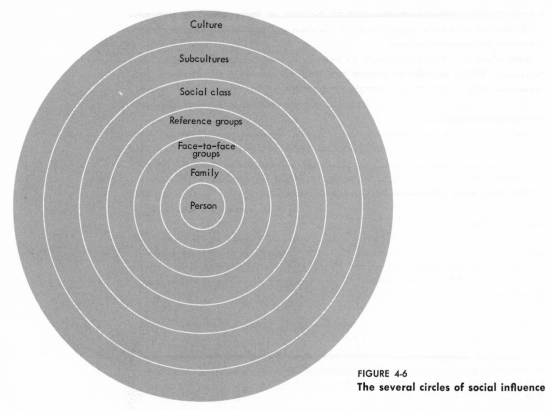

FIGURE 4-6
The several circles of social influence

field work in urban societies by men like Park [52] and Warner [53] contributed much to understanding the influence of society and culture. Research into the mechanisms of perception, conducted by early Gestalt psychologists like Wertheimer,[54] Köhler,[55] and Koffka,[56] eventually led to investigations of small-group influence on perception.

MARKETING APPLICATIONS OF VEBLENIAN MODEL. The various early streams of thought crystallized into the modern social sciences of sociology, social anthropology, and social psychology. Basic to them is the view that man's attitudes and behavior are influenced by several levels of society— culture, subcultures, social classes, reference groups, face-to-face groups, and family. These levels are illustrated in Figure 4-6. The challenge to the marketer is to determine which of these social levels are the most important in influencing the demand for his product.

Culture. The most enduring influences are cultural. Man tends to

[52] Robert E. Park, *Human Communities* (New York: Free Press of Glencoe, Inc., 1952).

[53] W. Lloyd Warner, *Social Life of a Modern Community* (New Haven, Conn.: Yale University Press, 1941).

[54] Max Wertheimer, *Productive Thinking* (New York: Harper & Brothers, 1945).

[55] Wolfgang Köhler, *Gestalt Psychology* (New York: Liveright Publishing Corp., 1947).

[56] Kurt Koffka, *Principles of Gestalt Psychology* (New York: Harcourt, Brace and Co., 1935).

assimilate his culture's mores and to believe in their absolute rightness until deviant elements appear within his own culture or until he confronts members of another culture.

Subcultures.   A culture tends to lose its homogeneity as the population increases. When people no longer are able to maintain face-to-face relationships with more than a small proportion of the population, smaller units or subcultures develop to help satisfy the individual's needs for more specific identity.

The subcultures are often regional entities, because the people of a region, as a result of frequent interactions, tend to think and act alike. But subcultures also take the form of religions, nationalities, fraternal orders, and other institutional complexes which provide a broad identification for people who may otherwise be strangers. Subcultures play a large role in attitude formation and are important predictors of values an individual is likely to hold.

Social class.   People become differentiated not only horizontally but also vertically through a division of labor. Society becomes stratified on the basis of wealth, skill, and power. Sometimes castes develop whose members are reared for certain roles. Sometimes social classes develop whose members are bound by a feeling of empathy with others who share similar values and economic circumstances.

Because social class involves different attitudinal configurations, it becomes a useful independent variable for segmenting markets and predicting reactions. Significant differences have been found among various social classes with respect to magazine readership, leisure activities, food imagery, fashion interests, and acceptance of innovations. A sampling of attitudinal differences in class is of interest.

> Members of the *upper-middle* class place an emphasis on professional competence, indulge in expensive status symbols, and more often than not show a taste, real or otherwise, for theater and the arts. They want their children to show high achievement and precocity and develop into physicists, vice-presidents, and judges. This class likes to deal in ideas and symbols.
>
> Members of the *lower-middle* class cherish respectability, savings, a college education, and good housekeeping. They want their children to show self-control and prepare for careers as accountants, lawyers, and engineers.
>
> Members of the *upper-lower* class try to keep up with the times, if not with the Joneses. They stay in older neighborhoods but buy new kitchen appliances. They spend proportionately less than the middle class on major clothing articles, buying a new suit mainly for an important ceremonial occasion. They also spend proportionately less on services, preferring to do their own plumbing and other work around the house. They tend to raise large families, and their children generally enter manual occupations. This class also supplies many local businessmen, politicians, sports stars, and labor-union leaders.

Reference groups.   Groups in which the individual has no membership but with which he identifies and to which he may aspire are called reference groups. Many young boys identify with big-league baseball players or astronauts, and many young girls identify with Hollywood stars. The activities of these popular heroes are carefully watched and frequently imitated. These reference figures become important transmitters of influence, although more along lines of taste and hobby than basic attitudes.

Face-to-face groups. Groups that have the most immediate influence on a person's tastes and opinions are face-to-face groups. This includes all the small "societies" with which he comes into frequent contact: his family, close friends, neighbors, fellow workers, fraternal associates, and so forth. His informal group memberships are influenced largely by his occupation, residence, and stage in the life cycle.

The powerful influence of small groups on individual attitudes has been demonstrated in a number of social-psychological experiments.[57] There is also evidence that this influence may be growing. David Riesman and his coauthors have pointed to signs which indicate a growing amount of *other-direction;* that is, a tendency for individuals to be influenced increasingly by their contemporaries in the definition of their values rather than by their parents and elders.[58]

For the marketer, this means that brand choice may increasingly be influenced by peer groups. For such products as cigarettes and automobiles, the influence of neighbors and associates is unmistakable.

The role of face-to-face groups has been recognized in recent industry campaigns attempting to change basic product attitudes. For years the milk industry has been trying to overcome the image of milk as a "sissified" drink by portraying its use in social and active situations. The men's-wear industry is trying to increase male interest in clothes by advertisements indicating that business associates judge a man by how well he dresses.

Family. Of all face-to-face groups, the person's family undoubtedly plays the largest and most enduring role in basic attitude formation. From them he acquires a mental set not only toward religion and politics, but also toward thrift, chastity, food, human relations, and so forth. Although he often rebels against parental values in his teens, he often accepts these values eventually. Their formative influence on his eventual attitudes is undeniably great.

Family members differ in the product messages they carry to other family members. Most of what parents know about cereals, candy, and toys comes from their children. The wife stimulates family consideration of household appliances, furniture, and vacations. The husband tends to stimulate the fewest purchase ideas, with the exception of the automobile and sporting equipment.

The marketer must be alert to what attitudinal configurations dominate in different types of families and also to how these change over time. For example, the parent's conception of the child's rights and privileges has undergone a radical shift in the last thirty years. The child has become the center of attention and orientation in a great number of households, leading some writers to label the modern family a "filiarchy." This has important implications not only for how to market to today's family, but also on how to market to tomorrow's family when the indulged child of today becomes the parent.

[57] See, for example, Solomon E. Asch, "Effects of Group Pressure Upon the Modification and Distortion of Judgment," in *Group Dynamics,* eds. Dorwin Cartwright and Alvin Zander (Evanston, Ill.: Row, Peterson & Co., 1953), pp. 151-52; and Kurt Lewin, "Group Decision and Social Change," in *Readings in Social Psychology,* eds. Theodore M. Newcomb and Eugene L. Hartley (New York: Henry Holt Co., 1952).

[58] David Riesman, Reuel Denney, and Nathan Glazer, *The Lonely Crowd* (New Haven, Conn.: Yale University Press, 1950).

The person. Social influences determine much but not all of the behavioral variations in people. Two individuals subject to the same influences are not likely to have identical attitudes, although their attitudes will probably converge at more points than those of two strangers selected at random. Attitudes are really the product of social forces interacting with the individual's unique temperament and abilities.

Furthermore, attitudes—in buying as in anything else—do not automatically guarantee certain types of behavior. Attitudes are predispositions felt by buyers before they enter the buying process. The buying process itself is a learning experience and can lead to a change in attitudes.

Alfred Politz noted at one time that women stated a clear preference for General Electric refrigerators over Frigidaire but that Frigidaire continued to outsell GE.[59] The answer to this paradox was that preference was only one factor entering into behavior. When the consumer preferring GE actually undertook to purchase a new refrigerator, her curiosity led her to examine the other brands. Her perception was sensitized to refrigerator advertisements, sales arguments, and different product features. This led to learning and a change in attitudes.

THE HOBBESIAN ORGANIZATIONAL-FACTORS MODEL

The foregoing models throw light mainly on the behavior of family buyers. But what of the large number of people who are organizational buyers? They are engaged in the purchase of goods not for the sake of consumption but for further production or distribution. Their common denominator is that they (1) are paid to make purchases for others and (2) operate within an organizational environment.

How do organizational buyers make their decisions? There seem to be two competing views. Many marketing writers have emphasized the predominance of rational motives in organizational buying.[60] Organizational buyers are represented as being most impressed by cost, quality, dependability, and service factors. They are portrayed as dedicated servants of the organization, seeking to secure the best terms. This view has led to an emphasis on performance and use characteristics in much industrial advertising.

Other writers have emphasized personal motives in organizational-buyer behavior. The purchasing agent's interest to do the best for his company is tempered by his interest to do the best for himself. He may be tempted to choose among salesmen according to the extent they entertain or offer gifts. He may choose a particular vendor because this will ingratiate him with certain company officers. He may shortcut his study of alternative suppliers to make his workday easier.

In truth, the buyer is guided by both personal and group goals, and this is the essential point. The political model of Thomas Hobbes comes closest of any model to suggesting the relationship between the two goals.[61] Hobbes held that man is "instinctively" oriented toward preserving and enhancing his own well-being. But this would produce a "war of every man

---

[59] Alfred Politz, "Motivation Research—Opportunity or Dilemma?", in Ferber and Wales, *op. cit.,* pp. 57-58.

[60] See Melvin T. Copeland, *Principles of Merchandising* (New York: McGraw-Hill Book Company, 1924).

[61] Thomas Hobbes, *Leviathan,* 1651 (London: G. Routledge and Sons, 1887).

against every man." Fear of this war leads men to unite with others in a corporate body. The corporate man tries to steer a careful course between satisfying his own needs and those of the organization.

MARKETING APPLICATIONS OF HOBBESIAN MODEL. The import of the Hobbesian model is that organizational buyers can be appealed to on both personal and organizational grounds. The buyer has his private aims; yet he tries to do a satisfactory job for his corporation. He will respond to persuasive salesmen, and he will respond to rational product arguments. However, the best "mix" of the two is not a fixed quantity; it varies with the nature of the product, the type of organization, and the relative strength of the two drives in the particular buyer.

Where there is substantial similarity in what suppliers offer in the way of products, price, and service, the purchasing agent has less basis for rational choice. Since he can satisfy his organizational obligations with any one of a number of suppliers, he can be swayed by personal motives. On the other hand, where there are pronounced differences among the competing vendors' products, the purchasing agent is held more accountable for his choice and probably pays more attention to rational factors. Short-run personal gain becomes less motivating than the long-run gain which comes from serving the organization with distinction.

The marketing strategist must appreciate these goal conflicts of the organizational buyer. Behind all the ferment of purchasing agents to develop standards and employ value analysis lies their desire to avoid being thought of as order clerks and to develop better skills in reconciling personal and organizational objectives.[62]

Summary

Marketing planning is inevitably based on a set of assumptions concerning what the buyer is like. If the view of the buyer or the buying process is oversimplified, the company may do a poor job or miss opportunities for doing a better job.

The buying process has five stages, all of which have significance for the marketer: a felt need, prepurchase activity, the purchase decision, product use, and postpurchase feelings. There are also various participants in the buying process, such in influencers, deciders, buyers, and users; they play various roles in family and industrial purchasing. Before a purchase is made, buying influences must be translated in the buyer's mind into purchasing responses. There have been many theories of how this happens—among them the Marshallian economic model, the Pavlovian learning model, the Freudian psychoanalytic model, the Veblenian social-psychological model, and the Hobbesian organizational-factors model.

It turns out that the "black box" of the buyer's mind, although

[62] For an insightful account, see George Strauss, "Tactics of Lateral Relationship: The Purchasing Agent," *Administrative Science Quarterly,* September 1962, pp. 161-86.

complicated, is not so black after all. Light is thrown in various corners by these models. Yet no one has succeeded in putting all these pieces of truth together into one coherent instrument for behavioral analysis. This, of course, is the goal of behavioral science.

Questions and Problems

1. Choose a product and analyze the behavior of buyers in the market for that product. Specifically, when, where, and how do they buy? How do they make their choices? Is some particular model especially useful for interpreting buyer behavior in this market?

2. The stage in the buying process called prepurchase activity has often been broken up into successive states of mind: awareness, knowledge, liking, preference, and conviction. Do you think each successive state is necessarily associated with a higher probability of purchase?

3. Name some factors which are likely to influence (a) the amount of family task specialization in purchasing and (b) the relative amount of authority held by the husband versus the wife in making major purchase decisions.

4. Indicate how various family consumption systems have been affected by the advent of television.

chapter 5

Market Measurement and Forecasting

The previous chapters in Part I examined different ways of looking at markets; that is, the type of market (consumer, business, international), some forces affecting markets (technology, distribution, and culture), the major segments within a market, and the attitudes, motivation, and behavior of individual buyers. Each level of analysis yielded another layer of information for appraising marketing opportunities, requirements, and risks.

For the most part, however, these analyses are highly qualitative. Marketing planning also requires conversion of the various qualitative understandings into quantitative estimates of specific demand by product, territory, and type of customer. This job has been called market measurement.

The discussion of market measurement in this chapter is divided into four sections. The first describes the vital role played by market measurement in the company's analysis, planning, and control processes. The second distinguishes among several concepts and steps needed for careful demand measurement and marketing planning. The third explores the major alternative methods of measuring demand. The last discusses how forecasts and forecasting methods can be evaluated in terms of their accuracy and costs.

Company Uses of Market Measurement

Market measurement describes the activity of developing quantitative estimates of demand. Figure 5-1 shows twenty-four types of demand measurement. Demand can be measured along at least four different product level dimensions, three different time dimensions, and two different space dimensions.

Each type of demand measurement serves a specific purpose. Thus a company might make a short-range forecast of the total demand for a particular product item to provide a basis for ordering raw materials, planning production, and scheduling short-run financing. Or it might make a long-range forecast of regional demand for its major product line to provide a basis for considering market expansion.

The various market measurements are used by the company to carry out three important management functions—the *analysis* of market opportunities, the *planning* of company efforts, and the *control* of marketing performance.

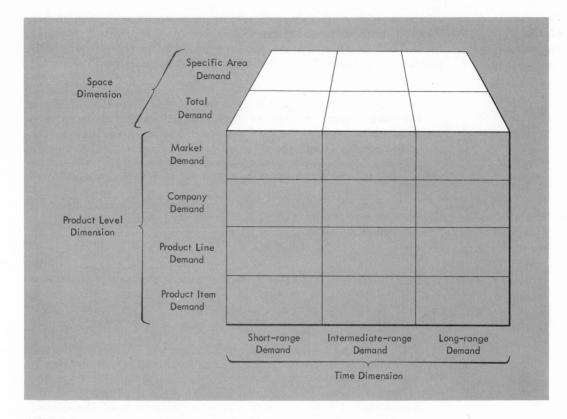

FIGURE 5-1
Twenty-four types of market measurement

ANALYSIS

Each company must make choices among the many markets or sub-markets open to it. The choice is greatly facilitated by quantitative estimates of demand in the various markets and market segments. The following situations illustrate the role of market measurement in the analysis of market opportunity:

> A large department store is trying to decide in which of five suburbs it should locate a branch department store. An estimate of company sales potential in each of these locations will be the guiding factor.
>
> An electronics manufacturer is trying to decide whether to produce a light portable television set. The company will be guided by the marketing research department's estimate of long-range total demand.
>
> An oxygen equipment manufacturer is trying to decide whether to broaden sales coverage to include surgical supply houses as well as fire departments. The company will be guided by an estimate of potential sales in this segment of the market.

PLANNING

After selecting its markets, the firm must carefully plan its marketing program. It must make short-run decisions involving the allocation and scheduling of its limited resources over many competing uses; it must make long-run decisions involving rates of expansion of capital equipment and funds. Both the short-run and the long-run decisions require quantitative estimates of demand. The following situations illustrate this:

> The sales manager of a hospital supply company wants to assign five new salesmen in the areas where they are most needed. He wants estimates of the expected growth of demand in the company's major territories to use as a basis for assigning the men.
>
> The advertising manager of an air conditioning company has to divide his budget between consumer and industrial advertising. He wants a short-run demand forecast for each sector to use as a basis for assigning the funds.
>
> The executive committee of a large utility company needs a long-range forecast of population and business expansion to use as a basis for planning future expansion.

CONTROL

The firm's actual performance in the market place takes on meaning when it is compared to measures of potential performance developed for products, territories, salesmen, and distributors. The use of these market measurements for control purposes is illustrated is the following situations:

> A large American television manufacturer was disappointed with its sales in Venezuela. The marketing research department was asked to develop a fresh estimate of company sales potential in Venezuela.
>
> The district sales manager of an insurance company wanted to subdivide a salesman's territory in which sales were unusually high. The salesman objected, arguing that the territory had only average sales potential and that the high level of sales reflected his superior sales ability. The sales manager asked his research staff to determine the sales potential of the territory.
>
> The vice-president of a tractor firm asked the research department to re-estimate the size of the potential market for a particular tractor which was selling better than expected.

Thus market measurement plays a central role in helping management analyze, plan, and control its efforts.

Major Concepts in Market Measurement

The field of market measurement is filled with a large, almost confusing number of terms. Company executives talk of sales forecasts, sales predictions, sales potentials, sales estimates, sales projections, sales-volume goals, sales quotas, and sales budgets. Many of these term are redundant; only three concepts are needed to discuss market measurement. They are *market demand, company demand,* and *company sales forecast.*

MARKET DEMAND

In evaluating marketing opportunities, the firm usually starts with the notion of market demand. It is not a simple concept, as the following definition makes clear:

Market demand for a *product class* is the *total volume* which would be *bought* by a defined *customer group* in a defined *location* in a defined *time period* under defined *environmental conditions* and *marketing effort*.

There are eight elements in this definition.

Product class. Market demand measurement requires a careful definition of the product or product class. The seller of tin cans has to define whether the relevant market to measure is the metal can market or the larger metal-glass container market. The seller of liquid detergents has to decide whether the relevant market to measure is the low-sudsing consumer liquid detergent market or the consumer liquid detergent market or the consumer liquid and powdered detergent market. These decisions depend on how the seller views the opportunities for penetrating adjacent markets.[1]

Total volume. Market demand can be measured either in physical volume terms, dollar volume terms, or both. The market demand for automobiles may be described as 9 million cars or $27 billion. The physical volume measure is useful when the product is relatively homogeneous. Its advantage is that historical sales are not distorted by changes in the value of the dollar. But if product homogeneity is lacking or shifting, the physical volume measure can be misleading. For example, 9 million cars can have vastly varying profit implications, depending upon the mix of high-priced and low-priced cars.

Market demand can also be expressed in relative rather than absolute volume terms. Thus the market demand for automobiles in Greater Chicago can be expressed as 270,000 cars or as 3 per cent of the nation's total demand.

Bought. In measuring market demand, it is important to define whether "bought" means the volume ordered, the volume shipped, the volume paid for, the volume received, or the volume consumed. For example, a forecast of new housing for the next year usually means the number of units which will be ordered, not completed (called housing starts). A forecast of passenger automobile sales can vary, depending upon whether the measure is the number of cars delivered to dealers or the number purchased by households.

Customer group. Market demand may be measured for the whole market or for any segment(s) of the market. Examples of the latter are a steel producer who estimates the volume to be bought separately by the construction industry and the transportation industry, or an airline which estimates the seat-miles to be bought by business travelers and vacation travelers.

Location. Market demand should be measured with reference to well-defined geographical boundaries. A forecast of next year's passenger automobile sales will vary depending upon whether the boundaries are limited to the United States or include Canada and/or Mexico. Market demand may be measured for cities, standard metropolitan areas, counties, states, regions, or countries.

Time period. Market demand should be measured with reference to a stated period of time. One can talk about the market demand for the next

---

[1] Economists use the concept of "cross-elasticity" to measure the relatedness of two markets. See Chapter 15, pp. 380-81.

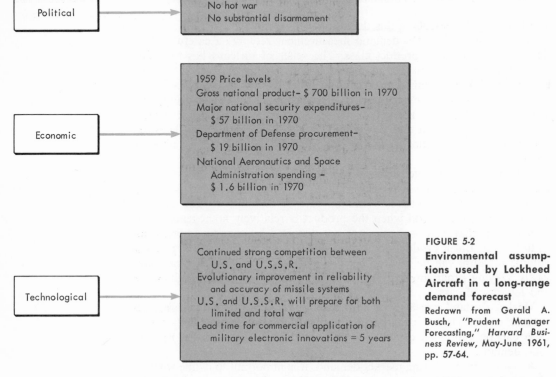

FIGURE 5-2

Environmental assumptions used by Lockheed Aircraft in a long-range demand forecast

Redrawn from Gerald A. Busch, "Prudent Manager Forecasting," *Harvard Business Review,* May-June 1961, pp. 57-64.

calendar year, or for the coming five years, or for 1975, and so forth. Generally speaking, the longer the forecasting interval, the more tenuous the forecast. Every forecast is based on a set of assumptions about environmental and marketing conditions, and the chance that some of these assumptions will not be fulfilled increases with the length of the period forecast.

Environmental conditions. Market demand is affected by a host of uncontrollable factors, such as technological breakthroughs, economic reversals, new legislation, and changes in taste. Different assumptions concerning the environmental conditions expected to prevail will lead to different estimates of market demand. Therefore it is important to list the set of environmental assumptions underlying any estimate of market demand. The environmental assumptions made by Lockheed Aircraft in 1960 in preparing its forecast of 1970 sales are reproduced in Figure 5-2.

Marketing effort. Market demand is also affected by controllable factors, particularly marketing programs developed by the sellers. Demand in most markets will show some elasticity with respect to industry price, promotion, product improvements, and distribution effort. Thus a market demand forecast also requires assumptions about future industry prices and marketing outlays.

MARKET DEMAND ILLUSTRATED GRAPHICALLY. The most important thing to realize about market demand is that it is not a single number, but

(a) Market demand as a function of price

Market demand per time period

(All other things equal)

Price

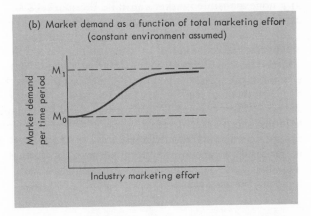

(b) Market demand as a function of total marketing effort
(constant environment assumed)

Market demand per time period

M_1

M_0

Industry marketing effort

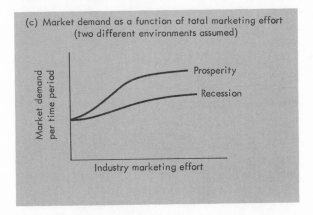

(c) Market demand as a function of total marketing effort
(two different environments assumed)

Market demand per time period

Prosperity

Recession

Industry marketing effort

FIGURE 5-3
Market demand

a function. One should recall the price-demand relationship found in all
elementary economics textbooks (see Figure 5-3a). Market demand per
time period is shown to vary inversely with the level of price. As for other
variables, such as environmental conditions, some set of them is assumed
implicitly and is further assumed to remain constant at the alternative price
levels.

Figure 5-3b represents a generalization of Figure 5-3a. Market demand is shown to vary with total industry marketing effort, not just price. Even at a zero level of marketing effort, there will be a minimum amount of market demand (M_0). At higher levels of industry marketing effort (more advertising, more salesmen, lower prices), market demand will also be higher. Still higher levels of marketing effort will not increase market demand very much. We can define a maximum level of market demand (M_1) called *market potential*. We can think of two extreme types of markets, the *expansible* and the *nonexpansible*. The expansible market, epitomized by markets for new products, is quite affected in its total size by the level of marketing expenditures. In terms of Figure 5-3b, the distance between M_0 and M_1 is relatively large. The nonexpansible market, epitomized by cigarettes or drugs, is not much affected by the level of marketing expenditures; the distance between M_0 and M_1 is relatively small. The firm selling in a nonexpansible market can take the market's size for granted and concentrate its marketing resources on getting a good share of the market.

Figure 5-3c brings out the fact that market demand depends on assumed environmental conditions as well as on the level of industry marketing effort. The top function shows market demand under the assumption of economic prosperity; the lower function shows market demand under the assumption of a recession, when the ability of marketing expenditures to stimulate sales is much less. Thus the analyst distinguishes between the position of the market demand function and movement along it. The sellers cannot do anything about the position of the market demand function; this is the result of uncontrollable environmental factors. The sellers influence their particular location on the function, however, in deciding how much to spend on marketing.

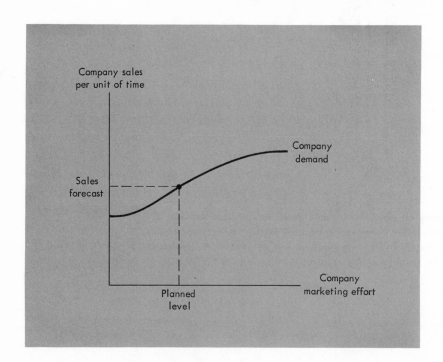

FIGURE 5-4
Company demand

The company's share of total market demand will depend upon the quality of its product and marketing effort relative to competitors. This varying share is expressed in the concept of company demand.

> *Company demand* is estimated company sales at alternative levels of company marketing effort.

A company demand function is illustrated in Figure 5-4. It resembles the market demand function of Figure 5-3b, except that it is specialized to the company situation. It shows company sales varying directly, but not proportionately, with its marketing effort.

A company's marketing effort affects both market demand and company demand. This is summarized in the following two propositions:

$$S = f(k_1m_1, k_2m_2, \ldots, k_im_i, \ldots, k_nm_n, a,b,c) \quad (1)$$

$$s_i = f(\frac{k_im_i}{k_1m_1 + k_2m_2 + \ldots + k_im_i + \ldots + k_nm_n}, a,b,c) \quad (2)$$

where

$$S = \text{market demand}$$
$$k_i = \text{company } i\text{'s marketing effectiveness per unit expenditure}$$
$$m_i = \text{company } i\text{'s total marketing expenditure}$$
$$k_im_i = \text{company } i\text{'s effective marketing expenditures}$$
$$a,b,c = \text{other factors}$$
$$s_i = \text{company } i\text{'s demand}$$
$$1,2, \ldots i, \ldots n = \text{subscripts referring to different sellers}$$
$$\text{(the first seller is 1, the last is } n)$$

Proposition 1 states that market demand is a function of the total effective marketing effort of all sellers, plus other factors. Proposition 2 states that company i's demand is a function of the magnitude and effectiveness of its marketing expenditures relative to the total industry marketing effort, plus other factors. If all firms were capable of the same effectiveness in spending a marketing dollar, then a firm's market share of total sales would be determined roughly by the proportion of its marketing expenditures to the total for the industry. This idea has been at the base of many investigations designed to explain the market share of different firms in an industry. One often reads of an attempt, for example, to correlate the market shares of different cigarette companies with the relative size of their advertising expenditures. This is not really a test of Proposition 2 because, first, differences in the effectiveness of different sellers' advertising expenditures are overlooked, and, second, other types of marketing effort, such as packaging or intrinsic product differences, are left out of the explanation. Although Proposition 2 is difficult to verify empirically, it provides a rough guide to what determines the sales of the ith firm.

In making its estimates of market and company demand, the firm in principle must estimate the likely magnitude and effectiveness of the marketing expenditures of all sellers. Some industries, such as cigarettes and copper, show relative stability in their marketing effort on a year-to-year basis. Surprise price cutting; establishment of new firms; or drastically changed products, advertising programs, or expenditure levels are unlikely. Market shares tend to persist for a long time, and the individual seller is fairly safe in extrapolating his current market share for short-range sales forecasting. Or if the seller's market share has been gradually rising over the years, he is fairly safe in adjusting the current market share upward according to the historical rate of change.

On the other hand, if the seller plans a drastically new program, he must consider competitive reactions in order to estimate the ultimate market share outcomes. Some industries, such as toys and women's apparel, are marked by a high mobility of firms and rapid changes in marketing tactics. In these cases, market shares are difficult to predict, and rather than extend the present market share, it is better to forecast on the basis of new assumptions.

COMPANY SALES FORECAST

Company demand describes estimated company sales at alternative planned levels of company marketing effort. It remains for management to choose one of the levels.[2] The chosen level of marketing effort implies a particular level of sales, which may be called the company sales forecast.

> The *company sales forecast* is the expected level of company sales based on a chosen marketing plan and assumed environmental conditions.

Too often the sequential relationship between the company sales forecast and the company marketing plan is confused. One frequently hears that the company should plan its marketing effort on the basis of forecast sales, implying

$$\text{Forecast} \longrightarrow \text{Plan}$$

The confusion arises because forecasts are prepared for various levels of product aggregation and time spans. The forecast-to-plan sequence is valid if "forecast" means an estimate of national economic activity, because the marketing expenditures (plan) of a single company has a negligible influence on gross national product. The sequence is also valid if "forecast" means an estimate of market demand where market demand is nonexpansible; i.e., where a company's plan does not influence the level of market demand. The sequence is not valid, however, where market demand is expansible, nor is the sequence valid if "forecast" means an estimate of company sales. In the last two instances, the correct sequence is

$$\text{Plan} \longrightarrow \text{Forecast}$$

The company sales forecast does not establish a basis for deciding on the amount and composition of marketing effort; quite the contrary, it is the *result* of an assumed blueprint for marketing action. The sales forecast must be viewed as a dependent variable which is affected, among other things, by the planned marketing activity of the firm.

The various company departments orient their planning around the sales forecast. The marketing department, of course, has already outlined its

---

[2] The theory of choosing the best level of marketing effort is described in Chapter 12, pp. 270-74.

general strategy of expenditures—this strategy was the original basis for developing the sales forecast. Marketing at this point has to fill in further details to make sure that the sales forecast is realized. Production, purchasing, personnel, and finance use the sales forecast to plan their respective operations.

OTHER CONCEPTS

The sales forecast is the last concept needed for market measurement purposes, although two further concepts can be mentioned in passing because they are derived from the sales forecast. One is the *sales quota*.

> A *sales quota* is defined as the sales goal set for a product line, company division, or company agent. It is primarily a managerial device for defining and stimulating sales effort.

The sales quota set by management is arrived at through a joint consideration of the sales forecast and the psychology of stimulating its achievement. The latter consideration generally leads to setting sales quotas which total to a slightly higher figure than the estimated sales forecast. It is hoped that by setting quotas on the high side, salesmen will exert extra effort. The sales quota is often accompanied by a remuneration plan in which bonus earnings are made available for sales overachievement.

The other concept is a *sales budget*.

> A *sales budget* is defined as a conservative estimate of the expected volume of sales and is used primarily for making current purchasing, production, and cash flow decisions.

The sales budget is arrived at through a joint consideration of the sales forecast and of the need to avoid excessive investment in case the forecast is not realized. The latter consideration generally leads to setting a sales budget slightly lower than the sales forecast.

Methods of Forecasting Demand

One of the most important aspects of market measurement is estimating the future demand for a product. Very few products or services lend themselves to easy forecasting. The few cases generally involve a product whose absolute level or trend is fairly constant and where competitive relations are nonexistent (public utilities) or stable (pure oligopolies). In the vast majority of markets, market demand and especially company demand are not stable from one year to the next, and good forecasting becomes a central factor in company success. The more unstable the demand, the more important is forecast accuracy and the more elaborate is forecasting procedure.

Forecasting methods range from the crude to the highly sophisticated. Many technical aspects fall in the province of experts. Yet there are compelling reasons for marketing management to possess some familiarity with the major alternative forecasting methods. This familiarity is necessary in order to understand the limitations of the current methods as well as whether better methods are available. Furthermore, forecasting is influenced by planning, requiring a continuous dialogue between marketing management and company forecasters. This dialogue is aided considerably when marketing management understands the basic forecasting techniques.

Six major methods of forecasting demand are discussed on the following pages.[3] The proliferation of forecasting methods should not be surprising, given the diversity of products, the variations in the availability, reliability, and types of information, and the variety of forecast objectives. Although six methods are discussed, there are actually only three information bases for building a forecast. The investigator can build his forecast on the basis of *what people say, what people do,* or *what people have done.*

The first basis—*what people say*—involves systematic determination of the opinions of buyers or of those close to them, such as salesmen or outside experts. It encompasses three methods: (1) surveys of buyer intentions, (2) composites of sales force opinions, and (3) expert opinion. Building a forecast on *what people do* involves another method: (4) putting the product to a market test to provide indications of future buyer response. The final basis—*what people have done*—involves analyzing, with mathematical and statistical tools, records of past buying behavior, using either (5) classical time series analysis or (6) statistical demand analysis. Each of these methods will be described, citing actual applications and underscoring its merits and limitations.

SURVEYS OF BUYER INTENTIONS

Forecasting is essentially the art of anticipating what buyers are likely to do under a given set of conditions. This immediately suggests that a most useful source of information would be the buyers themselves. Ideally, a list of all potential buyers would be drawn up; each buyer would be approached, preferably on a face-to-face basis, and asked how much he plans to buy of the stated product in the defined future time period under stated conditions. He would also be asked to state what proportion of his total requirements he intends to buy from the particular firm or at least what factors would influence his choice among suppliers. With this information, supposing it is both attainable and valid, the firm would seem to have an ideal basis for forecasting its sales.

Unfortunately, this method has a number of limitations in practice. Let us accept for the moment that the buyers could be identified and could and would convey valid information about their intentions. Would the value of this information be worth the cost of gathering it? In the case of consumer convenience goods, such as soda beverages, it would be prohibitively expensive to pay a personal call on every buyer. This objection is answered in part by taking a probability sample instead of a census. The cost can also be reduced by substituting telephone or mail interviewing for personal interviewing.

Would the buyers freely report their intentions? In many situations buyers would not confide their buying intentions. A purchasing agent

[3] For other classifications of forecasting methods, see Francis E. Hummel, *Market and Sales Potentials* (New York: The Ronald Press Company, 1961), p. 310; *Forecasting Sales,* National Industrial Conference Board, Business Policy Study No. 106, 1963, p. 109; Paul Stillson and E. Leonard Arnoff, "Product Search and Evaluation," *Journal of Marketing,* XXII (July 1957), 39.

might not want to reveal to a typewriter salesman how many machines his company has budgeted for purchase in the coming year. A Defense Department official would not reveal how many atomic weapons will be purchased. Such requests can be regarded as an invasion of privacy or secrecy.

Even if the buyers cooperated and a survey was not prohibitively expensive, the value of this method would depend ultimately on the extent to which the buyers have clearly formulated intentions and then carry them out. In regard to consumer convenience goods, buyers rarely reflect on the magnitude of their annual consumption or on how they divide their purchases among major brands. In regard to major consumer durables, such as appliances, furniture, and new housing, households are able to report their buying plans for the near term. Their intentions are based on expectations they have at the time of the survey concerning present and future business conditions as well as personal events affecting the family's financial status. For example, the family head's report of his intention to purchase a new car during the next six months may be based on his expectation of promotion. If the promotion does not materialize, or materializes but other canceling effects occur, such as a job transfer or family illness, this family head may not buy his car. Still, in the aggregate, as many families may experience favorable shifts in personal fortune as unfavorable shifts. What tends to weaken seriously the predictive value of intentions surveys are unanticipated shifts in general business conditions. Thus, if most consumers state their intentions in the context of expecting good business conditions to continue, an unexpected recession will reduce, if not destroy, the survey's usefulness.

When anticipations concerning general business conditions and personal events are met, the evidence seems to show that families do carry out their buying plans.[4] The proportion of automobile or house buyers tends to be higher among those who report a purchase intention than among those who do not. In general, surveys of consumer buying intentions have proved useful for short-range consumer durables sales forecasting.[5]

In the realm of industrial buying, intentions surveys regarding plant, equipment, and materials have been carried out by various agencies.[6] Various firms have also found it useful to carry out their own survey of customer buying intentions. The case of National Lead can be cited as an example.

[4] For an evaluation of consumer intention surveys and forecasting errors, see George Katona, *The Powerful Consumer* (New York: McGraw-Hill Book Company, 1960), chap. viii; James Tobin, "On the Predictive Value of Consumer Intentions and Attitudes," *Review of Economics and Statistics,* February 1959, pp. 1-11; and Francis T. Juster, *Anticipations and Purchases,* General Series, No. 79 (Princeton, N.J.: Princeton University Press, 1964).

[5] Surveys of consumer buying intentions are conducted by the U.S. Bureau of the Census on a quarterly basis and by the National Industrial Conference Board on a bimonthly basis. Numerous firms conduct their own consumer surveys to gain information on product purchase intentions and planned brand choices.

[6] The two best-known capital expenditures surveys are the one conducted by the U.S. Department of Commerce in collaboration with the Securities and Exchange Commission and the one conducted annually in the late fall by McGraw-Hill through its publication *Business Week.* Most of the estimates have been within a 10 per cent error band of the actual outcomes. This is a good record, considering that the business investment component of national income is highly variable.

The National Lead Company produces titanium, which is purchased in large quantities by the paint, paper, rubber, and hard-surface flooring industries. Therefore its demand is derived, and depends on the expected sales of the products in which titanium is an ingredient and on the expected input ratio of titanium in these products. Periodically its marketing research personnel visit a carefully selected sample of one hundred companies and interview the manufacturer's technical research director, the sales manager, and the purchasing director, in that order. The technical research director is asked about the rate of incorporation of titanium in the manufacturer's various products; the sales manager is questioned about the sales outlook for the company's products which incorporate titanium; and the purchasing director is queried about the total amount of titanium his company plans to purchase in relation to past purchases. On the basis of these interviews and supplementary information, National's marketing research department estimates the market demand for titanium and prepares a "most favorable" forecast and a "least favorable" forecast.[7]

A number of lessons can be drawn from this example. It illustrates the point that canvassing buyers for their opinions is a time-consuming and obviously expensive undertaking. At the same time, indirect as well as direct benefits are undoubtedly derived from this procedure. By interviewing the buyers, National Lead's analysts learn of new developments and modes of thinking which would not be apparent through published information. (Of course, this sounding function may also be performed by company salesmen.) Their visits may also promote National's image as a company which is concerned about buyers' needs. Another advantage of this method is that it yields subestimates for various industries and territories in the process of building an aggregate estimate. In contrast, some of the statistical-mathematical methods described later only yield an aggregate estimate which must then be broken down into subestimates for various operating units.

In summary, the appropriateness of the buyers' intentions survey method increases to the extent that (1) the buyers are few, (2) the cost of effectively reaching them is small, (3) they have clear intentions, (4) they follow out their original intentions, and (5) they are willing to disclose their intentions. As a result, it is of value for industrial products, for product purchases where advanced planning is required, and for new products where past data do not exist.

COMPOSITE OF SALES FORCE OPINION

Where it is impractical to make direct buyer inquiries, the company may decide to ask its salesmen for estimates. An example is the Pennsalt Chemicals Corporation.

In August, the field sales personnel are provided with tabulating cards to prepare their sales forecasts for the coming year. Individual cards are prepared for each product sold to each major customer, showing the quantity shipped to the customer in the previous six months. Each card also provides space in which the field salesmen post their forecasts for the coming year. Additional tab cards are also supplied for those customers who were not sold in the current six-month period but who were customers in the prior

[7] Adapted from *Forecasting Sales*, pp. 31-32.

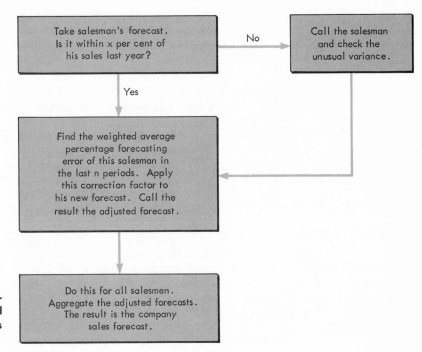

| Take salesman's forecast. Is it within x per cent of his sales last year? | No → | Call the salesman and check the unusual variance. |

Yes

Find the weighted average percentage forecasting error of this salesman in the last n periods. Apply this correction factor to his new forecast. Call the result the adjusted forecast.

FIGURE 5-5

How salesmen's estimates may be corrected to derive company sales forecast

Do this for all salesmen. Aggregate the adjusted forecasts. The result is the company sales forecast.

year; and finally, blank cards are provided for submitting forecasts of sales to new customers. Salesmen fill in their forecasts (on the basis of current prices) using their own informed judgment; in some divisions, they are also in a position to substantiate their forecasts by obtaining purchase estimates from their customers.[8]

It should be emphasized that very few companies use the salesmen's estimates without some adjustments. In the first place, salesmen can be biased observers. A salesman may be congenitally pessimistic or optimistic, or he may go to one extreme or another because of a recent sales setback or success. Furthermore, he is often unaware of larger economic developments and of company marketing plans which will shape future sales in his territory. Another biasing factor is that he may understate demand so that the company will set a low sales quota. In addition to possible biases, the individual salesman may not have the time or concern to prepare careful estimates.

In the light of these contaminating factors, why are salesmen's estimates used at all? There is the possibility that the over-and-under errors may cancel out, leaving a good aggregate forecast. Or a consistent bias in the forecast of individual salesmen may be recognized and a correction made. One possible method of correcting salesmen's estimates is shown in Figure 5-5.

The company may supply certain aids or incentives to the salesmen to encourage better estimating. Each salesman may receive a record of his past forecast compared with his actual sales, and also a set of company assumptions on the business outlook. Some companies will summarize

[8] *Ibid.*, p. 25.

individual forecasting records and distribute them to all salesmen. A tendency for salesmen to produce ultraconservative estimates to keep down their sales quota can be countered by basing territorial advertising and promotional expenditures on the salesmen's estimates.

Assuming these biasing tendencies can be countered, a number of benefits can be gained by involving the sales force in forecasting. Being closest to the customers, salesmen may have more knowledge or better insight into developing trends than any other single group. This is especially likely where the product is fairly technical and subject to a changing technology, as in the case of construction equipment. Second, because of their participation in the forecasting process, the salesmen may have greater confidence in the derived sales quotas, and this may increase their incentive to achieve them. Finally, a "grass roots" forecasting procedure results in estimates broken down by product, territory, customer, and salesman.

In summary, the appropriateness of the composite of sales force opinion method increases to the extent that (1) the salesmen are likely to be the most knowledgeable source of information, (2) the salesmen are cooperative, (3) the salesmen are unbiased or their biases can be corrected, and (4) there are some side benefits from the salesmen's participation in the forecasting procedure.

EXPERT OPINION

Another method of forecasting involves tapping the opinion of well-informed persons other than buyers or company salesmen, such as distributors or outside experts.

The automobile companies solicit estimates of sales directly from their dealers. These estimates are subject to the same strengths and weaknesses as salesmen estimates; like salesmen, distributors may not give the necessary attention to careful estimating; their perspective concerning future business conditions may be too narrow; and they may supply biased estimates to gain some immediate advantage.

Firms also tap outside experts for assessments of future demand. In effect, this happens when a firm uses or buys general economic forecasts or special industry forecasts prepared outside of the firm. Various public and private agencies issue or sell periodic forecasts of short- or long-term business conditions. While the experts are supplying what amounts to opinion, this "opinion" may be the joint outcome of specially conducted surveys among buyers and suppliers as well as statistical-mathematical analyses of past data.

An interesting variant of the expert opinion method is used by Lockheed Aircraft Corporation.[9] As a manufacturer of airframes and missiles, the company deals with a relatively small number of customers, each of which accounts for a relatively large percentage of sales. Therefore Lockheed's forecasting problem is to predict what each particular customer will order during the forecast period. The marketing research group works up a preliminary forecast on the basis of surveys and statistical-mathematical techniques. Independently, a group of Lockheed executives poses as dif-

---

[9] Gerald A. Busch, "Prudent Manager Forecasting," *Harvard Business Review,* May-June, 1961, pp. 57-64.

ferent major customers; in a hardheaded way they evaluate Lockheed's offering in relation to its competitors' offerings. A decision on what and where to buy is made for each customer. The purchases from Lockheed are totaled and reconciled with the statistical forecast to become Lockheed's sales forecast.

The use of expert opinion has several advantages and disadvantages. Its main advantages are: (1) forecasts can be made relatively quickly and cheaply, (2) different points of view are brought out and balanced in the process, and (3) there may be no alternative if basic data are sparse or lacking, as in the case of new products. The main disadvantages are: (1) opinions are generally less satisfactory than hard facts, (2) responsibility is dispersed, and good and bad estimates are given equal weight, and (3) the method usually is more reliable for aggregate forecasting than for developing reliable breakdowns by territory, customer group, or product.

MARKET TEST METHOD

The usefulness of opinions, whether those of buyers, salesmen, or other experts, depends upon the cost, availability, and reliability of this type of information. In cases where buyers do not plan their purchases carefully or are very erratic in carrying out their intentions or where experts are not very good guessers, a more direct market test of likely behavior is desirable. A direct market test is especially desirable in forecasting the sales of new product or the likely sales of an established product in a new channel of distribution or territory. Where a short-run forecast of likely buyer response is desired, a small-scale market test is usually an ideal answer.[10]

CLASSICAL TIME SERIES ANALYSIS

As an alternative to costly surveys or market tests, some firms prepare their forecasts on the basis of a statistical-mathematical analysis of past data. The underlying logic is that past data are an expression of real causal relationships which can be unearthed through quantitative analysis. To the extent that the discovered past relationships are stable, they can be used to predict future sales. Thus forecasting becomes an exercise in adroit backcasting.

A time series of past sales of a product should always be scrutinized for indications of possible future behavior. At one extreme are products, brands, and services whose sales move in a regular fashion, as in Figure 5-6a; examples would be the sale of telephone and electricity services and staple goods like salt. The relatively smooth growth (or decline) in the sale of such items reduces the forecasting problem to one of simple extrapolation. There is no need to search deeply for real relationships between sales and other factors, since the passage of time itself offers a good basis for prediction. Extrapolation then is an appropriate procedure as long as no important new development is anticipated.

At the other extreme are products whose sales seem to be influenced by a succession of nonrecurrent causes and events, as in Figure 5-6b. For example, weekly sales of a coffee brand are affected by every price change,

[10] Test marketing is discussed in some detail in Chapter 14, pp. 334-40.

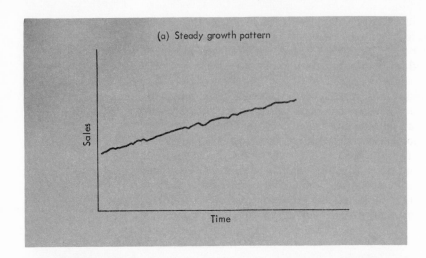

(a) Steady growth pattern

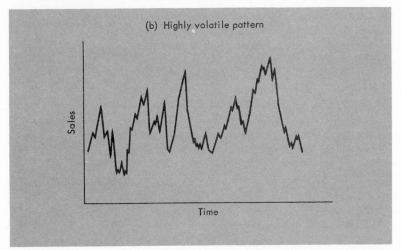

(b) Highly volatile pattern

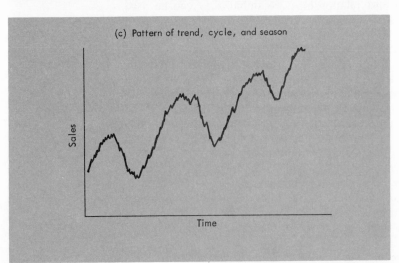

(c) Pattern of trend, cycle, and season

FIGURE 5-6
Three time series patterns

every in-store promotion, and every new advertising campaign. Many raw materials also show a highly variable sales pattern, where the variations stem from strikes, changes in weather, speculative buying or selling waves, price changes, and forays by substitute materials. In general, for products whose sales are continuously assaulted by erratic forces, extrapolative forecasting is not reliable. Neither classical time series analysis nor other statistical manipulations are of much help. This type of product presents the analyst with his major forecasting challenge, and he may have to turn to opinion methods for guesses as to future developments.

In between these two extremes are products whose past sales vary but in a largely systematic way, as in Figure 5-6c. Like the atom, this sales series can be split. Three different systematic forces can be distinguished.

The first force, *trend,* is the result of basic developments in population, capital formation, and technology. If the trend turns out to be statistically significant—that is, it has enough consistency to dispel the notion that it is a random artifact—then it becomes central in the preparation of a long-range forecast.

The second force, *cycle,* is seen in the wavelike movement of sales. Properly speaking, a cycle exists when the time series shows an undulation of a fairly constant amplitude and periodicity. Few if any business series exhibit pure cyclical behavior in this sense. A few, such as housing construction, hog sales, and pig iron sales, for example, exhibit approximate cyclical behavior. Many sales series are affected by swings in the level of general economic activity, which tends to be somewhat periodic.[11] Isolation of the cyclical component can be useful in intermediate-range forecasting.[12]

The final systematic force, *season,* refers to a consistent pattern of sales movements within the year. Although the term "season" suggests a distinct quarterly pattern induced by changes in the weather, it is used more broadly to describe any recurrent hourly, weekly, monthly, or quarterly sales pattern. The seasonal component may be related to weather factors, holidays, and/or trade customs. The seasonal pattern provides the investigator with a norm for forecasting short-range sales.

In addition to the three systematic forces of trend, cycle, and season, a time series also reflects nonrecurrent, *erratic* events, such as strikes, blizzards, fads, riots, fires, war scares, price wars, and other disturbances of the real world. These erratic components have the effect of obscuring the more systematic components, and the problem becomes one of starting with the original "noisy" time series and separating the underlying systematic forces from the erratic.

Classical time series analysis involves procedures for decomposing the original sales series (Y) into the components, T, C, S, and E (trend, cycle, season, and erratic events), respectively. According to one model, these components interact linearly; that is, $Y = T + C + S + E$, and according

[11] Products vary in their degree of "income sensitivity." See C. Winston and M. Smith, "Income Sensitivity of Consumption Expenditures," *Survey of Current Business,* January 1950, pp. 17-20.

[12] The most careful methodology for isolating and studying cyclical movements is that developed by the National Bureau of Economic Research. The procedure consists of dividing each cyclical pattern into nine stages and averaging the levels at each stage. See Arthur F. Burns and Wesley C. Mitchell, *Measuring Business Cycles* (New York: National Bureau of Economic Research, 1946).

to another model, they interact multiplicatively, that is, $Y = T \times C \times S \times E$. The multiplicative model makes the more realistic assumption that the seasonal and cyclical effects are proportional to the trend level of sales. T is stated in absolute values and C, S, and E are stated as percentages.

This is not the place to describe the methodology for decomposing a time series. The procedures are outlined in elementary business statistics textbooks.[13] The main caution is against mechanical extrapolation. The forecast is not simply a matter of putting together systematic components, but rather a creative and further act in itself. The systematic forces underlying past sales may not remain unchanged. Any one of the three components can take on a different form starting tomorrow; the past trend can be altered by the appearance of a competitive product; the cyclical pattern can be altered by new countercyclical government policies; the seasonal pattern can be altered by new counterseasonal company policies. A mechanical extrapolation ignores marketing plans, the effect of which has to be built into the final forecast. The impact of possible erratic forces can be conveyed by preparing an optimistic, pessimistic, and most likely forecast. The size of the forecast error band conveys to management a sense of how much confidence it can repose in the most likely forecast.

The classical time series method requires numerous calculations for isolating the original components. The firm which produces hundreds of products thus faces a formidable forecasting job. The computational burdens of classical time series analysis have been considerably ameliorated in recent times by the development of computer programs which decompose a given time series into its major systematic components.[14] On a modern computer, an entire time series analysis of ten years of monthly data can be performed in one or two minutes.[15]

STATISTICAL DEMAND ANALYSIS

Classical time series analysis treats past and future sales as a function of time, rather than of any real demand factors. Its main use is in markets where the underlying demand factors remain stable over time. Where this is not the case, it is much more desirable to try to discover the direct relationship between sales and real demand factors.

There are, of course, numerous real factors which affect the sales of any product. Statistical demand analysis is not an attempt to derive a complete set of factors but rather an attempt to discover the most important factors in the hope that they will explain a significant amount of the

[13] See F. E. Croxton and D. J. Cowden, *Practical Business Statistics,* 3rd ed. (Englewood Cliffs, N.J.: Prentice-Hall, Inc., 1960), chaps. xxviii to xxxi.

[14] See Julius Shiskin, *Electronic Computers and Business Indicators* (New York: National Bureau of Economic Research, 1957). For an application, see Robert L. McLaughlin, "The Breakthrough in Sales Forecasting," *Journal of Marketing,* XXVII (April 1963), 46-54.

[15] As an alternative to classical time series analysis, another method called *exponential smoothing* is coming into increasing use, specifically for short-range (weekly or monthly) forecasting. Because it can produce individual product forecasts quickly, easily, and cheaply, it is ideal where hundreds of items must be forecast. It is particularly useful for forecasting high-volume items which are in constant demand. See Peter R. Winters, "Forecasting Sales by Exponentially Weighted Moving Averages," *Management Science,* April 1960, pp. 324-42; or Robert G. Brown, *Statistical Forecasting for Inventory Control* (New York: McGraw-Hill Book Company, 1959).

variations in sales. The factors most commonly analyzed are prices, income, population, and promotion.

The procedure consists of expressing sales (Y) as a dependent variable and trying to explain sales variation as a result of variation in a number of independent demand variables X_1, X_2, ... X_n; that is

$$Y = f(X_1, X_2, \ldots, X_n)$$

For example, Kristian S. Palda found that the following demand equation gave a fairly good fit to the historical sales of Lydia Pinkham's Vegetable Compound between the years 1908 and 1960: [16]

$$Y = -3649 + .665X_1 + 1180 \log X_2 + 774X_3 + 32X_4 - 2.83X_5$$

where

Y = yearly sales in thousands of dollars
X_1 = yearly sales (lagged one year) in thousands of dollars
X_2 = yearly advertising expenditures in thousands of dollars
X_3 = a dummy variable, taking on the value 1 between 1908-1925 and 0 from 1926 on
X_4 = year (1908 = 0, 1909 = 1, and so on)
X_5 = disposable personal income in billions of current dollars

The five independent variables on the right helped account for 94 per cent of the yearly variation in the sale of Lydia Pinkham's Vegetable Compound between 1908 and 1960. To use it as a sales forecasting equation for 1961, it would be necessary to insert figures for the five independent variables. Sales in 1960 should be put in X_1, the log of the company's planned advertising expenditures for 1961 should be put in X_2, 0 should be put in X_3, the numbered year corresponding to 1961 should be put in X_4, and estimated 1961 disposable personal income should be put in X_5. The result of multiplying these numbers by the respective coefficients and summing them gives a sales forecast (Y) for 1961.

While this is not the place to outline the mathematics of deriving demand equations, the marketing executive should have certain basic understandings to appreciate their use and avoid their misuse. With the advent of high-speed computers, they are becoming increasingly popular as a means of forecasting, and many marketing researchers who are now deriving these equations may be unqualified to use them critically.

Basically, demand equations are derived by trying to fit the "best" equation to historical or cross-sectional data. The notion of fitting an equation to data can be conveyed by a simple example. Suppose a leading appliance manufacturer wants to determine the major factors affecting the sales (Y) of refrigerators. He suspects that the level of disposable personal income (X) is one of the most important factors. To check this hypothesis, he gathers annual data on refrigerator sales and DPI for four years (more years should actually be used) and plots them on the scatter diagram in Figure 5-7. The dots seem to show a positive relationship between refrigerator sales and DPI.

The natural thing to do at this point is to draw some straight or curved

[16] Kristian S. Palda, *The Measurement of Cumulative Advertising Effects* (Englewood Cliffs, N.J.: Prentice-Hall, Inc., 1964), pp. 67-68.

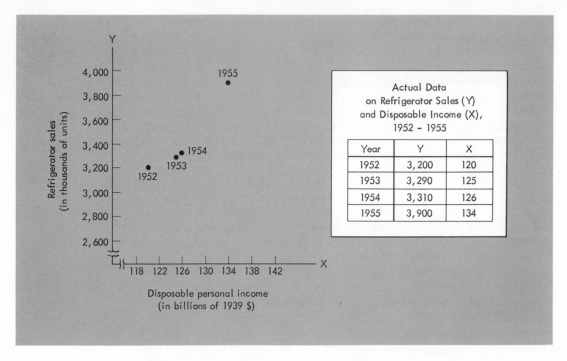

Actual Data on Refrigerator Sales (Y) and Disposable Income (X), 1952 – 1955		
Year	Y	X
1952	3,200	120
1953	3,290	125
1954	3,310	126
1955	3,900	134

FIGURE 5-7
Refrigerator sales and disposable personal income (DPI), 1952-1955

line going through these dots to express the underlying relationship. The line can be fitted visually, but this leads to the objection that its position would depend on the person's judgment. A mathematical criterion has been developed to meet the desire for objectivity; it is called the *least squares* criterion. According to this criterion, the best line is one which *minimizes the sum of the squared (vertical) deviations of the dots from the line.* The equation for this line can be derived through the use of formulas worked out for this purpose.

Its equation, if a straight line is fitted according to this criterion in Figure 5-7, turns out to be $Y = -3,164.8 + 52.3X$.[17] To check this, let DPI be 134 (1955 figure). According to the equation, refrigerator sales would be estimated at 3,843. Refrigerator sales were actually 3,900 in 1955, and so the estimate is fairly good. If the other DPI values are inserted, they will lead to fairly good estimates of actual sales.

The line is called a regression line, and its usefulness depends partly on how close the dots (representing the actual data) are to the line. If all the dots fall exactly on the line, it would be said that there is perfect positive correlation between sales and DPI. In other words, given DPI, sales could have been perfectly estimated. In virtually all actual cases, however, there

[17] The constant −3,164.8 represents the intercept of the line on the Y axis when X is zero. (Figure 5-7 does not show this intercept because only part of the X and Y axes are drawn.) The coefficient 52.3 represents the slope of the line. This slope says that a one billion dollar increase of DPI is associated with an average sales increase of 52.3 thousand refrigerators.

is never perfect correlation between sales and any one other variable or even set of variables.

The farther the dots are from the line, the less the correlation between the variables. If the dots are scattered randomly throughout the diagram, sales and DPI are described as uncorrelated; that is, DPI is of no help in estimating sales.

One is interested, then, both in deriving the "least squares" regression line for the scatter and in measuring the "goodness of fit," or correlation. Correlation is a measure which ranges from +1 (perfect positive correlation) to −1 (perfect negative correlation) with 0 representing no correlation. Correlation, when it does exist, must be interpreted cautiously. It is no proof of causality. All it indicates is that one series appears to be associated with another. This is why theoretical justification of variables found to be correlated statistically is always desirable.

In advanced statistical demand analysis, there are usually some changes from this simple example. Sales tend to be fitted not to a single variable (simple regression) but to several variables (multiple regression). The result is an equation such as Palda's with five independent variables. Curved lines, rather than straight ones, may be fitted. Note that in Palda's equation, sales were positively related not to advertising dollars but to the log of advertising dollars, to suggest diminishing returns to advertising. In some cases the equations become quite complex in form.[18]

That a demand equation shows a good fit is no guarantee of its forecasting usefulness. There are five major points to check before using the equation.

TOO FEW OBSERVATIONS. The predictive reliability of an equation depends on an excess of observations over variables. If the analyst can dig up only five years of past observation, he should not attempt to fit more than one independent variable. If he can find twenty past observations, he should not try to fit more than about five variables. The problem typically is that many product sales series are short and therefore the analyst cannot use more than a few independent variables.

[18] As an example of a complex equation, B. Slaten of the Econometric Institute developed in 1958 the following equation for forecasting refrigerator sales:

$$S = R + y \left\{ H_w \left[.0045 + .011 \left(\frac{I + 3\,C/P}{10^{.0217T} + 1.035} \right) \right] - .000016y \right\}$$

where

S = total new sales in thousands of units
R = computed replacement sales based on survival table in thousands of units
y = stock of refrigerators
H_w = wired homes
I = supernumerary income
C = consumer credit
P = price index of household furnishings
T = trend factor

This equation breaks refrigerator market demand into both a replacement demand (R), as measured by scrappage of old units, and new owner demand, as affected by the other factors listed. The study is described in Milton H. Spencer, Colin G. Clark, and Peter W. Hoguet, *Business and Economic Forecasting* (Homewood, Ill.: Richard D. Irwin, Inc., 1961), pp. 252-79.

MULTICOLLINEARITY. This is a technical term to describe a condition when some of the independent variables are not independent of each other. For example, sales are often fitted to both a population variable and an income variable. Both of these variables show a strong historical upward trend and hence are highly intercorrelated. If two independent variables move pretty much in the same way, it is hard to appraise their separate influence on sales as opposed to their joint influence, and their respective coefficients cannot be very meaningful. When multicollinearity is detected and strong, one of the variables should be dropped. Alternatively it may be possible to use both variables expressed in the form of first differences (yearly changes, rather than yearly levels), if it is found that these are less correlated.

AUTOCORRELATION OF RESIDUALS. This is another technical term, and it refers to a condition when the forecasting errors (or residuals) resulting from using the equation are not randomly distributed. For example, autocorrelation would exist for Palda's equation if sales were underpredicted for 1908-1914, overpredicted for 1915-1925, underpredicted for the next several years, and so forth. Such consistent underprediction followed by overprediction is called autocorrelation and indicates the omission of some systematic variable or variables from the equation. In theory, the residuals should reflect chance factors and should be distributed randomly through time. Autocorrelation suggests the need to search for further systematic variables. If they cannot be found, one option is to use lagged sales as an explanatory variable, and this is what Palda did. If the residuals are still autocorrelated, the autocorrelation should be taken into account in the next forecast.

TWO-WAY CAUSATION. A single demand equation implies a one-way direction of influence from the independent variables on the right to sales on the left. This would be true of such independent variables as temperature or DPI; they influence sales but are obviously not influenced by sales. What about such marketing variables as advertising or price? They both influence sales. However, they are also influenced by sales. Management often sets advertising on the basis of current or anticipated sales; the same can be said of price. The presence of two-way causation unfortunately means a single demand equation is not a good model; in fact, it can be shown mathematically that the coefficients estimated for the effects of advertising or price on sales are biased and unreliable. In such cases a system of two or more equations should frame the demand analysis.[19]

FORECASTING RELEVANCE. In the case of all statistical backcasting methods, the question must always be raised whether the equation is likely to apply to future conditions. Changes in environmental conditions and/or marketing policies in the industry may create a new set of relationships. The possible loss of relevance of an equation is dramatically illustrated in Figure 5-8. An equation in three independent variables was developed to explain the sales of electric refrigerators in the pre-World War II

[19] A good account of simultaneous equation model building and estimation is found in Stefan Valavanis, *Econometrics* (New York: McGraw-Hill Book Company, 1959).

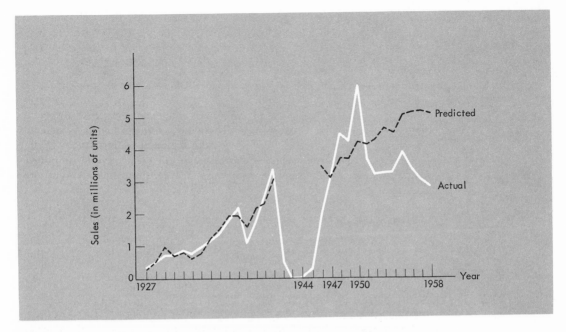

FIGURE 5-8

Annual manufacturers' domestic sales of electric refrigerators, 1927-1958

Redrawn from Erwin E. Nemmers, *Managerial Economics* (New York: John Wiley & Sons, Inc., 1962), pp. 111-12.

period. The equation gave a good fit to the prewar data as shown by the dotted line. If a manufacturer used the prewar equation in 1947, his forecast would have been good. During the next few years it was off the mark, mainly in magnitude rather than direction, and way off the mark in magnitude after 1950. This is a case where the coefficients of the old equation lost their relevance. Unfortunately there were too few years in the postwar period by, say, 1952 to permit a reliable refitting of the coefficients to the postwar data.

OVER-ALL EVALUATION OF STATISTICAL DEMAND ANALYSIS. Statistical demand analysis is an attempt to unravel the size and importance of real factors which affect the demand for a product. As such, it is a worthwhile pursuit whether or not it results in a highly reliable forecasting equation. It should increase company knowledge of demand factors. Very often the technique helps uncover relationships which cannot be found or measured in any other way. It stimulates the attempt to quantify demand factors and build better theories of demand in the industry. When the equation does forecast well, the analyst has an estimate of its probable error. He is also free to spend his time considering factors which in the next period may disturb the expected relationships.

On the other hand, the major danger is that the equation, if it has worked well in the past, may displace the exercise of independent judgment. New factors constantly come into play and must be assessed. The equation cannot incorporate qualitative factors. The equation is usually gross even in its handling of quantifiable factors. For example, the DPI variable reflects the level of income and not its distribution; yet the trend in income distribution may be quite important. Furthermore, it is often as hard to forecast certain independent variables as the dependent variable.

OTHER METHODS: GEOGRAPHICAL DEMAND

Around the basic methods of demand measurement just outlined, a great number of variations will be found in practice. The final choice of method is influenced by many factors, the more important of which are the availability and reliability of data, the degree of demand stability, and the type of product. It is not surprising therefore to find special procedures to meet such specific situations as forecasting new-product demand,[20] style-goods demand,[21] and individual-item demand.[22]

One important area of market measurement that may require special techniques is the estimation of demand by geographical area. These estimates are needed for analyzing geographical opportunities, planning the area allocation of marketing resources, and evaluating area marketing performance.

A method commonly used to estimate area demand is known as the *index method*. In the simplest form, area demand or opportunity is assumed to be directly related to a single factor, such as population. For example, population may be thought to be the key to area variations in the market demand for drug sales. If Texas has 5.3 per cent of the population, it might be assumed that Texas would be a market for 5.3 per cent of total drugs sold.

A single factor, however, is rarely a complete indicator of sales opportunity. Obviously, regional drug sales are also influenced by such factors as per capita income and the number of physicians per, say, ten thousand people. This leads to the desirability of developing a multiple-factor index, each factor being assigned a specific weight in the index.

One of the best-known, general-purpose, multiple-factor indices of area demand is published in the "Annual Survey of Buying Power" of *Sales Management* magazine. The index purports to reflect the relative buying power in the different counties and cities of the nation. *Sales Management's* index of the relative buying power of an area is given by:

$$M_i = .5y_i + .3r_i + .2p_i$$

where

M_i = percentage of total national buying power found in area i
y_i = percentage of national disposable personal income originating in area i
r_i = percentage of national retail sales in area i
p_i = percentage of national population located in area i

The magazine holds that these weights reflect market potential for many consumer goods that are neither low-priced staples nor high-valued luxury

---

[20] See Chapter 14, pp. 334-40.

[21] See David B. Hertz and Kurt H. Schaffer, "A Forecasting Method for Management of Seasonal Style-Goods Inventories," *Operations Research,* January-February, 1960, pp. 45-52; Carl Vreeland, "The Jantzen Method of Short Range Forecasting," *Journal of Marketing,* XXVII (April 1963), 66-70.

[22] See footnote 15.

goods. The weights, however, are not validated, and certainly vary in appropriateness for different products. Multiple regression has been used at times to find index weights.

It should be understood that area demand estimates, no matter how developed, reflect relative industry opportunities rather than relative company opportunities. Before using them as guides for allocating its marketing resources, the individual company would have to adjust the market potential estimates by factors left out of the index. In particular, the firm must take into consideration the intensity of competition in each area and its own facilities and competitive advantages in each area in developing its marketing targets and marketing plans. These in turn lead to area sales forecasts.

Improving Forecast Accuracy

No matter what forecasting system a company uses, it probably can be improved upon. The issue is one of the cost of improving the forecasts versus the savings from better forecasts.

Forecasting systems may be improved in two general ways. Sometimes it is a matter of collecting better data while retaining the present forecasting method. A company which conducts a mail survey of customers' intentions may get better results by increasing the sample size and/or using personal interviews. In other cases, it is a matter of supplementing or replacing the present forecasting method with a different, often more elaborate one. A company may be able to improve its short-range forecasting for individual items by supplementing the buyers' intentions survey with estimates derived through statistical demand analysis. It is easy to see how a forecasting system can be improved by a company which is willing to spend more.

The savings from better forecasting depend in part upon the costliness of inventory mistakes. Inventory mistakes occur when either too little or too much is carried. If too little is carried, the company loses the profit from sales lost through stockout. If too much is carried, the company bears an unnecessary cost through tying up its capital and risking obsolescence or perishability. A major purpose of forecasting is to enable the company to maintain more economical stock levels by anticipating demand more closely.[23]

The savings also depend upon how much the improved forecasting system can reduce the average forecasting error. The forecast error on any individual forecast can be expressed either as an absolute or percentage deviation of actual sales from forecast sales. The past errors can be averaged, preferably using the median, as an indication of average forecasting accuracy under the present system.

Many people consider a current forecasting system to be good if the average forecast error is plus or minus 2 per cent and to be adequate if it is plus or minus 5 per cent. These performance figures, however, do not mean much unless they are judged against other criteria. One criterion is the extent of sales variability. An average error of 5 per cent may be pretty

[23] The inventory problem is discussed in Chapter 17, pp. 433-39.

good if sales vary 15 per cent from period to period; it may be better than a 1 per cent average error if sales hardly vary at all.[24] Another criterion is the forecast accuracy which might be obtained under an optimal forecasting system for the particular product market. A 10 per cent average error for the present system may be quite satisfactory if it is unlikely to be much less under the best system; a 5 per cent average error may be bad if another system can bring down the forecast error to 1 per cent.

How much a company should invest in its forecasting operation must be decided separately for each case. Whatever system a company uses, it always pays to study past forecast errors, an analysis of which leads to two important benefits. By asking why the forecasts were in error, the analyst may discover systematic factors which can then be built into the forecasting procedure, and he can explain to management the probable error of the forecast so that management can proceed with this level of risk in mind.

In indicating the probable error, the forecaster should supply to management the explicit assumptions underlying each new forecast. The sales estimate will vary with the assumptions, and management may want an indication of expected sales under an alternative set of assumptions. Sometimes a sales estimate is very sensitive to small changes in assumptions; at other times it is not. The forecaster should make a sensitivity analysis. If the sales estimate is not very sensitive to small changes in assumptions, confidence in the forecast is increased.

Summary

No firm can conduct its business successfully without trying to measure the actual size of markets, present and future. Quantitative measurements are essential for the analysis of market opportunity, the planning of marketing programs, and the control of marketing effort. The firm may make many measures of demand, varying in the level of product aggregation, the time dimension, and the space dimension. In all its studies, however, the company should be clear about its demand measurement concepts, particularly the distinction between market demand, company demand, and the company sales forecast. The company may use one or any combination of at least six different forecasting methods: surveys of buyer intentions, sales force estimates, expert opinions, market tests, classical time series analysis, or statistical demand analysis. These methods vary in their appropriateness with the type of product and the availability and reliability of data. Probably every firm can improve its forecast accuracy by increasing its investment in data collection and/or better methodology. The question is

[24] For a standardized measure of forecasting accuracy which takes this into consideration, see McLaughlin, *op. cit.*, pp. 53-54.

one of spending enough but not too much and depends largely on the extent of improvements in planning and control which better forecasting would bring.

Questions and Problems

1. Two forecasters working for the same automobile manufacturer arrived at substantially different estimates of next year's demand. Does this variance imply that forecasting is largely guesswork?

2. A manufacturer of printing equipment makes estimates of sales by first asking the district sales managers for district forecasts. Describe how these initial forecasts may be refined at higher company levels through a check-and-balance system in order to arrive at a final companywide forecast.

3. A beverage company wants to use multiple regression to determine what factors explain state-to-state variations in the consumption of soft drinks. (a) What independent variables should be tested? (b) If the fitted regression equation "explains" most of the state-to-state variation in sales, does it follow that it is a good device for indicating relative market potential by state?

4. A manufacturer of women's hair products (home permanents, hair rinses, shampoos, etc.) wanted to determine the relative market potential for its products in each county of the United States. What three or four factors are most likely to belong in a weighted index of potential?

5. A marketing researcher sought a multiple regression equation to explain past sales in an industry. Good industry data on the dependent and independent variables only went back five years. He fitted the following equation:

$$Y = 5{,}241 + 31X_1 + 12X_2 + 50X_3$$

where

Y = yearly sales in thousands of dollars
X_1 = U.S. disposable personal income in billions of dollars
X_2 = U.S. population in millions of households
X_3 = time, in years away from $1960 = 0$

He was pleased to find that this equation accounted for 98 per cent of the yearly variations in industry sales. List any reservations you would have about using this equation in forecasting future industry sales.

2

Organizing for Marketing Activity

The makeup and needs of markets constitute the starting point for marketing planning. Accordingly, in the first part of this book, we looked at markets in various ways. We considered the problem of how marketing opportunity can be discerned in the face of considerable market complexity and continual shifts in the marketing environment.

We can now turn to the question of how a firm may respond optimally to the challenge of its marketing opportunities. This is our first look at the firm's controllable factors in contrast to the uncontrollable factors of market and marketing environment. Chapter 6, "Business Goals and Marketing Organization," examines the role played by a firm's business goals in orienting it to its environment; the chapter also examines how the firm organizes its human and other resources to achieve maximum effectiveness in the market place. Chapter 7, "Marketing Planning," considers planning as the active instrument by which the firm seeks to exploit its opportunities. Because marketing goals, organization, and plans evolve out of decisions, Chapter 8, "Marketing Decision Making," shows the application of modern decision theory to marketing decision making. Chapter 9, "Marketing Research," underscores the importance of systematic data collection and analysis as inputs into the marketing decision-making process. Chapter 10, "Marketing Models and Systems," describes the growing role of formal model building in dealing with complex marketing problems. Finally, Chapter 11, "Marketing Creativity," emphasizes the importance of creativity in expanding the firm's awareness of its opportunities and available strategies.

chapter 6

Business Goals and Marketing Organization

We now turn our attention to the company seeking to prosper and grow in the face of changing marketing opportunity. The company's problem is to make optimal adjustments of factors under its control to factors beyond its control, as illustrated in Figure 6-1.

The lowest dial represents the basic environmental factors affecting marketing: technology, marketing channels, culture, economics, and law. This dial turns slowly, and as it does, it wields its influence on the setting of the next dial representing markets and marketing opportunities. Together the first two dials, environment and markets, represent the major uncontrollables in the firm's situation.

The third dial shows the major company instruments available for defining a position in the larger marketing environment. The firm meets the marketing challenge by setting specific business goals, developing an effective organization, and formulating sound plans.

This dial constitutes a foundation for making the particular marketing adjustments shown on the fourth dial. Through decisions on products, prices, channels, physical distribution, advertising, and personal selling, the firm seeks the optimal attainment of its goals. Management's job is continuously to adjust the two top dials, its controllables, in response to basic shifts taking place in the two lower ones.

This first chapter of Part 2 is an exploration of how the firm adapts to the marketing environment through goal setting and organization. In the first section, we shall consider the character and variety of goals pursued by firms in their search for a "fit" with the environment. In the second section, we shall examine the marketing organization developed by firms to meet the marketing challenge.

Business Goals

In order to discuss principles of marketing organization and planning, it is desirable to start with a discussion of the basic ends toward which business firms are oriented. The purpose is to bring out the vital bearing of company business goals on marketing actions and planning.

The goal of an institution may seem obvious at first. Universities exist to produce and disseminate knowledge. Social welfare agencies exist to provide relief to the needy. Business firms exist to make a profit. But the answers are not really so simple. Even the top officers in a business firm may take different views of the company's goals. One officer might describe

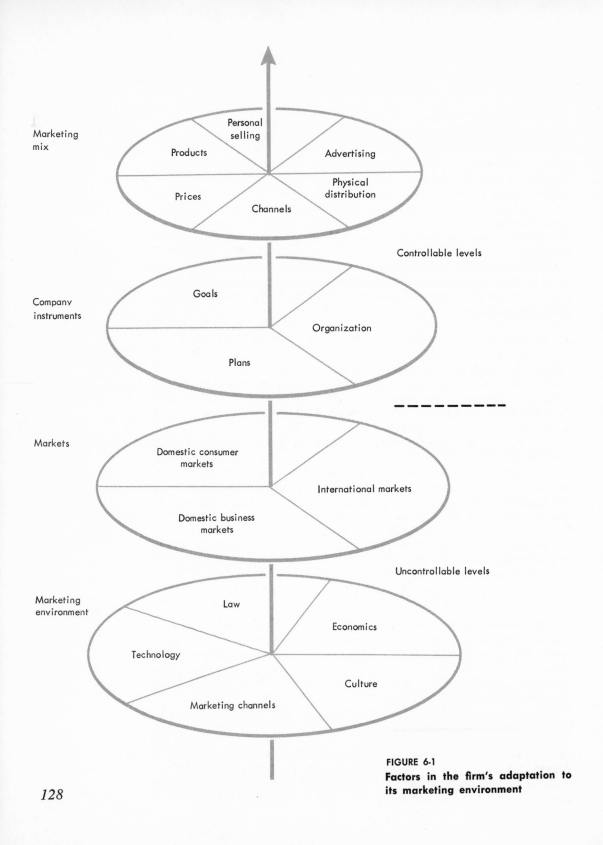

FIGURE 6-1
Factors in the firm's adaptation to
its marketing environment

the firm's goals as being "to produce widgets," another "to satisfy customer needs," and still another "to make profits." The same basic activity can give rise to a number of different goal interpretations.

IMPORTANCE OF GOALS

Management's interpretation of company goals has a feedback effect on present and future actions. If management sees the company's basic purpose as producing widgets, it concentrates on the task of producing good widgets. If management sees the company's basic purpose as satisfying certain wants in the market place, it concentrates on the various ways to satisfy these wants and not just on the production of widgets. If management sees the company's purpose as making profit, it concentrates on finding and exploiting profitable opportunities, regardless of products and markets.

The importance of developing management consensus on organizational goals cannot be overstated. When these goals are made explicit and are assimilated by the company's personnel, they can make several important contributions:

Organizational goals provide the ultimate criteria for resolving difficult company decisions.

Organizational goals are the basis for long-range planning.

Organizational goals produce consistency in the decentralized decision making of company executives.

Organizational goals provide employees with a sense of purpose that makes their work seem worthwhile.

ORGANIZATIONAL GOALS IN PRACTICE

Although the interpretation of organizational goals by individual executives affects company activity, company management often fails to work out a careful statement of its goals. In an exploratory survey of stated corporate objectives, it was found:

A number of firms cited their objectives in such broad terms that it was difficult to know what they had in mind other than to sound virtuous. Such statements as: ". . . our company's objective is to be the best in the industry," ". . . the company will strive for the most effective use of capital," and ". . . to serve the common good" are typical.[1]

Such statements are too vague to be of service in resolving difficult company decisions. And even if specific goals are mentioned, often there is no indication of their relative importance. Furthermore difficult company decisions will tend to set some company goals against others. If a decision means choosing among avowed company goals, how can they all be considered company goals?[2]

One way out of this dilemma is to recognize that organizational goals have the purpose of orienting company actions in the direction of organiza-

[1] Reported in an unpublished paper, "On the Setting of Corporate Objectives," by Harper W. Boyd, Jr., and Sidney J. Levy.

[2] A useful discussion of the multiplicity of company goals is found in Charles H. Granger, "The Hierarchy of Objectives," *Harvard Business Review*, May-June 1964, pp. 63-74.

tional survival and enhancement. All the groups which can affect the organization's survival and enhancement become relevant objects to be satisfied. Admittedly, company actions designed to increase the satisfaction of one group, such as employees, may diminish the satisfaction of another group, such as stockholders. The company therefore typically makes its decisions within a framework of constraints. *Recognizing that it cannot promote all groups' interests with the same decision, management focuses on different groups at different times, subject to providing minimum satisfaction levels for the other groups.* Thus goals and constraints are interchangeable. The constraint that is paramount any one time is called the dominant goal. But in a broader sense, it is the set of constraints which constitute the organization's goals.[3]

IS PROFIT MAXIMIZATION THE DOMINANT BUSINESS GOAL?

The constraint most often cited as the dominant business goal in a private enterprise economy is profits. Some hold, in fact, that firms always seek, or should seek, to maximize their profits above anything else. They advance at least three different arguments.

The first argument is that *profit maximization is the formal purpose for which companies are established.* It is held that those who supply venture capital are not interested in the particular project but in its prospective rate of return. For any given risk level, they will put their money into the projects that appear most profitable. Hired managers are therefore held to have a fiduciary obligation to the suppliers of capital to seek the maximum rate of profit and to put aside other goals.

The second argument is that *the competitive pursuit of maximum profits creates the greatest economic welfare.* In the classic rationale of competitive free enterprise, dating back to Adam Smith, profits are viewed as a reward for efficiency and value creation. The normal forces of competition are visualized as keeping the profits of an industry at a normal level reflecting the market value of capital and management resources. Individual firms hoping for better than normal profits have to seek them through the creation of innovations which either create more demand or reduce costs. The high profit from useful innovations testifies to their social value and to the need for additional resources to move into these areas. Capital is attracted into useful areas as a result of the high profits. In short, the pursuit by firms of maximum profits is held to lead to a high rate of growth and an efficient allocation of resources.

The third argument is that *profit maximization provides management with a relatively unambiguous criterion for business decision making in contrast to approaches calling for the simultaneous satisfaction of multiple company goals.* Management has only to estimate the expected profitability of alternative courses of action and adopt the course which appears superior in profits terms.

All three arguments have sufficient prima facie appeal to constitute an attractive case for profit maximization. *Profit maximization shall be used in this book as the major criterion for decision making.* At the same time,

---

[3] This interpretation of organizational goals is outlined in Herbert A. Simon, "On the Concept of Organizational Goals," *Administrative Science Quarterly,* June 1964, pp. 1-22.

we should be aware of some of its conceptual and methodological limitations.

In the first place, a keynote of modern capitalism is the rift between company stockholders and company managers. Berle and Means noted back in 1932 that the ownership of corporate stock tends to widen while control of corporate assets tends to narrow in the hands of a relatively few salaried managers.[4] Stockholders' and managements' goals tend to diverge. In particular, as management is liberated from the discipline of a small ownership group, it becomes much more interested in doing what is necessary to insure the survival of the corporation as an institution. This requires decision making which heeds the various pressure groups affected.

In the second place, high profits may signal superior economic performance, but they may also arise from collusion, monopoly, or predatory behavior. Furthermore, the unqualified pursuit of profits can cause important social dislocations and costs, such as industrial blight. If profits are to signal real gains in economic welfare, they must occur under competitive conditions where the firm's prices cover the social costs.

In the third place, profit maximization does not provide an unambiguous decision criterion. For one thing, all decisions are marked by risk; generally the higher profit opportunities are accompanied by higher risks. Therefore management must indicate its trade-off between expected profit and expected risk in order for the criterion to be operational. Another problem is that short-run profit maximization does not always coincide with long-run profit maximization. Naturally it is long-run profits which the firm seeks to maximize. Company actions which reduce the short-run level of profitability can be rationalized as increasing the long-run level of profitability. This is the argument for investing in corporate-image advertising, for proliferating customer services, for supporting community charities. But how can their prospective impact on long-run profits be estimated? It would seem that long-run profit maximization is an ingenious façade for pursuing a multiplicity of company goals.[5]

For these and other reasons, the doctrine that firms do, or should, maximize profits must be recognized as an oversimplification of practice and theory. The leading critic, Herbert A. Simon, has proposed the view that management tries to "satisfice" rather than maximize profits.[6] That is, modern corporate management pursues satisfactory profits. Management develops some conception of a desirable target level of profit, and this level serves as one of the constraints (goals) influencing its decisions. It searches among alternative moves until a satisfactory one is found, although more search might have led to a more optimal move.

Simon uses two types of evidence to back this view. He cites empirical studies of the pricing practices of large corporations, showing that they

[4] Adolph A. Berle, Jr., and Gardiner C. Means, *The Modern Corporation and Private Property* (New York: The Macmillan Company, 1932).

[5] The presence of ambiguity in the profit maximization criterion is debated in Fritz Machlup, "Marginal Analysis and Empirical Research," *American Economic Review,* September 1946, pp. 519-554; and Richard A. Lester, "Shortcomings of Marginal Analysis for Wage-Employment Problems," *American Economic Review,* March 1946, pp. 63-82.

[6] Herbert A. Simon, "Theories of Decision-Making in Economics and Behavioral Science," *American Economic Review,* June 1959, pp. 253-83.

seem to base their decisions on the concept of a target rate of return.[7] He also falls back on behavioral theory, particularly the concept that individuals and groups develop aspiration levels which are not related to their maximum performance capability but to other variables, such as normal performance and psychic income.

We have presented these qualifications to the concept of profit maximization so that it will not be used uncritically. Yet the concept unquestionably has useful explanatory and analytical properties. Many managements set their profit aspirations high enough to be tantamount to the pursuit of maximum profits. According to Henry Ford II:

> There is no such thing as planning for a minimal return less than the best you can imagine—not if you want to survive in a competitive market. It's like asking a professional football team to win by only one point—a sure formula for losing. There's only one way to compete successfully—all-out. If believing this makes you a greedy capitalist lusting after bloated profits, then I plead guilty. The worst sin I can commit as a businessman is to fail to seek maximum long-term profitability by all decent and lawful means. To do so is to subvert economic reason.[8]

Profits continue to provide the most widely shared and best single criterion for the analysis of decision alternatives. In spite of the difficulties in the concept, the profit criterion does discipline the analysis and provides a first approximation to the rough value of different courses of action. Other constraints can be brought in at the second stage of the analysis. Because of the universal importance of profit as a standard for business action, as well as its analytical power, much of the analysis of marketing decisions in this book will employ the profit standard to signify the rough values of various alternatives.

ORGANIZATIONAL GOALS AND PERSONAL GOALS

Organizations are collections of interacting groups and individuals who seek to achieve something for themselves as well as for the company. The personal goals of these individuals include more power, improved income, and so forth. These personal goals may obviously be a source of actions sometimes antithetical to company interests. Many illustrations of organizational suboptimization can be cited. Suppose a district sales manager notes that sales are far below his quota as the year's end approaches. Worried that his superiors may question him, he decides to stimulate distributors to make large purchases before the year ends. He does this by granting longer credit terms, to the extent within his authority, and in this way achieves his year's sales objectives. But from the company's point of view, inventory has simply been transferred from the company's warehouse to the distributors' shelves. And if the distributors are not able to move the merchandise on favorable terms in the next period, this action will probably alienate some good will in the channels. The district sales manager is trying to avoid the day of judgment, but in effect may only be postponing it.

---

[7] E.g., A. D. H. Kaplan, Joel B. Kirlam, and Robert F. Lanzillotti, *Pricing in Big Business* (Washington, D.C.: Brookings Institute, 1958).

[8] Henry Ford II, "What America Expects of Industry," in an address before the Michigan State Chamber of Commerce, October 2, 1962.

Suboptimizing behavior can occur in any department of the company. The task of management is to set incentives in such a way that the goals of departments and individuals coincide with the over-all interests of the firm. No organization can survive if it permits personal interests to dominate company interests, for then it would be a collection of independent entrepreneurs rather than an organization. The fact is that organizational goals would have to be invented if they did not exist.

There are, in fact, two different views on how organizational goals arise.[9] The first holds that the goals of the organization are imposed by its leader(s). In classic economic theory, each firm is assumed to be started and managed by an entrepreneur who defines the organization's goals. In the modern corporation this role is attributed to top management or to the stockholders.

The alternative view holds that organizational goals, rather than being imposed arbitrarily from above, develop out of consensus among the company personnel. The organization's goals are assumed to be shaped by a multitude of groups and to maintain continuity in spite of changes in top management. Top management's role is to put into words the felt consensus of the personnel.

Both views contain the seeds of truth. The attitudes of the firm's leaders will strongly affect the firm's actions. Yet they are effective only when rooted in a respect for the interests and understandings of the multiple groups that make up the organization. The importance of organizational consensus cannot be overstated. It is an "invisible hand" which guides company employees to harmonize their personal actions with company interests.

Marketing Organization

Organizational goals are a statement of the company's intended evolution. But the intended evolution does not fulfill itself automatically. Effective working arrangements must be established among the company's various actors (organization). And advanced decisions must be made on the future disposition of the company's resources (planning).

FORMAL PRINCIPLES OF ORGANIZATION

Whenever a group of people works together for a common set of goals, the problem of organization arises. Somehow their roles and relationships to the tasks and to one another must be defined. There are usually different ways to do this, and each alternative blueprint will carry a different implication for the group's potential effectiveness in realizing its goals. Here we shall review the major concepts in organizational design—*specialization, coordination,* and *authority*.

SPECIALIZATION. A business organization must perform many different tasks in the pursuit of its goals. Raw materials must be found and purchased; they must be converted into finished goods; customers must be

[9] See the discussion in Richard M. Cyert and James G. March, *A Behavioral Theory of the Firm* (Englewood Cliffs, N.J.: Prentice-Hall, Inc., 1963), pp. 26-43.

found and persuaded to buy these goods; the goods must be shipped; bills must be paid and collected; company assets and income must be reported periodically; and so forth.

Almost two centuries ago Adam Smith pointed out the great advantages that would come from each person's specializing in a narrow task.[10] His famous example involved a pin factory where one worker drew the wire, another straightened it, a third cut it, a fourth pointed it, and so on. He argued that specialization brings substantial gains in productivity, owing:

> first, to the increase of dexterity in every particular workman; secondly, to the saving of the time which is commonly lost in passing from one species of work to another; and lastly to the invention of a great number of machines which facilitate and abridge labour, and enable one man to do the work of many.[11]

To these may be added two other reasons for the gain. Men differ in their natural abilities, and it is therefore desirable for them to specialize; and specialization reduces the wasteful duplication of tools and facilities.

In modern business organizations, the functional areas of manufacturing, marketing, and finance provide the initial basis for the division of labor, and further task specialization occurs within each of these functional areas. In addition to specialization by tasks is specialization by roles, according to whether the work involves deciding, doing, planning, or advising. The *line-staff* distinction is an example of differentiating those who decide from those who advise.

COORDINATION. The advantages of specialization come at a price. The further it is pushed, the more serious is the problem of coordination. The danger is that while each part may work well individually, the whole organization may flounder and fall short of its purposes. Specialization creates the following problems:

Suboptimization, or the diminution of over-all company achievement because local goals are substituted for company goals. A specialist tends to lose sight of over-all company goals because he deals with problems in a local portion of the system. He shows a tendency to treat his own operations as ends rather than means. He finds difficulty in accepting other points of view. He builds up the position of his department at the expense of the organization.

Interdependency, or the increased dependence of each actor in the organization on the outputs of the other actors. The work of one specialist often cannot begin until the work of another specialist is finished. The performance of a company task is therefore at the mercy of each participating specialist.

Inconsistency, or the possible development of contradictory policies in different parts of the company. Each specialist develops policies which promote his local interests, and the sum of these may present an inconsistent picture.

Poor timing, or the danger that the various tasks may not achieve

[10] Adam Smith, *An Inquiry into the Nature and Causes of the Wealth of Nations,* 1776 (New York: P. F. Collier & Son Co., 1909), pp. 9-18.
[11] *Ibid.,* p. 13.

the proper coordination in time. Each specialist tends to schedule his own tasks to maximize his own convenience, and this may not coincide with good timing from the point of view of the over-all task.

These dangers of specialization make it clear that some mechanisms are necessary to harmonize the activities going on in different parts of the organization. The most common mechanisms for achieving coordination are *communication, committees,* and *coordinators*.

Communication is a precondition for the establishment of coordinated action. Various parties whose roles interact must be willing and able to make their purposes plain to each other. The communication system is effective to the extent that it is *open, bilateral, speedy,* and *accurate*. Communication is open when standard channels exist for communication without requiring special exertions. Communication is bilateral when information and advice is given as well as received by each party. Communication is speedy when messages can be transmitted in a reasonably short time. Communication is accurate when messages are not distorted in their formation or transmission.

Committees amount to a face-to-face consultation of various parties in a company whose interests are to be coordinated for some common purpose. They represent a forum for the exchange of information and opinion. They facilitate the development, coordination, and approval of plans. Committees seem to work best when they consist of similarly ranked individuals. They are a useful device for improving communication both within and between functional areas.[12]

Coordinators are persons who have been given the assignment to effect the coordination of specific areas or projects not ordinarily coordinated through conventional officers. Of increasing importance, for example, is the brand manager who has been given the responsibility of coordinating the various marketing efforts impinging on a brand. This responsibility, however, is generally not accompanied by commensurate authority, a fact which constitutes the major hurdle in effective coordination.

AUTHORITY.   Coordinated action cannot be left to the strict voluntarism of interacting company officers. If two executives cannot agree on an effort requiring coordinated action, an orderly process must be available for settling their differences. And even if they can agree, the terms may not necessarily be in the best interests of the company. All organizations therefore develop a structure of authority to insure coordination of the right type.

Authority is the power to issue and enforce orders. This power is necessary because all organizations operate on the principle of holding individual executives responsible for specific results. Such responsibility is realistic only if the executive has authority over those whose activities affect the results. This is summarized in the maxim that authority must be

---

12 There are strong advocates and strong critics of management through committees. Those who favor their use see them as a useful means to develop consensus and feel they lead to better decisions. Critics charge that they disperse responsibility, discourage initiative, slow down decision making, and lead to conservative decisions. See William H. Whyte, *Is Anybody Listening?* (New York: Simon & Schuster, Inc., 1952); and Rollie Tillman, Jr., "Committees on Trial," *Harvard Business Review,* May-June 1960.

commensurate with responsibility. Every organization contains a chain of command in which officers exercise authority over specific lower officers and are responsible to a higher officer. The familiar pyramidal organization chart expresses these formal relationships. Solid lines are used to show the authority relations among the various officers. Dotted lines are used to indicate areas of coordination without authority.

To build a good authority structure

In designing the authority structure of an organization, several principles have to be observed. The first is that *lines of authority should be unambiguous.* There is nothing more subversive of organizational effectiveness than overlapping authority. The second is that *authority and responsibility should fall along lines of related activities.* This is an application of the principles of specialization and coordination to the problem of authority. The third is that *the span of control should be balanced against the levels of control.* The span of control describes the number of different activities directly supervised by a particular officer. There are obviously limits to how many different activities an executive can oversee effectively. A smaller span of control will mean more levels of control. But this increases the number of decision intermediaries and therefore can increase the problems of coordination, communication, and control.

There are other issues of organizational design where the best principle is far from clear. Most important in this connection are the relative merits of *centralized versus decentralized* organization. The issue is essentially whether subunits should have extensive or limited authority and responsibility. Should each product division of Westinghouse, for example, have complete authority to set prices, determine advertising, and so forth, or should these decisions be made, or subject to review, at company headquarters? Centralization is based on the belief that headquarters is in the best position to make all or most of the decisions. Decentralization is based on the belief that local units can make better decisions on matters affecting them. In addition, it is felt that under decentralization local units tend to operate with more drive and creativeness. The difference between these two policies is sometimes described as management by system versus management by results.

HUMAN FACTORS IN ORGANIZATION

The principles of specialization, coordination, and authority play a central role in the creation of a sound formal organizational structure. However, every formal organization is overlapped by many informal relationships and groups which affect organizational performance to a considerable degree.

In the early days of the development of organizational theory (early 1900's), little attention was paid to informal relationships and groups. Organizational theory was dominated by men like Frederick Winslow Taylor and Frank Gilbreth who viewed organizational problems in terms of engineering concepts. They stressed the formal requirements of organization: division of labor, clear lines of authority, limited span of control. Taylor called his philosophy *scientific management* [13] and stressed the

---

[13] This term should be distinguished from *management science,* which is a more recent and more broadly conceived scientific movement in management theory. For Taylor's views, see his *Principles of Scientific Management* (New York: Harper & Bros., 1915).

development of efficiency standards through the rational analysis of the work task. Gilbreth developed the analysis of the work task into the fine art known as time-and-motion study. These developments mark positive and lasting contributions to management theory. The principles are increasingly being applied to marketing in the form of time-and-duty studies of salesmen and distribution operations.[14]

At the same time, scientific management was marked by a highly mechanical and authoritarian view of the worker. The worker was viewed as a passive instrument to be ordered around and molded into various assignments. The emphasis was placed on the job and not the man. It is this aspect of traditional organizational theory which came under the heaviest fire by subsequent writers.

The reaction crystallized in the early 1930's in the writings of men like Elton Mayo, F. J. Roethlisberger, William Foote Whyte, and Burleigh Gardner.[15] These early "industrial sociologists" explored the structure of human motivations and informal social relationships operating in the work situation. The famous Hawthorne experiments of Mayo brought out the importance of small group mores and norms in affecting productivity and job satisfaction.[16] More recently, research has proceeded in the same tradition to study informal relationships in selling groups. Retail sales personnel, for example, tend to develop informal rules as to a "fair" maximum effort, and the group exercises strong social sanctions against violators.[17]

The impact of these findings was to shift the stress away from formal organizational principles toward the improved management of human factors. *Human relations* became the magic word in organizational theory. Theorists and practitioners stressed the importance of human relations training programs to teach managers the principles of human motivation. They called for the replacement of authoritarian management practices by individual and group participation practices. Within the marketing operation, the human relations approach slowly but surely affected the handling of the sales force.

In more recent years, a feeling developed that the pendulum had swung too far in the human relations direction. Some felt that human relations had turned into a gospel rather than a balanced scientific perspective on the problem of achieving organizational efficiency. Writers like Chester Barnard, Herbert A. Simon, and James G. March have been developing a body of modern organizational theory which shows more integration of the formal and the human aspects of organization.[18] These writers approach the organization as a total system and lay particular stress on the decision

[14] For a summary, see Harold B. Maynard, *Industrial Engineering Handbook,* 2nd ed. (New York: McGraw-Hill Book Company, 1963), sec. 10, chap. 4.

[15] See, for example, F. S. Roethlisberger and William J. Dickson, *Management and the Worker* (Cambridge, Mass.: Harvard University Press, 1939); Elton Mayo, *The Social Problems of an Industrial Civilization* (Boston: Harvard Business School, 1945).

[16] Roethlisberger, *op. cit.*

[17] See George F. F. Lombard, *Behavior in a Selling Group* (Boston: Harvard Graduate School of Business Administration, Division of Research, 1955); and Cecil L. French, "Correlates of Success in Retail Selling," *American Journal of Sociology,* September 1960, pp. 128-34.

[18] Chester I. Barnard, *The Functions of the Executive* (Cambridge, Mass.: Harvard University Press, 1938); and James G. March and Herbert A. Simon, *Organizations* (New York: John Wiley & Sons, Inc., 1958).

making aspects. There is an analysis of its parts (such as formal and informal groups, status systems, and role perceptions), of its linkages (communication, information, and decision system), and its goals (goal multiplicity and satisficing).

THE MARKETING DEPARTMENT'S POSITION
IN THE ORGANIZATION

Our ultimate concern is to apply the preceding organizational principles to the problem of creating an effective marketing organization. Every firm resorts to specialization to gain the classic advantages propounded by Adam Smith. The typical organization is made up of different departments, such as manufacturing, marketing, and finance. But as we saw in Chapter 1, each specialized function has an impact on the buyers. Under the marketing concept, it is held desirable to coordinate the various impacts because the satisfaction gained by the customer is a function of the totality of stimuli, and not simply the stimuli managed by the marketing department proper. But typically, the chief marketing officer makes final decisions only on such matters as the use of the sales force, allocation of advertising funds, distributor relations, and marketing research. He shares with top management other customer-impinging decisions, such as pricing and product planning. Major decisions to reorganize the entire sales force, to develop new channels of distribution, or to penetrate new territories also are shared with top management. He only advises on certain other customer-impinging company activities, such as traffic and credit, where the final authority rests with other officers.

When the voluntary integration of the customer-impinging forces breaks down, the chief marketing officer becomes frustrated by his limited authority. He may seek the direct support of the president in his battles with other officers, or he may press for a new organization structure where he is given line command over the recalcitrant functions.[19]

Yet it is important for the marketing officer to appreciate the legitimate concerns of the other departments in the organization. Just as marketing stresses the customer's point of view, other departments must stress efficiency at their tasks. This results in a large number of conflicts with marketing, the chief ones being summarized in Table 6-1.[20]

Looking over the list, we can understand why many company officers resent the marketing concept. Marketing, in trying to mobilize the company's resources to develop customer satisfactions, often causes other departments to do a poorer job *in their terms*. Requests and pressures by the marketing department can increase product-design and material-purchasing costs, disrupt production schedules, increase accounting paper costs, and create budget headaches.

In some cases the hostility against the marketing concept erupts in costly power struggles and inconsistent departmental policies and actions. Unfortunately, it takes more than good intentions and communication among executives to resolve the basic conflicts. Good executive relations are essential, but the issues nevertheless remain real. As long as each department is judged not by over-all company contributions but by standards

[19] See Chapter 1, Figure 1-3b and c.
[20] The rest of this section is adapted from Philip Kotler, "Diagnosing the Marketing Takeover," *Harvard Business Review*, November-December 1965, pp. 70-72.

TABLE 6-1
Summary of organizational conflicts between marketing and other departments

Other departments	Their emphasis	Marketing emphasis
Engineering	Long design lead time	Short design lead time
	Functional features	Sales features
	Few models	Many models
	Standard components	Custom components
Purchasing	Standard parts	Nonstandard parts
	Price of material	Quality of material
	Economical lot sizes	Large lot sizes to avoid stockouts
	Purchasing at infrequent intervals	Immediate purchasing for customer needs
Production	Long production lead time	Short production lead time
	Long runs with few models	Short runs with many models
	No model changes	Frequent model changes
	Standard orders	Custom orders
	Ease of fabrication	Aesthetic appearance
	Average quality control	Tight quality control
Inventory	Fast moving items, narrow product line	Broad product line
	Economical levels of stock	Large levels of stock
Finance	Strict rationales for spending	Intuitive arguments for spending
	Hard and fast budgets	Flexible budgets to meet changing needs
	Pricing to cover costs	Pricing to further market development
Accounting	Standard transactions	Special terms and discounts
	Few reports	Many reports
Credit	Full financial disclosures by customers	Minimum credit examination of customers
	Low credit risks	Medium credit risks
	Tough credit terms	Easy credit terms
	Tough collection procedures	Easy collection procedures

related to the efficient performance of its own tasks, it has a real interest in adhering to these standards.

This suggests that *top* management should reduce its emphasis on departmental efficiency narrowly conceived and increase its emphasis on the development of interdepartmental policies and practices designed to advance over-all company interests. Each recurrent source of interdepartmental conflict should be examined objectively in terms of the company's interests, not the respective departments' interests. The ultimate standard is neither cost control nor customer satisfaction at any price. Just as production, engineering, finance, and the other departments should show more concern for keeping and cultivating the customer, marketing has to show more *restraint* in interrupting production schedules and multiplying product-design and material costs. Perhaps it might help if marketing's profit contribution were charged with some of the extra costs its actions create for other departments.[21]

[21] See Chapter 21, p. 563.

The chief marketing officer is responsible for managing a highly complex operation. Under him are specialists in such diverse activities as advertising, sales promotion, field selling, customer services, research, and planning. Under him may be further specialists in the various company products, in the various customer industries, and in the various geographical territories. He cannot personally supervise and coordinate all of these marketing employees. He must manage them through an organizational structure. A variety of alternative organizational structures exist for the management of marketing effort.

All marketing organizations must somehow accommodate to four basic dimensions of marketing activity: various *functions, products, regions,* and *customers*. These dimensions will be blended differently not only in different industries but by different firms within the same industry. This is because marketing organization structure is everywhere shaped by a host of unique factors, such as company goals, management's philosophy of organization, management's philosophy of marketing, the importance of different marketing tools, the types and numbers of products, and the character of competition. In addition, historical factors and current personnel count heavily in influencing the design of the company's marketing organization.

The resulting marketing organizations are often unique. All four dimensions are rarely given equal weight, and some may not even appear. Companies serving only one region will not build regional specialization into the marketing organization, and companies producing a single product will not build product managers into the organization. Even where all four dimensions are present, usually one or two dominate the others in importance. If the company's products are vastly different, products may become the fundamental framework for organizing the marketing effort; if the customers are vastly different in their buying methods and needs, customers may become the fundamental framework. The other dimensions may be built in on a subsidiary basis.

FUNCTION-ORIENTED MARKETING ORGANIZATION.   In the most common marketing organization the vice-president of marketing works through a set of managers who are specialized by function. Two examples of this type of organization are shown in Figure 6-2. Figure 6-2a shows five different functional specialties. Each functional manager carries out his responsibilities through a group of further specialists (not shown). For example, reporting to the marketing research manager may be someone in charge of market surveys, someone in charge of economic analysis and forecasting, and someone in charge of sales analysis. Or these subordinate specialists may be organized according to a different principle, such as territory for the manager of field sales.

That only five functional specialties are shown is arbitrary. In the selling of soap, for example, sales promotion may be of commensurate importance with advertising and managed separately because the required skills and knowledge are thought to differ. Other marketing functions may also be singled out for separate management. The decision depends on which are the most important in the marketing process for that firm.

The number of functional units reporting to the vice-president is subject,

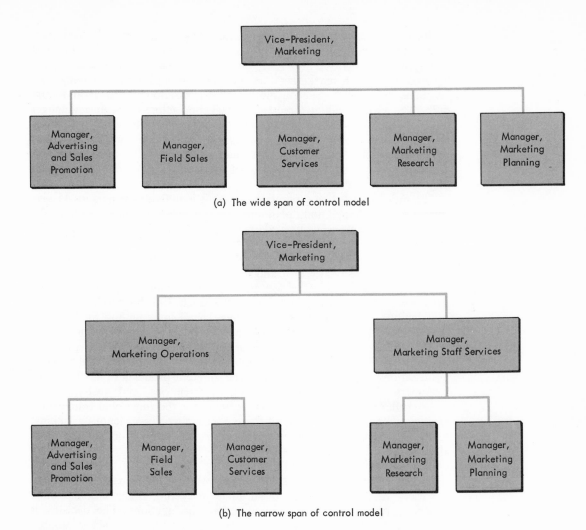

(a) The wide span of control model

(b) The narrow span of control model

FIGURE 6-2

Function-oriented marketing organization

however, to span-of-control limitations. As the number of separate managers reporting to the marketing vice-president increases, his time for supervising each is correspondingly reduced. According to traditional organizational theory, shrinking the time for individual supervision can lead to unfortunate consequences. Traditional organizational theory favors close supervision and hence a narrow span of control.

The traditional point of view has come under much criticism in recent years. Narrow spans of control increase the number of hierarchical levels and hence the number of administrators. Furthermore, a case can be made for loose supervision with more responsibility given to subordinates. Also there are many cases of successful companies, like Sears, using very wide spans of control. In general, clear evidence is lacking for the a priori superiority of either a narrow or broad span of control; much depends on the individual circumstances of each company.

Where it is felt desirable to have a narrow span of control but still preserve a function-oriented marketing department, the solution is to combine homogeneous functions into fewer groups. A basic division which might be used is between marketing line functions (doing) and marketing staff functions (planning). Such a marketing organization is shown in Figure 6-2b. The vice-president directs the marketing effort through a manager of operations and a manager of staff services. The marketing operations manager supervises personnel who execute specific programs related to advertising, field selling, and customer relations. The marketing staff services manager supervises personnel involved in researching and planning the marketing effort.

The rationale for this separation is that it is difficult for persons to give equal time to "doing" and "planning" and to be equally good at both. The operating executive is embroiled in daily crises and problems which detract from long-range thinking and planning. It is felt that the planning work gets done—and done better—by entrusting it to those who have specialized professionally in it and have time to do it. The major criticism of this separation is that the planners may do a poor job because they do not understand operating conditions well enough. But this can be overcome in a number of ways, such as having them spend some time in the field and having them consult regularly with marketing operations personnel.

The function-oriented marketing organization is based on the principle that there is more variance in the skills needed to handle different marketing functions effectively than to manage different products or territories or customers. When a company's products, territories, and customers are quite similar, an even stronger case is made for the functional framework. On the other hand, when any of these conditions is conspicuously lacking, a different organizational framework for the marketing effort may be more effective.

PRODUCT-ORIENTED MARKETING ORGANIZATION.   Companies producing a variety of products often build their marketing organization around product groups rather than around marketing functions. The decision is influenced by the extent of product heterogeneity and the sheer number of products. If the company product lines can benefit from specialized marketing programs or if the sheer number of products is beyond the capacity of individual salesmen to handle, a product-oriented marketing organization is a natural recourse.

Specialized product management can be built into a marketing organization in a number of ways. Figure 6-3a is appropriate for companies manufacturing highly diversified products; examples are General Electric, Du Pont, and Hunt's Foods and Industries. The major products are produced, marketed, and managed by separate divisions. Figure 6-3a shows the vice-president of marketing supervising a manager of corporate advertising, a manager of corporate marketing research and three divisional product marketing managers. The marketing manager for product (division) B manages in turn a function-oriented marketing department. Under him is a divisional advertising manager, field sales manager, and marketing research manager. They give all their attention to promoting the products of their division. At the same time, these functional specialists at the divisional level may work with, and may be answerable to, the correspond-

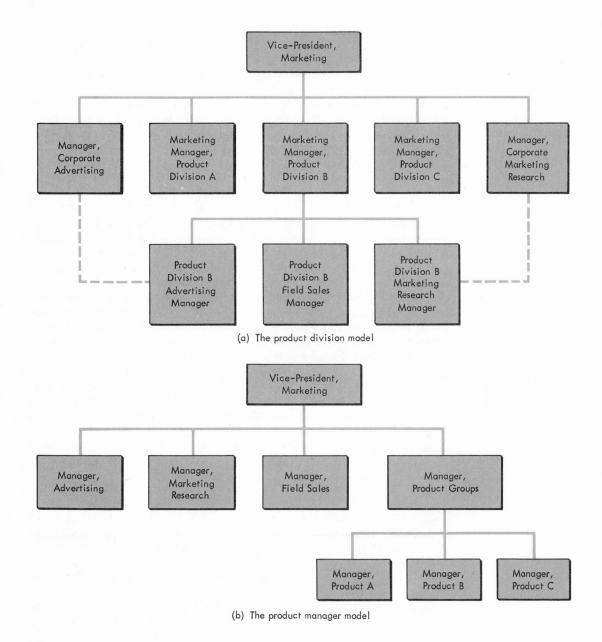

(a) The product division model

(b) The product manager model

FIGURE 6-3
Product-oriented marketing organization

ing functional managers at the corporate level as shown by the dotted lines in Figure 6-3a.

The desirability of carrying on advertising and marketing research at the divisional level in addition to the corporate level depends upon a number of factors. Economies may be gained by carrying out all staff functions at the corporate level. It minimizes the duplication of personnel, space, and equipment; it allows the hiring of a few extremely competent

143

administrators; and it makes possible better coordination of the separate product programs. On the other hand, the main danger is that the corporate level staff may lack sufficient acquaintance with the individual products and prepare unrealistic programs. If the advertising or marketing research problems of each product division are radically different, it would seem that divisional operations are called for. Figure 6-3a portrays these functions at both levels and makes no assumption about the division of labor or distribution of authority.

Figure 6-3b represents an alternative model of product specialization involving product or brand managers. It is found in companies or within divisions of companies where there are various products and it is felt desirable to give them individual attention. Many of the larger consumer-goods companies use the product manager concept. The product manager's major responsibility is to integrate the planning and marketing effort for his product. All the products are handled by a single sales force, and channels of distribution, distributor relations, shipping arrangements, and prices are generally decided at a higher level of management or in a different part of the marketing organization. The product manager is responsible for sales promotion, advertising, packaging, and product improvements for which he plans by soliciting the aid of specialists in these functional areas. Because the product manager has limited line authority, he spends much of his time trying to persuade sales managers and others to give his product a special push. His place in the organization is often ambivalent and generally characterized by responsibility without sufficient authority. In Figure 6-3b the separate product managers do not report directly to the vice-president of marketing but to a general product manager who in turn reports to the vice-president. The product managers are located in one limb of the organization and must find their way to the functional marketing specialists.[22]

REGIONALLY ORIENTED MARKETING ORGANIZATION. Companies selling over a wide area will almost always introduce regional specialization at some level in the marketing organization. Field sales is the marketing function typically organized on this basis. Under certain circumstances, the whole marketing organization may be structured along predominantly regional lines. If products and customer types are relatively homogeneous but the regions exhibit considerable differences, then regional specialization is usually desirable.

Figure 6-4 illustrates a regionally oriented marketing organization. Reporting to the marketing vice-president are three regional marketing managers and also a corporate-level advertising and marketing research manager. Reporting to each regional marketing manager are district sales managers and also a regional-level advertising and marketing research manager. Reporting to each district sales manager are salesmen who operate in separate territories making up the district.

The regional marketing manager is shown to supervise some marketing specialists as well as district sales managers. This enables him to plan regional advertising and conduct regionally oriented marketing research and sales analysis. The relation of the regional advertising and marketing re-

[22] The product manager concept is discussed in "Why Modern Marketing Needs the Product Manager," *Printers' Ink,* October 14, 1960, pp. 25-30.

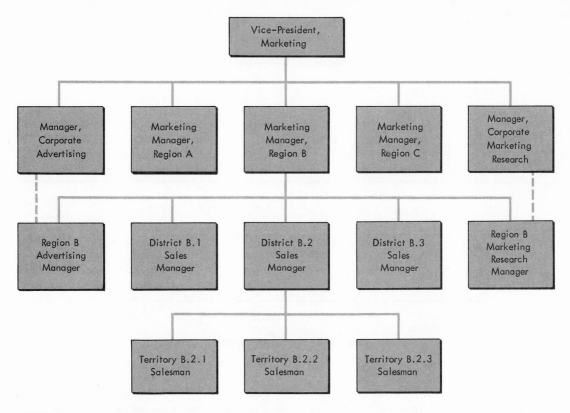

FIGURE 6-4
Regionally oriented marketing organization

search specialists and their counterparts at the corporate level raises the same issues discussed earlier in connection with the product-oriented organization; we have simply drawn dotted lines to indicate a relationship.

CUSTOMER-ORIENTED MARKETING ORGANIZATION.   Where the customers of a company fall into distinctly different groups in terms of buying practices or product interest, customer groups may be the desirable basis for the marketing organization. For example, a large cigarette company uses separate marketing managers for chain store sales, independent store sales, and vending machine sales, all reporting to the vice-president of marketing. A large steel fabricator uses separate marketing managers for railroad sales, home and office sales, construction industry sales, and public utility sales.

The general structure of such an organization is illustrated in Figure 6-5. Different customer-group marketing managers report to the marketing vice-president. In turn, each customer-group marketing manager supervises functional submanagers for advertising, field sales, and marketing research. As before, there are relations between the functional specialists at the corporate and customer-group level.

The major advantage of the customer-oriented marketing department is that it leads to greater expertise and effectiveness in marketing to differ-

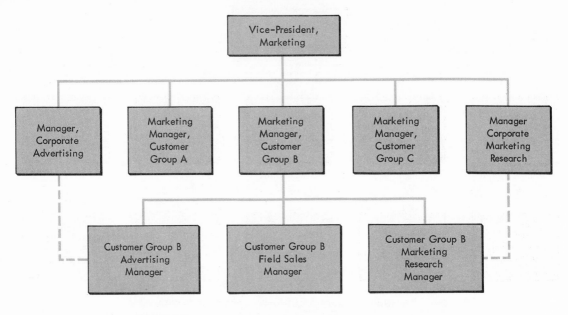

FIGURE 6-5
Customer-oriented marketing organization

ent customers. The salesmen, researchers, and advertising men specializing in industry B come to know more about the competitive forces at work in the industry and the industry's particular product requirements, service needs, and buying practices. They bring this knowledge to other departments in the company and press for a more customer-oriented marketing effort. The result typically is a finer attunement of over-all company effort to the varying needs of customers.

Yet a customer-group marketing organization is not feasible in all circumstances, even though it comes closest to expressing the spirit of the marketing concept. Some firms sell to a relatively homogeneous group of customers; while these customers exhibit individual differences, they do not show systematic group differences. In other cases, the firm's customers do fall into distinct groups (different industries, for example) but it may be too costly to specialize the sales forces or other marketing functions. If the customers in each group are widely dispersed, company salesmen would have to crisscross the country, increasing the travel and selling expense substantially over the alternative of territorially based salesmen. Or, certain customers might conduct multi-industry operations, and probably would be irritated by visits from several company salesmen, unless different purchasing agents of the customer were involved.

Thus, while customer-group management is the marketing organization principle most consonant with the marketing concept, it is not necessary or even desirable in all circumstances. A company can choose to design its marketing organization predominantly around functions, products, or regions, and still maintain the spirit of customer orientation by attending carefully to individual needs.

In practice, pure forms of marketing organizations are rarely found, each firm's marketing organization having evolved out of the rational factors cited here and a myriad of historical influences and factors peculiar to the company.[23]

Summary

In the efforts of firms to survive and prosper in an ever changing and challenging environment, business goals supply the framework for organization and planning. Firms typically try to satisfy several goals, some of which are in conflict. The task is not to pursue one goal and ignore others, but rather to develop a clear picture of their relative importance as constraints in the decision-making process. One of these goals, profits, is undoubtedly the most important, at least to the survival of the firm.

The goals are pursued through organized effort. Effective organization is built on the proper balancing of the principles of specialization, coordination, and authority, combined with an appreciation of the human factor. The position of the marketing department in the total organization is particularly difficult because of the types of conflicts which tend to occur between the logic of customer satisfaction and the cost minimization logic pursued by other departments. Organizational issues also arise with respect to the internal organization of the marketing department, and departments tend to be organized along those dimensions (functions, products, regions, or customers) which play the largest role in the company's marketing process.

Questions and Problems

1. "Few trends could so thoroughly undermine the very foundations of our free society as the acceptance by corporate officials of a social responsibility other than to make as much money for their stockholders as possible." Do you agree?

2. Suggest some criteria by which the usefulness of a stated company marketing objective can be evaluated.

3. "In 1945 he had been brought back to Millburgh and made Vice-President of sales. At fifty-three, J. Walter Dudley was probably the best-known man in the entire furniture industry. His memory for names and faces was phenomenal. At one Chicago Market . . . two bystanding salesmen had actually kept a count and heard him greet two hundred and eighteen furniture store owners and buyers by name before he was confronted by an individual whose name he did not know. There were hundreds of furniture merchants who would not have thought a market visit complete without having had the opportunity to

[23] The marketing organizations of some large American firms are illustrated in Hector Lazo and Arnold Corbin, *Management in Marketing* (New York: McGraw-Hill Book Company, 1961), pp. 79, 86-89.

shake hands with good old Walt Dudley."—Cameron Hawley, *Executive Suite* (Boston: Houghton Mifflin Company, 1952), pp. 133-34. Does J. Walter Dudley sound like the ideal vice-president of marketing?

4. In order to carry out a proposed national sales promotion, describe some of the departments whose efforts must be coordinated with those of the marketing department. Through what kind of planning device might these efforts be integrated?

chapter 7

Marketing Planning

In the preceding chapter we saw how a firm can exploit opportunities in the market place through the establishment of clear goals and an effective marketing organization. These two steps must take place before management can act purposefully and effectively. A third step must occur if company actions are to achieve a high degree of market impact. This step is planning.

This chapter views the problems and processes of marketing planning within the context of total company planning. The first section discusses the nature of planning: its meaning, variations in practice, major benefits, and organizational aspects. The second section contrasts four types of planning efforts: long-range, short-range, company-level, and marketing-level. The third section describes the six major steps in the planning process (diagnosis, prognosis, objectives, strategy, tactics, and control) as they apply to marketing planning. The last section describes how the new critical path techniques can be used by marketing management to improve the planning, scheduling, and control of specific marketing projects.

Nature of Planning

THE MEANING OF PLANNING

Planning is deciding in the present what to do in the future. It is the process whereby companies reconcile their resources with their objectives and opportunities.

All firms carry out some planning. The preparation of the annual budget represents planning. The determination of next year's advertising program (media, themes, monthly spending) represents planning. Decisions on new capital investments and financial borrowings represent planning. In all cases, the firm is deciding now how it will use its resources—men, materials, machines, and money—in the future.

VARIATIONS IN PLANNING PRACTICES

Although all firms plan, they vary considerably in how extensively, thoroughly, and formally they do it. Some managements are so embroiled in daily operations that they give little time to long-range thinking, let alone planning. Other managements go through the motions of some formal planning: written plans are prepared by individual departments, bound together, and filed away. Finally, some managements go through a full-fledged formal planning procedure, utilizing planning staffs, planning committees, and written documents. These firms are convinced that formal planning is the key to corporate survival in a world of rapid social change and intense competition. More than 700 companies are estimated to have formal planning staffs.[1]

Firms that do little formal planning may not make the best use of their opportunities and resources and may be the most vulnerable to changing markets. On the other hand, conclusive evidence is lacking that firms which do the most planning fare substantially better than the rest *because of their planning*. The facts are obscure because the firms which have developed the most extensive planning procedures are generally the larger ones, and the use of planning did not create their wealth. Still, most American companies probably err more in underplanning than in overplanning.

Planning is regarded with some suspicion in the pragmatic setting of business. Some executives of the old school argue that "pluck and luck" count for more than careful planning and claim that their firms are too successful to take the time out for planning. Yet planning does yield positive benefits, and though it can be carried to excess, this is usually not the problem. The problem is one of developing appropriate planning procedures and company-wide participation and enthusiasm in carrying them out.

BENEFITS OF PLANNING

The point of view taken here is that if good planning procedures are used, formal planning results in a number of distinct benefits to any firm seeking to grow and prosper in a rapidly changing environment. The use of planning:

> Encourages systematic thinking ahead by management
> Leads to a better coordination of company efforts
> Leads to the development of performance standards for control
> Causes the company to sharpen its guiding objectives and policies
> Results in better preparedness for sudden developments
> Brings about a more vivid sense in the participating executives of their interacting responsibilities [2]

ORGANIZATION FOR EFFECTIVE PLANNING

Good plans do not spring full-grown from the head of the company president nor emerge from a few meetings of a planning committee. Executives increasingly recognize that the benefits of planning come from carrying it out as *a continuous activity under centralized and professional supervision through many layers of participating management*.

In a growing number of companies, planning is being conducted along the lines of the model shown in Figure 7-1. An executive planning committee composed of the major company officers stands at the top of the process. This committee initiates the planning process in each period by setting forth specific objectives and guidelines.

Working with the planning committee and directly responsible for the

---

[1] "V.P. for the Future," *Time,* May 10, 1963, p. 89.
[2] See Melville C. Branch, *The Corporate Planning Process* (New York: American Management Association, 1962), pp. 48-49.

EXECUTIVE PLANNING COMMITTEE

(Sets objectives, guidelines; approves plans)

VICE-PRESIDENT OF PLANNING

(Bears planning responsibility and works with president and major officers)

PLANNING COORDINATOR & PLANNING STAFF

(Coordinates interdepartmental plans; develops research information)

DEPARTMENT HEADS

(Direct and coordinate intradepartmental plans)

FUNCTIONAL OFFICERS

(Develop departmental subplans)

FIGURE 7-1

The circular, participative nature of company planning

From a prose description in Bruce Payne, *Planning for Company Growth* (New York: McGraw-Hill Book Company, 1963), Chap. 2.

planning function is the vice-president of planning. The appointment of a vice-president of planning insures that long-range planning is a top management concern. It also avoids biasing planning toward any one company function, as might happen when it is entrusted to the financial vice-president or the marketing vice-president. The vice-president of planning works with the other major functional and divisional officers to clarify goals, programs, and needs.

Under the vice-president of planning is a planning coordinator and a professional planning staff. The planning coordinator supervises the planning staff and sees to it that the necessary research is carried out, that planning documents are received from the several parts of the company, and that conflicting programs are harmonized.

The actual plans are initially formulated by the separate department heads on the basis of the planning committee's goals and guidelines. Each department head puts together plans he has requested from his functional officers. These plans move up, and are screened and coordinated by the company planning staff. They are presented by the vice-president of planning to the planning committee, and further evaluations are made.

Some of the plans may be returned to department heads for amendment or further amplification; then they go back to the planning staff. Thus the planning process moves circularly through the organization, involving much participation and progressive refinement before final approval by the executive planning committee. Their approval means that the plan is regarded as realistic and that each department head accepts responsibility for the performance of his unit in meeting the plan's objectives.

151

Types of Planning

Planning is undertaken for a variety of purposes and under a variety of circumstances. A useful classification may be made on a time basis, in which long-range planning and short-range planning are distinguished. Long-range planning is undertaken to establish the basic direction of future company efforts and operations; the time horizon is at least a couple of years. Short-range planning is undertaken to program the company's efforts and operations for the immediate future, usually the coming year. A further distinction can be drawn between over-all company planning and marketing operations planning. Over-all company planning seeks to coordinate future actions in marketing, finance, production, purchasing, and other areas. Marketing planning seeks to coordinate the future operations within the marketing area.

LONG-RANGE COMPANY PLANNING

Long-range company planning involves developing the basic objectives and strategy to guide future company efforts. The long-range plan, therefore, provides the framework for both the annual plans and specific departmental plans.

Long-range planning may involve a time horizon of two or more years, although typically it uses a longer horizon of five to twenty years. In 1963, for example, the slogan at General Electric's planning center at Santa Barbara, California was "1970 starts today."

Historically, long-range planning concentrated on the problem of determining what facilities and financing would be needed to meet the expected growth in the company's existing product lines. More recently, because of the increased vulnerability of existing product lines to competitive attack, long-range planners consider as more primary the question of which markets the company should serve. They see the main mission of long-range planning to be the determination of attractive areas of new opportunities and the promulgation of programs for developing them. Facilities and finances are considered after these more basic determinations are made.

This new concept of planning is found, for example, at International Minerals and Chemical Corporation, a large manufacturer of fertilizers. According to their vice-president of corporate planning:

> We're not merely in the business of selling our brand of fertilizer. We have a sense of purpose, a sense of where we are going. The first function of corporate planning is to decide what kind of business the company is in. Our business is agricultural productivity. We are interested in anything that affects plant growth, now and in the future.[3]

As a result, "IMC is interested in population figures, use of land, plant pests, the cattle that feed on plants, and such far-out things as its new effort to find mineral deposits at the bottom of the seas." [4]

Such companies as General Electric, Procter & Gamble, Du Pont, and General Foods are impressed with the opportunities latent in the develop-

[3] Gordon O. Pehrson, as quoted by Edwin Darby, "Flavored Algae from the Sea?" *Chicago Sun Times,* February 3, 1965, p. 54.
[4] *Ibid.*

ment of new products and markets, and their planning starting point is the choice of product markets. Other companies turn to long-range product-market planning out of necessity because their basic markets are changing or unstable. Thus International Harvester, Boeing, and Standard Oil of Indiana have had to seek new markets because of the uncertainties and changes in their basic markets.

LONG-RANGE MARKETING PLANNING

The *long-range company plan* sets forth the company's long-range goals and strategies. Within this plan will be several functionally oriented plans, one of which is the long-range marketing plan. The marketing plan outlines the role and responsibilities which the marketing department assumes within the framework of the over-all company plan. It states how the company's marketing resources will be developed and allocated in the future.

The marketing vice-president formulates the marketing plan in roughly the same way as the over-all company plan is developed. In the larger companies, he will have a staff planner or coordinator. The marketing plan is built from separate plans submitted by the managers of the separate organizational units comprising the marketing department. The nature of the component plans depends on the way the marketing department is organized.

In a *function-oriented* marketing organization, a separate plan would be developed for each major marketing function. The major plans might include:

The *product mix* plan, which outlines contemplated product deletions, modifications, and additions, and their timing, in the effort to meet the firm's customer-target and volume-profit objectives.

The *product research and development* plan, which outlines the general objectives which will guide new research investments, the areas of concentration, and ways to achieve more efficiency in the management of product research and development.

The *sales force* plan, which outlines measures to enhance the effectiveness of the personal selling effort. Among the matters treated are territorial reorganization, planned increases in the size of the sales force, the scale of future compensation, and future incentive programs for stimulating effort.

The *advertising and sales promotion* plan, which outlines future advertising strategy and tactics in the areas of message, copy, and media, along with the planned allocations of funds to products, territories, and customers. It also outlines a strategy for sales promotion to prevent a hodge-podge of unrelated promotions conceived in haste.

The *distribution channels* plan, which outlines future company policies with respect to types and number of channels and channel management.

The *pricing* plan, which outlines principles and objectives to guide pricing during the planning period. Included are future price changes contemplated for major company products.

The *marketing research* plan, which outlines major future projects to study markets and the effectiveness of the company's marketing efforts.

The *physical distribution* plan, which outlines programs for improving the efficiency of stocking and moving the company's goods to its customers. Included are measures for improved inventory control, for relocating distribution points, and for choosing modes of transportation.

The *marketing organization* plan, which outlines desirable changes in the organization of the marketing department, its information and communication system, and its relations with other company departments.

In a *product-oriented* marketing organization, a separate plan would be developed for each major product by the respective product managers. Each product plan would establish long-run objectives for the particular product and a detailed program for achieving them. Individual sections on advertising, personal selling, marketing research, product improvement, and other tasks would specify the resources needed and how they might be correlated into a coherent marketing program to achieve the product objectives.

In a *regionally oriented* marketing organization, a separate plan would be developed for each major region by the respective regional marketing managers. Each regional plan would set sales objectives in that region and would outline a program for achieving them. The plan would take into consideration regional sales growth trends and likely competitors' efforts. Each regional plan would contain subsections on the amount of advertising, personal selling, and other resources needed and the means whereby they would be integrated to achieve the regional objectives.

In a *customer-oriented* marketing organization, a separate plan would be developed for each customer group by the respective customer-group marketing managers. Each customer-group plan would set company sales objectives for that customer group. The objectives would be based on a realistic program for improving the need satisfaction of that customer group through product improvements and improved services. Each plan would contain subsections on how much advertising, personal selling, and other resources would be needed and how they would be integrated into a coherent program for marketing to this group.

ANNUAL COMPANY PLANNING

Each year many companies prepare an annual operating plan. In principle, the annual operating plan is developed in the context of the company's long-range plan. This, of course, is not possible where the company has no long-range plan or where the long-range plan is too vague to guide the development of the annual operating plan. A long-range plan is necessary if the short-range plans are not to be a chaotic series of expedient solutions to short-run crises. Too often, short-run plans only reflect overreactions to last year's results and next year's problems, rather than the progressive implementation of a long-range plan.

The annual plan develops sales targets for the year and a budget for their accomplishment. There are two competing views as to how sales targets should be determined. The traditional view is that they should represent what management would like to accomplish. This implies that management will then develop and pursue whatever program is necessary to accomplish them. The major problem, of course, is that arbitrary sales targets may require a program so costly as to rob profits for the sake of volume. The new view is that sales targets should be developed after considering the various programs which might be devised and their likely sales consequences under the conditions that are expected to prevail.[5] The "best"

[5] See this point made by Leon Winer, "Are You Really Planning Your Marketing?" *Journal of Marketing,* XXIX (January 1965), 1-8.

of these programs, the one which projects to the best profit level, indicates the sales targets to be established. In this way, the sales targets and the program are simultaneously determined and coordinated. The plan amounts to a program of company actions which should result in specific sales results (adopted as the sales targets), providing the company's analyses and assumptions are satisfied by the subsequent events.

The budget is based on the contemplated program of company actions. These actions can be spelled out in terms of specific resource needs. The final budget represents the funds needed by each department to carry out the stated activities.

ANNUAL MARKETING OPERATIONS PLANNING

The marketing department details its role in the annual company effort in a component annual marketing plan. This annual plan, like the long-range one, consists of a set of separate, but coordinated, subplans. Each marketing subplan spells out carefully specific needed resources and their intended applications during the year. Marketing subplans are developed for each of the major functional areas in marketing and may also be developed for separate products, regions, and customer groups. The following two functional subplans would undoubtedly figure strongly in the annual marketing plan:

> The *advertising and sales promotion operating subplan* would outline the allocation over the months of requested advertising funds, by media, and would describe the advertising objectives and themes. It would contain plans for special advertising campaigns in connection with the introduction of new products or the penetration of new markets. It would also outline planned sales promotions, their timing, required resources, and expected costs.

> The *sales force operating subplan* would outline the program for hiring, training, and assigning salesmen during the coming year. It would schedule future sales meetings, trade-show participation, and planned sales penetrations. It would outline the sales incentive programs and their costs and would contain the sales quotas for each salesman and sales district.

These and other operating subplans are correlated by the vice-president of marketing and his staff. The final plan becomes the basis for the marketing department's budget request, which should show an *income side,* listing the physical volumes of the different products expected to be sold (the "sales targets"), and a *cost side,* showing the amount of advertising funds, salesmen, sales promotional materials, and other resources needed.

The Planning Process

Regardless of the type or level of planning, the planning process is composed of a series of steps. A convenient progression would be:

> *Diagnosis:* where is the company now, and why?
> *Prognosis:* where is the company headed?
> *Objectives:* where should the company be headed?

Strategy: what is the best way to get there?

Tactics: what specific actions should be undertaken, by whom, and when?

Control: what measures should be watched to indicate whether the company is succeeding? [6]

These six steps will be illustrated in the case of a manufacturer facing a drastic change in his markets.[7]

The case is that of the Arno Shoe Company (fictional name), which manufactures and sells a line of work shoes. Sales and profits have increased for several years, but recently have begun to decline. Company executives believe the rural market, on which the company has long depended for the bulk of its sales, is no longer large enough to make the company's present operation profitable. Company executives are currently engaged in developing a long-range plan and are considering the alternatives before them.

DIAGNOSIS

The planning process begins with an attempt by the company to size up its present market situation and the factors responsible for it. The size-up requires generating and interpreting data on absolute levels of company sales and market shares and their recent trends, by product, territory, and other breakdowns. Supplementary data on marketing costs, plant utilization, profit levels, and other variables are also required. Most of the necessary background data can be furnished by the controller and the marketing research director. Pains must be taken to make a careful analysis of the recent trends instead of relying simply on impressions.

Arno management feels that its decline in sales and profits is associated with a shrinking rural market. But other hypotheses can also explain the decline in sales. The agricultural industry may be in the grip of a temporary recession. Arno's sales force may be demoralized because their earnings have not kept up with the increased cost of living. Arno's prices may be too high. These and many other factors may be involved in the slackening of demand.

Clarification of the causes is primarily a job for marketing research. The marketing research department can conduct surveys among customers, dealers, and salesmen to discern what new attitudes are forming toward price, product styling, channels, and other marketing factors. The marketing research department can also make estimates of sales potential, and of sales results by product class, sales territory, and dealer size, to pinpoint the major areas of sales weakness.

PROGNOSIS

Besides correctly diagnosing its present position, the company must also estimate where it is likely to go if present company policies and market trends continue. What sales and profits can the Arno Company expect in

---

[6] Diagnosis and prognosis are sometimes combined in a stage called *situational analysis;* strategy and tactics are sometimes combined in a stage called *programming.*

[7] Adapted from Harper W. Boyd, Jr., Richard M. Clewett, and Ralph Westfall, *Cases in Marketing Strategy* (Homewood, Ill.: Richard D. Irwin, Inc., 1958), pp. 223-27.

x years by remaining in the work shoe industry and giving its main emphasis to rural markets? This answer would help management decide what kind of action is necessary in the present. If the future looks bright, then the company need not significantly alter its present policies; if the future looks bleak, then bold company action is required.

The premise underlying a prognosis is that the future is partly predictable; its seeds are in the present. The doctor anticipates what will happen to the patient on the basis of his present ailment and medical knowledge about its future course if unchecked. The progress of symptoms is less rigid in economic affairs, but not completely unknown. More assumptions have to be made, but this does not negate the value of a prognosis.

A systematic sales and profit prognosis consists of five steps. They will be illustrated by assuming that the Arno Company produces a single, homogeneous product called work shoes. The steps (plus a sixth one) are shown graphically in Figure 7-2 and are described below.

Projection of industry sales. Figure 7-2a shows the (hypothetical) forecast of industry sales over the planning period. Industry sales are related systematically to several variables. The aggregate demand for work shoes is related to real income, the number of blue-collar and farm workers, and various other factors. These factors and their respective importance may be evaluated through statistical demand analysis.[8] Future values of these factors can be estimated and used to forecast the likely course of the future aggregate demand for work shoes.

Forecast of company sales. The firm's present *market share* is a useful point of departure for forecasting future company sales. If its market share were to persist, then company sales could be determined from anticipated industry sales by a straightforward calculation. But the company need not assume that its market share will be constant. The company may lose ground because of increasingly keen competition or gain ground because of imminent company innovations or marketing expenditures. We shall assume here that the company can forecast the probable course of its market share. Then it is relatively simple to derive company sales from industry sales. (See Figure 7-2b.)

Forecast of company revenues, costs, and profits. The anticipated company sales volume in physical units can be used as a basis for making an estimate of future dollar profits. The first step is to forecast revenue, which would be the product of expected prices times expected unit sales. The second step, forecasting costs, involves estimating the resources the firm will use in production and distribution and the prices of these resources. The last step, calculating profits, is a simple subtraction, once the previous mammoth exercises have been completed. Figure 7-2c shows the (hypothetical) expected money levels of revenue, cost, and profits.

Forecast of investment. The ultimate indication of company achievement is not the absolute amount of profit, but the ratio of this profit to the value of the company's net investment. The rate of return on investment (ROI) is usually judged satisfactory if it matches or exceeds what is being earned by other firms in the same risk class. In estimating the future ROI, the company must envision what level of investment would be necessary

8 See Chapter 5, pp. 114-20.

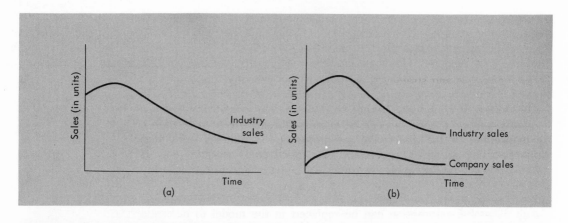

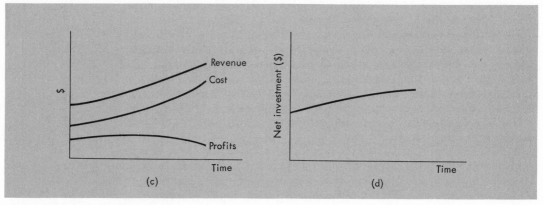

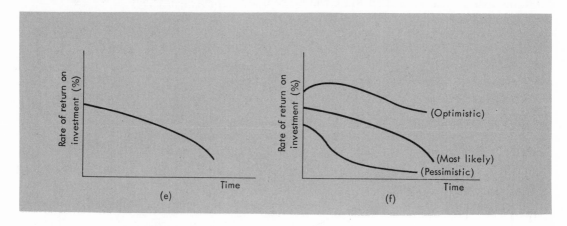

FIGURE 7-2
Steps in a prognosis of future company profits

to sustain the projected marketing program and sales volume. Figure 7-2d shows the (hypothetical) value of this investment.

Forecast of rate of return on investment (ROI). This last step is purely derivative from the two preceding steps. The combination of a large expected decline in profits and a small expected increase in investment accounts for the sharply declining ROI shown in Figure 7-2e. The prognosis according to Figure 7-2e is bleak enough to send a chill down every executive's back. If it is substantially correct, a radical revision of product-market objectives and strategy is warranted. The executive committee will want to know how much confidence it can place in this prognosis.

The degree of confidence cannot be expressed by confidence limits, as in random-sample theory, but can be expressed qualitatively in relation to the plausibility of the underlying assumptions. Assumptions were made about the future course of the economy, the effectiveness of Arno's policies, the reactions of competitors, and other variables. Presumably, the most plausible assumptions were adopted, and they are available for examination by the executive committee.

Any debatable assumption can be replaced in the model to determine what difference it would make in the forecast of ROI. If some executives believe the farm sector will shrink at the rate of only 1 per cent a year instead of 2 per cent, the new value can be substituted in the model to see whether the revised forecast ROI would be significantly more attractive. Sometimes a forecast is very sensitive to a change in assumptions, and other times it is not. The lower the sensitivity of the forecast to changes in key assumptions, the greater the confidence that can be felt by its users.[9]

Suppose three estimates of ROI are prepared, one based on the most plausible assumptions, another on highly optimistic assumptions, and the last on highly pessimistic assumptions. Suppose the results are those graphed in Figure 7-2f. It appears that even under highly optimistic assumptions, ROI will eventually decline; and if the pessimistic assumptions are borne out, then the firm would be in real trouble. As a result of the prognosis, which is a forecast of the future under the assumption of a continuation in present product-markets and policies, the Arno Company has cause for grave concern.

OBJECTIVES

If a company does not like the picture of where it is headed, it must redefine where it wants to go and how to get there. This does not mean that it has to change its basic goals or business philosophy, although this too may be involved. We have discussed the goals of business in the preceding chapter and will assume that the company is satisfied with the mix of basic company goals. *Objectives* in the context of a plan have the more specific meaning of (1) selecting the market areas for company action in the coming planning period and (2) establishing specific sales targets. The first may be called the *generic market objectives,* and the second may be called the *sales target objectives*.

Many companies fail to clarify the generic market(s) in which they operate, although this is pivotal in product-market planning. The concept of generic market attempts to shift management's view of the company as the producer of certain products to the company as an instrument for satisfying the needs of certain markets. If the Arno Company views its business as the manufacture of work shoes, its fate is linked to a particular

[9] See Richard B. Maffei, "Mathematical Models, Values of Parameters, and the Sensitivity Analysis of Management Decision Rules," *Journal of Marketing,* XXI (April 1957), 419-27.

product and not a set of generic and more durable market needs. On the other hand, if it considers that its business is to satisfy footwear needs, it gains a broader perspective of its opportunities and the nature of its resources.

In taking the broader view, Arno might single out the casual footwear market as one where new need satisfactions could be created. Some people want "airiness" (for which sandals excel), some want "ease of slipping on" (for which moccasins excel), and some want style combined with lightness and softness. Arno's skill in working with other leathers than cowhide may give it an advantage in entering this market. At least this is something for management to consider.

As for sales targets, they should be set realistically in terms of plausible programs for their achievement. A statement by Arno that it wants "to achieve a 30 per cent share of the casual shoe market in five years" may be more a reflection of wishful thinking than a sober appraisal of its capabilities. Sales targets should be set after alternative programs have been considered in conjunction with the environmental conditions expected to prevail in the future. The program which appears the most plausible then suggests the appropriate sales targets for the planning period.

STRATEGY

"Chess is a . . . game in which drifting from move to move is sure to lead to disaster. It is vitally important to form a plan of campaign." [10] The same must be said about business. A firm operates in a competitive environment and must make a competitive adaptation to its opportunities. The specific moves, which may be called tactics, must be guided by an over-all strategy. Strategy concerns itself with the over-all design for achieving the objectives, while tactics spells out the specific moves.

Strategy lays down the broad principles by which the company hopes to secure an advantage over competitors, an attractiveness to buyers, and a full exploitation of company resources. A particular marketing strategy for Arno might consist of the following tenets:

1. Develop the highest quality product possible
2. Charge a premium price
3. Advertise more heavily than competitors
4. Use salesmen who feel and exhibit a missionary drive

An alternative strategy might be:

1. Develop an average quality product
2. Charge a low price
3. Spend the same as competitors on advertising
4. Use more salesmen than competitors

One can readily appreciate the vast number of possible alternative strategies.[11]

How should a company select a strategy from the enormous array of

[10] H. Golombek, *The Game of Chess* (London: Penguin Books, 1954), p. 114.
[11] See Chapter 12, pp. 266-67.

possibilities? One philosophy holds that the company should imitate the strategy of its most successful rivals. If they use a high-price, high-advertising strategy, then this strategy must have merit. However, it does not prove that still another firm will be rewarded by the market for practicing this strategy. Such a strategy obviously gains a franchise among customers who can afford better prices and who are affected by advertising. Imitating this strategy would place the new firm into competition for that segment of the market in which its rivals are well entrenched.

An opposite philosophy holds that the company should develop a strategy which represents a dramatic departure from current rival strategies. If rivals are using a high-price, high-advertising marketing strategy, what may be called for is a low-price, medium-advertising strategy. This will position the company more strongly in a less well-cultivated market segment of customers who are price-conscious and not particularly impressed by advertising. In general, a deviant marketing strategy is likely to carry greater risks (because it is untried) but also the chance for greater gain (because it may meet unsatisfied market needs).

The best strategy cannot be casually determined. Finding it calls for the creative generation of alternatives, and their careful evaluation in the light of the unsatisfied needs of the market place and the strategies of competitors.

TACTICS

The objectives of a company indicate where it wants to be; the strategy indicates the intended route; the tactics indicate the particular vehicles it will use. For example, the strategic decisions on channels of distribution concern the types of channels to use and the intensity of coverage; the tactical decisions involve the selection of particular channel members and their particular responsibilities. In the area of personal selling, the strategic decisions concern the design of sales territories, the number of salesmen, and the principles for incentive and control; the actual selection of salesmen, their assignment to territories, and the particulars of the sales compensation plan are tactical decisions.

Although tactical decisions are not primary, they nevertheless are very important. Suppose the Arno Shoe Company decides to develop shoes for the casual footwear market (an objective). And it decides to produce a high-quality product, charge a premium price, and rely mainly on heavy advertising to develop its market (a strategy). And it designs a product which will give two years of normal wear, sell at $10.25, and be supported by an annual advertising budget of $820,000 concentrated about equally in television and magazines (the tactical decisions). The question now arises whether a different set of tactical values and allocations, but one consistent with the strategy decisions, would produce a higher sales volume and/or level of profits. For example, a price of $9.95 is not much different from $10.25 (both would be premium prices for casual shoes); yet the former might be far more effective because it doesn't quite sound like ten dollars. Or it may be more effective to spend two-thirds of the advertising budget in television and only one-third in print.

Tactical decisions are aided by conventional marketing research and some of the newer techniques in operations research. The latter provides models for thinking about the allocation of resources to different uses and the setting of values in an environment characterized by uncertainty.[12] Conventional marketing research provides the necessary data which must be plugged into these models to arrive at determinate and relevant solutions.

The plan itself generally passes over the underlying calculations and reasoning and states only the resulting tactics, or program. Typically, the program will be the most elaborate section of the plan. For each operating unit of the company (divisions and/or departments) there will be a statement of what resources will be made available, what specific actions are to be taken, when they are to be taken, and by whom they are to be taken. In other words, the tactics must be stated, budgeted, and scheduled.

CONTROL

The long-range plan represents the best vision of management, at the time of planning, of a proper set of objectives, strategies, and tactics. It is based on a detailed set of assumptions and expectations whose validity will only be revealed in the course of time. In fact, more often than not, events will occur during the planning period to invalidate some assumptions in the plan. This means two things. First, it means that the plan must include a control section which specifies the type of monitoring that will go on to check the plan's effectiveness and appropriateness. Second, it means that the company might prepare one or more contingency subplans to shorten its reaction time to new challenges.

The control section of a plan should set performance standards to be checked periodically to insure that the firm's strategy and tactics are leading to the achievement of company objectives. A set of performance standards is illustrated in Table 7-1. For example, management expects the

TABLE 7-1
Illustration of performance standards for monitoring the long-range plan

Year	Market share (%)	Dealers signing up (%)	Extent of product awareness (%)
1	1	5	3
2	2	10	5
3	4	20	20
4	7	35	50
5	10	60	70

marketing program to lead to a rising market share reaching 10 per cent by the end of the fifth year. It expects to sign up an increasing number of dealers amounting to 60 per cent of all dealers by the end of the period. It also expects consumer awareness of the new product to reach 70 per cent by the end of the period. Each year's expected gain is established on the basis of the planned allocation of marketing resources as scheduled over the five years.

These standards serve as a check on various parts of the program and on the program as a whole. For example, if only 2 per cent of the dealers

[12] See Chapter 10.

have signed up during the first year, doubt is cast on the particular strategy or tactics used in personal selling. If only 1 per cent of potential buyers are aware of the product at the end of the first year, doubt is cast on the effectiveness of the advertising message or media. (There is a question of how large the deviation must be before it is significant.) It is possible that the standards were set too high in terms of the resources allocated for their achievement. But this will not be known until the program is reviewed, which is, of course, the purpose of developing performance standards in the first place.

A small, but increasing, number of firms are beginning to formulate *contingency plans* along with the main plan. A contingency plan is designed to meet a different environment from the one assumed in the main plan. Ideally, the company should have a counter strategy ready for every major alternative development in the market place. In this way, the company would be able to react swiftly and effectively. But the problem is the large number of possible contingencies, and planning is too expensive a process to plan for all of them. It is usually necessary to limit the preparation of contingency plans to meet only the more critical contingencies, defined as those whose consequences could most disturb the firm and require the quickest competitive response. In practice, many top executives are satisfied just to prepare an effective main plan, let alone a number of contingency plans.

Planning and Scheduling Marketing Projects

Up to now, we have talked about planning the company's marketing operation for the purpose of achieving plan objectives for the coming year or a longer period. Another kind of planning is called for when the subject is a project. A project has a clear beginning, middle, and end. It generally calls for a set of constituent activities that are nonroutine, interdependent, and complex. Special budgeting and extra resources may be required, and completion dates tend to be critical.

Many examples can be cited of complex projects in the marketing area. They would include the introduction of a new product, the phasing out of an important old product from the product line, the opening of new retail outlets, the training of a large group of new salesmen, the reorganization of sales territories, the carrying out of a national consumer survey, the invasion of a new market, the execution of a special advertising campaign or national sales promotion, and the installation of a new goods-ordering system.

THE USE OF CRITICAL PATH ANALYSIS

Complex project planning has been aided immeasurably in recent years by a new tool known as *critical path analysis*. Planning and scheduling techniques actually have a long history, especially in production.[13] But *critical path analysis* represents a more powerful and versatile tool, com-

---

[13] See Martin K. Starr, *Production Management: Systems and Synthesis* (Englewood Cliffs, N.J.: Prentice-Hall, Inc., 1964), pp. 111-15.

bining three major ideas: the structuring of project activities in a network; the assignment of time and/or costs to constituent activities; and the concept of a critical path. The tool, or the variant of it known as PERT (Program Evaluation and Review Technique), was developed in 1958 by representatives of the Navy Special Projects Office, Lockheed Aircraft Corporation, and Booz, Allen & Hamilton, Inc., in connection with the expediting of the Navy's Polaris ballistic missile program. It is credited with shortening the original estimated project completion time of Polaris by two years.

Since this successful demonstration, the use of critical path analysis has spread rapidly through industry. The Defense Department became so impressed with the tool that it began to require critical path schedules to accompany the bids of leading contractors. To date, its major applications are found in R&D work, construction, and periodic maintenance projects. But it is also finding increasing application in new product introduction, advertising campaigns, and new store openings.[14]

Critical path analysis has several variants, such as PERT and CPM (Critical Path Method), but our emphasis will be on the basic ideas common to all.[15] These ideas shall be discussed in the context of a specific case dealing with the problem of developing and launching a new product.

The case is that of S. C. Johnson & Son, Inc.,[16] which in January 1956 was preparing to produce and market a new product (Glade) in the room deodorant line. The following timetable was developed:

March 12	Final selection of name
April 9	Complete package design
April 23	Order containers
May 7-21	Order new materials
June 1	Complete sales plans
June 18	Fill orders for test markets
July 2	Start test market
August 6	Fill orders for national sales
September 3	Begin national sales

By mid-April 1956, the company fell behind in production because of trade-mark difficulties and supplier trouble. A decision was made to postpone test marketing until October 1, 1956, and to go national in Septem-

---

[14] For a breakdown of present uses, see *The Management Implications of PERT* (Chicago: Booz, Allen & Hamilton, Inc., 1963), p. 20.

[15] Several articles offer the interested reader more detail. An excellent general introduction for the marketing reader is found in Yung Wong, "Critical Path Analysis for New Product Planning," *Journal of Marketing,* XXVIII (October 1964), 53-59. For a description of PERT, there is a good short article by Robert W. Miller, "How to Plan and Control with PERT," *Harvard Business Review,* March-April 1962, pp. 93-104, and a good handbook exposition by Harry F. Evarts, *Introduction to PERT* (Boston: Allyn and Bacon, Inc., 1964). For a discussion of CPM, see Borge M. Christenson and J. R. Greene, "Planning, Scheduling, and Controlling the Launching of a New Product Via CPM," in Wroe Alderson and Stanley J. Shapiro, *Marketing and the Computer* (Englewood Cliffs, N.J.: Prentice-Hall, Inc., 1963), pp. 178-201.

[16] The case is described more completely in "S. C. Johnson & Son, Inc. (A)," in Neil H. Borden and Martin V. Marshall, *Advertising Management: Text and Cases* (Homewood, Ill.: Richard D. Irwin, Inc., 1959), pp. 533-47.

ber 1957. But in July 1956, Johnson executives learned that Colgate had started to test market a similar new product (Florient). As a result, Johnson executives rescheduled their test market for September 1, 1956, and national sales introduction for January 1957. In late September 1956, after only one month of its own test marketing, Johnson executives learned that Florient was about to be introduced nationally. Fearing that Florient would capture the larger share of the market by being first, Johnson executives decided to start national marketing at once. Shipments began in October 1956, and Glade appeared in stores nationally by mid-December 1956. By November of the following year, Glade had gained 10 per cent of the total market; nevertheless, Johnson executives were not completely satisfied with the product's progress.

This case illustrates a number of principles about the management of complex marketing projects. First, it shows that a wide range of activities must be carried out and coordinated. Second, it shows that project completion time is at the mercy of such critical activities as getting the trademark approved and receiving materials from suppliers. Third, it shows that crash programming (which involves a revision of the timetable and extra costs) may be necessary because of unanticipated events, such as a competitor's introduction of the same product.

The Glade project occurred before the development and widespread use of critical path analysis. The delays in the project and other problems might have been minimized had this tool been available. Today critical path analysis is used to improve planning, scheduling, and control of new product introductions.

PLANNING THE PROJECT STRUCTURE

The first step in critical path analysis is to develop a project network structure. This is a hooking together of the many activities which make up a project. In the Glade case, the timetable represented the project structure. But a timetable is a primitive device because it implies that each activity starts only after the previous one is completed. It obscures the possibility of carrying on some of the activities simultaneously to reach an earlier completion date.

Activity is the key concept in critical path analysis. An activity is any action involving the use of *resources* and occurring over *time*. "Selecting a brand name" is an activity, because executive time and resources are invested in it. Of course, it could also be conceived of as a series of smaller activities, such as "collecting possible names," "getting consumer reactions to names," "making a final selection." Or it can be conceived of as part of the broader activity "developing product concept." The project planner has to determine what level of activity aggregation is the most suitable.

Each activity has a beginning and an end which are signified by *events*. An activity begins with the completion of some prior event and ends with its own completion.

The planning challenge is to enumerate all the constituent activities of a project and to combine them into an efficient network structure, showing in what order the activities are to be performed. In this latter connection, use is made of the distinction between activities in a *sequential* relationship and activities in a *concurrent* relationship. Two activities are in a sequential relationship if one must be completed before the other can begin. "Designing spray cans" must occur before "ordering spray cans" can begin. Two activities are in a concurrent relationship if one can be completed independently of the other. "Final selection of name" and "developing field sales plans" are in a concurrent relationship. The significance of this distinction is that project time can be cut down by making sure that activities in a concurrent relationship are scheduled concurrently and not sequentially.

What does a project network look like for a new product introduction? An illustration is given in Figure 7-3. The activities are represented as arrows with descriptive statements; and the events are represented as numbered circles (there are 63 events).[17] The network shows clearly which activities are related sequentially and which are related concurrently. Thus "initial screening" (between events 1 and 2) must take place before other activities. But once it is finished, five different concurrent activities can be started [(2,3), (2,4), (2,5), (2,6), (2,7)]. Further sequential and concurrent activities are listed, all flowing in the direction of consummating the terminal activity.[18]

SCHEDULING THE PROJECT

Marketing projects are typically carried out under great time pressure. We saw in the Glade case that Johnson's management moved up its dates when it learned that competition was preparing to introduce the same product. To shorten completion time requires a skillful project networking of activities and often the hiring of additional resources. The original and still most important use of critical path analysis is in showing how the activities and resources can be scheduled to increase the probability of meeting a given completion date.

Basic to estimating a completion time for the project as a whole are estimates by the participating executives of how long their individual jobs will take. The ease of estimating job completion times will vary. One can estimate more accurately the average time required to "receive raw materials" than to "complete test marketing." The estimating is left to the experienced company executive who has the responsibility.

Many department heads may be overly conservative about the time required to complete their job, since they do not want to be held responsible for delays. Other department heads may be overly optimistic, especially when they have a direct interest in the project and its completion time. The project supervisor must impress both types of executives with the need for estimates that are as accurate as possible. PERT allows for these biases to some extent by asking each executive for three figures: one indicating his most optimistic estimate, one his most pessimistic estimate, and a third his normal estimate, which is not necessarily midway between the other two. In this way, the executive feels protected and is apt to offer a

---

[17] The dashed arrows represent dummy activities, because they do not use up resources or take up time.

[18] Although the network flows toward the terminal event, the construction of the project network usually takes place in the opposite direction. First the terminal event is listed. Then activities which feed into this event are introduced. By reasoning backward and considering what must occur before each event can take place, the planner is less likely to overlook important activities.

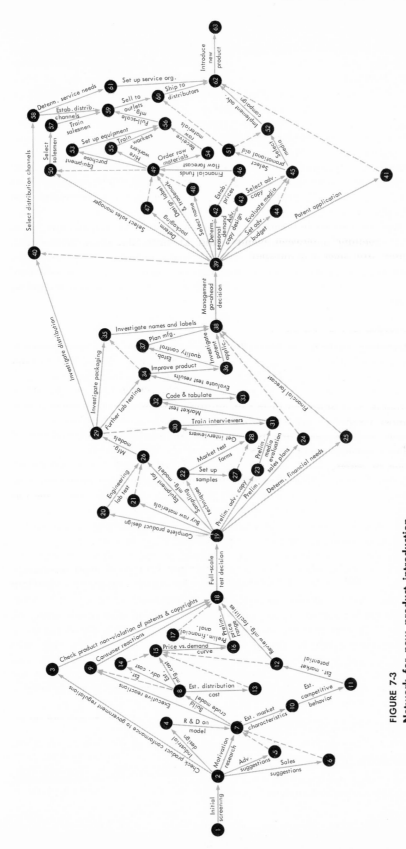

FIGURE 7-3

Network for new product introduction

Redrawn from Yung Wong, "Critical Path Analysis for New Product Planning," *Journal of Marketing,* XXVIII (October 1964), 55.

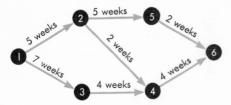

FIGURE 7-4
A project network showing estimated times

less biased estimate as to normal time. In any event, systematic biases by executives are eventually known through comparing their estimates with past performances and making allowances in future projects.

After all the normal duration times are estimated, they are added up for *each possible path* through the network (from the origin to the terminal event). The *critical path* is defined as that path (or paths) showing the greatest summation of time units.

The concept of the critical path can be illustrated through a simple example. Figure 7-4 shows a project involving six events. The normal estimated duration time is shown for each activity. It is necessary to trace through all the paths which may be traveled and to sum the total time each will take. There are three paths leading to the terminal event: (1,2,5,6), (1,2,4,6), and (1,3,4,6). On a *most likely time basis,* path (1,2,5,6) will take $5 + 5 + 2 = 12$ weeks; path (1,2,4,6) will take $5 + 2 + 4 = 11$ weeks; and path (1,3,4,6) will take $7 + 4 + 4 = 15$ weeks. This last path is, therefore, considered the *critical path.* Since it must be traversed and since it consumes the greatest sum of time, it sets the earliest most likely time for completion. Equally interesting is the fact that events along a noncritical path, such as (1,2,5,6), can take place later than estimated without necessarily delaying the 15-week estimate for the project as a whole. In other words, activities along noncritical paths have some slack in their required completion time.

The critical path is "critical" in two respects. Any delays in the actual time of completing any activity along the critical path will delay the total project by that amount of time. If "getting the trade-mark approved" is along the critical path and turns out to take five weeks instead of the estimated two weeks, every subsequent activity along the critical path is delayed in getting started by three weeks. The path is also critical in another respect. If the management finds the estimated completion time (here 15 weeks) to be too long, the critical path shows what activities must be expedited. And this opens an entirely new use of critical path analysis—the shortening of critical path time.

Activities can take a variable amount of time, depending on both uncontrollable and controllable factors. Uncontrollable factors include illnesses of key personnel, strikes which tie up shipments, and unexpected legal difficulties in clearing a trade-mark. Controllable factors include primarily the amount of money and resources made available to the executive responsible for the particular activity. The key point is that the company can shorten (up to a point) the duration of a critical activity, and hence total project completion time, by investing more money in it.

Computations to find the best schedule are usually carried out on a computer. On a large computer, it takes about a minute to find the time along the critical path for a project network of about 600 activities, and one gets the benefit of additional measures such as the earliest time and latest time for each activity on a dated basis as well as probability measures (in PERT). Furthermore, the computer makes it convenient to simulate alternative networks and costs and to revise schedules from time to time.

CONTROLLING THE PROJECT'S COURSE

The scheduling phase informs each company participant when he may begin his part of the work and how much time he has to finish it. As these activities are carried out, some will be finished earlier than expected and others, because of uncontrollable events and sometimes neglect, will not be finished when expected. These discrepancies between actual times and estimated times will accumulate to the point where it may become necessary to reschedule the remaining activities. This is especially true when the project is moving slower than scheduled and there are penalties. The project supervisor may want to take corrective action in the form of resource transfers from slack activities to critical activities. His control of the project is considerably facilitated by the availability of critical path analysis for updating and modifying the project's scheduling. The tool fits in nicely with the principle of management by exception whenever a deviation from a standard occurs.

BENEFITS OF CRITICAL PATH ANALYSIS

Critical path analysis contributes to all three phases of project management—planning, scheduling, and control. If it had been available to the Johnson executives in introducing Glade, certain problems might have been avoided or minimized. Critical path analysis would have highlighted the critical activities. It would have allowed the rapid computation of the effect of different resource transfers on project completion time. It would have allowed a revised schedule to be developed quickly when news of Colgate's action was received.

Critical path analysis can be used by all levels of marketing management for the conduct of projects under their control. The tool is easy to understand and yet powerful in its logic and derived measures. It encourages comprehensive planning and minimizes the chance of overlooking some activities. It highlights the interdependencies of intra- and interdepartmental activities. Various executives are made more aware of their responsibilities. They are led to think about assigned activities more carefully in terms of time and costs. There is more communication among them and understanding of each other's activities. All of these are by-products of critical path analysis and are as important as the benefits of developing better schedules.

Summary

Formal planning procedures are an instrumentality of growing importance in the competitive adaptation of the firm to its marketing environment. The marketing concept calls for integrated marketing effort aimed at well-defined customer groups for the purpose of achieving adequate volume and profits. Planning is the means whereby this clarity of company purpose is expressed and the integration of efforts is achieved.

Planning is becoming an increasingly professionalized aspect of management. Many companies have established elaborate procedures for developing long-range and short-range company and marketing plans. The planning process consists of determining where the company stands (diagnosis), where it is headed (prognosis), where it should go (objectives), how it should get there (strategy), what means it should use (tactics), and how it should measure its progress (control). Companies are also turning increasingly to the use of critical path analysis for the planning, scheduling, and control of specific marketing projects.

Questions and Problems

1. Although there is no universally agreed upon format for all company plans, every plan should contain at least three parts. What are they?

2. In developing the annual company plan, does the marketing plan have any logical priority in time before other departments develop their plans?

3. What skills and training should professional marketing planners have?

4. What kinds of suboptimizing practices often takes place in (a) setting sales targets and (b) setting departmental budgets?

5. The marketing department of a large company has to finalize its marketing plan by November 15. Participants at various stages in the planning process are top management, the marketing vice-president, the marketing research director, product planning managers, the field sales manager, and district sales managers. Develop the logical steps that might be involved from plan initiation to plan finalization and the likely duration of each step. How early should the process start in order to result in a finished plan by November 15?

chapter 8

Marketing Decision Making

As a firm adjusts its "controllables" of goals, organization, and plans, it must make an endless number of decisions. Decisions are the smallest unit of action. A decision may be defined as a conscious choice among alternative courses of action.

Every marketing executive is perpetually faced with the need to make decisions. They come in all sizes and shapes. Some decisions are *minor,* such as what type face to use on a new product; others are *major,* such as whether to produce the product at all. Some decisions are *recurrent,* such as selecting media and setting sales quotas; other decisions are *rare,* such as changing the advertising agency or reorganizing the sales force. Some decisions involve relatively *little risk,* such as hiring a new salesman; other decisions involve *great risk,* such as hiring a new vice-president of marketing.

In this chapter, we shall examine major concepts and tools useful in the making of marketing decisions. The first section describes the special characteristics of marketing decisions. The second section briefly sketches the behavioral aspects of decision making as background for the more normative aspects. The third section presents a normative model for decision making and illustrates it in the context of a marketing problem. The final section explores the question of handling efficiently the large inflow of problems requiring decision.

Special Characteristics of Marketing Decisions

A firm's marketing decisions are among the most crucial it makes: they define its field of operations in the environment; they determine sales; and they have a lasting effect on its image. Over time, they absorb an increasing amount of company dollars relative to other decisions. Increasingly, the cost of doing business is the cost of marketing.

COMPLEXITY OF MARKETING DECISIONS

Marketing decisions as a class are more difficult to make scientifically than decisions in other functional areas. The postwar period has been marked by the development of practicable operations research models for capital budgeting, traffic, inventory, and production problems. No comparable development of practicable models has occurred for advertising, pricing, or new-product problems. The fundamental reason is that marketing phenomena, in contrast to production or finance phenomena, for example, are more behavioral than technical and tend to exhibit unusually complex properties.

Consider, for example, the determination of the "best" size promotional budget. The following eight complex effects can be singled out as obstacles to a straightforward solution of this problem: [1]

Nonlinear effects. Higher expenditures on promotion do not necessarily mean proportionately higher sales. Sales may increase proportionately more at low levels of advertising expenditure than at high levels.

Threshold effects. Promotion may have no effect unless a certain minimum amount, called the threshold level, takes place.

Carryover effects. The sales impact of promotional expenditures tends to take place through time rather than immediately.

Decay effects. Customer goodwill built up by past promotional expenditures will tend to decay over time in the absence of further promotion.

Marketing-mix interaction effects. The sales impact of promotional expenditures depends upon the levels and mix of the other elements in the marketing program.

Environmental interaction effects. The sales impact of promotional expenditures depends upon the level of general economic activity, attitudes in the market place, and other environmental factors.

Competitive effects. The sales impact of promotional expenditures depends upon competitors' current programs and their responses to the company's program.

Quality effects. The sales impact of promotional expenditures depends on the unique content, presentation, and placement of the promotion.

As a result of these complex effects and the problems of estimating them empirically, the company that is about to spend money on promotion has only a vague idea of what it can expect. And the vagueness that exists before the expenditure is likely to linger on after the money is spent. This is in sharp contrast to the improving techniques of premeasuring and postmeasuring the value of investments in facilities and equipment.

This might sound like a case for intuitive decision making in marketing. Not at all! The complexity of marketing phenomena is no argument for the abandonment of analysis; if anything, it is an argument for better analysis.

SCIENTIFIC STUDIES OF THE DECISION-MAKING PROCESS

Progress may be slow in marketing, but nevertheless it will be made. A major hope comes from the formal study of decision-making processes by a growing number of scholars hailing from such diverse disciplines as economics, anthropology, mathematics, social psychology, and neurology. A science of decision making is evolving with two specific branches.[2] One

---

[1] For an alternative discussion, see R. P. Willett, "A Model for Marketing Programming," *Journal of Marketing,* XXVII (January 1963), 40-45.

[2] See the excellent review articles by Ward Edwards, "The Theory of Decision Making," *Psychological Bulletin,* 1954, pp. 380-417; and "Behavioral Decision Theory," *Annual Review of Psychology,* 1961, pp. 473-98.

branch is called *behavioral decision theory* and focuses on how decisions are actually made. The scientists in this branch have conducted numerous experiments to observe how people actually go about solving problems and making decisions. These experiments have ranged from asking a person to think aloud as he tries to solve a problem in symbolic logic,[3] to observing two subjects engaged in an economic bargaining process,[4] to recording the bets people are willing to make in different hypothetical situations.[5] Besides conducting experiments, scientists have asked subjects for case histories of particular decisions. They have also been active in analyzing the environment in which decisions are made.

The other branch, called *normative decision theory,* deals with analyzing how decisions *should* be made in order to maximize the achievement of some objective(s). There is a long speculative tradition in economics concerned with how demand and cost functions may be utilized to arrive at optimal decisions, especially for price and output.[6] Traditionally, these economic decisions were analyzed under the assumption of perfect knowledge of the demand and cost functions and the reactions of competitors. The increasing awareness of monopolistic competition and oligopoly shifted attention to the problem of uncertainty and also to the growing role of variables other than price such as advertising, quality, and service. It was recognized that new models for decision making were needed.

In the postwar period four factors in particular stimulated the growing interest of executives in improved models for decision making. The first factor is that *the modern corporation is called upon to make a larger number of important decisions per time period with an ever shorter lead time.* This reflects the intensification of competitive effort and the increased innovative activity of firms. The second factor is *the appearance of powerful new mathematical tools, such as mathematical programming, queuing theory, and Markov processes.*[7] These tools have increased the likelihood of finding solutions to some very difficult problems. The third factor is *the increased availability of timely and accurate data.* For example, it took over thirty months for the U. S. Bureau of Commerce to prepare its *Statistics on Income* for 1946; for 1960, it took only sixteen months on a considerably greater number of returns. A fourth factor is *the development of high-speed electronic computers.* Without the computer, much of the data would take years to process, and many of the mathematical models would be too difficult to solve because of sheer calculation time.[8]

---

[3] See Allen Newell and Herbert A. Simon, "Computer Simulation of Human Thinking," *Science,* December 22, 1961, pp. 2011-17.

[4] Lawrence E. Fouraker and Sidney Siegel, *Bargaining Behavior* (New York: McGraw-Hill Book Company, 1963).

[5] D. Davidson, P. Suppes, and S. Siegel, *Decision Making: An Experimental Approach* (Stanford, Calif.: Stanford University Press, 1957).

[6] See Chapter 15, esp. pp. 353-57.

[7] See Chapter 10.

[8] The incredible calculating speed of modern computers has been the subject of many jokes. A *New Yorker* cartoon showing some scientists puzzling over the output of a computer bore the caption: "It would have taken 500 mathematicians 500 years to make a mistake like this."

Decision-Making Behavior

Although most of this chapter deals with normative decision making, it is important to recognize the many nonrational aspects of the process. Like every other human activity, decision making is influenced by the forces of culture, organization, and personality.[9]

CULTURAL INFLUENCES

Decision-making patterns are influenced by variations in child training, methods of formal education, the values placed on thought versus action, and other cultural factors. Two broad types of culture can be distinguished for their differential impact on decision-making style. An Apollonian culture values deliberateness, thought, and delayed gratification; a Dionysian culture values spontaneity, impulse, and immediate gratification.[10] Simple societies show a predominant cultural orientation, but within a complex modern society, such as our own, both strains can be found. They can be seen in the contrasting "wise sayings" of our culture:

Apollonian	*Dionysian*
Look before you leap.	He who hesitates is lost.
Thought is the key to success.	You can only confuse yourself by thinking of all that might happen.
He who lives in hope will die starving.	Lady Luck decides the turn of the card.
Where men feel sure, they are bound to be mistaken.	Certainty alone brings peace of mind.

ORGANIZATIONAL INFLUENCES

Decision making is also influenced by a host of *organizational* factors. The following statement of a leading executive brings this out:

A corporation is a social institution. . . . It is an institution that tends to develop within it pressure groups and empire builders. It develops taboos, prejudices, policies, and rules of thumb. It develops sacred cows and scapegoats. It has pride in every corner. Instead of being oriented toward the conquest of some aspects of the external environment, it has an inclination toward introspection; it is overly concerned with its own internal problems of communication, organization, and lines of command. The energies of the more talented, more aggressive, more ambitious employees often seem to be taken up with internal problems of power, prestige, and position.[11]

Thus decisions within an organization must take into consideration factors which may at first seem alien to the issue at hand. Purely rational concerns must be mixed in a cauldron seething with human emotions,

---

[9] Most of the discussion of models of buyer behavior in Chapter 4 applies also to executive decision-making behavior.

[10] Friedrich Nietzsche, *The Birth of Tragedy,* 1872 (New York: Doubleday & Company, Inc., 1956).

[11] Thomas M. Ware, "An Executive's Viewpoint," *Operations Research,* January-February 1959, p. 3.

ambitions, and institutional concerns. The following excerpt gives much of the flavor of organizational forces in marketing decision making:

> I was sitting in a meeting in which the advertising manager, John Smith, made an hour-and-a-half presentation on the new advertising campaign. He was very persuasive. He showed Starch studies, quoted the number of subscribers that the magazines would reach and kept referring to the fact that he was "within budget." A few questions were asked, but only to clarify a monetary figure or a meaning.
>
> When the presentation was over, the president and the general manager commented, "Sounds good, John . . . looks very impressive." At this point, I mentioned the fact that in Nebraska the Company's dealer distribution was very sparse and yet we were spending the same amount on consumer advertising in Nebraska as we were in the other states. John Smith got excited and said that if we are going to do an ad campaign, we couldn't discriminate among territories. The sales manager then interjected the comment that most of the money spent on advertising was a waste anyway. The argument continued and then John mentioned he was late for an appointment. He left, and so did everyone else. The advertising budget for the year stood approved.

PERSONALITY FACTORS

Whereas culture and organization define two broad influences on the outcomes of decisions, personality defines the unique turn given to the decision by the decision maker's own aspirations, temperament, and philosophy. In one study, subjects were asked to make bets. Those who made more conservative bets were found to score higher on need achievement, theoretical and aesthetic values, and fear of failure compared to those who made more risky bets.[12]

Personal as well as personality factors also enter into decision making, as the following case illustrates:

> The vice-president of a medium-sized firm advised the president not to develop a new product proposal because the company might lose as much as $10 million if the project failed. The president decided to go ahead anyway. He was not impressed with the size of the possible loss, because the issue was one of the probability of the project's failing, and in his mind this was very small. A major consideration in his mind, however, was that this product would bring in enough sales to put the company into the $100 million sales class, one of his long-time dreams.

A Normative Model for Decision Making

The preceding examples stress the cultural, organizational, and personality factors which enter into and shape decision processes. This does not mean, however, that models for rational decision making have no place in executive thinking. Most executives want their decision making to be characterized by orderly processes of analysis. They perceive the

---

[12] A. Scodel, P. Ratoosh, and J. S. Minas, "Some Personality Correlates of Decision Making Under Conditions of Risk," *Behavioral Science,* January 1959, pp. 19-28.

need for breaking down complex problems into basic elements. They want to know how to evaluate uncertainties and structure alternatives. While they may base a decision on organizational or personal considerations, they do want to know how to determine the right action *in principle*. They have a manifest interest in models which will increase their chances of discerning the best course of action.

In recent years, a model for rational decision making has been evolving that promises to tie together many of the facets of formal decision making. The decision-making process is conceived to consist of six steps. They are:

Defining the problem, objectives, and constraints
Distinguishing major decision alternatives
Identifying key uncertainties
Gathering relevant data
Estimating the value of alternative outcomes
Choosing the best alternative as defined by the objectives

Some have called this the "decisioning" process, to distinguish it from deciding, which is only the last step. To concentrate on the last step would do an injustice to the turbulent, lengthy, and vital process preceding the decision. The various steps will be discussed in terms of the following marketing problem:

> The Dayton Company is a large capital-goods producer that has just developed a machine which would be of special interest to small manufacturers. Until now, Dayton has sold chiefly to large manufacturers. Its present sales force is fully occupied in attending to the large accounts. Therefore Dayton is considering hiring some new salesmen to contact smaller manufacturers. How many salesmen should be hired?

DEFINING THE PROBLEM, OBJECTIVES, AND CONSTRAINTS

The first prerequisite of problem solving is that the problem be correctly defined. As W. S. Gilbert noted, "Things are seldom what they seem/Skim milk masquerades as cream." In the Dayton case, is the problem simply how many salesmen to hire? Is the company sure that it wants to use direct selling instead of (say) manufacturers' representatives? Does the company actually belong in this new market segment in terms of its resources and experience? What is the company really after?

Dayton's new product may have been developed for a number of reasons. The firm may have spotted an unsatisfied market need and believes it has the right resource mix for exploiting it. Perhaps the firm wants a product which would provide counterseasonal employment of the production facilities. Perhaps the firm intends to use the new product as a bait item for its other products. The specific objective makes a difference in trying to decide how many salesmen to hire.

Often, not one but several objectives are sought by the company, some of which are in conflict. For example, it is usually difficult to satisfy simultaneously the objectives of high current profits and of high future growth. High current profits could be realized by hiring a small number of salesmen to canvass the most promising accounts. High future growth could be realized by hiring a larger number of salesmen to win over the market before competition can develop a rival product. When objectives are in conflict, the decision maker might select one as paramount and try to maximize it, subject to satisfying minimum levels of the other objectives.

DISTINGUISHING MAJOR DECISION ALTERNATIVES

Defining the problem and objectives carefully leads the decision maker to a better grasp of what courses are open to him. If only one course of action is available, then there is no decision problem. A decision problem implies alternatives, and it is the alternatives which help orient the search for information and the character of the evaluation.

Listing alternatives is hardly a routine matter. At this stage creativity plays a most important part. There are usually many ways to frame the range of choices open to a firm. This can be quickly appreciated in considering the Dayton Company problem. If the problem is one of how many salesmen to hire, Dayton can hire 0 or 1 or 2 or 13 or 55 or 83 salesmen. The alternatives, or *solution space,* seem to consist of the whole set of positive integers. On the other hand, if the problem is how to sell the product, the alternatives may include direct selling, selling through manufacturers' representatives, selling the product rights to another firm, and selling entirely through direct mail without any sales force. In other words, the company's possible maneuvers and opportunities with respect to the new product are manifold, as a careful definition of the problem reveals.

Suppose the company has given thought to all major selling methods but direct selling and found them to be wanting. Then it is legitimate to confine attention to the direct-sales-force alternative. Although the solution space would then seem to consist of all the positive integers, most of them must be ruled out as *infeasible.* For example, the firm may not have the resources to hire and train more than 20 salesmen. And even among the alternatives that are technically feasible, only a few of them may be *reasonable.* The potential size of the market may make it unreasonable to hire more than 15 men. Furthermore, there is no need to examine all 15 possible alternatives. Examining a smaller regularly spaced set may provide all the information needed. If expected profits are estimated for 1, 5, 9, and 13 salesmen, a pattern may emerge indicating where the profit function might attain its maximum level.

The choice is not always between simple numerical alternatives. The firm may wish to conceptualize more complex alternatives, such as hiring two salesmen now and five next month or hiring five salesmen now and two next month. Although both alternatives involve hiring seven salesmen, they are distinct alternatives if management considers that the temporal order of hiring the seven men makes a difference. The first alternative involves a smaller initial outlay and a chance to observe the pattern of sales results before additional salesmen are hired. The second alternative may be more appropriate if a competitor is about to enter the market at the same time.

IDENTIFYING THE KEY UNCERTAINTIES

Decision alternatives are listed in order to compare their respective outcomes in terms of the company's objectives. But the outcomes are not

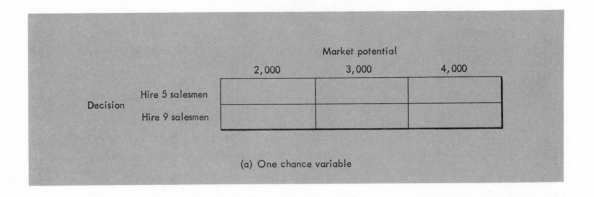

(a) One chance variable

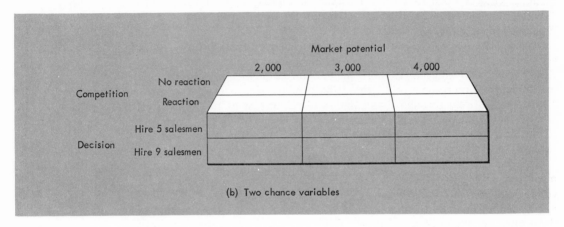

(b) Two chance variables

FIGURE 8-1

Outcome matrix for decision problem on size of sales force

solely a function of the decisions. An outcome depends upon the decision and the unknown states of certain *chance variables*. Among the chance variables which influence the outcomes in this problem are the number of potential accounts, the reaction of competitors, and the level of economic activity.

Suppose Dayton has narrowed down its alternatives to two, that of hiring five or nine salesmen. Suppose, further, that market potential is considered the most important chance variable and its state is assumed to be one of the following: 2,000 machines, 3,000 machines, or 4,000 machines. For this simple case, it is possible to show in tabular form the relationship between decisions, possible levels of market potential, and outcomes, as illustrated in the *outcome matrix* in Figure 8-1a. The decision alternatives are listed on the left-hand side and the possible states of the chance variable are listed at the top. Each cell represents the outcome(s) of the conjunction of a particular decision and a particular state of nature. The problem of expressing these outcomes will be discussed shortly.

In more realistic cases, there are not one but several chance variables. To illustrate the matrix where there are two chance variables, assume the outcome would also be affected by whether or not a major competitor decides to produce a similar machine. Dayton's new outcome matrix is illustrated in Figure 8-1b. The outcome matrix is a three-dimensional figure consisting of 12 possible outcomes (2 decisions × 3 levels of market potential × 2 competitive reactions).

Figure 8-1 represents the casting of the decision problem in essentially *tabular* form. An alternative graphical technique providing more flexibility in certain situations involves structuring the problem in the form of a *decision tree,* illustrated in Figure 8-2.[13] The decision alternatives are listed at the far left. Branches are used to depict the set of possible events that could follow each decision. In Figure 8-2, the branches proliferate at two successive chance event stages. Finally, further branches are shown representing the company's major decision alternatives in the light of the preceding events.

GATHERING THE RELEVANT DATA

In many accounts of the decision-making process, data gathering is often listed as the first or second step. In this account, however, formal research is postponed until there has been a careful definition of problem, alternatives, and unknowns. The reason for this is that data gathering is very expensive. To ask the research department to gather any and all data connected with a problem is inefficient. They may end up gathering data on something other than the real problem, on infeasible alternatives, or on irrelevant variables. By taking the time first to make a careful analysis of the problem, the informational needs are considerably clarified, and there is a greater chance of finding what is needed at a much lower cost.

In the course of gathering information, it is quite possible that new insights will develop and lead the company to return to the earlier steps and restructure the problem. There is nothing rigid about this model of the decision process. Each step interacts with previous and subsequent steps, and a considerable amount of back-and-forth play is expected. Each step has the potentiality of *serendipity,* "the pleasant discovery of unexpected things." This is particularly true during the data-gathering phase.

In the Dayton example, the prior structuring of the problem, alternatives, and chance variables will at least emphasize the need for information about:

> The number of potential buyers
> The state of competitive offerings and intentions in this market
> The number of calls the average salesman can make in the period

Even when better defined, these questions still will not be easy to answer. But knowing the right questions is half the battle.

[13] The tree diagram is more flexible where the problem involves a sequence of decisions rather than a single decision and/or where there are more than three chance variables affecting decision alternatives in different ways. See John F. Magee, "Decision Trees for Decision Making," *Harvard Business Review,* July-August 1964, pp. 126-38.

The decision maker's task would be simple if each decision alternative produced a determinate and known outcome. The decision maker could then rank the various outcomes and adopt the alternative that led to the most desirable one. Unfortunately, there are at least three complications.

In the first place, *an outcome is probabilistic rather than determinate*. An outcome is a joint function of the decision and many events beyond the control of the firm. In the second place, *each outcome has several dimensions*. It will affect company profits, cash flow, personnel relations, company image, and other company objectives. In the third place, *the outcome takes place through time and not at a point in time*. A major decision can create reverberations that continue into the distant future.

The challenge to the decision maker is twofold. He must anticipate the major possible outcomes of each decision and develop a method for reducing diverse outcomes to some common denominator.

The first task is *scientific* in that the decision maker is required to evaluate as objectively as possible the impact of a decision on an ongoing behavioral system. This requires an understanding of consumer, competitor, channel, and sociopolitical processes. It also involves an appreciation of the various nonlinearities, lags, and interactions within the behavioral system.

The second task is *normative* in that some way must be found to reduce the complex outcomes of each decision to a single value reflecting the outcomes' desirability. To accomplish this, the decision maker must make a number of arbitrary simplifications. First, he must restrict the consideration of consequences to some definite time period. This time period may be called the *planning horizon*. In introducing a new product, for example, the decision maker may want to limit his evaluation of consequences to the first five years, feeling that consequences beyond this period are too speculative to consider. Second, the decision maker must use the over-all company objectives specified in the first stage of the decision process to determine which outcomes matter. If the company is singularly after the maximization of profits, then the decision maker need not concern himself with the implications of different decisions for cash flow and personnel relations except where they have clear feedback effects on profits. If the company has multiple objectives, the decision maker must weigh the set of outcomes by the weights of the various objectives in order to arrive at some index of desirability.

Higher index numbers would reflect more desirable states. Index numbers have the drawback, however, of not signifying the expected level of return. Whenever possible, it is desirable to place a dollar return or rate of return in each cell. In Figure 8-3, hypothetical estimates of profit have been introduced in the Dayton example.

The matrix is now called a *payoff matrix*, because the outcomes are all reduced to the common denominator of profit. The profit estimates have to be developed from assumptions about product price, production costs, effect of number of salesmen on sales, and selling costs. It is assumed that each figure represents the *present value of the discounted future earnings flow* expected from the conjunction of a particular decision and a particular market potential.

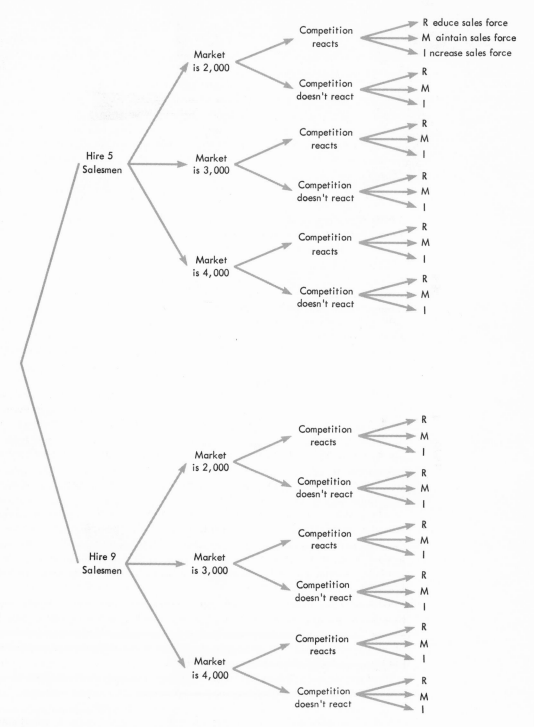

FIGURE 8-2
**Decision tree for decision problem on size of
sales force**

	Market potential		
	2,000	3,000	4,000
Hire 5 salesmen	-$20,000	$50,000	$60,000
Hire 9 salesmen	-$40,000	$40,000	$70,000

Decision

FIGURE 8-3
Payoff matrix for decision problem on size of sales force

CHOOSING THE BEST ALTERNATIVE

If Dayton management knew with certainty the actual states of all chance variables, then it would immediately recognize the best alternative. For example, if market potential for the new machine was 3,000 units, then management would choose to hire five salesmen, assuming it had confidence in the payoff measures of the outcomes. If market potential was 4,000, it would hire nine salesmen. Decision making under *certainty,* that is, where the actual states are known, does not pose any problem.[14]

But, typically, management will not know with certainty what states of nature prevail. Therefore, a decision can lead to one of several outcomes, as in Figure 8-3. Hiring five salesmen can result in a loss of $20,000 and a profit up to $60,000, depending upon the true but unknown level of market potential. Hiring nine salesmen can result in profits ranging from −$40,000 to +$70,000. It should be noted that this decision presents the possibility of either gaining more or losing more than in the other decision. On what basis is the choice to be made?

There is, strictly speaking, no one best criterion for decision making where perfect knowledge is absent. One of the principal discoveries of decision theorists is that several different criteria may be used. The choice among them is partly a matter of management predilection and partly a matter of the nature of the missing knowledge. In the latter case, three different states of imperfect knowledge can be distinguished. These states are known as *risk, uncertainty,* and *ignorance.* Risk is a state of imperfect knowledge in which the decision maker apprehends the different possible outcomes of a decision and feels he knows their probabilities. In uncertainty, the decision maker apprehends the different possible outcomes of a decision but lacks any feeling for their probabilities. Ignorance is a state of imperfect knowledge in which the decision maker cannot even apprehend the possible outcomes, let alone their probabilities.

[14] Although most decision problems in business are accompanied by uncertainties, a number exist for which the actual states of nature are relatively known, making the problem primarily one of computation. Thus the problem of which plants should ship to which warehouses is computationally complex but not uncertain, nor is uncertainty involved in the problem of blending nutrients for an animal feed to minimize cost.

The distinguishing of risk, uncertainty, and ignorance is done for theoretical convenience rather than to imply that there are sharp breaks in the level of imperfect knowledge. The level of imperfect knowledge falls along a continuum. The decision maker applies these distinctions primarily to ascertain the appropriate criteria for decision making. The major alternatives are known as *expected monetary value criterion, expected utility value criterion, criterion of pessimism* and *criterion of optimism*.[15]

EXPECTED MONETARY VALUE CRITERION. In situations of risk, especially where the firm is likely to make many decisions of the same kind and where the worst outcomes are not too bad, the decision maker is likely to choose the course of action which would maximize *expected monetary value* (EMV). Suppose these assumptions applied in the Dayton case and the decision maker had reason to believe, on the basis of a preliminary market survey, that there is a 20 per cent chance that the market potential is 2,000 units, a 30 per cent chance that it is 3,000 units, and a 50 per cent chance that it is 4,000 units. If he hired five salesmen, he would face a 20 per cent chance of losing $20,000, a 30 per cent chance of earning $50,000, and a 50 per cent chance of earning $60,000. If he made this decision on a repeated basis and the odds and payoffs remained the same, he would expect to earn on the average $41,000 ($-$20,000 $\times$ 0.2 + $50,000 $\times$ 0.3 + $60,000 $\times$ 0.5). Likewise, if he hired nine salesmen, the expected monetary value would be $39,000 ($-$40,000 $\times$ 0.2 + $40,000 $\times$ 0.3 + $70,000 $\times$ 0.5). The expected monetary value of the first decision (hiring five men) is slightly higher than that of the second decision (hiring nine men). This is true in spite of the fact that the decision maker expects a market on the high side according to his probabilities. His optimism about the size of the market is not quite strong enough.

EXPECTED UTILITY VALUE CRITERION. Now suppose Dayton drops the assumption that this decision will be made on a repeated basis. The company does not introduce a new product very often, nor are the same alternatives always considered, nor are the same chance variables likely to be involved. This is a one-shot decision-making situation. Suppose the loss of $20,000 by Dayton would be disappointing, but the loss of $40,000 would threaten its solvency. Although $40,000 is just twice the loss of $20,000, it may present more than twice the threat. The point is that utility or disutility (the gain or loss in satisfaction) is not necessarily proportional to profits, especially where the stakes are high. As profits increase, utility also increases but at a diminishing rate; and as losses increase, disutility increases at an increasing rate. However, utility is fairly proportional to profits within the "normal" profit-loss range. Therefore, for decisions whose consequences occur in the normal profit range, EMV is an appropriate criterion. For decisions whose profit consequences can have a large impact on the firm's stability, a substitution of utility values for dollar figures would be desirable.

Suppose the decision maker considered the dollar stakes listed in

15 See, for example, David W. Miller and Martin K. Starr, *Executive Decision and Operations Research* (Englewood Cliffs, N.J.: Prentice-Hall, Inc., 1960), chap. 5.

	Market potential		
	2,000	3,000	4,000
Hire 5 salesmen	-1.20	1.00	1.05
Hire 9 salesmen	-4.00	0.90	1.08

Decision

FIGURE 8-4
Utility matrix for decision problem on size of sales force

Figure 8-3 to be very high. He would then prefer to make the decision on the basis of maximizing expected utility rather than expected monetary value. He would have to replace the profit figures in Figure 8-3 by their utility values.[16] Let the utility values be those shown in Figure 8-4. Again suppose the decision maker assigns the same probabilities (0.2, 0.3, and 0.5 respectively) to the three possible levels of market potential. The expected utilities of the two decision alternatives would be:

$$U(5) = (-1.20) \times 0.2 + (1.00) \times 0.3 + (1.05) \times 0.5 = +0.585 \quad (1)$$
$$U(9) = (-4.00) \times 0.2 + (0.90) \times 0.3 + (1.08) \times 0.5 = +0.010 \quad (2)$$

While the first decision has only a slightly greater EMV than the second decision, it has a considerably greater expected utility value (EUV). Both criteria therefore lead to the same decision, but the second one, that of maximizing expected utility, makes the case even more convincing. In effect, the possible loss of $40,000 with the second decision (in contrast to $20,000) counts for more than the possible gain of $70,000 (in contrast to $60,000).

CRITERION OF PESSIMISM. If the decision maker at Dayton has no convictions as to the relative probability of the three market potential levels, he is dealing with a situation of uncertainty rather than risk. Assuming this is a once-only decision and the stakes are high, a common criterion is to choose the course of action which would *minimize* the size of the *maximum* possible loss.[17] Hiring five men would satisfy this criterion in that the loss is not likely to exceed $20,000, whereas it might be as large as $40,000 if the other alternative is chosen.

The conservative criterion has been called the *criterion of pessimism* because it concentrates on the prospect that "nature" or competition may

---

[16] In Chapter 2 of his *Probability and Statistics for Business Decisions* (New York: McGraw-Hill Book Company, 1959), Robert Schlaifer describes how an executive can explicate his utility function by making choices in a series of hypothetical betting situations.

[17] See Chapter 10, pp. 232-34.

be malevolent. The possible size of the gain does not influence the choice so much as the possible size of the loss.

CRITERION OF OPTIMISM. The opposite criterion in a state of uncertainty would call for making the decision that could maximize the maximum possible reward (called the *maximax* rule). This criterion would lead Dayton to hire nine salesmen. While some managements occasionally prefer to go after the highest reward, these are the exception rather than the rule.

OTHER CRITERIA. Decision making in situations of ignorance is the most difficult to handle in any analytical fashion. The decision maker should try to convert the situation into one of uncertainty through marketing research. In such situations, the only criteria are caution and a determination to act in such a way as to avert an excess of postdecision regret.

EVALUATION OF OVER-ALL DECISION-MAKING MODEL

The foregoing model spells out a sequence of logical steps for trying to arrive at a decision. The steps are listed only to indicate that there are several distinct activities which make up the process of decision making and that the order somehow represents a movement closer to a solution. It would be a mistake to think that the decision maker must proceed unidirectionally and rigidly through these steps. In practice, steps may be reversed, skipped, or returned to several times as new difficulties or inspirations arise.

The criticisms of this model have been of two kinds. One class of criticism says that the model goes too far in formalizing the decision-making process and requires too much talent, omniscience, and funds on the part of the decision maker.[18] The other class of criticism says that the model does not go far enough because it deals with essentially the single decision, rather than the multistage decision problem.[19] The ultimate issue here is whether the model is logical and useful. It has been described in considerable detail because it is felt that a large and growing number of marketing executives will find this a useful way to think about marketing problems.

One further point that deserves clarification is the relationship between the executive and the detailed implementation of the decision-making process. The executive is the decision maker in the sense that he does the "deciding." But in most situations, he does not do most of the "decisioning," namely the preliminary work leading up to the decision. This work is done by analysts on his staff. The relationship between the executive and his analyst has been succinctly described by a leading analyst:

> I think it can best be described as a continuing dialogue between the policymaker and the systems analyst, in which the policymaker . . . asks for alternative solutions to his problems, while the analyst attempts to clarify the conceptual framework in which the decisions must be made, to define

[18] This criticism has been voiced by David Braybrooke and Charles E. Lindblom, *A Strategy of Decision* (New York: Free Press of Glencoe, Inc., 1963), p. 113.
[19] See Edwards, "Behavioral Decision Theory," *op. cit.*, p. 474.

alternative possible objectives and criteria, and to explore in as clear terms as possible (and quantitatively) the cost and effectiveness of alternative courses of action.[20]

Efficiency in Decision Making

The model of the decision-making process shows how a marketing executive might proceed to solve a particular problem. The challenge, however, lies not only in knowing how to solve particular problems but also in finding the time to handle all the marketing problems that arise. At the beginning of any day the marketing executive's in-basket will contain a number of unsolved problems, and new ones will be added during the day. With much effort, the executive may dispose of as many problems as were added; with proper management techniques, he may even be able to reduce the backlog of problems awaiting decision.

The marketing executive must fight a tendency which has been called Gresham's Law of Planning; that is, for easy problems to be preoccupying and to drive the harder ones away from resolution.[21] The executive needs some orderly procedures for making sure that each problem receives the time and attention it deserves. One systematic way to handle the incessant flow of problems is illustrated in Figure 8-5.

DELEGATABLE PROBLEMS

The marketing executive first asks whether a particular problem can be delegated to someone else in the organization (Box 1). For example, customers' requests for additional product specifications may be routed to the industrial engineer for reply. Branch sales office requests for tactical guidance can be delegated to the marketing planning officer. Delegating problems is the fastest way to get rid of them. Yet this must be done with discretion if these problems are to be satisfactorily resolved.

PROGRAMMABLE PROBLEMS

If the problem is not delegatable, the executive asks whether it is of a sufficiently routine and repetitive character to justify an investment in developing a decision model (Box 2). These may be called programmable problems, and over time an increasing number of problems are likely to become programmable.[22] In the marketing area, examples would include routine ordering decisions, routine pricing decisions, credit extension decisions, and traffic decisions.

The decision model can take the form of a *decision rule*, a *logical flow diagram*, or a *mathematical model*.

DECISION RULE.   A decision rule is an explicit statement of how a deci-

[20] Alain Enthoven, Deputy Assistant Secretary of Defense for Systems Analysis, quoted in "The Whizziest Kid," *Time*, June 28, 1963, p. 18.

[21] For experimental evidence, see James G. March, "Business Decision Making," *Industrial Research*, Spring 1959. The original law was named after Sir Thomas Gresham (1519-1579), who advanced the thesis that a cheaper currency would tend to drive a dearer currency out of circulation.

[22] Herbert A. Simon, *New Science of Management Decision* (New York: Harper & Row, Publishers, 1960), p. 5.

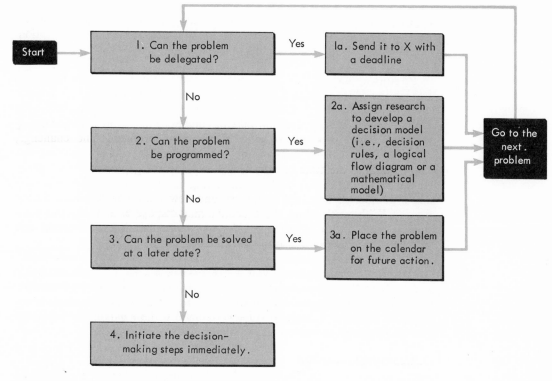

FIGURE 8-5
A procedure for managing problems

sion is to be made in a particular type of situation. In the area of pricing, for example, the decision rule might be: "Set price to obtain a 15% rate of return on investment." An alternative decision rule might be: "Add a 10% markup to high turnover items (as defined) and a 20% markup to low turnover items." It is important to distinguish between the form of the *decision rule* and the *decision parameters*. A decision parameter is a specific number found in the rule, such as 15% in the first rule. It is important that both the rule *and* the parameter be well chosen.

LOGICAL FLOW DIAGRAM. A logical flow diagram is a sequence of decision rules in diagram form for handling more complex situations. Figure 8-3 itself is a logical flow diagram, and many others are found throughout this book. The various decision boxes of such a diagram are connected in a flow pattern and are related to each other through two fundamental operations. One of these is called *branching*. Branching takes place when a question is posed at a certain step of the decision process and its possible answers are expressed as alternative branches leading away from the box. The other operation is called *looping*. Looping takes place when certain answers to a question require the decision maker to return to an earlier decision step. Logical flow diagrams offer the advantage of making the decision process explicit and easy to understand without knowledge of higher mathematics.[23] They are coming into increasing use to express normative routines for decision making and behavioral descriptions of the apparent mental processes of decision makers.

MATHEMATICAL MODELS. A mathematical model often has to be set up for the more complex but programmable problems. There is an increasing number of practicable mathematical models for problems in the area of media selection, new product evaluation, and store location determination. These models may be cast in logical flow diagram form for computer solution.

NONPROGRAMMABLE PROBLEMS

By delegating certain decisions and programming others, the executive may be able to increase the amount of time he can give to the nonprogrammable problems. These are novel, important, and infrequent problems for which an original decision model must be constructed. Examples of such problems are whether to go into private branding, whether to cut prices, and whether to expand the sales force. All of these problems require a fresh structuring of alternatives, an identification of the key uncertainties, and an evaluation of the probabilities and likely payoffs.

A major decision problem is likely to involve the company in expensive preliminary data collection and analysis. One of the decision maker's ancillary tasks is to decide how much time, expense, and effort should be expended in trying to reduce the uncertainty surrounding a problem. Naturally the more serious the possible consequences of the decision and/or the greater level of uncertainty, the greater the desirable investment in problem analysis and data collection. The executive should determine in a preliminary way how long the problem might take to solve. He can then work backwards from the decision deadline date to determine when research on the problem should be started. Sometimes the decision-making steps have to be initiated immediately (Box 4), and sometimes they can be initiated at a later date (Box 3a).

Summary

Marketing decisions are among the most important and difficult decisions faced by the business firm. The job of marketing is to stimulate sales profitably. Yet the sales-creating instruments at the firm's disposal tend to have complicated effects on sales, namely, nonlinear effects, threshold effects, carry-over effects, decay effects, marketing-mix interaction effects, environmental interaction effects, competitive effects, and quality effects. Data for estimating these effects may be poor or nonexistent.

Since marketing decisions are made under conditions of highly imperfect knowledge, they require careful definition and analysis. Scientists from various disciplines have developed insights into

[23] See William F. Massy and Jim D. Savvas, "Logical Flow Models for Marketing Analysis," *Journal of Marketing,* XXVIII (January 1964), 32-37.

decision making, both how it is influenced by cultural, organizational, and personality factors and how it can be conducted more rationally.

A model for normative decision making consists of six steps representing a movement toward the final decision—defining the problem, objectives, and constraints; distinguishing the major alternatives; identifying the key uncertainties; gathering the relevant data; estimating the value of alternative outcomes; and choosing the best alternative. Used flexibly, this model can be very useful in stimulating the creative and analytical abilities of the decision maker. The busy marketing executive can expedite his decision making through classifying his inflowing problems as delegatable, programmable, and nonprogrammable, and handling them accordingly.

Questions and Problems

1. Take an actual marketing decision you are personally acquainted with, and analyze the cultural, organizational, and personality factors which entered into it.

2. Decision making, although engaged in by all men, is excelled in by only a few. Is the good decision maker born or made?

3. When asked how he made business decisions, a leading executive said: "It is like asking a pro baseball player to define the swing that has always come natural to him." Another leading executive said: "There are no rules." (a) Do remarks like these fly in the face of using a formal approach to decision making? (b) Do you think that the normative decision model is inconsistent with a creative approach to marketing decision making? (c) Does it seem to demand too much from decision makers or not enough? (d) Is the advantage of formal decision making that two company decision makers approaching the same problem are likely to arrive independently at the same decision?

4. A marketing decision maker evaluates two alternative marketing strategies and estimates their expected rates of return to be 8 per cent and 12 per cent, respectively. Which strategy should be chosen if this decision is to be made many times? Which strategy should be chosen if this decision is to be made only once?

5. Which marketing decision would you make in the following case, and what does it indicate about the utility of money in your mind: (a) a sure payoff of $100,000, or (b) an equal chance of winning either $300,000 or nothing?

6. Where the decision maker has no knowledge or intuition about which of several states of nature might be true, is it logical to assign equal probabilities to them? Would you advocate some other solution?

7. In each of the following marketing situations, describe whether it is likely to be characterized primarily by certainty, risk, uncertainty, or ignorance: (a) introducing a radically new product; (b) choosing among three applicants for the job of salesman; (c) determining which carrier to use for shipping goods; (d) forecasting sales in a fairly stable industry.

8. For each of the following marketing decisions suggest a decision rule which might be in common use: (a) setting a price on new merchandise;

(b) determining the size of the advertising budget; (c) setting salesmen's quotas; (d) determining whether a product should be dropped; (e) determining how much to stock; (f) determining whether to mark down merchandise; (g) forecasting next year's sales; (h) responding to a decline in market share.

chapter 9

Marketing Research

Marketing decision making today calls for highly specialized marketing analysis and information. When firms were small and their markets limited, management knew their customers directly through the experience of selling to them. Firms now blanket such large market areas that casual observation of customers is not sufficient. Many firms do not even sell directly to their final customers, relying instead on lengthy channels of distribution. As a result, a growing number of companies has recognized the need for a specialized operation devoted to the collection and analysis of data on marketing problems. This operation is known as marketing research.

This chapter examines the contributions of marketing research to the management of marketing activities. It is divided into five sections. The first defines the meaning and scope of marketing research activities. The second describes the four major steps making up the marketing research process: problem definition, model construction, data collection, and data interpretation. The third section examines the four major data-collection strategies: secondary source research, observation, experimentation, and interviewing. The fourth section discusses the evaluation of research results, particularly through the use of Bayesian statistical decision theory. The final section discusses and presents illustrations of two important characteristics of marketing research: scientific method and creativity.

Meaning and Scope of Marketing Research

MEANING OF MARKETING RESEARCH

Marketing research is defined by the American Marketing Association as "the systematic gathering, recording, and analyzing of data about problems relating to the marketing of goods and services." [1] This is a good description of marketing research in most American companies, for marketing research is mainly an activity involving data collection and data analysis.

In a small but growing number of companies, the conception of marketing research is expanding to include two additional emphases. The first is that marketing research involves the *analysis of the problem as*

---

[1] *Marketing Definitions: A Glossary of Marketing Terms,* compiled by the Committee on Definitions of the American Marketing Association, Ralph S. Alexander, Chairman (Chicago: American Marketing Association, 1960), pp. 16-17.

well as the data. The real nature of the marketing problem is not always obvious, and even after it is determined, the difficult task of structuring a meaningful model for its analysis remains. The second is that marketing research is undertaken to *improve decision making and control, not just to have data about company marketing problems.* The AMA definition states the major activities making up marketing research but is not clear on the ends. In this book, the term is defined as follows:

> *Marketing research* is systematic problem analysis, model building, and fact finding for the purposes of improved decision making and control in the marketing of goods and services.

THE SCOPE OF MARKETING RESEARCH

It is not surprising that the conception of marketing research is undergoing change when we realize that formal company marketing research departments made their appearance only fifty years ago, and then on a very small scale. The number of marketing research departments has soared since the Twenties. Every five-year period has been marked by the formation of more *new* marketing research departments than in the immediately preceding five-year period.[2] Over half of all companies today have formal marketing research departments, and half of these departments were formed during the last decade.

The continuous growth of marketing research has been accompanied by a continuous expansion in the range of projects undertaken by marketing researchers. Nothing tends to throw more light on what a profession is than what its practitioners do. Table 9-1 lists thirty-four different marketing research activities carried on by firms along with the percentage of all responding companies carrying on each activity.

The seven most common activities are development of market potentials, market share analysis, determination of market characteristics, sales analyses, competitive product studies, new product acceptance and potential, and short-range forecasting, in this order. On the other hand, less than half of the surveyed firms did their own research on advertising effectiveness or carried out any marketing operations research.

The day-to-day activities of the typical marketing research department tend to fall into three categories.

ROUTINE INFORMATION GATHERING AND ANALYSIS. Much of any department's energy goes into collecting and analyzing current data to keep executives posted on market developments and the company's marketing efficiency. Some department staffers may spend their time clipping pertinent articles from periodicals; others prepare and examine market-share statistics; still others analyze the movements of company sales by territory, product, and other breakdowns.

ROUTINE PROBLEM ANALYSIS. Another large part of any department's effort goes into preparing routine analyses of fairly standard problems. The department is asked to develop sales forecasts, or estimate geo-

[2] For the status of marketing research in the United States, see Dik Warren Twedt, ed., *A Survey of Marketing Research: Organization, Functions, Budget, Compensation* (Chicago: American Marketing Association, 1963).

TABLE 9-1

193
*Marketing
Research*

Research activities of 1,660 companies

Type of research	Per cent doing
Advertising	
Motivation research	30
Copy research	37
Media research	47
Studies of ad effectiveness	48
Other	12
Business economics and corporate	
Short-range forecasting (up to 1 yr.)	62
Long-range forecasting (over 1 yr.)	59
Studies of business trends	58
Profit and/or value analysis	53
Plant and warehouse, location studies	44
Diversification studies	49
Purchase of companies, sales of divisions	44
Export and international studies	39
Linear programming	35
Operations research	29
PERT studies	18
Employee morale studies	32
Other	7
Product	
New product acceptance and potential	63
Competitive product studies	65
Product testing	57
Packaging research design or physical characteristics	45
Other	7
Sales and market	
Development of market potentials	68
Market share analysis	67
Determination of market characteristics	67
Sales analyses	66
Establishment of sales quotas, territories	57
Distribution channels and cost studies	52
Test markets, store audits	37
Consumer panel operations	27
Sales compensation studies	44
Studies of premiums, coupons, sampling deals	29
Other	6

Source: Dik Warren Twedt, ed., *A Survey of Marketing Research: Organization, Functions, Budgets, Compensation* (Chicago: American Marketing Association, 1963), p. 41.

graphical market potentials, or find out how customers feel about the company's products. The techniques called for by these problems are fairly standard and usually do not require much modification to serve the purpose. The main challenge is one of designing an economical research plan for getting the information.

NONROUTINE PROBLEM ANALYSIS. Marketing research departments also get or initiate problems which require a more creative research approach because of their uniqueness or importance. The department may have to estimate what would happen to sales and profits if the company dropped its franchised dealers, or if it introduced a radically new sales compensation plan, or if it doubled its advertising budget. In such cases, much time has to be spent in conceptualizing the problem and determining or inventing appropriate techniques. Because the problem is nonroutine, there is a greater need for the exchange of ideas between the executive and the marketing researcher.

MANAGEMENT'S USE OF MARKETING RESEARCH

The growth in the number of marketing research departments might leave the impression of extremely rapid acceptance of marketing research by American business. Yet this impression must be qualified. About 45 per cent of the responding companies reported no formal marketing research department. Furthermore, companies with formal departments gave them smaller budgets than the budgets allotted to advertising and research and development. William R. Davidson, past president of the AMA, concluded: ". . . the typical corporation's investment in marketing research is minimal . . . and it indicates a reluctance within industry to invest in research dealing with people, markets and marketing to the extent that would seem to be called for by corporations that espouse the so-called modern marketing concept." [3]

What are the factors which have stood in the way of greater acceptance of marketing research?

A NARROW CONCEPTION OF MARKETING RESEARCH. Many executives see marketing research as only a fact-finding operation. The marketing researcher is supposed to design a questionnaire, choose a sample, carry out interviews, and report results, often without being given a careful definition of the problem or of the decision alternatives before management. As a result, some of the fact finding fails to be useful. This reinforces management's idea of the limited good which can come from marketing research.

UNEVEN CALIBER OF MARKETING RESEARCHERS. Some executives view marketing research as little better than a clerical activity and reward it as such. In these cases, less able individuals are attracted into its ranks, and their weak training and deficient creativity are reflected in their output. The disappointing output reinforces management prejudice against expecting too much from marketing research. Management continues to pay low salaries, perpetuating the basic difficulty.

OCCASIONAL ERRONEOUS FINDINGS BY MARKETING RESEARCH. Many executives want conclusive information from marketing research, although most of the time marketing processes are too complex to yield more than highly conditional information. The problem is complicated by the low budgets often given to marketing researchers to get the information. Executives become disappointed, and their opinion of the worth of marketing research is lowered. In the television industry, for example, some executives:

---

[3] William R. Davidson, "Marketing Renaissance," in *Toward Scientific Marketing,* ed. Stephen A. Greyser (Chicago: American Marketing Association, 1964), p. 10.

have little confidence in the value of market research—and possibly for good reason. There have been several widely publicized examples in the industry where research (poor in quality, to be sure) produced wrong answers. An outstanding failure was the very low estimate for the potential market for a 14-inch portable set. . . . General Electric executives rejected the conclusions reached by marketing research and demonstrated that a very large market existed. R.C.A. has had numerous experiences, it is said, in which consumers expressed preferences for particular kinds of designs and features, but did not buy them when they were put on the market.[4]

INTELLECTUAL DIFFERENCES. Intellectual divergences between the mental sets of businessmen and researchers often get in the way of productive relationships. A marketing research executive listed four such conflicts:

Management demands	*Research offers*
Simplicity (Can't you just ask "yes" or "no"?)	Complexity (The variability of response indicates . . .)
Certainty (It is or it isn't)	Probability (Maybe)
Immediacy (Now)	Futurity (It appears that by the end of the year . . .)
Concreteness (Aren't we number one yet?)	Abstraction (Our exponential gain indeed appears favorable) [5]

What is needed is a gradual education about each other's needs and capabilities.

The Marketing Research Process

The major role of marketing research is to aid the marketing executive in solving marketing problems. Although each problem is unique, the professional marketing researcher goes through certain general steps to aid in the solution of a problem. These steps make up what is known as the marketing research process. The four major steps are *problem definition, model construction, data collection,* and *data interpretation.* These steps will be illustrated in connection with the following case: [6]

> The Consolidated Packing Company (fictional name) is a leading firm in the food-canning business with sales of around $270 million. Its brand name is found on canned fruits and vegetables and a variety of frozen foods. Although the brand name is highly regarded by consumers, management recently has become concerned about the growth of private brands. Large food chains are increasingly selling products under their own label, often

---

[4] Alfred Oxenfeldt, *Marketing Practices in the TV Set Industry* (New York: Columbia University Press, 1964), pp. 78-79.

[5] Leslie A. Beldo, "Introduction to Attitude Research and Management Decisions," in *Effective Marketing Coordination,* ed. George L. Baker (Chicago: American Marketing Association, 1961), p. 584.

[6] Adapted from Ralph Westfall and Harper W. Boyd, Jr., *Cases in Marketing Management* (Homewood, Ill.: Richard D. Irwin, Inc., 1961), pp. 178-81.

at several cents less than national brands. The product is often identical, in many cases coming from a national brand producer under contract. The lower store price of the private brand reflects the facts that chain-store distribution is more efficient and chains spend much less on advertising their own brands. Consumers seem to be gradually turning to private brands because of the price differential. Consolidated has been approached by some of the chains to contract some of its output for private branding. This is a tempting solicitation, especially because the firm has excess capacity.

It is evident that Consolidated is facing a major policy decision. The vice-president of marketing calls the marketing research director into his office. He tells him to launch a study of private brands.

PROBLEM DEFINITION

The first step in the conduct of research calls for a careful definition of the problem. If the problem is stated vaguely, if the wrong problem is stated, or if the uses of the research are not made clear, then the researcher has a difficult time designing an effective and efficient research plan. He can make an important contribution by getting management to define clearly what the decision context is for the research assignment.

In the Consolidated case, the marketing research director has a right to feel uneasy about the assignment. It is too general. All kinds of information can be gathered on the private brand issue: a survey of consumer attitudes toward national versus private brands; a five-year forecast of the likely share of private brands of the total canned food business; or profit trends among food canners who supply private brands, to cite only a few examples.

The difficulty is that while each of these studies is likely to produce interesting information, none may help management come any closer to a policy decision. Suppose a consumer attitude study showed that 60 per cent of the housewives believe national brands are of a higher quality than private brands. How does this affect the company's decision? What if the percentage had turned out to be 20 per cent or 80 per cent? There is something sterile about a fact which is not made part of a larger model for decision making.

This kind of research assignment can be called exploratory or fact-oriented, in contrast to decision-oriented. Exploratory research is mostly warranted in situations where the company's ignorance of the issues is substantial, and it may uncover much that is interesting. Yet the research effort is generally more efficient when the problem and alternatives are well-defined. This is because the cost of research is generally related to the total amount of information gathered, while the value of research is associated only with the proportion of information which is useful. The useful proportion is the information that helps management narrow down the alternatives and make a better estimate of their payoffs.

For Consolidated, the alternatives of practical interest may be:

The company can continue its present policies without any change.

The company can lower its prices in an attempt to narrow the price differential.

The company can increase its total advertising in an effort to shift the demand curve to the right.

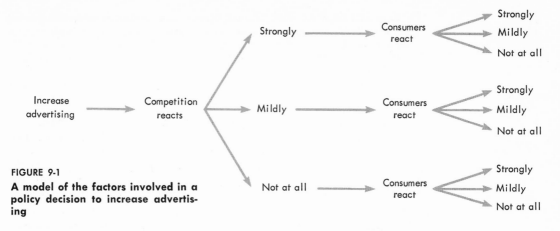

FIGURE 9-1
A model of the factors involved in a policy decision to increase advertising

The company can produce a small amount for private branding to the extent that it has excess capacity.

The company can discontinue its national brands and enter into full-scale production for private branding.

Management wants to adopt one of these alternatives, and the role of research is to clarify the profit and risk implications of each alternative. Instead of exploratory research for general information, there is decision-oriented research for specific information.

MODEL CONSTRUCTION

The second step in the research process is to develop a significant structure or model relating various factors to each of the possible policy alternatives.

Consider the third alternative, that of the company's meeting the private brand challenge by substantially increasing its advertising spending. Figure 9-1 shows one way to structure the factors affecting the payoff of the third alternative. The diagram shows Consolidated making a personal move to increase advertising. The next move is made by competition, and will be a strong reaction, a mild one, or none at all. This is followed by consumers reacting in either a strong or mild way or not at all.

Figure 9-1 is highly oversimplified in that it does not state the new level of advertising expenditure, nor distinguish between the reactions of independent food outlets and the chains, nor spell out the level of reactions in dollars and cents. But it does show how the consequences of a decision alternative may be modeled. Another decision alternative for Consolidated, such as converting to full-scale private brand production, would require a different modeling of the uncertainties.[7]

DATA COLLECTION

The third step calls for collecting the data specified in the model of the problem. For example, the model for the third alternative indicates that management needs information on how its competitors and customers are likely to react to an intensified advertising campaign.

[7] Model construction is explored more thoroughly in Chapter 10.

Predicting the responses of competitors and customers are two of the most difficult research problems in marketing.[8] Yet this information is needed, and it is the researcher's responsibility to develop an effective data-collection plan. Data-collection procedures are discussed later on in this chapter.

DATA INTERPRETATION

The last step calls for analyzing the data so as to arrive at conclusions regarding the relative merits and risks of the various policy alternatives. Management would ideally like to see the project culminate in a clear ranking of the policy alternatives. The marketing research director may be able to rank the policy alternatives according to the estimated payoffs, but he should also show how these estimates would be affected by alternative assumptions.

In presenting a less than conclusive report, the marketing research director admittedly treads a dangerous line. If the report is too inconclusive, management may feel that they have learned nothing new in spite of the time and resources devoted to the study. If the report is too conclusive, the marketing research director virtually pre-empts the decision-making function. Either extreme is a risk for the research director and his job.

Alternative Data-Collection Strategies

Of the four steps in the marketing research process, data collection tends to consume the most time and effort in the typical marketing research department. Since the results of marketing research depend critically on the data, the marketing executive should have a working knowledge of the major characteristics and limitations of the different ways of gathering data.

The information needed for a problem may or may not presently exist. Data that are already assembled are called *secondary data*. Data that the firm must gather for the first time are called *primary data*. The three major ways to generate primary data are observation, experimentation, and interviewing.

SECONDARY DATA

The researcher first tries to find the data he needs in existing sources. If he succeeds, he has saved time and expense. However, existing data are not always relevant, accurate, or complete enough for his purpose. Secondary data are often gathered for different purposes than the researcher may have in mind. Nevertheless, secondary data are often very useful. The two requirements for the researcher are that he be familiar with the major sources of data and that he know how to use them critically.

MAJOR SOURCES OF EXISTING INFORMATION. Three general sources of existing information are company files, marketing research services, and open publications.

Company files. The researcher in a large company is aware that much

[8] See Chapter 15, pp. 369-75.

information is contained in various company files, such as accounting reports, detailed sales information, and special studies. The researcher should not ignore this source, nor should he overlook the possibility that useful data may exist in the files of his distributors, advertising agency, trade association, or other companies.

Marketing research services. Information is also available from marketing research firms who sell it on a fee basis. Various product, brand, and advertising studies are available from organizations such as A. C. Nielsen Company, Market Research Corporation of America, Audits & Surveys Company, Social Research, Inc., Gallup-Robinson, Daniel Starch, and others.

Open publications. Open publications are probably the most frequently used sources of information. An open publication is any book or magazine available to companies through libraries or purchase. The most important types are *government publications* and *commercial* and *trade publications.*[9]

USING EXISTING INFORMATION CRITICALLY. Information in published sources is collected for a variety of purposes and under a variety of conditions which may render some of the data of limited usefulness. Often, the marketing researcher is so gratified to find some information he has been looking for in published form that he forgets to evaluate it critically. When the accuracy of the information is uncertain, its use can do more harm than if the researcher never found it. Marketing researchers and executives should check these data for four important qualities:

Impartiality. Impartiality is a quality not so much of the data as of the person or organization supplying it. The researcher generally can assume that government statistics and the data furnished by the larger commercial organizations are free from any conscious slant or bias. On the other hand, some of the data published by private organizations, such as trade associations and chambers of commerce, may be selected to cast the organization, industry, or area in a favorable light. The issue may not be one of conscious fabrication but of the selection of statistical measures and samples which create a one-sided picture.[10]

Validity. Validity raises the question of whether a particular number or series is a relevant measure for the researcher's purposes. A historical series of official steel prices would not be a completely valid measure of the actual prices paid for steel, because the steel market has been characterized by unreported gray prices in different periods. Company data on shipments to various regional warehouses may not be a completely valid measure of sales in each region, because often warehouses transship stock to other regions to meet unanticipated surges in demand.

Reliability. Reliability raises the question of how precisely sample data reflect the universe from which they are drawn. A randomly drawn sample of 4,000 housewives is likely to give a more accurate picture than a random

---

[9] For an annotated description of these publications, see Harper W. Boyd, Jr. and Ralph Westfall, *Marketing Research: Text and Cases,* rev. ed. (Homewood, Ill.: Richard D. Irwin, Inc., 1964), chap. 7. Also see Steuart Henderson Britt and Irwin A. Shapiro, "Where to Find Marketing Facts," *Harvard Business Review,* September-October 1962, pp. 44 ff.

[10] The classic account of these dangers is found in Darrell Huff, *How to Lie with Statistics* (New York: W. W. Norton & Company, Inc., 1954).

sample of 400 housewives. Before using reported studies, management should examine the sample size and the degree of precision it implies.

Homogeneity. Homogeneity raises the question of whether a given set of numbers is internally consistent. A time series on an industry's total advertising expenditures would not be homogeneous if the number of reporting units varied over time or if the definition of advertising costs varied.

While a researcher cannot evaluate all secondary information for impartiality, validity, reliability, and homogeneity, he should do this for the more critical information inputs. When the data's quality is in doubt, he must seriously consider whether the existing data should be used or fresh data collected.

PRIMARY DATA THROUGH OBSERVATION

When the data for a marketing problem are not found in any existing source, the company must engage in original data collection. This calls for some form of contact with company customers (actual and potential), middlemen, salesmen, competitors, or other primary information sources. The contact can take one of three forms: the informational source can be observed, or involved in a controlled experiment, or interviewed. Here, we shall consider observation as a method.

Partial answers to many marketing research questions can often be developed through observing the particular marketing processes at work.

> Two investigators recently set up a hidden television camera in the ceiling of a Pittsburgh supermarket to follow the movements of shoppers through the store. The objective was to develop generalizations on the customer flow pattern which might lead to the rearrangement of merchandise to increase customer convenience and purchases.
>
> Another supermarket study involved stationing a hidden movie camera behind a particular canned goods display to record the eye movements of shoppers. The objective was to determine how shoppers scan the brands.
>
> An investigator used a concealed tape recorder to record how different department store television salesmen answered his inquiry about buying a particular television set. The objective was to determine the typical sales arguments used and the degree of sales enthusiasm for the product.
>
> Investigators observing a special display of foam rubber pillows in a department store checked the number of persons passing by, the number who stopped to look at the display, the number who handled the product, and the number who purchased it. The objective was to evaluate the effectiveness of the display.

Thus the observational method can be used to study sales techniques, customer movements, and customer responses among other things. Its main advantage is that it generally leads to a more objective picture of overt behavior than can be expected from relying on people's accounts of how they behave. Observation avoids the problem of response bias.

The method may, however, introduce two new biases militating against an accurate picture of behavior. It assumes that the investigators are accurate and diligent observers. Instruments such as tape recorders and cameras are usually included just for the reason of improving observational accuracy. The method also assumes that the act of observing the marketing process does not change the behavior of those being observed. This is the reason for trying to observe behavior through concealed means. Nevertheless, it yields little or no information about what is taking place under the skin of the people being observed. Their state of mind, their buying motives, their images are not revealed through this method. Even their incomes and education may not be obvious. This, coupled with the frequent costliness of the observational method resulting from the extensive time investigators must spend waiting for particular actions to take place, makes it desirable to consider other primary data-collecting strategies.

PRIMARY DATA THROUGH EXPERIMENTS

One of the major weaknesses of the observational method is that there is little or no control over the behavior or environment being observed. Behavior is observed in its natural setting with all the unique and uncontrollable factors that may attend it. Therefore, plain observation can rarely be counted on to yield conclusive proof of cause-and-effect relationships in marketing.

In order to test hypotheses about the effects of particular marketing stimuli on behavior, some controls must be introduced. The *experimental method* consists of introducing selected stimuli into a controlled environment and systematically varying them. To the extent that extraneous factors are eliminated or controlled, the observed effects can be related to the variations in the stimuli. The purpose of control is to eliminate competing hypotheses which might also explain the observed phenomena.

Many of the important decisions facing the marketing executive cannot be settled by secondary research, observation, or by surveying the opinions of customers or experts. Consider such common marketing problems as:

What is the best method for training salesmen?
What is the best remuneration plan for salesmen?
What is the best shelf arrangement for displaying a product?
What is the effectiveness of a point-of-purchase display?
What package design should be used?
Which copy is the most effective?
What media are the most effective?
Which version of a product would consumers like best?

For such questions, experimental design may be the most reliable and fruitful way to find the answers.

A MODEL FOR EXPERIMENTS IN MARKETING. The nature and problems of conducting marketing experiments can be understood best by thinking of an experiment as a system in which a number of inputs affect subjects and result in a number of outputs. This "systems" view of an experiment is illustrated in Figure 9-2. Each of the elements of an experiment is discussed below.

Subjects. The subjects of an experiment are the units that are being acted upon and whose responses are solicited. In marketing experiments the subjects may be consumers, stores, sales territories, and the like. Be-

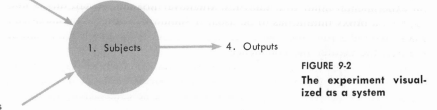

2. Experimental inputs

1. Subjects

4. Outputs

3. Environmental inputs

FIGURE 9-2
The experiment visualized as a system

cause people are the ultimate subjects of marketing experiments, special techniques and precautions must be observed.[11] Some of the main problems are:

> *Instrumentation,* or the problem of finding instruments that are sufficiently precise to measure changes in awareness, preference, or purchase behavior.
>
> *Matched groups,* or the problem of developing groups of comparable subjects before the experiment begins.
>
> *Uniformity,* or the problem of insuring comparable exposure of the subjects to the same environmental inputs during the experiment.
>
> *Reactive bias,* or the problem of obtaining authentic behavior from people who are conscious of their participation in an experiment.

Experimental input. The experimental input is the variable whose effect is being tested. In marketing experiments, the experimental input may be price, packaging, display, a sales incentive plan, or some other marketing variable.

Environmental inputs. Environmental inputs are all the factors affecting the experiment save the experimental input and the subjects. In marketing experiments, environmental inputs may include competitors' actions, weather changes, uncooperative dealers.

Fortunately, many environmental inputs do not make a difference in the results. And of those which make a difference, some may be controllable, or at least measurable. The real danger comes from undetected environmental inputs or detected inputs whose effects cannot be controlled or measured.

Two precautions can be taken. One is to use a sample of sufficient size so that the effect of exceptional environmental inputs is swamped by the normal inputs. The other is to set up a control group, namely, a group equivalent to the experimental group and differing only in not receiving the experimental input. The theory of the control group is that it catches all the effects of the uncontrolled inputs and therefore provides a measure for adjusting the contaminated experimental outputs.

Experimental outputs. The results of the experiment are called experimental outputs. In marketing experiments, the results may come in the form of changes in sales, attitudes, or behavior.

Sales are the ultimate output of interest in appraising the effect of

---

[11] An excellent discussion of the control problems posed by people in experiments is found in Donald T. Campbell and Julian C. Stanley, "Experimental and Quasi-Experimental Designs for Research on Teaching," in *Handbook of Research on Teaching,* ed. N. L. Gage (Chicago: Rand McNally, 1963), pp. 171-246.

marketing stimuli. The marketing experimenter should strive to submit an experimental input to a *sales test* whenever possible. Where this is not possible, a proxy output has to be used. It should be highly correlated with sales, and, as a rule, the closer the proxy output is to the criterion output (sales), the greater the confidence.

Assuming good control was exercised in designing the experiment, the outcomes represent information about the effectiveness of the experimental inputs. In principle, decision rules should be established in advance of the experiment to guide the ensuing interpretation. Consider the following decision rule: "If a sales difference of a certain size or greater takes place between two types of packages, the company should produce the more popular package; if the sales difference is less than a certain size, then either package can be used; and if the sales difference falls in between the two specified sizes, a second experiment should be conducted before acting." The actual choice of the critical sales differences requires an examination of the error characteristics of the available decision rules, the economic losses implied by various possible errors, and the prior convictions of the decision maker. These are the ingredients in a Bayesian statistical analysis undertaken to find the best decision rule.[12]

THE VARIETY OF EXPERIMENTAL DESIGNS. The discussion of experimentation in marketing has pointed to a number of hazards. But many hazards also attend the interpretation of results in observational research and survey research. This discussion has a purely constructive purpose, to increase the sensitivity of executives concerning the variables that need to be controlled in an experiment. Control itself is achieved through better experimental design.

Experimental design deals with the problem of deciding on the number of subjects, the length of the experiment, and the types of controls. These are of course technical problems and best left to the trained researcher. Nevertheless, some of the major alternatives will be described here, primarily because it will help the executive appreciate the range of possibilities and the probable cost of good experimentation in marketing.

Suppose a manufacturer of quality power mowers finds sales disappointing and believes they may be helped by the development of a point-of-purchase cutaway display. The contemplated display is expensive, however, and the manufacturer would like to try it out first on a limited basis to be sure that it stimulates more sales and profits than it costs. The following experiments can be designed, ranging from the simple to the complex:

Simple time-series experiment. A simple experiment would consist of selecting some dealers, auditing their sales for a few weeks, introducing the display, and measuring their subsequent sales.

Recurrent time-series design. Alternatively, the display can be introduced for a few weeks, removed, reintroduced, removed, and so forth, each time noting the sales change and averaging the results. The averaging should eliminate the effects of unique events.

Before-after with control group design. Alternatively, two matched groups of dealers can be selected and their sales audited for a few weeks before the display is introduced. Then the display can be introduced only into the stores of the first group of dealers while sales are audited for both groups. The average sales for the experimental and control groups are then compared, and the difference is tested for statistical significance.

Factorial design. Alternatively, the experiment can be set up to test other marketing inputs in addition to the point-of-purchase display. Testing only one experimental input at a time is often inefficient.[13] Suppose the firm wants to test three displays, three prices, and three types of guarantee, or 27 possible combinations of experimental inputs. By getting the cooperation of some multiple of 27 dealers, it is possible to estimate the separate effect of different displays, prices, and guarantees, and also their interactions.[14]

Latin square design. The preceding experiment involved testing 27 different combinations of experimental inputs. If interaction among the experimental inputs is not thought to exist, there is a design known as a simple Latin square which can yield fairly good estimates of the separate effects of input on the basis of testing only nine experimental combinations. This reduces considerably the scale and cost of the many-factor experiment.[15]

THE FUTURE OF THE EXPERIMENTAL METHOD IN MARKETING.   Experimentation in marketing will never be as easy as it is in the physical sciences or even in the agricultural sciences. Yet the experimental method remains the only research method for verifying cause-and-effect relationships in marketing. The existence of hurdles emphasizes that special experimental designs and precautions should be exercised, not that experiments should be dismissed.

The number of actual bona fide experiments carried out in marketing to date is quite small. Executive resistance is based on such factors as skepticism, lack of time for carrying out experiments, difficulties in securing cooperation, and cost. In spite of these deterrents, there is evidence of increasing use of marketing experiments. Scott Paper Company and Du Pont have pioneered large-scale experiments for testing the effectiveness of advertising.[16] Experiments have also been conducted in stores, where the experimental inputs have been displays or shelf-space arrangements.[17] The experimental method has also proved useful for testing such product

[13] "It was a long held scientific doctrine that good experimental procedure was to study one variable at a time holding all others constant. . . . Such a procedure is not only quite wasteful of time and resources, but provides insufficient information. If there is an interaction . . . it would never be discovered by this method. The correct method is to determine the effects . . . and their interactions *simultaneously* in a single well-planned experiment." R. J. Jessen, "A Switch-Over Experimental Design to Measure Advertising Effect," *Journal of Advertising Research*, March 1961, pp. 15-22.

[14] For an example of the statistical analysis, see Kenneth P. Uhl, "Factorial Design —Aid to Management," *Journal of Marketing*, XXVI (January 1962), 62-66.

[15] This and the previous designs are described in more detail in Boyd and Westfall, *Marketing Research*, pp. 95-124. *(see also, Banks.)*

[16] See, for example, James C. Becknell, Jr., and Robert W. McIsaac, "Test Marketing Cookware Coated with 'Teflon,'" *Journal of Advertising Research*, September 1963, pp. 2-8.

[17] See Peter L. Henderson, James F. Hind, and Sidney E. Brown, "Sales Effects of Two Campaign Themes," *Journal of Advertising Research*, December 1961, pp. 2-11; Keith Cox, "The Responsiveness of Food Sales to Supermarket Shelf Space Changes," *Journal of Marketing Research*, May 1964, pp. 63-67.

features as taste and color.[18] The test marketing of new products is another area where principles of experimental design are (or should be) used.[19]

PRIMARY DATA THROUGH SURVEYS

The most common method of generating new marketing information is through surveys. Compared with either direct observation or experimentation, surveys yield a broader range of information and are effective for a greater number of research problems. Surveys can produce information on socioeconomic characteristics, attitudes, opinions, motives, and overt behavior. Surveys are an effective way of gathering information for planning product features, advertising copy, advertising media, sales promotions, channels of distribution, and other marketing variables.

Because surveys are so commonplace, there is a tendency to think that planning, executing, and interpreting them requires little training. Questions are written up, people are asked to respond, and the responses are summarized. The truth of the matter is that a good survey requires expert planning. Each step in developing survey information is subject to special problems, and the handling of these problems distinguishes the skilled researcher from the unskilled. The major steps in conducting a survey are deciding on the research objectives; developing the research strategy; gathering the data; and interpreting the data.

RESEARCH OBJECTIVES. All research projects should start with a clear statement of objectives. Surveys in particular can go in an almost unlimited number of directions. To prevent all kinds of questions from being asked, clear informational objectives should be developed and put in writing, if possible. Every effort should be made to state the objectives in specific terms.

RESEARCH STRATEGY. The research director faces many alternative ways to collect the information that will satisfy the research objectives. He must decide among *survey methods, research instruments,* and *sampling plans.* His decisions with respect to these three elements constitute his *research strategy.*

Suppose a company wants to draw a sample of people and interview them about their attitudes toward the company's products. There are a large number of possible research strategies. Table 9-2 shows four of the more common ones. The first strategy is to collect a limited amount of information by making telephone calls to a small sample of households chosen in a systematic way from the telephone directory. The second strategy is to send mail questionnaires to a group of magazine subscribers. The third strategy is to take a large-scale national probability sample. The fourth strategy is to carry out some depth interviewing with a small group of product users. Other permutations of these elements are possible, and this is why the research director's skill, experience, and judgment count heavily in the ultimate usefulness and cost of the collected information. The

---

[18] See Norman T. Gridgeman, "A Tasting Experiment," *Applied Statistics,* June 1956, pp. 106-12.

[19] For an excellent exposition and evaluation of the experimental method in marketing, see Seymour Banks, *Experimentation in Marketing* (New York: McGraw-Hill Book Company, 1965).

TABLE 9-2

Some alternative research strategies

Elements of the strategy	Strategy 1	Strategy 2	Strategy 3	Strategy 4
Survey method	Telephone interviews ↓	Mail interviews ↓	Personal interviews ↓	Personal interviews ↓
Research instrument	with a few factual questions ↓	with a 2-page questionnaire ↓	with many questions ↓	with projective tests ↓
Sampling plan	to a small sample of households chosen as every thousandth name in telephone directory	to all subscribers to a magazine	to a large sample of subjects chosen on a national probability sampling basis	to a dozen people found using the product

three research strategy elements of survey method, research instrument, and sampling plan are discussed below.

Survey method. Each of the three major survey methods—telephone interviews, mail questionnaires, and personal interviews—has advantages and disadvantages. Telephone interviewing stands out as the best method of the three for gathering quickly needed information. It has the advantage over a mail questionnaire of permitting the interviewer to talk to one or more persons and to clarify his questions if they are not understood. The response rate for telephone interviewing seems to be a little better than for mail questionnaires. The two main drawbacks of telephone interviewing are that only people with telephones can be interviewed (this used to be a more serious disadvantage) and only short, not too personal interviews can be carried out.

The mail questionnaire may be the best way to reach persons who would not give personal interviews or who might be biased by interviewers. It is typically the least expensive of the three methods. On the other hand, mail questionnaires require simple and clearly worded questions and are usually slow in returning to survey headquarters. The response rate to mailed questionnaires is typically low.

Personal interviewing is the most versatile of the three methods. The personal interviewer can ask more questions and can supplement the interview with personal observations. These advantages come at a high cost, however. Personal interviewing is the most expensive method and requires much more technical and administrative planning and supervision. In a real sense, companies turn to telephone interviewing or mail questionnaires as a second choice out of cost consideration.

Research instrument. The research instrument is chiefly influenced by the type of information sought and the method by which it is to be gathered. A short questionnaire is usually prepared when a few answers are sought over the telephone. A one- or two-page, attractively printed questionnaire is more appropriate for mailing. A long, objective questionnaire and/or a set of psychological or projective tests may be used in personal interviewing.

The construction of good questionnaires calls for considerable skill. A professionally marketing researcher can usually spot several errors in a casually prepared questionnaire, and these errors can invalidate some of the information. Errors turn up even in professionally prepared questionnaires, because questionnaire construction is still a fine art, not a science. There are only rules of thumb, not formulas, for preparing a good questionnaire.[20]

The more common errors arise in connection with the *types of questions asked,* the *form and wording of the questions,* the *sequencing of the questions,* and the *layout of the questionnaire.*

The most common errors in regard to the *types of questions asked* are the inclusion of questions which cannot be answered, or would not be answered, or need not be answered, and the omission of other questions which should be answered. Examples include:

> What is your husband's favorite brand of golf balls? (How do I know?)
>
> What TV programs did you watch a week ago Monday? (How would I remember?)
>
> How many pancakes did you make for your family last year? (Who counts?)
>
> Tell me your exact income. (None of your business.)
>
> Can you supply me with a list of your grocery purchases this month? (I've got better ways to spend my time.)

Each question should also be checked to determine whether it is necessary in terms of the research objectives. The form should avoid questions which are just interesting (except for one or two to start the interview on a good basis) because they lengthen the session and try the respondent's patience.

Even when the types of questions have been decided upon, their *form and wording* can make a substantial difference to the response. For most information, one has the option of using an open-ended or close-ended question. An open-ended question is one to which the respondent is free to answer in his own words. Examples are: "Why did you buy that brand?"; "What is your opinion of stainless steel razor blades?"; "Do you think the salesmen are doing an effective sales job?" A close-ended question is one in which the possible answers are prescribed. The respondent may be asked to respond in one of two ways (dichotomous questions), to check one of several answers (multiple-choice questions), to place marks along a scale (scaling questions), and so forth. The choice between open-ended and close-ended questions affects the thoughtfulness of responses, the costs of interviewing, and the quality of the subsequent analysis.

Even after the form of the question is determined, the *choice of words* calls for considerable care. All the following questions suffer from faulty wording:

> Do you drink beer regularly? (Vague wording—what does "regularly" mean?)
>
> What methodology do you employ to develop future projections? (Stilted wording—better to ask "How do you forecast sales?")

20 The interested reader should see Stanley L. Payne's classic work on the subject of wording questions, *The Art of Asking Questions* (Princeton, N. J.: Princeton University Press, 1951).

Do you like frappes? (Regional wording—in many parts of the country, people wouldn't recognize that "milkshake" is intended.)

Do you think it is right as a loyal American citizen to buy foreign products which put Americans out of work? (Biased wording.)

In general, the designer should strive for simple, direct, unambiguous, and unbiased wording. A good rule is always to pretest the questions on a sample of respondents before they are used on a wide scale.

Other "do's" and "don'ts" arise in connection with the *sequencing of questions* in the questionnaire. The lead questions should create interest, if possible. Open questions are usually better here. Difficult questions or personal questions should be used toward the end of the interview, in order not to create an emotional reaction which may affect subsequent answers or cause the respondent to break off the interview. Questions which may reveal the brand or sponsor should also be asked toward the end. As for the body of neutral questions, they should be asked in as logical an order as possible in order to avoid confusing the respondent. Classificatory data on the respondent are usually asked for last, because they tend to be less interesting and are on the personal side.

The final category of rules for questionnaire construction arises in connection with its *physical form and layout*. Questionnaires which the respondent will see—those mailed or used in personal interviewing—should have an attractive and professional appearance. The respondent will tend to make a different judgment of the survey's importance according to whether the questionnaire is (say) mimeographed on cheap paper or printed in tricolor with a neat layout. Attractiveness is especially important for mailed questionnaires, where no interviewer is present to sell the respondent on answering the questions. The form should also be designed to provide sufficient room for ease of answering and handling by respondent and editors.

Sampling plan. The third element of research strategy is a sampling plan. The sampling plan answers three questions: who is to be surveyed (sampling unit); how many are to be surveyed (sample size); and how they are to be selected (sampling procedure). These may be determined after the survey procedure and research instrument have been chosen, or simultaneously with the other decisions, or sometimes before them.

Perhaps the basic issue is "who is to be surveyed." The proper *sampling unit* is not always obvious from the nature of the information sought. In a survey designed to uncover attitudes toward breakfast cereals, should the primary sampling unit be the housewife, the husband, the children, or some combination of the three? Where the roles of influencers, deciders, users, and/or buyers are not combined in the same person, the researcher must determine not only what information is needed but also who is most likely to have it.

After the sampling unit is decided upon, the next issue is *sample size*. In general, larger samples give more reliable results than smaller samples.[21]

---

[21] Although appearing obvious, this statement must be qualified in at least two respects: If the respondents give biased answers, then the information will not be more reliable simply because the sample is larger; also, if a smaller sample is selected and interviewed more carefully, and a larger sample is chosen and interviewed less carefully, then the smaller sample may be more reliable. This is a perennial choice facing the researcher with a fixed research budget.

However, it is not necessary to sample the whole universe or even a substantial part of it to achieve satisfactory precision. Samples amounting to less than 1 per cent of the whole population can often give good reliability, given a creditable sampling procedure.[22] Furthermore, the research objective may not be to establish accurate estimates of some variables, but rather to gain general information and product clues. In exploratory research, very small samples suffice. Much insight about marketing processes and attitudes can be gained from a sample of fewer than 100 persons. In motivation research studies, where the objective is to probe latent product and company attitudes, fewer than 30 depth interviews usually suffice to uncover the full range of product meanings.

Sampling procedure also depends upon the research objective. For exploratory research, nonprobability sampling procedure may be adequate. However, to make an accurate estimate of population characteristics, a random (probability) sample of the population should be drawn. Everyone in the universe should have an equal (or known) chance of being selected for the sample. Different types of persons tend to appear in the sample in rough proportion to their frequency in the population.

Random sampling allows the calculation of confidence limits for sampling errors. If certain conditions are met, it is possible to place a specified degree of confidence on the precision of the sample estimates. One could say "the chances are ninety-five in a hundred that the interval 'five-to-seven bottles' contains the true number of bottles purchased annually by the typical user of Brand X."

Unfortunately, random sampling is almost always more costly than nonrandom sampling.[23] The reasons are several. Random sampling requires finding or developing a list of all the members of the universe; it involves selecting a sample through the use of random numbers; it involves sending interviewers to all parts of the city, region, or nation to find the chosen subjects; it means that the interviewers must call back several times where these respondents are difficult to reach; and other cost-producing factors. In contrast, a nonrandom sampling procedure eliminates the need for listing, for extensive travel, and for expensive call-backs. It only requires finding persons who have the stipulated characteristics and interviewing them.

Some marketing researchers feel that the extra cost of using probability sampling could be better spent in other ways.[24] Specifically, more of the money of a fixed research budget could be spent in designing better questionnaires and hiring better interviewers to reduce response and non-

[22] For samples which are already "large enough" to yield close confidence limits, further increases in sample size will not add much to the precision of the estimates. Sampling precision depends more on the absolute number of units sampled than on the absolute size of the sample universe.

[23] As an example of the cost of random sampling, the National Opinion Research Center charges (as of 1963) $51,000 to conduct 1,500 interviews (with 10-11 open-ended items) selected through probability sampling. This is a cost of $34 per interview. (See *Survey Research Service,* a brochure prepared by the National Opinion Research Center, Chicago, 1963).

[24] Peter G. Peterson and William F. O'Dell, "Selecting Sampling Methods in Commercial Research," *Journal of Marketing,* XV (October 1950), 182-89.

sampling errors which can be just as fatal as sampling errors.[25] This is a real issue, one which the marketing researcher and marketing executives must carefully weigh. Much depends upon whether the sampling or the nonsampling error poses the greater threat to the accuracy of the particular study.

FIELD DATA-COLLECTION PROCEDURES. After the research strategy has been formulated and approved by management, the research department must supervise, or subcontract, the actual task of collecting the data. This phase is generally the most expensive and the most liable to error. Consider, for example, the steps and precautions taken by Alfred Politz in carrying out extensive personal interviewing.

> *A Study of Four Media* was the result of visits by interviewers to the homes of some 8,060 people whose households had been chosen for investigation after rigorous probability analysis of the entire population. . . . Home-office statisticians, working from Census data and detailed maps of each area, gave Politz's interviewers instructions as to exactly which houses were to be visited, and no substitutions were permitted. If the occupants of the house or apartment were not at home, or were too busy for such nonsense, the interviewer was under instructions to try again and again, at least eight times per house, until he received either his interview or a flat rejection. . . .
>
> Of the 8,060 households in the original Politz sample, 7,141 were willing to cooperate at the beginning. The interviewing proceeded over a period of a year, with each household visited six times by the interviewers, and at the end, 5,236 families had survived all six interviews. The final data were drawn from 99,052 visits which accomplished 33,686 completed interviews. The cost of the survey has been variously estimated, but $350,000 is regarded as rock-bottom minimum and $650,000 as likely. . . .
>
> Politz employed 207 interviewers steadily on this project for more than one year. . . . They were selected only after careful screening (one of the major qualifications was an ability to speak the "canned" comments in a natural way), and subjected to intensive training by 35 instructors who traveled back and forth across the country to work with them . . . While the interviewing was proceeding, supervisors checked the work by calling or visiting respondents and sending them stamped, addressed postcards on which to comment on interviewer and interview. In short, every precaution was taken to ensure maximum possible accuracy.[26]

The typical company survey is conducted on a much smaller scale, but the same four major problems arise:

Not-at-homes. When an interviewer does not find anyone at home he can either call back later or substitute the household next door. The latter is the less expensive alternative because the interviewer will not have to

---

[25] Ferber and Hauck believe that response errors in survey research are generally more serious than nonresponse errors. See Robert Ferber and Matthew Hauck, "A Framework for Dealing with Response Errors in Consumer Surveys," in *The Marketing Concept in Action,* ed. Robert M. Kaplan (Chicago: American Marketing Association, 1964), pp. 533-40.

[26] Martin Mayer, *Madison Avenue, U.S.A.* (New York: Harper & Row, Publishers, 1958), pp. 184-87.

travel back to the same block. The only problem is that there is no easy way to learn whether the adjacent household resembles the original one precisely, because no data were collected on the original. The substitution may be biasing.

Refusal to cooperate.   After finding the designated individual at home, the interviewer must interest the person in cooperating. If the time is inconvenient or if the survey appears phony, the designated person may not cooperate. Even if the vast majority of persons cooperated, the lack of cooperation by a minority, for whatever reason, could bias the sample results.

Respondent bias.   The interviewer must also encourage accurate and thoughtful answers. Some respondents may give inaccurate or biased answers in order to finish quickly or for other reasons.

Interviewer bias.   Interviewers are capable of introducing a variety of unconscious biases into the interviewing process, through the mere fact of their age, sex, manner, or intonation. In addition, there is the problem of conscious interviewer bias or dishonesty. Interviewers face a great temptation to fill their quota of interviews as quickly or as cheaply as possible. This can be done by not making the required number of call-backs or claiming refusals to cooperate, or, in extreme cases, actually falsifying an interview.[27]

All of these field collection problems threaten to reduce the value of the findings in one way or another. Most of them can be avoided or minimized by spending more money and employing more sophisticated incentive and checking devices.

PROCESSING AND INTERPRETING THE DATA.   The final phase of a survey is to distill the essentials from the reams of data turned in by the interviewers. This calls for tabulating, classifying, and cross-classifying the responses. This work formerly required weeks of labor, but now can be performed quickly and accurately with the aid of electronic data-processing equipment.

Not only must the essentials be distilled, but they must be presented properly to management. A 200-page report brimming with graphs, tables, and ponderous explanations may impress management, but it is unlikely to motivate them. The major findings should be summarized at the beginning of the report. The more technical aspects of the study should be described later so that they do not burden the reading and yet are available to those executives who are interested.

In short, the gathering of primary data by the survey method is not a novice's task. Skill and experience are called for in stating the research objectives, developing the research strategy, collecting the data, and analyzing the results. Whenever the firm prepares to get primary marketing data —whether through a survey, observation, or experimentation—the greatest care and planning is required if the results are to be useful.

[27] A good survey of this problem is presented in Harper W. Boyd, Jr., and Ralph Westfall, "Interviewer Bias Revisited," *Journal of Marketing Research,* February 1965, pp. 58-63.

Evaluation of Research Results

The results of a research project are not always conclusive. When the results are inconclusive, management must decide whether to make a decision now or to spend further money collecting data. There are two different schools of thought on when to cut off data collection and make a final decision. The two are known, respectively, as the Bayesian and traditional schools of statistical decision theory.[28]

The Bayesian mode of thinking about the value and cost of information is becoming increasingly popular among business executives, combining as it does a way to blend objective information with executive judgment.[29] This section will describe and contrast the Bayesian and traditional approaches to making decisions about information.

BAYESIAN APPROACH

The essentials of the Bayesian mode of reasoning will be illustrated with the following example:

> The management of a company which produces hair tonics is trying to decide whether to add an antidandruff ingredient to its brand to enhance the product's sales. The ingredient increases the cost of the product, and the question is whether sales will increase sufficiently to cover the extra cost. Company management estimates that a 5 per cent increase in sales will be necessary to cover the extra costs of ingredients and promotion.

The company can act in one of three ways. Management can decide to add the ingredient, decide not to add it, or postpone the decision pending a study of likely consumer response. Recognizing the major alternatives is the first step in structuring the decision problem.

The next step is to estimate the expected value (or payoff) of each alternative. If management decides to add the ingredient, it will make or lose money, depending on how much sales increase in relation to the new breakeven cost. If management decides to reject the ingredient, it will not lose or gain any actual dollars. If management decides to carry out consumer research, it will spend so many actual dollars in order to increase the chances of making the right decision.

The payoffs of the three alternatives clearly hinge on the true, but unknown, value of the expected sales increase. How, then, can management decide on the best alternative? If the sales increase would be substantial, it would be a mistake to drop the ingredient or even spend money in marketing research to find this out. If the sales increase would be low, it would be a mistake to add the ingredient or even to carry out marketing research to discover this.

The Bayesian solution to this problem is to ask management for an *intuitive probability distribution* of the possible levels of sales increase. This distribution would show the probabilities in management's mind of attaining different levels of sales because of the new ingredient. Suppose

[28] The Bayesian school takes its name from the Reverend Thomas Bayes, a Presbyterian minister and mathematician who lived in England in the early part of the eighteenth century. A probability theorem developed by Bayes plays a central role in the theory. *(see Sellafor)*

[29] See "Math and Intuition = Decision," *Business Week,* March 24, 1962, pp. 54 ff.

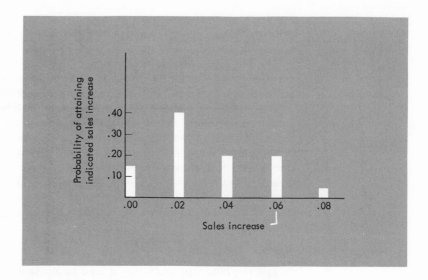

FIGURE 9-3
An intuitive probability distribution for use in Bayesian decision making

the distribution is the one illustrated in Figure 9-3.[30] It shows that management believes that the new ingredient will increase sales somewhere between 0 and 8 per cent (no one believes it will lead to a sales decline). The modal expected sales increase is 2 per cent, and the mean expected sales increase is 3.2 per cent.

If only the mean or modal expected sales increase is considered, management should reject the ingredient. The probability distribution reflects more skepticism than optimism. It should be noted, however, that management believes that there is one chance in four that the new ingredient would push sales up by 6 or more per cent. The best decision is, therefore, not so simple. The profits on introducing the new ingredient may be great enough to justify the gamble.

At this point, the Bayesian analyst uses management's intuitive probability distribution to make a series of calculations estimating the value of the three alternatives. The mathematical details can be found in a number of good expositions.[31] Suppose the analysis shows the best alternative to be that of developing marketing research information through a limited market test. Specifically, the company is advised to test-market its hair tonic with and without the antidandruff ingredient in comparable markets.

Suppose the market test is conducted and sales turn out to be 7 per cent higher where the ingredient has been added. The Bayesians suggest that new calculations be made which blend the sample results with prior management convictions into a new *posterior* probability distribution using Bayes' theorem. This new probability distribution is used to evaluate what the company should now do. Here the Bayesians emphasize that there

[30] When there is more than one decision maker, special techniques are required to average their separate judgments into one group probability distribution. See Norman Dalkey, "An Experimental Application of the Delphi Method to the Use of Experts," *Management Science,* April 1963, pp. 458-67.

[31] See Jack Hirshleifer, "The Bayesian Approach to Statistical Decision: An Exposition," *Journal of Business,* October 1961, pp. 471-89; Harry V. Roberts, "Bayesian Statistics in Marketing," *Journal of Marketing,* XXVII (January 1963), 1-4.

are again *three* choices, not just two, for the new computations may indicate that management should adopt the ingredient, reject the ingredient, or run another market test.

The last alternative is likely to be adopted in this example. When prior skepticism is followed by favorable sample information, the Bayesian calculation usually points to the desirability of more information.

If a further market test confirms the previous market test, the Bayesian calculation is likely now to favor adding the antidandruff ingredient, for the more positive the sample evidence, the more weight it should have in relation to management's initial judgment. On the other hand, if the subsequent market test contradicts the earlier market test, management's skepticism is again renewed. A new Bayesian calculation will reveal whether further test marketing should be conducted or the ingredient dropped. The over-all decision process of the Bayesian approach is illustrated on the left of Figure 9-4.

TRADITIONAL APPROACH

The Bayesian approach might lead to no sampling, a single sample, or repeated sampling. In contrast, the traditional approach typically calls for the collection of some information. No weight is given to management's prior convictions. The traditional decision process is shown on the right of Figure 9-4. Management is asked how much risk it is willing to assume with respect to each possible type of wrong decision (Error Type 1: accepting the ingredient when it should be rejected; Error Type 2: rejecting the ingredient when it should be accepted). These risk levels allow calculation of critical values so that whatever the sample result, there is a clear terminal action which should be taken. The field sample is then taken, the results are tabulated, the critical value is read, and the corresponding terminal decision is made, subject to a known risk. It is unlikely that the company will take another sample unless the first sample leads to suspicious or borderline results.

Scientific Method and Creativity in Marketing Research

The marketing research process—problem definition, model construction, data collection, and data interpretation—can be conducted with various degrees of skill. The best marketing research has two characteristics: scientific method and creativity.

THE SCIENTIFIC METHOD IN MARKETING RESEARCH

Scientific method is one of several ways of going from doubt to belief about some debatable proposition. Suppose management is considering the proposition that a particular advertising campaign which has just been presented by its advertising agency will create substantial sales. Is this true? According to Cohen and Nagel, men have tended to resolve such questions in four different ways.

1. *The method of tenacity.* The proposition is believed or disbelieved simply as a function of the long-term general attitude of the executive toward advertising.

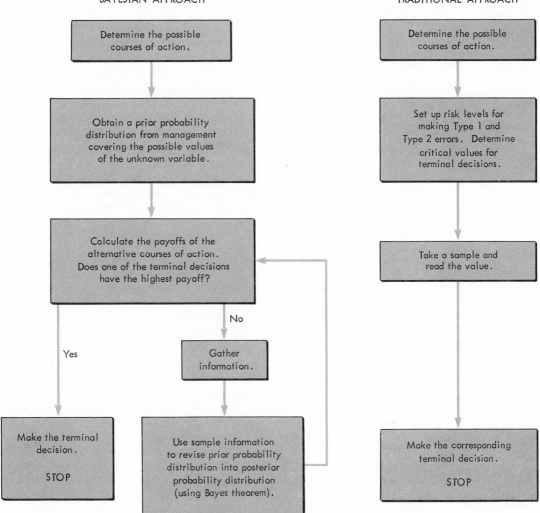

BAYESIAN APPROACH   TRADITIONAL APPROACH

FIGURE 9-4

Contrast between the Bayesian and traditional approaches to statistical decision making

2. *The method of authority.* The proposition is believed or disbelieved by an appeal to authority, either that of the agency or some independent expert in advertising.

3. *The method of intuition.* The proposition is believed or disbelieved on the basis of the intuitive appeal of the particular advertising campaign as outlined.

4. *The method of science.* The proposition is believed or disbelieved on the basis of the best available empirical evidence for and against it.[32]

[32] Morris R. Cohen and Ernest Nagel, *An Introduction to Logic and Scientific Method* (New York: Harcourt, Brace and Company, 1934), pp. 193-96.

The first three methods for settling doubts have in common a dependence on human opinion and willfulness. They involve trying to settle a proposition about the real world with a subjective measuring rod. In contrast, the scientific method encourages the establishment of belief on the basis of objective evidence outside of the particular observer and available to all observers. The method calls for the purging of preconceptions, the development of systematic inductive evidence, and the interpretation of this evidence according to strict canons of logic.

The physical scientist is in a very good position to generate evidence which meets these high standards. He is often able to control virtually all the extraneous variables except the ones he wants to examine. The marketing researcher, on the other hand, can only create highly limited experiments subject to very weak controls. Marketing actions and decisions, therefore, are made with much less scientific support. Nevertheless, the scientific method of the physical sciences represents a worthy model for the marketing researcher, as shown in the following two examples.

MAIL ORDER RETURNS.[33] A small mail order house was suffering from a high rate (30 per cent) of merchandise return. Management asked the marketing research director to try to uncover the causes of the high return rate and to recommend what might be done to reduce it. The research director proceeded to analyze statistically various characteristics of the returned orders, such as the geographical locations of the customers, the sizes of the returned orders, and the type of merchandise returned. In this he used multiple regression techniques. One hypothesis he formulated was that the longer the customer waited for ordered merchandise, the greater the probability of its return. His subsequent regression analysis of the historical data confirmed this hypothesis. He ventured the prediction that the return rate would fall if the company speeded up its delivery time. The company did this, and his prediction proved correct. The researcher had solved the problem through the following four steps, often regarded as the scientific method: observation, formulation of hypothesis, prediction, and testing.[34]

NEW GASOLINE MARKETING METHOD.[35] In the early 1950's, the Sun Oil Company was the last of the major oil companies to merchandise a single grade of gasoline. Management wondered how much longer it could retain the single-grade policy in light of the trend toward heavier compression engines. Management appointed an operations research task force composed of social and physical scientists, together with operating and administrative personnel to consider this problem.

Their first action was to identify the major alternatives facing the company. The following four alternatives were considered: (1) retaining only a single grade and gradually shifting the octane upward; (2) marketing a

[33] Horace C. Levinson, "Experiences in Commercial Operations Research," *Operations Research,* August 1953, pp. 220-39.

[34] See James H. Lorie and Harry V. Roberts, *Basic Methods of Marketing Research* (New York: McGraw-Hill Book Company, 1951), chap. 3.

[35] James S. Cross, "Operations Research in Solving a Marketing Problem," *Journal of Marketing,* XXV (January 1961), 30-34.

regular and a premium grade; (3) marketing a regular, premium, and a superpremium grade; and (4) marketing several grades by custom blending them at the pump. The last alternative, custom blending, represented a radically new concept in gasoline marketing. It involved meeting each car's octane requirement through a single pump which blended the fuel mix on the spot.

Custom blending had to be checked for technical and marketing feasibility before it could be included as a legitimate alternative. After two years of intensive research, the technical problems of custom blending were licked. The marketing problem was to determine how consumers would react to custom blending. The company arranged for its first market test in southeastern United States. Using experimental and control stations, Sun Oil found that custom blending increased both the volume of sales and the proportion of sales made to high-priced, high-octane requirement cars.

The final task consisted of evaluating the likely rate of return for each of the four policy alternatives. The custom blending alternative turned out to have the highest probable payoff, and management decided to adopt it. This project was characterized throughout by objectivity and attention to evidence. Only after determining in a detached scientific way whether custom blending was better than the other alternatives did management decide to make a decision in its favor.

THE CREATIVE FACTOR IN MARKETING RESEARCH

The scientific method is one of the characteristics of good marketing research. There is an additional ingredient which can transform the research from being competent to being outstanding. That ingredient is creativity. Two examples of creative marketing research are described below:

INSTANT COFFEE.[36] When instant coffee was first introduced, housewives complained that it did not taste like real coffee. Yet in blindfold tests, many of these same housewives could not distinguish between a cup of instant coffee and a cup of real coffee. This indicated that much of their resistance was psychological. But exactly what underlay their resistance? The researcher decided to design two almost identical shopping lists, the only difference being that regular coffee was on one list and instant coffee on the other. The regular coffee list was given to one group of housewives and the instant coffee list was given to a different, but comparable, group. Both groups were asked to guess the social and personal characteristics of the woman whose shopping list they saw. The comments were pretty much the same with one significant difference; a higher proportion of the housewives whose list contained instant coffee described the subject as "lazy, a spendthrift, a poor wife, and failing to plan well for her family." These women obviously were imputing to the fictional housewife their own anxieties and negative images about the use of instant coffee. The instant coffee company now knew the nature of the resistance and could develop a campaign to change the image of the housewife who serves instant coffee.

[36] Mason Haire, "Projective Techniques in Marketing Research," *Journal of Marketing,* XIV (April 1950), 649-56.

MAGAZINE READERSHIP.[37]   People who are interviewed in their homes about their current magazine subscriptions report reading *Harper's, Atlantic Monthly,* and the *New Yorker* with a higher frequency than seems plausible in terms of the circulation figures for these magazines. The hypothesis has been put forth that many people claim to read these magazines to gain prestige in the eyes of the interviewer. From a research point of view, the task is to determine the percentage of people who claim readership although they do not actually read these magazines. Among the possible approaches is to ask them to describe a recent article or to ask to see a copy of the magazine. The research director in this case thought up a less embarrassing ruse. A few weeks after the interviewing, he sent solicitors to the homes which had claimed to read these magazines to collect magazines for charities. These pickups were examined outside the home, and only a fraction actually included the previously mentioned magazines.

In general, marketing research problems, especially the less routine ones, can be handled with different degrees of deftness. There is room for inspiration at every stage: in tracking down the true problem, building a model, developing the means of getting the data, and analyzing the data. Good marketing research has aspects of both art and science.

Summary

Marketing research has been expanding rapidly in the United States as a means of coping with the growing size of markets and sums of money involved in marketing decisions. Marketing research requires the systematic definition of problems, construction of models, collection of data, and interpretation of results in the interests of improving marketing decision making and control. Data collection is most efficiently conducted when the marketing problem and variables are carefully defined. The marketing researcher's job is to gather the required data through secondary sources or through primary means such as observation, experimentation, or survey research. The marketing executive should understand the strengths and weaknesses of these alternative data collection methods in order to use the information critically. Ultimately he will blend the information with his prior judgments in a way suggested by the Bayesian approach. He recognizes that research has both scientific and creative aspects which affect the results.

Questions and Problems

1. (a) Suggest how a liquor company might estimate the amount of liquor consumed in a legally dry town. (b) Suggest how a research organization might estimate the number of people who read given magazines in a doctor's office. (c) Suggest six different ways in which a sample of men can be gathered to be interviewed on their usage of hair tonics.

[37] See A. B. Blankenship, "Creativity in Consumer Research," *Journal of Marketing,* XXV (October 1961), 34-38.

2. What is the major issue (impartiality, validity, reliability, homogeneity) that is likely to come up in the following uses of secondary data: (a) Using a time series of disposable personal income (in current dollars) to indicate the historical trend in consumer purchasing power; (b) Using the reported gross national products of different nations to compare their levels of national output; (c) Using a local chamber of commerce study on the average income of the community; (d) Using a man-in-the-street sample to estimate the proportion of men who own dinner jackets.

3. A marketing research department is asked to carry out twenty different research projects, but it only has funds for ten. Suggest how the research department might rank the twenty proposals in terms of relative payoff.

4. What is the major weakness of the simple time-series experimental design? the recurrent time-series design? Are you convinced that more complex experimental research designs can handle the complexity of marketing processes?

5. Suppose an experiment calls for developing two matched groups of housewives. How should the groups be formed? What if the groups appear different after they are chosen?

6. "A manufacturer of automobiles is testing a new direct-mail approach B versus a standard approach A. An experiment is conducted in which each of the two approaches is tried out on random samples of size n (sample size 2n in total) from a large national mailing list. Suppose that n = 100,000 so that 200,000 is the total sample size of the experiment. During a three-month period, approach B has 761 sales and A has 753." What decision should be made? List the alternatives and the rationale of each.

7. Suppose a company is considering whether to develop and introduce a new product whose payoff will depend upon the true but unknown state of the economy. The research director estimates the following payoffs depending upon the state of the economy: prosperity, $2,000,000; recession, $300,000. Top management believes that there is a .8 probability of prosperity and a .2 probability of a recession. What is the most that the company should be willing to pay for an accurate forecast? Why?

8. Suppose a research director evaluates several different alternatives facing a company and estimates the expected payoff and risk of each. Show how his findings might be presented in a diagram.

chapter 10

Marketing Models and Systems

The marketing research process was defined earlier as involving the four steps of problem definition, model construction, data collection, and data interpretation. Data collection and interpretation have traditionally played the largest role in marketing research. More recently, increased attention is being paid to model construction, especially in connection with solving nonroutine marketing problems. The growing literature in this field suggests that the marketing executive will find it increasingly desirable to use, discuss, and initiate operations research studies in marketing. Fortunately, the basic ideas and the major marketing applications are easy to describe.

This chapter is divided into four sections. The first describes the nature and scope of model-building efforts in marketing. The second contrasts various types of models, such as descriptive and decision models, and quantitative and verbal models. The third describes the five types of models that have the most promising applications in the marketing area: allocation models, game models, brand-switching models, waiting-line models, and simulation models. The final section discusses the contributions computers are making to information processing and problem solving in marketing.

The Nature and Scope of Model Building in Marketing

The term "model" has become very fashionable in marketing and is often used interchangeably with the term "theory." A useful distinction, however, can be drawn between the two terms. "Theory" can be used to describe the body of basic and substantive knowledge in a field. A model, on the other hand, represents a particular construction using theory which is designed to serve an instrumental purpose. A model can be developed to explain how advertising works, to forecast sales, to select sites, and so forth. A model requires only the specification of primary variables and an explicit statement of their interrelationships.

Models have been formulated for the economic system (Keynes), the human psyche (Freud), and the evolution of man (Darwin). The *organization chart* is a model of the firm's formal authority structure, the *profit and loss statement* is a model of the firm's revenue and cost flows, and the *normal curve* is a model of the distribution of the characteristics of many populations. In addition to these explicit models, people carry countless models in their heads regarding the behavior of various real-world systems.

Experienced marketing executives may be said to carry very good models of marketing processes in their head.

THE GROWTH OF MODEL BUILDING IN MARKETING

Historically, there has been a tendency to contrast marketing research and model building in marketing. In 1955 John A. Howard characterized the marketing researcher's task in the following way:

> He concerns himself with obtaining market data for certain kinds of management decisions—specifically, these are "effect" data: the effect of an advertising campaign on sales, the effect of changing the geographical distribution of the sales force, the effect of a new package, the effect of a price change, or the effect of a different trade channel.

In contrast, Howard said that the task of the operations researcher was to build mathematical models, adding:

> The newer models were making such severe data demands on the marketing researcher that . . . if all operations analysts were shot at sunrise tomorrow, company market researchers would live longer and be happier.[1]

It is becoming clear, as time passes, that this distinction is overdrawn. Model building and data estimation are not in the separate domains of operations researchers and marketing researchers, respectively. Aspects of each appear in both.[2] Even in defining marketing research as the job of estimating "effects," it is clear that some analytical structure must be used or assumed. The historical bias of marketing research lies not in the absence of model building but in the failure to develop it profoundly. Increasingly, marketing scholars are recognizing the parallel importance of both model building and data estimation. Wroe Alderson made this point in 1962:

> The use of systematic marketing analysis in the United States is scarcely more than 50 years old. Over that entire period the market analyst has struggled with two fundamental research problems. One is to get the facts and the other is to analyze the facts in a way that is helpful to executive judgment. During most of the 50-year history of research, it concentrated on the first task of obtaining the marketing facts. . . . Marketing analysis is now moving into a new stage of methodological awareness. . . . The key concept . . . is that of the explicit analytical model. . . . It would be a mistake to assume that quantitative models contribute only to the analytical rather than the data side of problem solving. . . . The very term "quantitative model" suggests the combination of empirical data with the logical structure of the system which the model represents. Instead of perpetuating the argument between the fact finders and the logicians, the new emphasis on explicit quantitative models holds out the hope that these separate contributions can now be successfully integrated.[3]

[1] John A. Howard, "Operations Research and Market Research," *Journal of Marketing,* XX (October 1955), 143.

[2] The relationship between marketing research and operations research is explored in more detail in Philip Kotler, "Quantitative Analysis in Marketing Research Courses," in *Reflections on Progress in Marketing,* ed. L. George Smith (Chicago: American Marketing Association, 1964), pp. 651-63, esp. pp. 657-60.

[3] Wroe Alderson, "Introduction," in Ronald E. Frank, Alfred A. Kuehn, and William F. Massy, eds., *Quantitative Techniques in Marketing Analysis* (Homewood, Ill.: Richard D. Irwin, Inc., 1962), pp. xi-xvii.

Marketing is one of the last of the functional business areas to undergo model-building efforts. Most of the business models grew out of operations research on military problems during World War II. The operations researchers who sought solutions to problems of supply, bombing, and strategy were primarily mathematicians. When the war ended, military problems lost their urgency, and some of the researchers turned their attention to some classic business problems.

Problems in the field of production and inventory control were the first to be examined. There are several reasons for this. The early postwar period was characterized by a large pent-up demand, and the main concern was to find ways of increasing output. Several years would pass before the main concern would turn to finding markets. Also production and inventory problems were more tractable than marketing problems. The actions and sentiments of human beings count for less on a highly automated production line than in the market place. And the major variables in such problems as scheduling the use of machines and maintaining adequate inventories are quantitative; the variables are price, cost, quantity, and time. Furthermore, the theory of production had attained a more coherent and satisfactory development in the hands of economists than the theory of demand. Much of economic theory revolved around the theory of the firm and particularly the concept of a production function (relating output to productive inputs). Statisticians before and after the war had made some progress in measuring this function.

Problems of physical distribution—location, routing, inventory—also received early attention by operations researchers. They have a quantitative character and invite mathematical analysis. One of the most publicized early applications in the area of routing concerned the mathematical determination of shipping schedules for the H. J. Heinz Company.[4] This company manufactured ketchup in six plants and distributed it to about seventy warehouses around the country. The company's plant capacity on the West Coast exceeded that region's market requirements, while the reverse was true in the East. Therefore, the total freight bill could not be minimized by simply shipping output from each plant to the warehouse nearest to it. The problem of finding a shipping schedule that minimized total freight cost was translated into linear programming terms, and the computer was able to deliver a better schedule at a faster speed than experienced company personnel could hope to emulate.

Early operations research breakthroughs on problems of production and physical distribution did not surprise marketing practitioners, because the emphasis in these business problems was quantitative. Marketing problems were thought to involve too many qualitative factors. Yet marketing studies of a mathematical character began to appear in the late 1950's, dealing with such topics as advertising budgeting, sales force allocation, and pricing strategy. The trickle turned into a stream, and by the early 1960's a bibliography listing over 200 marketing articles of a quantitative character as well as several different collections of readings had been pub-

[4] See Alexander Henderson and Robert Schlaifer, "Mathematical Programming: Better Information for Better Decision Making," *Harvard Business Review,* May-June 1954, pp. 73-100.

lished.[5] Furthermore, the Marketing Science Institute was formed in 1962   *223*
to abet scientific research into marketing, and the American Marketing   *Marketing Models*
Association, in a separate move, launched the new *Journal of Marketing*   *and Systems*
Research.

THE VALUE OF MARKETING MODELS

Model building in marketing is far from receiving universal acceptance.
Those who are closest to the market place where the actual battles are
fought tend to be the most skeptical. They are continually impressed with
the seeming uniqueness of each marketing situation. They express four
types of criticisms of model building in marketing:

Models oversimplify marketing reality

Marketing reality keeps changing faster than the model is changed

Marketing data often are poor or nonexistent

Models have not yet been demonstrated to lead to superior decision making
in marketing

Some of these criticisms show a misunderstanding of the purposes of
model building. While there are formidable problems in developing useful
models of marketing processes, model-building efforts are expected to
lead to three benefits.

EXPLICATION.   Much of the personal thinking of executives about
marketing problems is characterized by vagueness, intuition, and highly
personal frames of reference. Model building's major contribution lies in
explicating otherwise obscure assumptions and relationships. The model
spells out a conception of how a particular phenomenon works. Debate
can be focused on specific assumptions and relationships. Communication
is facilitated. The model clarifies the data that are needed. The model can
be used experimentally to probe the probable consequences of different
courses of action.

EVENTUAL USEFULNESS.   Models have to mature. As one analyst put it:

The model from which these results were derived (a model for the budgeting of advertising) is relatively complex when viewed in its entirety. This
research was begun some seven years ago with a very simple model—a
model which has been modified and extended repeatedly in the light of
additional evidence.[6]

[5] Robert D. Buzzell, *A Basic Bibliography on Mathematical Methods in Marketing*
(Chicago: American Marketing Association, 1962); Frank M. Bass, Robert D. Buzzell,
Mark R. Greene, William Lazer, Edgar A. Pessemier, Donald L. Shawver, Abraham
Shuchman, Chris A. Theodore, and George W. Wilson, eds., *Mathematical Methods
and Models in Marketing* (Homewood, Ill.: Richard D. Irwin, Inc., 1961); Ronald E.
Frank, *et al., op. cit.;* Wroe Alderson and Stanley Shapiro, eds., *Marketing and the
Computer* (Englewood Cliffs, N.J.: Prentice-Hall, Inc., 1962); and Ralph L. Day, ed.,
Marketing Models, Quantitative and Behavioral (Scranton, Pa.: International Text-
book Company, 1964).

[6] Alfred A. Kuehn, "How Advertising Performance Depends on Other Marketing
Factors," *Journal of Advertising Research,* March 1962, pp. 2-10.

Models are susceptible of cumulative development, and as they mature, they are often far superior to any lay analysis of the same marketing problem.

SERENDIPITY. The value of a model is not to be judged solely on whether it yields an operational model for marketing decision making and problem solving. The by-products of model-building effort are often just as important. The effort helps to clarify what is known and what remains unknown. Often it stimulates new hypotheses. The unexpected things that may be learned in the course of building a model may be of the most value.

Classification of Models

The marketing executive is in a much better position to understand and evaluate marketing models when he is aware of the major types of models. The variety of model types is illustrated in Figure 10-1 and discussed on the following pages.

DESCRIPTIVE AND DECISION MODELS

Models can be classified according to whether their purpose is description or decision making. A *descriptive model* purports to describe things as they are. It contains no value judgment about the phenomena being de-

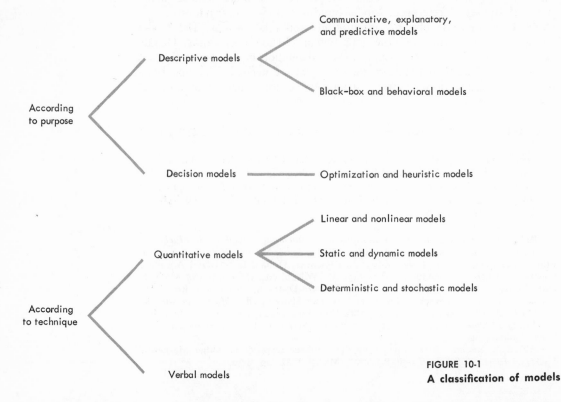

FIGURE 10-1
A classification of models

picted, its only concern being to bare the underlying operations of the system. A *decision model* purports to probe how things should be. It is a formulation developed for the purpose of evaluating the merits of different actions.[7]

DESCRIPTIVE MODELS. Descriptive models can be subclassified in different ways. Two different classifications are described below.

Communicative, explanatory, and predictive models. John A. Howard made these distinctions.[8] A *communicative model* describes the structural arrangements of the elements in a system. A road map is a model in this sense, and so is the description of the communication process.[9] An *explanatory model* describes the causal relationships among a restricted set of elements in a system. For example, in the economist's model of price determination under pure competition an explanation is offered, on the basis of simple assumptions about the response of buyers and sellers to price changes, of how prices and outputs are determined in a free, competitive market. A *predictive model* describes the causal relationships among a comprehensive set of elements in a system. The Keynesian model of national income determination is an example of this insofar as it has been shown capable of yielding useful predictions of short-term business movements.

"Black-box" and behavioral models. Robert D. Buzzell distinguished between "black-box" models and behavioral models.[10] A *black-box model* is one which links together two or more variables without postulating the specific mechanisms that relate them. The inputs and outputs are known, but the contents of the box connecting them is left "black" or unspecified. A *behavioral model* attempts to specify the intervening behavioral factors and sequences occurring between the reception of stimuli and its crystallization in action. The interest centers in explicating exactly what occurs when customers are exposed to certain marketing stimuli or competitors face certain marketing challenges.

Single equations are a good example of black-box models. The analyst sets up an equation where sales is represented as a function of advertising, price, consumer incomes, and other factors. The equation may show a statistically significant fit to historical data and be useful in prediction, but it is generally not very satisfying from an explanatory point of view. The exact and complex relationships and feedbacks are not indicated by the equation.

Many *sales experiments* are also of the black-box model variety. The

[7] The distinction between *descriptive* and *decision* models has gone by many names. *Positive* and *normative* models: Milton Friedman, *Essays in Positive Economics* (Chicago: University of Chicago Press, 1953); *systems* and *goal* models: William Lazer, "The Role of Models in Marketing," *Journal of Marketing,* XXVI (April 1962), 9-14; and *behavioral* and *optimization* models: William F. Massy and Frederick E. Webster, Jr., "Model Building in Marketing," *Journal of Marketing Research,* May 1964, pp. 9-13.

[8] Howard, *op. cit.,* p. 144.

[9] See Figure 18-1, p. 455.

[10] Robert D. Buzzell, *Mathematical Models and Marketing Management* (Boston: Harvard University Graduate School of Business Administration, Division of Research, 1964), pp. 206-26.

research director selects a set of presumably comparable cities and introduces a different level of advertising in each. He later observes the level of sales in each city and develops a mathematical relationship between sales and advertising. The relationship may take the form of the familiar S-curve.[11] But this curve is just a gross description of market response to market stimuli, devoid of any behavioral explanation.

Behavioral models, on the other hand, often take the form of simulation models. In one developed by the writer, 100 simulated customers make individual brand choices each week among three competing brands of coffee.[12] Their brand choices are influenced by their socioeconomic characteristics, past brand choices, interim exposure to advertising, and in-store perception of competing prices, deals, and displays. This is a behavioral model because it specifies relationships among customer characteristics, attitudes, and reactions.

Cyert and March created a behavioral model to explain how department store buyers make ordering and pricing decisions.[13] The model used logical-flow diagrams to represent what buyers said they did when they were making decisions. When tested on a computer, the model predicted more than 90 per cent of the actual prices set.

Although black-box models can be effective and sufficient for many uses, behavioral models are more ambitious ventures. They represent the aspiration to develop an actual theory of the behavioral dynamics of firms and markets.

DECISION MODELS. Decision models are also of various kinds. Most are of a postwar vintage, having largely developed out of the investigations of operations researchers and statistical decision theorists. A notable exception is the breakeven-point model which has been used by businessmen for over a generation to make decisions about introducing and retaining products. The distinguishing characteristic of decision models is that they all contain an evaluational element, some criterion for distinguishing the value of different states or solutions. Two of the standard decision models with particular relevance to marketing are allocation models and game-theory models, which are described later on.

Decision models are subclassified into *optimization* and *heuristic* models. An *optimization model,* the class most used in operations research to date, is one for which computational routines exist for finding the best solution. Thus if a problem is stated in linear programming terms, a "best" solution to the problem as stated is automatically guaranteed.

A *heuristic model* is one for which computational routines are not available for finding the best solution, but which offers other advantages. The model may be a much more flexible and complex statement of the problem, one which may avoid the restrictive assumptions of a linear programming statement of the problem. To use this model, the analyst applies *heuristics,* defined as rules of thumb which tend to shorten the time required to find a reasonably good solution. The heuristics may amount to the common-

---

[11] See Figure 12-2b, p. 272.

[12] Philip Kotler, "The Competitive Marketing Simulator—A New Management Tool," *California Management Review,* VII, No. 3 (Spring 1965), 49-60.

[13] Richard M. Cyert and James G. March, *A Behavioral Theory of the Firm* (Englewood Cliffs, N.J.: Prentice-Hall, Inc., 1963), chaps. 7 and 8.

sense procedures used by actual decision makers in their problem solving. For example, in a model to determine good warehouse locations, an heuristic used may be "Only consider locations in large cities." This may exclude a perfectly good location in a small city but the savings in having to check far fewer cities is expected to compensate for the omission. It is hoped that the solution arrived at through a rich modeling of the problem may be better than the "best" solution arrived at through a simplified optimization modeling of the problem.[14]

INTERDEPENDENCE OF DESCRIPTIVE AND DECISION MODELS. While it is useful to distinguish between descriptive models and decision models, it is also important to appreciate their interdependence. The marketing executive's ultimate interest lies in decision models for determining price, advertising, sales-force appropriations, and other marketing variables. But it is becoming increasingly apparent that decision models must incorporate better descriptive models of the behavioral relationships in the problem. Thus, in creating a media decision model, one has to have better descriptive models of the relationship between advertising exposures, consumer attitudes, and consumer responses. Or, in creating a retail facilities planning model, one has to have better descriptive models of the relationship between customer waiting times and customer store switching behavior. Or in creating a game model, one has to have better descriptive models of the relationship between possible company moves and probable competitor reactions. In general, the development of effective decision models depends on the development of better descriptive models.

QUANTITATIVE AND VERBAL MODELS

Many models are quantitative, but this is not an essential characteristic of models. A model is called quantitative when the variables and their relationships are expressed in mathematical language. Otherwise, the model is verbal.

QUANTITATIVE MODELS. Quantitative models can be subclassified in many ways. The major subclassifications are described below.

Linear and nonlinear models. A *linear model* is one where all the relationships between variables are expressed as straight lines. This means that a unit change in one variable has a *constant* marginal impact on a related variable. The advertising-sales relationship would be linear if every $100 increase in advertising created a $1,000 increase in sales, no matter how much had already been spent. This, of course, is dubious, because increasing or diminishing returns to advertising are likely to be found at different points in the relationship. It is also likely that other marketing inputs, such as price and sales call time, do not relate to sales in a thoroughly linear way. The assumption of linearity is generally useful only as a first approximation for mathematical convenience. It may be a good approximation, but marketing models will eventually have to incorporate more nonlinear relationships.

Static and dynamic models. A *static model* centers on the ultimate

[14] See Alfred A. Kuehn, "Heuristic Programming: A Useful Technique for Marketing," in *Marketing Precision and Executive Action,* ed. Charles H. Hindersman (Chicago: American Marketing Association, 1962), pp. 162-70.

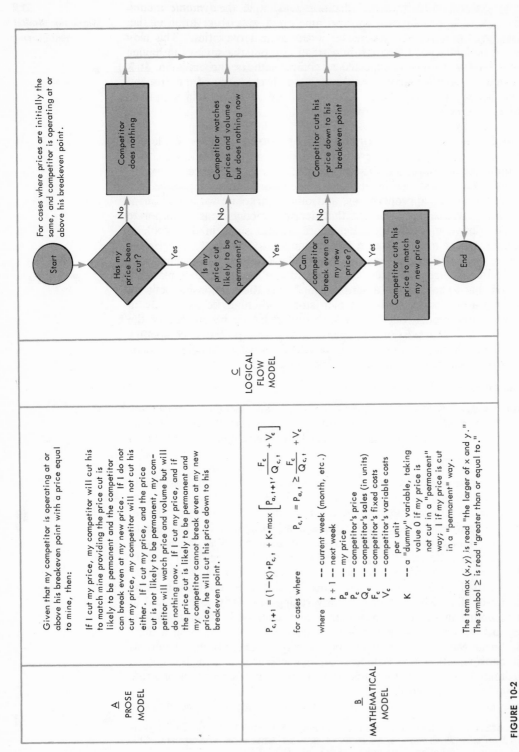

FIGURE 10-2

Three models of a competitor's reaction to a price cut

Redrawn from William F. Massy and Jim D. Savvas, "Logical Flow Models for Marketing Analysis," *Journal of Marketing*, XXVIII (January 1964), 32.

state (or solution) of a system, independent of time. A *dynamic model* brings time explicitly into its framework and allows the observation of the movement of the state (or solution) of the system over time. The elementary demand-supply diagram in beginner economics courses represents a static model of price determination, in that it indicates where price and output will be in equilibrium without indicating the path of adjustment through time. Most competitive game models are also static, in that they indicate what a player should do without indicating how he should react to subsequent developments. Brand-switching models are dynamic, in that they become the basis for predicting period-to-period changes in customer states.

Deterministic and stochastic models. A *deterministic model* is one in which chance plays no role. The solution is determined by a set of exact relationships. The linear programming model for determining blends (oils, animal feeds, candies) is deterministic because the relationships are exact and the cost data are known. A *stochastic model,* on the other hand, is one where chance or random variables are introduced explicitly. Econometric models of national income determination are often stochastic to provide for random shocks and external disturbances. Brand-switching models are also stochastic, in that customer's brand choices are regulated by probabilities.

VERBAL MODELS. Models in which the variables and their relationships are described in prose rather than mathematically are *verbal models*. A familiar verbal model in marketing describes purchasing disposition as passing through six stages:

> . . . advertising should move people from *awareness* . . . to *knowledge* . . . to *liking* . . . to *preference* . . . to *conviction* . . . to *purchase*.[15]

Another verbal model is the one elaborated by Everett Rogers to explain the stages in the acceptance of innovations.[16] Many logical-flow diagrams are also essentially verbal models of processes. Figure 10-2 shows the same model cast in three different forms: in prose, in mathematical terms, and in logical-flow diagram terms.

Are quantitative models better? When quantitative and verbal models are compared, it is often implied that the former are more desirable. This is the implication of Lord Kelvin's famous dictum:

> When you can measure what you are speaking about and express it in numbers, you know something about it; or when you cannot measure it, when you cannot express it in numbers, your knowledge is of a meager and unsatisfactory kind. It may be the beginning of knowledge, but you have scarcely in your thought advanced to the stage of a science.[17]

There are indeed many advantages of trying to express models in the

---

[15] Robert J. Lavidge and Gary A. Steiner, "A Model for Predictive Measurements of Advertising Effectiveness," *Journal of Marketing*, XXV (October 1961), 59-62.

[16] See Chapter 14, p. 343.

[17] Sir William Thomson (Lord Kelvin), *Popular Lectures and Addresses* (London: The Macmillan Company, 1889), vol. 1, p. 73.

powerful language of mathematics. Consider this thoughtful summary of the advantages.

> First, the rigors of translating from verbal to symbolic form requires much clarification (and generalization) and frequently a great deal of fuzziness is rubbed off in the translation. This may result in immediate qualitative gains in understanding. Second, even within a single social science (and to a high degree among social sciences), the specialized sub-disciplines have jargons of their own that reduce the interchange of ideas. Reduction of all to a common language may reveal interrelations previously not known to any of them. Third, verbal theorizing is much more at the mercy of intuition than is mathematical analysis. Finally, mathematics is tremendously more efficient than prose theorizing. Verbal theory is pick and shovel; mathematics is steam shovel. The superiority in efficiency is so great that the difference ceases to be one of degree and becomes one of kind.[18]

At the same time, not all models can be cast in mathematical form, and if they could, many would lose something. For mathematics as a language suffers from one great limitation; it lacks *nuance*. Just as mathematics can plumb to certain depths of analysis that prose cannot achieve, prose can soar to heights of understanding that mathematics cannot reach. A good psychoanalyst uses a verbal model of human behavior that cannot be expressed in any set of mathematical equations, however complex. A good marketing executive uses a verbal model of his markets which cannot be completely captured in any set of equations. A great many models are intrinsically verbal. All that can be asked is that the language be as explicit and consistent as possible.

Useful Marketing Models

Not all models developed by operations researchers have direct relevance to problems in the marketing area. There are elaborate scheduling and assembly-line balancing models for production problems and portfolio selection and capital budgeting models for financial problems, but they have only peripheral relevance to marketing problems. However, the detailed development of other operations research models is already leading to promising uses in marketing problem solving. Of the five models described, all are mainly quantitative; two—allocation and game-theory models—are decision models, and three—waiting-line, brand-switching, and simulation models—are descriptive.[19]

ALLOCATION MODELS

An allocation model helps the decision maker allocate scarce resources so as to maximize some given objective(s). In marketing, the scarce resources may be salesmen who are too few to make all the desirable calls or advertising dollars which are too limited to produce adequate exposure.

[18] Paul G. Craig, "An Introduction to Economic Models," an unpublished workshop paper in the Institute of Basic Mathematics with Applications to Business, Harvard University, March 1960.

[19] This material is adapted from Philip Kotler, "The Use of Mathematical Models in Marketing," *Journal of Marketing,* XXVII (October 1963), 31-41.

The problem is to find the one "best" way to allocate or *program* these resources in terms of specified objectives and constraints.

Mathematical programming is the best-known mathematical format for handling a large class of allocation problems. It calls for expressing the decision maker's objective(s) in the form of a mathematical function whose value is to be optimized. Various constraints are also introduced, in the form of equations and/or inequalities. These constraints reduce the number of admissible alternatives. A mathematical procedure called the "simplex algorithm" searches among the alternatives to find the one that optimizes the value of the objective function.

In *linear programming,* the objective function and all the constraints are expressed as straight-line relationships.[20] The term *nonlinear programming* is reserved for a problem formulation where either some constraint(s) or the objective function, or both, are not linear. One example is *quadratic programming,* which uses a second-degree curve for some of the constraints or objective function, or both. Nonlinear programming problems are much harder to solve.

Integer programming is a variant so named because the optimal solution is constrained to consist of integer number answers. For example, suppose X_1 represents how many salesmen should be hired. If the answer is *not* constrained to be an integer, it could be a mixed decimal such as 9.4. What does it mean to hire 9.4 salesmen? Should the answer be "rounded" to 9 salesmen or 10 salesmen? The solution is not obvious, and the decision may involve a difference of thousands of dollars. Integer programming is a way of avoiding the ambiguities of fractional answers.

Dynamic programming, the most complicated of the programming variants, is applied to problems where a series of *consecutive, interdependent* decisions have to be made. Purchasing decisions, for example, must be made throughout the year; today's decision must be made in terms of what it implies for the decision choices in the next period, which in turn will affect the decision choices in the following period, and so on. The marketing executive must look at the whole horizon of decisions and choose that decision sequence which implies maximization of profits for the given time horizon.[21]

Some specialized versions of the programming model are useful in a marketing context. The Heinz Company case discussed earlier utilized a version called the *transportation model.* This model defines the existence of several *origins* (such as warehouses) and *destinations* (such as stores), and the unit cost of shipping from every origin to every destination. Furthermore, the amount of goods available for shipment from each warehouse and the amount of goods ordered by each retail store are specified. The problem is to find, under the given constraints, which warehouses should ship their goods to which stores, in order to minimize total transportation costs. A sample problem is shown in Figure 10-3. The reader can try to find the least-cost shipping allocation by trial and error. Mathematical

[20] Applications of linear programming to the marketing-mix problem are described in Chapter 12, pp. 279-81, and to the media-selection problem in Chapter 18, pp. 477-78.

[21] For an application to the problem of allocating sales effort to different territories, see Andrew Vazsonyi, *Scientific Programming in Business and Industry* (New York: John Wiley & Sons, Inc., 1958), pp. 219-27.

Warehouse	Store 1	Store 2	Store 3	Warehouse availabilities
A	$5	$3	$6	300
B	$2	$9	$4	200
C	$3	$7	$8	600
D	$6	$1	$4	500
Store requirements	200	1,000	400	1,600

FIGURE 10-3

Unit shipping costs from various warehouses to various stores

analysis would show that the least-cost shipping allocation would be $5,800. *$4,800.*

The *assignment model* is a variant of the transportation model, with promising applications to other problems. In the assignment model, the number of origins *equals* the number of destinations, and each origin is associated with *only one* destination. For example, the problem might be to find the optimal assignment of four salesmen to four territories, where estimates have been made of the expected sales of each salesman in each territory.[22] The solution is fairly straightforward in this problem but requires more advanced mathematical techniques when the number of salesmen and territories grows.

Another problem is known as the *"traveling-salesman"* problem. Suppose a salesman must make calls in *n* cities. This means that there are *n factorial* possible routes. The problem is to find the one route which minimizes either the total time or total cost of travel. The problem is becoming increasingly manageable with advanced mathematical analysis and high-speed computers.[23]

In general, allocation models hold great promise for aiding in the solution of such important marketing problems as media selection, allocation of sales force, determination of the best product line, site location, and selection of channels of distribution.

GAME MODELS

Game theory is the name given to the systematic investigation of rational decision making in the context of uncertainty concerning the moves of competitors. It will be illustrated in terms of the following simple example:

Suppose Row and Column are the managers of two competing supermarkets. Every week, Row and Column must choose some item to promote as the "Special of the Week." Neither one knows in advance what the other

[22] See Chapter 19, pp. 515-16.

[23] See John D. C. Little, Katta G. Murty, Dura W. Sweeney, and Caroline Karel, "An Algorithm for the Traveling Salesman Problem," *Operations Research,* November-December 1963, pp. 972-89; and Robert L. Karg and Gerald L. Thompson, "A Heuristic Approach to Solving Traveling Salesman Problems," *Management Science,* January 1964, pp. 225-48.

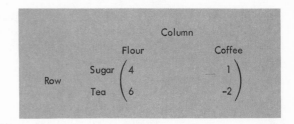

FIGURE 10-4
Payoffs to Row resulting from various decision combinations

is going to feature. However, each can roughly estimate the profit that would result from every pair of possible choices. Row estimates his payoffs to be those shown in Figure 10-4.

Figure 10-4 is interpreted as follows. If Row featured sugar and his competitor featured flour, Row would gain 4 (say in hundreds of dollars); that is, more of the marginal customers will "flow" to his store, and the profit derived from this extra trade is estimated as 4. And Column will lose 4. If Row featured sugar and his competitor featured coffee, Row would gain only 1 and Column would lose 1. If Row featured tea and his competitor featured flour, then Row would gain 6 and Column would lose 6. However, if Row featured tea and Column featured coffee, Row would lose 2 and Column would gain 2.

If Row is to adopt one item and feature it week after week, which should it be? If he chooses sugar, he will gain at least 1 each week and possibly 4; with tea, he may lose as much as 2. He will probably choose sugar. Column, using the same reasoning, can lose as much as 6 each week with flour, but no more than 1 each week with coffee. He will probably chose coffee. By seeking to minimize their maximum possible loss (the criterion of pessimism), they both will adopt choices which in this case are in mutual equilibrium. Neither could gain more by making a different move.

Sometimes the solution will not be in equilibrium, and each could gain by surprising the other. The best strategy would be for each to determine his weekly decision randomly, using the mix of probabilities which will leave him best off in the long run.[24]

The Row and Column example illustrates one of the simplest types of games: *a two-person, zero-sum game.* Only two players are involved, and they transfer a fixed sum of money between each other. The term "zero-sum" is used because in each play the sum of one player's gain (positive) and the other player's loss (negative) is zero. More interesting, but at the same time more difficult mathematically are the *three-or-more person, nonzero-sum games.* The three-or-more-person feature allows the formation of coalitions where certain players can gain more by not acting independently. The nonzero-sum feature refers to the fact that competitive actions may expand the size of the market (that is, the total stakes) in addition to shifting market shares.

Game models have been designed for a variety of situations, especially military and political, and some have interesting possible marketing applications. One is a game of timing involving two duelists (competitors), who, at a signal, begin to approach each other at some constant uniform

[24] See question 3 at end of chapter.

rate. Each has only one available bullet (a new product) and is free to fire it whenever he wishes, with the knowledge that his chance of hitting the opponent improves as the distance narrows. When should the duelist fire? [25]

Another game involves distributing an army over several battlefields, with the knowledge that each battlefield is "won" by the side which has disposed more troops in that battlefield. How should an army distribute its troops (or a company distribute its salesmen or advertising funds) in this situation? [26]

To date, game models do not have much predictive power. They do, however, suggest a useful analytical approach to such competitive problems as pricing, sales-force allocation, and advertising outlays. They may help to clarify the strategic implications of such moves as surprise, threat, and coalition.[27]

Game theory should be distinguished from *operational gaming*. The latter term describes the modeling of a game around a realistic situation, where the participants actually make decisions (often in teams) and where the results of their interacting decisions are reported and become the data inputs for the next round of decisions. A large number of management and marketing games have been developed and used in both formal management training programs and in research settings.[28]

BRAND-SWITCHING MODELS

Marketing executives watch their *market share* at least as carefully as they watch the level of profits. Present customers can never be taken for granted. The firm's customers are incessantly bombarded by competitors' promotions and price deals.

The attitude of marketing executives toward brand switching is quite simple: the switching-out rate must be slowed down, and the switching-in rate must be increased. The factors affecting brand choice must be analyzed, and this knowledge applied where possible in order to alter existing brand-switching rates.

Switching rates can be estimated from data showing the individual brand choices made over time by a representative panel of consumers. Suppose three brands are involved, A, B, and C. We can ask what proportion of those who bought A in the last period purchased A again and what proportions switched to B and C. The proportions for each product can be conveniently exhibited in matrix form. Figure 10-5 is a hypothetical example.

Note that each row adds up to 1.00. In the first row of those who purchased brand A in the last period, 70 per cent bought A again, 20 per cent bought B, and 10 per cent bought C. Thus, A retained 70 per cent of its previous customers and lost 30 per cent, with twice as many of its

---

[25] See R. Duncan Luce and Howard Raiffa, *Games and Decision* (New York: John Wiley & Sons, Inc., 1957), pp. 453-55.

[26] See Lawrence Friedman, "Game-Theory Models in the Allocation of Advertising Expenditures," *Operations Research,* September-October 1958, pp. 699-709.

[27] See Martin Shubik, *Strategy and Market Structure* (New York: John Wiley & Sons, Inc., 1959).

[28] J. F. McRaith and Charles R. Goeldner, "A Survey of Marketing Games," *Journal of Marketing,* XXVI (July 1962), 69-72.

$$\begin{array}{c} \\ \text{From} \end{array} \begin{array}{c} \\ A \\ B \\ C \end{array} \begin{array}{ccc} & \overset{\text{To}}{} & \\ A & B & C \\ \begin{pmatrix} .70 & .20 & .10 \\ .17 & .33 & .50 \\ .00 & .50 & .50 \end{pmatrix} \end{array}$$

FIGURE 10-5
A brand-switching matrix

previous customers going to B as C. Thus B poses a more competitive threat to A than does C. The other two rows are interpreted similarly.

We have seen where A's ex-customers go. Where do new customers come from? This is revealed by column A, rather than row A. Note that A picks up 17 per cent of the customers lost by B, and none lost by C. This is further evidence that A and B are in close competition.

The brand-switching matrix provides information about:

> The *repeat purchase rate* for each brand, indicated by the diagonal numbers. Under certain assumptions, the repeat purchase rate can be interpreted as a measure of brand loyalty.
>
> The *switching-in and switching-out rate* for each brand, represented by the off-diagonal numbers.

But that is not all. If the switching rates are likely to remain constant, at least for the short run, the matrix becomes a useful tool in forecasting both the magnitude and speed of change in future market shares on the basis of present market shares. Even where the switching rates change, if they change in a predictable way, a forecast of market shares is possible.

In this connection, important research is taking place to determine how switching rates are affected by price and promotion changes. Some of the products which have been studied in terms of brand-switching rates are margarine, frozen orange-juice concentrate, and instant and regular coffee.[29]

WAITING-LINE MODELS

Waiting appears in many marketing situations. Customers wait for service, and companies wait for both customers and deliveries. Waiting is of interest because it imposes a cost. The customer who waits in a supermarket line bears a cost in terms of more desirable alternative uses of her time. If she regards the waiting time as excessive, she may leave and buy elsewhere, and the cost of her waiting could be shifted to the supermarket.

While waiting time imposes a cost, so does the effort to reduce waiting time. The supermarket might reduce waiting time by adding more counters or personnel, or both. The decision problem is one of balancing the cost of lost sales against the cost of additional facilities. In marginal terms, the supermarket should increase its servicing facilities up to the point where

---

[29] For an excellent review of the brand-switching literature, see John U. Farley and Alfred A. Kuehn, "Stochastic Models of Brand Switching," in *Science in Marketing*, ed. George Schwartz (New York: John Wiley & Sons, Inc., 1965), pp. 446-64.

the cost of an additional facility would just overtake the profits lost due to customer impatience.

The decision problem is illustrated graphically in Figure 10-6. The higher the average waiting time in the system, the greater the cost of lost sales (1), but the lower the cost of facilities and personnel (2). The two cost curves are added vertically to derive a combined cost curve (3). The lowest point on this combined cost curve indicates the optimal waiting time to be built into the system (W_1) and the optimal investment in service facilities (F_1). The lowest point can be found graphically or through differential calculus if appropriate cost equations can be found.

The cost of additional facilities is not difficult to measure, but it is very difficult to measure the value of lost sales which take place due to customer impatience. In the first place, people vary considerably in their attitudes toward waiting. In the second place, customer impatience is a function of the difference between anticipated and actual waiting time, and anticipated waiting varies by situations. Also, customers who feel impatient may not abandon the store if alternative stores are no better.

Waiting-line theory, also called queuing theory, is not designed to answer *how much* waiting time *should* be built into a system. This is primarily an economic question as shown in Figure 10-6. The theory is designed instead to handle two preliminary questions: What amount of waiting time may be expected in a particular system? How will this waiting time change as a result of particular alterations in the facilities?

The waiting time depends on four dimensions of the system:

The interarrival time. The time between arrivals into the system has a probability distribution which can be estimated from frequency data. The mean, standard deviation, and other characteristics of interarrival time can then be derived from the probability distribution.

The service time. The time between the initiating of a service and its completion can also be viewed as having a probability distribution.

The number of service facilities. The greater the number of service facilities, the shorter the waiting time.

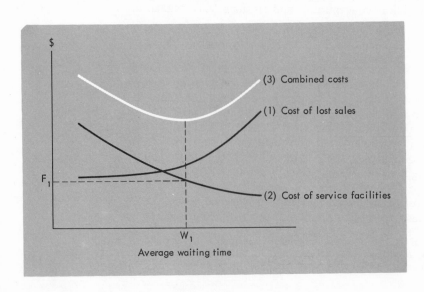

FIGURE 10-6

**System costs as related
to average waiting time**

The service method. Usually customers are serviced in the order in which they arrive (called first-in, first-out). But other methods are service to the most "important" customers first; service for the shortest orders first; and service at random.

When these four dimensions are specified for a particular system, it is possible to estimate queuing characteristics, such as expected waiting time, expected queue length, and the variability of waiting time and queue length. For certain simple queuing situations, it is possible to derive these answers mathematically; for more complicated systems, estimates can be derived through *simulation*.

If the existing system breeds long queues, the decision maker can simulate the effects of different hypothetical changes. In the case of a supermarket with a serious queuing problem on Saturdays, four possible attacks are indicated by the dimensions. The supermarket can try to influence its customers to do their shopping on other days; this would have the effect of increasing the time between arrivals on Saturdays. The supermarket can decrease the service time, by employing baggers to aid the cashiers. More service channels can be added. Or some of the channels can be specialized to handle smaller orders.

Most of the literature about queuing deals with facility planning for telephone exchanges, highways and toll roads, docks and airline terminals. Yet retailing institutions such as supermarkets, filling stations, and airline ticket offices also face critical queuing problems, and marketing executives of such organizations can be expected to show increased interest in waiting-line models.[30]

SIMULATION MODELS

Many marketing situations are too complicated and dynamic to be represented by a standard mathematical model. An increasingly promising way to deal with complex marketing processes is through simulation. The following definition is quoted at length because it states well the main characteristics of simulation.

> *Simulation.* A general method of studying the behavior of a real system or phenomenon; the method usually involves the following features: (1) devising a model or set of mathematical and logical relations, which represents the essential features of the system; (2) carrying out step-by-step computations with these relations which imitate the manner in which the real system might perform in real time. Typically, the real system is subject to chance elements, and this leads to the inclusion of probabilistic characteristics in the model. In systems of complexity, a high-speed digital computer may be programmed to carry out the sequence of computations (also a simulation may involve both a computer and persons imitating certain human functions in a system). An important advantage of simulation is that the system can be studied under a wide variety of conditions which might be expensive or impossible to apply directly to the real system. Simulation is an important tool for a great variety of problems, particularly where ordinary mathematical solution is not possible, or where intangibles of human judgment

[30] See Robert B. Fetter and John L. Enos, "Waiting-Line Theory," in *The Frontiers of Marketing Thought and Science,* ed. Frank M. Bass (Chicago: American Marketing Association, 1958), pp. 157-64.

are involved. . . . Examples include (1) the functioning of a business firm, (2) the diffusion of neutrons in a nuclear reactor, and (3) the problem-solving behavior of a human being.[31]

There are six different types of simulation models which are germane to work in marketing. They are described in the following paragraphs.[32]

ENTERPRISE MODELS. This type of model is used to investigate how the existing information and decision systems *within* an enterprise system affect the flows of material, men, machines, and money. A model of the existing system is constructed and then experimented with in the hope of finding alternative information-decision rules and arrangements that improve various flows according to specified criteria.

Two somewhat different simulation approaches have attracted major attention in this area. The first is called Industrial Dynamics and is associated with Jay W. Forrester of the Massachusetts Institute of Technology.[33] Forrester has been interested chiefly in the phenomenon of *amplification;* that is, the intensification of certain flows caused by various system delays and the lack of decision coordination in the firm. His estimates on delays come largely through fitting curves to historical company records. The other approach is associated with studies done at the Graduate School of Industrial Administration at Carnegie Institute of Technology.[34] The Carnegie approach differs with Forrester's in being more behavioral; it utilizes actual observations of business practice and behavioral propositions drawn from economics and social science to model the behavior of component units.

The major deficiency in these enterprise models from the point of view of marketing analysis lies in their generally oversimplified approach to sales determination. Sales typically are treated as an exogenous input characterized by a specified trend, seasonal pattern, cycle, and random disturbances. This allows the analyst to concentrate on studying enterprise responses. Forrester later recognized that the magnitude and timing of sales are affected partly by company marketing decisions. He specifically examined how poor timing of advertising expenditures could cause undesirable amplifications in some of the enterprise flows.[35]

Charles Bonini's enterprise model is the most advanced in a marketing sense in that he made actual sales a function of the type of salesman, the pressure he worked under in the current period, the sales potential of his district, the market trend, prices, and a random element.[36] But he did not

[31] William Karush, *The Crescent Dictionary of Mathematics* (New York: The Macmillan Company, 1962), pp. 243-44.

[32] The following section is adapted from Philip Kotler, "The Competitive Marketing Simulator—A New Management Tool," *California Management Review,* VII, No. 3 (Spring 1965), 49-60, by permission of the Regents of the University of California.

[33] Jay W. Forrester, *Industrial Dynamics* (New York: John Wiley & Sons, Inc., 1961).

[34] See Cyert and March, *op. cit.;* and Charles P. Bonini, *Simulation of Information and Decision Systems in the Firm* (Englewood Cliffs, N.J.: Prentice-Hall, Inc., 1963).

[35] Jay W. Forrester, "Advertising: A Problem in Industrial Dynamics," *Harvard Business Review,* March-April 1959, pp. 100-110.

[36] Bonini, *op. cit.*

incorporate advertising, product attributes, and some other important mix elements.

In general, most enterprise models lack an adequate description of marketing processes from two points of view: first, they tend to postulate only a few marketing-mix variables and treat them in a gross way. Second, they make no specific allowance for competitive interactions; company sales are made a direct function of company decisions and the economic climate. These deficiencies are remedied in other types of models.

MARKETING-MIX MODELS. This type of model is used to investigate the impact of alternative company marketing strategies on sales and profits. The models which come closest to serving this purpose are those incorporated in business games. Although business games are designed primarily for educational purposes, their potential use as a research tool is being recognized increasingly. For example, the researcher could dispense with live players and program explicit competitive strategies for each decision unit. The implications of alternative programmed strategies can be investigated through simulation.[37]

Virtually all business games provide that some marketing decisions be made by the players. But the marketing function is highly simplified in the typical game. The players set a price, determine separate budgets for advertising and personal selling, and possibly allocate those budgets over three or four products and/or regions. Such games are of insufficient marketing complexity for realistic simulation. An exception is the Carnegie Tech Management Game, modeled after the household detergent industry.[38] It calls for decisions on advertising, distribution, prices, product development, and various types of market information. The M.I.T. Marketing Game goes even further in defining a complex marketing environment.[39] Modeled around electric floor polishers for household use, this game requires the players to determine product quality, price, dealer margins, channels of distribution (including number and types of dealers), market area, advertising expenditures, advertising media and appeals, the number and disposition of salesmen, and promotion within the retail store.

The major shortcoming of these games from the point of view of a genuine marketing simulation lies in their superficial treatment of the market. Instead of modeling the behavior of different types of buyers, the games use an aggregate function to describe the whole market's response. Thus, even those games which boast of an environmentally rich marketing function fail to supply an environmentally rich market. For this we must turn to market models.

MARKET MODELS. A market model is a hypothetical sample universe of customers on which the effects of alternative marketing mixes can be tested. Some examples are described below:

The Simulmatics Corporation created, for the purposes of evaluating

[37] See Chapter 12, pp. 284-86.

[38] Kalman J. Cohen, William R. Dill, Alfred A. Kuehn, and Peter R. Winters, *The Carnegie Tech Management Game* (Homewood, Ill.: Richard D. Irwin, Inc., 1964).

[39] Peter S. King, William F. Massy, Arnold E. Amstutz, and Gerald B. Tallman, "The M.I.T. Marketing Game," in *Marketing: A Maturing Discipline,* ed. Martin L. Bell (Chicago: American Marketing Association, 1960), pp. 83-102.

media schedules, a sample universe of 2,944 hypothetical persons alleged to represent a cross-section of the American population. One hundred and forty different types of persons are defined by cross-classification on sex, age, type of community, employment status, and education. Several representatives of each type are located at ninety-eight sampling points in the United States. This population is exposed to a given media schedule over a hypothetical year and the computer tabulates which individuals are exposed and produces summary charts on their characteristics.[40]

At Wisconsin, Guy Orcutt and his co-workers developed a demographic model consisting initially of 10,000 individuals having an age, sex, marital distribution, etc., resembling that found in the United States in 1950. The computer makes passes through this population—each pass representing a hypothetical month—to determine births, marriages, divorces, and deaths. Ultimately Orcutt will attribute economic decision-making functions to these hypothetical individuals.[41]

Over 300 retailers are modeled in the Pitt-Amstan Market Simulator. Their business is awarded to competing wholesalers on the basis of their characteristics and the wholesalers' relative marketing efforts.[42]

COMPETITIVE-RESPONSE MODELS. These models are designed to explore the likely reactions of competitors to each other's moves. Cyert and March developed an elaborate duopoly model in which each duopolist forecasts the behavior of his competitors, estimates his own demand and costs, specifies a profit goal, and evaluates different marketing plans.[43] If no marketing plan meets his profit goal, he looks harder for possible cost savings, or considers new demand stimulants, or lowers his profit goal. His searching ends when he finds some plan which will attain his profit goal. The model was simulated with specific parameters, and the designers managed to generate competitor profit ratios and market shares which agreed in a rough way with observed values arising from the competition between the American Can Company and the Continental Can Company between 1913 and 1956.

There also exist oligopoly models describing the likely reactions of competitors to price changes initiated by one of the oligopolists. But hardly any models have been developed which specify the likely reactions of competitors to other types of marketing challenges initiated by a particular oligopolist, such as an improvement in product quality, a change in packaging, increased advertising activity, or the use of premiums.

DISTRIBUTION MODELS. These models deal with channel and logistical problems. Kalman Cohen designed a model which imputed specific price and purchasing behavior to different channel members in the shoe, leather, and hide industry.[44] His objective was to see whether the attributed

---

[40] *Simulmatics Media-Mix: Technical Description* (New York: The Simulmatics Corporation, October 1962).

[41] G. H. Orcutt, M. Greenberger, J. Korbel, and A. M. Rivlin, *Microanalysis of Socioeconomic Systems: A Simulation Study* (New York: Harper & Row, Publishers, 1961).

[42] W. B. Kehl, "Techniques in Constructing a Market Simulator," in Bell, *op. cit.,* pp. 85-102.

[43] Cyert and March, *op. cit.,* pp. 83-97.

[44] Kalman J. Cohen, *Computer Models of the Shoe, Leather, Hide Sequence* (Englewood Cliffs, N.J.: Prentice-Hall, Inc., 1960).

micro-behavior of channel members would produce industry price and sales time series similar to those actually observed in the industry.

With a somewhat different objective, Balderston and Hoggatt developed a model based on the West Coast lumber industry in which the behavioral units were suppliers, wholesalers, and customer firms.[45] The wholesalers were brokers who attempted to match suppliers and customers. The brokers' major costs arose from searching, ordering, and confirming orders. A major purpose of the simulation was to examine the effects of changes in the availability and cost of information on the survival and efficiency of participant firms.

Physical distribution aspects of marketing channel arrangements also have been simulated. Gerson and Maffei have described a computer model for evaluating a system of up to 40 warehouses, 4,000 customers, and 10 factories.[46] The objective is to explore the cost of proposed alterations in the existing number and locations of factories and warehouses. Simulation is proposed as a more flexible instrument than linear programming, although it does not provide a systematic procedure for determining the "best" solution.

COMPREHENSIVE MARKETING MODELS. These are models which incorporate all or most of the foregoing components for the purpose of creating a comprehensive tool for the investigation of marketing strategy. Specifically, a comprehensive marketing model would contain a model of the enterprise, the channels, the competitors, the environment, and the customers. Such a grand marketing simulator could be used to explore the effects of alternative marketing-mix decision rules and varying strategies of market segmentation.[47]

Role of the Computer in Marketing

Management's efficiency in information processing and problem solving has been tremendously enhanced by the recent development of high-speed electronic computers. The speed of these machines has enabled problems to be solved in minutes which had formerly taken several man-days or -weeks of calculation. The calculating power of these machines has enabled users to achieve a depth of analysis formerly beyond their reach. Properly utilized, these machines cannot fail to extend the capacity of executives to make more and better decisions.

Marketing executives are just beginning to recognize the many and diverse uses to which the computer can be put in the area of marketing. Some examples of the computer's role as information processor and problem solver are described in this final section.

[45] Frederick E. Balderston and Austin C. Hoggatt, *Simulation of Market Processes* (Berkeley, Calif.: University of California, Institute of Business and Economic Research, 1962).

[46] Martin L. Gerson and Richard B. Maffei, "Technical Characteristics of Distribution Simulators," *Management Science,* October 1963, pp. 62-69. A less technical exposition is described in Harvey N. Shycon and Richard B. Maffei, "Simulation—Tool for Better Distribution," *Harvard Business Review,* November-December 1960, pp. 65-75.

[47] See Chapter 12, pp. 284-86.

The computer is an information processor to the extent that it classifies, counts, stores, and prints out needed bits of information. It is an instrument par excellence for preparing sales reports and facilitating statistical survey work, among other things.

SALES REPORTS.   Sales reports are based on the original orders from salesmen and customers in the field. These orders contain the name of the customer, the name of the salesman, the name of the sales territory, and the items ordered, along with their quantities and prices. The original orders are typed on special billing–key-punching equipment that produces paper copies of the order as well as key-punched cards for each item ordered. The key-punched cards are read into the computer, which reports back items that can be satisfied out of inventory and items that have to be back ordered. An invoice is prepared on the basis of this information. At the end of each period, the accumulated deck of item cards can be used to print out a number of useful reports. The cards can be sorted by *salesman* for the purpose of comparing individual salesman weaknesses and strengths. They can be sorted by *customer* or *type of customer* for the purpose of identifying new opportunities and problems relating to customers. They can be sorted by *item* or *product* for the purpose of discerning fast movers and slow movers.

Sales information can also be sorted on multiple classifications, such as *items sold by territory*. This is regularly done by Catalina, Incorporated, a sportswear firm. Catalina processes current swimming suit sales information on a computer to learn about regional patterns in sizes, colors, and other characteristics. As a result, it can answer whether Texas women are large (the answer is no) or whether New England women prefer conservative colors (the answer is yes).[48]

STATISTICAL SURVEYS.   Another important information-processing use of the computer arises in connection with *statistical survey work*. A market survey might involve anywhere between a few hundred to many thousands of interviews. Interviewers send in their reports, and the surveying firm faces a tremendous task in cross-tabulating and summarizing the results. It formerly took weeks simply to sort and count the responses to various questions. This would delay the firm's marketing decision and also add the danger that the information would be less representative by the time the analysis was completed. Today these same interviews are key-punched on cards, and the computer can be programmed to prepare various tables from this information in a matter of hours.

PROBLEM-SOLVING USES IN MARKETING

The computer is a problem solver to the extent that it can perform sophisticated operations on raw data and yield solutions to a complicated inquiry. Some examples are given below.

SALES FORECASTS.   Here the company is interested in estimating likely sales over some future time period. This problem is typically solved by

[48] "Think," *Glamour Magazine,* July 1962.

decomposing the past pattern of sales into trend, seasonal, and cyclical components. In the past, the sheer calculations involved in time-series analysis occupied a great deal of the potential time available to marketing research departments. Today this work is painlessly performed by computers. The output comes out faster, has a higher probability of being free from error, and is generally more sophisticated. A large number of firms have switched from the use of a fixed seasonal index to the fresh calculation each month of a changing seasonal.[49] Other large firms have adopted exponential smoothing forecasting methods, which allow new forecasts to be made for hundreds or even thousands of products in a matter of minutes.[50]

DEMAND ANALYSIS.   The objective of demand analysis is to determine for the sales of a particular product the relative roles played by its own price, competitors' prices, per capita income, and other real factors. The major tool in demand analysis has been the multiple regression equation. Before the advent of high-speed computers, much time would be required to find the best fitting equation to a set of variables, and, as a result, most analyses were confined to simple linear equations in three or four variables. Today standard computer programs can try different nonlinear fits in dozens of variables at relatively lightning speeds.

OTHER PROBLEM-SOLVING USES.   New problem-solving uses of the computer in the area of marketing evolve each year in connection with operations research breakthroughs. Practicable computer programs have already been formulated and are in use in the following areas:

The selection of advertising media (see pages 477-82)
The routing of goods from factories to warehouses to distributors (see page 231)
The routing of traveling salesmen (see page 232)
The determination of good warehouse locations (see page 429)
The formulation of an efficient time schedule for the activities involved in developing and launching new products (see pages 163-69)
The determination of optimal inventory policies respecting how much to order and when to order (see pages 434-38)

In time, the development of practicable computer programs can also be expected in the following areas:

Routine ordering and pricing of goods
The annual and monthly determination of the optimal amounts to spend on advertising
The allocation of advertising funds geographically and by product line
The allocation of personal selling effort geographically
The determination of good retail locations
The selection of advertising themes

It is important to emphasize that it is the mathematical model, not the computer, which represents the breakthrough in each case. However,

---

[49] See Chapter 5, footnote 14.
[50] See Chapter 5, footnote 15.

many of the models require such complicated and extensive calculations that they would be fruitless without the high-speed calculating power of computers.

OTHER MARKETING USES

The computer's versatility in the marketing area is by no means limited to enhancing management's ability at information processing and problem solving. It is also an able management trainer, dispatcher, and even merchandiser. It performs as a *management trainer* by being the instrument for putting people through highly intense experiences in competitive business decision making. Games have been designed for retailing (service stations, department stores, supermarkets, automobile dealerships), salesforce management, and product management.[51] The computer performs as a *dispatcher* when it is incorporated in warehousing operations to provide greater speed and accuracy in filling orders. The automated warehouse is the prime example of this growing use of the computer.[52] The computer performs as a *merchandiser* to the extent that it actually vends products or facilitates in the purchase of products. Vending equipment has been called the silent salesman and is constantly being improved upon to handle a large variety of goods and to make complicated transactions, such as money changing. Computers are also being used to recommend insurance policies to clients, fertilizers to farmers, etc., to improve the company's service image. A rather unusual use of computing equipment in a merchandising capacity has appeared during the Christmas season in certain large metropolitan department stores. The shopper who does not know quite what to buy for someone describes vital statistics about the person (age, sex, relationship, and interests), as well as the desired price range for the purchase. These facts are key-punched on a card, and in 25 seconds the computer produces a list of a dozen suggestions along with their prices and location in the store.

Thus, the computer has many roles to play in the future of marketing.[53] It will be used as an information processor, a problem solver, a management trainer, an automatic dispatcher, and a merchandiser. This does not mean that it is to be embraced uncritically, however. Electronic data-processing equipment is extremely expensive whether it is bought or rented. Furthermore, the results give an aura of precision which should be guarded against. Any innovation can be perverted by unintelligent use. The secret is for man to remain smarter than the machine.

Summary

Marketing processes are exceedingly complex, and to some this suggests the futility of formal model-building efforts in marketing. To others, it supplies the major reason for them. The purpose of model construction is to identify the most important elements and relationships in the phenomena being

---

[51] See this chapter, footnote 28.
[52] See Chapter 2, footnote 51.
[53] For additional illustrations, see "Computers Begin to Solve the Marketing Puzzle," *Business Week,* April 17, 1965, pp. 114 ff.

studied. Models explicate the processes, allows their experimental manipulation, lead to new insights, and tend to mature over time into useful explanatory and predictive tools.

In the marketing area, the most useful mathematical models seems to be those set up to deal with problems of allocating marketing resources, dealing with competitors, anticipating customers' brand switching, and studying the characteristics of waiting lines. Marketing processes that are too complicated to represent and solve by mathematical deduction can be modeled in their own terms and studied fruitfully through simulation. In all these efforts, the computer is an important adjunct in easing the computational burdens. The computer is showing a variety of uses in marketing, including information processing, problem solving, management training, goods dispatching, and even merchandising.

Questions and Problems

1. List and discuss the major criteria for judging models.

2. Which is more likely to advance the cause of science in marketing, a concentration on the simpler marketing problems where existing mathematical models might be applied effectively or a concentration on the more complex problems in marketing in the hope of eventually developing the needed techniques?

3. For the following games, what strategy would you adopt if you were R?

	C_1	C_2	C_3
R_1	6	5	7
R_2	7	4	8
R_3	−3	2	1

	C_1	C_2	C_3
R_1	3	6	7
R_2	5	4	8
R_3	−3	2	1

4. Some marketing men view the emergence of mathematical model building in marketing with hostility. They will make the following statements: (a) We don't use models. (b) Models are typically unrealistic. (c) Anyone can build a model. (d) A model is of no help unless you can get the data. How would you answer these objections?

5. As time passes, marketing executives will make increasing use of the computer as an aid to decision making. (a) Suggest some types of information which the marketing executive of the future will retrieve on a push-button basis from the computer. (b) Suggest some types of recurrent marketing analyses which the computer will perform. (c) Suggest some types of decision making which the computer will perform.

6. With the emergence of operations research in marketing, large companies are trying to determine the proper organizational relationship between marketing research activities (MR) and marketing operations research (MOR). Describe five alternative conceptions.

chapter 11

Marketing Creativity

Previous chapters have stressed the use of organizational and analytical techniques in managing marketing activity. Our discussion would be incomplete if we did not say something formally about the creative dimensions of marketing management.

The first section of this chapter explores the major areas of marketing management calling for creative effort; the second section examines the nature of creativity; and the final section presents an overview of the major techniques for stimulating creativity, with examples drawn from marketing.

The Need for Creativity in Marketing

Creativity is a valuable ingredient in every facet of business, but it plays its most conspicuous role in the marketing area. The firm is pitted against other firms in a never ending struggle to win the attention and patronage of highly elusive customers. Conventional marketing strategy is likely to lead only to conventional sales results. To achieve exceptional results, companies must develop creative ideas which, in the realm of products, advertising, merchandising, and sales presentation, distinguish their offerings from those of competitors.

CREATIVITY IN PRODUCT DEVELOPMENT

The increased capability of competitors to imitate or improve upon a company's products has shortened considerably the typical product's life span. As a result, companies have to rely on the continuous development of new products to insure steady earnings. This in turn requires organizational arrangements and techniques that are effective in producing new product ideas.

In this connection, a list of thought-provoking questions like the one reproduced in Table 11-1 can be helpful in stimulating new ideas. Other techniques discussed later in the chapter (attribute listing, forced relationships, morphological analysis, and brainstorming) have direct relevance in assisting the search for profitable new products.

CREATIVITY IN ADVERTISING

Creativity is such an important input into the advertising process that the industry has appropriated the term to describe the personnel who

TABLE 11-1
Questions that spur ideas for new and improved products

Put to other uses?	New ways to use as is? Other uses if modified?
Adapt?	What else is this like? What other idea does this suggest? Does past offer parallel? What could I copy? Whom could I emulate?
Modify?	New twist? Changing meaning, color, motion, sound, odor, form, shape? Other changes?
Magnify?	What to add? More time? Greater frequency? Stronger? Higher? Longer? Thicker? Extra value? Plus ingredient? Duplicate? Multiply? Exaggerate?
Minify?	What to subtract? Smaller? Condensed? Miniature? Lower? Shorter? Lighter? Omit? Streamline? Split up? Understate?
Substitute?	Who else instead? What else instead? Other ingredient? Other material? Other process? Other power? Other place? Other approach? Other tone of voice?
Rearrange?	Interchange components? Other pattern? Other layout? Other sequence? Transpose cause and effect? Change pace? Change schedule?
Reverse?	Transpose positive and negative? How about opposites? Turn it backward? Turn it upside down? Reverse roles? Change shoes? Turn tables? Turn other cheek?
Combine?	How about a blend, an alloy, an assortment, an ensemble? Combine units? Combine purposes? Combine appeals? Combine ideas?

Source: Alex F. Osborn, *Applied Imagination*, 3rd rev. ed. (New York: Charles Scribner's Sons, 1963), pp. 286-87.

dream up and execute the ideas for an advertisement. These people are hired primarily because they are creative. Each has his own technique for producing advertising ideas. Many rely on free association; others skim a dictionary; some go to an art museum or the client's factory. Some soak up the product and marketing data supplied by the research department and let it incubate, expecting a flash of inspiration to come eventually, perhaps during a casual conversation or while riding to work.

Agencies often provide broad rules to guide their creative men in developing new ideas. For example, David Ogilvy, a founder of the large advertising agency of Ogilvy, Benson & Mather, developed the prescription "To attract women, show babies or women; to attract men, show men." [1] His agency followed this rule in developing the highly successful "The Man in the Hathaway Shirt" and "The Man from Schweppes." But certainly all the rules in the world cannot substitute for creative inspiration. And some of the best advertisements arise from breaking the rules.

Although the term "creative men" is applied only to those in the agency who produce advertisements, it would be wrong to think that the job of placing the ads, which falls to the media men, is noncreative. Advertising history is full of examples of advertising coups which were brought about because an advertisement was placed in new types or combinations of media. For example, men's clothes were almost always advertised in men's magazines like *Esquire* until someone saw the possibilities of advertising them in women's magazines, on the premise that the wife may be a prime

[1] Martin Mayer, *Madison Avenue, U.S.A.* (New York: Harper & Row, Publishers, 1958), p. 126.

mover in making the husband's wardrobe grow. Burma-Shave created an indelible name for itself with the inspiration to use billboard sequences in the countryside.

CREATIVITY IN MERCHANDISING

The term "merchandising" is used in many ways. Here it will be used to describe the decisions made on where and how to sell the product. In this sense, merchandising includes the choice of channels, the packaging of the product, its pricing, and its sales promotion. This is an area in which one creative idea can make millions of dollars for a company. We have only to think of such major merchandising innovations as self-service, discount selling of national brands, trading stamps, and national credit cards. Those who developed these ideas first earned their investments many times over.

Very often a daring change in channel strategy is just what is needed to propel the sales of a product. This is what happened when the Conn Organ Company decided to merchandise organs through department and discount stores, thus drawing more attention to them than they ever enjoyed in the small music stores where they had always been merchandised.[2] A daring new channel was exploited when a group decided to merchandise books through the mails in the now famous Book-of-the-Month Club. Other sellers, perceiving the success of the Book-of-the-Month Club, developed Record-of-the-Month clubs, Candy-of-the-Month clubs, and dozens of others.

There are many examples of products which enjoyed fantastic success because of a creative idea for packaging them. This happened when ice cream was switched from paper cartons to plastic containers, when liquid bubble bath was packaged in a series of Walt Disney plastic characters, and when beer was packaged in easy-to-open pop-top containers.

The area of sales promotion thrives on new ideas. Consider such ideas as one-cent sales, money-back-for-labels, and premium giveaways. In the last case, much creative energy is spent in trying to discover new types of premiums with a fresh appeal. When the Leo Burnett advertising agency thought of packaging a dozen small bars of soap in an apothecary jar, the jars turned out to be very popular with housewives, and the sales of the soap zoomed.

CREATIVITY IN SALES PRESENTATION

The salesman is faced with the problem of getting into buyers' offices and convincing them within a small amount of time to place an order with his firm. The salesman's success will depend on hundreds of factors, including his personality, the buyer's mood, and the intrinsic qualities of the product. One factor that makes a difference is the sales message and how it is presented to the buyer. Many companies have found it useful to have their salesmen brainstorm for new approaches to the sale of their products. These sessions not only lead to new ideas on what to say but also to ideas on visual aids, props, and advertising specialty items which often help boost sales substantially.

[2] Walter Talley, "Marketing R & D," *Business Horizons*, Fall 1962, pp. 31-40.

What Is Creativity?

Creativity is *the development of new or original ideas that have value to a significant group of other persons.*[3] It is the value of the ideas that distinguishes creativity from the broader notion of imagination. Everyone has imagination; everyone visualizes new events or new combinations—fantasies, dreams, wishful thinking all represent the workings of imagination. But unless these things are tamed, embodied, and communicated in a way that gives satisfaction to others, they are only rumblings in the private world of the individual. They are imaginative products but not creative products.

TWO TYPES OF CREATIVITY

In examining various expressions of creative effort, we can start by distinguishing between *aesthetic creativity* and *problem-solving creativity*. The first is exemplified by writers and artists. Their creative products are extensions of their own personalities and embodiments of their personal responses to the nature of the world. The second is exemplified by scientists and businessmen. Their creative products are solutions to problems. The creativity is stimulated by externally defined goals, such as the need to explain something or to find a way of doing something better. As stated by Hoopes:

> . . . a theory is needed to explain certain phenomena in nature. The Einstein who produces such a theory has created an original product, but it is not an extension of himself in the sense that a Beethoven symphony *is* Beethoven.[4]

In many cases, the two types of creativity merge. The advertising copywriter is assigned to develop an advertisement which meets certain specifications about media and message. But within this problem-solving framework, the truly creative copywriter will leave the stamp of a highly personal vision and form of expression. This interaction between the two types of creativity should be remembered, although here we will deal primarily with creativity directed at problem solving.

THE CREATIVE PROCESS

How do creative products come about? Many discussions of creativity tend to leave the impression that the creative person simply gets a sudden flash of illumination and this is what constitutes the creative process. Unfortunately, this omits much that occurs before and all that must occur after an inspiration to transform it into a creative product. The creative problem-solving process is much more complicated. As described by Braybrooke and Lindblom:

> When a man sets out to solve a problem, he embarks on a course of mental activity more circuitous, more subtle, and perhaps more idiosyncratic than

[3] See Morris I. Stein, "Creativity as an Intra- and Inter-Personal Process," in *A Source Book for Creative Thinking,* eds. Sidney J. Parnes and Harold F. Harding (New York: Charles Scribner's Sons, 1962), pp. 85-94.

[4] Townsend Hoopes, "Creativity: Key to Organizational Renewal," *Business Horizons,* Winter 1963, p. 40.

he perceives. If he is aware of some of the grosser aspects of his own problem solving, as when he consciously focuses his attention on what he has identified as a critical unknown, he will often have only the feeblest insight into how his mind finds, creates, dredges up—which of these he does not know—a new idea. Dodging in and out of the unconscious, moving back and forth from concrete to abstract, trying chance here and system there, soaring, jumping, backtracking, crawling, sometimes freezing on point like a bird dog, he exploits mental processes that are only slowly yielding to observation and systematic description.[5]

The scientific study of the creative process which Braybrooke and Lindblom allude to is just in its infancy. While psychologists for many years have studied such mental processes as thinking, learning, and motivation, they have only recently begun to try to unravel the apparently greater mysteries of creativity.[6] One thing they have done is to examine the characteristics of people who are generally regarded as creative: their intelligence, personality, and other traits. They have developed some important findings, which we shall describe shortly. Another thing they have done is to break the creative process into a series of stages. Although the creative mind "soars and jumps and backtracks," distinct developments occur during the creative process that can be described as stages.

One of the earliest and most useful classifications of stages was developed by Graham Wallas in 1926.[7] He saw the creative process as consisting of:

1. *Preparation:* the stage in which the problem is investigated from all directions
2. *Incubation:* the stage during which the individual is not consciously thinking about the problem
3. *Illumination:* the stage during which the "happy idea" occurs, together with the psychological factors that immediately preceded and accompanied its appearance.
4. *Verification:* in which the validity of the idea is tested, and the idea is reduced to exact form.[8]

This classification makes two important points. It highlights the fact that the creative person assimilates material related to the problem and makes some effort to solve it before the flash of illumination occurs. It also highlights the fact that illumination must be followed by verification and additional refinement to yield a creative product.

This last point lies at the bottom of Joseph Schumpeter's well-known distinction between inventions and innovations.[9] A tremendous amount of work typically must take place to convert an invention into a socially useful product or innovation. Part of the creative process is having the patience to persevere. Edison himself defined genius as 1 per cent inspira-

---

[5] David Braybrooke and Charles E. Lindblom, *A Strategy of Decision* (New York: Free Press of Glencoe, Inc., 1963), p. 1.

[6] For an annotated bibliography on scientific studies of creativity see Morris I. Stein and Shirley J. Heinze, *Creativity and the Individual: Summaries of Selected Literature in Psychology and Psychiatry* (New York: Free Press of Glencoe, Inc., 1960).

[7] Graham Wallas, *The Art of Thought* (New York: Harcourt, Brace & Co., 1926).

[8] Described by Stein, *op. cit.,* p. 86.

[9] Joseph Schumpeter, *The Theory of Economic Development* (Cambridge, Mass.: Harvard University Press, 1934).

tion and 99 per cent perspiration. Edison first got the inspiration for the phonograph during the Civil War, but it was not until 1877 that he developed a workable model.[10] King Camp Gillette conceived of the razor blade in 1899, but it took five years of tinkering before he was able to manufacture a successful blade.[11] The creative process depends on doggedness as much as on inspiration.

Morris I. Stein would add another stage after verification called "communication of results." [12] In a complex society, the creative idea depends upon various intermediaries if it is ever to find its way to those who constitute a receptive audience. Among the important intermediaries in the innovation process are large firms, agents, professional organizations, art and drama critics, and newspapers.

A somewhat different, though overlapping classification, has been popularized in recent years by Alex F. Osborn, one of the founders of the large advertising agency, Batten, Barton, Durstine & Osborn. Osborn is the father of "brainstorming," and has probably done more than any other contemporary to show how people can stimulate their latent creativity. He sees creative problem solving as involving the following stages:

1. Fact-Finding
    a) *Problem-definition:* Picking out and pointing up the problem.
    b) *Preparation:* Gathering and analyzing the pertinent data.
2. Idea-Finding
    a) *Idea-production:* Thinking up tentative ideas as possible leads.
    b) *Idea-development:* Selecting from resultant ideas, adding others and re-processing by means of modification, combination, et cetera.
3. Solution-Finding
    a) *Evaluation:* Verifying the tentative solutions by tests and otherwise.
    b) *Adoption:* Deciding on and implementing the final solution.[13]

This differs from Wallas' scheme in emphasizing a more deliberate effort to develop a satisfactory solution to a problem. Wallas talks about illumination, which implies waiting for the happy flash of inspiration. Osborn talks about idea production, which implies the generation of as many ideas as possible so that a few "inspired" ones result. Osborn also has explored in great detail the varying mechanism that can expedite each stage of the creative process.

Stimulating Creativity in People

Because marketing organizations thrive on the development of new ideas, every marketing department has a vested interest in creative personnel. Developing a satisfactory level of creativity in the organization is really a threefold problem. It calls for hiring a sufficient number of people who are exceptionally creative; tapping the latent creativity of the

[10] Alex F. Osborn, *Applied Imagination,* 3rd rev. ed. (New York: Charles Scribner's Sons, 1963), p. 346.
[11] John E. Arnold, "Useful Creative Techniques," in Parnes and Harding, *op. cit.,* pp. 258-59.
[12] Stein, *op. cit.,* p. 90.
[13] Osborn, *op. cit.,* p. 111.

average person on the staff, who generally operates far below his capacity; and removing organizational inhibitions to creativity.

SELECTING UNUSUALLY CREATIVE PEOPLE

While creativity in problem solving is latent in many men, some possess it to an unusual degree. At the very top stand a few men like Galileo, Freud, and Edison, whose every act gave testimony to a boundless creativity. There are thousands of others, in every field of endeavor, who distinguish themselves by generating a disproportionately high number of new ideas. One study of seven diverse fields showed that the top 10 per cent of contributors produced approximately 50 per cent of the total output.[14] The firm's problem is to recognize these men in advance of their contributions. This raises the question of whether there are any common traits possessed by highly creative people.

A number of studies have explored the relation of creativity to such factors as age, I.Q., and personality. The typical procedure has been to take a sample of people in a field who are regarded by their peers as highly creative and study their characteristics through tests and other means.

AGE. Age appears to be an important factor, especially in certain fields and with respect to producing the highest-quality work. Harvey Lehman's classic study in this area showed that the years of the most creative production seem to be under 30 for chemistry and poetry, 30-34 for mathematics, physics, botany, and symphonies, 35-39 for astronomy, physiology, opera, and philosophy, and over 40 for novels and architecture.[15] Lehman also found that the rate of good production, as opposed to the rate of highest production, continues through the middle years and declines only gradually with the onset of old age. Our interest is in the age at which creativity is most fervent in the business field, and especially marketing, but unfortunately no substantial studies have been reported in this area.

INTELLIGENCE. Intelligence does not appear to be strongly correlated with creativity, although intelligence is a necessary prerequisite for creative work in the more difficult fields, such as nuclear physics. One investigator found virtually no relationship between the performance of research scientists on intelligence tests and their creativity on the job.[16] In another study, the investigator found a low positive correlation (.40) over the whole range of intelligence and creativity, but for I.Q.'s above 120, the amount of intelligence seemed to be a negligible factor in creativity.[17]

PERSONALITY TRAITS. Certain personality traits seem to be shared

[14] Wayne Dennis, "Variations in Productivity Among Creative Workers," *Scientific Monthly,* April 1955, pp. 277-78.

[15] Harvey C. Lehman, *Age and Achievement* (Princeton, N.J.: Princeton University Press, 1953), p. 326.

[16] H. G. Gough, "Techniques For Identifying the Creative Research Scientist," in Institute of Personality Assessment and Research, *The Creative Person* (University of California and University Extension, Liberal Arts Department, 1961), p. III-8.

[17] Frank Barron, "Creative Vision and Expression in Writing and Painting," in Institute of Personality Assessment and Research, *The Creative Person,* p. II-10.

by creative people according to various studies. Berelson and Steiner summarized the various studies of the personalities of creative individuals in the following two propositions:

1. Highly creative people show a preference for, and interest in, complexity and novelty; they have intrinsic interest in situations that require some resolution, rather than those that are cut-and-dried.
2. Highly creative people are more likely than others to view authority as conventional rather than absolute; to make fewer black-and-white distinctions; to have a less dogmatic and more relativistic view of life; to show more independence of judgment and less conventionality and conformity, both intellectual and social; to be more willing to entertain, and sometimes express their own "irrational" impulses; to place a greater value on humor and in fact to have a better sense of humor; in short, to be somewhat freer and less rigidly controlled.[18]

These are some of the guidelines which management might use to identify persons of more than average creativity. Management must be aware, however, that some of these men may act in an unorthodox manner in the context of business. They are more free-wheeling and may be less responsive and sometimes hostile to authority, company traditions, and status. This is a price which management may have to pay if it wants to nurture creativity. Too often in the past, management hired men and judged them by the degree to which they possessed conventional and conforming qualities.[19] But these qualities may tend to breed only conventional results.

DIRECT STIMULANTS TO CREATIVITY

In addition to trying to recruit highly creative individuals the firm must do a better job of tapping the creative talents latent in everybody. In spite of individual differences in the inherited potential for creativity, most persons usually are capable of more creativity than they exercise. The stimulation of creativity is both an intrapersonal and an interpersonal matter. Techniques exist whereby the individual alone or the individual in a group can be stimulated to be more creative.

TECHNIQUES FOR STIMULATING SELF-CREATIVITY. Individuals have sought in various ways to stimulate their own creativity. Some of the ways used by artists are almost bizarre:

. . . in order to produce a state of inspiration, Schiller kept rotten apples in his desk; Shelley and Rousseau remained bareheaded in the sunshine; Bossuet worked in a cold room with his head wrapped in furs; Milton, Descartes, Leibniz and Rossini lay stretched out; Tycho Brahe and Leibniz secluded themselves for very long periods, Thoreau built his hermitage, Proust worked in a cork-lined room, Carlyle in a noise-proof chamber, and Balzac wore a monkish working garb; Grétry and Schiller immersed their feet in ice-cold water; Guido Reni could paint, and de Musset could write poetry, only when dressed in magnificent style; Mozart, following exercise;

18 Bernard Berelson and Gary A. Steiner, *Human Behavior: An Inventory of Scientific Findings* (New York: Harcourt, Brace, and World, Inc., 1964), pp. 229-30.
19 See William H. Whyte, Jr., *The Organization Man* (New York: Simon and Schuster, Inc., 1956), p. 429.

Lamennais, in a room of shadowy darkness, and D'Annunzio, Farnol and Frost only at night.[20]

As for stimulating problem-solving creativity, the individual can benefit by understanding the stages of the creative process, as described earlier, and the mechanisms available at each stage. The individual must seek to define the problem better, to ask questions, to digest some data, to "free associate," and to rub various ideas together. Three specific techniques have a direct application to the problem of creating ideas for new products.

Attribute listing. Developed by Robert P. Crawford of the University of Nebraska, this technique involves listing the attributes of an object and then modifying different attributes in the search for a new combination that will improve the object. The typical problem used to illustrate this technique is that of devising a better screwdriver.[21] The first step is to list the attributes which completely define the existing type of screwdriver, such as round, steel shank; wooden handle, riveted to it; wedge-shaped end for engaging slot in screw; manually operated; and torque provided by twisting action. The next step is to imagine a change or many changes in each attribute which might improve need satisfaction. For example, the round shank could be changed to a hexagonal shank, so that a wrench could be applied to increase the torque; the wooden handle could be replaced by a plastic handle to cut down breakage and danger from electrical shock; the end could be modified to fit different types of screw heads; electric power could replace manual power; or the torque could be produced by pushing.

Forced relationships. Developed by Charles S. Whiting, the technique relies upon listing a lot of ideas and then considering each one in relation to every other one as a means of stimulating the idea-production process. For example, a manufacturer of office equipment who is seeking new product ideas might list separate items he manufactures, such as a desk, bookcase, filing cabinet, and chair.[22] He starts by free-associating about the relationship between a desk and a bookcase. This may lead him to visualize the possibility of designing a desk with a built-in bookcase; here there are several possibilities, such as collapsible book ends built into the far corner of the desk or rigid book shelves in the back of the desk. Then he considers the relationship between a desk and a filing cabinet and may get the idea of replacing two desk drawers by a filing cabinet drawer. He goes systematically through the list considering all the combinations and may add even new and bizarre items to the list to stimulate his imagination.

Morphological analysis. Morphology means structure, and the technique is one of structural analysis. Developed by Fritz Zwicky of Aero-Jet Corporation, the method consists of singling out the most important dimensions of a problem and then examining all the relationships among them. Suppose the problem or need is described as that of "getting something from one place to another via a powered vehicle." [23] One dimension of this problem is the type of vehicle to use; this suggests such possibilities

[20] H. B. Levey, "A Theory Concerning Free Creation in the Inventive Arts," *Psychiatry*, 1940, pp. 229-93. Quoted in Stein, *op. cit.*, p. 87.

[21] See Arnold, *op. cit.*, p. 255.

[22] Osborn, *op. cit.*, pp. 213-14.

[23] Arnold, *op. cit.*, pp. 256-57.

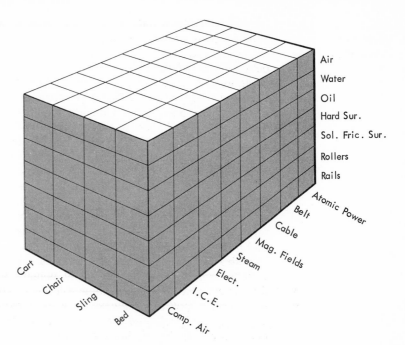

Air
Water
Oil
Hard Sur.
Sol. Fric. Sur.
Rollers
Rails

Atomic Power
Belt
Cable
Mag. Fields
Steam
Elect.
I.C.E.
Comp. Air

Cart
Chair
Sling
Bed

FIGURE 11-1

Morphological analysis for the problem of getting something from one place to another via a powered vehicle

Redrawn from John E. Arnold, "Useful Creative Techniques," in *A Source Book for Creative Thinking,* Sidney J. Parnes and Harold F. Harding, eds. (New York: Charles Scribner's Sons, 1962), p. 256.

as a cart, chair, sling, or bed. A second independent dimension is the medium in which the vehicle operates; this suggests such possibilities as air, water, oil, hard surface, rollers, rails, a solid frictionless surface. A third dimension is the power source, suggesting such possibilities as compressed air, internal combustion engine, electric motor, steam, magnetic fields, moving cables, moving belt, atomic power. Assume that these three dimensions or variables completely describe the problem. They can be combined into the three-dimensional figure shown in Figure 11-1, consisting of 224 (4 × 8 × 7) cells. The next step is to let the imagination loose on each cell. Some cells turn out to be quite familiar; a cart-type vehicle, powered by an internal combustion engine and moving over hard surfaces, is the automobile. Some of them turn out to be absurd or impractical; a sling-type vehicle moving through oil, powered by a moving belt. Some may turn out to be novel and represent just the inspiration sought.

TECHNIQUES FOR STIMULATING GROUP CREATIVITY.   Persons can also be stimulated to greater creativity through certain types of organized group experiences. Some people get their best ideas during committee meetings while listening to others speak. However, conventional committee meetings are not the best medium for loosening and energizing the latent creativity in people. Two group techniques in particular have been notably successful in stimulating idea generation through group interactive processes. They are known as "brainstorming" and "operational creativity," respectively.

Brainstorming.   The word coined by Alex Osborn describes an activity which has appeared in many places, especially in the advertising business, in which men collaborate to "storm" a problem. It is a creative conference

255

for the sole purpose of producing a lot of ideas. Over the years, Osborn and his followers have discovered many things which help to increase the output of these sessions. Generally the group size should be limited to between six and ten, preferably six or seven. It is not a good idea to include too many experts in the group, because they tend to have a stereotyped, pre-set way of looking at a problem. The problem should be made as specific as possible, and there should be no more than one problem. The session should last about an hour, and may be held at almost any time of the day, although the morning is often the most effective time.

As the system works in Osborn's advertising agency, BBD&O,[24] almost every field office contains one or more brainstorming groups, men who meet when ideas are needed on a new problem. The group has a chairman. When a client brings in a problem, the chairman notifies the members of the brainstorming group of the problem, in brief and specific terms, and schedules a meeting to take place in the next day or two. The purpose of outlining the problem before the meeting is to stimulate some preparation and idea incubation. When the meeting takes place, the chairman starts with "Remember now, men, we want as many ideas as possible—the wilder the better, and remember, no *evaluation.*" The ideas start to flow, one idea sparks another, and within the hour over a hundred or more new ideas may find their way into the tape recorder. For the conference to be maximally effective, Osborn believes the following four rules must be observed.

1. *Criticism is ruled out.* Adverse judgment of ideas must be withheld until later.
2. *Free-wheeling is welcomed.* The wilder the idea, the better; it is easier to tame down than to think up.
3. *Quantity is wanted.* The greater the number of ideas, the more the likelihood of useful ideas.
4. *Combination and improvement are sought.* In addition to contributing ideas of their own, participants should suggest how ideas of others can be joined into still another idea.[25]

Operational creativity. An alternative technique, also called "synectics," was developed by William J. J. Gordon while he was affiliated with the consulting firm of Arthur D. Little. Gordon felt the main weakness of the Osborn brainstorming session was that it produced solutions too quickly before a sufficient number of perspectives were developed. Gordon decided that instead of defining the problem specifically, as Osborn would do, he would define it so broadly that the men would have no inkling of the specific problem.

One of the problems, for example, required designing a vaporproof method of closing vaporproof suits worn by workers who handled high-powered toxic fuels.[26] Conventional devices for closing suits, such as zippers, buttons, and snaps were inadequate. Osborn would have described the problem in just this form to a brainstorming group. Gordon, on the other hand, would have kept the specific problem a secret and instead

24 This account is adapted from Arnold, *op. cit.,* pp. 260-62.
25 Osborn, *op. cit.,* p. 156.
26 John W. Lincoln, "Defining a Creativeness in People," in Parnes and Harding, *op. cit.,* pp. 274-75.

sparked a discussion of the general notion "closure." This might lead to images of different closure mechanisms such as bird nests, mouths, or thread. As the group exhausted the initial perspectives, Gordon would gradually interject facts that further defined the problem. The group then had new fields to discuss. Only when Gordon sensed that the group was close to a good solution would he describe the exact nature of the problem. Then the group would start to refine the solution. These sessions would last a minimum of three hours, and often longer, for Gordon believed that fatigue played an important role in unlocking ideas.

Gordon described five themes which guided these idea-conception conferences:

1. *Deferment*. Look first for viewpoints rather than solutions.
2. *Autonomy of object*. Let the problem take on a life of its own.
3. *Use of the commonplace*. Take advantage of the familiar as a springboard to the strange.
4. *Involvement/detachment*. Alternate between entering into the particulars of the problem and standing back from them, in order to see them as instances of a universal.
5. *Use of metaphor*. Let apparently irrelevant, accidental things suggest analogies which are sources of new viewpoints.[27]

The idea-conception conference is followed by implementational conferences to turn the idea into a reality. They take the form of research conferences, consultations, and experimentation. Through these conferences, the Synectics Group develops, in addition to a finished product, recommendations on methods of manufacture and sale. The manufacturer who has turned over a difficult problem to the group gets back a complete package.

INHIBITORS OF CREATIVITY

The firm that wishes to encourage creativity must avoid attitudes and procedures that repress it. One of these is running an organization in an authoritarian manner; another is evaluating ideas before they have a chance to blossom.

An *authoritarian organization* centralizes power and decision making in the hands of a few men and encourages all others to perform their tasks in the way they have been performed in the past. Such companies value tradition, obedience, and group solidarity above individual creativity. The ideal seems to be that the organization should run like a well-oiled machine. However, like a well-oiled machine, it always remains what it is and lacks the capacity to grow into something better. The latent creativity in people atrophies in such an atmosphere. Their ideas are not encouraged and have no where to go. As a result, men devote all their energy to conforming and being a better conformist than the next one. Thought and action become stereotyped, rigid.

Creativity is also inhibited by a *premature evaluation of ideas*.[28] Men in business tend to respect a judicial capacity, a capacity for discriminating between good and bad ideas, a capacity to make sound decisions. They are

[27] Lincoln, *op. cit.*, p. 274.
[28] The following account is adapted from Osborn, *op. cit.*, pp. 40-42.

heard to compliment a man for having an unerring judgment more often than for having a soaring imagination. Even the educational system represents mainly a training of the judicial faculty rather than the creative one. The significance of this is that, to a large extent, a judicial frame of mind does not mix well with a creative frame of mind. The judicial mind is largely negative; it tries to identify weaknesses; its end is to render a verdict. In contrast, the creative mind is largely positive; it tries to remove weaknesses; its end is to produce a better idea. Creativity needs encouragement, not judgment. When men feel their ideas are being evaluated on the spot, they tend to become more careful and more self-critical. They block their own free flow of ideas. This is why many committee meetings produce relatively few ideas. Everyone sits in a judicial frame of mind. Every new idea is immediately examined for loopholes, for inadequacies. No one wants to stick his neck out. People are willing to express only safe ideas, well-thought-out ideas. But this robs the group of the stimulus of many ideas, both good and bad. All ideas are fertile; they give birth to further, and often better ideas.

The main danger in an organization is that as the organization perfects its judicial mind, it may stifle its creative mind. The research of Dr. E. Paul Torrance of the University of Minnesota has indicated that as knowledge and judgment expand, imagination tends to contract.[29] Since judgment expands with age and must be exercised every hour of the day, special efforts must be made to preserve creativity through exercise and through a willingness to separate the periods of judgment from the periods of creativity. In Osborn's words:

> . . . in most creative efforts there is no need for any decision as to relative merits of our ideas *until* we come to the question of which one, if any, is to be used. At this time we should be as cold in our criticism as we have been warm in our enthusiasm during the creative process.[30]

Summary

Good judgment is one of the most respected attributes in a businessman, but this is not enough to pull a company above a standard of average performance. The company which has outstanding marketing management is one whose marketing executives have, in addition to good judgment, the knack of producing fresh and good ideas in the realm of products, advertising, merchandising, and salesmanship.

Most people operate far below their creative potential. In fact, there is evidence that as the judicial faculties are improved, the creative faculties tend to wither in the absence of concrete measures to keep them exercised and active. There are definite ways to stimulate the creative faculties. Techniques such as attribute listing, forced relationships, and morphological analysis have proved value in stimulating the person's imagination. Brainstorm-

---

[29] Quoted in Osborn, *op. cit.,* p. 40.
[30] Osborn, *op. cit.,* p. 42.

ing and operational creativity are highly effective in pulling out a large number of ideas from a group. The marketing organization which hopes to be creative must see its job as that of using direct stimulants to creativity, removing organizational inhibitions to creativity, and seeking out people who are endowed with high creativity. The importance of creativity in the recipe for marketing success is being increasingly recognized and evidenced in the growing number of schools and business firms which are developing and sponsoring formal courses on the subject.[31]

Questions and Problems

1. A candy store chain is seeking ideas for a new sales promotion campaign. Show how morphological analysis might be used to generate a large number of ideas for a campaign.

2. "Just as the necessities of World War II led to such lasting innovations as the jet plane and the aerosol spray, the $5 billion-a-year exploration of space has started a beneficent fallout of commercial products and processes that promises profound effects on the economy and on U.S. life." Try to imagine some of the new products and processes which might be developed as by-products of the space program.

3. "Discussions of merchandising practices in the oil industry have often proceeded from the premise that the existing distributive channel structure for gasoline is a millstone around the industry's neck." Can you think of innovations for improving the distribution of automobile fuel or for improving the profitability of service stations?

4. "A consumption system is a series of steps which incorporate the use of one or more products plus various actions by one or more consumers relative to solving a given problem." Name some consumption systems which are common to households and some of the product innovations which arose to ease the consumers' tasks.

[31] See, for example, Sidney J. Parnes, "The Creative Problem-Solving Course and Institute at the University of Buffalo"; Harry L. Hansen, "The Course in Creative Marketing Strategy at Harvard Business School"; and George I. Samstad, "General Electric's Creative Courses"—all in Parnes and Harding, *op. cit.,* pp. 305-39.

3

We now turn to the specific areas of marketing planning and decision making as distinct from the management factors affecting the firm's adaptation to its marketing opportunities.

The first need is to develop a broad view of the various marketing instruments and their interrelationships. This is done in Chapter 12, "Theory of Marketing Programming," which discusses the major principles for making decisions on the level, mix, allocation, and strategy of marketing effort. Chapter 13, "Product Policy Decisions," introduces the concept of the product mix as the basis for planning the other marketing policies and discusses decisions to drop or modify products in the mix. Chapter 14, "New Product Decisions," extends the previous discussion to the decisions involved in successfully introducing new products. Chapter 15, "Price Decisions," considers the major decisions a firm faces setting the initial price on a product, initiating a price change, reacting to a competitive price change, and pricing a whole product line. Chapter 16, "Channel Decisions," examines the problem of developing effective trade channels, particularly choosing among types of channels, determining number of channel members, establishing contractual arrangements and motivations, and reacting to channel changes. Chapter 17, "Physical Distribution Decisions," considers opportunities to improve service and/or reduce costs in the area of physical distribution through better decisions on types of transportation and levels and locations of inventories.

Chapter 18, "Advertising Decisions," considers how the company can effectively promote its products through decisions on the size, allocation, message content, and media for its advertising effort. Chapter 19, "Sales Force Decisions," examines the problems in developing an effective sales force through improving decisions on selecting, training, assigning, motivating, and controlling salesmen, as well as developing better sales territories. Finally, Chapter 20, "Marketing Decisions and the Law," discusses how decisions on each of the marketing instruments are constrained by legal and political considerations developed for the protection of business and consumers.

Planning the Marketing Program

chapter 12

Theory of Marketing Programming

We are now ready to examine how marketing management, following its analysis and selection of target markets, may proceed to develop marketing programs. This involves determining the level, mix, and allocation of marketing resources in the pursuit of marketing objectives.

To a large extent, the theory of marketing programming involves the application of standard principles of economics, particularly marginal analysis, to determine optimal levels and employment of marketing resources. Although the theory is still evolving and many problems remain unsolved, the work of men like Chamberlin, Verdoorn, Alderson, Mickwitz, and many others marks a good beginning toward conceptual foundations for a distinct theory of marketing programming.[1]

The chapter is divided into five parts. The first part develops foundational concepts for the theory of marketing programming. The remaining parts discuss in turn the principles of finding the optimal level, allocation, mix, and strategy of marketing effort.

Major Concepts of Marketing Programming

At least seven terms must be defined in a careful discussion of how marketing management can make its programming decisions. They are *demand variables, marketing decision variables, marketing mix, marketing strategy, marketing effort, marketing allocation,* and *market response.* Each is discussed below.

DEMAND VARIABLES

The ultimate purpose of the firm is to employ its resources in a way that will lead to the maximum attainment of company objectives. Company objectives may include many things, but among them will be a high level of profits. Profits themselves are the result of how well the firm succeeds in generating a good relationship between company sales and company costs. It is the task of management to generate a profitable level of sales.

---

[1] Edward H. Chamberlin, *The Theory of Monopolistic Competition* (Cambridge, Mass.: Harvard University Press, 1933); P. J. Verdoorn, "Marketing from the Producer's Point of View," *Journal of Marketing,* XX (January 1956), 221-35; Wroe Alderson, *Marketing Behavior and Executive Action* (Homewood, Ill.: Richard D. Irwin, Inc., 1957); and *Dynamic Marketing Behavior* (Homewood, Ill.: Richard D. Irwin, Inc., 1965); and Gösta Mickwitz, *Marketing and Competition* (Helsingfors, Finland: Centraltrycheriet, 1959).

Company sales are affected by a host of variables, some beyond and some within management's control. For our purposes, *any factor that affects company sales will be called a demand variable*. The sale of home air conditioners, for example, is affected by such demand variables as:

Number of households in warm climates
Number of warm months a year
Attitudes toward air conditioning
Level and distribution of income
Average cost of electricity
Average prices of air-conditioning units
Payment terms
Industry promotion and extent of distribution
Product features and quality
Sales effort
Number of competitors
Skill of competitors

It is fruitful to recognize that demand variables can be classified into certain broad categories. One useful classification is described below.

Customer variables. Company sales are affected by the number of buyers in the market and by their incomes, motives, needs, attitudes, and purchasing habits. A company can do very little to alter these customer variables. Its task is to use market analysis and forecasting to learn how to make the most profitable adaptation to them.

Environmental variables. Company sales are affected by environmental variables which transcend particular markets, such as the level of economic activity, the character and course of legislation, and the pattern of weather. These variables are also beyond the control of individual companies, and the task is again one of profitable adaptation through careful forecasting and planning.

Competitive variables. Company sales are affected by the policies of other companies producing similar and substitute products. Although a company generally has little control over the actions of competitors, it can seek to anticipate them and to plan accordingly.

Marketing decision variables. Company sales are affected by product quality, price, promotion, and distribution. Given customer characteristics, environmental characteristics, and the actions of competitors, the final level of company sales will depend upon the company's marketing program.

MARKETING DECISION VARIABLES

Of the four categories of demand variables just listed, it is marketing decision variables that play the central role in the theory of marketing programming. They are the tools of the firm's control, however limited, over sales.

A *marketing decision variable* (or *marketing instrument, marketing tool*) is any factor under the control of the firm which may be used to stimulate company sales.

At one time, firms had comparatively few tools for influencing sales.

The eighteenth and nineteenth centuries were characterized by small businesses, local competition, homogeneous products, little branding, and little advertising. Economists, in their analysis of competition, limited their attention to price. As firms and markets grew in size, however, other marketing decision variables increased in competitive importance. In the 1930's some formal analyses began to appear of the role of such nonprice variables as quality, advertising, and service.[2] The trend moved away from a theory of competitive prices toward a theory of competition, in which all instruments of competition were considered.[3] Companies even began to consider their image and the appearance of their plant as marketing decision variables.

The large variety of marketing decision variables led scholars to search for a classification that would facilitate discussion, analysis, and decision making. One useful classification was formulated by Albert W. Frey, who proposed that they be divided into:

1. The offering (product, packaging, brand, price, service)
2. Methods and tools (distribution channels, personal selling, advertising, sales promotion, and publicity) [4]

The distinction largely rests on the difference between *what* the customer is offered and *how* it is offered. The offering embraces those factors which the customer perceives as enhancing the value he receives, while methods and tools are designed primarily to create awareness and interest in these values.

More recently, William Lazer and Eugene Kelley developed the following three-factor classification of marketing decision variables:

1. Goods and service mix
2. Distribution mix
3. Communications mix

According to Lazer and Kelley:

> The *goods and service mix* is concerned with all the ingredients which comprise the bundle of utilities that consumers purchase. This includes such items as the product per se, the package, branding, labeling, warrantees, and services accompanying the product. The *distribution mix* has two major components: (1) Channels of distribution, including all the middlemen and facilitating agencies involved in getting goods and the title to goods to consumers; and (2) Physical distribution, which is concerned with transporting, warehousing, storing, and handling goods. The *communications mix* is concerned with all the persuasive and informational ingredients that are employed in communicating with the market place. Included are personal selling, advertising, sales promotion, merchandising, and special sales aids.[5]

[2] Chamberlin, *op. cit.*

[3] Mickwitz, *op. cit.*

[4] Albert W. Frey, *Advertising,* 3rd ed. (New York: The Ronald Press Company, 1961), p. 30.

[5] William Lazer and Eugene J. Kelley, *Managerial Marketing: Perspectives and Viewpoints,* rev. ed. (Homewood, Ill.: Richard D. Irwin, Inc., 1962), p. 413.

E. Jerome McCarthy popularized a fourfold classification of marketing decision variables which he calls the "Four P's":

1. Product
2. Place

3. Promotion
4. Price [6]

This is essentially the same classification as the preceding one, with price pulled out and given explicit treatment. McCarthy's classification is especially useful from a pedagogical point of view. Nevertheless, the feeling remains that some other classification, still to be born, will develop better conceptual distinctions among the large variety of marketing decision variables.

MARKETING MIX

From the broad array of marketing decision variables, the firm selects some for active use. At any point in time, the firm can be considered to be using some mix of marketing decision variables.

> *Marketing mix* refers to the amounts and kinds of marketing variables the firm is using at a particular time.[7]

The notion of a marketing mix can be conveyed conveniently in the form of vector notation. Suppose the firm produces a product currently priced (P) at $20 and backed by an annual advertising budget (A) of $20,000 and distribution expenditures (D) of $30,000. The company's mix at time t can then be summarized as

$$(\$20, \ \$20{,}000, \ \$30{,}000)_t$$

In more general terms, the company's marketing mix at time t is

$$(P, \ A, \ D)_t$$

One can readily see that a company's current marketing mix is selected from a great number of possibilities. Suppose the company's price is constrained by competitive factors to lie somewhere between $16 and $24 (to the nearest dollar) and both its advertising and its distribution expenditures are constrained by budget limitations to lie somewhere between $10,000 and $50,000 (to the nearest $10,000) each. In other words, the company can choose one of nine possible prices and one of five possible budgets for advertising and distribution respectively, or 225 ($9 \times 5 \times 5$) marketing-mix combinations in all. There would be many more had the choices not been limited to such discrete values. The large number of possible marketing mixes makes it quickly apparent why the optimal marketing mix is so hard to discover.

MARKETING STRATEGY

Marketing mixes have to be changed from time to time in response to new factors in the marketing picture. The firm can react to environmental

[6] E. Jerome McCarthy, *Basic Marketing: A Managerial Approach,* rev. ed. (Homewood, Ill.: Richard D. Irwin, Inc., 1964), pp. 38-40.
[7] For the origin of the concept of marketing mix, see Neil H. Borden, "The Concept of the Marketing Mix," in *Science in Marketing,* ed. George Schwartz (New York: John Wiley & Sons, Inc., 1965), pp. 386-97.

changes in an expedient or in a systematic fashion. In the latter case we postulate the existence of a marketing strategy.

> A *marketing strategy* is a set of principles, or decision rules, that adjust $(P, A, D)_t$ from period t to period $t + 1$, for all t.

Marketing strategies differ according to the elements of the environment they emphasize, the nature and complexity of the response, and the objectives they embody. In a later section we shall distinguish among nine types of marketing strategies and describe how their differing profit-generating capacities can be appraised through simulation.[8]

MARKETING EFFORT

Each particular marketing mix implies a certain amount of effort the company is making for the purpose of generating sales. Thus it can be said unambiguously that the marketing mix ($20, $20,000, $30,000)$_t$ represents a great amount of marketing effort than the mix ($20, $10,000, $30,000)$_t$, because the company is spending $10,000 more on advertising while holding the settings of the other marketing instruments constant.

> *Marketing effort* is a summary term for the value of all the company inputs into the marketing process for the purpose of stimulating sales.

A company's marketing effort can be described in terms of its *level* and *effectiveness*. *Level* refers to the total amount of marketing effort. In principle, the level is measurable in dollars; that is, marketing inputs represent the using up of scarce resources which have a cost. The total cost (or value) of the resources used up in this way represents the company's level of marketing effort. The company's *marketing budget* comes close to being the monetary equivalent of the level of marketing effort. However, it omits certain actions which also express marketing effort, and, as a result, the marketing budget usually understates total marketing effort. For example, a planned reduction in price is tantamount to an increase in marketing effort. So is an R&D investment to improve the quality of a product. Ideally these actions represent alternative uses of funds for the purpose of stimulating sales and should be monetized.

The *effectiveness* of the marketing effort refers to how ably the funds are employed. Implicit is the notion that there is a maximally effective way to use the funds, which may be described as unity. Admittedly it is very hard to measure effectiveness in practice. Low effectiveness is usually signaled before the fact by noting that competitors seem to be doing better with the same budget or after the fact when a new executive seems to produce much more with the same budget.

Company sales thus depend on the level of the company's market effort adjusted by its effectiveness. A company can increase its sales in only two ways. If effectiveness is below unity, the company could concentrate on improving the employment of its present funds. This may mean switching advertising themes, revising sales territories, or changing marketing chan-

[8] See pp. 284-86.

nels. If, however, the company is doing the best job possible with its given funds, it must increase the budget size in order to increase its sales.

MARKETING ALLOCATION

Marketing management must not only set an over-all level of marketing effort but must also determine how to distribute it.

> *Marketing allocation* describes the company's division of its market effort among its products, customer segments, and sales areas.

Earlier we said that the over-all company marketing mix may be represented by $(P, A, D)_t$; that is, a price, advertising budget, and distribution budget at time t. If the company has more than one product, customer type, and sales area, it faces a problem of allocation. Management must decide on the marketing mix for each customer type for each product in each territory. Suppose it sets a price of $20, an advertising budget of $5,000, and a distribution budget of $10,000 for product i selling to customer type j in area k at time t. This can be represented as:

$$(\$20, \$5,000, \$10,000)_{i,j,k,t}$$

Further assignments of effort are made to all the other combinations of customer types, products, and areas. The totality of these assignments constitutes the company's marketing effort.

There are obviously millions of ways to break up the given marketing budget. The problem of determining the optimal allocation is extremely difficult. What the notation is designed to emphasize is that company sales are a function not only of the total mix and level of marketing effort but also of their allocation over the different customer segments, products, and sales areas.

MARKET RESPONSE

All the decisions embodied in the marketing program—decisions on level, allocation, mix, and strategy—are guided by assumptions regarding probable market response.

> *Market* (or *sales*) *response* refers to the behavior of sales in response to alternative levels, allocations, and mixes of marketing effort.

Market response may be used to describe the behavior of an individual buyer, a market segment, or the whole market. The most fruitful level of aggregation depends upon the problem being analyzed, the availability of data, and the number and size distribution of buyers.

Individual buyer level. Figure 12-1 shows the hypothetical responses of two different industrial purchasing agents to the number of calls they receive per year by a company salesman. Buyer A will not make any purchases from the company if the salesman makes fewer than three calls a year. He will buy a hundred units a year from the company if he gets somewhere between three and ten calls a year. He will buy 125 units a year if the salesman makes more than ten calls a year. He is responsive (in jumps) to increased marketing effort.

Buyer B buys an amount that varies directly with the number of calls

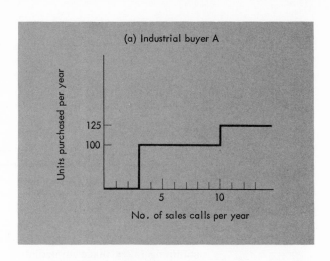

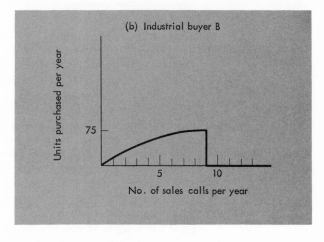

FIGURE 12-1
Hypothetical buyer response to sales calls

per year he receives from the company's salesman, up to nine calls. Beyond nine calls a year, however, he gets impatient about the time the salesman takes up and drops him.

Individual buyer sales response functions are very difficult to determine. If the salesman is making five calls to both A and B, he knows that he gets yearly orders for 100 and 75 units, respectively. What he does not know is how the orders would change if he decreased or increased his calls. He does not know that buyer A would not change his orders for minor decreases or increases in the number of sales calls, while buyer B would change his orders, but not substantially. Generally, the individual salesman is left on his own to guess at the probable shape of the function for each buyer.

Segment level. When there are many buyers and the problem is one of allocating over-all marketing effort (not just sales calls), the analysis of market response is usually made on a market segment level. In this type of analysis, it is assumed that each distinguishable segment of the market has a distinct sales response function; that is, it is a distinct segment because it responds uniquely to marketing mix and effort. Instead of buyer A and buyer B, as in Figure 12-1, there is segment A and segment B. It is likely, however, that segment sales response functions will be smoother because each is really an aggregate of many individual buyers whose idiosyncrasies are averaged out while their commonalities remain.

Whole market level. When it comes to deciding on the over-all level of marketing effort, the analysis is usually based on a conception of the total market response function. Since the curve summarizes all buyers' responses to changes in the level of marketing effort, it is likely to be a smooth function. Furthermore, it may be possible to construct these functions less on guesswork and more on fact through multivariate analysis of past data and data furnished by market experimentation.

Carry-over effects. A major difficulty in the concept of the market response function is the problem of lagged or carry-over effects. The difficulty becomes clear if we contrast responses to production inputs and marketing inputs. If a sheet of metal is placed under a stamp press, the stamping takes place immediately or with a known delay. However, if an advertisement is placed in a magazine, its effect is not likely to be immediate. It represents a tiny deposit in the awareness of the viewer, and many additional exposures, plus other influences, may have to occur before there is a noticeable behavioral response. Marketing inputs, in other words, tend to have their effects distributed or carried over through time.

The carry-over effect of marketing inputs must be taken into consideration in the planning and evaluation of marketing and other company efforts. The fact that the sales response to a new marketing campaign takes place through time means that the company need not immediately fill the channel pipelines with all the goods it expects to sell. It also means that sufficient time must elapse before the total impact of a campaign can be evaluated. Many marketing actions and expenditures are thus in the nature of investments rather than current expenses. They build up capital in the form of company reputation and brand loyalty. Even if the company suddenly reduced its promotional expenditures drastically, its sales would continue for a while at roughly the same level and then decay slowly.

Given the significance of the carry-over effect, the real need is for better ways to conceptualize and measure it. A number of good theoretical and empirical papers have appeared on the subject.[9] To some extent the carry-over effect may be measurable through multivariate analysis of past data, although actual experiments appear even more promising for getting at carry-over effects.

Having defined several terms in the theory of marketing programming, we may now examine the major programming issues.

The Optimal Level of Marketing Effort

Consider a company that is trying to decide how much money to budget for marketing effort. In principle, the company needs information on how the total market would respond to different levels of marketing effort.

9 Roy N. Jastram, "A Treatment of Distributed Lags in the Theory of Advertising Expenditure," *Journal of Marketing,* XX (July 1955), 36-46; Kristian S. Palda, *The Measurement of Cumulative Advertising Effect* (Englewood Cliffs, N.J.: Prentice-Hall, Inc., 1964); and Donald S. Tull, "The Carry-over Effect of Advertising," *Journal of Marketing,* XXIX (April 1965), 46-53.

Some rather complicated statistical and/or experimental procedures may be required to learn this.[10] Here we shall confine ourselves to some general propositions about the likely shape of the sales response function.

SHAPE OF THE SALES RESPONSE FUNCTION

The first proposition is that *increases in the company's marketing effort will produce increases in company sales*. Even this has to be qualified. We are assuming that other things (such as the expenditures of competitors) do not change in the meantime, that the marketing effort is efficiently managed and directed, and that the market is not saturated.

The second proposition is that *the relationship between the sales volume and marketing effort is not linear throughout*. Two different conceptions of the likely shape of the sales response function can be found in the literature. They are contrasted in Figure 12-2. The curve in Figure 12-2a shows the rate of sales increase as always diminishing. This general pattern may be represented by any of the mathematical functions indicated in the figure. The rationale for this curve is as follows: The first marketing dollar will be spent in the best possible way. The second marketing dollar will be spent in the second best way. Successive marketing dollars will be applied in successively less productive ways, and this accounts for the continuously diminishing rate of sales increase.

The curve in Figure 12-2b shows sales initially increasing at an increasing rate and then increasing at a decreasing rate. This general pattern may also be represented by either of the mathematical functions shown in the figure. The rationale for this curve is as follows: Small amounts of marketing effort are not very effective in the market place. They may create some brand awareness and even some brand preference, but are insufficient to motivate widespread purchasing. They are below the threshold level. But additional doses of marketing effort capitalize on the preconditioning and bring about substantial purchasing action.

The curves, in spite of their differences, are alike in holding that eventually a diminishing rate of sales growth can be expected. There are a number of reasons for this. First of all, at a given point in time, there tends to be an upper limit to the total potential demand for any particular product. The easier sales prospects are sold first; the more recalcitrant sales prospects remain. As the upper limit is approached, it becomes increasingly expensive to stimulate further sales. In the second place, as a company steps up its marketing effort, its competitors are likely to do the same, with the net result that each company experiences increasing sales resistance. In the third place, if sales were to increase at an increasing rate throughout, natural monopolies would result. A single firm would tend to take over in each industry because of the greater level of its marketing effort. Yet this is contrary to what we observe in industry.

FINDING THE OPTIMAL MARKETING EFFORT

Now suppose a company managed to determine the approximate shape of its sales curve and it resembled b in Figure 12-2. Where is the point

[10] See R. J. Jessen, "A Switch-over Experimental Design to Measure Advertising Effect," *Journal of Advertising Research*, March 1961, pp. 15-22; and Richard E. Quandt, "Estimating Advertising Effectiveness: Some Pitfalls in Econometric Methods," *Journal of Marketing Research*, May 1964, pp. 51-60.

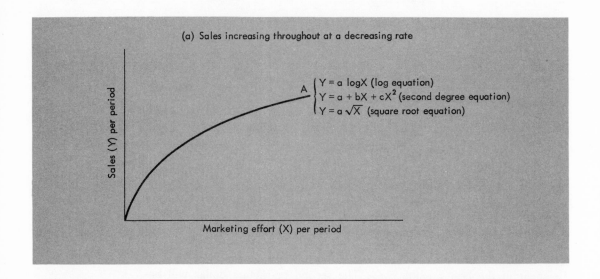

(a) Sales increasing throughout at a decreasing rate

Sales (Y) per period

$$A \begin{cases} Y = a \log X \text{ (log equation)} \\ Y = a + bX + cX^2 \text{ (second degree equation)} \\ Y = a \sqrt{X} \text{ (square root equation)} \end{cases}$$

Marketing effort (X) per period

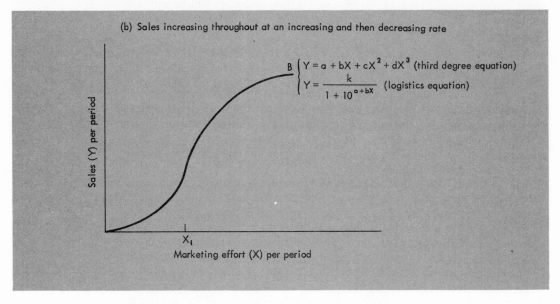

(b) Sales increasing throughout at an increasing and then decreasing rate

Sales (Y) per period

$$B \begin{cases} Y = a + bX + cX^2 + dX^3 \text{ (third degree equation)} \\ Y = \dfrac{k}{1 + 10^{a+bX}} \text{ (logistics equation)} \end{cases}$$

X_1

Marketing effort (X) per period

FIGURE 12-2
Alternative conceptions of the sales response function

of optimum marketing effort? It might seem that this would be where the last increment of effort produces the greatest *rate* of increase in sales. This would take place at the *inflection point* on curve b whose abscissa value is X_1.[11] But this criterion does not really make sense. In the first place, the important thing is not the rate of revenue increase itself but rather the relation of the rate of revenue increase to the rate of cost in-

[11] The inflection point of a curve is the point at which the *rate* of increase (or decrease) changes from increasing to decreasing, or vice versa.

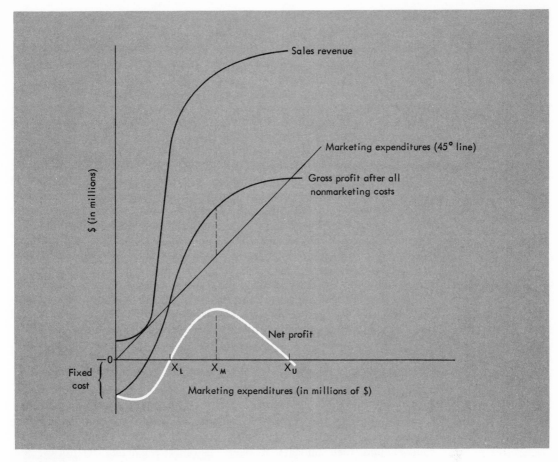

FIGURE 12-3
Relationship between sales, marketing expenditures, and profits

crease; that is, the relation of marginal revenue to marginal cost. In the second place, the criterion would suggest that virtually no marketing effort be expended if sales response was described by curve a, since the greatest rate of sales increase takes place with the first dollar.

Using sales curve b as the basis, some further curves have to be developed to clarify the location of the point of optimum marketing effort. The derived curves are shown in Figure 12-3. First, all nonmarketing costs (mainly material, manufacturing, and administration costs) are subtracted from the *sales revenue curve* to derive the *gross profit curve*. Next the marketing-mix expenditures are drawn in such a way that a dollar on one axis is projected as a dollar on the other axis. This amounts to a 45° line when the axes are scaled in identical dollar intervals. The *marketing expenditures curve* is then subtracted from the *gross profit curve* to derive the *net profit curve*. There are positive net profits with marketing expenditures between X_L and X_U, which could be defined as the rational range of marketing expenditure. The net profit curve is seen to rise to a maximum

273

at X_M. Therefore the marketing expenditure which would maximize net profit is $\$X_M$.

The same solution can be explained in the marginal language of economists. Net profits are maximized at the point where the marginal cost of marketing effort just equals the gross profit derived from the marginal sales increase.[12] This is a useful way of looking at the problem because it implies that a decision on total marketing expenditure can be made without having to know the shape of the entire sales curve. Suppose a marketing budget of $1 million is proposed. Is this optimal? Management can consider this question by pondering what would be gained by raising the budget another $100,000. What would be the best way to spend the additional $100,000, and what increment in sales would it probably generate? What would be the gross profit on this increment of sales? If the expected gross profit exceeds $100,000, then the company would do well to consider the higher budget. In fact, it should apply the same reasoning to consider the spending of a further $100,000. On the other hand, if the marginal gross profit was expected to be less than $100,000, the company would do well to consider reducing the budget below the proposed $1 million. Admittedly, the estimate of marginal sales is crucial and yet highly subjective. But this weakness would exist regardless of the reasoning used in setting the marketing budget. The important thing is to use a model that offers the correct framework for considering the problem.

The Optimal Allocation of Marketing Effort

A company can use one of two opposite approaches to determine the allocation of its marketing budget. It may first decide on a total marketing budget and then allocate it over customer segments, territories, and products. Or it may arrive at the total marketing budget at the end of a process of examining carefully how much should be spent in different segments. For expositional convenience, we shall assume that the planning process starts with a total budget. Our interest will center on how this budget may be optimally subdivided among market segments. For convenience, we shall consider these segments to be sales territories.

ALLOCATION IN PRACTICE

Businessmen generally use one of two rules of thumb to allocate the total marketing budget over sales territories. The first holds that company marketing effort ought to be proportional to industry sales in the different territories ("industry size" rule). If the industry sells twice as much in territory C as in territory D, the company feels it should spend twice as much in territory C as D. The implicit assumption is that territorial opportunity is proportional to present territorial sales.

The other rule holds that company marketing effort ought to be proportional to present company sales in the different territories ("company size" rule). The implicit assumption is that territorial opportunity for a

---

[12] Graphically, this is where the tangent to the gross profit curve shows the same slope as the marketing expenditure curve.

particular company depends upon its present facilities and penetration into each market, not on total industry demand in each market.

Either rule serves the purpose of developing a tentative, initial schedule of allocations. However, neither goes far enough, and both are really wrong in principle. The "industry size" rule leads a company to allocate effort to every geographical area where customers are found. Thus its funds are spread thin, with the result that it may make no special impact on any particular areas. The "company size" rule leads a company to stabilize its present position in each area. It will remain weak where it is now weak and strong where it is now strong. This ignores the possible advantages of strengthening or terminating its position where it is weak or further strengthening its position where it is strong.

In practice, the tentative allocations arrived at by these size rules should be adjusted by *ad hoc* estimates of competitors' intentions, territorial trends, and other modifiers of opportunity. Thus, if it is known that competitors are stepping up their efforts in territory C, the company may prefer to concentrate on territory D rather than go through a bloody, profitless fight to maintain position in C. Or if sales in D are low but historically rising and sales in C are high but historically falling, the company may want to modify any allocation based strictly on a "size" rule of thumb.

Basically, size rules for allocation are wrong because they confuse "average" and "marginal" sales response. Firms ought to allocate their funds on the basis of marginal response and not average response. Figure 12-4 shows the difference between the two and the fact that there is no reason to assume they are correlated. The two dots in the figure show present company sales and marketing expenditures in the two territories. Company sales are $40,000 in C and only half, or $20,000 in D; the company spends $3,000 on marketing in both territories. The average sales response to a dollar of marketing effort is thus greater in C than in D; it is 40/3 as opposed to 20/3, respectively. It might seem therefore desirable to shift

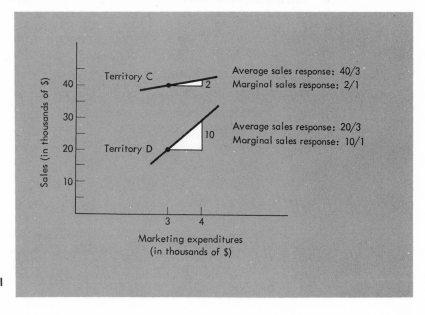

FIGURE 12-4
**Average and marginal
sales response**

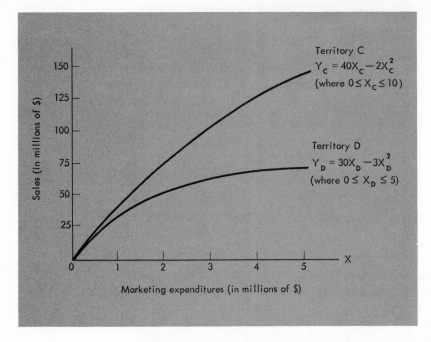

FIGURE 12-5

Sales response functions in two company territories

funds out of D into C where the average response is greater. Yet the real issue is one of the marginal response. The marginal response is represented by the *slope* of the sales function through the points. A higher slope has been drawn for D than C. The respective slopes show that another $1,000 of marketing expenditure would produce a $10,000 sales increase in D and only a $2,000 sales increase in C. Clearly, marginal response, not average response, should guide the allocation of marketing funds. Marginal response is not indicated by average response but by a separate appraisal of the opportunities for using additional funds in the various territories.

ALLOCATION IN THEORY

Let us illustrate the theory of allocation with the simple case of a company that sells in two territories. Assume that the sales response curves for both territories are the ones illustrated in Figure 12-5. Now suppose the company sets a total marketing budget of $6 million. What division of this budget between territories C and D would maximize total company sales?

Let X_C and X_D represent the amount of marketing funds to be allocated to territories C and D respectively. We know that these expenditures are to equal $6 million; i.e.,

$$X_C + X_D = 6 \qquad \text{(1) budget constraint}$$

Furthermore, we know that the optimum allocation would have the following property: it would not pay to switch a dollar from one territory to the other. This is another way of saying that the marginal sales response would be equal in each territory. Now the marginal sales response is graphically interpreted as the slope of a tangent to the sales curve at a

276

given point. Or in mathematical terms, the marginal sales response is given by the *first derivative* of the sales curve.[13] The first derivative of the sales curve $Y_C = 40X_C - 2X_C^2$ is

$$\frac{dY_C}{dX_C} = 40 - 4X_C \qquad \text{(2) marginal sales response, territory } C$$

and the first derivative of the sales curve $Y_D = 30X_D - 3X_D^2$ is

$$\frac{dY_D}{dX_D} = 30 - 6X_D \qquad \text{(3) marginal sales response, territory } C$$

At the optimum allocation, the two first derivatives (or marginal sales responses) would be equal, or

$$\frac{dY_C}{dX_C} = \frac{dY_D}{dY_D}$$
$$40 - 4X_C = 30 - 6X_D \qquad \text{(4) equal marginal effectiveness constraint}$$

We are seeking to find two unknowns which satisfy the two independent constraints (1) and (4). Under normal circumstances, a unique solution is defined by two unknowns and two equations. Substituting (1) into (4) we have

$$40 - 4X_C = 30 - 6(6 - X_C)$$
$$40 - 4X_C = 30 - 36 + 6X_C$$
$$10X_C = 46$$
$$X_C = 4.6$$
$$X_D = 1.4$$

The optimal allocation consists of spending $4.6 million in territory C and $1.4 million in territory D. We could have guessed that more would be spent in C because of the steeper ascent of this curve. Total sales with this allocation will be:

$$Y_C = 40(4.6) - 2(4.6)^2 = \$141.68$$
$$Y_D = 30(1.4) - 3(1.4)^2 = \underline{36.12}$$
$$\$177.80$$

No other allocation can be expected to produce as much as $177.80 million worth of sales.

This solution indicates that the optimal *marketing expense/sales ratios* differ between the two territories. The ratios are:

Territory C: $\dfrac{\text{Marketing expense}}{\text{Expected sales}} = \dfrac{4.6}{141.68} = 3.25\%$

Territory D: $\dfrac{\text{Marketing expense}}{\text{Expected sales}} = \dfrac{1.4}{36.12} = 3.88\%$

This is an important observation. It confirms the fact that "size" rules of thumb do not automatically lead to the optimal allocation. The optimal allocation requires that the *marginal* (not the average) *marketing expense/*

[13] The first derivative is a function showing the instantaneous rate of change occurring at every point on the "parent" function. See any calculus text.

marginal sales ratios be the same for all territories. In the example, these ratios are, for an extra spent $1 (in millions):

Territory C:

$$\frac{\text{Marginal marketing expense}}{\text{Marginal sales response}} = \frac{\$1}{40 - 4(4.6)} = \frac{1}{21.6} = 4.63\%$$

Territory D:

$$\frac{\text{Marginal marketing expense}}{\text{Marginal sales response}} = \frac{\$1}{30 - 6(1.4)} = \frac{1}{21.6} = 4.63\%$$

Our example has been couched in terms of two territories, but it can easily be generalized to n sales territories.[14] Suppose the company develops an approximate idea of the sales curve for each territory. There will be n sales curves represented by n equations. From these, n marginal sales response equations can be found by taking the first derivatives. Now these n marginal equations must all be set equal to each other under optimal allocation. This results in $n - 1$ equality relationships. One more equation is supplied by the condition that the sum of the allocations must add up to the total marketing budget. This makes n equations and since there are n unknowns, under normal circumstances, a unique, maximizing allocation will be yielded by the simultaneous solution of the n equations.[15]

The Optimal Mix of Marketing Effort

We saw in the last section that any level of marketing effort, whether or not it is optimal, can be divided optimally among segments of the market. Given the amount that will go to a segment, the task is now to divide this amount optimally among the various marketing instruments or, to put it another way, to determine the optimal marketing mix for the segment.

The formal conditions for an optimal marketing mix have been stated in a number of ways. Dorfman and Steiner explored the conditions for simultaneous equilibrium of price, advertising, and product quality.[16] They proved mathematically that these instruments are set optimally when

Price elasticity of demand	=	Marginal value product of advertising	=	Quality elasticity of demand times price markup over average cost of production

The intuitive rationale for these equalities is not easy to explain, except to say they represent derivations based on the "marginal revenue equals

---

[14] The basic article on this subject is J. A. Nordin's "Spatial Allocation of Selling Expense," *Journal of Marketing,* VII (January 1943), 210-19. The mathematical analysis is generalized to more than two territories in John A. Howard, *Marketing Management: Analysis and Planning,* rev. ed. (Homewood, Ill.: Richard D. Irwin, Inc., 1963), pp. 475-79.

[15] If the sales response functions are too irregular to be represented by standard equations, convex or dynamic programming techniques can be used. See Andrew Vazsonyi, *Scientific Programming in Business and Industry* (New York: John Wiley & Sons, Inc., 1958), pp. 202-08, 219-27.

[16] See Robert Dorfman and Peter O. Steiner, "Optimal Advertising and Optimal Quality," *American Economic Review,* December 1954, pp. 826-36.

marginal cost" rule for optimality, so familiar to economics students. P. J. Verdoorn stated the rule more intuitively in the following statement based on his own mathematical derivations:

> In an optimum position the additional sales obtained by a small increase in unit costs are the same for all non-price instruments and at the same time equal to the additional sales accompanying a corresponding decrease in unit prices.[17]

The implementation of the rules for finding the optimal marketing mix depends upon having estimates available of marginal sales responses to different marketing instruments. Usually there are not enough past data to do anything more than estimate historical point elasticities. The major recourse at the present time is to use informed executive judgment about the magnitude of the relevant elasticities.

FINDING THE OPTIMAL MIX THROUGH MATHEMATICAL PROGRAMMING

Mathematical programming provides an alternative framework for finding the optimal marketing mix. We shall develop a simple example to show how linear programming may be used in principle to solve simultaneously the optimal allocation of effort between two market segments as well as the optimal mix of effort for each segment. After the example is presented, some of the problems and limitations of the method will also be described.

> The Oxite Company produces a portable oxygen unit and sells it to two types of distributors—fire equipment distributors and surgical supply houses. Oxite's profit margin varies between the two types of distributors because of differences in selling costs, typical order sizes, and different credit policies. On the basis of a distribution cost analysis, the company estimates that the current profit margins are $15 and $10, respectively.
>
> The company's sales are generated by a combination of personal sales-force calls and selective media advertising. The company has four trained salesmen on its payroll, representing 4,000 hours of available customer "contact" time during the next six months. Furthermore, the company has allotted $14,000 toward advertising during the next six months.
>
> An examination of past data indicates that a unit sale to a fire equipment distributor requires about a half-hour sales call and $1 worth of advertising, while a unit sale to a surgical supply house requires a quarter-hour sales call and $2 of advertising.
>
> The company would like to achieve sales of at least 3,000 units in each customer segment. It will accept any allocation of its marketing resources which will maximize profits providing these minimum sales levels are achieved.
>
> The company's problem is to determine how much sales it should seek to develop in each customer segment to maximize its total profits. The actual amount of sales in each territory will depend upon the mix of advertising and selling resources it applies in each segment, both of which are limited. Offhand, it would seem that the company should seek more sales to fire equipment distributors because of the higher profit margin. But selling to fire equipment distributors consumes relatively more sales-force time per unit sold and the limited call time may be a bottleneck.

[17] Robert Ferber and P. J. Verdoorn, *Research Methods in Economics and Business* (New York: The Macmillan Company, 1962), p. 535.

To solve this problem, the first step is to state all the conditions in a compact mathematical form. We shall now proceed to do this. We can distinguish between the firm's objective and the firm's operating constraints.

The objective is to maximize total profits by establishing optimal sales target volumes and marketing mixes for the two customer segments. Let:

X_1 = sales target volume (in units) for fire equipment distributors
X_2 = sales target volume (in units) for surgical supply houses

Since every unit sold to a fire equipment distributor and a surgical supply house will yield $15 and $10 net profit, respectively, total profits will be

$$\text{Profits} = 15X_1 + 10X_2 \qquad \text{(1) profit function}$$

This is called the *objective function,* which the firms wishes to maximize.

Now each possible target sales volume requires a different amount of personal selling and advertising effort. The marketing input requirements and constraints for different sales levels can be expressed mathematically. The sales force, for example, has 4,000 hours of selling time available during the next six months. The estimated amount of selling time consumed will be

$$\tfrac{1}{2}X_1 + \tfrac{1}{4}X_2$$

that is, ½ hour (on the average) for every unit sold to fire equipment distributors and ¼ hour for every unit sold to surgical supply houses. (The numbers ½ and ¼ are called the marketing input coefficients.) The expected amount of selling time cannot exceed the available amount, which is 4,000 hours. Therefore

$$\tfrac{1}{2}X_1 + \tfrac{1}{4}X_2 \leqq 4,000 \qquad \text{(2) sales force constraint}$$

This is the first constraint. We employ a "less-than-or-equal to" sign to indicate that the estimated selling time cannot exceed 4,000 hours.

Similarly, unit sales to fire equipment distributors and surgical supply houses require $1 and $2 of advertising, respectively; i.e.,

$$X_1 + 2X_2$$

But the total amount of advertising cannot exceed $14,000; i.e.,

$$X_1 + 2X_2 \leqq 14,000 \qquad \text{(3) advertising budget constraint}$$

In addition to these constraints, the company has decided that it must strive to sell at least 3,000 units in each segment. This is stated as

$$X_1 \geqq 3,000$$
$$X_2 \geqq 3,000 \qquad \text{(4) minimum sales quota constraints}$$

At this point, the solution technique of linear programming (called the "simplex method") is used to find the values of X_1 and X_2 which maximize the profit function (1) while satisfying the constraints (2), (3), and (4). Here we shall simply state the solution.[18] The Oxite Company should divide its total marketing effort between the two segments so as to

---

[18] Because it involves only two unknowns, this problem can be solved by graphical means or by the simplex method. For a simple account, see R. Stansbury Stockton, *Introduction to Linear Programming* (Boston: Allyn and Bacon, Inc., 1960).

try to sell 6,000 units to the fire equipment distributors and 4,000 units to surgical supply houses. This will result in $130,000 profit. To attain sales of 6,000 units to fire equipment distributors will require 3,000 sales calls (because a half-hour call is required for each sale) and $6,000 of advertising (because one dollar of advertising is required for each call); i.e., (3,000, $6,000). To attain sales of 4,000 units to surgical supply houses will require 1,000 sales calls and $8,000 of advertising; i.e. (1,000, $8,000). These allocations just exhaust the total of the company's marketing resources. No other allocation of marketing resources can produce more profit.

This example shows how a problem in determining the best allocation and mix of marketing effort can be stated and solved in linear programming terms. The example used only two market segments, two marketing instruments, and four constraints (two of which were superfluous), but it is obvious that larger problems can be handled.

At the same time, the limitations of a linear programming statement of this problem should be appreciated. The main obstacles standing in the way of more fruitful marketing applications of linear programming are non-linearities, marketing-mix interactions, and the lack of reliable data. The nonlinearities in real-world relationships may in some cases be compensated for by use of more advanced forms of mathematical programming, such as quadratic programming, integer programming, and dynamic programming. The presence of marketing-mix interactions is more serious. And the problem of data would remain serious even if a nonlinear, interactive statement of the problem could be formulated. The major recourse may be to plug in the estimates of experienced executives. It may be that the solution will not be very sensitive to reasonably different estimates of the data. In any event, the hope is that the insights gained through a mathematical programming approach will more than repay the trouble and cost.

The Optimal Marketing Strategy

Up to now, we have talked about developing an optimal marketing program for today's situation. It should consist of a level, allocation, and mix of marketing effort that maximizes present company objectives in the light of today's market and environmental conditions. But these conditions change over time. There is need to adjust the marketing program in response to various temporal forces: seasons, cyclical changes, and changes in the stage of the product life cycle.

By *marketing strategy* we mean a set of principles for adjusting the marketing program to changing conditions. Marketing strategy acts as an over-all plan that comprehends various possible developments and states the principles for meeting them. In this section, we shall examine one particular temporal force, product life cycle, and discuss possible adjustments of marketing effort and mix to it.

CHANGING IMPORTANCE OF DIFFERENT MARKETING INSTRUMENTS

The theory of the competitive value of different marketing instruments at different stages in the product life cycle has received its most advanced

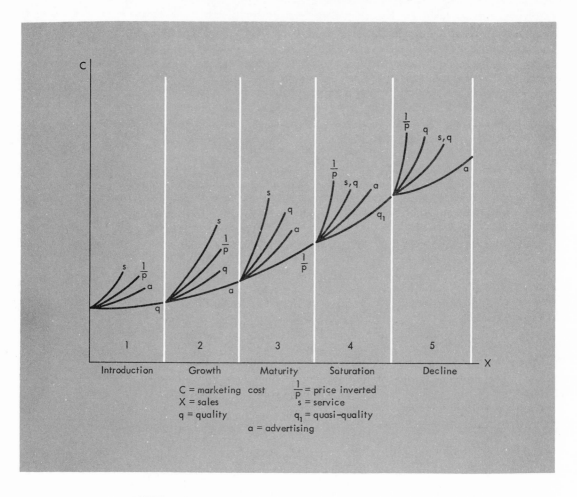

FIGURE 12-6

Elasticity of marketing instruments in different stages of a product's life cycle
Redrawn from Gösta Mickwitz, *Marketing and Competition* (Helsingfors, Finland: Centraltry-ckeriet, 1959), p. 88.

treatment in the hands of the Finnish economist Gösta Mickwitz.[19] His analysis of the changing elasticity of five competitive instruments—product quality, advertising, price, service and quasi-quality (packaging)—is summarized in Figure 12-6. Each of the five panels in Figure 12-6 represents the product at a different stage in its life cycle, (introduction, growth, maturity, saturation, decline).[20] The C axis represents an increase in marketing cost, and the X axis represents the corresponding increase in sales. The slope of each line represents the responsiveness of sales (X) to an increase in that marketing instrument's input (C) at that stage in the product life cycle. Looking at stage 1, we see that quality has, according to Mickwitz, the largest impact on sales. For a very small increase in the cost of more quality, sales increase substantially. The more nearly horizontal the

[19] Mickwitz, *op. cit.*
[20] For definitions, see Chapter 13, p. 291.

line, the greater that instrument's impact on sales. The next most important instrument at stage 1 is advertising, followed by price. The least important instrument is service, indicating that an investment in increased service at the product introduction stage is not likely to increase sales by very much.

By stage 2, the early adopters have already purchased the product, and the firm faces increased buyer resistance. Advertising now becomes the most potent marketing instrument while quality slips to second place. Price and service elasticity are still low.

In stage 3, most of the price-insensitive buyers have already tried the product. Furthermore, new firms have entered the market, and the competition for customers is keen. The industry now makes an effort to draw in the price-sensitive buyers by lowering price. Price is considered the instrument with the highest elasticity at this stage, followed by advertising, quality, and service.

By stage 4, the active price competition of stage 3 has led to a low price, and there is little remaining price elasticity. Sellers try to increase the differentiation of their product. Packaging becomes important. However, the slope of even the packaging curve is high and shows that a fairly substantial investment is needed to generate more sales. Next in importance are advertising, quality, and service, which have about the same capability of increasing sales.

By stage 5, there is less to be gained through further packaging investments. The problem is one of finding new product uses and advertising them. Quality and service investments will have some impact on sales, and price cuts will have virtually no impact.

Mickwitz does not present evidence for these propositions. He deduced them through theory and casual observation. Nevertheless, the import of his analysis is unquestionably valid. Competitive requirements and conditions are continually changing over the product life cycle and therefore warrant periodic changes in the relative use of different marketing instruments.

TESTING MARKETING STRATEGIES

Is there any way for a company to determine in advance which of several alternative long-run marketing strategies is likely to be the most effective? Three different techniques have been proposed for developing a preliminary evaluation: *field experimentation, mathematical analysis,* and *simulation.*

FIELD EXPERIMENTATION.   It would be ideal if the firm could try out a strategy in the real world, then wind the environment back to its initial conditions, and try out another strategy. Since this cannot be done, the next best thing is to try to find two or more sales territories, similar in initial conditions and likely to be exposed to the same subsequent events. The firm can pursue a different strategy in each territory (with replications) and compare the results. Needless to say, there are formidable problems of comparability, control, and interpretation, in addition to the high cost of marketing experiments.

MATHEMATICAL ANALYSIS.   Conceivably the performance characteristics of different strategies can be analyzed mathematically. Environmental events might be represented by probability distributions and a mathematical analysis conducted to evaluate the properties of the different strategies, as well as an optimal strategy. Unfortunately total marketing processes, in contrast to specific marketing problems, are generally too complex to represent and solve through manageable equation systems.

SIMULATION. A third way to deal with complex systems and processes is through simulation. Computer simulation suggests itself as the most promising tool in this connection.

Computer simulation was used by this writer to examine what would happen when two competitors introduced a new product at the same time and employed different marketing strategies over the product life cycle.[21] The market was one which exhibited classic S-shaped growth, a regular pattern of seasonal variation, and responsiveness to the total level, mix, and allocation of competing companies' marketing efforts. The new product, an inexpensive portable tape recorder, was introduced simultaneously by the two firms at $t = 0$. Market acceptance was rapid at first and then tapered off; by the sixtieth month ($t = 60$) the product was in the market saturation stage of the product life cycle.

Firm i's marketing mix at time t was given by $(P, A, D)_{i,t}$. The issue of marketing strategy is one of developing a set of decision rules which would adjust $(P, A, D)_{i,t}$ to $(P, A, D)_{i,t+1}$, for all t. The following nine general classes of marketing strategy were distinguished:

1. *Nonadaptive.* A strategy in which the initial marketing mix is held constant throughout the product's life cycle.
2. *Time-dependent.* A strategy which provides for prescheduled changes in the marketing mix to take place through time.
3. *Competitively adaptive.* A strategy in which firm i adjusts its marketing mix to the marketing mix changes made by firm j in the previous period.
4. *Sales-responsive.* A strategy in which the firm adjusts its marketing mix on the basis of its sales in the previous period(s).
5. *Profit-responsive.* A strategy in which the firm adjusts its marketing mix on the basis of its profits in the previous period(s).
6. *Completely adaptive.* A strategy which produces monthly changes in the company's marketing mix in response to all current developments, including the passage of time, changes in own and competitor's sales and profits, and changes in the competitor's marketing mix.
7. *Diagnostic.* A strategy which produces changes in the marketing mix only after distinguishing among possible causes of current developments.
8. *Profit-maximizing.* A strategy which would maximize the firm's profits.
9. *Joint profit-maximizing.* A strategy which would maximize total industry profits under collusion.

Two specific examples of these strategies are described to illustrate the approach:

[21] Philip Kotler, "Competitive Strategies for New Product Marketing over the Life Cycle," *Management Science,* December 1965, pp. 104-119.

$$P_{i,t} = 5 \ (.95)^t + 15$$

Price initially stands at \$20 and falls at a decreasing rate to \$15 as time goes to infinity.

$$A_{i,t} = 1.01 \ A_{i,t-1}$$
$$D_{i,t} = 1.01 \ D_{i,t-1}$$

Advertising and distribution expenditures are increased 1 per cent each period.

The objective of the pricing decision rule is to earn an initial premium by selling the product to the less price-sensitive, more affluent customers. Further sales gains are made by gradually reducing the price to stimulate sales among more price-sensitive segments of the market. The price is never permitted to fall below \$15 which represents unit variable production costs (say \$10) plus some margin (say \$5) which, at planned sales levels, would cover overhead and yield some profit. Advertising and distribution expenditures are increased each month by 1 per cent to take advantage of the expected continuous growth in the market.

Example of a competitively adaptive strategy

$$P_{i,t} = \ .95 \ P_{j,t-1}$$

Firm i sets its price at 95 per cent of firm j's previous price.

$$A_{i,t} = 1.02 \ A_{j,t-1}$$
$$D_{i,t} = 1.02 \ D_{j,t-1}$$

Firm i sets advertising and distribution expenditures at 102 per cent of firm j's expenditures in the previous period.

Here the firm seeks to "out-appeal" its rival in every possible way, in the interest of achieving the larger market share. It sets its price 5 per cent below the rival's price in the last period and sets its advertising and distribution expenditures 2 per cent above its rival.

Altogether, 13 different specific strategies were developed for testing. Given this number of strategies, it is possible to form 78 pairs.[22] The procedure consisted of simulating each of the 78 possible competitive strategy confrontations over a 60 month period. For example, one confrontation consisted of one duopolist using the specific time-dependent strategy shown above and the other using the specific competitively adaptive strategy shown above for 60 months. The print-out provided a month-by-month description of the marketing mix of each duopolist, the level of total industry sales, each firm's sales and market share, and each firm's profits. In addition, the monthly profits of each duopolist were cumulated with compound interest, and the total was posted at the end of 60 months of play.

The profit and market share results of the 78 simulations were summarized and analyzed. Subject to a number of qualifications, it was possible to answer the following questions:

Which of the 13 specific strategies was the best to adopt if the firm

[22] Since there were 13 specific strategies, 78 unique confrontations could be simulated, according to the combinatorial formula $_{13}C_2 = 13!/2!11!$.

wanted to guarantee a minimum return regardless of what its competitor did? (The best minimax strategy was a completely nonadaptive one.)

Which strategy subjected the firm to the greatest amount of risk? (One of the competitively adaptive strategies was ruinous. It led to the largest market share but at substantial losses.)

Which strategy offered the chance of greatest profit? (A profit-responsive strategy was best.)

If the rival's strategy is known in advance with certainty, what is the firm's best strategy? (The best strategy varied with the firm's objectives.)

In this way computer simulation permitted a preliminary evaluation to be made of alternative marketing strategies.

Summary

After a firm analyzes its marketing opportunities and selects its marketing targets, it faces the task of developing an effective marketing program. The marketing program is a set of policy decisions on the level, allocation, and mix of marketing effort. This chapter has examined the basic principles underlying the making of these decisions. Several concepts are basic to marketing programming: demand variables, marketing decision variables, marketing mix, marketing strategy, marketing effort, marketing allocation, and market response. And there are various useful principles for determining the optimal level, allocation, and mix of present marketing effort, as well as the optimal marketing strategy for adjusting the program through time. Theory is continuing to evolve in this area, and should eventually culminate into practical rules for developing the marketing program.

Questions and Problems

1. The statement is made in the text that "a planned reduction in price is tantamount to an increase in marketing effort." How can the price reduction be monetized into its equivalent in increased marketing effort?

2. List as many specific marketing actions to stimulate sales as you can think of available to (a) supermarkets; (b) airlines.

3. What difficulties are there in a two-factor classification of all marketing decision variables into the offering and the marketing tool mix?

4. How many different marketing mixes could be formulated given a dozen marketing activities which could each be performed at five different levels?

5. Develop a long-range plan for marketing a new line of electric can openers, indicating for each stage in the product's life cycle (introductory, growth, maturity, saturation, and decline) the major objective and the likely policy on price, quality, advertising, personal selling, and channels.

6. Suppose the quantity sold (Q) of an item depends upon the price charged (P), the level of advertising expenditure (A), and the level of distribu-

tion expenditure (D). Develop a hypothetical equation (a) where the marginal effect of each marketing variable is uninfluenced by the level of the other marketing variables; (b) where the marginal effect of each marketing variable is influenced by the level of the other variables.

7. The solution to the linear programming problem on pp. 279-81 was stated without proof. Can you show how the solution can be found through graphical methods?

chapter 13

Product-Policy Decisions

In this chapter, we turn to one of the most crucial factors in the company's marketing effort: the products it develops to meet customer needs. The company's products are the foundation of the marketing program. The choice of products affects the choice of trade channels, promotional media and messages, physical distribution arrangements, and other significant dimensions of the marketing program.

Product policy not only affects the rest of the marketing program but is a variable in its own right, determining the company's position in the market place. Decisions on the width and depth of the company's product mix significantly affect buyer interest. Buyer interest is also affected by company decisions on modifying, dropping, and adding individual products.

This chapter examines the major decisions faced by companies in the area of product policy. The first section presents some basic product concepts and distinctions useful in the analysis of product-policy problems. The second section examines the influence of a product's characteristics on product policy and marketing strategy. The third section examines how the product-mix decision is affected by company objectives. The final two sections develop analytical approaches to the product-modification and product-elimination decisions, respectively. The new-product decision is analyzed separately in the next chapter.

Basic Product Concepts

Product-policy decisions are shaped by a multitude of factors, including the basic nature of the firm's business, its objectives, its resources, and its opportunities. As a prelude to discussing these decisions, we shall first define some concepts.

WHAT IS A PRODUCT?

The idea of a product seems intuitive; yet there is a real problem in knowing exactly what it embraces. Consider a camera. Viewed physically, it is an air-filled assembly of metal or plastic parts surrounding a lens. It may come with a case, accessories, and instructions, all packaged in an attractive box bearing a bright brand trade mark. To the buyer, the company's product is composed of these elements plus the services the seller and manufacturer make available as part of the purchase.

But the camera as a product is more than the bundle of physical parts and company services. The buyer sees the camera as a means of satisfying certain needs and desires. The camera promises him pleasure, nostalgia, a form of immortality. It may be a means of expressing artistic or craftsmanship instincts. It can be a symbol of status and a means of relating to other people.

Therefore we shall find it useful to define a *product* as:

> a bundle of physical, service, and symbolic particulars expected to yield satisfactions or benefits to the buyer.

Product policy in its broadest sense would comprehend all decision making that affects what customers see as the firm's offer.

ITEMS, LINES, AND THE PRODUCT MIX

Most companies today are multiproduct organizations. Whether large or small, whether in manufacturing, wholesaling, or retailing, a company generally handles a multitude of products and product varieties. In 1965, for instance, the average supermarket handled 6,800 items, American Optical Company manufactured 30,000 different items, and General Electric handled over 250,000 items.

The proliferation of products within the typical company means that product-policy decisions are made at three different levels of product aggregation:

> *Product item:* A specific version of a product that has a separate designation in the seller's list.
> *Product line:* A group of products that are closely related either because they satisfy a class of need, are used together, are sold to the same customer groups, are marketed through the same types of outlets, or fall within given price ranges.
> *Product mix:* The composite of products offered for sale by a firm or a business unit.[1]

For example, the Kodak Instamatic 100 is a product item; Eastman Kodak's cameras are a product line; Eastman Kodak's cameras, photographic supplies, chemicals, plastics, and fibers are its product mix.

WIDTH, DEPTH, AND CONSISTENCY OF THE PRODUCT MIX

The *width* of the product mix refers to *how many different product lines are found within the company*. The Bissell Company until recently produced only one product line, carpet sweepers. General Electric, on the other hand, produces transformers, light bulbs, toasters, radios, jet engines, and scores of other product lines. The measured width of the product mix depends on the definitions established for product-line boundaries.

The *depth* of the product mix refers to the *average number of items offered by the company within each product line*. The Toni Company, for example, produces its Home Permanent Waves in nine versions to accommodate different hair types and styles and produces its Deep Magic Skin Creme in two versions to accommodate regular and dry skin. These

---

[1] The last two definitions are taken from *Marketing Definitions: A Glossary of Marketing Terms,* compiled by the Committee on Definitions of the American Marketing Association, Ralph S. Alexander, Chairman (Chicago: American Marketing Association, 1960).

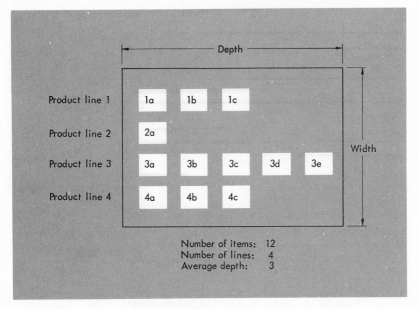

Product line 1 — 1a 1b 1c

Product line 2 — 2a

Product line 3 — 3a 3b 3c 3d 3e

Product line 4 — 4a 4b 4c

Depth

Width

Number of items: 12
Number of lines: 4
Average depth: 3

FIGURE 13-1

Conceptual representation of a product mix

and other product-line depths can be averaged to indicate the typical depth of the company's product mix.

The *consistency* of the product mix refers to *how closely related the various product lines are in end use, production requirements, distribution channels, or in some other way.* Contrast the product mixes of General Electric and Hunt Foods & Industries, Inc. In spite of the large number of General Electric's lines, there is an over-all consistency in that most products involve electricity in one way or another. Hunt, on the other hand, produces tomato products, paint, matches, magazines, metal and glass containers, and steel.

All three dimensions of the product mix have a market rationale. Through increasing the width of the product mix, the company hopes to capitalize on its good reputation and skills in present markets. Through increasing the depth of its product mix, the company hopes to entice the patronage of buyers of widely differing tastes and needs. Through increasing the consistency of its product mix, the company hopes to acquire an unparalleled reputation in a particular area of endeavor.

The concepts of width, depth, and consistency are related to those of product item, lines, and mix. Figure 13-1 illustrates these relationships for a hypothetical company's product mix. The mix consists of four different lines of products with an average depth of three products to a line.

The figure helps clarify the major issues in product policy. Product policy at the level of the product item involves the issues of whether to modify, add, or drop product items. Product policy at the level of the product line involves the issue of whether to deepen or shorten an existing line. Product policy at the level of the product mix involves the issue of whether to drop or add a whole line.

PRODUCT LIFE CYCLE

Figure 13-1 presented a picture of a company's product mix at a point in time. Over time, this mix will undoubtedly change; new items and

290

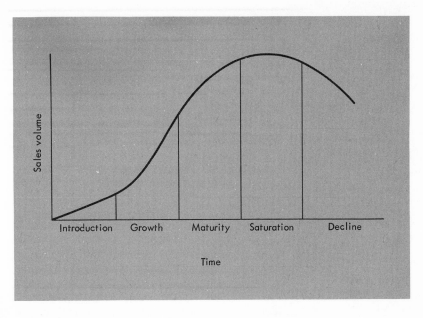

FIGURE 13-2
Stages in the product life cycle

lines will be added and old ones dropped. This is because current company products cannot hold their market positions indefinitely.

The lifetime sales of many branded products reveal a typical pattern of development, known as the *product life cycle,* which is illustrated in Figure 13-2. Five stages can be distinguished.

> *Introduction.* The product is put on the market; awareness and acceptance are minimal.
>
> *Growth.* The product begins to make rapid sales gains because of the cumulative effects of introductory promotion, distribution, and word-of-mouth influence.
>
> *Maturity.* Sales growth continues but at a declining rate because of the diminishing number of potential customers who remain unaware of the product or who have taken no action.
>
> *Saturation.* Sales reach and remain on a plateau marked by the level of replacement demand.
>
> *Decline.* Sales begin to diminish absolutely as the product is gradually edged out by better products or substitutes.

The product life cycle concept is advanced as a useful idealization rather than a rigid description of all product life histories.[2] It should be understood that there is nothing fixed about the length of the cycle or of its various stages. According to Joel Dean, the length of the product life cycle is governed by the rate of technical change, the rate of market acceptance, and the ease of competitive entry.[3] Each year, some new dress styles are introduced in the knowledge that their whole life cycle may span only a year or a season. On the other hand, new commercial air-

[2] See Arch Patton, "Top Management's Stake in the Product Life Cycle," *The Management Review,* June 1959, pp. 9-14, 67-71, 76-79.

[3] See Joel Dean, "Pricing Policies for New Products," *Harvard Business Review,* November-December 1950, p. 28.

craft are introduced in the expectation that they will enjoy good sales for at least a decade.

Furthermore, products have been known to begin a new cycle or to revert to an earlier stage as a result of the discovery of new uses, the appearance of new users, or the invention of new features. Television sales exhibited a history of spurts as new sizes of screens were introduced, and color television may well put television sales back into a rapid growth stage.

Despite these difficulties, the concept of the product life cycle remains very useful in that it reminds us of three important phenomena:

> *Products have a limited life.* They are born at some point, may (or may not) pass through a strong growth phase, and eventually degenerate or disappear.
>
> *Product profits tend to follow a predictable course through the life cycle.* Profits are absent in the introductory stage, tend to increase substantially in the growth stage, slow down and then stabilize in the maturity and saturation stages, and all but disappear in the decline stage.
>
> *Products require a different marketing (as well as production and financial) program in each stage.* Management must be prepared to shift the relative levels and emphasis given to price, advertising, product improvement, and other marketing elements during different stages in the product life cycle.[4]

Product Characteristics and Marketing Strategy

It is important to recognize that a product's characteristics have a substantial influence on the design of the marketing program. For example, the fact that cameras have a moderate unit value, are capable of technical variation, are purchased on a "one-shot" basis, and are durable leads manufacturers to develop a large variety of cameras, to search continuously for new product features, to develop selective to intensive distribution, and to place about equal emphasis on advertising and personal selling.

The substantial influence of a product's characteristics on marketing strategy has led marketing scholars to search for meaningful ways to classify products. The thought is that a good classification can help the marketer determine more accurately appropriate product and marketing policies. We shall examine some alternative product classifications and their marketing implications.

CONSUMERS' AND INDUSTRIAL GOODS

The most venerable classification is that of consumers' goods and industrial goods:

> *Consumers' goods:* goods destined for use by ultimate consumers or households, and in such form that they can be used without commercial processing.

---

[4] See Chapter 12, pp. 281-83. Also see Theodore Levitt, "Exploit the Product Life Cycle," *Harvard Business Review,* November-December 1965, pp. 81-94.

Industrial goods: goods which are destined to be sold primarily for use in producing other goods or rendering services. . . . They include equipment (installed and accessory), component parts, maintenance, repair and operating supplies, raw materials, fabricating materials.[5]

Many goods fall exclusively into one or the other category (toothpaste is always a consumers' good, and jet engines are always an industrial good). Other goods may have both consumer and industrial destinations (paper, diamonds, and typewriters). The basic reason for the distinction is that industrial buyers differ somewhat in their buying motives, habits, and skills from consumer buyers.[6] To the extent these differences exist, the marketing strategies for industrial and consumers' goods are likely to show some over-all differences.

CONVENIENCE, SHOPPING, AND SPECIALTY GOODS

Consumers' goods have been subclassified for many years into convenience, shopping, and specialty goods.[7] The most recent American Marketing Association definitions are:

Convenience goods: Those consumers' goods which the customer usually purchases frequently, immediately, and with the minimum of effort in comparison and buying. Examples are tobacco products, soap, newspapers, magazines, chewing gum, small packaged confections, and many food products.

Shopping goods: Those consumers' goods which the customer, in the process of selection and purchase, characteristically compares on such bases as suitability, quality, price, and style. Examples are millinery, furniture, dress goods, women's ready-to-wear and shoes, used automobiles, and major appliances.

Specialty goods: Those consumers' goods with unique characteristics and/or brand identification for which a significant group of buyers are habitually willing to make a special purchasing effort. Examples are specific brands and types of fancy goods, hi-fi components, certain types of sporting equipment, photographic equipment, and men's suits.[8]

Whereas the previous classification was based on who the buyers are, this one is based on how they buy the product. The idea is that the amount and character of the buyers' shopping effort for the product have an important bearing on marketing strategy. If cameras are bought as a specialty good, the manufacturer might adopt selective or exclusive distribution and direct his promotion to loyal segments of the market. If cameras are bought as a shopping good, then the manufacturer might instead adopt the latest product features, price competitively, develop widespread distribution, and place most of the emphasis on advertising.

The classification does give rise to some ambiguities, and many redefini-

[5] Committee on Marketing Definitions, *op. cit.*

[6] See Chapter 2, pp. 20-22.

[7] The classification was first developed by Melvin T. Copeland, "Relation of Consumers' Buying Habits to Marketing Methods," *Harvard Business Review*, April 1923, pp. 282-89.

[8] Committee on Marketing Definitions, *op. cit.*

tions and revisions have been proposed over the years in the interest of rendering the marketing strategy implications of these concepts clearer.[9]

DURABLES, NONDURABLES, AND SERVICES

Another classification of goods may be made among durables, non-durables, and services.

> *Durable goods:* Tangible goods which normally survive many uses.
> *Nondurable goods:* Tangible goods which normally are consumed in one or a few uses.
> *Services:* Activities, benefits, or satisfactions which are offered for sale.[10]

These distinctions are based both on the rate of consumption and on the tangibility of the product, which in turn have implications for marketing strategy. Products that are consumed fast and purchased frequently (non-durables and services) are likely to be made available in many locations, command a small margin, and develop strong brand loyalty. Durable products, on the other hand, are likely to be shopping or specialty goods, need more personal selling, command a higher margin, and require more seller guarantees.

RED, ORANGE, AND YELLOW GOODS

It has been thought that some of the anomalies between the classification of products and the supposed appropriate market strategy result from consideration of too few characteristics. Each product embodies a multitude of characteristics, some of which work at cross purposes. With this in mind, Leo V. Aspinwall in 1958 proposed a product classification based on a more extensive list of five product characteristics which he held led to contrasting policies for promotion and distribution: [11]

> *Replacement rate:* the rate at which a good is purchased and consumed by users in order to provide the satisfaction a consumer expects from the product.
> *Gross margin:* the difference between the paid-in cost and the final realized sales price.
> *Adjustment:* the amount of services applied to goods in order to meet the exact needs of the consumer.
> *Time of consumption:* the measured time of consumption during which the good gives up the utility desired.
> *Searching time:* the measure of average time and distance from the retail store.

On the basis of these characteristics, Aspinwall used arbitrary color designations to define three categories of goods:

> *Red goods:* Goods with a high replacement rate and a low gross margin, adjustment, time of consumption, and searching time. (Example: many food products)

[9] See Louis P. Bucklin, "Retail Strategy and the Classification of Consumer Goods," *Journal of Marketing,* XXVII (January 1963), 50-55.
[10] Committee on Marketing Definitions, *op. cit.*
[11] Leo V. Aspinwall, "The Characteristics of Goods Theory," in *Managerial Marketing: Perspectives and Viewpoints,* rev. ed., eds. William Lazer and Eugene J. Kelley (Homewood, Ill.: Richard D. Irwin, Inc., 1962), pp. 633-43.

Orange goods: Goods with a medium score on all five characteristics. (Example: men's suits)

Yellow goods: Goods with a low replacement rate and a high gross margin, adjustment, time of consumption, and searching time. (Example: refrigerators)

Aspinwall suggested that a scoring system could be set up so that any particular good could be rated on a scale from zero to one hundred on the basis of the total amount it contained of the five characteristics. Red goods would score on the low end of the scale, and yellow goods would score on the high end.[12] He held that the product's score would indicate the desirability of using direct as opposed to indirect methods of distribution; the higher the product's score, the more desirable is direct distribution. The product's score is supposed to indicate desirable policies in other marketing areas as well.

Aspinwall's basic notion that it takes several characteristics to define an appropriate marketing strategy for a good has received further elaboration by others. Gordon E. Miracle classified goods into five categories based on the following nine product characteristics: unit value, significance of each individual purchase to the consumer, time and effort consumers spend purchasing, rate of technological or fashion change, technical complexity, consumer need for service, frequency of purchase, rapidity of consumption, and extent of usage.[13]

His Group I goods, for example, consisted of goods which scored very low on the first six characteristics and very high on the last three characteristics; examples were cigarettes, candy bars, razor blades, and soft drinks. He postulated that the following marketing strategies would tend to characterize Group I goods:

Product policy: only one, or a few varieties

Marketing channel policy: intensive distribution

Promotional policy: almost complete reliance on consumer advertising

Pricing policy: stable prices not subject to much control by seller

Goods in his Group V scored very high on the first six characteristics and very low on the last three; examples were electric generators and specialized machine tools. Miracle postulated that these goods would be marketed through policies at the opposite end of the spectrum from those shown for Group I goods. While Miracle's elaboration of Aspinwall's scheme still gives rise to some marketing strategy anomalies, it represents the kind of cumulative theorizing that will ultimately lead to a very useful product classification.

Company Objectives and the Product Mix

The previous section showed how product characteristics have a strong influence on product and marketing strategy. Management's long-run ob-

[12] In scoring, the inverse of the replacement rate is used. Thus a high replacement rate means a low number of points.

[13] Gordon E. Miracle, "Product Characteristics and Marketing Strategy," *Journal of Marketing,* XXIX (January 1965), 18-24.

jectives also have a strong influence on product and marketing strategy. These objectives shape the firm's product mix, determine the attention paid to individual products, and influence their marketing programs. The following paragraphs examine how a company's mix of objectives regarding profits, sales stability, and sales growth affects and is affected by its product mix.

PROFITS

The amount of profit a company can realize depends ultimately upon its product mix. Its current product mix will generate a certain level of sales and profits. The firm's product mix, in fact, tends to set the upper limit for the firm's potential profitability, while the quality of its marketing program tends to determine how closely this upper limit is reached. The two sources of profit improvement are, therefore, adjustments in the product mix and adjustments in the marketing strategy.

The current relative profit contributions of individual products are not likely to be reflected by their relative sales. High-volume products tend to carry small gross margins. The profit contributions should be measured by the differences between the revenues brought in by the individual products and their respective traceable costs. These differences are the products' contributions to profit and overhead.

Figure 13-3 shows the profit-overhead contributions of ten products of a hypothetical company, expressed as percentages of the total. The first, or best-ranking product, contributes 28 per cent of all the profit and overhead. The first four products contribute 83 per cent of all the profit and overhead. This picture is quite typical. Generally, a small proportion of a company's products accounts for a high proportion of its profits.

The variation of individual product-profit contributions has at least two important implications for product-mix planning. The first implication is that the company has to devote a major part of its effort to protecting and enhancing the market position of its top four products. If product 1 meets some unexpected market reversal, then 28 per cent of the total contribution to overhead and profits is endangered. The second implication is that the company may be able to increase its average level of profits by dropping some of the bottom six products, especially those which absorb a lot of company time and resources in relation to the profits they generate. This is a very complicated decision, however, and will be analyzed in a later section.[14]

STABILITY

Many managements adopt the objective of reasonably stable sales from period to period. High sales variability can be quite costly to the firm. It means that the company has to invest in facilities for peak demand or carry higher inventories to meet peak demand. It means that the company may have to pay more interest on its money because of the greater risk that it may not be able to cover its interest payments in periods of low sales. It increases the number of wrong decisions in forward planning because sales are more difficult to forecast.

A company would therefore want to consider how alternative adjustments of its product mix are likely to affect the stability of sales revenue.

[14] See pp. 302-312.

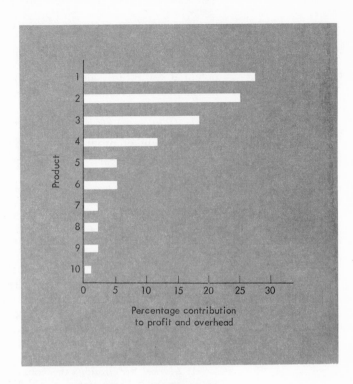

FIGURE 13-3
Profit-overhead contribution of different company products

To dramatize the problem, suppose the company's present product mix generates highly variable sales. Four different products are under review as possible additions to the product mix. The first product promises highly stable sales. The second product is unrelated to the current products and would produce sales subject to about the same amount of variability as now exists. The third product's sales are expected to show high positive correlation with present total sales. The fourth product's sales are likely to show high negative correlation with present total sales. Which product addition would do the most to stabilize total product sales?

Since the first product's sales are highly stable, the addition of this product would not alter the existing level of variability. Since the second product's sales are uncorrelated with current sales, the addition of this product would increase slightly the level of sales variability. Since the third product's sales are positively correlated with sales arising from the current product mix, the addition of this product would increase substantially the level of sales variability. Only the fourth product, whose sales are negatively correlated with current total sales, would decrease over-all variability. In fact, if a new product were found whose expected sales equaled in magnitude present total sales and showed perfect negative correlation with them, the addition of this product would produce a new pattern of total sales that would be perfectly stable. The main point is that the objective of sales stability imposes certain constraints on which products might be added or deleted.

GROWTH

Another objective emphasized by a large number of companies is rising sales through time. The rate of sales growth depends upon where various

297

products in the company's current mix are in their respective life cycles and what plans are made for product additions and deletions.

Peter Drucker described how every company's product mix reveals the potential for future sales growth through the proportions of its products in each of the six following categories:

1. *Tomorrow's breadwinners*—new products or today's breadwinners modified and improved.
2. *Today's breadwinners*—the innovations of yesterday.
3. *Products capable of becoming net contributors if something drastic is done.*
4. *Yesterday's breadwinners*—typically products with high volume, but badly fragmented into "specials," small orders, and the like.
5. *The "also rans"*—typically the high hopes of yesterday that, while they did not work out well, nevertheless did not become outright failures.
6. *The failures.*[15]

The company whose current product mix consists largely of "yesterday's breadwinners" and "also rans" is headed for trouble, no matter how attractive its current sales level appears.

For the company that is committed to a high rate of growth, four basic *product-market strategies* are available. Ansoff has described these strategies as follows:

1. *Market penetration:* the company seeks increased sales for its present products in its present markets through more aggressive promotion and distribution.
2. *Market development:* the company seeks increased sales by taking its present products into new markets.
3. *Product development:* the company seeks increased sales by developing improved products for its present markets.
4. *Diversification:* the company seeks increased sales by developing new products for new markets.[16]

Thus a sales growth objective can be implemented through a variety of product-market strategies.

THE OPTIMAL PRODUCT MIX

The company's objectives are the basis for defining the optimal product mix. The company's current product mix is said to be optimal if no adjustment would enhance the company's chances of achieving its objectives. If the company's objective is primarily profit maximization, then the product mix is optimal if profits could not be improved by deleting, modifying, or adding products. If the company's objective is primarily sales growth, then the product mix is optimal if it yields a rate of sales growth that could not be profitably enhanced by any product-mix changes. Typically there are many objectives, and this complicates the problem of defining an optimal product mix.

[15] Peter Drucker, "Managing for Business Effectiveness," *Harvard Business Review,* May-June 1963, p. 59.

[16] H. Igor Ansoff, "Strategies for Diversification," *Harvard Business Review,* September-October 1957, pp. 113-24.

It is generally easier to recognize the symptoms of suboptimality than to state positively the characteristics of an optimal mix. Any of the following conditions suggests that a current product mix might be less than optimal:

> Excess productive capacity on a chronic or seasonally recurring basis.
> Disproportionately high percentage of total profits from a few products.
> Insufficient product width to exploit sales-force contacts efficiently.
> Steadily declining sales or profits.

Here we will present a management science perspective on the problem of achieving an optimal product mix. We shall distinguish between the static and dynamic optimal product-mix problem.

STATIC OPTIMAL PRODUCT-MIX PROBLEM.   The static optimal product-mix problem can be described in the following way: given n product possibilities, choose m of them (when $m < n$) such that profit (or some other objective) is maximized subject to certain constraints being satisfied. This problem is found in a number of situations. Retailers and wholesalers typically have to ration scarce shelf space among a large competing set of products, candy manufacturers have to decide on the best mix of candies to produce and package, and companies facing equipment or labor shortages have to decide which products to produce.

Under certain conditions the problem may be solvable through mathematical programming, the most important condition being no demand and cost interactions among the various products being considered. This condition is rarely satisfied in practice.

DYNAMIC OPTIMAL PRODUCT-MIX PROBLEM.   This is the problem of timing deletions and additions to the product mix in response to changing opportunities and resources so that the product mix remains optimal through time. Conceptually, it requires re-solving the static product-mix problem periodically because the constraints of the problem change or are expected to change.

Although little work has been done on this problem, computer simulation offers the greatest hope of some breakthrough. Management is interested in what will happen to profits, sales stability, and sales growth as the product mix is changed. A logical approach would be to investigate possible sequences and timings of planned product deletions and additions over some future time period. This approach would require assumptions about the future behavior of sales, costs, and profits for individual products and groups of products.

The computer's contribution would consist of making rapid calculations of profit, stability, and growth characteristics of the many different possible transformations of the product mix through time. By simulating sales and profit patterns of alternative product-mix changes, it would provide management with informative estimates of the expected payoffs and risks of different product-mix strategies.

The Product-Modification Decision

In the remainder of this chapter we shall discuss questions dealing with the management of products in the current mix. Some of these products require periodic modification if they are to remain competitive. Other products pass on to the stage where further product modification could not help; they are candidates for elimination. We shall examine these two product-decision areas separately.

A product modification is any deliberate alteration in the physical attributes of a product or its packaging. It will be distinguished from alterations made in the marketing program for the product.

Some products are not capable of being modified. Many chemicals and raw materials are what they are, and virtually all seller competition in these fields focuses on merchandising differentiation rather than product differentiation. But most products are capable of substantial and sometimes infinite variation in their physical attributes. Here is where the manufacturer is faced with real product-variation alternatives which can critically affect over-all sales. The manufacturer will want to review periodically whether anything can be gained through product modification.

A number of factors may prompt the manufacturer to alter his product. He may want to take advantage of a *new technological development*. Thus, razor-blade manufacturers turned to stainless steel once certain technical problems were solved. He may have to modify his product out of *competitive necessity;* the annual restyling of automobiles is a prime example of this. He may want to rejuvenate a product whose sales are slipping; many manufacturers commission new packaging for their products when newer and brighter competitor brands threaten their sales.

What kinds of product modifications can the manufacturer consider? Since products have such attributes as color, size, material, functional features, styling, and engineering, any one or combination of these attributes could be candidates for change. The following paragraphs examine three especially important and contrasting product-modification strategies: quality improvement, feature improvement, and styling improvement.

QUALITY IMPROVEMENT

A strategy of quality improvement aims at increasing the reliability and durability of the product through better materials or engineering. It can be rewarding as a strategy provided that (1) the product is capable of significant and perceivable variations in quality and (2) a sufficient number of buyers are motivated by quality considerations.

Quality improvements may be undertaken in a number of different circumstances. A manufacturer's sales may be suffering because of the product's reputation for low quality. Other manufacturers may not want to be left behind by competitors. Still others pursue quality improvement as a marketing objective; their purpose is to attain a position of dominance in the segment of the market most concerned with product quality.

In the last instance, the firm gains and loses certain things. A premium-quality producer often finds it easier to identify potential customers, because income or other customer variables tend to be correlated with an interest in quality. Consequently the firm can develop a more precise and coherent marketing program in terms of advertising copy and media, sales-force calls, service, and pricing. On the other hand, the premium-quality producer gives up some marketing flexibility. The firm is not free to reduce the quality of its product in order to reduce costs. It must continue to make investments in quality improvement to maintain its leadership. If the quality-interested segment of the market does not grow fast enough, or is invaded by new competitors, the firm is in a vulnerable position. If it seeks a defensive foothold in other segments of the market, through introducing product versions of a lower quality, it does this at some risk to its image. The ramifications of this loss of flexibility should be well thought out by any firm contemplating a premium-quality strategy.

FEATURE IMPROVEMENT

A strategy of feature improvement aims at increasing the number of real or fancied user benefits. It involves redesigning the product so that it offers more convenience, safety, efficiency, or versatility.

A good illustration is found in the evolution of lawn mowers. The introduction of power was designed to increase the speed and ease of cutting grass. Manufacturers then worked on the problem of engineering better safety features in view of the increased power. Some manufacturers have now built in conversion features so that the lawn mower doubles as a snow plow. All of these feature improvements are quite distinguishable from quality improvements on the one hand and styling improvements on the other.

John B. Stewart has outlined five advantages flowing from a strategy of feature improvement:

1. The development of new functional features is one of the most effective means of building a company image of progressiveness and leadership.
2. Functional features are an extremely flexible competitive tool because they can be adapted quickly, dropped quickly, and often can be made optional at very little expense.
3. Functional features allow the company to gain the intense preference of preselected market segments.
4. Functional features often bring the innovating company free publicity.
5. Functional features generate a great amount of sales force and distributors' enthusiasm.[17]

The chief disadvantage is that feature improvements are highly imitatable; unless there is a permanent gain from being first, the investment in original innovation may not be justified.

STYLE IMPROVEMENT

A strategy of style improvement aims at increasing the aesthetic appeal of the product in contrast to its functional appeal. Much of the annual modification of automobiles amounts to style competition rather than functional-feature competition. In the case of packaged food and household products, where the opportunities for product styling and featuring are minimal except for color and texture variations, manufacturers place

---

[17] John B. Stewart, "Functional Features in Product Strategy," *Harvard Business Review,* March-April 1959, pp. 65-78.

their greatest emphasis on package styling, treating the package as an extension of the product.

The outstanding advantage of a style strategy is that each firm may achieve its own unique identification and secure some durable share of the market on the basis of that identification. Whereas quality differences allow products to be ranked from low to high and functional features allow products to be classified as either possessing or not possessing a feature, style differences are usually not scalable on any single dimension. Fords, Plymouths, and Chevrolets look different and so do Remingtons, Smith-Coronas, and Royals. And there can be little disputing in the area of taste.

Yet styling competition brings in its wake a number of problems. First, it is very difficult to predict whether people (and what people) will like a new style. Liking tail fins or sculptured automobile chassis is largely a psychological phenomenon unrelated to a person's income, geographical residence, or other overt characteristics. Second, style changes usually are thoroughgoing; companies discontinue the old style in introducing the new one. The company therefore risks losing some of the customers who liked the old style in the hope of gaining a larger number of customers who like the new one.

OPTIMAL PRODUCT MODIFICATIONS

The three strategies of product modification were contrasted as if they were mutually exclusive. In practice, a firm generally pursues some mixture of all three strategies. Just to maintain its competitive position the firm must incorporate the latest developments in quality, styling, and functional features. At the same time, each firm may specialize in one strategy in order to achieve leadership in that area.

Since product modifications involve risks, the company should consider maneuvers that help reduce risk. One risk-reduction policy is to modify the product gradually rather than abruptly. Another risk-reduction policy is to continue the old product alongside the new. A third risk-reduction policy is to make adequate investments in marketing research in order to improve estimates of the sales impact of the contemplated product modification.

The Product-Elimination Decision [18]

Businessmen tend to neglect the subject of product elimination in comparison with the attention they give to product modification and new-product development. Many sick or marginal products never die; they are allowed to continue in the company's product mix until they "fade away." In the meantime, they consume considerable resources which may be more fruitfully employed elsewhere. As a result, these marginal products lessen the firm's profitability and reduce its ability to take advantage of new opportunities.

[18] This section is adapted from Philip Kotler, "Phasing Out Weak Products," *Harvard Business Review,* March-April 1965, pp. 107-18.

Every weak-selling product that lingers in a company's line constitutes a costly burden—one whose magnitude businessmen often do not realize. They are complacent as long as the revenues of the weak product cover at least the direct costs of producing it, and are relieved if the revenues cover most of the overhead.

The cost of sustaining a weak product in the mix is not just the amount of uncovered overhead and profit. No financial accounting can adequately convey all the hidden costs. Thus:

> The weak product tends to consume a disproportionate amount of management's time.
>
> It often requires frequent price and inventory adjustments.
>
> It generally involves short production runs in spite of expensive setup times.
>
> It requires both advertising and sales-force attention that might better be diverted to making the "healthy" products more profitable.
>
> Its very unfitness can cause customer misgivings and cast a shadow on the company's image.

Furthermore, as if the hidden costs were not burden enough, the biggest cost imposed by carrying weak products may well lie in the future. By not being eliminated at the proper time, these products delay the aggressive search for replacement products; they create a lopsided product mix, long on "yesterday's breadwinners" and short on "tomorrow's breadwinners"; they depress present profitability and weaken the company's foothold on the future.

The tremendous savings that can be effected by product-pruning programs are dramatized in the following two cases:

> Hunt, a medium-sized canner, began to cut its thirty-some-odd lines in 1947. By 1958 it had only three products: fruit cocktail, tomato products, and peaches. Within these lines, Hunt reduced the variety offered. For example, in peaches Hunt packed only one grade (choice) in one type of syrup (thick). This simplification was apparently very successful for Hunt. Its sales increased from $15 million in 1947 to $120 million in 1958. By that time it had the top brand in tomato sauce and tomato paste and was second in peaches and catsup. In addition to cutting down on the number of lines, Hunt also began a diversification program by buying out nonrelated companies, such as a manufacturer of matches.[19]

> After a survey one company with annual sales of $40,000,000 eliminated sixteen different products with a total volume of $3,300,000. It also made a number of improvements in methods of handling the products retained. . . . Over the next three years the company's total sales increased by one-half and its profits by some twenty times. Among the many factors contributing to these spectacular increases, top executives have stated that dropping unsatisfactory products was one of the most important.[20]

[19] Ralph Westfall and Harper W. Boyd, Jr., *Cases in Marketing Management* (Homewood, Ill.: Richard D. Irwin, Inc., 1961), p. 181.

[20] Charles H. Kline, "The Strategy of Product Policy," *Harvard Business Review,* July-August 1955, p. 100.

In view of the costs of carrying weak products, why does management typically shy away from product-pruning programs? Certainly sentimentality, as R. S. Alexander suggests, is a part of the aversion to product abandonment: "But putting products to death—or letting them die—is a drab business, and often engenders much of the sadness of a final parting with old and tried friends. The portable, six-sided pretzel polisher was the first product The Company ever made. Our line will no longer be our line without it." [21]

There are, in fact, many reasons for this aversion, logical as well as sentimental.

Sometimes it is expected, or hoped, that product sales will pick up in the course of time when economic or market factors become more propitious. Here management thinks that poor performance is due to outside factors which will change.

Sometimes the fault is thought to lie in the marketing program, which the company plans to revitalize. It may be felt that the solution lies in reviving dealer enthusiasm, increasing the advertising budget, changing the advertising theme, or modifying some other marketing factor.

Even when the marketing program is thought to be competent, management may feel that the solution lies in product modification. Specifically, the thinking might be that sales could be stimulated through an upgrading of quality, styling, or features.

When none of these explanations exists, a weak product may be retained in the mix because of its alleged contribution to the sales of the company's other products. The weak product may provide the salesman with an entrée to important accounts. It may be used as bait to attract interest in the rest of the line. It may be the sacrificial lamb in full-line merchandising to court those buyers who like to obtain their "nuts and bolts" from the same supplier.

If none of these functions is performed by the weak product, then the retention rationale may be that its sales volume at least covers "out-of-pocket" costs, and the company may temporarily have no better way of keeping its fixed resources employed. Any sales receipts above out-of-pocket costs make some contribution to overhead charges. Unless another product is available to make an even larger contribution to overhead, the weak product ought to be retained in the short run until a decision has to be made on renewing a major fixed resource.

The foregoing are all logical arguments for retaining weak products in the mix. But there are also situations where the persistence of weak products can be explained only by the presence of vested interests, management or consumer sentiment, or just plain corporate inertia. A lot of people inside and outside an organization grow to depend on a particular product. Among them are the product manager, the employees, and certain customers. Eliminating a product from the mix is organizationally disruptive. Personnel may have to be shifted or released. In such cases sentiment becomes a powerful factor in the decision-making process and often explains the slow decay of many weak products.

[21] R. S. Alexander, "The Death and Burial of 'Sick' Products," *Journal of Marketing,* XXVIII (April 1964), 1.

Those in the organization whose interests may be adversely affected by a product's elimination may engage in practices designed to conceal its weakness. Through hard selling, the product may be pushed into the dealers' stocks although the consumer "pull" is known to be feeble. To postpone the day of judgment, the product manager may use some of his budget to stimulate sales in artificial ways. While these and other ruses may conceal the true facts from top management for a period of time, they cannot work indefinitely.

CURRENT ABANDONMENT PRACTICES

The vast majority of companies, including some of the most progressive in industry, have not established orderly procedures for pruning their products. Such action is usually undertaken either on a *piecemeal* basis, e.g., where the product's money-losing status is incontrovertible, conspicuous, and embarrassing, or on a *crisis* basis, where the precipitating event may be a financial setback, a persistent decline in total sales, piling inventories, or rising costs.

But neither piecemeal pruning nor crisis pruning is really a satisfactory practice. Each leaves too many dated products lingering in the lineup for too long. Each leads to hasty "hatchet" jobs under improvised standards. Each is abrupt and possibly traumatic to the morale of some people inside and outside the company.

A somewhat more systematic approach has been described as follows:

A major manufacturer of consumer durables . . . makes a review every six months of all products whose profitability is less than the corporate average; for each such product, the manager responsible is requested to recommend action for improving earnings or elimination of the product.[22]

Although faults can be found with this approach, it represents a step in the right direction. It provides a standard for appraisal; it communicates a performance objective; it inspires the preparation of plans; and it sets a day of judgment. These features constitute the beginning of a control system for the problem of weak products.

A PERIODIC PRODUCT REVIEW SYSTEM

A company that wishes to maintain a strong product mix must commit itself to the idea of a periodic product review. Such a review can be expected to accomplish two objectives:

Increase over-all company profits through identification of products requiring modification or meriting elimination from the mix in the light of changing conditions.

Provide a periodic incentive for better performance on the part of executives who share product responsibility.

An over-all view of a practical control system is charted in Figure 13-4. The first two parts (*creation stages*) take place when it has been decided that a control system should be installed. The *operational steps,* 1 through

[22] See D'Orsay Hurst, "Criteria for Evaluating Existing Products and Product Lines," in *Analyzing and Improving Marketing Performance,* Management Report No. 32 (New York: American Management Association, 1959), p. 91.

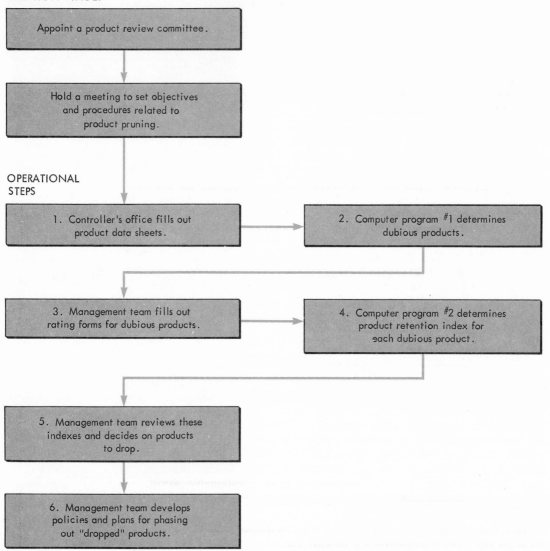

CREATION STAGES

Appoint a product review committee.

Hold a meeting to set objectives and procedures related to product pruning.

OPERATIONAL STEPS

1. Controller's office fills out product data sheets.

2. Computer program #1 determines dubious products.

3. Management team fills out rating forms for dubious products.

4. Computer program #2 determines product retention index for each dubious product.

5. Management team reviews these indexes and decides on products to drop.

6. Management team develops policies and plans for phasing out "dropped" products.

FIGURE 13-4

Creation and operation of annual product review system
Figures 13-4 through 13-7 are redrawn from Philip Kotler, "Phasing out Weak Products," *Harvard Business Review*, March-April 1965, pp. 107-18.

6, represent the system as it is reactivated annually thereafter for product-pruning purposes.

CREATION STAGES.   Product pruning is not a task to be entrusted to any one man or department in the organization. There are too many parties involved and too many honest differences of opinion on appropriate criteria.

Therefore, the first creation stage is the appointment of a management

306

team to assume responsibility for this problem. Because important policy questions are involved, as well as potentially large savings, the product review committee should consist of high-level executives. A representative corporate team could include executives from the following departments:

Marketing—to provide views on marketing strategy, customer relations, competitive developments, and future sales outlook.

Manufacturing—to describe any scheduling, manufacturing, or inventory problems connected with the products.

Purchasing—to discuss estimates of future costs of materials.

Control (accounting and finance)—to offer data on past sales, costs, and profits and also to develop the implications of product abandonment for cash flow and over-all corporate rate of return.

Personnel—to speak about the feasibility of reassignment for company personnel who would be affected by product-abandonment decisions.

Research and development—to report on replacement products being developed which might utilize the physical and human resources affected by abandonment decisions.

The second creation stage is to have the committee hold a series of meetings to develop objectives and set up procedures.

OPERATIONAL STEPS. The product control system established by the management team can take numerous forms, one of which is the six-step system exhibited in Figure 13-4.

Step 1: Product sheet. The product review process should be reactivated at about the same time each year, generally after an accounting period. The controller's office takes the first step by preparing a data sheet for every company product. A sample product data sheet is shown in Figure 13-5. This sheet summarizes key statistics about the product for the last several years. The exact number of years and the particular statistics depend on the nature of the business, the availability of various types of information, and the judgment of the management team as to what data might indicate that the product is of questionable worth.

The purpose of the data sheet is to provide the informational basis for judging whether the product is in a good state of health or merits further study for an abandonment decision. It is not assumed that the data sheet contains sufficient information for making the abandonment decision. The use of two stages in the decision is necessary because it takes much less information to detect whether a product is weak than to make a judgment on whether it should be dropped.

Step 2: Determining candidates. The challenge is to develop a computer program that can "intelligently" scan the product data sheets (in the form of key-punched cards) for signs of weakness in much the same way the management team would. The best approach is to ask the executives what they look for and to embody these principles in computer decision rules.

A very simple program of decision rules is shown in Figure 13-6, which raises five critical questions—more could be listed—about recent trends in sales, market share, gross margin, and overhead coverage. These trends can be calculated from the product data sheets obtained in Step 1. The

```
         Product No. _____

         Model No._____

         Date _____

                                 Past years
                            3      2      1     Current

         Industry sales      $ _____
         Company sales       $ _____
         Physical volume       _____
         Unit total cost     $ _____
         Unit variable cost  $ _____
         Price               $ _____
         Cyclical adjustment factor _____
         Overhead burden       _____


         Comments: _____
```

FIGURE 13-5
Sample product data sheet
Source: See Figure 13-4

questions are hooked in series so that a product must earn a negative answer to all questions to avoid an investigation of its status. Each company sets the K values it regards as critical for placing a product on the dubious list.

Step 3: Rating form. After the computer has produced a list of the dubious products, the management team meets to review the list. The major purposes of the meeting are for the team members to sense the overall pattern and magnitude of the company's weak-product problem, to remove from the list products which their good sense, as opposed to the computer's intelligence, tells them do not belong there, and to implement a formal product rating device. A formal rating device is quite essential if abandonment decisions are to be guided by consistent and explicit standards.

A product rating form incorporating a number of important considerations is shown in Figure 13-7. This form calls for assigning a *rating value* to each dubious product on seven different scales. In this area, some of the scales are unavoidably subjective. Each scale ranges from zero to one, with zero representing strong grounds for eliminating the product and one representing strong grounds for retaining the product.

The first scale, for instance, calls for evaluating the future market potential of the product. A product that is becoming hopelessly obsolescent —for example, a detergent that is not able to clean modern synthetic fabrics as well as it cleans cotton and linen—would be rated close to zero on this scale.

308

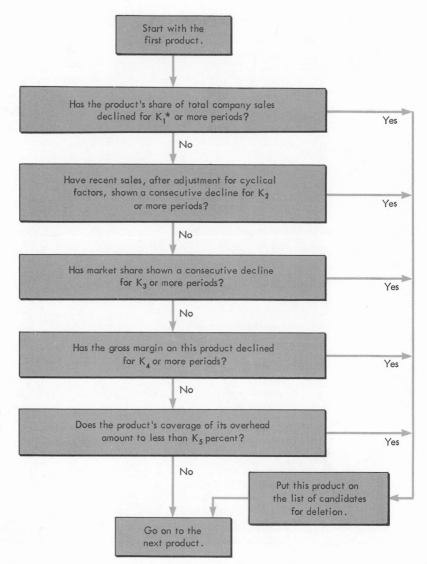

FIGURE 13-6

Flow chart of computer program #1 decision rules

Source: See Figure 13-4

* The K's are chosen by the management team. For example, if the team sets $K_1 = 3$, then management thinks that 3 or more periods of sales decline should put a product on the dubious list.

The flowchart contains the following text:

Start with the first product.

Has the product's share of total company sales declined for K_1* or more periods? — Yes

Have recent sales, after adjustment for cyclical factors, shown a consecutive decline for K_2 or more periods? — Yes

Has market share shown a consecutive decline for K_3 or more periods? — Yes

Has the gross margin on this product declined for K_4 or more periods? — Yes

Does the product's coverage of its overhead amount to less than K_5 percent? — Yes

Put this product on the list of candidates for deletion.

Go on to the next product.

Since management may not consider all scales to be equally important, each scale is also assigned a *weight value*. These weight values are presumably agreed on early in the creation stage and remain constant for all product judgments.

The product rating form serves as a discussion guide for each product case and helps to highlight the informational needs. Ultimately the committee must agree on a question-by-question rating value for each dubious product. A few meetings may have to be held before the necessary information is available or sufficient consensus develops.

Step 4: Retention index. When this work is completed, the product rating form can then be processed to yield a single number, the "product-

Product No. _____

Model No. _____

Date _____

Weight (W)

Rating (R)

____ 1 What is the future market potential for this product?

.0 .2 .4 .6 .8 1.0
Low   High

$W_1 R_1 =$

____ 2 How much could be gained by product modification?

.0 .2 .4 .6 .8 1.0
Nothing   A great deal

$W_2 R_2 =$

____ 3 How much could be gained by marketing strategy modification?

.0 .2 .4 .6 .8 1.0
Nothing   A great deal

$W_3 R_3 =$

____ 4 How much useful executive time could be released by abandoning this product?

.0 .2 .4 .6 .8 1.0
A great deal   Very little

$W_4 R_4 =$

____ 5 How good are the firm's alternative opportunities?

.0 .2 .4 .6 .8 1.0
Very good   Very poor

$W_5 R_5 =$

____ 6 How much is the product contributing beyond its direct costs?

.0 .2 .4 .6 .8 1.0
Nothing   A great deal

$W_6 R_6 =$

____ 7 How much is the product contributing to the sale of the other products?

.0 .2 .4 .6 .8 1.0
Nothing   A great deal

$W_7 R_7 =$

_____

Product retention index*

FIGURE 13-7
Seven-scale product rating form
Source: See Figure 13-4

retention index," indicating the degree of product desirability. (The fate of some products may already have been decided in the course of the management team's discussion of the ratings in Step 3.) This single number will be the sum of the weighted ratings on the product rating form.

The sum can range from a maximum value of 7, if the product shows superior grounds for being retained on all counts, to a minimum value of 0, if the product shows minimal grounds for retention on all counts. Although the single number can be obtained by using a desk calculator, when many dubious products are involved it is best to enter the rating values on a mark-sensing card and to use the computer to calculate the index numbers. Thus Computer Program #2 normally consists of a straight-forward calculation of products and sums.

Step 5: Abandonment decisions. When the indexes are ready, the product review committee again convenes to make a final judgment on which products to drop. The committee may have already established a retention index number between 0 and 7 so that any dubious product receiving an index number below it would almost unquestionably be dropped from the line. Any product which scores less than one out of a possible seven points, for example, must be judged as having very little potential, imposing a large burden on executive time, and contributing very little to profits or to the sale of other company products. There is little reason for retaining such a product.

Products whose indexes exceed the established retention value number have more than minimum justification on one or more criteria, but the management team must examine these individual cases carefully. Product-retention indexes supply a formal, albeit subjective, basis for ranking the dubious products in order of the strength of the arguments for retention.

Generally speaking, products with lower indexes will be weaker, and management will want to concentrate on these. At the same time, it is entirely possible that the committee members may decide to drop a product with a higher index value than another which they decide to retain. The indexes serve as a guide rather than as a final verdict. They are designed to aid in the systematic consideration of product intangibles and not to replace judgment.

Another reason exists for not using this retention index or any other formal device too mechanically. Various products in the line have joint demands and/or joint cost and manufacturing relationships. Management must consider the total effect on its business operations of dropping any set of products. The particular set may spell too great a weakening of the company's position in a certain market, may place too great a strain on some company personnel, or may lead to costly idling of particular facilities.

Step 6: Phasing out. One step remains after management has decided which products to drop; this is the formulation of phasing-out policies and plans for the individual products being dropped. For each product, management must determine its obligations to the various parties affected by the decision. Management may want to provide for a stock of replacement parts and service to stretch over the expected life of the most recently sold units. It may want to find a manufacturer willing to take over the discontinued product.

Some of the products can be dropped quite easily with little repercussion, while other product eliminations will require an elaborate phasing-out plan. Where the product involved has enjoyed major distribution, management should consider preparing a critical path program (such as PERT) to ensure efficiency in its phasing out.[23] The program should show when various parties are to be notified about the decision and when various asset-disposal efforts should be made. The objective is to let the news

[23] See Chapter 7, pp. 163-69.

disseminate in a pattern that does not handicap the company's efforts to dispose of the product and yet does not lead some parties to feel they were unfairly treated.

Summary

The product situation in the United States is so fluid and competitive that no company can maintain the desired level of profits, stability, and growth without making periodic adjustments in its product mix. Products must be dropped, added, and modified if the firm is to maintain a viable position in the market place.

To understand the major product-policy decisions faced by the firm, certain analytical concepts and distinctions need to be grasped: the meaning of a product; the distinction between a product item, line, and mix; the distinction between the width, depth, and consistency of the product mix; and the concept of the product life cycle.

Product characteristics have implications for product policy and marketing strategy that are suggested by different goods' classifications: whether consumers' or industrial goods; convenience, shopping, or specialty goods; durable, nondurable, or service goods; or red, orange, or yellow goods. Company objectives with respect to profits, sales stability, and sales growth also affect product policy and marketing strategy. Management science techniques offer an increasing opportunity to determine formally the optimal product mix for given management objectives.

The decision must often be made to modify a product; it may involve quality improvement, feature improvement, or style improvement, and each of these has its own arguments. And it may be necessary to eliminate a product. The costs of carrying weak products are often great, yet management may resist abandonment decisions for a number of reasons. A computer-management system for spotting and eliminating weak products is one way of dealing efficiently with the problem.

Questions and Problems

1. "As a firm increases arithmetically the number of its products, management's problems tend to increase geometrically." Do you agree?

2. On the principle that the characteristics of the product affect the appropriate marketing mix, compare how personal selling, advertising, technical service, product quality, and delivery might differ as between a commodity and a manufactured good.

3. "A rough rule of thumb in many companies has been that 80 per cent of volume comes from 20 per cent of the product line. In reality, these figures often may be running 90 per cent of volume from 10 per cent of prod-

ucts." Can you think of any logical reason for these numbers to add up to 100 per cent?

4. Does the ranking of a company's products according to their relative profit contribution (see Figure 13-3) indicate the best way to allocate the marketing budget to these products? If yes, how should the budget be allocated to the products? If no, why?

5. Prove the proposition stated in the text that if a firm adds a new product whose sales are uncorrelated with the sales of existing products, the absolute amount of sales variability is increased.

6. A firm is trying to decide how much quality to build into a new machine tool. Illustrate diagrammatically the logic of determining the optimal quality decision.

7. On the matter of when to eliminate a weak product, there are often sharp differences of opinion among accountants, economists, and sales managers. Describe their respective views.

chapter 14

New-Product Decisions

U. S. businesses are increasingly recognizing that the key to their survival and growth may lie in the continuous development of new and improved products. Gone is the confidence that established products will continue to maintain strong market positions indefinitely. There are too many competitors with fast-moving research laboratories, ingenious marketing techniques, and large budgets standing ready to woo away customers. Customers themselves are not always loyal or invulnerable to competitors' enticements.

The major problems and decisions in new-product development are taken up in this chapter. The first section describes the costs and dilemmas of new-product development. The second section describes four major ingredients in the successful management of innovation—effective organizational arrangements, experienced new-product development management, a sophisticated research and development operation, and sound analytical criteria for decision making. The next six sections take up the major criteria and decision-making techniques for each step in the innovation process—idea gathering, screening, business analysis, product development, test marketing, and commercialization. The last section describes the consumer-adoption process and its implications for the successful marketing of the new product.

"New products" for our purposes will mean "products new to the company." This definition embraces original products, major modifications of existing products, duplications of competitors' products, and product-line acquisitions, all of which involve assimilation of something "new" into the product mix.[1]

The New-Product Development Dilemma

Under modern conditions of competition, it is becoming increasingly risky not to innovate. Consumers and industrial customers want and expect a stream of new and improved products. Competition will certainly do its best to meet these desires. Continuous innovation seems to be the only way to avert obsolescence of the company's product line.

[1] For a useful classification of types of "newness," see the market-technology grid in Samuel C. Johnson and Conrad Jones, "How to Organize for New Products," *Harvard Business Review,* May-June 1957, pp. 49-62.

At the same time, it is extremely expensive and risky to innovate. The main reasons are: (1) Most product ideas which go into product development never reach the market; (2) many of the products that do reach the market are not successful; and (3) successful products tend to have a shorter life than new products once had.

HIGH ATTRITION RATE OF NEW PRODUCTS.   A large number of products and product ideas which cost the firm good money never reach the market place. They are casualties of the innovation process. The company discovers belatedly that they are technically infeasible, they would cost too much to develop, or their market was overestimated.

How many ideas must a firm generate for each idea that eventually culminates in a successful new product? The Management Research Department of Booz, Allen & Hamilton studied this question for 51 companies and summarized its findings in the form of a decay curve of new product ideas." [2] The curve is reproduced as Figure 14-1. Of every 58-odd ideas, about 12 pass the initial screening test showing them to be compatible with company objectives and resources. Of these, some 7 remain after a thorough evaluation of their profit potential. About 3 survive the product-development stage, 2 survive the test-marketing stage, and only 1 is commercially successful. Thus, about 58 new ideas must be generated to find 1 good one.

HIGH RATE OF MARKET FAILURE.   Of those products introduced into the market, how many achieve commercial success? The estimates vary widely. Booz, Allen & Hamilton's study of 366 recently marketed products places the failure rate at 33 per cent (10 per cent clear failures and 23 per cent doubtful).[3] A Ross Federal Research Corporation report places the failure rate as high as 80 per cent, based on a study of the products introduced by 200 leading packaged-goods manufacturers.[4] A study by the New York industrial design firm of Lippincott and Margulies places the rate as high as 89 per cent.[5] These discrepancies arise from different samples and different definitions of an unsuccessful product, but all the studies concur that a significant and probably substantial percentage of new products fail.

SHORTER LIFE SPANS OF SUCCESSFUL PRODUCTS.   Even when a new product turns out to be a commercial success, rivals are so quick to follow suit that the new product is typically fated for only a short happy life. As told by Fred J. Borch of General Electric:

> The honeymoon cycle of a new product is becoming shorter and shorter. We introduced the GE automatic toothbrush just two years ago. There are now 52 competitors. Our slicing knife, a product that we introduced ap-

[2] *Management of New Products,* 4th ed. (New York: Booz, Allen & Hamilton, Inc., 1965), p. 9.
[3] *Ibid.,* p. 11.
[4] Quoted in John T. O'Meara, Jr., "Selecting Profitable Products," *Harvard Business Review,* January-February 1961, p. 83.
[5] Quoted in Burt Schorr, "Many New Products Fizzle, Despite Careful Planning, Publicity," *Wall Street Journal,* April 5, 1961.

proximately one year ago, now competes with seven others and at least that many more manufacturers are preparing to enter the marketplace.[6]

The race to be first on the market sometimes assumes grotesque proportions. Alberto-Culver was so eager to beat a new Procter & Gamble shampoo to market that it developed a name and filmed a TV commercial before it even developed its own product.[7] Yet, the market does not always go to the swift. Monsanto, the first company to produce soap for automatic washers, eventually decided to withdraw rather than compete with the gigantic budgets of the soapmakers. Du Pont, a giant in its own right, often drops a product when two major competitors have established themselves in the market. Lestoil Products watched its sales climb to $25 million with its new liquid cleanser. Then Lever Brothers, Procter & Gamble, and later Colgate jumped into this market, and Lestoil's sales slipped so badly that at one point it stopped paying dividends.

Thus management finds itself in a dilemma; it must develop new products; yet the odds weigh heavily against their success. New-product development can be as risky a course as doing nothing. The answer still must lie in new-product development, but conducted in a way that reduces the risk of failure.

FIGURE 14-1

Decay curve of new-product ideas (51 companies)

Redrawn from *Management of New Products*, 4th ed. (New York: Booz, Allen & Hamilton, Inc., 1965), p. 9.

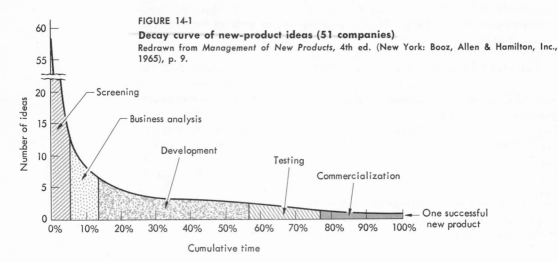

Ingredients in the Successful Management of Innovation

The risk can never be completely taken out of new-product development, but specific practices may increase the likelihood of successful innovation.

[6] Fred J. Borch, "Tomorrow's Customers," Speech at the Sales Executive Club of New York, September 15, 1964.

[7] This illustration and some of the following ones were reported in *Time*, March 29, 1963, p. 83.

The first ingredient of successful innovation is an effective organizational structure for processing new ideas and following them through. Many different organizational arrangements are found in practice. In companies not geared for continuous innovation, a new-product idea appears somewhere, and either an individual or an *ad hoc* committee is assigned to follow it through. Depending on the energy of the individuals and the cooperation they receive from other parts of the company, the product may or may not ever see the light.

In companies where new-product ideas are considered with some frequency, a more or less permanent committee is usually found, often consisting of key executives from marketing, finance, production, and engineering. A small professional staff may be appended to this committee to aid the executives. The great advantage of the committee arrangement is that it leads to interdepartmental decision making and joint responsibility. Its major shortcoming is that professionalized new-product management is usually inadequate or not given enough authority.

In those companies where new products are the lifeblood of the business, management has increasingly turned to the development of a "new product" or "product-planning" department. The department is placed in the charge of a special officer who is generally given substantial authority and access to top management. An analysis of 56 such departments by Booz, Allen & Hamilton, Inc., showed that the new-product department manager reported in 48 per cent of the cases to the chief executive, in 30 per cent of the cases to the top marketing officer, in 13 per cent of the cases to the top research and development officer, and in 9 per cent of the cases to other executives.[8] The department's major responsibilities typically included:

Recommending new-product objectives and program
Planning exploration activities
Making screening decisions
Developing specifications
Recommending development of new products
Coordinating testing and precommercialization
Directing interdepartmental teams in all stages

These departments are typically small (4 to 6 men) because their main function is not to do the work of new-product development but to help those who are doing the work (usually a product team organized around each product under development). The nucleus of the team is often formed at the product-development stage. As the product evolves, the major burden shifts from one area of competence to another, but the continuity is maintained.

The new-product development department is not necessarily the best organizational form for all companies. Much depends upon company size, the nature of the industry, and the degree of company orientation toward innovation. But the departmental organization is likely to provide for the

[8] *Management of New Products,* p. 21.

most continuous follow-up, coordination, and expertise in cases where continuous innovation is a major activity of the company.

EXPERIENCED AND PROFESSIONAL MANAGEMENT

The second ingredient of successful innovation is experienced new-product development management. The job calls for more than general administrative skill. The ideal executive would have an engineering background, an interest in new scientific developments, a strong research sense, creative marketing vision, good leadership qualities, a taste for risk, and impeccable judgment. Some of these qualities undoubtedly have to be compromised if anyone is to be found. Yet the important point is that expertise is developing in this field and that top management should hire men with a view toward their professional qualifications.

ABLE RESEARCH STAFF

The third ingredient is the presence of able research personnel. Many different types of research must take place during the innovation process. *Marketing research* determines the numbers, types, and likely responses of potential buyers. *Economy research* finds materials and product design features that keep production costs low without sacrificing market appeal. *Product performance research* tests progressive mock-ups of the product to discover any possible shortcomings. *Packaging research* develops packaging with maximum appeal within the bounds of economy. All of these forms of research have become quite specialized. For the company wishing to keep the risk of product failure small, a large part of the answer lies in recruiting qualified research personnel.

SOUND PROCEDURES AT EACH STAGE OF THE INNOVATION PROCESS

Six stages of the innovation process can be distinguished: *idea generation, screening, business analysis, product development, test marketing,* and *commercialization.*[9] Each stage involves the trinary decision of whether the project should go on to the next stage, whether it should be abandoned, or whether further evidence should be collected. The decision often is an act of faith, but some analytical principles exist to reduce the risk of making wrong decisions. In the remainder of this chapter, we will discuss principles of decision making and evaluation at each stage of the new-product development process.

Idea Generation

Every new product starts off as an idea. But as we have seen, most ideas never become products. A large number of ideas must be generated in order to insure finding a few good ones.[10] In fact, the greater the

[9] Adapted from *Management of New Products.*

[10] A 1950 study by the investment firm J. H. Whitney & Company reported that of 2,100 new-product propositions, only 17 were considered to be meritorious enough to develop. This study is quoted in Paul Stillson and E. Leonard Arnoff, "Product Search and Evaluation," *Journal of Marketing,* XXII (July 1957), 33-39.

number of ideas generated, the better the best ones are likely to be.[11]

Many companies do nothing formally about generating product ideas. They rely on the spontaneous appearance of ideas from customers, distributors, salesmen, and others.

Companies with a major interest in product innovation or diversification cannot, however, rely on informal and spontaneous processes of idea generation. An increasing number are recognizing the advantages of seeking out new areas of risk systematically. The expectation is that organized management of the idea flow will lead to more and better ideas.

ORGANIZED MANAGEMENT OF THE IDEA FLOW

When there is no formal management responsible for gathering ideas, many useful ideas are lost forever to the company. This is shown in Figure 14-2a. Ideas are continually being generated by forces in the environment—customers, technology, and competitors—but few of them reach the company. Ideas are also being generated by persons within the company—executives, company scientists, and salesmen—but many of them are lost.

The picture is quite different if systematic procedures are installed to gather ideas from the environment and within the company. Figure 14-2b shows how the appointment of someone responsible for idea gathering is likely to increase the quantity and quality of product ideas available to the firm. Such a person would have three responsibilities:

Search. He would conduct an active search in the environment for good product ideas.

Stimulation. He would encourage company personnel to develop and send ideas to his office.

Enhancement. He would reroute the ideas to logical parties in other parts of the company for feedback and idea enhancement.

SOURCES OF NEW-PRODUCT IDEAS

The major sources of new-product ideas are customers, scientists, competitors, company salesmen, and top management.

Customers. An increasing number of companies are turning to their customers for new ideas. Sometimes they simply pay more attention to the "why dontcha?" mail from customers. General Food Corporation receives over 80,000 spontaneous letters annually from housewives and other consumers.[12] When letters began to come in complaining about cereal boxes (they were too tall to stand upright in kitchen shelves, they tipped easily, etc.), the company gave them consideration, and this led to the development of new compact boxes.

Sometimes the company arranges for a group of consumers to gather together and discuss the merits and shortcomings of a product. Out of one such discussion with a group of men, Kimberly-Clark Corporation got the

[11] This conclusion follows if it is assumed that the *quality* of potential product ideas tends to be normally distributed. The company is chiefly interested in the few ideas found in the high-quality end of the distribution. If the company relies on a "random drawing" of ideas, the probability of discovering the extreme ones increases with the number of draws.

[12] See "Helpful Consumers," *Wall Street Journal,* June 2, 1965, pp. 1, 20.

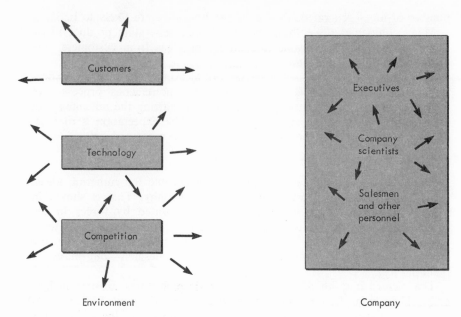

(a) Before management of the idea process

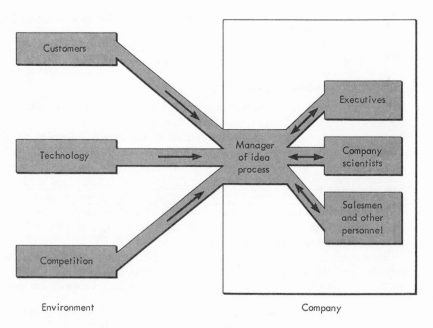

(b) After management of the idea process

FIGURE 14-2
The idea generation process

suggestion that paper tissues should be made larger; this led to the eventual introduction of "Man-Size" Kleenex.[13]

Free-wheeling brainstorming sessions are also highly productive of new ideas. Alex Osborn described one such panel where the question was: "What new products not now available are needed in the home?" Among the ideas mentioned were:

Bed sheets with double-strength weave in the center where the weave first weakens

Suction cups on the bottom of egg beaters to prevent skidding in bowl

Venetian blinds so constructed that the slats in the upper or lower half may be opened or closed independently of the other half.

Switches for door bells so you can turn them off when children are asleep or when you don't want to be disturbed.

Within 40 minutes, the group of 12 men and women produced 136 ideas.[14]

Scientists. Advances in technology are another major environmental source of product ideas.[15] Research in solid-state physics underpins the revolution in radio and television products, research in plastic chemistry underlies the revolution in packaging many products, and synthetic fiber research underlies the revolution in clothing. Recognizing the potential contributions of basic research, companies such as Du Pont, International Business Machines, and American Telephone and Telegraph (Bell Laboratories) make large annual investments to advance the state of knowledge. Other companies remain content to establish applied research laboratories which seek new applications for the basic technologies developed elsewhere.

Competitors. The company must also watch the new products being developed by its competitors. Marketing intelligence can come from the trade and from salesmen. After competitive products have been introduced, their sales performance can be carefully audited through research services.

Company salesmen. Company salesmen are a particularly good source of product ideas. They have first-hand experience with customers' unsatisfied needs and complaints. They often are the first to learn of competitive developments. An increasing number of companies are trying to use more systematic procedures for tapping the ideas of salesmen.

Top management. Top management is in the best position to define the kinds of ideas needed by the company. The product areas to explore are suggested by the company's strengths and weaknesses. Starting from its *strengths,* the company might search for product additions which

Constitute complementary products. (A washing machine manufacturer might add a dryer to the line.)

Utilize the same channels. (A manufacturer of upholstered furniture might add a line of floor lamps.)

Utilize the same raw materials, production facilities, technology, or know-how. (A manufacturer of work shoes made of pig skin might add a line of casual sneakers.)

[13] *Ibid.,* p. 1.

[14] Alex F. Osborn, *Applied Imagination,* 3rd rev. ed. (New York: Charles Scribner's Sons, 1962), p. 174.

[15] See Chapter 2, pp. 26-30.

Exploit by-products of the production process. (A meat processor might go into the manufacture of soap.)

Or the company might search for products that would mitigate company *weaknesses,* such as

Highly seasonal sales. (A bathing suit manufacturer might go into the production of ski outfits.)

Highly cyclical sales. (An appliance manufacturer might merge with a food producer.)

Product losing out to substitutes. (A manufacturer of razor blades might go into the production of electric razors.)

Screening

The main purpose of the first stage in the product-addition process is to increase the number of good ideas. The main purpose of all the succeeding stages is to *reduce* the number of ideas. The company is not likely to have the resources or the inclination to develop all of the new-product ideas, even if they were all good. And they will not all be equally good. Evaluation and decision now enter the picture. The first idea-pruning stage is screening.

A SCREENING PROCEDURE

The purpose of screening is to eliminate from further consideration those product ideas that are dissonant with either company objectives or resources. Figure 14-3 shows a screening procedure for considering new product proposals one at a time. The first task is to determine whether the product is compatible with the company's objectives. Four objectives are mentioned—profit, sales stability, sales growth, and company image—and others could be added. A strong negative answer to any one of these questions can disqualify the product idea from further consideration. The second task is to determine whether the product is compatible with the company's resources; in the illustration, capital, know-how, and facilities are used. If any of these resources is lacking, the question is asked whether it is obtainable at a reasonable cost. A strong negative answer to any of these questions will also disqualify the product idea from further consideration. Product ideas that pass all these tests move on to the third stage, that of business analysis.

PRODUCT-IDEA RATING DEVICES

Many of the ideas can be eliminated through the process shown in Figure 14-3, but there is an additional problem for the firm which generates a large number of product ideas each period. Proposals have to be ranked against one another, and the most attractive subset within the company's resources must be chosen. Management needs a rating instrument for this purpose.

Checklists are a favorite company instrument for systematizing product evaluations in the screening stage. Table 14-1 shows how two alternative product ideas fared in an evaluation by a large materials processor. Nine

Is the idea any good?

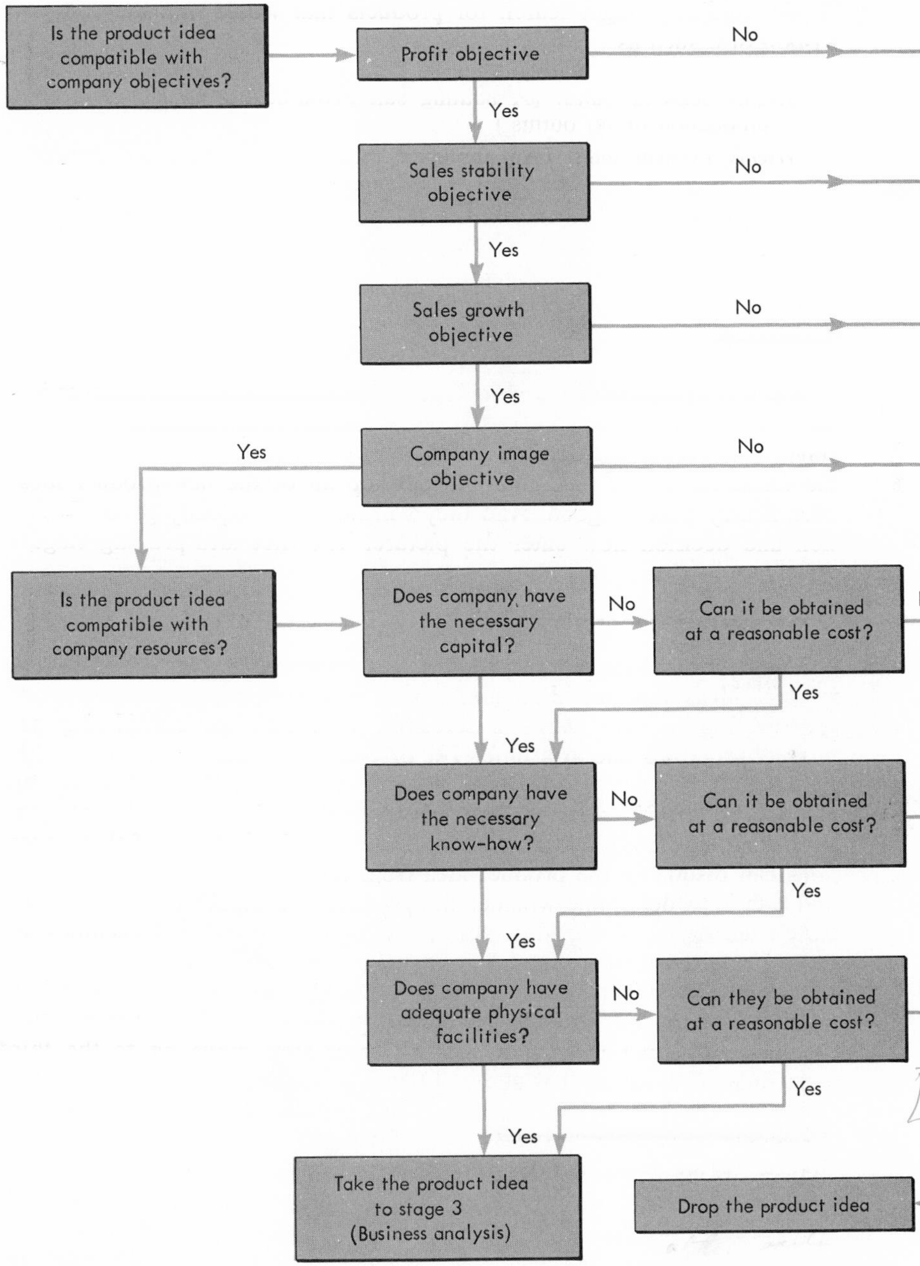

FIGURE 14-3

A screening procedure

what about adding a department to sell good ideas that normally fall out for other reasons?

TABLE 14-1

Examples of summary product appraisals by a large materials processor

Case A: A Generally Favorable Pattern

	Rating				
	Very good	Good	Fair	Poor	Very poor
Sales volume	✓				
Type and number of competitors	✓				
Technical opportunity	✓				
Patent protection		✓			
Raw materials		✓			
Production load		✓			
Value added		✓			
Similarity to major business				✓	
Effect on present products			✓		

Case B: A Generally Unfavorable Pattern

	Rating				
	Very good	Good	Fair	Poor	Very poor
Sales volume	✓				
Type and number of competitors					✓
Technical opportunity				✓	
Patent protection					✓
Raw materials		✓			
Production load				✓	
Value added		✓			
Similarity to major business	✓				
Effect on present products	✓				

Source: Charles H. Kline, "The Strategy of Product Policy," *Harvard Business Review,* July-August 1955, pp. 91-100.

significant factors were considered, and each was rated on a five-point scale from very good to very poor. The first product showed a generally favorable pattern while the second product showed a generally unfavorable pattern. If the nine factors were assumed to be equally important, the first product idea was obviously a better one than the second product idea. Were the profiles less extreme, however, a ranking judgment would be more difficult to make. It would be necessary to introduce some quantification technique.

The checklist could be easily converted into a device for producing numerical ratings of product proposals. An example is reproduced in Table 14-2. At the left is a listing of factors deemed to be significant in screening the product. At the right, instead of a collection of adjectives from very poor to very good, there is an eleven-point numerical scale ranging from .0 to 1.0. A rating of .0 means that the company is likely to perform very ineffectively on that factor, while a rating of 1.0 means that the company is likely to perform very effectively on that factor. In order to derive a single over-all index of the product's merit, weights are assigned to show the relative importance of each factor in contributing

TABLE 14-2
Evaluation matrix—product fit

Sphere of performance	(A) Relative weight	(B) Product compatibility values											Rating (A × B)
		.0	.1	.2	.3	.4	.5	.6	.7	.8	.9	1.0	
Company personality and goodwill	.20							√					.120
Marketing	.20										√		.180
Research and development	.20								√				.140
Personnel	.15							√					.090
Finance	.10										√		.090
Production	.05									√			.040
Location and facilities	.05				√								.015
Purchasing and supplies	.05										√		.045
Total	1.00												.720*

* Rating scale: .00–.40 poor; .41–.75 fair; .76–1.00 good. Present minimum acceptance rate: .70. Source: Barry M. Richman, "A Rating Scale for Product Innovation," *Business Horizons,* Summer 1962, pp. 37-44.

to product success. In the example, weights are chosen that sum to one.

The decision maker proceeds by placing a ✔ after each performance factor in the column expressing his best estimate of company adequacy. After this is done, each factor's value is multiplied by the factor weight, and the product of the two is placed in the last column. The numbers in the last column are totaled, and the sum is used as an index of the product's relative merit. A product idea that was extremely inappropriate for company development on all counts would achieve an over-all score of 0.00; an extremely appropriate product idea would score 1.00. The company establishes some ranges for product-idea acceptance, such as the ones shown at the bottom of Table 14–2. The hypothetical product in the illustration, because it scored .72, would probably move on to detailed consideration in the next stage.

This basic rating device is capable of additional refinements; whether it is advisable to introduce them is largely a matter of how much more would be gained.[16] The purpose of the product screening stage might be missed if the devices became too elaborate. It costs a company money and valuable executive time to review product proposals. Since over half of the proposals are likely to be eliminated at this stage, the company has an interest in rapidly screening out ideas that do not have prima facie appeal.

The checklist, or its quantitative equivalent, is a quick way to review systematically the merits and drawbacks of different proposals. Generally speaking, product ideas that emerge with high over-all ratings should be moved into the business analysis stage, and product ideas with intermediate ratings should be reviewed once more. This system is likely to work well on the average, although undoubtedly it may occasionally lead to wrong judgments especially where the proposed product is quite new or risky. Companies should avoid using it mechanically. It is designed to aid in the systematic judgment of product intangibles, not to replace judgment.

[16] See, for example, the rating method proposed by O'Meara, *op. cit.,* pp. 83-89.

The purpose of this stage is to develop a model of how the product idea is likely to affect sales, costs, and profits over a stipulated time period. The nature of this stage has been described by a research executive at Hercules Powder:

> Once we have anything we can name—a new product, perhaps, or a new process—we build a business model. . . . The model is built on the same accounting principles that Hercules used in its day-by-day operations. It contains the same type of data as would be used for a request for a capital appropriation. Into it go estimates for plant costs, costs for service facilities, and working capital to get total operating assets required. Estimates for costs of raw materials, conversion, packaging, warehousing, and depreciation provide total manufacturing costs. To this are added charges for sales costs and corporate overhead to determine total cost of sales. Also going into the model are data on prices and volume . . . to obtain a return on operating investment. . . . Also plugged into the analysis are such factors as research and development costs, time required for completion, and the chances of success.[17]

The only weakness in this otherwise good statement lies in the "wooden" treatment of sales costs. In making a breakeven analysis or a rate-of-return analysis (the two are related), many firms overlook the functional relation between marketing expenses and sales. But the dual role of marketing effort as both a cost and a sales stimulant must be incorporated in the analysis. Specifically, the business executive must estimate the profit consequences of alternative ways to market the product. The manner in which this may be done will be illustrated in terms of the following example: [18]

> The ABC Electronics Company is a small manufacturer of transistors and clock radios, and is now engaged in reviewing other electronic products for possible addition to the product line. One possibility is a small portable tape recorder. Small, novelty tape recorders have appeared recently on the market, retailing at prices between $20 and $50. The company's marketing research department surveyed the market and found that interest in this type of unit is substantial and growing.
>
> An executive committee is appointed to examine the potential profitability of this product. The production department estimates that $60,000 would have to be invested in specific new equipment and facilities and that this investment would have an estimated life of five years. The accounting department submits that the product would have to absorb $26,000 a year of general overhead to cover the value of supporting facilities, rent, taxes, executive salaries, cost of capital, etc. The marketing department advises that the product be supported initially with an advertising budget of approximately $20,000 and a distribution budget of approximately $30,000 and furthermore that it should be priced at approximately $18 f.o.b. factory with no quantity discounts. Finally, the various operating departments estimate that the new product would involve a direct material and labor cost of $10 a unit.

[17] Robert Cairnes, quoted in "Winds of Change in Industrial Chemical Research," *Chemical and Engineering News,* March 23, 1964, p. 99.

[18] This section is adapted from Philip Kotler, "Marketing Mix Decisions for New Products," *Journal of Marketing Research,* published by American Marketing Association, February 1964, pp. 43-49.

In the light of these estimates, should the ABC Electronics Company develop this new product? Is the marketing mix proposed by the marketing department sound?

BREAKEVEN ANALYSIS

The first step in the business analysis of a new-product idea is to estimate how many units would have to be sold in order to cover costs. The number of units is called the breakeven volume. This volume is estimated by analyzing how total revenue and total cost vary at different sales volumes.

Total revenue at any particular sales volume is that volume times the unit price adjusted by allowances for early payment, quantity purchases, and freight. The adjustments are fairly straightforward, and total revenue as a function of sales volume is generally simple to estimate.

The total cost function is more difficult to estimate. Total costs often bear a nonlinear relationship to output. But as a practical matter, a linear total cost function is usually sufficient to use for the normal range of output variation.

The total cost function is composed of variable and fixed cost elements. In the example, variable costs are assumed to be constant at $10 a unit. The following fixed costs are found in the example. The tape recorder requires additional fixed investment of $60,000 with an estimated life of five years. On a straight-line basis, this amounts to an annual depreciation cost of $12,000. The new product is also charged $26,000 a year for its share of general overhead. This figure presumably represents a long-run estimate of the opportunity value of the corporate resources required to support this new product. In addition, the company is considering an annual expenditure of $20,000 on advertising and $30,000 on distribution. Fixed costs therefore add up to $88,000 ($12,000 + $26,000 + $20,000 + $30,000).

The breakeven volume now can be estimated. At the breakeven volume (Q_B), total revenue (R) equals total cost (C). But total revenue is price (P) times the breakeven volume, and total cost is fixed cost (F) plus the product of unit variable cost (V) and breakeven volume. In symbols:

$$R = C$$

$$P{\cdot}Q_B = F + V{\cdot}Q_B$$

Combining similar terms, and solving for Q_B, we find

$$Q_B = \frac{F}{P - V}$$

$P - V$ is the difference between price and unit variable cost and is called the unit contribution to fixed cost. It is $8 in the example. The company would have to sell 11,000 units ($88,000 ÷ $8) to cover fixed costs.

At this point it would be useful to express the breakeven volume (Q_B) not as a constant but rather as a function of the elements in the marketing mix. The breakeven volume will vary with the product price and the amount of marketing effort devoted to the new product:

$$Q_B = \frac{\$12,000 + \$26,000 + A + D}{P - \$10} = \frac{\$38,000 + A + D}{P - \$10}$$

where

P = unit selling price to wholesaler
A = advertising budget
D = distribution budget

In the first four columns of Table 14-3, eight alternative marketing programs are listed for this product along with their implied breakeven volumes. Thus with mix #1, the company has to sell 9,667 tape recorders to break even; with mix #5, the company could sell as few as 4,143; with mix #4, the company has to sell as many as 23,000 to break even. This high sensitivity of the breakeven volume to the marketing-mix decision must not be overlooked.

Different marketing mixes not only imply different breakeven volumes, but also differences in the sensitivity of profits to *deviations* from the breakeven volume. For example, the breakeven volume is approximately the same for mixes #1 and #8. Yet the high-price, high-promotion character of #8 promises greater losses or greater profits for deviations from the breakeven volume. There are higher fixed costs under mix #8, but once they are covered, additional volume is very productive of revenue because of the high price.

DEMAND ANALYSIS

Breakeven analysis is not a sufficient technique for identifying the optimal marketing mix. It indicates what volumes have to be achieved but does not indicate what volumes are likely to be achieved. Missing is an account of how various elements in the marketing mix will affect the actual volume of sales.

Ideally the company requires a demand equation showing sales as a function of price, advertising, distribution, and other important marketing-mix elements. Such equations are difficult to derive for established products where there are historical data, let alone for new-product ideas where there are no historical data. Yet on the basis of whatever market information is gathered, the executives can be asked to estimate the most likely sales volume (Q) with each marketing mix. The fifth column in Table 14-3 shows a (hypothetical) expected sales volume for each of the eight marketing mixes. It should be noted that sales are expected to move inversely with price and directly with the amounts spent on advertising and distribution. However, increased promotion is expected to increase sales at a diminishing rate.

THE OPTIMAL MARKETING MIX AND IMPLIED PROFITS

At this point, the expected volume (Q) and the breakeven volume (Q_B) can be compared for each mix. The results are shown in column 6 of Table 14-3. The greatest extra volume ($Q - Q_B$) is achieved with mix #1. But extra volume is not a sufficient indicator of the best mix. The extra volume must be multiplied by the unit value ($P - V$). A high-price mix delivering a small extra volume may be superior to a low-price mix delivering a large extra volume. Therefore $Z = (P - V) \cdot (Q - Q_B)$ has to be calculated for each marketing mix. These results are shown in column 7 of Table 14-3.

Z is a measure of the profits expected from different marketing mixes. Of the mixes shown in Table 14-3, mix #5 appears to promise the largest

TABLE 14-3
Comparison of expected volume (Q) and breakeven volume (Q_B) for various marketing mixes

| Mix # | Marketing mix | | | Breakeven volume (Q_B) | Expected volume (Q) | Volume above breakeven (Q − Q_B) | Profits (Z)* |
	Price (P)	Advertising (A)	Distribution (D)				
	(1)	(2)	(3)	(4)	(5)	(6)	(7)
1	$16	$10,000	$10,000	9,667	12,400	2,733	$16,398
2	16	10,000	50,000	16,333	18,500	2,167	13,002
3	16	50,000	10,000	16,333	15,100	−1,233	−7,398
4	16	50,000	50,000	23,000	22,600	−400	−2,400
5	24	10,000	10,000	4,143	5,500	1,357	18,998
6	24	10,000	50,000	7,000	8,200	1,200	16,800
7	24	50,000	10,000	7,000	6,700	−300	−4,200
8	24	50,000	50,000	9,857	10,000	143	2,002

*$Z = (P - V)(Q - Q_B)$, where V = unit variable cost.

[handwritten annotations]
PROFITS
PRICE
VARIABLE UNIT COST
BREAKEVEN VOLUME
EXPECTED VOLUME

amount of profit. This mix calls for the product to be sold at a high price with little promotional support. This strategy often is used when a company believes its product has been smartly designed and essentially sells itself.

The estimated profit is a short-run measure of the project's financial attractiveness and as such is subject to a number of qualifications.[19] It cannot be a long-run measure because it leaves out long-run developments in costs, competition, market response, and economic fluctuations. But because of the substantial uncertainties surrounding new-product introductions, the company is mainly interested in whether the short-term profit potential looks good enough to develop the product.

In summary, the purpose of the business-analysis stage is to take product ideas found compatible with the company's objectives, needs, and resources and to make a careful analysis of their potential risk and profitability. Detailed information on costs and on the size and nature of the market has to be gathered at this stage. Because marketing effort influences both costs and sales, estimates should be made for different conceptions of the product's attributes and marketing mix. The estimated profit potential using the best marketing mix becomes the basis for judging whether the company should develop the new product.

Product Development

Product ideas appearing sound from a business point of view can now be turned over to the research and development department. This is an important step in at least three ways. It marks the first attempt to develop the product in a "concrete" form. Up to now, it has existed only as an idea, or perhaps as a drawing, or a very crude mock-up. Second, it represents a very large investment which is likely to dwarf the idea-evaluation costs incurred in the earlier stages. Much time and many dollars go into trying to develop a technically feasible product. And finally, it provides an answer as to whether the product idea can be translated into a technically and commercially feasible product. If not, the company's investment up to now is lost except for any by-product information gained in the process.

ENGINEERING

The challenges in the product-development stage vary with the type of product. In the case of a *manufactured durable good,* an idea that has passed the business-analysis stage is typically turned over to engineering for the development of prototypes. The objective is to arrive at a prototype that is trouble-free, designed for economical manufacture, and appealing to the customers. Many different versions may have to be tried before a satisfactory one is found.

The experience of the Bissell Company illustrates the problems at this stage. In 1959, the company developed a prototype for a combination electric vacuum and floor scrubber:

[19] *Ibid.,* pp. 45-48.

. . . four were left with the research and development department for continued tests on such things as water lift, motor lift, effectiveness in cleaning, and dust bag design. The other eight were sent to the company's advertising agency for test by a panel of fifty housewives. The research and development department found some serious problems in their further tests of the product. The life of the motor was not sufficiently long, the filter bag did not fit properly, and the scrubber foot was not correct. Similarly, the consumer tests brought in many consumer dissatisfactions that had not been anticipated: the unit was too heavy, the vacuum did not glide easily enough and the scrubber left some residue on the floor after use.[20]

CONSUMER PREFERENCE TESTING

In the case of a *consumer nondurable good,* such as a food product, the product-development stage consists largely of consumer preference testing of different product characteristics to find the most appealing combination in consumer terms. "Engineering"-type tests play a minor role, their purpose being to make sure the preferred product characteristics are built into the product safely and effectively.

Consumer preference testing is carried out by the manufacturer of jams trying to determine the best level of sweetness to build into his product,[21] by the detergent manufacturer trying to determine the best level of sudsiness,[22] and by the manufacturer of food-wrapping material trying to determine the best width to offer.[23] In all of these cases, the manufacturer is seeking to discover the distribution of consumer preferences for different levels of a particular product attribute.[24] Knowledge of this distribution becomes the basis for better product development.

Various methods have been proposed for determining the distribution, including paired comparisons,[25] multiple choices,[26] and ranking procedures. This is not the place to examine the merits of the different methods. Whichever method is used, it should be employed within the framework of good experimental design. The experimental subjects should be separated into significant groups; equivalent subjects should be assigned to experimental and control groups on a random basis; precautions should be taken against order, time of day, and other biases; and incentives should be provided for subjects to respond accurately and seriously.

After estimating the preference distribution for a particular product attribute, the firm has to decide which segment of the market it could serve most profitably. It must avoid committing the "majority fallacy." [27]

[20] Ralph Westfall and Harper W. Boyd, Jr., *Cases in Marketing Management* (Homewood, Ill.: Richard D. Irwin, Inc., 1961), p. 365.

[21] See Norman Theodore Gridgeman, "A Tasting Experiment," *Applied Statistics,* June 1956, pp. 106-12.

[22] See Alfred A. Kuehn and Ralph L. Day, "Strategy of Product Quality," *Harvard Business Review,* November-December 1962, especially pp. 106-07.

[23] See Purnell H. Benson, "A Short Method for Estimating a Distribution of Consumer Preference," *Journal of Applied Psychology,* October 1962, pp. 307-13.

[24] In practice, the problem is more complicated in that the manufacturer is trying to determine an optimal *set* of characteristics rather than an optimal *single* characteristic. Since various characteristics are likely to interact, it is not simply a matter of varying one at a time while holding the others constant. A factorial experimental design is required in these circumstances.

[25] See Kuehn and Day, *op. cit.;* and Gridgeman, *op. cit.*

[26] Benson, *op. cit.*

[27] See Chapter 3, p. 58.

Since many of the competitors are probably selling to the major segment of the market, the company might look for the relatively neglected segments. By estimating potential sales in these segments and the cost of serving them, the company can determine the most lucrative segment(s) of the market and develop its product accordingly.

PACKAGING

Another part of the product-development process is packaging design. Packaging design should be distinguished from product styling, although they have many things in common.

PACKAGING OBJECTIVES.   Until recently, packaging has been considered a minor element in the marketing mix for a product. The two traditional packaging concerns of manufacturers are product *protection* and *economy*. The manufacturer wants packaging that will protect the product during its long passage from the factory through the distributors to the final customers. At the same time, the manufacturer wants to keep packaging costs down because packaging is viewed in many quarters as a straightforward cost without any substantial marketing consequences.

A third packaging objective that comes closer to considering the consumer is *convenience*. This means such things as offering size options and packages that are easy to open.

Over the years, a fourth packaging objective has received increasing recognition from manufacturers, particularly those in the consumers' goods field. This is the *promotional* function of packaging. Various factors account for the growing recognition of packaging as an independent and potent selling tool.

Self-service.   An increasing number of products are sold on a self-service basis as a result of the spread of supermarkets and discount houses. Instead of confronting a salesman, the consumer first confronts a package. The package must now perform many of the sales tasks. It must attract attention, describe the product's features, give the consumer confidence, and make a favorable over-all impression.

Consumer affluence.   The steady rise in American incomes has caused consumers to attach increasing importance to nonprice features. They are willing to pay a little more for convenience, appearance, dependability, and prestige. Packaging is an important vehicle for projecting these qualities.

Integrated marketing concept.   Companies are increasingly trying to endow their brands with distinctive personalities. These personalities are conveyed through the general company image, through advertising messages and media, and through the choice of brand name. It does not make sense to stop short at packaging. Packaging must support and reinforce the brand personality the company is trying to build.

Innovational opportunity.   Packaging is an area where innovation per se can bring large sales gains. One has only to think of pop-top and aerosol cans, boil-a-pak dinners, and plastic-animal bubble-bath containers to appreciate this.

For all these reasons, manufacturers are taking increased interest in the promotional aspects of packaging. Things are being packaged for the consumer which never were packaged before: hardware screws, men's socks, toy rubber balls, linens, and other goods. Some companies base their whole advertising campaign on the merits of their packaging rather than on those of their product.

PACKAGING DECISIONS.   Developing the package for a new product requires a large number of decisions, in which representatives from marketing and production participate along with technical specialists.

The first task is to establish the *packaging concept.* The packaging concept is a definition of what the package should basically *be* or *do* for the particular product. Should the main function(s) of the package be to offer superior product protection, introduce a novel dispensing method, suggest certain qualities about the product or the company, or something else? The following case demonstrates the development of a packaging concept:

> General Foods developed a new dog-food product in the form of meat-like patties. Management decided that the unique and palatable appearance of these patties demanded the maximum in visibility. Visibility was defined as the basic packaging concept, and management considered alternatives in this light. It finally narrowed down the choice to a tray with a film covering.[28]

Once the packaging concept is defined, a host of further decisions must be made on the component elements of the package design—*size, shape, materials, color, text,* and *trade-mark.* Each element presents a large number of options. Decisions must be made between use of the corporate name or another name, between much text or little text, between cellophane and other transparent films or a paper, plastic, or laminate tray. Furthermore, each packaging element must be developed in harmony with the other packaging elements; size suggests certain things about materials, materials suggest certain things about colors, and so forth. The packaging elements also must be guided by decisions on pricing, advertising, and other marketing elements.

Even after the package is designed, most companies put it through a number of tests before it is finalized. *Engineering tests* are conducted to assure that the packaging stands up under normal conditions. *Visual tests* are conducted to assure that the script is legible and the colors harmonious. *Channel tests* are conducted to assure that dealers find the packages attractive and easy to handle. And *consumer tests* are conducted to assure favorable consumer reaction.

In spite of these precautions, a packaging design occasionally gets through with some basic flaw that is discovered belatedly:

> Sizzl-Spray, a pressurized can of barbecue sauce developed by Heublein, Inc., a distiller and food processor, had a potential packaging disaster that was discovered in the market test. Reports J. G. Martin, Heublein's chairman: "We thought we had a good can, but fortunately we first test marketed the product in stores in Texas and California. It appears as soon as the cans got warm they began to explode. Because we hadn't gotten into national distribution, our loss was only $150,000 instead of a couple of million." [29]

[28] See "General Foods—Post Division (B)," Case M-102, Harvard Business School, 1964.

[29] "Product Tryouts: Sales Tests in Selected Cities Help Trim Risks of National Marketings," *Wall Street Journal,* August 10, 1962, p. 1.

By now it becomes clear why developing a package for a new product may cost a few hundred thousand dollars and take from six months to a year to finalize.[30] According to a traditional view of the functions of packaging, it may seem an excessive amount. But to those who recognize the promotional potency of packaging, it is a very small investment indeed.

OTHER DEVELOPMENT ACTIVITIES

Other activities must take place in the product-development stage, among them, formulation of a preliminary advertising program, selection of a brand name, and application for patents and copyrights. All of these things must be readied for the impending test, however limited, in the market place.

Test Marketing

Up to this time the reaction of potential buyers to the new product has not been tested under normal marketing conditions. Potential customers may have been asked to react to one or more product features and to comment on the packaging and advertising appeals. But this is essentially artificial. Test marketing is the stage where the entire product and marketing program is tried out for the first time in a small number of well-chosen and authentic sales environments.

Not all companies choose the route of test marketing. A company officer of Revlon, Inc., stated:

> In our field—primarily higher-priced cosmetics not geared for mass distribution—it would be unnecessary for us to market test. When we develop a new product, say an improved liquid makeup, we know it's going to sell because we're familiar with the field. And we've got 1,500 demonstrators in department stores to promote it.[31]

The decision to test market is related to the degree of confidence the manufacturer has in the new product. In Bayesian language, it is a matter of comparing the "expected value of immediate action" and the "expected value of first sampling and then acting." Suppose in a particular case, it is estimated that test marketing would cost $100,000. Suppose the company has estimated that it may lose at most $2 million if the product fails. If management felt the odds of this product's failing were one in 100, then its expected loss for going national would only be $20,000 (2,000,000 × 1/100). Thus the expected loss from immediately going national is only one-fifth of the sure loss of $100,000 if the company pays for a market test.

If management thought the product had only an even chance of succeeding—and only 50 per cent of new products are clear successes, according to the Booz, Allen & Hamilton study—then paying $100,000 for a market test makes good sense. The company is paying a small sum of money to protect its interest in a much larger sum. Test marketing is a form of risk control.

[30] J. Gordon Lippincott and Walter P. Margulies, "Packaging in Top-Level Planning," *Harvard Business Review,* September-October 1956, pp. 46-54.
[31] "Product Tryouts," *op. cit.*

Test marketing is more frequently used by consumer-goods manufacturers than industrial-goods manufacturers. Industrial-goods manufacturers get their new-product feedback in more informal ways. When an industrial concern develops a new product, its sales representatives usually take it around to a sample of prospective buyers to learn their reactions. Often they pick up ideas and suggestions which lead the company to rework the product. When the company is finally satisfied that a sufficient number of prospective customers like the product in its latest form, the company adds the product to its catalog and prepares to sell it nationally. Thus "test marketing" in industrial situations amounts in reality to a "market probe."

The test marketing of new consumer products is a much more organized and grandiose proposition. The normal test runs between $25,000 and $250,000, mostly in fees for marketing research and advertising.[32] Typically these figures do not include production and physical distribution expenses, since they are expected to be covered by test sales. The test may involve three to six different cities and run from six weeks to as much as two years, depending on how long it takes to establish the repurchase rate.

REASONS FOR TEST MARKETING

Test marketing is expected to yield several benefits. The primary motive for testing is to *improve knowledge of potential product sales*. If product sales fall below breakeven expectations in the test markets, then the company may be a lot wiser.[33] For a relatively small amount of money, it has averted the expense and embarrassment of a national product fiasco.

A second motive for test marketing is to *pretest alternative marketing plans*. In the spring of 1960, Colgate-Palmolive used a different marketing appeal in each of four cities to test market a new soap product.[34] The four approaches were:

An average amount of advertising coupled with free samples distributed door to door

Heavy advertising plus samples

An average amount of advertising linked with mailed redeemable coupons

An average amount of advertising with no special introductory offer

Colgate found that the third alternative generated the best sales. Subject to certain qualifications, it gained some evidence on the relative merits of different marketing mixes.

The testing of basic market interest and the testing of alternative marketing mixes are the two basic motives for test marketing. Some other benefits may also be derived. Sometimes the company may discover a product fault that escaped its attention in the product-development stage. The example of Heublein was reported in the preceding section. The company may also pick up valuable clues to distribution-level problems. Its salesmen can observe how channel agents react to the new product and

[32] "Product Tryouts," *op. cit.*
[33] This is a big "maybe." If the test markets were not chosen with sufficient care, results may lead the company to withdraw a product that would have succeeded nationally, or to launch a product nationally that meets failure.
[34] "Product Tryouts," *op. cit.*

how they merchandise it to ultimate customers. And the company may gain a richer understanding of the various groups making up the market. This improved perception of market segments should enable the company to bring various aspects of its marketing program into finer focus.

PROCEDURES FOR TEST MARKETING

If these various benefits are to be realized, the company must get the best advice it can in laying out its test-market plans. Test marketing is rapidly approaching the state of a science, or at least a highly developed art. Large companies like Procter & Gamble and General Foods have accumulated considerable experience, and generally develop their test plans internally. Companies with less experience generally rely on advertising agencies, specialized consultants, or large marketing services like A. C. Nielsen Company. In the following pages, the major decisions and factors in test marketing are discussed. They concern the number of test cities to use, the selection of the cities, the length of the test run, the type of information to collect, and the action to take on the basis of test results.

HOW MANY TEST CITIES?

Great variation is found in the number of cities used in market tests. When 102 firms were recently asked how many test cities they use, almost half used fewer than four cities.[35] Is this number sufficient for projecting results on a national basis?

In deciding on the number of test cities, the two basic considerations are *representativeness* and *cost*. Unfortunately they work at cross-purposes. Results can be expected to be more representative as the sample size is increased. Additional cities allow the company to set up better experimental controls, test more alternative mixes, and probe more carefully for regional differences. But, setup and auditing fees increase with the number of cities. The benefits of including an additional city must exceed the cost of including it. In general, a larger number of cities should be used: the greater the maximum possible loss and/or the probability of loss from going national; the greater the number of alternative marketing plans and/or the greater the uncertainty surrounding which is best; the greater the number of regional differences; and the greater the chance of calculated test-market interference by competitors.

WHICH CITIES?

In spite of much press agentry, no single city in the United States can be considered a perfect replication in miniature of the nation as a whole. There are, however, some cities which typify aggregate national characteristics better than others and some cities which are more typical of their regions than others. It is not surprising, therefore, that certain cities have become popular for test-marketing purposes. Some of the favorites for national testing are Syracuse, New York; Dayton, Ohio; Peoria, Illinois; and Des Moines, Iowa; some favorites for regional testing are Richmond, Virginia; Portland, Oregon; San Diego, California; and Springfield, Mas-

[35] *Printers' Ink,* April 13, 1962, p. 22. This was a special issue devoted to test marketing. The author has relied on this source for some of the statistics.

sachusetts.[36] The popularity of Syracuse was explained by one agency that audits market tests.

337
New-Product
Decisions

> It has a relatively good cross-section of ethnic groups, and not any one group dominates. There's a broad economic spectrum with a sizable middle class. The city is surrounded by typical American suburbs and, beyond them, by satellite farm communities. Syracuse is fairly stable; it isn't a one-industry town that can be hit hard by abnormal swings in the economy. Moreover, a large element of the population is cosmopolitan and critical partly because of the presence of Syracuse University and partly because large plants there hire sophisticated technical and managerial personnel. These people are hard to convince a new product is worth buying, but if you can convince them you usually can convince the nation.[37]

Each company must define its own test-city selection criteria. One company restricts its choice of test cities to those with several industries, good media coverage, cooperative chain stores, average competitive activity, and no evidence of being overtested. Additional test-city selection criteria may be introduced because of the special characteristics of the product. For example, small luxury items, such as expensive wallets and specialty perfumes, have no market in most cities. They are sold through fine stores found in a handful of cities, and this considerably limits the city-selection problem. As another example, Patio Foods wanted to test market a new line of frozen Mexican dinners. The number of eligible cities shrank quite rapidly because the criteria included the incidence of travel to Mexico, the existence of a Spanish-language press, and the retail sales of prepared chili and frozen Chinese food. In general, each product may call for additional criteria beyond the regular guidelines used by the company.

HOW LONG SHOULD THE TEST RUN?

Market tests have lasted anywhere from a few months to several years.[38] The test duration is decided in each case by the peculiar circumstances surrounding it. Although many factors must be considered, three stand out as having prime importance: the average repurchase period, the competitive situation, and the cost of test marketing.

The first factor is the product's *average repurchase period*. This refers to the length of time that normally elapses before the purchaser restocks the product. The new product or brand may have gotten into his hands as a free sample, or on a special deal, or as an impulse purchase. Asking him for his opinion after he uses it is not an adequate substitute for observing his next purchase. Even one repurchase observation is hardly enough. After using it once, the consumer may buy his former brand to make a comparison. Or he may buy the new product a few times in succession and then drop it out of dissatisfaction. Therefore it is desirable to observe a few repurchase periods. This is no great obstacle for products

---

[36] A list of the 36 most popular testing cities can be found in *Printers' Ink,* April 13, 1962.

[37] "Product Tryouts," *op. cit.*

[38] When *Printers' Ink* queried 102 firms on how long they thought tests should run, 18 per cent felt that one to two months was sufficient, 16 per cent named two to four months, another 18 per cent named six months, and 24 per cent named one to two years. *Printers' Ink,* April 13, 1962, p. 22.

with short repurchase periods. But it is a major problem for new products with long repurchase periods, when the company may have to run the test for one or two years or rely on postpurchase interviewing.

The second factor influencing the length of the market test is the *competitive situation*. A company wants the market test to last long enough to get useful information but not so long that competitors are given a chance to catch up. The right duration is difficult to ascertain. Lever Brothers took a year to test a new pancake-syrup concept using butter (Mrs. Butterworth). During this time, General Foods, maker of the Log Cabin brand, is alleged to have audited Lever's sales in Cleveland and Indianapolis. Both companies managed to introduce buttered syrup nationally at about the same time. Commented an industry spokesman: "Lever's long test undoubtedly kept it from getting the jump on its competition. If General Foods hadn't come in at about the same time, Lever would now have a larger share of the market." [39]

The third factor of prime importance in setting a length for the market test is *cost*. The total costs of test marketing vary directly with the test's duration. The expenses of auditing the sales results and supervising the test continue through the test period. The company also bears the opportunity costs of not introducing the product earlier.

The decision maker faces the same dilemma in setting the length of the test that he faced in choosing the number of cities. Test results are generally more informative as the test is extended through time, but test costs, both direct and competitive, tend to increase with the test's length.

WHAT INFORMATION SHOULD BE COLLECTED DURING THE TEST?

In laying plans for a market test, the planner must decide what sales and other information is required to evaluate the new product's strengths and weaknesses. He must then make arrangements with the company's marketing research department and outside commercial services to gather this information.

PRODUCT SHIPMENTS DATA. Various kinds of information can be obtained, differing in value and cost. Perhaps the least informative and least costly are data about product shipments to test markets. Product shipments are made in response to dealers' orders for new stock. But because of reporting lags and inventory level changes, weekly changes in shipment figures do not necessarily reflect weekly changes in the rate of retail sales.

STORE AUDITS. In order to keep abreast of the actual movement of retail sales, it is necessary to arrange for periodic store audits. The company has the option of buying reports from a regular commercial service or arranging for special auditing.

A. C. Nielsen Company conducts bimonthly store audits (food outlets, drug stores) for major product categories. The report summarizes store sales and inventories for the major competitive brands. This service is of limited usefulness in test marketing, however, because it is only conducted bimonthly and the data may not be available for some weeks afterward.

[39] "Product Tryouts," *op. cit.*

Furthermore, sales information gained through store audits does not reveal anything about the characteristics of the buyers, such as the proportion of new buyers to repeat buyers.

CONSUMER PANELS. Information on buyer characteristics can sometimes be obtained when the new product is purchased by members of consumer panels. The Market Research Corporation of America receives a purchase diary each week from 7,500 different households scattered in various parts of the United States. Each household reports all its grocery purchases, by brand, size, price, and special deal (if any). MRCA rearranges this information according to product class. If the company has introduced a new brand of coffee, it can purchase information on the coffee-brand purchase sequences of the sample of households in the test areas. From these data, the firm can estimate how much repeat purchasing of its brand is taking place, from what particular brands it is gaining customers and to what particular brands it is losing customers, what types of customers are showing the most interest in the new brand, and so forth. In addition, the firm can process the data into a Markov model for forecasting future market shares on the basis of the early brand-switching and -staying rates.[40]

BUYER SURVEYS. The company may also want to obtain direct data on buyer attitudes and reactions to the new product. This involves getting the names of a sample of new buyers and arranging to interview them. The following plan was used by a company that was introducing a new after-shave lotion:

> It was proposed that retailers be induced to procure names and addresses of all purchasers of the new item until names of about 600 purchasers in each city were obtained. This could be done by offering clerks in retail outlets 10¢ for each purchaser's name secured. Six weeks after their purchases, these consumers would be contacted by investigators who would disguise their interest in after-shave lotions through a series of questions concerning other products. During the interview attention would finally be centered on after-shave lotions.[41]

These interviews provided data on the characteristics of the buyers and their verbal reactions to after-shave lotions in general and the new brand in particular.

All told, the more information the company collects, the better its chances are that it will make the right decision; at the same time, costs increase with the amount of information bought. The right amount and types of information must be decided on the basis of the test-market objectives, the market risks, and the information costs.[42]

[40] See Louis A. Fourt and Joseph W. Woodlock, "Early Prediction of Market Success for New Grocery Products," *Journal of Marketing*, XXV (October 1960), 31-38; Benjamin Lipstein, "Tests for Test Markets," *Harvard Business Review*, March-April 1961, pp. 74-77; William D. Barclay, "Probability Model For Early Prediction of New Product Market Success," *Journal of Marketing*, XXVII (January 1963), 63-68.

[41] Harper W. Boyd, Jr., and Ralph Westfall, *Marketing Research: Text and Cases* (Homewood, Ill.: Richard D. Irwin, Inc., 1956), p. 613.

[42] For a Bayesian approach to deciding what type of market information to gather, see Frank M. Bass, "Marketing Research Expenditures: A Decision Model," *Journal of Business*, January 1963, pp. 77-90.

A company makes an investment in a market test in order to achieve a rough indication of the product's probable sales performance on a national basis. The test results are a major factor in the subsequent decision.

Some of the possible actions the company can take on the basis of the test results are shown in Figure 14-4. If product sales in the test markets are substantial, the company will in all probability launch the new product nationally. If test sales fall in a middle range, indicating neither clear success nor clear failure, the company has a number of options, the most likely being to conduct further tests. If product sales are poor, the company again has some options, the most likely being to drop the product, provided it does not suspect the test markets of being unrepresentative or the product of having faults that can be corrected.

Commercialization

Only a handful of product ideas originating at the idea-generation stage survive the successive stages of screening, business analysis, product development, and test marketing. Each product that does is ripe for commercial introduction. By now the company has apparently gained the necessary confidence in the product's future. The product's profit outlook looks good in relation to its risk.

What is involved in introducing the product commercially? Among other things, the company must finalize all the attributes of product and

FIGURE 14-4
Alternative decisions following test market results

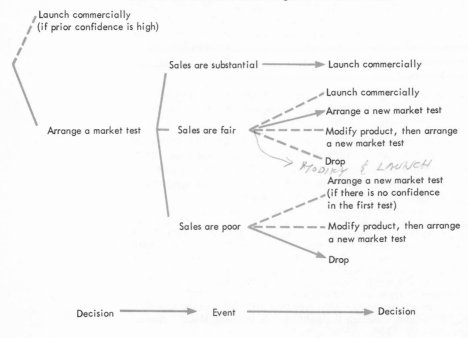

package. It must invest in new equipment and facilities to make large-scale production possible. It must hold meetings with the sales force to create skills and enthusiasm for handling the product. It must arrange a complete advertising and promotion program with its agency.

All of these steps involve expenditures that rapidly dwarf those incurred up to this stage. For example, to introduce a major new household detergent into the national market may require $10 million for advertising and promotion alone.[43] The company cannot expect to operate in the black for the first year or two. Even the largest companies have to go to the money market to finance ventures of this size.

The product generally is not introduced all at once on a national scale. Instead it is introduced into the prime markets first and gradually into secondary and tertiary markets.[44] The *rate of planned market expansion* is governed by a number of factors. If the test-market results are very encouraging and if it appears that the product will be a big money-maker, the company would undoubtedly try to introduce the product on a crash basis. An additional incentive would exist in the case of a highly copyable product if competition was rushing into the same market. However, the company can move no faster than its resources permit. There is the question of how fast it can expand its production facilities and train its sales force. There is the further question of how much capital it can raise to finance the desired rate of market expansion.

Companies that are not completely confident in their new product will want to move more slowly into new markets. In doing so, they recognize that they may be limiting their gain for the sake of being able to limit their loss. They cannot take advantage of national media discounts. They risk an outpacing by competition. But they feel that it is prudent to hold down costs until signs of the product's probable performance become more definite.

Whether the company introduces its new product gradually or on a national basis, it needs to schedule the product's commercial introduction carefully. The smooth coordination and progression of the hundreds of activities making up the commercialization stage warrant the use of some advanced planning and scheduling technique such as PERT.[45]

The company must decide important questions of strategy in guiding its new product through the introductory and later stages of its life cycle. At the business-analysis stage, the company presumably decided on a tentative marketing program for introducing the product. It tested this and alternative programs at the test-marketing stage to improve its estimates of their relative effectiveness. By the time the company is ready to launch the product commercially, events having to do with competition or the state of the economy may lead the firm to revise its basic marketing strategy. It may decide on a "low-price, high-promotion" mix in order to capture as large a share of the market as early as possible. Or it may decide in favor of a "high-price, medium-promotion" mix to recover its investment as quickly as possible. Whatever decision it makes at this stage, it will

[43] See "Guerrilla War on Soap Giants," *Business Week,* August 29, 1964, p. 51.
[44] For an analysis of the problem of ranking alternative market areas for expansion, see William R. King, "Marketing Expansion—A Statistical Analysis," *Management Science,* July 1963, pp. 563-73.
[45] See Chapter 7, pp. 163-69.

undoubtedly have to make further revisions as changes occur in costs, sales, competition, market saturation, and economic activity.

The Consumer-Adoption Process

The *consumer-adoption process* begins where the *firm's innovation process* leaves off. It deals with the process by which potential customers come to learn about the new product, try it, and eventually adopt or reject it. The manufacturer's problem is to understand this process so that he can bring about early mass awareness and trial usage. The *consumer-adoption process* should be distinguished from the *consumer-loyalty process,* which is the concern of the established product manufacturer.

The consumer-adoption process has come under increasing study by social scientists and others interested in understanding the general process by which an innovation becomes diffused through the society. This area of study promises to shed light on what determines the rate of acceptance of a new idea. Because an understanding of the adoption process is vital in formulating marketing strategy for a new product, the main concepts and propositions in this field will be examined.[46]

CONCEPTS IN INNOVATION DIFFUSION

The vocabulary of the field is apt to be confusing, and so it is best to start with some definitions. The central concept is that of an *innovation.* While this term has been used in many ways, in this context it refers to any idea in the way of a good or service which is *perceived* as new by someone. The idea may have had a long history, but it is still an innovation to the person who sees it as being new. Examples of innovations under this definition would be electric typewriters, language laboratories, a new brand of soap, smoking pipes for women, charge accounts, stainless steel razor blades, sauna baths, and Cinerama.

These innovations are assimilated into the social system over time. *Diffusion process* is the name given to "the spread of a new idea from its source of invention or creation to its ultimate users or adopters." [47] The *adoption process,* on the other hand, focuses on "the mental process through which an individual passes from first hearing about an innovation to final adoption." *Adoption* itself is a decision by an individual to use an innovation regularly.

The differences among individuals in their response to new ideas is called their *innovativeness.* Specifically, innovativeness is "the degree to which an individual is relatively earlier in adopting new ideas than the other members of his social system." On the basis of their innovativeness, individuals can be classified into different *adopter categories.* (These will be discussed on pp. 343-46.

Individuals also can be classified in terms of their influence on others with respect to innovations. *Opinion leaders* are "those individuals from

---

[46] The consumer adoption process represents a specialized application of principles of buying stages and learning described in Chapter 4 ("Buyer Behavior"). I am indebted to Everett M. Rogers' *Diffusion of Innovations* (New York: Free Press of Glencoe, Inc., 1962) for the account that follows.

[47] See Rogers, *ibid.,* for this and following definitions.

whom others seek information or advice." Individuals or firms who actively seek to change other people's minds are called *change agents.*

PROPOSITIONS ABOUT THE CONSUMER-ADOPTION PROCESS

The stage is now set for examining the main generalizations drawn from hundreds of studies of how people accept new ideas.

STAGES OF THE ADOPTION PROCESS. The first proposition is that *the individual consumer goes through a series of stages of acceptance in the process of adopting a new product.* The stages are classified by Rogers as:

1. *Awareness:* the individual becomes cognizant of the innovation but lacks information about it.
2. *Interest:* the individual is stimulated to seek information about the innovation.
3. *Evaluation:* the individual considers whether it would make sense to try the innovation.
4. *Trial:* the individual tries the innovation on a small scale to improve his estimate of its utility.
5. *Adoption:* the individual decides to make full and regular use of the innovation.[48]

This particular version of the process evolved largely out of studies of the adoption of new agricultural methods and products by farmers. An individual farmer is likely to hear about a new development, say a new fertilizer, from his newspaper or radio, from local merchants, or from other farmers. This information remains in the back of his mind until something happens to increase his interest. He may read about a special price on the new fertilizer or hear a second merchant praising it. When his interest is aroused enough, the farmer undertakes to inquire systematically into the benefits of the new fertilizer. He discusses it with other farmers and dealers and perhaps agricultural scientists. He evaluates this information prior to the time he has to purchase fertilizer and may decide either to stick with his old fertilizer or to give the new fertilizer a try. If he tries the new fertilizer on a limited scale and the results please him, he will probably decide to use it regularly. At that point, we say that he has *adopted* the new fertilizer. Adoption is thus the last phase of a complicated learning process.

The value of this model of the adoption process is that it requires the innovator to think carefully about new-product acceptance. Depending on the product, one or more stages may be critical in moving the buyer toward purchase. The manufacturer of electric dishwashers may discover that many housewives are frozen in the interest stage; they cannot jump the gap to the trial stage, because of their uncertainty and the large investment. But these same housewives would be willing to use an electric dishwasher on a trial basis for a small fee. Recognizing this, the manufacturer may wish to institute a trial-use plan with option to buy. In general, by considering the stages in the movement toward purchase, the innovating firm may be able to spot potential problems and opportunities.

INDIVIDUAL DIFFERENCES IN INNOVATIVENESS. The second proposi-

[48] *Ibid.,* pp. 81 ff.

tion is that *people differ markedly in their penchant for trying new products*. In each product area, there are apt to be leaders and early adopters. Some women are the first to adopt a new Parisian style and bring it back to Podunk, U.S.A. Some are the first to adopt new small appliances, such as blenders, electric toothbrushes, and infrared broilers. Some doctors are the first to prescribe new medicines,[49] and some farmers are the first to adopt new farming methods.[50]

By the same token, other individuals tend to adopt innovations much later. This has led to a classification of people into adopter categories on the basis of their relative earliness in adopting an innovation. The classification is shown in Figure 14-5.

The adoption process is represented as following a normal (or near normal) distribution when plotted over time. After a slow start, an increasing number of people adopt the innovation, the number reaches a peak, and then it diminishes as fewer individuals remain in the nonadopter category. The use of the normal distribution is supported by both empirical and theoretical studies.[51]

Convenient breaks in the distribution are used to establish adopter categories. Thus innovators are defined as the first 2½ per cent of the individuals to adopt a new idea, the early adopters are the next 13½ per cent who adopt the new idea, and so forth. Although this partitioning in terms of unit standard deviations is somewhat arbitrary (given that innovativeness is a continuous dimension), the model does provide the standardization needed to facilitate comparisons of different studies of product adoption.

No break is established between early and late laggards, because research has not produced any clear grounds for differentiation. Thus the categorization is somewhat asymmetrical. In addition, the figure leaves out the whole group of nonadopters, those who never adopt the new idea.

Rogers has tried to characterize the five adopter groups in terms of ideational values.[52] The dominant value of innovators is *venturesomeness;* they like to try new ideas, even at some risk, and are cosmopolite in orientation. The dominant value of early adopters is *respect;* they enjoy a position in the community as opinion leaders and adopt new ideas early but with discretion. The dominant value of the early majority is *deliberateness;* these people like to adopt new ideas before the average member of the social system although they rarely are leaders. The dominant value of the late majority is *skepticism;* they do not adopt an innovation until the weight of majority opinion seems to legitimize its utility. Finally, the dominant value of the laggards is *tradition;* they are suspicious of any changes, mix with other tradition-bound people, and adopt the innovation only because it has now taken on a measure of tradition itself.

The marketing implication of the adopter classification is that an in-

[49] See James Coleman, Elihu Katz, and Herbert Menzel, "The Diffusion of an Innovation Among Physicians," *Sociometry,* December 1957, pp. 253-70.

[50] See J. Bohlen and G. Beal, *How Farm People Accept New Ideas,* Special Report No. 15 (Ames, Iowa: Iowa State College Agricultural Extension Service, November 1955).

[51] Rogers, *op. cit.,* pp. 156-57.

[52] *Ibid.,* pp. 168 ff.

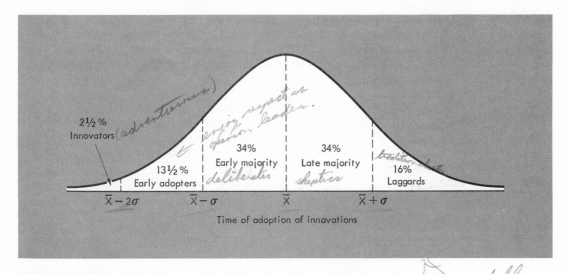

FIGURE 14-5

Adopter categorization on the basis of relative time of adoption of innovations
Redrawn from Everett M. Rogers, *Diffusion of Innovation* (New York: Free Press of Glencoe, Inc., 1962), p. 162.

novating firm should direct its communications to those people who are likely to be early in adopting the innovation; messages reaching late adopters and laggards are wasted. Of the two early groups, innovators and early adopters, the latter are more important. Innovators tend to learn about new ideas and adopt them regardless of directed promotion; they do not tend to enjoy much influence over noninnovators; and they are a small group. Early adopters on the other hand are generally looked to for advice and information. Change agents try to seek them out to speed the diffusion process. The two practical problems are: how can early adopters be identified, and how can they be reached?

The identification of early adopters is not easy. So far no one has demonstrated the existence of a general personality factor called innovativeness. Individuals tend to be innovative in certain areas and laggard in others. We can think of a businessman who dresses conservatively but who delights in trying unfamiliar cuisines. The firm's problem is to identify the characteristics of those who are likely to be early adopters in its product area. The probability of being an early adopter may turn out to be related to easily identified economic or educational or social or personality characteristics. For example, studies show that innovative farmers are likely to be better educated and more efficient than noninnovative farmers.[53] Innovative housewives, those who are the first to try new food products, are more gregarious and usually of a higher social status than noninnovative housewives.[54] Furthermore, certain communties as a whole, especially those with higher than average mobility, tend to be more ready

[53] For a summary of these studies, see Rogers, *op. cit.*, p. 176.
[54] Elihu Katz and Paul F. Lazarsfeld, *Personal Influence* (New York: Free Press of Glencoe, Inc., 1955), pp. 234 ff.

345

to accept new ideas.[55] The innovativeness of some communities is an important though neglected factor in selecting test markets. On the basis of these and other studies, Rogers offered the following hypotheses about early adopters, keeping in mind they would have to be checked freshly for each product area:

> The relatively earlier adopters in a social system tend to be younger in age, have higher social status, a more favorable financial position, more specialized operations, and a different type of mental ability from later adopters. Earlier adopters utilize information sources that are more impersonal and cosmopolite than later adopters and that are in closer contact with the origin of new ideas. Earlier adopters utilize a greater number of different information sources than do later adopters. The social relationships of earlier adopters are more cosmopolite than for later adopters, and earlier adopters have more opinion leadership.[56]

Once the characteristics of early adopters are identified, a marketing communications program can be developed for the new product calculated to reach and interest these people. The known media habits of these people can be used to increase the effectiveness of the company's advertising. The company can also supply samples to community leaders and utilize store demonstrations to attract the early adopters.

ROLE OF PERSONAL INFLUENCE.   The third proposition is that *personal influence plays a very large role in the adoption of new products.* By *personal influence* is meant the effect of product statements made by one person on another's attitude or probability of purchase. Katz and Lazarsfeld reported:

> About half of the women in our sample reported that they had recently made some change from a product or brand to which they were accustomed to something new. The fact that one third of these changes involved personal influences indicates that there is also considerable traffic in marketing advice. Women consult each other for opinions about new products, about the quality of different brands, about shopping economies and the like. . . .[57]

Although personal influence is an important factor throughout the diffusion process, its significance is greater in some situations and for some individuals than for others. Personal influence seems to be more important in the evaluation stage of the adoption process than in the other stages. It seems to have more influence on the later adopters than the earlier adopters. And it appears to be more important in risky situations than in safe situations.[58]

Recognizing the role of personal influence can make an important contribution to marketing planning. It tempers one's enthusiasm about media advertising's being able to do the whole job. It underscores the desirability

[55] For evidence of the relation between mobility and innovativeness, see Reuben Cohen, "A Theoretical Model for Consumer Market Prediction," *Sociological Inquiry,* Winter 1962, pp. 43-50.
[56] Rogers, *op. cit.,* p. 192.
[57] Katz and Lazarsfeld, *op. cit.,* p. 234.
[58] Rogers, *op. cit.,* pp. 219-23.

of creating advertising messages designed to supply early adopters with ways of verbalizing their opinions to others. It highlights the importance of designing a good product.

INFLUENCE OF PRODUCT CHARACTERISTICS ON THE RATE OF ADOPTION. The fourth proposition is that *the character of the innovation itself affects the rate of adoption.* Innovations are known to have widely varying rates of adoption, some taking hold in a few months and others requiring many decades. What are the major product characteristics accounting for these differences?

Five characteristics seem to have an especially important influence on the adoption rate.[59] The first is the innovation's *relative advantage,* or the degree to which it appears superior to previous ideas. The greater the perceived relative advantage, whether in terms of higher profitability, reliability, or ease of operation, the more quickly the innovation will be adopted.

The second characteristic is the innovation's *compatibility,* or the degree to which it is consistent with the values and experiences of the individuals in the social system. Innovations that are compatible with favorably held ideas are likely to be adopted more quickly.

Third is the innovation's *complexity,* or the degree to which it is relatively difficult to understand or use. The more complex innovations are likely to take a longer time to diffuse, other things being equal.

Fourth is the innovation's *divisibility,* or the degree to which it may be tried on a limited basis. The evidence of many studies indicates that divisibility helps to increase the rate of adoption. There is also evidence that earlier adopters may need more divisibility than later adopters, because they take more risk.

The fifth characteristic is the innovation's *communicability,* or the degree to which the results are observable or describable to others. Innovations that lend themselves to better demonstration or description of advantage will diffuse faster in the social system.

Has the firm any control over the characteristics of its new product so that it can speed up the rate of adoption? The answer is yes, within certain limits. The five listed characteristics carry important implications for *product design, promotion,* and *merchandising.*

As for *product design,* the firm should create a product with maximum relative advantage over the products it supersedes, maximum compatibility with the adopter's values, and minimum complexity. These characteristics occasionally conflict. Mechanical equipment can often be made more versatile at the price of greater complexity. A rear, air-cooled engine in automobiles increases certain efficiencies, but is not favorably regarded by many Americans. There is no simple formula; there are only guidelines for maximizing the contribution of product design to the acceleration of product acceptance.

As for *promotion,* the firm must design its communications to maximize the potential customers' understanding and interest. The firm cannot take for granted that customers will perceive the new product's advantages in their true magnitude. These advantages must be verbalized and ac-

[59] *Ibid.,* chapter 5.

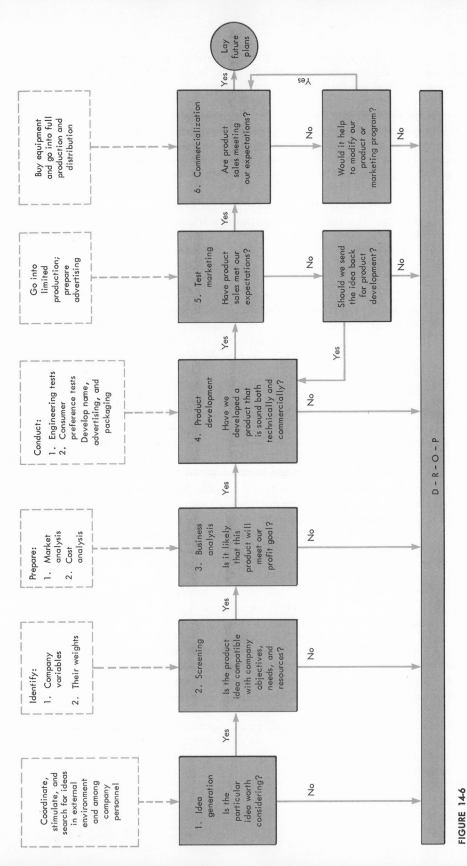

FIGURE 14-6
Summary of the new-product development decision process

centuated. Where the product would appear complex, the communications must emphasize its simplicity. Where the product would appear radically different, the communications must emphasize its harmony with the adopter's value system.

As for *merchandising,* various characteristics can be tapped to accelerate the rate of product acceptance. Consider divisibility. In introducing new consumer nondurables, the firm might distribute free samples or develop small sizes to increase the rate of trial. In introducing large appliances or equipment, the firm might provide a rental arrangement with option to buy.

Summary

If Rip Van Winkle had fallen asleep in 1940, he would be astonished upon awaking in the Sixties at the changes that had taken place in the American market place. He would confront and have to puzzle out such innovations as frozen foods, television, aerosol cans, high fidelity equipment, synthetic fabrics, electric blankets, wonder drugs, and automatic clothes dryers, to name but a few. He would learn that American society's major orientation was change.

Innovation takes place at such a rapid pace because manufacturers see profit opportunities in it and because increasingly affluent consumers covet it. There is growing recognition among businessmen that this is a race to be joined . . . or lost.

New-product development however is not a primrose path. The risks of innovation are as great as the rewards. A large percentage of new products fail in the market place, and a still larger number have to be dropped, at great cost, before commercialization. The secret of successful innovation lies in developing effective organizational arrangements, professional new-product management, a sophisticated research operation, and sound analytical criteria for decision making.

We have viewed the new-product development process as consisting of six stages, which, with their corresponding criteria, are summarized in Figure 14-6. New-product ideas, which mark the beginning of the process, move through a series of stages involving screening, business analysis, product development, test marketing, and commercialization. The purpose of each successive stage is to produce a judgment as to whether the idea should be further developed or dropped. The company should seek decision criteria for each stage which minimize the chances of poor ideas moving forward and good ideas being rejected. The last stage, commercialization, involves the introduction of the products that have passed the previous tests; it is benefited by marketing planning and strategy based on an understanding of the consumer-adoption process.

Questions and Problems

1. The new-product development process starts with a search for good ideas. Suggest some concepts which define a company's search effort.

2. Complained a research executive: "Would fluorocarbon resins, nylon, or polyethylene have come out of a screening formula—or a check list, for that matter? The important things are intuition and judgment. Research is a creative art." Is this a valid argument against formal screening devices? Can you name any advantages of using formal screening devices?

3. Hardly a marketing forum takes place anywhere in this country without some speaker's complaining about the high failure rate of new products. Yet statistical estimates of the new-product failure rate vary widely. How would you define new-product failure, and how would you propose the rate be measured?

4. A shaving cream manufacturer is planning to introduce a new after-shave lotion. Research indicates that light blue is the favored color by a strong margin. Does it follow that light blue should be adopted?

5. (a) The eight marketing mixes in Table 14-3 are a small sample from a very large number of mixes which could be used to launch the new tape recorder. How were they formed? Describe the marketing philosophy of each mix in words.

(b) What refinements might be made in the model described for the business-analysis stage?

6. (a) Expected profit and risk are two major dimensions for determining whether to introduce a new product nationally. Can you develop a diagram using these two dimensions to show how critical limits might be set up by a firm before a market test to guide its decision after the test?

(b) Suppose a firm finds that the test-market results are borderline and concludes that the product would probably yield a below-average return. It has sunk a lot of money into the development of the product. Should it introduce the product nationally or drop it?

(c) State the two opposing risks that a firm faces when it bases its new-product decision on test-market results. How can it reduce these risks?

(d) In the Colgate test marketing of its new soap (described in the text) the third marketing mix yielded the highest sales. Does this mean that it should be preferred to the other mixes if the product is launched nationally?

7. Do all adopters of new products pass through all five stages of the adoption process?

chapter 15

Price Decisions

Of all the marketing variables that may influence the potential sales of a product, price has received the most attention from professional economists. Some marketing executives also attach a great deal of importance to price. An even larger number, however, regard pricing as one of the less important concerns in the effective marketing of their products.[1]

This chapter will discuss the role of pricing in contemporary marketing and the major pricing decisions faced by the firm. The first section presents a brief historical analysis of the changing position of pricing in the total marketing program. The second describes the economic theory of setting prices and some of its limitations. The third section describes the leading practical methods in use for setting prices. The fourth and fifth sections discuss respectively the decision to initiate a price change and the decision to react to a price change initiated by a competitor. The final section considers pricing for the entire product line.

Pricing in the Marketing Mix

For over 150 years, economists have emphasized the price variable in describing the level of demand.[2] What accounts for this strong emphasis, why is it changing, and how important is price today as a factor in competitive marketing?

REASONS FOR PRICE EMPHASIS

There are historical, technical, and social reasons for the predominant attention paid to pricing in the past. The historical reason lies in the character of the economy when economists like Adam Smith and David Ricardo first began to develop systematic economic theory. The typical nation's output consisted of raw materials (including foodstuffs) and

---

[1] See Jon G. Udell, "How Important Is Pricing in Competitive Strategy?" *Journal of Marketing,* XXVIII (January 1964), 44-48. Udell sent questionnaires to a sample of 200 producers of industrial and consumer goods, seeking to determine the rated importance of price versus other marketing policy variables in competitive strategy. Udell concluded: "It appears that business management did not agree with the economic views of the importance of pricing—one-half of the respondents did *not* select pricing as *one of the five most important* policy areas in their firm's marketing success."

[2] Microeconomic theory and general equilibrium theory, even to this day, are largely price theory. For example, see James N. Henderson and Richard E. Quandt, *Microeconomic Theory* (New York: McGraw-Hill Book Company, 1958).

finished consumer goods. Items like wheat, cotton, sugar, and basic clothing were highly standardized, and little effort was made to differentiate them through branding, packaging, or advertising. The major variable differentiating competitive offerings was price. Price took on additional sensitivity as a marketing variable because of the low level of per capita income. Frugality had to be cultivated by households just to meet subsistence requirements.

The technical reason is that price has more tractable properties from the point of view of analysis. Prices are quantitative, unambiguous, and unidimensional, whereas product quality, product image, customer service, promotion and similar factors are qualitative, ambiguous, and multidimensional. It is easier to speculate about what consumers would do if price rose by 5 per cent than if quality rose by 5 per cent; in fact, it is not even easy to define what is meant by a quality improvement of 5 per cent.

The social reason is that the price mechanism affords an elegant rationale for the efficiency of a competitive free enterprise system. Prices act as signals by which potential buyers and sellers can rationally decide how to allocate their scarce resources. Flexible prices are viewed as an ideal mechanism for clearing markets of gluts and shortages. In the presence of a glut, sellers tend to cut their prices. The reduced prices encourage more purchasing and less production, both of which help clear the glut. In the presence of a shortage, prices rise, discouraging buying and encouraging production, both of which help alleviate the shortage. The rate at which these adjustments take place depends on how quickly the price changes, how fast the news is disseminated, and how rationally the market participants behave. The main point is that a competitive system characterized by flexible prices leads, in principle, to maximum economic efficiency.[3]

GROWING RECOGNITION OF NONPRICE VARIABLES

More recently, a small but growing number of economists have begun to pay more systematic attention to the role played by nonprice variables in the sale of goods. One of the earliest formal inclusions of nonprice variables—in this case quality and advertising—appeared in 1933 in E. H. Chamberlin's *Theory of Monopolistic Competition.*[4] His book and some of those which followed gave formal recognition to *new variables in household consumption* and *new patterns of business competition* that actually had been apparent for several decades.

Under the influence of rising incomes, households were spending less time in home manufacture. Their purchase mix shifted from such goods as flour, fresh peaches, and cotton yarn to bread, canned peaches, and manufactured sweaters. An increasing number of durable goods, such as refrigerators, gas stoves, radios, and automobiles, were also becoming available to the average household. Many of the new goods could be differentiated on functional or stylistic grounds, or at least psychologically differentiated through branding, packaging, and advertising.

The symbolic aspect of pricing became increasingly important. The

---

[3] *Ibid.*, pp. 202 ff.

[4] Edward H. Chamberlin, *The Theory of Monopolistic Competition* (Cambridge, Mass.: Harvard University Press, 1933).

price tag no longer always functioned in the expected manner; the sale of certain goods could be stimulated more effectively through higher rather than lower prices. This could happen for two different reasons. In some cases, the higher price increased the snob appeal of the goods. In other cases, the higher price increased the customer's confidence that he was getting good quality.[5]

On the seller's side, many industries and areas were increasingly dominated by a few large firms, resulting in a mutual awareness and sensitivity to one another's pricing. Firms increasingly recognized that not much is gained in reducing a price if other firms do the same thing. Indeed, if total industry demand is fairly inelastic, as is the case with many consumer nondurables (gasolines, foodstuffs, etc.), price competition tends to cut into the profits of all the firms concerned. Price wars, skirmishes, and just normal price competition, because of the low returns and great risks involved, are to be avoided. Many sellers prefer to conduct the battle along nonprice lines.

SITUATIONS WHERE PRICE DECISIONS ARE OF GREAT IMPORTANCE

Is it to be concluded then that the typical firm does not face major pricing problems? Definitely not. Pricing remains a very complex issue in many firms. Firms outside of those selling standardized products in highly competitive markets or in highly oligopolized markets enjoy varying degrees of price latitude, and hence are faced with pricing decisions.

Pricing is a problem in four general types of situations. It is a problem *when a firm must set a price for the first time*. This happens when the firm develops or acquires a new product, when it introduces its regular product into a new distribution channel or geographical area, or when it regularly enters bids on new contract work. Pricing is a problem *when circumstances lead a firm to consider initiating a price change*. This happens when a firm begins to doubt whether its price is right in relation to its demand and costs. It can also be triggered by a sudden change in demand or costs. It also happens on a more regular basis in firms which periodically introduce temporary price deals to stimulate the trade or final buyers. Pricing is a problem *when competition initiates a price change*. The firm has to decide whether to change its own price and if so, by how much. Finally, pricing is a problem *when the company produces several products that have interrelated demands and/or costs*. The problem is one of determining optimal price relationships for the products in the line.

Price Setting in Theory

DEVELOPMENT OF THEORETICAL PRICING MODEL

Economists have developed a simple, yet elegant model of how to set a price. The model has the properties of logical consistency and optimization, but it represents a severe simplification of the pricing problem as it is confronted in practice. There is value, however, in examining it because

---

[5] See D. S. Tull, R. A. Boring, and M. H. Gonsior, "A Note on the Relationship of Price and Imputed Quality," *Journal of Business*, April 1964, pp. 186-91.

it provides some fundamental insights into the pricing problem and because its very limitations help bring out the complex issues involved in pricing.

The model assumes a profit-maximizing firm that has knowledge of its demand and cost functions for the product in question. The demand function describes the expected level of quantity demanded per period (Q) for various prices (P) that might be charged. Figure 15-1 presents two conceptions of the shape of the demand function which are popular with economics instructors. The first function is linear; the second is curvilinear. Both are negatively sloped to indicate that less will be bought at higher prices (the law of demand). Suppose the firm is able to determine through statistical demand analysis [6] that its demand function is described by the following linear equation: [7]

$$Q = 1,000 - 4P \qquad \text{(1) demand equation}$$

The cost function describes the expected level of total cost (C) for various quantities per period (Q) that might be produced. It is customary to distinguish between total fixed costs (those which do not vary with the level of output) and total variable costs (those which do vary with the level of output). In the simplest case, the total cost function can be described by the general linear equation $C = d + eQ$ where d is total fixed cost and e is unit variable cost. Suppose the company derived the following cost equation for its product:

$$C = 6,000 + 50Q \qquad \text{(2) cost equation}$$

With the preceding demand and cost equations, the pricing executive is almost in a position to determine the best price. He only needs two more equations, both definitional in nature.[8] First, total revenue (R) is defined as equal to price times quantity sold; i.e.,

$$R = PQ \qquad \text{(3) revenue equation}$$

Second, total profits (Z) are defined as the difference between total revenue and total cost; i.e.,

$$Z = R - C \qquad \text{(4) profit equation}$$

[6] See Chapter 5, pp. 114-20.

[7] It is understood that this equation is relevant exclusively in the positive quadrant and not too close to the two axes. Thus it does not make sense to ask what would be sold at a price of —$5 or at a price exceeding $250. (Why?) This is not surprising. Many of the familiar equations in physics, such as those describing the tension of a spring or the motion of a pendulum, break down or lose accuracy when the inputs take on extreme values. Equations are useful ways to summarize relationships among variables whose values are in the normal range.

[8] Equations serve a variety of purposes. Demand equations are *behavioral* in that they attempt to summarize the average behavior of people in response to variations in a price stimulus. Cost equations are *technological* in that they attempt to relate the cost of inputs in a technological process to the amount of output. Revenue and profit equations are *definitional;* they state relations which are true by definition. Other equations (not shown here) are *institutional* when they express a social or political artifact, such as the relationship between income taxes and income, e.g., $T = .2Y$, where $T =$ amount of tax, $Y =$ amount of income. See Robert S. Weinberg, "The Uses and Limitations of Mathematical Models for Market Planning," in *Mathematical Models and Methods in Marketing*, eds. Frank M. Bass, *et al.* (Homewood, Ill.: Richard D. Irwin, Inc., 1961), pp. 4-8.

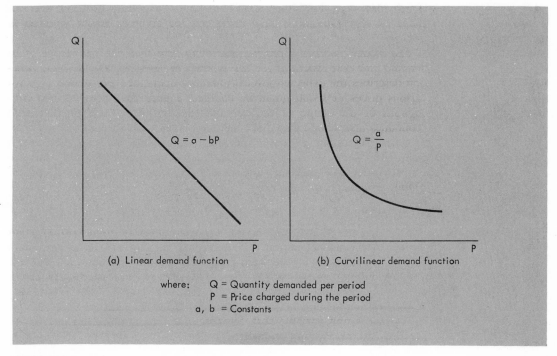

(a) Linear demand function   (b) Curvilinear demand function

where: Q = Quantity demanded per period
         P = Price charged during the period
      a, b = Constants

FIGURE 15-1

Two conceptions of the shape of the demand function

Note: In keeping with a longstanding tradition in economics, the P and Q axes are reversed in most textbooks. Here they are shown with the independent variable (price, in this case) on the horizontal axis, following the usual mathematical convention.

With these four equations, the pricing executive is in a position to solve for the profit-maximizing price. (The reader should try this before reading on.)

The executive is essentially trying to determine the relationship between profits (Z) and price (P). The four equations have to be solved simultaneously in order to find the single relationship between Z and P. It is best to start with the profit equation (4). The derivation is as follows:

$$Z = R - C$$
$$Z = PQ - C$$
$$Z = PQ - (6,000 + 50Q)$$
$$Z = P(1,000 - 4P) - 6,000 - 50 (1,000 - 4P)$$
$$Z = 1,000P - 4P^2 - 6,000 - 50,000 + 200P$$
$$Z = -56,000 + 1,200P - 4P^2 \qquad \text{(5) profit equation}$$

Total profits turn out to be a quadratic (i.e., second degree) function of price. By inserting different possible values of price, the pricing executive can graph the relationship between profits and price. The graph, illustrated in Figure 15-2, is a hatlike figure (a parabola), and profits seem to reach their highest point ($34,000) at a price of $150.

The same conclusion could be reached without the aid of graphing by using calculus to solve equation 5 for the price that would maximize

355

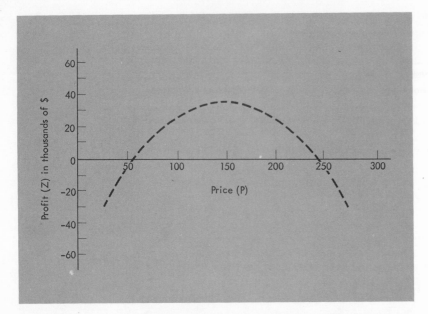

FIGURE 15-2
Relationship between profits (Z) and price (P)

profit.[9] The typical economics textbook uses a still different route to arrive at the same conclusion. Instead of working with total revenue and total cost, the economist often works with marginal revenue and marginal cost. Marginal revenue is the change in total revenue that occurs with a one-unit change in output. Marginal cost is the change in total cost that occurs with a one-unit change in output. If the marginal revenue from a unit increase in output exceeds the marginal cost, then the change should be made. Output should be increased until marginal cost equals marginal revenue.[10]

Although it is often not made clear, this theoretical model is based on

[9] The first derivative of $Z = -56,000 + 1,200P - 4P^2$ is $dZ/dP = 1,200 - 8P$. Setting this equal to 0 and solving for P, we find $P = \$150$.

[10] Marginals are essentially the first derivatives of total functions. For the example above, marginal revenue and marginal cost are respectively

$$\frac{dR}{dQ} = -\tfrac{1}{2}Q + 250$$

$$\frac{dC}{dQ} = 50$$

The next step is to set marginal revenue equal to marginal cost and solve:

$$-\tfrac{1}{2}Q + 250 = 50$$
$$Q = 400$$

Thus marginal revenue and marginal cost are equal at an output of 400 units. The price at which this output can be sold is determined through the demand equation:

$$Q = 1,000 - 4P$$
$$400 = 1,000 - 4P$$
$$P = \$150$$

Very often this exposition is carried out in the form of a diagram illustrating four curves: marginal revenue, marginal cost, average revenue, and average cost. The economist locates the point on the output axis above which marginal revenue and marginal cost are equal. He then uses the average revenue curve to find the price which will sell this output. See Paul A. Samuelson, *Economics, An Introductory Analysis,* 5th ed. (New York: McGraw-Hill Book Company, 1961), p. 531.

several highly restrictive assumptions, which severely limit the model's applicability to actual pricing problem. They are:

The firm's objective in setting a price is to maximize the short-run profits on the particular product.

The only party to consider in setting the price is the firm's immediate customers.

The price can be set independently of the levels set for the other marketing variables.

The demand and cost equations can be estimated with sufficient accuracy.

These assumptions shall be examined in turn.

THE PROBLEM OF OBJECTIVES

The theoretical pricing model assumes a single product for which the seller is trying to determine the price that would maximize current profits. Current profits rather than long-run profits are at issue because of the use of stable demand and cost assumptions. In reality, demand can be expected to change over time (as a result of changes in tastes, population, and income), and cost can be expected to change over time (as a result of changes in technology and input prices). Pricing to maximize long-run profits would have to utilize projections of the likely long-run course of demand and cost. A more sophisticated model would be required to solve the problem of pricing optimally over the product's life cycle.

A limitation of quite another sort is that profit maximization, whether current or long-run, is not always the immediate pricing objective of a firm. It may be the ultimate goal, but conceptions of the means for achieving it may differ. At least five different objectives of a more concrete sort can be found in practice.[11]

MARKET PENETRATION OBJECTIVE. Some companies set a relatively low price in order to stimulate the growth of the market and to capture a large share of it. Any of several conditions might favor setting a low price: [12] (1) The market appears to be highly price-sensitive; that is, many additional buyers would come into the market if the product were priced low. (2) The unit costs of production and distribution fall with increased output. (Whenever a product is favored by scale economies, it is desirable to give serious consideration to all measures that would stimulate sales, including a low price.) (3) A low price would discourage actual and potential competition.

MARKET-SKIMMING OBJECTIVE. Some firms seek to take advantage of the fact that some buyers always stand ready to pay a much higher price than others because the product, for one reason or another, has high present value to them. The objective of skimming pricing is to gain a premium from these buyers and only gradually reduce the price to draw in the more price-elastic segments of the market. It is a form of price

[11] For a documentation of pricing objectives, see the Brookings study by A. D. H. Kaplan, Joel B. Dirlam, and Robert F. Lanzilloti, *Pricing in Big Business* (Washington, D. C.: Brookings Institute, 1958).

[12] See Joel Dean, *Managerial Economics* (Englewood Cliffs, N.J.: Prentice-Hall, Inc., 1951), pp. 420 ff.

discrimination over time rather than over space. It makes good sense when any of the following conditions are present: (1) There is a sufficiently large number of buyers whose demand is relatively inelastic. (Were the company to set a low price initially, it would forego the potential premium from this segment of the market.) (2) The unit production and distribution costs of producing a smaller volume are not so much higher that they cancel the advantage of charging what some of the traffic will bear. (3) There is little danger that the high price will stimulate the emergence of rival firms. (Where barriers to entry are high, because of patents, high development costs, raw material control, or high promotion costs, the innovating firm can proceed with relative safety to pursue a market-skimming pricing policy.)[13]

EARLY CASH RECOVERY OBJECTIVE. Some firms seek to set a price that will lead to a rapid recovery of cash. They may be either strapped for funds or regard the future as too uncertain to justify patient market cultivation.

SATISFICING OBJECTIVE. Some companies describe their pricing objective as the achievement of a satisfactory rate of return. The implication is that although another price might produce an even larger return over the long run, the firm is satisfied with a return that is conventional for the given level of investment and risk. Target pricing (see pp. 363-64) is an example of this.

PRODUCT-LINE PROMOTION OBJECTIVE. Some firms seek to set a price that will enhance the sales of the entire line rather than yield a profit on the product by itself. This has often been called loss-leader pricing, although if it succeeds in enhancing total profits by increasing sales of the entire line, it should more properly be called profit-leader pricing.

THE PROBLEM OF MULTIPLE PARTIES

In addition to taking a narrow view of pricing objectives, the theoretical pricing model assumes that the only significant group to consider in the pricing of a product is the firm's customers. But in reality, several parties have to be considered simultaneously in setting the price.

INTERMEDIATE CUSTOMERS. The firm must think through its pricing not only for its ultimate customers but for its intermediate customers as well. Some companies in fact set a price for distributors and allow them to set whatever final price they wish. This is done where it is thought that each distributor is in the best position to determine the price suited to local conditions and to set it high enough to provide sufficient selling incentive. The disadvantage is that the manufacturer relinquishes control over the final price. The other approach is for the manufacturer to deter-

---

[13] A high initial price offers two other advantages. First, it leaves room for reducing the price if a mistake has been made; this is always easier than increasing a price if it had been set too low initially. Second, a high price may create an impression of a superior product. A home permanent kit, originally marketed at 39¢ in dimestores, did not sell. It caught on when it was repriced at $1.98 and marketed through drugstores.

mine the final price and how much of a distributor's margin is necessary to provide sufficient distributor incentive. The distributors must recognize that the important incentive variable is not the difference between the distributor's and final price (the margin) but rather the margin times the sales stimulated by the particular final price.

RIVALS. The theoretical pricing model did not consider competitive reactions explicitly. It can be argued that whatever assumption is made about competitive reactions can be incorporated in the shape of the demand function, but this treatment of competitive reaction is too implicit and static. The price set by the manufacturer influences the rate of entry of new rivals and the pricing policies of existing rivals. The traditional demand curve is too summary a way to represent the dynamic reactions and counter-reactions occasioned by a pricing policy.

SUPPLIERS. The company's suppliers of materials, funds, and labor also must be considered in setting the price. Many suppliers interpret the product's price as indicating the level of the firm's revenues (and profits) from the product. Labor unions will act as if a high price, or price increase, constitutes grounds for higher wages. Farmers believe they deserve higher cattle prices if retail meat prices are high. The firm's bank often feels uneasy if the firm's price is on the low side. Thus various supplier groups may have to be considered by the firm in setting a price.

GOVERNMENT. Another price-interested party is the government. Under the Robinson-Patman Act, the seller cannot charge different prices to comparable customers unless the price differences are based strictly on cost differences. Under the Miller-Tydings Act, the seller may or may not be able to require retailers to sell his branded product at a uniform list price, depending upon the state laws.[14] Public utilities must justify their rates before regulatory commissions. The steel industry must move cautiously with price increases because of the government's interest in price stability. At various times, pricing in the meat, drug, and heavy equipment industries has been subject to government pressure. The prices of agricultural goods and of imported goods are affected by agricultural and tariff legislation respectively. And various state and local governmental units pass legislation and rulings affecting the prices that can be set by sellers.

OTHER COMPANY EXECUTIVES. Price is a concern of different parties within the company. The sales manager wants a low price so that his salesmen can "talk price" to customers. The controller likes to see a price leading to an early payout. The price makes an important difference in copy and media tactics to the advertising manager. The production scheduling manager is interested because the price will affect the rate of sales. These and other executives in the organization can be expected to have strong views on where to set the price.

THE PROBLEM OF MARKETING-MIX INTERACTION

The theoretical pricing model also assumes that other marketing variables are held at some constant level while the effect of price on sales is being

[14] See Chapter 20, pp. 541-43.

examined. This is evident in the usual treatment of the demand function as a relationship only between quantity demanded (Q) and price (P). But this begs the whole question of how optimal values can be set on advertising, personal selling, product quality, and other marketing variables before price is set. As emphasized throughout this book, the several marketing variables have to all be considered simultaneously to arrive at the optimal mix. This task is missing or assumed away in the theoretical pricing model.

THE PROBLEM OF ESTIMATING DEMAND AND COST FUNCTIONS

Grave statistical problems handicap the determination of actual demand and cost functions. In the case of a new product, there is no experience upon which to base these estimates. Unless data are available on a similar, established product, estimates are likely to take the form of soft facts and guesses rather than hard facts. Data on established products are usually not much more satisfactory.

Johnston has described the major econometric techniques for estimating cost functions from existing data.[15] Demand functions are more difficult to determine because several of the variables are not quantifiable; they are typically highly intercorrelated; both demand and cost have been shifting during the period; and the random errors tend to be large. Because some of the "independent" variables are also dependent (sales depends on advertising, and advertising depends upon sales), a system of simultaneous equations rather than a single equation estimate of demand seems to be required.[16] Finally, even were these hurdles to be overcome, there are always lingering doubts about whether the relationships measured from historical data apply to today's situation.

Since the demand and cost equations are estimated with an unknown degree of error, the criterion of maximizing profits may have to be replaced with the criterion of maximizing *expected* profits (where probability distributions are put on the estimated functions) or the criterion of maximizing the minimum possible gain. In any situation of risk and uncertainty, the pricing executive will want to see how sensitive the theoretically calculated price is to revisions in the estimated data.

Price Setting in Practice

The fault with the economist's pricing model is not one of illogic but of oversimplification. It assumes that short-run profit maximization is the paramount objective, that customers are the only interested party, that the other marketing variables can be set optimally before price is set, and that accurate estimates can be made of demand and costs. The pricing models used in practice also for the most part tend to be based on a limited view of the pricing problem and opportunities. They tend to emphasize one of the factors, such as cost, demand, or competition, to the neglect of the

[15] See Jack Johnston, *Statistical Cost Analysis* (New York: McGraw-Hill Book Company, 1960).

[16] See Richard E. Quandt, "Estimating Advertising Effectiveness: Some Pitfalls in Econometric Methods," *Journal of Marketing Research*, May 1964, pp. 51-60.

other factors. Nevertheless they meet some of the more practical requirements for price determination in the presence of imperfect information
and multiple parties. We shall examine cost-oriented, demand-oriented,
and competition-oriented pricing.

COST-ORIENTED PRICING

A great number of firms set their prices largely or even wholly on the
basis of their costs. Typically, all costs are included, including a usually
arbitrary allocation of overhead made on the basis of expected operating
levels.

MARKUP PRICING. The most elementary examples of this are markup
pricing and cost-plus pricing. They are similar in that the price is determined by adding some fixed percentage to the unit cost. Markup pricing
is most commonly found in the retail trades (groceries, furniture, clothing,
jewelry, and so forth) where the retailer adds predetermined but different
markups to various goods he carries. Cost-plus pricing is most often used
to describe the pricing of jobs that are nonroutine and difficult to "cost"
in advance, such as construction and military weapon development.

Markups vary considerably among different goods. Some common
markups in department stores are 20 per cent for tobacco goods, 28 per
cent for cameras, 34 per cent for books, 41 per cent for dresses, 46 per
cent for costume jewelry, and 50 per cent for millinery.[17] In the retail
grocery industry, items like coffee, canned milk, and sugar tend to have
low average markups, while items like frozen foods, jellies, and some
canned products have high average markups. In addition, quite a lot of
dispersion is found around the averages. Within the category of frozen
foods, for example, one study showed the markups to range from a low
of 15 per cent to a high of 213 per cent.[18]

Many hypotheses have been advanced to explain the variations in
markups within selected product groups. Lee E. Preston conducted a
detailed study to examine how much of the markup dispersion within
common grocery-product groups could be explained by three commonly
used rules of thumb:

> Markups should vary inversely with unit costs.
> Markups should vary inversely with turnover.
> Markups should be higher and prices lower on reseller's (private) brands
> than on manufacturer's brands.[19]

Using multiple regression analysis with 5 per cent levels of significance,
he could only conclude that "some of the . . . rules of thumb were followed to some extent in some of the product groups." In one product
group a single rule helped explain 61 per cent of the variance in percentage
markups, and in two groups a combination of two rules helped explain

---

[17] *Departmental Merchandising and Operating Results of 1962* (New York: National Retail Merchants Association, 1963), pp. 16, 20, 28.
[18] See Lee E. Preston, *Profits, Competition, and Rules of Thumb in Retail Food
Pricing* (Berkeley, Calif.: University of California Institute of Business and Economic Research, 1963), p. 31.
[19] *Ibid.*, pp. 29-40.

over 60 per cent. Evidently store managers used at least rough rules of thumb to avoid "getting lost" in a maze of individual pricing decisions. But the principal finding was that a large amount of variation remained unexplained and was probably due to erratic decisions, random factors, and frequently better adaptations to the current market than could be provided by the rules.

Does the use of a rigid customary markup over cost make logical sense in the pricing of products? Generally, no. Any model that ignores current demand elasticity in setting prices is not likely to lead, except by chance, to the achievement of maximum profits, either in the long run or short run. As demand elasticity changes, as it is likely to do seasonally, cyclically, or over the product life cycle, the optimum markup should also change.[20] If markup remains a rigid percentage of cost, then under ordinary conditions it would not lead to maximum profits.

Under special conditions, however, a rigid markup at the right level may lead to optimum profits. The two conditions are that average (unit) costs must be fairly constant over the range of likely outputs and price elasticity must be fairly constant for different points on the demand curve and over time. The reader should try to supply intuitive arguments for these conditions.[21]

[20] For example, housing contractors generally price by marking up their estimated costs by some percentage. But they show a willingness to accept a lower percentage when demand falls, as in the winter. In a study of the pricing policies of a sample of 88 small businesses, William Haynes found that most of the firms did not adhere strictly to rigid markups but modified them under different circumstances. See William W. Haynes, *Pricing Decisions in Small Business* (Lexington: University of Kentucky Press, 1962).

[21] The argument proceeds as follows. It can be shown that price (P) and marginal revenue (MR) are related in the following way:

$$MR = \left(1 + \frac{1}{e}\right) P \tag{1}$$

where
e = price elasticity of demand

(See George Stigler, *The Theory of Price,* rev. ed. [New York: The Macmillan Company, 1952], pp. 37-38.) Now, profits are maximized when marginal revenue is equated to marginal cost. Therefore, applying (1), the optimality condition is

$$MC = \left(1 + \frac{1}{e}\right) P \tag{2}$$

Suppose average costs are constant (Special Condition 1). Then $AC = MC$, and the condition for optimality is

$$AC = \left(1 + \frac{1}{e}\right) P \tag{3}$$

(3) can be arranged algebraically to yield a formula for the optimal markup. From (3),

$$\frac{P}{AC} = \frac{1}{1 + \dfrac{1}{e}} = \frac{e}{e + 1}$$

Subtracting $\dfrac{AC}{AC}$ from both sides and simplifying,

$$\frac{P - AC}{AC} = \frac{e}{e + 1} - 1 = \frac{1}{e + 1}, \text{ or}$$

$$\text{Markup} = \frac{1}{e + 1} \tag{4}$$

Both conditions—fairly constant costs and fairly constant elasticity—are apt to characterize many retailing situations. This may explain why fairly rigid markups are in widespread use in retailing and why this may not be inconsistent with optimal pricing requirements. In manufacturing, however, it is less likely that the two special conditions obtain, and here fixed markup pricing is more difficult to justify on logical grounds. In particular, marginal costs are likely to differ from average costs because of scale economies. When manufacturers set prices on the basis of average costs, they are not likely to arrive at the profit-maximizing price.

Still, markup pricing remains popular for a number of reasons. First, there is generally less uncertainty about costs than about demand. By pinning the price to unit costs, the seller simplifies his own pricing task considerably; he does not have to make frequent adjustments as demand conditions change. Second, where all firms in the industry use this pricing approach, their prices are likely to be similar if their costs and markups are similar. Price competition is therefore minimized, which would not be the case if firms paid attention to demand variations when they priced. Third, there is the feeling that cost markup pricing is socially fairer to both the buyer and the seller. The seller does not take advantage of the buyer when his demand becomes acute; yet the seller earns a fair return on his investment. Thus the popularity of a cost-oriented approach to pricing rests on considerations of administrative simplicity, competitive harmony, and social fairness.

TARGET PRICING. A common cost-oriented approach used by manufacturers is known as *target pricing,* in which the firm tries to determine the price that would give it a specified target rate of return on its total costs at an estimated standard volume. This pricing approach has been most closely associated with General Motors, which has publicly stated that it prices its automobiles so as to achieve a long-run average rate of return of 15 to 20 per cent on its investment.[22] It is also closely associated with the pricing policies of public utilities, which have a large investment and are constrained by regulatory commissions in view of their monopoly position to seek a fair rate of return on their costs.

The pricing procedures used in target pricing can be illustrated in terms of the breakeven chart in Figure 15-3. Management's first task is to estimate its total costs at various levels of output. The total cost curve is shown rising at a constant rate until capacity is approached. Management's next task is to estimate the percentage of capacity it is likely to operate at in the coming period. Suppose the company expects to operate at 80 per cent of capacity. This means that it expects to sell 800,000 units if its capacity is 1,000,000 units. The total cost of producing this volume, according to Figure 15-3, is $10,000,000. Management's third task is to specify a target

---

According to (4), the optimal markup is inversely related to price elasticity. If brand price elasticity is high, say 5.0, as it might be in the case of *branded* sugar, then the optimal markup is relatively low (16⅔ per cent). If brand elasticity is low, say 0.5, as it might be in the case of branded frozen pastry, the optimal markup is relatively high (66⅔ per cent). Furthermore, if the price elasticity remains fairly constant over time (Special Condition 2), then a fairly rigid markup would be consistent with optimal pricing.

[22] Kaplan, *et al., op. cit.,* pp. 48-55; 131-35.

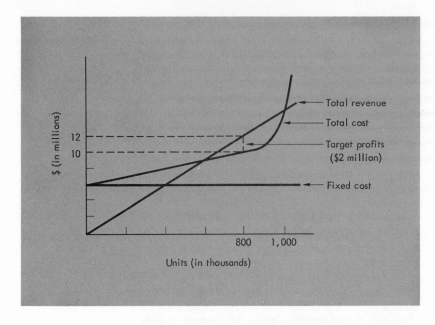

FIGURE 15-3
Breakeven chart for determining target price

rate of return. If the company aspires for a 20 per cent profit over costs, then it would like absolute profits of $2,000,000. Therefore one point on its total revenue curve will have to be $12,000,000 at a volume of 80 per cent of capacity. Another point on the total revenue curve will be $0 at a volume of zero per cent of capacity. The rest of the total revenue curve can be drawn between these two points.

Where does price come in? The slope of the total revenue curve is price. In this example, the slope is $15 a unit. Thus if the company charges $15 a unit and does manage to sell 800,000 units, it will attain through this price the target rate of return of 20 per cent or $2,000,000.

Target pricing, however, has a major conceptual flaw. The company used an estimate of sales volume to derive the price, but price is a factor that influences sales volume! A price of $15 may be too high or too low to move 800,000 units. What is missing from the analysis is a demand function, showing how many units the firm could expect to sell at different prices. With an estimate of the demand curve and with the requirement to earn 20 per cent on costs, the firm could solve for those prices and volumes that would be compatible with each other. In this way, the firm would avoid setting a price which failed to generate the estimated level of output.

DEMAND-ORIENTED PRICING

Cost-oriented approaches rely on the idea of a standard markup over costs and/or a conventional level of profits. Demand-oriented approaches look instead at the intensity of demand. A high price is charged when or where demand is intense, and a low price is charged when or where demand is weak, even though unit costs may be the same in both cases. This may seem like profit-maximizing pricing, but reasons will be given shortly why the two are not always equivalent.

is price discrimination, in which a particular commodity is sold at two
or more prices.[23] Price discrimination takes various forms, according to
whether the basis is the customer, the product version, the place, or the
time. Examples of each will be presented.

Pricing that discriminates on a *customer basis* is illustrated in the retail
selling of automobiles and major appliances. A car buyer may come into
an automobile showroom and pay the list price for the automobile. Ten
minutes later, another car buyer may hold out for a lower price and
pay it.[24] The automobile may be identical in both cases, and the marginal
cost of the transaction may be identical; yet the seller has managed to
extract a higher price from one buyer than from the other. The occurrence
of price discrimination among customers may indicate different intensities
of demand or variation in consumer knowledge. Charging different prices
to different customers calls for strong nerves and considerable adroitness
on the part of the seller, for it is potentially disruptive of customer relations.

Pricing that discriminates on a *product version basis* occurs when
slightly different versions of a product are priced differently but not proportionately to their respective marginal costs. An example would be the
sale of an electric dishwasher with a $5 formica top for $180 and the same
dishwasher with a $10 wooden top for $220. The higher premium for the
latter dishwasher reflects not so much the extra production cost as the
extra psychological demand. Manufacturers, however, do not always mark
up the more costly version at a disproportionately higher price. In many
cases, the price discrimination is reversed to encourage the buyer to trade
up, thereby increasing total dollar sales.

Pricing that discriminates on a *place basis* is also quite common, since
place is a form of utility. The pricing of theater seats is a case in point.
Although all seats cost virtually the same to install, theater managements
price seats differently because of different intensities of demand for the
various locations. If a relatively high price is charged for all seats, the
front would be filled, but many back seats would be empty. If a relatively
low price is charged, people would queue early in order to get the better
seats on a first-come first-served basis. Different prices are charged so that
each customer pays close to the maximum of what he is willing to pay.
The theater is filled, and theater revenue is maximized.

Pricing that discriminates on a *time basis* also takes many forms. The
demand for a product is likely to vary in intensity over the business cycle,
over the seasons, by the day, and sometimes by the hour. Public utilities,
in their pricing to commercial users, typically vary their prices according
to the day (week end versus weekday) and even the time of day. Not
long ago an economist advocated that public transportation services be

[23] A more rigorous definition says that price discrimination is the sale of a particular commodity at two or more prices which do not reflect a proportional difference in marginal costs. (Stigler, *op. cit.,* pp. 214-20). For this reason, the common
practice of granting price discounts to customers placing larger orders is not treated
as a form of price discrimination.

[24] For data on the wide variations in prices paid for the same car, see Allen F.
Jung, "Price Variations among Automotive Dealers in Metropolitan Chicago,"
Journal of Business, January 1960, pp. 31-42.

priced higher at peak hours than at off-hours.[25] Generally speaking, the firm whose costs are largely fixed can gain by varying prices according to temporal variations in demand.

For price discrimination to be possible in the first place, whether by customer, product version, place, or time, certain conditions must exist.[26] First, the market must be segmentable, and the segments must show different intensities of demand. Second, there should be no chance that the members of the segment paying the lower price could turn around and resell the product to the segment paying the higher price. Third, there should be little chance that competitors will undersell the firm in the segment being charged the higher price. Finally, the cost of segmenting and policing the market should not exceed the extra revenue derived from price discrimination.

Price discrimination may or may not lead to long-run profit maximization. Charging what different parts of the traffic will bear may maximize short-run receipts but may injure customer relations in the long run. In this connection, the automobile manufacturers in the immediate postwar period did not raise prices to the full extent they could have on the basis of demand, but many of the independent dealers, instead of rationing the scarce automobiles on a first-come, first-served basis, sold the cars to the highest offerers of illegal premiums. This antagonized both the buyers who paid the premiums and those who were by-passed, and may have hurt these dealers after supply caught up with demand.

COMPETITION-ORIENTED PRICING

When a company sets its prices chiefly on the basis of what its competitors are charging, its pricing policy can be described as competition-oriented. It is not necessary to charge the same price as competition, although this is a major example of this policy. The competition-oriented-pricing firm may seek to keep its prices lower or higher than competition by a certain percentage. The distinguishing characteristic is that it does *not* seek to maintain a rigid relation between its price and its own costs or demand. Its own costs or demand may change, but the firm maintains its price because competitors maintain their prices. Conversely, the same firm will change its prices when competitors change theirs, even if its own costs or demand have not altered.

GOING-RATE PRICING. The most popular type of competition-oriented pricing is where a firm tries to keep its price at the average level charged by the industry. Called *going-rate* or *imitative pricing,* it is popular for several reasons. Where costs are difficult to measure, it is felt that the going price represents the collective wisdom of the industry concerning the

---

[25] This recommendation was not made in the spirit of deriving premiums from those whose demand for public transportation was more intense—those who travel to work—but rather to try to stimulate housewives and others to shift their trips from rush-hour periods to nonrush-hour periods. In this way, the existing transportation capacity would be utilized more evenly through the day, and there would be less need for equipment to meet peak demand. See William S. Vickrey, "A Proposal for Revising New York's Subway Fare Structure," *Operations Research,* February 1955, pp. 38-68.

[26] See Stigler, *op. cit.,* pp. 215 ff.

price that would yield a fair return. It is also felt that conforming to a going price would be least disruptive of industry harmony. The difficulty of knowing how buyers and competitors would react to price differentials is still another reason for this pricing.

Going-rate pricing primarily characterizes pricing practice in homogeneous product markets, although the market structure itself may vary from pure competition to pure oligopoly. The firm selling a homogeneous product in a *highly competitive market* has actually very little choice about the setting of its price. There is apt to be a market-determined price for the product, which is not established by any single firm or clique of firms but through the collective interaction of a multitude of knowledgeable buyers and sellers. The firm daring to charge more than the going rate would attract virtually no customers. The firm need not charge less because it can dispose of its entire output at the going rate. Thus, under highly competitive conditions in a homogeneous product market (e.g., food, raw materials, and textiles) the firm really has no pricing decision to make. In fact, it hardly has any significant marketing decisions to make. The major challenge facing such a firm is good cost control. Since promotion and personal selling are not in the picture, the major marketing costs arise in physical distribution, and here is where cost efficiency may be critical.

In *pure oligopoly,* where a few large firms dominate the industry, the firm also tends to charge the same price as competition, although for different reasons. Since there are only a few firms, each firm is quite aware of the others' prices, and so are the buyers. A certain grade of steel is likely to possess the same quality whether it is produced by Inland or Bethlehem, and so the slightest price difference would favor the lower-price firm unless service or contractual relationships are sufficient to overcome this. The observed lack of price competition in these industries has been explained on the basis of the individual oligopolist's demand curve's having a kink in it at the level of the present prices. The demand curve tends to be elastic above the kink because other firms are not likely to follow a raise in prices; the demand curve tends to be inelastic below the kink because other firms are likely to follow a price cut.[27] An oligopolist can gain little by raising his price when demand is elastic or lowering his price when demand is inelastic, and this is held to explain much of the price timidity in these markets.

This does not mean that the going price in an oligopoly market will be perpetuated indefinitely. It cannot, since industry costs and demand change over time. Usually, the industry takes collective action to raise the price, or in rarer cases, to lower the price. This is not done through official channels, for that would be illegal. Typically, one firm assumes the role of price leader. The others follow any change in price by the leader. Of the twelve general price increases in the steel industry between World War II and 1960, United States Steel led in eleven cases, thus maintaining the position of price leader that began in the days of Judge Gary.[28] Occasionally, the pattern of leadership is more diffused; of thirteen price increases in the aluminum industry between 1950 and 1958, Alcoa led in

[27] Price elasticity is defined on p. 370.
[28] See Leonard W. Weiss, *Economics and American Industry* (New York: John Wiley & Sons, Inc., 1961), p. 294.

nine, Kaiser in two, and Reynolds and Aluminium Limited in one apiece.[29]

In markets characterized by *product differentiation,* the individual firm has more latitude in its price decision. Product differences, whether in styling, quality, or functional features, serve to desensitize the buyer to existing price differentials.[30] Firms try to establish themselves in a pricing zone with respect to their competitors, assuming the role of either a high-price firm, a medium-price firm, or a low-price firm. Their product and marketing program are made compatible with this chosen pricing zone or vice versa. They respond to competitive changes in price to maintain their pricing zone.

SEALED-BID PRICING. Competitive-oriented pricing also dominates in those situations where firms compete for jobs on the basis of bids, such as original equipment manufacture and defense contract work. The bid is the firm's offer price, and it is a prime example of pricing based on expectations of how competitors will price rather than on a rigid relation based on the firm's own costs or demand. The objective of the firm in the bidding situation is to get the contract, and this means that it hopes to set its price lower than that set by any of the other bidding firms.

Yet the firm does not ordinarily set its price below a certain level. Even when it is anxious to get a contract in order to keep the plant busy, it cannot quote a price below marginal cost without worsening its position. On the other hand, as it raises its price above marginal cost, it increases its potential profit but reduces its chance of getting the contract.

The net effect of the two opposite pulls can be described in terms of the *expected profit* of the particular bid. Suppose a bid of $9,500 would yield a high chance of getting the contract, say .81, but only a low profit, say $100. The expected profit with this bid is therefore $81. If the firm bid $11,000, its profit would be $1,600, but its chance of getting the contract might be reduced, say to .01. The expected profit would be only $16. Table 15-1 shows these and some other bids and the corresponding expected profits.

One logical bidding criterion would be to state the bid which would maximize the expected profit. According to Table 15-1, the best bid would be $10,000 for which the expected profit is $216.

The use of the expected-profit criterion makes sense for the large firm which makes many bids and is not dependent on winning any particular contract. In playing the odds, it should achieve maximum profits in the long run. The firm which bids only occasionally and/or may need a particular contract badly will probably not find it advantageous to use the expected-profit criterion. The criterion, for example, does not distinguish between a $1,000 profit with a .10 probability and a $125 profit with an .80 probability. Yet the firm which wants to keep production going is likely to prefer the second contract to the first. In other words, the dollar value of expected profits may not reflect the utility value.

---

[29] *Ibid.,* pp. 211-12.

[30] Other factors which desensitize buyers to price differentials are differences in personal selling, service, and buyer information. See Richard D. Sampson, "Sense and Sensitivity in Pricing," *Harvard Business Review,* November-December 1964, pp. 99-105.

TABLE 15-1
Effect of different bids on expected profit

Company's bid	Company's profit	Probability of getting award with this bid (assumed)	Expected profit
$ 9,500	$ 100	.81	$ 81
10,000	600	.36	216
10,500	1,100	.09	99
11,000	1,600	.01	16

The chief obstacle to the use of formal bidding theory is guessing the probability of getting the contract at various bidding levels. This estimate requires information about what the competitors are likely to bid. Here lies the problem, because competitors keep their intentions as secret as possible. Therefore the company has to rely on conjecture, trade gossip, or past bidding history.

The theory of competitive bidding has received considerable refinement in the hands of applied mathematicians. Not only the standard situation but also special situations have been explored, such as that of a company that wants to bid simultaneously on a number of contracts and yet cannot afford to win them all.[31] The major problem remains that of obtaining reliable data to insert into the model.

Initiating Price Changes

Pricing is not only a difficult decision when a price is being set for the first time but is also challenging when the firm is about to initiate a price change for one reason or another. The firm may be considering a *price reduction* in order to stimulate demand, to take advantage of lower costs, or to shake out weaker competitors. Or it may be considering a *price increase* in order to take advantage of tight demand or to pass on higher costs. Whether the price is to be moved up or down, the action is sure to affect buyers, competitors, distributors, and suppliers, and may interest government as well. The success of the move depends critically on how the parties respond. Yet their responses are among the most difficult things to predict in business. Hence, any contemplated initiated price change carries great risks.

This section will concentrate on the principles of estimating the reactions of buyers and competitors. Similar principles apply to estimating the reactions of other parties.

BUYERS' REACTIONS TO PRICE CHANGE

The traditional analysis of buyers' reactions to price change is based on assuming that all buyers learn of the price change and take it at face value. The magnitude of their response to the price change is described by the concept of *price elasticity of demand*.

[31] See C. W. Churchman, Russell L. Ackoff, and E. Leonard Arnoff, *Introduction to Operations Research* (New York, John Wiley & Sons, Inc., 1957), pp. 559-73.

PRICE ELASTICITY OF DEMAND. This term refers to the ratio of the percentage change in demand (quantity sold per period) caused by a percentage change in price.[32] A price elasticity of one means that sales rise (fall) by the same percentage as price falls (rises). In this case, total revenue is left unaffected. A price elasticity greater than one means that sales rise (fall) by more than price falls (rises) in percentage terms; in this case, total revenue rises. A price elasticity less than one means that sales rise (fall) by less than price falls (rises) in percentage terms; in this case, total revenue falls.

Price elasticity of demand gives more precision to the question of whether the firm's price is too high or too low. From the point of view of maximizing *revenue,* price is too high if demand is elastic and too low if demand is inelastic. Whether this is also true for maximizing *profits* depends on the behavior of costs. If unit costs are constant over a wide range of possible outputs, it is true, but if unit costs change with the scale of production, it may not be true.[33]

Price elasticity is extremely difficult to measure in practice. There are definitional as well as statistical hurdles. Definitionally, price elasticity is not an absolute characteristic of the demand facing a seller but rather a conditional one. Price elasticity depends on the magnitude of the contemplated price change. It may be negligible with a small price change (one below the threshold level) and substantial with a large price change. Price elasticity also varies with the original price level. A 5 per cent increase over current prices of $1 and $1.20 respectively, may exhibit a quite different elasticity. Finally, long-run price elasticity is apt to be different from short-run elasticity. Buyers may have to continue with the present supplier immediately after his price increase because choosing a new supplier takes time, but they may eventually stop purchasing from him. In this case, demand is more elastic in the long run than in the short run.[34] Or the reverse may happen; buyers drop a supplier in anger after he increases prices but return to him later. The significance of this distinction between short-run and long-run elasticity is that the seller will not know how wise his price change is for a while.

In addition to the need for a careful definition of elasticity in each situa-

[32] In symbols,

$$E_{qp} = \frac{\dfrac{Q_1 - Q_0}{Q_0}}{\dfrac{P_1 - P_0}{P_0}} = \frac{relative\ change\ in\ quantity}{relative\ change\ in\ price}$$

where

E_{qp} = elasticity of quantity sold with respect to a change in price
Q_1 = quantity sold per period after price change
Q_0 = quantity sold per period before price change
P_1 = new price
P_0 = old price

[33] Suppose unit costs are higher at reduced production levels and that demand is relatively inelastic. The firm can increase its total revenue by raising its price. But in doing this, sales may decline enough to increase unit costs to the point where the higher total revenue may be more than offset by higher total costs.

[34] Stigler suggests that demand is generally more elastic in the long run because the short run is marked by the difficulty of rapid adjustment, the existence of market imperfections, and the presence of habit. Stigler, *op. cit.,* pp. 45-47.

tion, major statistical estimation problems face the firm wishing to evaluate it. In fact, different techniques have evolved, none completely appropriate or satisfactory in all circumstances. The whole problem can be brought into focus by considering the following case:

> One of the telephone companies in the Bell chain is considering a rate reduction. After the war, the number of telephone connections climbed rapidly with the housing boom and the increase in incomes. In more recent years, the rate of new connections has begun to taper off. One of the company's important sources of income is the extension (or second) phone which it installs in a home for an extra monthly charge of 75 cents. The company noticed that the percentage of homes with one or more extension phones was approaching a stable level of around 30 per cent. The company had been using heavy promotion to sell families on second phones, but the advertising stimulation appeared to be showing diminishing returns. There was some evidence that many families whose dwelling units were large resisted two phones because the 75 cents monthly charge seemed too high to them. The company was wondering how many additional extension phones would be ordered if the charge were reduced to 50 cents.

A telephone company does not have any competitive reactions to worry about in contemplating a price change. The company can proceed directly to the task of estimating the likely reactions of the ultimate customers. In this case, it wants to know if the number of extensions would increase enough to offset and exceed the reduced revenue resulting from cutting the price. There are at least four different ways to proceed:

Direct attitude survey. The company can interview a sample of potential extension users as to whether they would add another phone if the monthly service charge were lowered to 50 cents. The percentage who said yes could then be applied against the known total number of potential users (those who live in apartments or homes with more than three rooms, according to one definition) to find the number of extra extensions this would mean.

Statistical analysis of relationship between price and quantity. This can take the form of either a historical or cross-sectional analysis. A historical analysis consists in observing how extension usage was affected in the past by rate reductions. A cross-sectional analysis consists in observing how extension usage varies with the rates charged by different companies in the Bell System.

Market test. The company can offer a representative sample of potential users the chance to have an extension phone for 50 cents a month if they act on the offer within a specified time period. The percentage who take advantage can then be applied against the known number of potential users.

Analytic inference. The company can conjecture how many additional families are likely to find a second phone worth-while at the lower price. The issue of a second phone is one of convenience versus cost. The company can segment the market into dwelling units of different sizes and different income levels. A family in a large home with a good income would tend to be more receptive to a second phone. The company can estimate how many families in this segment are without second phones and apply the probability that they would acquire the phone at the reduced rate. This can be done for all the segments to build up an estimate.

These are the major approaches to estimating demand elasticity.[35] They work with different degrees of success in different circumstances, and sometimes two or more of the approaches may be undertaken simultaneously for additional confirmation. In practical situations, the task is not one of estimating the absolute level of elasticity so much as whether it differs substantially from the breakeven level where nothing would be gained through a price change. This level is an elasticity of one if constant unit costs can be assumed. The breakeven level of elasticity can be translated into the actual number of new extensions which would have to be ordered to make up for the loss in revenue from reducing the rate on all present extensions from 75 to 50 cents a month. Suppose this number is 5,000 in the Bell case; i.e., 5,000 more extensions would have to be sold to restore Bell's total revenues. If Bell has reason to believe that the rate reduction would easily stimulate at least 5,000 new extension installations, and probably more, then it is academic whether the number is 8,000, 10,000 or some other number. The problem is one of estimating whether elasticity is sufficiently greater or less than the breakeven level and not necessarily how much greater.

Another point to be borne in mind is that elasticity is a measure of total market response and not every individual buyer's response. The market consists of many types of people with varying demand reactions. Some respond strongly to a price change, some respond mildly, and some do not respond at all. Elasticity is largely a function of the size of the price-sensitive segment in relation to the total market. The characteristics of this segment should be identified to facilitate estimation of its size and to guide the subsequent directing of promotion to target customers.

PERCEPTUAL FACTORS IN BUYERS' RESPONSE.   In discussing elasticity, it was assumed that price changes would be interpreted in a straightforward manner. However, this may not be satisfied in practice. Although economists have tended to ignore perceptual factors, they constitute an important intervening variable in explaining responses to price changes. In the Bell case, this turned out to be particularly true. In a direct attitude survey, potential extension users were asked what they thought the extension service cost. Over 80 per cent of the respondents named a price above 75 cents a month, in some cases as high as $2.00. The amount of price misinformation was profound, and this could have been an important deterrent of purchase. The policy implication is quite interesting. It means that *bringing people closer to an understanding of the correct price would be tantamount to a price reduction.* If a housewife thought the monthly charge was a $1.00 and then learned that it was only 75 cents, this is tantamount to a price reduction *in her mind* of 25 per cent. As an alternative to reducing the monthly rate to 50 cents the company might gain more through sponsoring an advertising campaign that clarified the current price.

This is only one example of a perceptual factor intervening between

---

[35] Still other approaches are outlined in Edgar A. Pessemier, "A New Way to Determine Buying Decisions," *Journal of Marketing,* XXIV (October 1959), 41-46; and Wayne A. Lee, "Techniques for Pretesting Price Decisions," in *Pricing: The Critical Decision,* Marketing Division Report No. 66 (New York: American Management Association, 1961).

the price change and the reaction to it. In general, people may not always put the most straightforward interpretation on a price change when it occurs. A price reduction may symbolize any number of things: [36]

That the item is about to be superseded by a later model.

That the item has some fault and is not selling well.

That the firm is in financial trouble and may not stay in business to supply future parts.

That the price will come down even further and it pays to wait.[37]

That the quality has been lowered.

A price increase may also be given unorthodox interpretations:

That the item is very "hot" and may be unobtainable unless it is bought soon.

That the item represents an unusually good value and could not yield a profit at the old price.

The main point is that perceptual factors in all these cases lead buyers to react to the price change in a way opposite to the one intended.

COMPETITORS' REACTIONS TO PRICE CHANGES

A firm contemplating a price change normally has to worry about competitors' as well as customers' reactions. Generally speaking, competitors' reactions are important where the number of firms is small, the product offering is homogeneous, and the buyers are discriminating and informed. When it is important, the firm contemplating a price change must incorporate an estimate of competitors' reactions into the analysis.

How can the firm estimate the likely reaction of its competitors? Let us assume at first that the firm faces only one large competitor. The likely behavior of this competitor can be approached from two quite different starting points. One is to assume that the competitor has a set policy for reacting to price changes. The other is to assume that the competitor treats each price change as a unique challenge and considers afresh his self-interest. Each assumption has quite different research implications, which are explored below.

If the competitor has a set price-reaction policy, there are at least two different ways to fathom it—through inside information and through statistical analysis. Inside information can be obtained in many ways, some quite acceptable and others verging on cloak-and-dagger methods.[38] One of the more respectable methods is hiring an executive away from a com-

---

[36] See Alfred R. Oxenfeldt, *Pricing for Marketing Executives* (San Francisco: Wadsworth Publishing Company, 1961), p. 28.

[37] Economists use the concept of elasticity of expectations to convey this possibility. The elasticity of expectations is the ratio of the future expected percentage change in price to the recent percentage change in price. A positive elasticity means that buyers expect a price reduction (increase) to be followed by another reduction (increase).

[38] "Marketing intelligence" is the term used for the more respectable methods and "industrial espionage" for the less respectable methods. See William J. Guyton, "A Guide to Gathering Marketing Intelligence," *Industrial Marketing,* March 1962, pp. 84-88.

petitor. In this way the firm acquires a rich source of information on the competitor's thought processes and patterns of reaction. It may even pay to set up a unit of former employees whose job is to think like the competitor.[39] But information on the thinking of a competitor can also come through sources other than present or former employees of the competitor. The intelligence operation should embrace customers, the financial community, suppliers, dealers, and the business community at large.

A set policy toward meeting price changes may also be discovered through a statistical analysis of the firm's past price reactions. In this connection, we can employ the concept "conjectural price variation" (V), defined as the ratio of the competitor's reactive price change to the company's previous price change. In symbols: [40]

$$V_{A,t} = \frac{P_{B,t} - P_{B,t-1}}{P_{A,t} - P_{A,t-1}}$$

where

$V_{A,t} =$ the change in competitor B's price during period t as a proportion of company A's price change during period t

$P_{B,t} - P_{B,t-1} =$ the change in competitor B's price during period t

$P_{A,t} - P_{A,t-1} =$ the change in company A's price during period t

The last observed $V_{A,t}$ can be used by the company as an estimate of the probable reaction of the competitor. If $V_{A,t} = 0$, then the competitor did not react last time. If $V_{A,t} = 1$, then the competitor fully matched the company's price change. If $V_{A,t} = \frac{1}{2}$, then the competitor only matched half of the company's price change; and so forth. However, it could be misleading to base the analysis only on the last price reaction. It would be better to average several of the past V terms, giving more weight to the more recent ones because they are reflections of more current policy. A possible estimate of future competitive price reaction ($V_{A,t+1}$) might be

$$V_{A,t+1} = .5V_{A,t} + .3V_{A,t-1} + .2V_{A,t-2}$$

where three past conjectural price variation terms are combined in a weighted average.[41]

The statistical method makes sense only on the assumption that the competitor has a fairly consistent price-reaction policy. Otherwise it would be better to base the whole analysis on a quite different assumption, that

[39] There is at least one company that has set up this type of unit. See Gerald A. Busch, "Prudent Manager Forecasting," *Harvard Business Review,* May-June 1961, pp. 57-64. The major powers in the cold war apparently have set up "enemy" units staffed with their own people.

[40] The concept of conjectural variation has been used for a long time in oligopoly-duopoly theory. See William Fellner, *Competition Among the Few* (New York: Alfred A. Knopf, Inc., 1949). The concept was applied to output (rather than price) changes in Richard M. Cyert and James G. March, *A Behavioral Theory of the Firm* (Englewood Cliffs, N.J.: Prentice-Hall, Inc., 1963), chap. 5, especially pp. 88-90.

[41] If there is any indication that the competitor's price reactions are asymmetrical (i.e., he doesn't meet price increases in the same way as price decreases), then the estimate for a contemplated price increase should be based only on past reactions to increases. A number of other refinements can also be introduced.

the competitor decides afresh on each occasion of a price increase what reaction would be in his best interest. If this is so, an analysis must be made of how the competitor perceives his self-interest. His current financial situation should be researched, his recent sales, the basis of his customer appeal, and his corporate objectives. If evidence points to a market share objective, then the competitor is likely to match the price change. If evidence points to a profit maximization objective, the competitor may react on some other policy front, such as increasing his advertising or improving his product's quality. The job again is to get into the mind of the competitor through inside and outside sources of information.

The problem is complicated because each price change occurs under unique circumstances, and the competitor, just like the customers, is capable of putting quite different interpretations on it. His reaction will be based on his interpretation, and this makes it all the more important to see it through his eyes. The competitor's reaction might differ depending on whether he thinks the price change is temporary or permanent. He may take a price reduction either to mean:

The company is trying to steal the market from him

The company is not doing well and is trying to improve its sales

The company is hoping that the whole industry will reduce its prices in the interests of stimulating total demand

Since the competitor's reaction will be based on what *he thinks* is motivating the company's price change, his reaction may be quite different than the company expects.

Because of the uncertainty surrounding competitive reaction, it is becoming increasingly popular to talk not about what the competitor is most likely to do but about the probabilities governing his different possible reactions. These probabilities are necessarily subjective; they represent the firm's best judgment based on past experience and current information about the competitor. These probabilities, along with probabilities of different levels of customer reaction, can be incorporated into a decision-tree analysis to guide the decision maker as to whether to initiate the contemplated price change. This approach will be illustrated shortly.

When there is more than one important competitor, the company must proceed in the same way to anticipate each competitor's likely reaction. If all competitors are likely to behave alike, this amounts to analyzing only a typical competitor. If the competitors cannot be expected to react uniformly because of critical differences in size, market shares, or policies, then separate analyses are necessary. If it appears that a few competitors will match the price change, there is good reason to expect the rest will also match it. In general, the presence of more than one competitor usually does not complicate the principles of analysis, although it does increase the amount of information, time, and effort required for appraisal.

USING DECISION THEORY FOR PRICE CHANGES

An example will now be given of how one firm proceeded to analyze the merits of a contemplated price reduction. This example shows how the various uncertainties about customers' and competitors' reactions can be integrated into a model for decision making and what procedures might be used to gather the required information.[42]

A large company had been selling a plastic substance to industrial users for several years and enjoyed 40 per cent of the market. The management became worried about whether its current price of $1 per pound could be maintained for much longer. The main source of concern was the rapid buildup of capacity by its three competitors and the possible attraction of further competitors by the present price. Management saw the key to the problem of possible oversupply in further market expansion. The key area for market expansion lay in an important segment of the market that was closely held by a substitute plastic product produced by six firms. This substitute product was not as good, but it was priced lower. Management saw a possible solution in displacing the substitute product in the recalcitrant segment through a price reduction. If it could penetrate this segment, there was a good chance it could also penetrate three other segments which had resisted the displacement.

The first task was to develop a decision structure for the problem in which all components would be related. This meant defining the objectives, policy alternatives, and key uncertainties. It was decided that the objective would be to maximize the present value of future profits over the next five years. Management decided to consider the four alternatives of maintaining the price at $1.00 or reducing the price to $0.93, $0.85, and $0.80, respectively. The following were considered among the key uncertainties that had to be evaluated:

How much penetration in the key segment would take place without a price reduction?

How will the six firms producing the substitute plastic react to each possible price reduction?

How much penetration in the key segment would take place for every possible price reaction of the suppliers of the substitute plastic?

How much would penetration into the key segment speed up penetration into the other segments?

If the key segment were not penetrated, what was the probability that the company's competitors would initiate price reductions soon?

What would be the impact of a price reduction on the decision of existing competitors to expand their capacity and/or potential competitors to enter the industry?

The data-gathering phase consisted mainly in asking key sales personnel to place subjective probabilities on the various possible states of the key uncertainties. Meetings were held with the sales personnel to explain the concept of expressing judgments in the form of probabilities. The probabilities were filled out on a long questionnaire. For example, one question asked for the probability that the producers of the substitute product would retaliate if the company reduced its price to $0.93 per pound. On the average, the sales personnel felt that there was only a 5 per cent probability of a full match, a 60 per cent probability of a half match, and a 35 per

[42] The case was described and analyzed by Paul E. Green, "Bayesian Decision Theory in Pricing Strategy," *Journal of Marketing*, XXVII (January 1963), 5-14.

cent probability of no retaliation. They were also asked for probabilities for the $0.85 and $0.80 case. The sales personnel indicated, as expected, that the probability of retaliation increased with an increase in price reduction.

The next step was to estimate the likely payoffs of different courses of action. A decision-tree analysis revealed that there were over 400 possible outcomes. For this reason, the estimation of expected payoffs was programmed on an electronic computer. The computer results indicated that in all cases a price reduction had a higher expected payoff than *status quo* pricing, and, in fact, a price reduction to $0.80 had the highest expected payoff. To check the sensitivity of these results to the original assumptions, the results were recomputed for alternative assumptions about the rate of market growth and the appropriate cost of capital. It was found that the ranking of the strategies was not affected by the change in the assumptions.

The analysis clearly pointed to the desirability of some price reduction in preference to the *status quo*. The last step belongs to management, to decide on the basis of this analysis as well as other factors that may have eluded analysis, whether to initiate the price reduction and, if so, by how much.

Meeting Price Changes

The previous section took the point of view of the firm considering whether to change its price. It was seen that a major determinant of its decision is the expected reaction of its competitors. Now the problem will be analyzed from the point of view of the reacting firm. How can a firm that has just witnessed a price change by a competitor decide on its best course of action?

In some market situations the firm has no choice but to meet a competitor's price change. This is particularly true when the price is cut in a homogeneous product market. Unless the other firms meet the price reduction, most buyers will choose to do business with the lowest-price firm, other things being equal.

When the price is raised by a firm in a homogeneous product market, the other firms may or may not meet it. They will comply if the price increase appears designed to benefit the industry as a whole. But if one firm does not see it that way and thinks that it or the industry would gain more by standing pat on prices, its noncompliance can make the leader and the others rescind any price increases. This happened in 1962 when Inland Steel refused to match the price increases of U.S. Steel and most other steel companies; in a matter of days, prices returned to their former level.

In nonhomogeneous product markets, a firm has more latitude in reacting to a competitor's price change. The essential fact is that buyers choose the seller on the basis of a multiplicity of considerations: service, quality, reliability, and other factors. These factors desensitize many buyers to minor price differences. The reacting firm has a number of options: doing nothing and losing few or many customers, depending upon the level of customer loyalty; meeting the price change partly or fully; countering with modifications of other elements in its marketing mix.

The firm's analysis could take the form of estimating the expected pay-offs of alternative possible reactions. In doing this, the answers to the following questions will take on special importance in deciding how to react:

> Why did the competitor change his price? Was it to steal the market, to meet changing cost conditions, or to evoke a calculated industry-wide price change to take advantage of total demand?
>
> Is the competitor intending to make his price change temporary or permanent?
>
> What will happen to the company's market share (and profits) if it ignores the price change? Are the other companies going to ignore the price change?
>
> What is the competitor's (and other firms') response likely to be to each possible reaction?

All of these questions enter directly or indirectly in the structuring of objectives, alternatives, and uncertainties, in the gathering of information, and in the estimation of payoffs.

An extended analysis of company alternatives is usually not feasible at the time of a price change. The competitor who initiated the price change may have spent considerable time in preparing for this decision, but the company that must react may have only hours or days before some decisive position must be taken. The analysis and information are necessarily below the standard usually required for determining such an important decision as a price reaction. About the only way to place such decisions on a surer footing is to anticipate their possible occurrence in advance and to prepare a program for reaction. An example of such a program to meet a possible price cut is shown in Figure 15-4.

If a price cut has occurred, the firm asks a number of questions. First it asks whether the competitor's price cut is likely to affect the firm's sales significantly *and* be permanent. If *both* conditions are satisfied, the firm will consider some form of reaction. The firm asks whether there are any workable alternatives to dropping price. If not, and if a price reduction would not damage the firm's brand image, it cuts its price to that of the competitor or to its own breakeven point, whichever is higher. However, nonprice reactions may appear more attractive to the firm, in which case the particular nonprice reaction is geared to the magnitude of the competitor's price cut; the more substantial the price cut, the more substantial the nonprice reaction. The possibility of dropping the product is even introduced. Provision is made to evaluate the effectiveness of the nonprice reaction, and if it appears effective, nothing else is done until the competitor makes a new move.

The reaction program illustrates how a firm might plan in advance to meet the price moves of a competitor. The actual program would have to be more detailed in providing for responses to price increases as well, in outlining the occasions for fractional price matches as well as full price matches, and in defining criteria for judging whether a nonprice reaction is preferable to a price reaction.

Reaction programs for meeting price changes are likely to find their greatest application in industries where price changes occur with some frequency and where it is important to react quickly. Examples could be

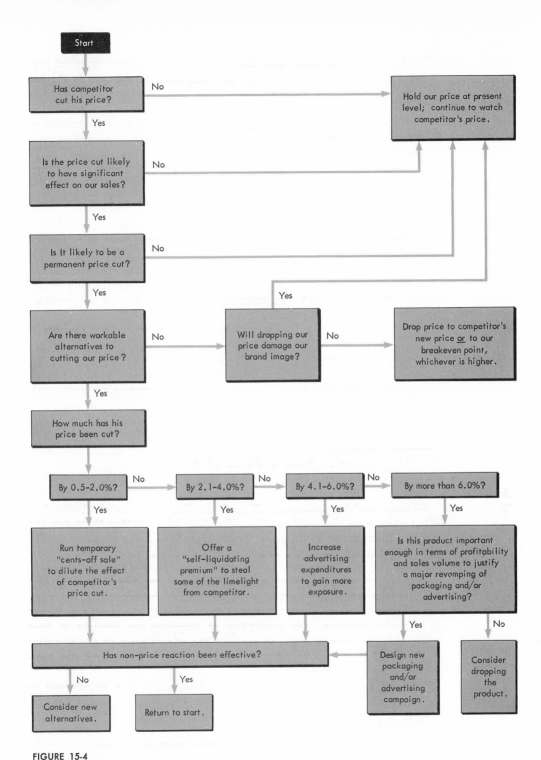

FIGURE 15-4

Decision program for meeting a competitor's price cut

Redrawn, with modifications, from an unpublished paper by Raymond J. Trapp, Northwestern University, 1964.

found in the meat-packing and lumber industries. A pilot study was conducted in one such industry by William Morgenroth to determine whether the decision maker's thought processes in reacting to price changes could be spelled out in the form of a computer program.[43] After observing a pricing executive in action over an extended period of time and querying him about his procedure, Morgenroth was eventually able to develop a program in the form of a binary flow chart which predicted price reactions with a high degree of accuracy. The program involved comparisons of market shares, anticipations of how the other firms would react, queries about the intentions of the district office, comparisons of nearby market prices, and built-in delays. The program incorporated the personal biases and organizational influences taking place in the price-reaction situation and in this sense was a realistic simulation of the pricing process in use. At the same time it could serve as a tool for investigating the effectiveness of alternative price-reaction rules.

Product-Line Pricing

The problem of setting a price or changing a price on an individual product has been examined. Some of the preceding logic must be qualified when the product is a member of a product line. In the latter case, the true quest is for a set of mutual prices which maximizes the profits of the line. This quest is made difficult because various company products are interrelated in demand and/or cost and are subject to different degrees of competition.

INTERRELATED DEMAND

Two products are interrelated in demand when the price (or some other element of the marketing mix) of one affects the demand for the other. Economists use the concept of "cross-elasticity of demand" to express the interaction.[44] A positive cross-elasticity means that two goods are *substitutes,* a negative cross-elasticity means that two goods are *complements,* and a zero (or low) cross-elasticity means that two goods are *unrelated* in demand. If a television manufacturer lowered the price of his color television sets, this would decrease the demand for his black and white sets (substitutes), increase the demand for the components of his color sets (complements), and probably would not affect the demand for his pocket radios. Before changing the price of any single item in his line, the seller should consider the various cross-elasticities to determine the over-all impact of his move.

The most conspicuous examples of substitutes in a product line are the various versions manufacturers offer of a product. The practice of offering different versions of a product is especially prevalent in the automobile industry and in most consumer appliance industries. The buyer is able to get higher quality, better styling, or extra features by paying more; and

[43] William M. Morgenroth, "A Method for Understanding Price Determinants," *Journal of Marketing Research,* August 1964, pp. 17-26.

[44] Technically, the cross-elasticity of demand (E_c) is the percentage change in quantity sold of product B associated with a percentage change in price of product A.

the seller is able to attract a wider range of buyer types and possibly gain by inducing buyers to "trade up" to the more expensive versions.[45] The manufacturer's problem is how to price these versions to achieve the greatest over-all revenue.

INTERRELATED COST

Two products are interrelated in cost when a change in the production of one affects the cost of the other. By-products and joint products are related in this sense. If the production of ham is cut down, so will the production of pork be cut down. As a result, the unit cost of the pork that is produced will rise because the overhead is spread over fewer units. More generally, any two products using the same production facilities are inter-related on the cost side even if they are not joint products. This is largely because accounting practice requires a full allocation of costs. The sig-nificance of all this is that if the company increases the price of A, for example, and causes its sales to fall, the cost of the other products, assum-ing they are not complementary goods, will be higher. Thus management must examine the cost interactions before it changes the price of a single product in the line.

EFFECT OF COMPETITION

Various products in a company line are exposed to different degrees of competition. The seller may have little latitude in pricing products in his line where existing or potential competition is keen, and he will have vary-ing degrees of price discretion in the other cases. Therefore the structure of prices for the products in the line should not simply be proportional to costs, however measured, for this would overlook profit opportunities that are associated with taking advantage of different degrees of competition.

Take advantage of competitor's pricing to affect a "trade-up"

ALTERNATIVE PRODUCT-LINE PRICING PRINCIPLES

In practice, costs have provided the usual starting point for determining the prices of interrelated products in the line. Even here there seems to be considerable disagreement over which costs should be used. The three most popular cost bases are full costs, incremental costs, and conversion costs. The price structures resulting from using these respective cost bases are illustrated for a hypothetical soap manufacturer in Table 15-2.

The soap manufacturer makes two different types of specialty soap. The second soap requires more labor cost but less material cost per bar than the first soap. The second bar also takes more manufacturing support and overhead than the first. The specific costs per bar are shown in Table 15-2a.

The first pricing principle calls for pricing the soaps proportionately to their full costs. Since both soaps have the same full costs, they will bear the same price (here 42 cents because of a 20 per cent markup). The chief criticism against using full cost is that the allocation of overhead unavoidably involves some arbitrariness. Therefore the resulting prices

[45] Sometimes the line will include a super "prestige" model for the sake of pro-moting the rest of the line. One of the manufacturers of medium-priced men's hats promoted a $50 hat to improve the rest of the line's over-all quality image. The major automobile manufacturers produce some very high-priced models on which they often just break even to promote the company's image.

TABLE 15-2

Illustration of alternative product-line pricing principles

(a) *Product-line cost structure*

	Soap 1	Soap 2
1. Labor cost	.10	.15
2. Material cost	.20	.10
3. Overhead cost	.05	.10
Full cost (1 + 2 + 3)	.35	.35
Incremental cost (1 + 2)	.30	.25
Conversion cost (1 + 3)	.15	.25

(b) *Alternative product-line prices*

	Markup	Soap 1	Soap 2
1. Full cost pricing	20%	.42	.42
2. Incremental cost pricing	40%	.42	.35
3. Conversion cost pricing	180%	.42	.70

take on a partly arbitrary character. As a result, the company may be blinded to profit opportunities that would exist if the prices of the two soaps were not geared so tightly to the recovery of a somewhat arbitrary overhead burden.

The second pricing principle calls for setting prices that are proportional to incremental costs. The underlying theory is that the company should charge customers proportionately to the extra costs it has to bear in supplying additional units of the two soaps. In the example, supplying an additional unit of soap 2 imposes less additional cost than supplying another unit of soap 1. The net effect of pricing on an incremental cost basis is to shift sales toward the soap that absorbs more company overhead.[46]

The third pricing principle calls for setting prices that are proportional to conversion costs. Conversion costs are defined as the labor and company overhead required to convert purchased materials into finished products. Conversion costs thus amount to the "value added" by the firm in the production process; it can be found by subtracting purchased material costs from the allocated full costs. The argument that has been advanced for using conversion costs is that the firm's profits should be based on the value its own operations add to each soap. The net effect of pricing on a conversion cost basis is to shift sales toward the soap that has more material cost. This pricing principle economizes on the use of scarce company resources, such as labor and machines. Other than this, there is no particular economic justification for choosing certain elements of cost to bear the profit markup rather than others; furthermore, this basis again involves arbitrary allocations of overhead.

[46] The principle of marking up incremental costs is analyzed and defended for retail pricing in Malcolm P. McNair and Eleanor G. May, "Pricing for Profit, A Revolutionary Approach to Retail Accounting," *Harvard Business Review,* May-June 1957, pp. 105-22. The problems encountered in making a functional analysis of incremental costs and inducing stores to use this technique are described by Peggy Heim, "Merchandise Management Accounting: A Retail Experiment in Explicit Marginal Calculation," *Quarterly Journal of Economics,* November 1963, pp. 671-75.

As stated earlier, costs represent a starting point for developing the pricing structure, but they hardly represent sufficient criteria. Incremental costs provide the lower limit to individual product pricing (except in special circumstances, such as loss leading). But a *uniform* markup over incremental or any other costs is fallacious in that it ignores the different cross-elasticities, competitive conditions, and life-cycle characteristics of each product. Model building in this area has not yet progressed to a stage where the cost, demand, and competitive factors are blended to produce a set of determinate prices. Mathematical programming and simulation represent the most promising mathematical techniques for reaching the future solution of the complex problems of product-line pricing.

Other Problems

Other pricing problems not treated here are of special concern in certain situations. Clothing retailers regularly mark down the prices of fashion merchandise as the season progresses, and the problem of the appropriate size and timing of the markdown(s) is a question of substantial interest.[47] Manufacturers of food products regularly offer price deals (cents-off on branded food products), and are concerned with the problem of seasonal timing and magnitude.[48] The psychology of pricing is of great interest to other sellers, who are concerned with whether sales are really stimulated by prices ending in odd figures, such as $9.95 instead of $10.00.[49] Retailers are particularly interested in "sales" or "loss-leading" pricing, although there is little to turn to in the way of theory. Some manufacturers are concerned with how to price to different distributors and customers and particularly whether a policy of resale price maintenance makes sense.

Pricing is an acute concern in particular industrial situations, such as where there is production overcapacity (gasoline industry), where forms of distribution are rapidly changing (the advent of the discount house in retailing), where competition is keen (appliance industry), and where jobs must be bid for (military and private construction industry). In these and other situations, price decisions require skill and experience, and the companies involved would gain from developing pricing specialists within the company.[50] At the same time, prices must be set as part of a total marketing strategy covering channels, promotion, personal selling, and other marketing variables, and pricing executives must make their decisions in this broader context.

[47] A markdown pricing model is described in Cyert and March, *op. cit.,* pp. 140-46. Also see Sterling D. Sessions, "Sales/Stock Ratios: Key to Markdown Timing," in *New Research in Marketing,* ed. Lee E. Preston (Berkeley, Calif.: University of California Institute of Business and Economic Research, 1965), pp. 57-69.

[48] See Alfred A. Kuehn, "Effectiveness of Consumer Deals and Advertising," in *Toward Scientific Marketing,* ed. Stephen A. Greyser (Chicago: American Marketing Association, 1964), pp. 233-40; and Ronald E. Frank and William F. Massy, "Short Term Price and Dealing Effects in Selected Market Segments," *Journal of Marketing Research,* May 1965, pp. 171-85.

[49] Dean reports some evidence that odd prices do not stimulate more sales. See Dean, *op. cit.,* pp. 490-91. For a demand curve interpretation of odd prices (and other pricing policies), see Edward H. Hawkins, "Price Policies and Theory," *Journal of Marketing,* XVIII (January 1954), 233-40.

[50] Oxenfeldt has discussed the main factors determining the size and type of pricing department needed to carry out the pricing function. See Oxenfeldt, *op. cit.,* p. 19.

Summary

In spite of the increased role of nonprice factors in the modern marketing process, price remains an important element and especially challenging in certain types of situations.

In setting a price, a firm can draw guidance from the theoretical pricing model of the economists. The model suggests how the firm can find the short-run profit maximizing price when estimates of demand and cost are available. The model, however, leaves out several factors that have to be considered in actual pricing situations, such as the presence of other objectives, multiple parties, marketing-mix interactions, and uncertainties surrounding the estimates of demand and cost. In practice, companies tend to orient their pricing toward either cost (as in markup pricing and target pricing), demand (as in price discrimination), or competition (as in going rate pricing and bidding).

When a firm considers changing its established price, it must carefully consider customers' and competitors' reactions. The probable reaction of customers is summarized in the concept of price elasticity of demand. There are several ways to estimate price elasticity and some problems in interpreting it, but it is a key input in the determination of how much would be gained by the price change. Competitors' reactions also must be taken into account, and they depend very much on the nature of the market structure and the degree of product homogeneity. Competitors' reactions may be studied either on the assumption that they flow from a set reaction policy or that they flow from a fresh appraisal of the challenge each time. The firm initiating the price change must also consider the probable reactions of suppliers, middlemen, and government.

The firm that witnesses a price change must try to understand the competitor's intent and the likely duration of the change. If swiftness of reaction is desirable, the firm should pre-plan its reactions to different possible pricing developments.

Pricing is complicated when it is realized that various products in a line typically have important demand and/or cost interrelationships. Then the objective is to develop a set of mutual prices which maximize the profits on the whole line. Most companies develop tentative prices for the products in the line by marking up either full costs, incremental costs, or conversion costs and then modifying these prices by individual demand and competitive factors.

Questions and Problems

1. Does an "early cash recovery" pricing objective mean that the firm should set a high rather than low price on its new product?

2. The statement was made that a firm might set a low price on a product to discourage competitors from coming in. Are there any situations (aside from antitrust reasons) when a firm might deliberately want to attract competitors into a new market and set a high price for this reason?

3. Four different methods of estimating the price elasticity of demand for extension telephones were described in the text. What are the limitations of each method?

4. Haloid-Xerox developed a new office copying machine called the 914. The machine was more expensive than competitive machines but offered the user superior copy and lower variable costs: 1 cent per copy as opposed to between 4 to 9 cents for competing processes. The machine cost around $2,500 to produce, and management was considering pricing it at either $3,500 or $4,500. How could it estimate unit sales at the two alternative price levels?

5. Bell and Howell was the first company to develop an electric-eye camera by combining a regular $70 camera with a $10 electric-eye mechanism. What price do you think might be charged for the new camera?

6. A group of people were asked to choose between two raincoats, one bearing a brand label and a higher price and another bearing a store label and a lower price. The two coats happened to be identical, but the customers were not told this. If customers were completely knowledgeable, (a) what percentage would choose the higher-priced coat? (b) What percentage do you think actually chose the higher-priced coat?

chapter 16

Channel Decisions

In today's economy, most producers do not sell their goods directly to the final users. Between them and the final users stands a host of marketing intermediaries performing a variety of functions and bearing a variety of names: brokers, agents, wholesalers, jobbers, cooperatives, retailers, and so forth. Not all of these are used in every industry, and producers within the same industry are known to employ different intermediaries for distributing similar products. The important point is that particular goods may usually be brought to the ultimate users in more than one way.

Two aspects of channel decisions place them in the important policy-decision areas facing top management. The first is that *the channels chosen for the company's products intimately affect every other marketing decision.* The firm's pricing decisions depend upon whether it seeks a few franchised high-markup dealers or mass distribution; the firm's advertising decisions are influenced by the degree of cooperation from channel members; the firm's sales-force decisions depend upon whether it sells directly to retailers or uses manufacturers' representatives. This does not mean that channel decisions are always made prior to other decisions, but rather that they exercise a powerful influence on the rest of the mix. Channel decisions impose important limitations on the possible configurations of the other elements in the mix.

The second reason for the significance of channel decisions is that *they involve the firm in relatively long-term commitments to other firms.* When an automobile manufacturer signs up independent franchised dealers to merchandise his automobiles, he cannot easily replace them with company-owned outlets if conditions change. When a drug manufacturer relies heavily on retail druggists for the distribution of most of his products, he must heed them when they object to his merchandising through chain stores. There is a powerful tendency toward *status quo* in channel arrangements. Therefore management must choose its channels with an eye toward tomorrow rather than today.

This chapter is divided into four sections. The first considers the nature and role of marketing channels and intermediaries. The second considers the major issues in designing a new channel system. The problem is viewed as one of determining channel objectives and constraints, distinguishing major channel alternatives, and evaluating the alternatives in terms of economic, control, and adaptive criteria. The third section considers the major issues in selecting, motivating, and evaluating specific channel members. The final section examines the problems of modifying parts or the whole of an existing channel system to improve channel performance.

Every producer seeks to link together the set of marketing intermediaries that best fulfill the firm's objectives. This set of marketing intermediaries is called the *marketing channel* (also trade channel, channel of distribution). According to Ralph Breyer, "a trading channel exists once the terms of the franchises or agreements spanning the whole gap from producer to consumer are concluded between concerns assumed to possess the necessary marketing capabilities." [1] The relationship among the participating concerns is symbiotic in that they are usually dissimilar but work together for mutual advantage. Cooperation is the dominant theme among the members of a marketing channel, but at times conflict is no less pronounced.

TYPES OF CHANNELS

Marketing channels range from the simple to the complex. Some examples of alternative channel arrangements are shown in Figure 16-1.

The first channel consists of the direct sale of goods by producers to ultimate users. Direct marketing occurs in the following situations:

A manufacturer of cosmetics employs saleswomen to sell to housewives on a door-to-door basis

A manufacturer of heavy machinery solicits business directly from user firms

A custom tailor takes orders for suits from customers who come into his establishment

An apple orchard invites the public to pick their own apples at a flat price per bushel

A mail-order house fills the direct orders of ultimate customers

All of these cases are marked by the absence of independent selling intermediaries (middlemen) between the producer and the ultimate buyer.[2]

The second marketing channel shows one selling intermediary between the producer and the ultimate customer. If he is a *broker,* his function is to find prospects and either consummate the sale (though he does not take title to the goods) or turn the prospects over to the manufacturer. If he is a *manufacturers' sales agent,* his function is to require his sales force to spend some of their time soliciting business for the producer. The agent generally carries some goods on consignment and may provide ancillary services such as financing or installation. If the middleman is a *retailer,* his function is to purchase the producer's goods and resell them at a profit. The retailer typically deals with many more producers than an agent and therefore is less closely involved with any one producer.

[1] Ralph F. Breyer, "Some Observations on 'Structural' Formation and the Growth of Marketing Channels," in *Theory in Marketing,* Reavis Cox, Wroe Alderson, and Stanley J. Shapiro, eds. (Homewood, Ill.: Richard D. Irwin, Inc., 1964), p. 165.

[2] However, there may be nonselling, i.e., *facilitating intermediaries* who perform some vital function(s) in the consummation of the transaction. Anyone other than the producer or final user who supplies transportation, storage, or financing services would be considered a facilitating intermediary. But these facilitating intermediaries are generally not used to define the marketing channel; the channel is generally conceived of as a linkage of selling intermediaries.

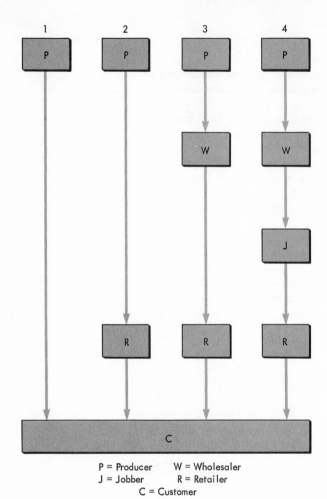

P = Producer   W = Wholesaler
J = Jobber   R = Retailer
        C = Customer

FIGURE 16-1
Examples of different marketing channels

The third marketing channel in Figure 16-1 shows two different and vertically related selling intermediaries. The most common example of this two-stage marketing channel consists of wholesalers and retailers standing between the producer and final customers. This is known as the linkage P-W-R-C. Wholesalers and retailers are generally utilized in industries where there are several producers and a large number of final customers who generally buy the product in small quantities.

The last illustrated marketing channel consists of three selling intermediaries. An example of this is found in the meat-packing industry, where a jobber usually intervenes between the wholesalers and the retailers. The linkage is then P-W-J-R-C. The jobber buys from wholesalers and sells to the smaller retailers, who generally are not serviced by the large wholesalers.

Higher-stage marketing channels are also found, but with less frequency. From the producer's point of view, the problem of control increases with the number of stages. This is so, even though the producer typically deals only with the stage just below him.

Why is the producer generally willing to delegate some of the selling job to intermediaries? The delegation usually means the relinquishment of some control over how the products are sold and to whom they are sold. The producer appears to be placing the firm's destiny in the hands of intermediaries.

Since producers are free in principle to sell directly to final customers, there must be certain unchallengeable advantages or necessities for using middlemen. Some of the major factors are:

Many producers lack the financial resources to embark on a program of direct marketing. (For example, General Motors' new automobiles are marketed by over 18,000 independent dealers; even as the world's largest corporation, General Motors would be hard pressed to raise the cash to buy out its dealers.)

Direct marketing would require many producers to become middlemen for the complementary products of other producers in order to achieve mass distributional efficiency. (For example, the P.K. Wrigley Company would not find it practical to establish small retail gum shops throughout the country or to sell gum door to door or to sell gum by mail order. It would have to tie gum in with the sale of many other small products and end up in the drugstore and foodstore business. It is much easier for Wrigley to work through the existing and extensive network of privately owned distribution institutions.)

Those producers who have the required capital to develop their own channels often can earn a greater return by increasing their investment in other aspects of their business. (If a company is earning a 20 per cent rate of return on its production operations and foresees only a 5 per cent rate of return on investing in direct marketing, it would not make sense to put money toward vertically integrating its channels.)

The use of middlemen largely boils down to their superior efficiency in the performance of basic marketing tasks and functions. Marketing intermediaries, through their experience, their specialization, their contacts, and their scale offer the producer more than he can usually achieve on his own.

Figure 16-2 shows just one source of the economies effected by the use of middlemen. Part a shows three producers using direct marketing to reach each of three customers. This system requires nine different contacts. Part b shows the three producers working through one middleman, who in turn contacts the three customers. This system requires only six contacts. In this way the use of middlemen cuts down on the amount of work that must be done.

From the point of view of the economic system, the basic role of marketing channels is to transform the heterogeneous supplies found in nature into meaningful goods assortments desired by man. According to Wroe Alderson:

> The materials which are useful to man occur in nature in heterogeneous mixtures which might be called conglomerations since these mixtures have only random relationship to human needs and activities. The collection of goods in the possession of a household or an individual also constitutes a heterogeneous supply, but it might be called an assortment since it is re-

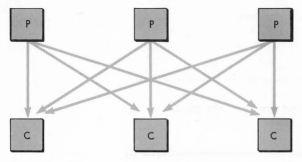

Number of contacts = P x C = 3 x 3 = 9

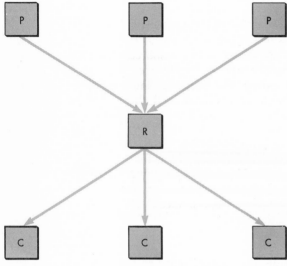

Number of contacts = P + C = 3 + 3 = 6

FIGURE 16-2

How a middleman effects an economy of effort

lated to anticipated patterns of future behavior. The whole economic process may be described as a series of transformations from meaningless to meaningful heterogeneity.[3]

The chief functions of selling intermediaries are to assemble the lines of many producers into an assortment of potential interest to buyers and to break bulk so as to meet the scale of need of the customer. Alderson has summarized this role in the statement that "the goal of marketing is the matching of segments of supply and demand."[4]

The matching of segments of supply and demand requires the carrying out of a number of specific marketing functions. These functions have been variously classified by different writers. The following list of functions was defined by McGarry:

[3] Wroe Alderson, "The Analytical Framework for Marketing," *Proceedings—Conference of Marketing Teachers from Far Western States* (Berkeley: University of California Press, 1958).

[4] Wroe Alderson, *Marketing Behavior and Executive Action: A Functionalist Approach to Marketing Theory* (Homewood, Ill.: Richard D. Irwin, Inc., 1957), p. 199.

1. Contactual—the searching out of buyers and sellers
2. Merchandising—the fitting of the goods to market requirements
3. Pricing—the selection of a price high enough to make production possible and low enough to induce users to accept the goods
4. Propaganda—the conditioning of the buyers or of the sellers to a favorable attitude toward the product or its sponsor
5. Physical distribution—the transporting and storing of the goods
6. Termination—the consummation of the marketing process [5]

It is not a question of whether these functions must be performed in order to bridge the gap between producer and customer—they must be—but rather who is to perform them. All of the functions have two things in common: they use up scarce resources, and they can often be performed better through specialization. To the extent that the producer performs them, his costs go up and his prices have to be higher. In delegating some of these tasks to middlemen, the producer's costs and prices are lower, but the middleman must add a charge to cover the use of scarce resources. The issue of who should perform various channel tasks is largely one of relative efficiency and effectiveness. To the extent that specialist intermediaries achieve economies through their scale of operation and their know-how, the producer can gain through transferring some of the channel functions to their charge.[6]

A major point to keep in mind is that marketing functions are more basic than the institutions that at any given time appear to perform them. Changes in the number of channel stages and/or types of selling intermediaries largely reflect the discovery of more efficient ways to combine or separate the economic work that must be carried out if meaningful assortments of goods are to be presented to customers.

THE QUESTION OF CHANNEL LEADERSHIP

We have been viewing channel decisions from the vantage point of the producer in search of distributional effectiveness. This perspective is still the most relevant because most extant channels are dominated by the producers. At the same time, it should be recognized that some channels are "captained" by participants other than the producer. At one time, wholesalers stood as the dominant link in many channels:

Wholesalers had enjoyed a rather large measure of control over marketing

---

[5] Edmund D. McGarry, "Some Functions of Marketing Reconsidered," in *Theory in Marketing,* eds. Reavis Cox and Wroe Alderson (Homewood, Ill.: Richard D. Irwin, Inc., 1950), pp. 269-73.

[6] Many social critics of the distribution system fail to grasp this point. In observing that a good part of the final price of many products goes to middlemen, they conclude that the middleman is an exploitative entity in the process of moving goods from producer to consumer. They overlook the fact that the economic work performed by middlemen—making contact, stocking goods, shipping goods, and so forth—has to be performed somewhere in the channel. The producer's price is artificially low because he does not perform this work. One of the reasons he doesn't choose to perform this work is that the middlemen, through specialization, may perform it for less. Thus middlemen generally bring down the final cost of goods. Middlemen's charges are close to their costs if there is heavy competition among them. When certain middlemen do begin to cost too much, new channel innovations usually develop to replace them.

. . . from the earliest times. Direct descendant [*sic*] of colonial importers, they grew up with the country and waxed wealthy and powerful in their growth. It was the wholesalers who were the big businessmen of the early nineteenth century. . . . These wholesalers were able to dominate the puny manufacturing industries of the early industrial revolution. They provided about the only means of disposing of the manufacturers' output. They had access to greater stores of capital and often were able to finance nascent manufacturers. Retailers were largely of the general store type and had to depend on wholesalers for such manufactured goods as they handled. Wholesalers kept pace in the changing patterns of trade from rural to urban markets, and from general line to specialty merchandising as long as such changes were slow. Thus, with the growth of cities, retail shops developed which were able to specialize in groceries, in drugs, in dry goods, in hardware, in shoes, and in clothing. Wholesalers followed or, perhaps more accurately, kept pace with these changes, and retained their dominant role in the marketing structure until well into the twentieth century.[7]

More recently, many channels have been lorded over by retailing giants such as A&P or Sears. A&P's power over producers was at one time so large that it inspired a series of antitrust suits against the company.[8] Sears provides the example of a retailer who not only controls the channels for many products which pass through it, but even is responsible for bringing into existence some manufacturing firms to fill gaps in its assortments. The development of dominant retailers largely reflects the existence of economies of scale and assortment in distribution exceeding those available in production. The emergence of powerful associations of middlemen who also dominate certain channels, another recent development, reflects the opportunities for a collectivization of power by middlemen to countervail the strength of individual producers.[9]

Nevertheless, the producer remains the dominant member in a great number of marketing channels. Furthermore, it is easier to appreciate the major issues in channel design and management by starting from his vantage point and looking toward the market.

Channel-Design Decisions

CHOOSING CHANNELS OR BEING CHOSEN?

In developing channels of distribution, producers always have to struggle with what is ideal and what is available. In the typical case, a new firm starts as a local or regional operation seeking sales in a limited market. Since its capital is likely to be small, it usually utilizes existing intermediaries. Furthermore, the number of actual middlemen in any local market is apt to be limited: a few manufacturers' sales agents, a small number of wholesalers, an established set of retailers, a few trucking companies,

[7] U.S. Temporary National Economic Committee, Monograph No. 17, *Problems of Small Business,* by John H. Cover *et al.* (Washington, D.C.: Government Printing Office, 1941), pp. 159-60.

[8] U.S. v. New York Great Atlantic & Pacific Tea Co., 67 F. Supp. 626 (1946). This case is discussed by M. A. Adelman, *A & P: A Study of Price-Cost Behavior and Public Policy* (Cambridge, Mass.: Harvard University Press, 1959).

[9] See John K. Galbraith, *American Capitalism, The Concept of Countervailing Power,* rev. ed. (Boston: Houghton Mifflin Company, 1956).

and a few warehouses. The best way to market may be a foregone conclusion; the problem may be to get the available middlemen to handle the producer's line.

If the new company is successful, it may branch out to new markets. Again, the producer will tend to work through the existing intermediaries, although this may mean using different types of marketing channels in different areas. In the smaller markets, the producer may deal directly with the retailers; in the larger markets, he may work only through distributors. In rural areas, he may work with general-goods merchants; in urban areas, he may work with limited-line merchants. In one part of the country, he may grant exclusive franchises because the merchants are accustomed to work this way; in another part of the country, he may sell through any and all outlets willing to handle his merchandise. In this way, the producer's channel system evolves as an expedient adaptation to local opportunities and conditions. An example of this adaptation to local conditions is found in the set of marketing channels used by the Maytag Company, a well-known manufacturer of major appliances.[10]

> Maytag products are bought by households through a national network of approximately 15,000 retailers. It is in the linkages between the company and the retailers where structural differentiation has occurred from region to region. For example, Maytag retailers in New Orleans, Louisiana, deal directly with Maytag Company salesmen. Their orders are shipped from the nearest public warehouse carrying a stock of Maytag products. These retailers are billed directly by Maytag and must pay full cash upon delivery. Maytag retailers in Portland, Maine, are also called upon by Maytag Company salesmen. But their orders are sent to a primary dealer for the area who does no selling of his own. The primary dealer buys Maytag appliances by the carload on his own account and ships out orders as they are received from Maytag salesmen. The primary dealer functions as a warehouser and title holder of Maytag products and also extends credit to the retailers. Maytag retailers in Philadelphia, Pennsylvania, are not called upon by Maytag salesmen but by the salesmen of an independent franchised distributor for that area. This distributor is a regular wholesaler who maintains Maytag stocks in his own or public warehouses, grants credit and service, and adjusts complaints.

a case of adaptation to local environment

These diverse channel patterns are responses to local conditions and opportunities rather than the implementation of a channel blueprint fully conceived by a company when it begins its operations. Even if a master plan existed, the passage of time itself would call for major adjustments. Existing marketing channels and institutions can be counted upon to undergo change; markets shift, products change, and innovations in distribution occur. Channel design is, therefore, a recurrent problem for established companies and one of the most crucial developmental hurdles for the producer who is first getting started.

Channel design is a problem which can be considered fruitfully in decision-theory terms. The major steps in designing an effective channel system consist in determining the channel objectives and channel con

[10] See Ralph Westfall and Harper W. Boyd, Jr., *Cases in Marketing Management* (Homewood, Ill.: Richard D. Irwin, Inc., 1961), pp. 481-88. The channels are being described as of 1961.

straints; distinguishing the major feasible channel alternatives; and evaluating the channel alternatives.

DETERMINING CHANNEL OBJECTIVES AND CONSTRAINTS

The starting point for the effective planning of channels is a clear determination of which markets are to be the target of the company's marketing effort. In principle, the choice of markets is not a problem of channel design but precedes it. It is part of the determination of over-all company product-market objectives. In practice, however, the choice of markets and choice of channels are interdependent. The company may discover that markets it would like to serve cannot be served profitably with the available channels.

> An example is provided by a producer of gypsum wallboard who defined his market target as all contractors and dry-wall applicators. But this producer could not get lumber yards to handle his product since existing lumber yards were tied to existing competitors. This led him to change his market target to large tract builders who would prefer to deal directly with him as a producer rather than through lumber yard intermediaries. Thus the choice of market target was re-determined after the consideration of channels.[11]

Nevertheless, it can generally be assumed that market targets are spelled out during the corporate planning process and channel design is the problem of finding the best means to reach these markets. In a narrow sense, "best" can be interpreted to mean the determination of structural and functional linkages to the market which would maximize the producer's revenue for a given distribution cost or which would minimize his costs of achieving a given revenue. In a broader sense, the producer's objectives are shaped by unique factors in his situation which influence what is desirable and what is possible. Each producer shapes his specific channel objectives from major situational constraints stemming from the customers, products, intermediaries, competitors, company policies, and the environment. The implications of each factor for channel-design objectives will be discussed briefly.

CUSTOMER CHARACTERISTICS. Channel design is greatly influenced by such characteristics of the customers as their number, geographical distribution, purchase frequency and average quantities bought, and susceptibility to different selling methods.

When the *number* of customers is large, producers tend to use long channels with many middlemen on each level. The importance of the number of buyers is modified somewhat by their degree of *geographical dispersion*. It is less expensive for a producer to sell directly to 500 customers who are concentrated in a few geographical centers than to sell them if they are scattered over 500 locations. Even number and geographical dispersion are further qualified by the *purchasing pattern* of these buyers. Where the ultimate customers purchase small quantities on a frequent basis, lengthier marketing channels are desirable. The high cost of filling small and frequent orders leads manufacturers of such products as hardware,

---

[11] See Richard H. Buskirk, *Cases and Readings in Marketing* (New York: Holt, Rinehart & Winston, Inc., 1961), pp. 108-9.

tobacco, drug sundries, and the like to rely chiefly on wholesalers. At the same time, these same manufacturers may also bypass their wholesalers and sell direct to certain larger customers (retail chains and cooperative associations) who can place larger and less frequent orders. The buyers' *susceptibilities to different selling methods* also influence channel selection. For example, a growing number of furniture retailers prefer to make selections at trade shows, and this has increased the popularity of this channel.

PRODUCT CHARACTERISTICS. Each *product* is a bundle of attributes. Some attributes, such as product color and hardness, may have no bearing on channel design; other attributes, such as perishability, bulk, degree of product standardization, service requirements, and unit value, often have very important implications for channel design.

Perishable products, such as fresh produce, dairy and bakery products, and fresh seafood, usually require more direct marketing because of the dangers associated with delays and repeated handling. Products that are *bulky,* i.e., heavy or large in relation to their value, such as building materials or soft drinks, usually require channel arrangements which minimize the shipping distance and the number of handling turnovers in the movement from producer to ultimate customers. *Unstandardized* products, such as custom-built machinery and specialized busines forms, are usually sold directly by company salesmen because of the difficulty of finding middlemen with the requisite technical knowledge. Products requiring installation and/or maintenance *services,* such as various types of machines, usually are sold and maintained directly by the company or by dealers given exclusive franchises. Products of *high unit value* are often sold through a company sales force rather than through middlemen; although a company sales force is an expensive means of selling, the high unit value of these goods means the sales cost is often a low percentage of the sales price. Thus, product attributes play an important role in influencing channel objectives with respect to channel length, the desired degree of exclusivity in middleman operation, and the particular functions to be borne by the middlemen.

MIDDLEMAN CHARACTERISTICS. Channel design also takes into account the strengths and weaknesses of different types of intermediaries in handling various tasks. For example, manufacturers' representatives are able to contact customers at a relatively low cost per customer because the total cost is shared by several clients. But the selling effort per customer during the contact is often less intense than if the company's salesmen were doing the selling. In general, intermediaries differ in their aptitude for performing such functions as transit, advertising, storage, and contact, as well as in their requirements for credit, return privileges, training, and frequency of shipment. In addition to these behavioral differences, the number, locations, size variations, and product assortments of intermediaries differ and affect the design of channels.

COMPETITIVE CHARACTERISTICS. The producer's channel design is also influenced by the channels competitors use. The producers in some industries want their products to compete in or near the same outlets carrying the competitors' products. Thus food producers want their brands to be displayed next to competitive brands, and this means using the same middlemen. In some industries, competitors utilize exclusive distributors for their products, and the firm may be led to do the same. The marketing channels used by competitors sometimes define what the producer wants to avoid rather than imitate. For example, Avon decided not to compete with other cosmetics manufacturers for scarce and inconspicuous positions in retail stores and established instead a very profitable door-to-door selling operation.

COMPANY CHARACTERISTICS. A company's channels are also influenced by characteristics peculiar to the company, such as its size, financial strength, product mix, past channel experience, and over-all marketing policies.

The company's over-all *size* in the industry determines the extent of its markets and the size of its larger accounts; it also determines its ability to secure the cooperation of intermediaries it elects to use. Its *financial strength* determines which marketing tasks it can handle and which ones to delegate to intermediaries. A financially weak company, for example, tends to employ commission methods of distribution and tries to enlist intermediaries able and willing to absorb some of the inventory, transit, and customer-financing costs. Its *product mix* influences its unique pattern of channels. The wider the company's product mix, the greater the ability of the company to deal with its customers directly. The greater the average depth of the company's product mix, the more it is likely to favor exclusive or selective dealers. The more consistent the company's product mix, the greater the homogeneity of its marketing channels.

The *past channel experience* of the company and its executives affects channel design. The experience of working through certain types of intermediaries tends to develop channel preferences. For example, many old-line producers of kitchen hardware who sold directly to retail food stores have resisted relinquishing control to the rack jobber. Similarly, many national-brand appliance manufacturers boycotted discount houses until it was clear that these middlemen were accounting for a large and growing volume. Present company *marketing policies* also shape the choice of channels. A policy of speedy delivery and service to ultimate customers affects the functions the producer wants intermediaries to perform, the number of final-stage outlets and stocking points, and the type of transportation system used. A policy of heavy advertising leads the producer to seek intermediaries willing to handle displays and join in cooperative advertising programs. A policy of uniform retail prices leads the producer to limit distribution to those final-stage sellers who will cooperate in maintaining list prices.

ENVIRONMENTAL CHARACTERISTICS. Channel design is further influenced by such environmental factors as economic conditions and the law. Where *economic conditions* are depressed, producers want to move their goods to market in the way that is least expensive for final customers. This often means shorter channels and dispensing with inessential services that add to the final price of the goods. *Legal regulations and restrictions* also affect channel design. Through a host of federal and state statutes and judicial and administrative decisions, the law has sought to prevent certain channel arrangements which "may tend to substantially lessen competition or tend to create a monopoly." The most sensitive areas have to do with agreements by manufacturers not to sell to certain types of outlets, attempts by a manufacturer to offer his line to dealers on condition they do not carry competitive lines, attempts by a manufacturer to force his full line through dealers, arbitrary action by a manufacturer in the withdrawal or refusal to renew dealer franchises, and attempts to set up territorial restrictions which substantially lessen competition.[12]

DISTINGUISHING THE MAJOR CHANNEL ALTERNATIVES

After specifying the channel objectives and constraints, the next step in channel design is to distinguish the channel alternatives facing the firm. Channel design is a problem when there is more than one way to move the product toward the final markets.

Channel design has several dimensions. When all are considered, the producer faces many different possible channel alternatives. A channel alternative is fully specified only after the following decisions have been made:

The basic *types of business intermediaries* who will be involved in selling and facilitating the movement of the goods to the market

The *number of intermediaries* who will be used at each stage of distribution

The particular *marketing tasks* of the participating intermediaries

The *terms and mutual responsibilities* of the producer and intermediaries

TYPES OF INTERMEDIARIES. In many industries, virtually all competitors use the same types of intermediaries; the firm does not really face alternatives. In other industries producers use quite different but well-defined alternative marketing channels; here the firm faces real alternatives. There are also cases where individual producers manage to develop completely new channel intermediaries. Some of the different and often novel channel alternatives are illustrated in the following cases:

Industrial testing equipment.[13] A manufacturer of test equipment for public utilities developed a new product that had considerably broader appeal. The product was an audio device that could help detect poor mechanical connections in any machinery with moving parts. The company executives felt that this product would have a market in all industries where electric, combustion, or steam engines were either used or manufactured. This meant such industries as aviation, automobile, railroad, food canning, construction, and oil. The problem was how to reach these diverse industries in an effective way. The following channel alternatives came out of management discussions:

Rely mainly on the present sales force and a heavy program of direct-mail and trade-magazine advertising.

Expand the company sales force and assign each salesman to a large industrial center where he is to contact all these industries.

---

[12] See Chapter 20, pp. 553-55.

[13] Adapted from David E. Faville, *Selected Cases in Marketing Management* (Englewood Cliffs, N.J.: Prentice-Hall, Inc., 1961), pp. 98-101, by permission of the Board of Trustees of the Leland Stanford Junior University.

Rely mainly on several manufacturers' agents, each of whom specializes in a different industry and a different region of the country.

Rely mainly on mill supply houses (wholesalers) who would undertake a limited amount of promotion and carry stocks in their warehouses. The company could gain national coverage by selecting five to fifteen of these supply houses as exclusive distributors.

Outdoor furniture.[14]   A medium-sized manufacturer of upholstered pads for outdoor furniture was organized to sell goods both to retailers and to companies manufacturing frames for garden furniture. In choosing its channels, one of the prime considerations was the fact that its business was seasonal (seven months of concentrated selling effort). It considered the following four channel alternatives for reaching its customers:

Company salesmen.

Manufacturers' representatives.

Joint venture. Other companies in the outdoor furniture field were also dissatisfied with the previous two alternatives, and there was the possibility that a half-dozen companies producing complementary goods might band together and hire salesmen to represent only these companies.

A subsidiary selling organization. The company could expand its sales force and form a subsidiary selling organization which would take on complementary lines of some other manufacturers as well as off-season lines to provide full employment throughout the year.

FM car radios.[15]   A new manufacturer of FM car radios visualized the following four channel alternatives for merchandising his product:

He could try to arrange an exclusive contract with some automobile manufacturer. This manufacturer would install only his brand on factory-ordered installations.

He could seek automobile dealers who were willing to carry his brand.

He could work through the customary channel, that of seeking distributors who would get his product into the many retail auto-radio shops.

He could market directly to consumers in large cities by establishing several installation sites and arranging with local FM stations to promote the product in return for a commission on each sale.

The preceding cases illustrate that a producer often faces several alternatives in the choice of types of intermediaries. Not only do conventional channel arrangements keep reappearing, but also more innovative examples, such as the joint venture, the selling subsidiary, and the use of FM stations as intermediaries.

NUMBER OF INTERMEDIARIES.   The number of intermediaries to use at each stage is influenced by the degree of market exposure sought by the company. Three degrees of market exposure can be distinguished.

Intensive distribution.   Producers of convenience goods and common raw materials generally seek *intensive distribution;* that is, the stocking of

---

[14] *Ibid.*, pp. 144-48.
[15] Adapted from Buskirk, *op. cit.*, p. 115.

their product in as many outlets as possible. The dominant factor in the marketing of these goods is their place utility. The producers of cigarettes, for example, try to enlist every possible retail outlet and device to create maximum brand exposure and convenience. This policy has culminated in the use of over 1,000,000 outlets, which is about as intensive as distribution can get.

Exclusive distribution. Some producers deliberately limit the number of intermediaries handling their products. The extreme form of this is *exclusive distribution,* a policy of granting outlets exclusive rights to distribute the company's products in its territory; it often goes along with *exclusive dealing,* where the manufacturer requires the dealers not to carry competing lines. This is found at the retail level with respect to the distribution of new automobiles, some major appliances, and some brands of women's apparel. But why would a manufacturer want to limit his products' market exposure? Obviously, he must be gaining other advantages in giving up some exposure. Through granting exclusive distribution privileges, the producer hopes to gain a more aggressive selling effort and be able to exercise more direct controls over intermediaries' policies on prices, promotion, credit, and various services. Exclusive distribution also tends to enhance the prestige or image of the product and allow higher markups.

Selective distribution. Between the two extreme policies of intensive distribution and exclusive distribution stands a whole range of intermediate arrangements which have been called *selective distribution.* Selective distribution involves the use of more than one but less than all the intermediaries who are willing to carry a particular product. It is used by both established companies with good reputations and by new companies seeking to get distributors by promising them selective distribution. The producer does not have to dissipate his efforts over a lot of outlets, many of which would be marginal. He can develop a good working understanding with the selected intermediaries and expect a better than average selling effort. In general, selective distribution enables the producer to gain adequate market coverage with more control and less cost than intensive distribution.

A producer will want to carefully consider these different strategies of market exposure and their implications for sales, costs, and degree of control. Sometimes the nature of the product, the market, or competitive practices clearly dictates one of these choices; at other times, all alternatives may be feasible.

SPECIFIC MARKETING TASKS OF CHANNEL MEMBERS. Every producer faces a certain set of tasks in moving his goods to the target markets. The role of intermediaries is not to increase the number of these tasks but to perform them more efficiently. Looking at a channel as a sequence of tasks rather than a linkage of business entities makes it immediately apparent that every producer faces a large number of alternatives, even when there is little choice regarding the basic types of intermediaries and the best degree of market exposure.

To show how many channel alternatives open up when the channel problem is conceived in terms of marketing tasks, assume that the following four tasks have to be performed:

T = transit, the work of transporting the goods toward the target markets

A = advertising, the work of informing and influencing buyers through advertising media

S = storage, the work of carrying an inventory out of which orders are filled

K = contact, the work of searching for and negotiating with buyers over terms

It may be further assumed that each intermediary can perform one or more of these tasks.

Suppose the maximum length of the channel structure under consideration is P-W-R-C. Now consider one of the potential stages, say R (for retailers), and the possible tasks that R may perform. For example, an R intermediary can participate in all four tasks; it can be responsible for transit, for some advertising, for some storage, and for contactual work (TASK). Or an R intermediary can be responsible for advertising and contact, but not for storage or transit (OAOK).[16] Still another possibility is to dispense with the R stage (OOOO). If all the possible task allocations to retailers were enumerated, there would be sixteen.[17]

OOOO	TOOO	TAOO	TASO	TASK
	OAOO	TOSO	TAOK	
	OOSO	TOOK	TOSK	
	OOOK	OASO	OASK	
		OAOK		
		OOSK		

For the moment, assume all of these possibilities make sense; i.e., it is meaningful for a retailer to handle any combination of the above mentioned tasks and still be a retailer. Likewise, assume that the producer can also perform any of sixteen possible task combinations (including no marketing tasks) and the same with the W (for "wholesaler") intermediary. Since one of these sixteen functional patterns will be borne by the producer, one by the W stage, and one by the R stage and assuming each stage could choose its task pattern independently of the other stages, there are 4,096 (16^3) different marketing channel arrangements from which to choose.

Let us look at one arbitrary channel arrangement from the set of 4,096:

$$\frac{P}{\text{TAOO}} \longrightarrow \frac{W}{\text{TOSO}} \longrightarrow \frac{R}{\text{OAOK}}$$

In this channel, the producer limits his marketing work to shipping the goods as they are produced and to advertising the product. The inventory is held by the marketing intermediary W, who also takes responsibility for further shipment. W is therefore a warehouse agent (a facilitating intermediary) rather than a full-service wholesaler. The final intermediary R is

[16] In fact, an important trend in appliance distribution is for retailers only to carry display models; customer orders are forwarded to the manufacturer who ships them out of a central inventory. See "Building a Faster Track from Factory to Home," *Business Week,* February 16, 1963, pp. 45-46.

[17] The number of possible task allocations to a marketing intermediary where there are n tasks is 2^n.

responsible for further advertising (perhaps on a cooperative basis with the producer) and the contactual work.

A different marketing channel is implied by the pattern

$$\frac{P}{TOSO} \longrightarrow \frac{W}{OOOO} \longrightarrow \frac{R}{OAOK}$$

Here the producer is reduced to a private-brand operator who produces, stocks, and ships on order, the W intermediary is eliminated, and the R intermediary assumes the complete selling function. This is the marketing channel developed by mail-order houses for many of its products.

Many of the 4,096 marketing channel patterns have to be ruled out as implausible or involving too much channel conflict. An example would be:

$$\frac{P}{OOOK} \longrightarrow \frac{W}{OOOK} \longrightarrow \frac{R}{OOOK}$$

The main problem here is that all three levels are engaged in contacting the final customer. Each stage is discouraged by witnessing the larger customers being grabbed up by the preceding stage. When all three participants engage in a search for customers, channel conflict is highly likely.

Some other combinations can be ruled out because they may be uneconomic, illegal, or unstable. As a result, the number of really feasible alternatives in task assignments may be quite small and manageable.[18]

TERMS AND RESPONSIBILITIES OF CHANNEL MEMBERS. In conceiving the tasks to be performed by different types of intermediaries in the channel, the producer must also determine the mix of conditions and responsibilities which must be established among the channel members to get the tasks performed effectively and enthusiastically. The "trade relations" mix is capable of many variations and introduces a still further dimension of alternatives.

The main elements in the trade relations mix are the *price policies, conditions of sale, territorial rights,* and *the specific services to be performed by each party.*

Price policy is one of the major elements in the trade relations mix. The producer usually establishes a list price and then allows discounts from it to various types of intermediate customers and possibly for various quantities purchased. In developing his schedule of discounts, the producer must proceed carefully for at least two reasons. First, different types of intermediate customers have strong feelings about the discounts they and others are entitled to. For example, small retailers who buy through wholesalers resent a producer who allows the large retail chains to buy direct at the wholesaler's discount; whereas the larger retailers resent not being allowed better terms on the basis of their quantity purchases. Thus the

---

[18] For a somewhat different approach to the number of alternatives latent in channel design, see F. E. Balderston, "Design of Marketing Channels," in Cox, Alderson, and Shapiro, *Theory in Marketing,* esp. pp. 179-80. Balderston uses an illustration involving three marketing functions (F_1, F_2, F_3) and three possible levels in the channel structure where they may be performed (S_1, S_2, S_3). The major difference is that he assumes that each function can be performed only by one level, while here it has been assumed that each function can be performed to some extent at each level. For his 3 by 3 case, under his assumption he derives 27 alternatives (3^3).

discount schedule is a potential source of channel conflict. Second, the Robinson-Patman Act forbids price discrimination between different buyers of the same goods where the discrimination may tend to lessen competition, except where the price differences are proportional to *bona fide* differences in the costs of selling to the different buyers. Therefore the producer must be able to justify the discounts he offers to different buyers.[19]

Conditions of sale are the second element of the trade relations mix. The most important conditions relate to the payment terms and to producer guarantees. Most producers grant a discount from the distributor's invoice price for early cash payment. For example, "2 per cent in 10 days, net 30" means that the distributor can deduct 2 per cent from the invoice price if he pays within 10 days, or otherwise the full cash price would be payable within 30 days. The particular terms can play an important role in the producer's costs and distributor's motivation, because they indicate the extent to which the producer will finance the distributor's inventories. The producer may also extend certain guarantees to the distributor regarding defective merchandise or price declines. The offer of a guarantee against price declines may be necessary to induce the distributors to buy in large quantities rather than on a hand-to-mouth basis.

Distributors' territorial rights are a third element in the trade relations mix. A distributor wants to know where the producer intends to enfranchise other distributors. He also would like to receive full credit for all sales taking place in his territory, whether or not they were stimulated through his own efforts.

Mutual services and responsibilities are a fourth element of the trade relations mix. These are likely to be comprehensive and well-defined in franchised- and exclusive-agency channels where the relation between producer and distributor is close. For example, the Howard Johnson Company provides the restaurant leaseholders with the building, promotional support, a record-keeping system, training, and general administrative and technical assistance. In turn, the leaseholders are supposed to meet company standards regarding physical facilities, comply with new promotional programs, furnish requested information, and buy specified food products. In contrast, where the producer goes after more intensive distribution, he may supply distributors only occasionally with some promotional materials and some technical services. The distributor in turn is less willing to furnish an accounting of his efforts, an analysis of customer buying differences, or cooperation in distributing promotional materials.

EVALUATING THE MAJOR CHANNEL ALTERNATIVES

By this time, the producer's review of his major situational factors (customers, products, available middlemen, competition, company, and environment) has helped shape the objectives and constraints governing the design of his channels. He has also spelled out the major channel alternatives in terms of feasible permutations of the basic types of intermediaries which may be used, the possible degrees of market exposure, the possible allocations of marketing tasks among the channel members, and the different trade relations mixes. Each alternative is presumably a well-conceived and specific route he may take to the final customer. His

---

[19] See Chapter 20, pp. 541-42.

problem is to decide which of the mutually exclusive plausible alternatives would satisfy best the long-run objectives of the firm.

Each channel alternative must be evaluated for its over-all enterprise implications. At least three different criteria should be included in the evaluation. The first is *economic;* i.e., what does each channel alternative imply in the way of sales, costs, and profits? The second is related to *control;* i.e., what does each channel alternative imply in the way of possible sources of channel conflict? The third is *adaptive;* i.e., what does each channel alternative imply about the firm's flexibility in meeting new competitive and distributional challenges?

ECONOMIC CRITERIA.   Of the three, economic criteria are the most important, since the firm is not pursuing channel control or adaptibility as such but is pursuing profits. True, channel harmony and adaptability have implications for long-run profit, but the more outstanding a channel alternative seems from an economic point of view, the less important seem its potentialities for conflict and rigidity. Therefore an evaluation of channel alternatives should start with an estimation of their respective implications for sales, costs, and profits.

To illustrate the economic analysis, a concrete and familiar pair of channel alternatives will be examined—the choice between a company sales force and the use of a manufacturers' sales agency.

> Assume that the company wishes to reach a large number of retailers in a certain region of the country. Suppose an adequate company sales force would require hiring and training ten salesmen who would operate out of a branch office in the region. They would be given a good base pay along with the opportunity for further earnings through a commission plan. The other alternative would be to use a reputable manufacturers' agency in the region who has developed extensive contacts with these retailers through the other lines he carries. The agent has thirty salesmen in his organization and would receive a fixed percentage of the sales price of each unit he sold.

The problem is that each system of distribution is likely to produce a different level of sales and costs. The better system is not the one producing the greater sales nor the one producing the lesser costs, but rather the one that produces the best relationship between the two.

The analysis should begin with an estimate of *sales* under each system, because some costs will be dependent upon the level of sales. Will more sales be produced through the use of company salesmen or the sales agency? When the question is posed in the abstract, most marketing managers answer that company salesmen sell more. Many reasons are given for this generalization. A company salesman concentrates only on the company products; he is better trained to sell the company's products; he is more aggressive because his future depends on the company; he is more successful with customers because they prefer to deal with company personnel. But these are abstract arguments, and the facts facing the producer are always concrete. It is conceivable that the sales agent's operation could produce as many as or more sales than a company-sponsored sales effort. Why?

In the first place, the hypothetical producer is considering representation by ten company salesmen versus thirty sales agency salesmen. The sheer difference in the number of salesmen may lead to more sales through the agency. In the second place, the agency's salesmen may be just as aggressive as the company salesmen in representing the company's products. This depends on how much pay incentive the line offers them in relation to the other lines they represent. The company can influence the degree of enthusiasm felt by agents as well as company salesmen by manipulating the terms. In the third place, it is not unconditionally true that customers prefer to deal with company salesmen over agents. Where the product and terms are standard, the customers may be quite indifferent. They may prefer dealing with the agent who represents a wider assortment of goods instead of dealing with a company salesman representing a single line. In the fourth place, one of the chief assets of the sales agent is the extensive contacts he has built up over the years, while a company sales force would have to cultivate contacts from scratch. The agency can often produce more sales for the manufacturer, at least in the beginning.

Thus the relative sales impacts of a company sales force versus a sales agency are impossible to predict in the abstract and even quite difficult to settle in the concrete. It is necessary to review the two actual proposals in detail.

The estimates of relative sales impact can come out of a theoretical analysis of the two specific channel proposals, a polling of company management, a field test under actual operating conditions,[20] or some combination of these.

Once sales have been estimated, the next step is to estimate the costs of the two channel systems. Only costs that are variable with each particular channel and level of sales should be considered. If the company has been using both types of marketing channels, a fairly good estimate of the respective costs can be made through a standard distribution cost analysis of existing data.[21] If the company is new, then speculative estimates have to be made. In either case, the probable cost differences between the two channels generally can be estimated more reliably than the likely sales differences.

The last step in the economic analysis of the two channels consists of bringing together the estimates of sales and costs, either in the form of a *breakeven analysis* or a *rate-of-return analysis*.

A hypothetical *breakeven chart* is shown in Figure 16-3. The costs of each channel vary with the sales level. The fixed costs of engaging a sales agency are obviously lower than those of conducting a branch sales operation. On the other hand, costs rise faster with additional sales through a sales agency than through company salesmen. The reason is that sales agents get a larger fixed percentage of sales than company salesmen, who are only on part commission.

Looking at the chart, there is one sales level (S_B) at which distribution

[20] Charles H. Sevin reports a case where a manufacturer facing these channel alternatives set up a test area to try out each alternative. At the end of a year, sales had risen by 24 per cent in the area canvassed by the sales agent and 31 per cent in the area served by company salesmen operating out of a branch house. These differences are specific to that company's situation, however, and should not be thought of as typical. Charles H. Sevin, *How Manufacturers Reduce Their Distribution Costs* (U.S. Department of Commerce, Economic Series No. 72, 1948), pp. 48-53.

[21] See Chapter 22, pp. 586-92.

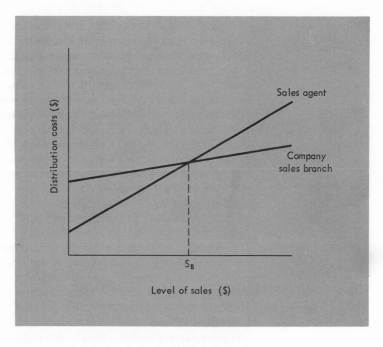

FIGURE 16-3
Breakeven cost chart for the choice between a sales agency and a company sales branch

cost would be the same for the two channels. Now suppose there was no reason to believe that either channel was better at producing sales. Then the chart could be read in a straightforward manner. The sales agency would constitute a superior channel at any volume of sales lower than S_B, and the company sales branch would constitute a superior channel at any volume of sales higher than S_B. This analysis accords with common observations of the circumstances under which the two channels have been used. Sales agents tend to be engaged by smaller firms, or by larger firms in their smaller territories, because in both cases the sales volume is too low to justify a fixed investment in a company sales force.

If it cannot be assumed that both channels produce the same sales, it is better to make a straightforward *rate-of-return* analysis. For each channel, the ratio R_i would be determined, where

$$R_i = \frac{S_i - C_i}{C_i}$$

where

R_i = rate of return associated with marketing channel i
S_i = estimated sales associated with using channel i
C_i = estimated costs associated with using channel i

R_i is an estimate of the rate of return expected on the costs of using channel i. All other things being the same, the channel emerging with the higher R_i is preferred.

CONTROL CRITERIA. The evaluation of the economics of sales agents versus company salesmen provides a rough guide to the probable economic superiority of one channel over the other. The evaluation must now be broadened by a consideration of the motivational, control, and conflict aspects of the two channel alternatives.

The use of sales agents can give rise to a number of control problems. The central fact is that the sales agent is an independent businessman. Therefore he is primarily interested in maximizing his own profits. This sometimes can lead to suboptimization from the producer's point of view. The sales agent is more concerned with promoting the image of his organization than his clients'. He often does not cooperate with the client's sales agent in an adjacent territory although the cooperation may benefit the client. He concentrates his calls on the customers who are most important to him in terms of his total assortment of goods rather than on the customers who are most important to the client. He may not take the time to master the technical details concerning the client's product nor show care in using client promotional material. Altogether, the use of sales agents comes at the price of creating certain problems of control. The degree of control the producer can achieve affects the economic results, and indeed should be considered in the economic evaluation of this channel alternative. But control should also be considered separately where the company wishes to attain other objectives than just the purely economic, such as knowing that its policies will be pursued faithfully.

The control aspects of a channel are broader than suggested in reviewing the sales agent example. Where the producer is considering a complicated channel alternative, the following issues should be considered:

Vertical relations in the channel. How will the various levels in the channel interact? Here there are two opposing dangers. At one extreme, the self-interests of two or more levels may be so diametrically opposed that they are always in conflict at the expense of the producer. At the other extreme, the self-interests of two or more channel levels may be so alike that they collude to force concessions from the producer.

Horizontal relations in the channel. How will the members located at a particular level in the channel interact? At one extreme, their self-interests may clash, as when territorial or business boundaries are not clear. At the other extreme, they may form an association to gain power at the expense of the producer, as the automobile dealers did.[22]

Interchannel conflict. Will the different marketing channels established by a producer be in too much conflict? For example, watch manufacturers have a difficult time pleasing both small retailers and discount outlets.

Legal conflict. Will the channel contain any questionable features that might involve the company in a legal suit? For example, a producer who plans to set up exclusive distribution should first determine its legal status.

ADAPTIVE CRITERIA. Suppose a particular channel alternative appears superior from an economic point of view and poses no particular problem of control. One other criterion should be considered—that of the producer's freedom to adapt to changing conditions. Each channel alternative involves some duration of commitment and loss of flexibility. When a department store chain builds a unit in a shopping center, it generally commits itself for 20 to 30 years. During this time, many changes may occur in distribution to make its outlet obsolete: the decline of shopping

---

[22] "Why Auto Dealers Want a Law," *Business Week,* January 18, 1958, pp. 75-76.

centers, the emergence of highly automated vending, the growth in popularity of mail or telephone ordering, etc. Exclusive dealerships also involve a long commitment. An appliance firm that franchises retail outlets to deal exclusively in its products can withdraw from these outlets only slowly, although distributional and merchandising methods may be changing rapidly. This is because dealers who commit their capital to this relationship want contractual assurance of some continuity.

In general, the less certain the future seems to be, the less favorable are channel alternatives involving long commitments. A channel alternative involving a long commitment must appear to be greatly superior on economic grounds in order to be considered.

Channel-Management Decisions

After a company has determined its basic channel design, individual middlemen must be *selected, motivated,* and periodically *evaluated.*

SELECTING CHANNEL MEMBERS

Each producer finds himself somewhere between two extreme positions respecting the recruitment of middlemen for his proposed channel operation. Some producers have no trouble finding specific business establishments to join the channel. Their proposal attracts more than enough dealers either because of the great prestige enjoyed by the firm or because the specific product (or line) appears to be a good money-maker. For example, Ford had no trouble attracting 1,200 new dealers for its Edsel. In some cases, the promise of exclusive or selective distribution will influence a sufficient number of middlemen to join the channel. The main problem for the producer who is fortunate enough to get all the middlemen he needs is one of selection. He must decide on what characteristics of middlemen prospects provide the best indication of their competence.

The other extreme position is where a producer chooses a channel alternative for which he has to work hard to line up the desired number of qualified middlemen. For example, the producer of a new soft drink finds it very hard to get shelf space in food outlets. Of course, the producer must have some chance of succeeding, or else the channel alternative should never have been considered. In the end he may have to accept whatever middlemen he can get, although he should initiate his recruitment effort among the more desirable middlemen. His recruitment effort should be based on a plan tailored to the psychology of the middlemen. Some plans are based on a strategy of *pulling* the product through the middlemen. The producer can advertise heavily to the final customers in the hope that they will ask the middlemen for the merchandise. Other recruitment plans are based on a strategy of *pushing* the product into the middlemen. This involves a well-designed sales presentation by the producer emphasizing the potential profitability in carrying the product, supplemented by good terms, and even something as persuasive as free merchandise or a gift.

Whether the producer finds it easy or difficult to recruit middlemen, he should determine what characteristics distinguish the better middlemen from the poorer ones. Even where the producer's aim is intensive distribution, he may not want his product associated with weak or faltering distributors. The critical characteristics vary with each type of intermediary, but in general, the producer wants to evaluate the middleman's number of years in business, his growth record, his solvency, his cooperativeness, and his reputation. If the middleman is a sales agent, the producer also wants to evaluate the number and character of other lines he carries, whether he is adequately staffed to give sufficient attention and know-how to the new line, and the turnover record of his salesmen. If the middleman is a department store being considered for exclusive distribution, the producer wants to evaluate the store's location, future growth potential, and type of clientele. In each case, the producer has to define the criteria that count most in discriminating the better dealers from the poorer ones.

MOTIVATING CHANNEL MEMBERS

Middlemen must not only be selected and signed up, but they must also be motivated to do their best job. The factors and terms that led them to join the channel provided some of the motivation, but these must be supplemented by continuous supervision and encouragement from the producer. The producer must not only sell through the middlemen but to them. The question of motivation is a complex one, since there are grounds for both cooperation and conflict between the producer and his distributors.

The job of stimulating channel members to good performance must start with the psychology and behavioral characteristics of the particular middlemen. Many a middleman has been criticized, according to McVey:

> for failure to stress a given brand, or for the poor quality of his salesmen's product knowledge, his disuse of suppliers' advertising materials, his neglect of certain customers (who may be good prospects for individual items but not for the assortment), and even for his unrefined systems of record keeping, in which brand designations may be lost.[23]

However, what are shortcomings from the producer's point of view may be quite understandable from the middleman's point of view. McVey listed the following four propositions to help understand the middlemen:

> The middleman is not a hired link in a chain forged by a manufacturer, but rather an independent market. . . . After some experimentation, he settles upon a method of operation, performing those functions he deems inescapable in the light of his own objectives, forming policies for himself wherever he has freedom to do so. . . .
>
> [The middleman often acts] primarily as a purchasing agent for his customers, and only secondarily as a selling agent for his suppliers. . . . He is interested in selling any product which these customers desire to buy from him. . . .
>
> The middleman attempts to weld all of his offerings into a family of items which he can sell in combination, as a packaged assortment, to individual customers. His selling efforts are directed primarily at obtaining orders for the assortment, rather than for individual items. . . .
>
> Unless given incentive to do so, middlemen will not maintain separate sales records by brands sold. . . . Information that could be used in product development, pricing, packaging, or promotion-planning is buried in non-standard records of middlemen, and sometimes purposely secreted from suppliers.[24]

[23] Phillip McVey, "Are Channels of Distribution What the Textbooks Say?" *Journal of Marketing*, XXIV (January 1960), 61-64.
[24] *Ibid.*

Although these are generalizations, they serve as a provocative departure from otherwise stereotyped thinking about the purpose and performance of middlemen. The first step in motivating others is to see the situation from their viewpoint.

The producer must steer a careful course between overmotivating and undermotivating his distributors. Overmotivation occurs when the producer's terms are more generous than they have to be to secure a particular level of cooperation and effort from the distributors. The result may be high sales for the producer but low profits. Undermotivation occurs when the producer's terms are too anemic to stimulate more than a token effort by distributors. The result is low sales and low profits. The producer's problem is to determine how much effort and what kind of effort he should expend in motivating the trade.

The basic level of motivation among distributors is established by the original trade relations mix. If the distributors are still undermotivated, the producer has two alternatives. He can improve the distributors' margins, extend better credit terms, or do any one of a number of things that alter the trade relations mix in favor of the distributor. Or he can apply artificial means to stimulate greater distributor effort by using any of a host of familiar devices, ranging from nagging the distributors until they either produce or quit, running dealers' trade shows and pep rallies, sponsoring sales contests for distributors and their salesmen, and increasing advertising directed at both the ultimate customers and the trade.

Whether the stimulation is provided at the level of the trade relations mix and/or in supplementary form, the producer must carefully interpret how the distributors perceive things from their vantage point. There are so many points of conflict latent in channel relations that it is often hard for the producer to put his finger on the real problem when he confronts a lack of cooperation. A basic problem is that the downward communication of the producer is usually better than the upward communication of the distributor. The producer must do what he can to improve the feedback he gets from his marketing channels.

EVALUATING CHANNEL MEMBERS

Besides selecting and motivating channel members, the producer must periodically evaluate their performance. Where an individual channel member's performance is seriously below standard, it is necessary to determine the underlying causes and to consider the possible remedies. The producer may have to tolerate the unsatisfactory performance if dropping or replacing the middleman would lead to even worse results. But if there are attractive alternatives to the use of this middleman, then the producer should require the middleman to reach a certain level of performance within a stated time period or face the consequence of being dropped from the channel.

Much grief can be avoided if standards of performance and sanctions are agreed upon at the very beginning between the producer and the channel members. These should be reduced to writing for the mutual protection of both parties. The areas posing the greatest need for explicit agreement on middleman responsibilities concern sales intensity and coverage, average inventory levels, customer delivery time, treatment of damaged and lost goods, cooperation in company promotional and training programs, and middleman services owed to the customer.

In addition to developing contractual bases for the performance responsibilities of the middleman, the producer might issue periodic sales quotas to define current performance expectations. Automobile manufacturers and many appliance dealers not only set quotas for total units to be sold but often for types of units. In some cases, these quotas are treated only as guides; in others, they represent serious standards. Some producers list the sales of various middlemen after each sales period and send the rankings out. This device is supposed to motivate middlemen at the bottom of the list to do better for the sake of self-respect (and continuing the relationship) and middlemen at the top to maintain their performance out of pride.

A simple ranking of the middlemen by level of sales is not really a logical measure. Middlemen face varying environments over which they have different degrees of control; the importance of the producer's line in their assortments also varies. If middlemen's performances are to be compared, there are better measures than gross sales.

One useful measure is to compare each middleman's sales performance against his own performance in the previous period. The average percentage of improvement (or decline) for the group can be used as the norm. Evaluation and motivation efforts can then be concentrated on the middlemen who perform below the group mean. An investigation of the situational factors in each case where a middleman lags behind the group may uncover certain valid factors: a decline in local economic activity, the unavoidable loss of an important customer, the loss or retirement of some key salesman, etc. Some of these factors can be remedied in the next period, or at least do not require immediate action against the middleman. In other cases, poor performances will not be traceable to valid situational factors, but rather to neglect of the line, failure to cooperate in promotional or training programs, or selling techniques that alienate customers. These are the middlemen with whom discussions must be held and understandings reached about future performance.

Another useful measure is to compare each middleman's performance not against his previous performance, but against a quota established for him based on an analysis of the sales potential in his territory.[25] After each sales period, middlemen are ranked according to the ratio of their actual sales to their sales potential. Investigatory and motivational effort can then be focused on those middlemen who have underachieved. Where valid reasons cannot be found for underachievement, company management must discuss with these middlemen what future steps are to be taken.

Channel-Modification Decisions

The major channel decisions discussed so far have been the design of the original channel system, and the selection, motivation, and evaluation of individual channel members. But the producer must do more than design a good system and set it into motion. Every so often it becomes apparent that the system or parts of it may require modification to meet new conditions in the market place.

[25] See Chapter 5 for methods of measuring sales potential.

This fact recently struck a large manfacturer of major household appliances who had been marketing exclusively through franchised dealers. A relative loss in market share made the producer take stock of at least the following distributional innovations that had taken place since the original channel was designed:

> An increasing share of major brand appliances were being merchandised through discount houses.
>
> An increasing share of major appliances were being sold on a private-brand basis through large mail-order department stores.
>
> A new market was developing in the form of volume purchases by tract home builders who preferred to deal directly with the retailers.
>
> Household door-to-door solicitation of orders was being undertaken by an increasing number of dealers and competitors.
>
> The only independent dealers who still remained strong were those located in small towns, and rural families increasingly were making their purchases on special trips to the big cities.

These and other developments in the ever changing distribution scene led this manufacturer to undertake a major review of possible channel changes.

In discussing the revision of company marketing channels, three different levels should be distinguished. At the operating level, the change could involve adding or dropping individual channel members. At the specific market planning level, the change could involve adding or dropping particular market channels. At the corporate systems planning level, the change could involve a totally new way to conduct business in all markets.

ADDING OR DROPPING INDIVIDUAL MIDDLEMEN

Channel changes that come up for consideration most often involve adding or dropping individual middlemen. The decision usually requires a straightforward incremental analysis. The economic question is what would the firm's profits look like with this middleman and without this middleman. The actual estimation may be quite difficult although the solution is clear in principle. On the other hand, an incremental analysis would not suffice where the decision on an individual channel member would have repercussions on the rest of the system. A large automobile manufacturer's decision to grant another dealer franchise in a metropolitan area affects the demand, costs, and morale of the other dealers. The new dealer's sales in the city can hardly be taken as an adequate indication of the total effects of his being added to the system.

Sometimes a producer contemplates dropping not an isolated middleman or two but all middlemen who fail to bring their unit sales above a certain level within a certain period. This happened when a large manufacturer of motor trucks selling through a network of franchised dealers noted that at least 5 per cent of its dealers were selling fewer than three or four trucks a year. According to the controller's calculation, it cost more for the company to service these small dealers than the sale of three or four trucks was worth. If the issue were a matter of dropping a few of these weak dealers, then an incremental analysis would probably indicate that company profits would rise. But the decision to drop most of these dealers could have such large repercussions on the system as a whole that an incremental analysis would not suffice. Such a decision would raise the unit costs of producing trucks, since the overhead would have to be spread over fewer trucks; some men and equipment would be idled; some business in the markets where the smaller dealers were cut out would go to competitors; and other company dealers might be made insecure by the decision. Nothing short of a detailed, total systems simulation would be adequate for comprehending all the effects.

ADDING OR DROPPING A MARKETING CHANNEL

A producer sometimes faces the question of whether he is reaching a particular market in the best way. It may be an important geographical market where the buying patterns have been undergoing dynamic change while the company's distribution channels have remained static. It may be a particular customer type (such as large retail chains) who must be given the goods at lower cost or be lost to competition. In such cases, the producer must think of amending his channels in a particular market although his over-all system and philosophy of distribution remain unchanged.

The pivotal consideration for analysis is once again whether the contemplated change will be confined to this market or have repercussions on the total system. In the former case, a simple breakeven or rate-of-return analysis could be made of the present and proposed systems. In the latter case, the nature of the repercussions would have to be determined, and the decision would call for a systems-level analysis.

THE "PRIVATE-BRAND" PROBLEM. An illustration of the issues at this level of channel decision making is afforded by the "private-brand" problem. Manufacturers of well-known branded products occasionally are approached by powerful wholesalers or retail chains to produce some output for them under the latter's private label. Thus Whirlpool produces automatic washing machines and dryers under Sears' Kenmore name; and Smith-Corona produces electric typewriters under Sears' Tower name. The brand manufacturer in effect is being asked to add another channel to reach the same market.

The manufacturer quickly realizes that this new channel can have significant repercussions on the sales of its branded product through its regular channels. If the same customers patronize both the regular and the new channel, they are apt to compare the products. Often, the producer's brand sells for more than the private brand, because the latter is bought in larger quantities on better terms and involves less distribution and promotion expense. The price difference and customer awareness that the two products are identical or similar may lead to a shift in sales from the existing channel to the new channel. This can provoke some of the middlemen in the existing channel to withdraw, causing a further shift of sales in favor of the private brand. Soon the manufacturer may find that most of his output is being sold under the private-brand label and indeed that he is losing money on his own brand. He then faces the choice of stepping up his promotional expenditures or reducing the price on his branded product or dropping the brand. He is increasingly dependent upon the large middleman, who in turn may press him for better terms. The manufacturer cannot very well refuse lest the large middleman who now takes a good part of his output drop him in favor of another producer. In the end, he may be reduced to a link in a chain forged by the powerful middleman (rather than the other way around), and depend entirely on the middleman's bounty for the profits he enjoys.

Note that the producer also courts trouble if he refuses the original solicitation for a private brand. He must face the prospect that an increasing number of buyers may move toward private brands because of the price differential or because of the middleman's reputation for quality and service. He must face the prospect that some competitor may sign up on terms which give the middleman an even better leverage in the market place and that this middleman may drop his brand. It seems that he is exposed to considerable risk whether he produces or refuses to produce the private brand.

The type of analysis required for making this difficult decision is first to structure all the alternatives (there are more than two) and then to estimate their respective payoffs in terms of the firm's long-run objectives. When this problem faced a large producer of branded baked goods, he discerned a number of alternatives, ranging from outright refusal to qualified refusal (offering to institute a system of price differentials so that his brand would be available at a lower cost to volume purchasers), to qualified acceptance (offering to produce a lower-quality version of his products) to outright acceptance. The alternatives were analyzed carefully in a decision-theory framework, including an evaluation of the probabilities of different countermoves by the soliciting middleman, other middlemen, and competitors, as well as an estimate of the likely monetary impacts of these different developments. While much of the data was highly conjectural, the decision-theory framework offered a way of systematically analyzing a most difficult problem.[26]

REVISING THE OVER-ALL SYSTEM OF DISTRIBUTION

The most difficult "channel change" decision, fortunately one that does not have to be made very often, involves the revision of the over-all system of distribution. Here the firm is sailing into uncharted waters, and if the decision is wrong, the whole enterprise may flounder. This type of decision is exemplified by the major appliance manufacturer mentioned earlier who, witnessing the growth of discount and private-brand sales, could no longer safely ride on a system involving exclusive distribution. It is also faced periodically by automobile manufacturers when they consider replacing independent dealers with company-owned dealerships. These are decisions made at the highest level, decisions which not only may change the channels, but necessitate a revision of most of the marketing-mix elements and policies to which the firm is accustomed.

Such decisions have so many ramifications that any quantitative modeling of the problem can only be a first approximation. Techniques of analysis are sorely lacking in the area of evaluating total channel systems. Certain new approaches are being experimented with, although it will be years before manufacturers begin to use them in an extensive way. The greatest promise seems to lie in system simulation; that is, developing a

[26] See Robert D. Buzzell and Charles C. Slater, "Decision Theory and Marketing Management," *Journal of Marketing*, XXVI (July 1962), 7-16.

computer model of the existing system and studying the consequences of systematic alterations in the model.[27]

A CONCEPTUAL APPROACH TO THE PROBLEM OF CHANNEL MODIFICATION [28]

In analyzing the desirability of changing a channel, the task is basically one of determining whether the channel is in equilibrium. A channel is in equilibrium when there is no structural or functional change that would lead to increased profits. A structural change is one involving the addition or elimination of some level in the channel. A functional change is one involving the reallocation of one or more channel tasks among the channel members. The channel is likely to undergo change only when it is in disequilibrium; that is, when it provides an opportunity for gain through a structural or functional modification.

A simple example will convey the concept of channel disequilibrium. Assume there is a channel of the producer-wholesaler-retailer type (P-W-R) and each channel member seeks to maximize his own profits. The retailer looks at his cost function from the wholesaler and his demand function from the market and makes the set of decisions on price, advertising, and distribution which will maximize his profits. Likewise the wholesaler looks at his cost function from the producer and his derived demand function from the retailers and makes the marketing decisions which will maximize his profits. Finally, the producer considers his own cost function and the derived demand function from the wholesalers and makes the marketing decisions which will maximize his profits. A conceptual picture of the input-output relationships in the channel is shown in Figure 16-4.

Each box represents a channel member at one of the levels in the channel. Each channel member makes a set of decisions on price, advertising, and distribution (P,A,D). For simplicity, assume that these decisions only affect the previous stage. Thus the producer makes decisions $(P,A,D)_3$ which influence the quantity ordered by the wholesaler (Q_3). The producer calculates his net profits (Z_3) by subtracting his costs from his revenue from the wholesaler. In the same fashion, each channel member makes an independent set of decisions which influence his revenue and cost and bring about a particular net profit.

Looking at the channel as a whole, a set of independent decisions is made $[(P,A,D)_1, (P,A,D)_2, (P,A,D)_3]$ which results in some total channel profit $(Z_1 + Z_2 + Z_3)$. The concept of channel disequilibrium can now be defined precisely. The channel is in disequilibrium if there exists an alternative set of decisions $[(P,A,D)_1, (P,A,D)_2, (P,A,D)_3]$ * which would result in a different total channel profit $(Z_1 + Z_2 + Z_3)$ * such that $(Z_1 + Z_2 + Z_3)$ * is greater than $(Z_1 + Z_2 + Z_3)$. If this is the case, the channel presents an opportunity for increased profit. But the alternative decisions are not likely to be made as long as the channel members make their decisions independently. The greater the difference between $(Z_1 + Z_2 + Z_3)$ * and $(Z_1 + Z_2 + Z_3)$, the greater will be the

[27] See Chapter 10, pp. 237-41.

[28] This section leans heavily on some pioneering model building by Stanley Stasch, in *A Method of Dynamically Analyzing the Stability of the Economic Structure of Channels of Distribution,* an unpublished doctoral dissertation, School of Business, Northwestern University, 1964.

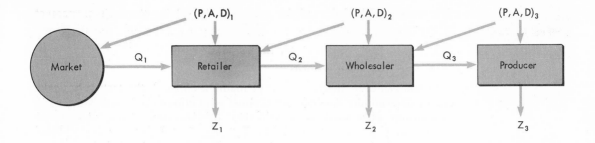

where

$(P, A, D)_i$ = the price, advertising, and distribution decisions of channel member i

Q_i = the quantity ordered per period by channel member i

Z_i = the profits per period of channel member i

FIGURE 16-4

Conceptual picture of the profits in a marketing channel

Redrawn, with modifications, from Stanley Stasch, *A Method of Dynamically Analyzing the Stability of the Economic Structure of Channels of Distribution,* an unpublished doctoral dissertation, School of Business, Northwestern University, 1964, p. 63.

incentive of the channel members to pursue joint planning or for some channel to absorb one or more of the others to achieve the extra profits from integrated decision making.

The producer is usually in a good position to spot and take advantage of channel disequilibrium. The type of model building for examining proposed channel modifications, however, is quite complex and beyond the scope of this book.[29]

Summary

Marketing channel decisions are among the most complex and challenging decisions facing the firm. Each firm usually confronts a number of alternative ways to reach the market. Marketing channels differ significantly in their capabilities for creating sales, in their costs of operation, and in their susceptibility to control. Once they are chosen, the firm must usually adhere to them for a substantial period of time. Furthermore, the chosen channels intimately affect the development of the other parts of the marketing program.

Good channel design should proceed with a clarification of channel objectives, alternatives, and likely payoffs. The objectives are conditioned by the particular characteristics of customers, products, middlemen, competitors, company, and environment. The alternatives are usually many because of the variety of types of intermediaries, the different possible inten-

[29] See Stasch, *ibid.*

415

sities of market coverage, the various ways in which channel tasks can be allocated among channel members, and the many possible trade relations mixes. Each feasible alternative way to reach the market has to be spelled out and evaluated according to economic, control, and adaptive criteria.

After the basic design of the channel is determined, the firm faces the task of effective channel management. It has to select particular firms to work with or find business firms willing to work with it. It has to supplement the motivations provided to channel members through the trade relations mix by special incentives and supervision. It has to periodically evaluate the performance of individual channel members against their own past sales, other channel members' sales, and, possibly, sales quotas.

Because markets and the marketing environment are continually changing, the firm must be prepared to make channel revisions: individual members may be dropped or added, the channels in specific markets may be modified, and sometimes the whole channel system may have to be redesigned. Evaluating a proposed channel change may be approached through incremental analysis if only the particular unit or channel is affected; it may require a systems-level analysis if the change is likely to affect other units. In the latter case, system simulation may be the most efficient way to determine the channel's equilibrium. The greater the disequilibrium in a channel, the more apparent it will be to observers that channel modification would lead to increased profits.

Questions and Problems

1. If there are five producers and five customers in a market, how many contacts would have to be made (a) without a middleman? (b) with a middleman? What are the general formulas?

2. Explain how the characteristics of (a) peaches and (b) cement affect the channels for them.

3. Suggest some alternative channels for (a) a small firm which has developed a radically new harvesting machine and (b) a small plastic manufacturer who has developed a picnic pack for keeping bottles and food cold.

4. What are the major drawbacks of each of the four alternatives described for (a) the manufacturer of outdoor furniture and (b) the FM car radio manufacturer?

5. Is the following channel pattern plausible? What kinds of institutions are implied?

$$\frac{P}{OOOK} \longrightarrow \frac{W}{OASO} \longrightarrow \frac{R}{TAOO}$$

6. Produce a checklist of questions for rating prospective applicants for a distributorship.

7. Discuss the long-run implications for competition in an industry where vendors extend larger discounts to the larger buyers.

chapter 17

Physical Distribution Decisions

Throughout the years, the term "marketing" has connoted two different but related processes, the first dealing with the *search for and stimulation of buyers* and the second with the *physical distribution of goods*. With the increased competition for markets, marketing executives have devoted the bulk of their time to the search and stimulation function. Their attention has been given over to developing a mix of products, prices, promotion, and channels which would keep demand high and growing. They have viewed physical distribution, or the logistics of getting goods to the buyers, as a supportive and subsidiary activity.

More recently, several developments have awakened management's interest in the logistics problem and led them to wonder whether they were not overlooking many opportunities, not only for cost saving but also for improved demand stimulation.

One of the alerting factors is the steady climb in the bill for such physical distribution services as freight, warehousing, and inventory. Freight and warehousing bills are rising as a result of increased labor and equipment costs. The inventory bill is rising because buyers are tending to place smaller orders more frequently, and manufacturers are tending to expand the width and depth of their lines. Many executives have been shocked to learn that the total costs of storing, handling, and moving their products are anywhere between 15 and 30 per cent of sales.[1]

Authorities in increasing numbers argue that substantial savings can usually be effected in the physical distribution area, which has been variously described as "the last frontier for cost economies"[2] and "the economy's dark continent."[3] There is much evidence of uncoordinated physical distribution decisions resulting in suboptimization. Not enough use is being made of modern decision tools for determining economic levels of inventories, better transshipment schedules, and better plant, warehouse, and store locations.

Management is increasingly recognizing that physical distribution policies are a potent instrument in the demand-stimulation process. Companies are able to effect stronger patronage by offering more than competitors in the way of service or by cutting prices through succesfully reducing physical distribution costs.

[1] Richard E. Snyder, "Physical Distribution Costs," *Distribution Age,* December 1963, pp. 35-42.

[2] Donald D. Parker, "Improved Efficiency and Reduced Cost in Marketing," *Journal of Marketing,* XXVI (April 1962), 15-21.

[3] Peter Drucker, "The Economy's Dark Continent," *Fortune,* April 1962, pp. 103, 265, 268, and 270.

For all these reasons, the physical side of marketing is attracting grow-ing attention. In this chapter many of these points will be amplified. The first section describes the scope and components of a company's physical distribution system. The second discusses the objectives of a physical distribution system. The third considers major alternative designs of the physical distribution system and the means of evaluating them in the light of company objectives. The fourth and fifth sections describe the special nature and problems of inventory and location decisions, respectively. The sixth section considers organizational responsibility for physical dis-tribution, particularly how much centralization in this area is desirable and where it should be positioned in the organization.

The Scope and Components of a Physical Distribution System

SCOPE OF PHYSICAL DISTRIBUTION

Discussions of physical distribution are hampered because the term is used in many ways. The failure to distinguish particularly between what we shall call here the broad and the narrow views of physical distribution produces much of the confusion.

In the broad view, physical distribution starts with the location of original materials and labor inputs required in the productive process and stretches to the location of final consumer markets. It becomes co-extensive with the basic marketing task, according to Wroe Alderson, of bridging the gap between the unassorted supplies found in nature and the assortment needs found in man.[4] This perspective is particularly pertinent to the firm planning to enter a new product market. Having as yet no investment in suppliers, factories, warehouses, middlemen, or final markets, it is in a position to consider all of them as variables in designing its physical distribution system. Final markets are generally the best starting point for planning the new system. The company selects its final target markets and then works backwards to an appropriate system of middle-men, an appropriate warehousing system, and appropriate plant locations.

The narrow view of physical distribution starts with the fact that going concerns have much less freedom in choosing the components of their physical distribution system. Most things are "givens" rather than "vari-ables." Such companies are saddled with a set of suppliers, factories, ware-houses, middlemen, and final markets. In time, of course, they can liquidate their commitments. As a practical matter, however, they are not free in the short run to make radical changes in their system for distributing goods. These firms must seek physical distribution economies through improving the efficiency of their system rather than revising it.

The difference between the broad and the narrow perspective of physical distribution underlies the confusion between *channel of distribution* deci-sions and *physical distribution* decisions. The broad perspective would make channels of distribution just one aspect of the larger problem of physical distribution. In terms of the narrower perspective, however, the two are separate problems. We shall adopt the narrower perspective of the

[4] See Chapter 16, pp. 389-90.

established company that has already solved its channel of distribution problem. Decisions have already been made on the kinds of marketing intermediaries to use, the intensity of market coverage, and the mix of dealer margins, services, and so forth. These channel decisions are assumed to be prior to the making of physical distribution decisions. For any given choice of channels, a subsequent decision can be made on optimal physical distribution policies. This will be our view, although in principle, channel alternatives and physical distribution alternatives should be considered simultaneously.

COMPONENT ACTIVITIES IN PHYSICAL DISTRIBUTION

What are the component activities of physical distribution management, and how are they related? A useful conception developed by Wendell Stewart is reproduced in Figure 17-1. Eleven different activity "cogs" make up the physical distribution system. The whole system centers on the inventory management cog. Inventory is the link between the customers' orders and the company's manufacturing activity. Customers' orders draw down the inventory level, and manufacturing activity builds it up. Manufacturing activity requires an inflow of raw materials into the company, and this involves inbound freight and receiving operations. Finished goods then flow off the assembly line, involving packaging, in-plant storage,

FIGURE 17-1

Activity cogs in a distribution system
Redrawn from Wendell M. Stewart, "Physical Distribution: Key to Improved Volume and Profits," *Journal of Marketing,* XXIX (January 1965), 66.

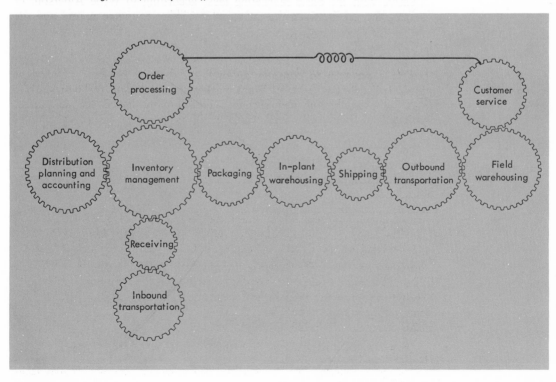

shipping-room activities, outbound transportation, field warehousing, and customer delivery and service.

The various activities are highly interactive in time. Each activity depends upon the preceding one, and therefore upon all preceding ones. The time it takes to fill a customer's order depends upon the time it takes to develop or find stock, to package and bring the goods to the shipper, and for the shipper to transport it to the buyer. The extent to which these activities are well managed and coordinated has an important effect on the buyer's attitude toward doing business with the seller.

The Physical Distribution Objective

Many companies state their physical distribution objective as *getting the right goods to the right places at the right time for the least cost.* Unfortunately, this provides little actual guidance. No physical distribution system can simultaneously maximize customer service and minimize distribution cost. Maximum customer service implies such policies as large inventories, premium transportation, and many warehouses, all of which raise distribution cost. Minimum distribution cost implies such policies as slow, cheap transportation, low stocks, and few warehouses.

The physical distribution objective can be defined more carefully by introducing the notion of an *efficient system.* System efficiency is a matter of the ratio of a system's output to its input. By clarifying what the outputs and inputs are in a physical distribution system, we can come closer to defining a clear objective for such a system.

LEVEL OF SERVICE (OUTPUT)

A basic output of a physical distribution system is the *level of customer service,* typically defined in terms of the "number of days" delivery. For example, when Pillsbury revised its physical distribution system in the late 1950's, it defined its objective to be "third-morning rail delivery anywhere in the U.S." [5] Some companies define the level of service as the "percentage of customers who should get their orders in X days." Others think in terms of a system that holds down the fraction of backorders to a certain level. Actually, there are many components in the customer service level (e.g., product availability, order cycle time, stockout percentages, delivery frequency, and delivery reliability), and a more complex "level of service" variable could be formulated.[6]

How does the company determine a desirable level of customer service? In many cases, it simply uses the standard set by competitors. If it offers a lower level of service than the prevailing one, it is in danger of losing patronage unless there is some compensatory element in its marketing mix. If it offers a higher level of service than the prevailing one, the competitors may increase their service level in self-defense, and all companies would be stuck with higher costs. Any advantage would be temporary, especially if it is an effective advantage.

[5] "New-Fangled Routes Deliver the Goods—Faster and Cheaper," *Business Week,* November 14, 1959, p. 110.

[6] William B. Saunders, "Designing a Distribution System," *Distribution Age,* January 1965, pp. 32-36.

The company's decision on the service level must rest ultimately on an analysis of probable customer—and competitor—response to alternative levels of service. Sometimes a slight increase in customer service can produce a good gain in customer patronage—say 15 per cent—whereas a major costly increase may produce only a slightly higher gain—say 20 per cent. The value customers place on service is admittedly one of the hardest things to evaluate in marketing. Nevertheless, it can sometimes be measured with a little ingenuity. One investigator was able to estimate how the percentage of returned merchandise to a mail-order house varied with the length of the delay in shipment.[7] Even where the estimates are rough, one can use sensitivity analysis to find out how much difference any estimate would make in the choice between physical distribution alternatives.

In addition to setting up an *average* level of customer service, firms often have to evaluate the impact of proposed increases or decreases in service levels to specific customers. The decision process for this problem has to be modeled separately in each case. Consider a national can manufacturer who operates many local plants because cans are a low-cost, low-price product that has a relatively high transportation cost when shipped assembled, being mostly "air." Suppose some of his plants appear uneconomic, and he is considering closing them. Much depends upon whether customers in the affected areas would accept a longer delivery time, switch business to a competitor's local plant, or manufacture their own cans. A self-explanatory flow diagram showing how the company might analyze probable customer reactions to the elimination of a local plant is given in Figure 17-2.

COST OF SERVICE (INPUT)

A company bears certain costs, of which freight, inventory, and warehousing are the main ones, in providing its present level of customer service. Often the total bill is not known because companies typically lack centralized management and accounting of their physical distribution activities. These costs, however, must be measured, through special auditing procedures if necessary, as a prerequisite for evaluating distributional efficiency.

The present system can be said to be efficient if no reorganization of logistical inputs could reduce the costs *while maintaining the present service level*. Many companies think their physical distribution system is efficient because each decision center—inventory, warehousing, and traffic—appears to do a good job of keeping down its own costs. However, this is an area where the sum of distributional costs is not necessarily minimized by a set of uncoordinated efforts to minimize the separate costs. As stated by Donald D. Parker:

> Pressures are applied by top management which encourage the separate functional units to control and reduce their costs of operation. Cost reduction becomes the primary way for these functional units to call attention to themselves. . . . As a result, when decisions are made about transportation, warehousing, packaging, inventory levels . . . they are based on an analysis of alternatives within that specific function, without regard for the possible effects upon other closely related functions. Functional costs are

[7] See Chapter 9, p. 216.

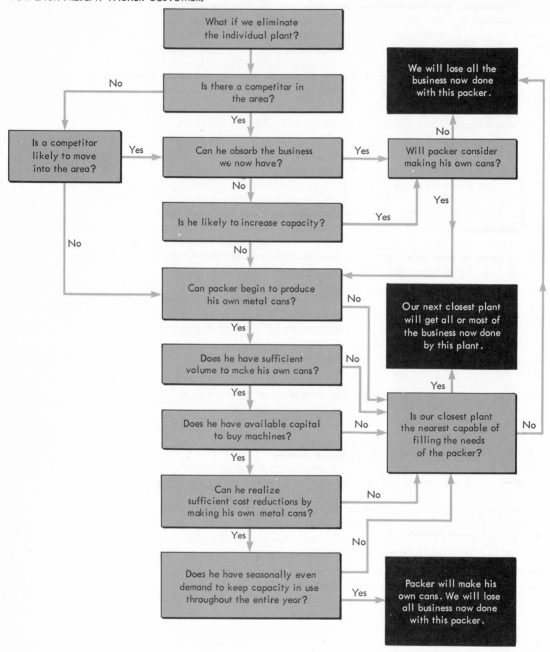

REPEAT FOR EACH PRESENT
CUSTOMER OF THE PLANT

FIGURE 17-2
The decision by a metal can manufacturer to eliminate a local plant
From an unpublished paper by Jeffrey Pope, Northwestern University, 1963.

considered, but the all-important total cost of the related functions is ignored.[8]

Various physical distribution costs interact, often in an inverse way:

The traffic manager favors railroad shipments over air shipments whenever possible. This reduces the company's freight bill. However, because the railroads are slower, this ties up company capital longer, delays customer payment, and may cause customers to buy from competitors offering more rapid service.

The shipping department uses cheap containers to minimize shipping costs. This leads to a high damage rate of goods in transit and the loss of customer good will.

The inventory manager favors holding low inventories to reduce total inventory cost. However, this results in many stockouts, backorders, accompanying paper work, special production runs, and high-cost fast-freight shipments.

The import is that since physical distribution activities are highly interrelated, decisions must be made on a total system basis.

THE OBJECTIVE

We are now ready to define the objective of physical distribution design. A unique physical distribution system consists of a set of decisions on the number, location, and size of warehouses; freight policies; and inventory policies. Each possible physical distribution system implies a total distribution cost, as given by the expression:

$$D = T + FW + VW + S$$

where

D = total distribution cost of proposed system
T = total freight cost of proposed system
FW = total fixed warehouse cost of proposed system
VW = total variable warehouse costs (including inventory) of proposed system
S = total cost of lost sales due to average delivery delay under proposed system [9]

The choice of a physical distribution system calls for examining the total distribution cost associated with different proposed systems and selecting the system that minimizes total distribution cost.

Major Alternatives in Physical Distribution Strategy

A firm faces a large number of alternatives in designing its physical distribution system. The variety increases in number and complexity as we

[8] Parker, *op. cit.,* p. 17.
[9] Adapted from Alfred A. Kuehn and Michael J. Hamburger, "A Heuristic Program for Locating Warehouses," *Management Science,* July 1963, pp. 657-58.

go from a firm with a single plant serving a single market to a firm with multiple plants and multiple markets. For this reason, we shall start with the single-plant, single-market case.

SINGLE PLANT, SINGLE MARKET

The vast majority of the 300,000 manufacturers in the United States are single-plant firms doing business in single markets. The single markets served may be a small city, as in the case of small bakeries and printing firms, or a region, as in the case of local breweries and boat manufacturers.

Does the single-plant firm generally locate in the midst of its market? It often does, for the cost of serving a market increases with the distance. The distant firm has to absorb higher outbound freight costs and would appear to be at a competitive disadvantage.

Yet in some cases there are offsetting economies in locating a plant at some distance from the market. The higher market transportation cost may be offset by lower costs of land, labor, energy, or raw materials. Two examples demonstrate this.

> A small pickler serving the Chicago market located his plant in the midst of a cucumber-growing region 200 miles from Chicago. This gave him better control over crop selection. His labor costs were lower because pickling and packing were done only in certain months, when farmers had surplus time on their hands. Finally, the acreage for his plant cost only a fraction of what it would have cost near the city.

> A meat-processing company built its plant near a cattle auction market in a small town. This eliminated the need to pay shipment costs on the whole steer when only 45 per cent of its weight has market value.

The merits of locating a plant near the market or near its sources can rarely be resolved in the abstract; it depends mainly on relative transfer and processing costs.[10] A substantial change in certain costs could upset the balance of advantages. Many textile and shoe manufacturing firms moved out of New England to the South chiefly because of lower labor costs in the South. This decision could be folly if southern labor becomes unionized and demands the northern pay scale. The firm choosing between two alternative plant sites must carefully weigh not only present alternative costs, but expected future alternative costs.

SINGLE PLANT, MULTIPLE MARKETS

The firm with a single plant and selling in a dispersed set of markets has a choice of several physical distribution strategies. Consider a midwestern manufacturer who has been selling in the Midwest but now wishes to expand his operation into the East. He can serve the eastern market in at least four alternative ways:

> *Direct shipment* to customers on the East Coast from the Midwest plant.
> *Carload shipments to a warehouse* on the East Coast.
> *Fabricated parts shipment to an assembly plant* on the East Coast.
> *Establishment of a manufacturing plant* on the East Coast.

[10] For a brief description of the pure theory, see John A. Howard, *Marketing Management: Analysis and Planning,* rev. ed. (Homewood, Ill.: Richard D. Irwin, Inc., 1963), pp. 220-22.

Any proposed system of physical distribution must be evaluated in terms of both customer service and cost. A cursory look at the direct shipment proposal leaves the impression that it would score poorly on both of these counts. In the first place, direct shipment would seem to imply slower delivery than shipments to the customer from an eastern-based warehouse. Secondly, direct shipment would seem to imply more cost, because the typical customer order is likely to be smaller than carload size. Carload rates (CL) are often 50 per cent lower than less than carload rates (LCL).

But whether direct shipment does involve these disadvantages depends upon a number of things. It is conceivable that direct shipment from a distant plant could effect *faster* delivery than shipment from a nearby warehouse. A Kansas City manufacturer of colored, flavored ice cream cones learned that his customers in the East could receive shipments sooner by air freight direct from Kansas City than by truck shipments out of New York City.[11] Furthermore, direct shipment of less than carload orders must always be measured against the cost of maintaining warehoused inventories in the East. The decision on whether to use direct shipment depends on such factors as the nature of the product (its unit value, perishability, and seasonality), the required speed and cost of delivery, the size and/or weight of the typical customer order, and the geographical distance and direction.

What is being compared to warehoused inventories in the East is not direct shipment in the abstract, but some particular mode of direct shipment. The cost of direct shipment varies with selection of waterways, railroad, motor carrier, airfreight, or some combination. Figure 17-3 shows how the cost of different modes of transportation may be compared. If the company tended to receive eastern orders for shipments weighing less than ten pounds on the average, it could minimize transportation cost by using airfreight. If eastern orders averaged between ten and thirty-five pounds, motor freight would be the preferred alternative. Finally, if the average-size order exceeded thirty-five pounds, shipment by rail would minimize the freight bill.[12]

This analysis is incomplete because each transportation alternative implies a different average delivery time. We can assume a higher cost of lost sales for longer delivery delays. Thus the slower modes of transportation cost less freight-wise but more sales-wise. These two diverging cost functions of delivery time are shown in Figure 17-4. By adding the two cost curves vertically, we can find a total cost curve. The total cost curve tends to be U-shaped, and by projecting its minimum point down to the days-of-delivery axis, we can estimate the optimum delivery delay, D. This delay has the property that the marginal savings in freight from a slightly longer delay would just equal the marginal costs of lost patronage.

This analysis highlights the need for an over-all systems approach to physical distribution decisions. Suppose the company's average-size ship-

---

[11] See Ralph Westfall and Harper W. Boyd, Jr., *Cases in Marketing Management* (Homewood, Ill.: Richard D. Irwin, Inc., 1961), pp. 488-91.

[12] The firm may also face the decision whether to rent or to own transit facilities. For example, the midwestern company could hire a common motor carrier or could purchase a truck to make its shipment to the East. If it could arrange with an eastern manufacturer to rent its return capacity, the buy option might be the more attractive.

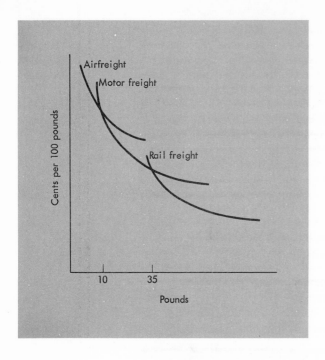

Cents per 100 pounds

Airfreight

Motor freight

Rail freight

10   35

Pounds

FIGURE 17-3

Shipping cost as a function of average weight and type of transportation

ment to the East weighed 50 pounds. According to Figure 17-3, rail transportation would be the most economical medium. But rail transportation is relatively slow and would increase the cost of lost sales (Figure 17-4). It might therefore be better to use a motor carrier and absorb a higher freight bill in order to reduce lost sales. But even before this conclusion could be reached, the inventory cost implications of different modes of shipment would have to be considered.

BULK SHIPMENTS TO A WAREHOUSE NEAR THE MARKET.   Instead of direct shipments to eastern customers, the firm may find it less expensive to make bulk shipments to a regional warehouse in the East and to fill customer orders from that regional warehouse. The savings would arise mainly because of the substantial difference between carload and less than carload shipping rates. Suppose the midwestern manufacturer expects to sell 5,000 units annually in the East, and virtually all of the individual orders call for less than carload shipments. Assume that the shipping cost is $8 per unit on a carload basis, and $12 per unit on a less than carload basis. The cost of shipping the 5,000 units directly to customers at less than carload rates would be $60,000 (5,000 × $12). The cost of shipping carloads to a warehouse would be $40,000 (5,000 × $8). This represents a gross cost saving of $20,000.

From this, we have to subtract the cost of local delivery from the warehouse to the customer and the cost of warehousing. Suppose the typical local delivery charge is $1 a unit; then local delivery charges of $5,000 (5,000 × $1) must be subtracted from the gross savings, leaving savings of $15,000. Suppose the average unit stays in the warehouse one week

426

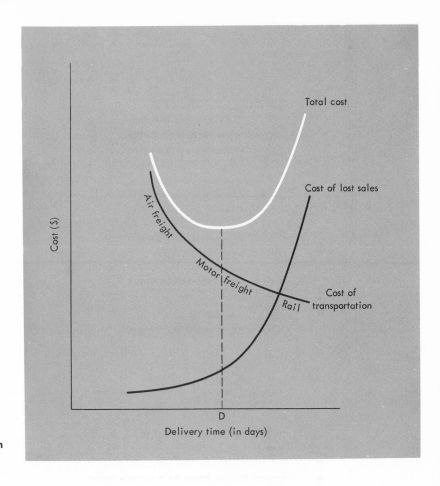

Total cost

Cost of lost sales

Air freight

Motor freight

Rail

Cost of transportation

Cost ($)

D

Delivery time (in days)

FIGURE 17-4
**Total cost as a function
of delivery time**

before shipment and the warehouse charge per unit per week is $2, including handling, insurance, and all other charges. Then the annual warehousing bill would be $10,000 (5,000 × $2), leaving net savings of $5,000. Given these assumed figures, the midwestern manufacturer could save $5,000 a year by making bulk shipments to a warehouse in the East as an alternative to direct shipments to customers.

To this possible freight savings should be added another advantage accruing from the use of a market-located stocking point. A regional warehouse typically makes it possible to make faster deliveries to customers and thereby increase customer patronage. In general, the optimizing rule for adding regional warehouses is simple enough. A regional warehouse should be added *if the freight savings and increased patronage resulting from faster delivery exceed the incremental costs of operating the warehouse.*

The midwestern manufacturer faces another decision, whether to lease warehouse space or develop a company-owned warehousing facility. The leasing alternative provides more flexibility and less risk, and is the preferred alternative in the majority of cases. The other alternative, private ownership of distribution warehouses, would make sense only for markets

427

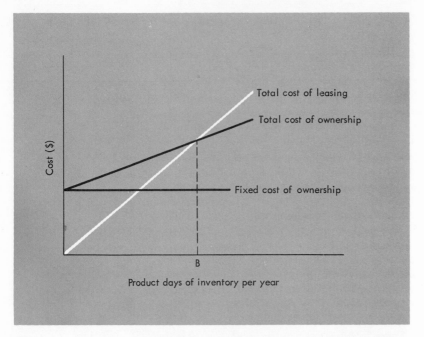

FIGURE 17-5
Breakeven analysis for the decision whether to lease or own a warehouse

where volume is large and demand stable. These two principles both emerge from considering the breakeven characteristics of this decision. For this we can turn to Figure 17-5.

Suppose leasing imposes a cost that was strictly proportional to the annual inventoried volume. (In practice, there may be a minor fixed charge, but for all practical purposes, the total cost of leasing can be described by a curve starting at the origin.) Alternatively, the firm that owns a warehouse must bear substantial fixed costs. The firm ties up a certain sum of money in the land, building, and handling equipment. It loses the opportunity return on this capital. It bears the annual depreciation expenses on the building and equipment. It pays taxes, insurance, and utility bills, which are primarily fixed in nature. Even labor may be a primarily fixed cost if most of the men report regardless of fluctuations in the level of warehouse activity.

According to Figure 17-5, warehouse ownership is the more economical alternative *if the average inventory level exceeds B, and exceeds it most of the time.* That is, regional demand must be sufficiently high and stable to warrant an inventory level exceeding B. For this reason, large companies like Lever Brothers and Pillsbury usually own regional warehouses. For smaller companies or companies with more variable demand, warehouse ownership may carry too much risk or burden. Such a company, in bad times, would have to divest itself of the warehouse or be forced to enter into competition for warehouse business, for which it may have neither the resources nor skills. An intermediate solution in the presence of volatile demand is for the company to combine owned and leased space, where the owned space supplies the capacity needed for the slowest season.

We have been discussing the *bulk shipment to warehouse* alternative as if only one warehouse were involved. The larger companies, leaving our small midwestern manufacturer aside, must consider a whole system

428

of regional warehouses, or stocking points, to serve a national market. Maytag, a large manufacturer of home laundry equipment, had in 1959 over 100 regional stocking points.[13] Instead of sending small-volume orders of washing machines to over 15,000 different dealers, the company sent carload shipments to its various stocking points. In this way, it can promise speedier delivery and also save considerably on freight costs.

But an extensive regional warehouse system raises a number of new problems. One question is whether the company has established the "best" number of stocking points. That is, should there be 50, 100, or 150 stocking points? A second question concerns the best geographical location for the stocking points. This question, however, is not independent of the first question. Both the number of stocking points and their locations have to be considered simultaneously in the search for an optimum distribution system. A third question concerns the proper inventory levels to maintain at the various regional locations. A company using a multiple stocking-point system inevitably carries a larger total inventory than one using a single stocking point. Each warehouse in the system must carry a broad mixture of company products, including slow moving items as well as high turnover ones. Each warehouse has to carry safety stocks in addition to ordinary demand stocks. As a result, more items are carried than would ordinarily be carried in a centralized inventory system.[14]

In view of the complex characteristics of a multiple stocking-point system, how can management proceed to determine the optimal design? Paper and pencil calculations are exceedingly inadequate, and only a few gross alternatives can be evaluated. A major breakthrough is now being promised through the application of model-building techniques. Gerson and Maffei have described a computer simulation program for evaluating a system of up to 40 warehouses, 4,000 customers, and 10 factories.[15] This program can be used to estimate quickly the cost of alternative arrangements in the existing number and locations of factories and warehouses. The major drawback of simulation is that it does not provide a systematic method of moving toward the optimal arrangement. Some operations researchers have been working with linear programming and heuristic programming techniques and have produced useful results.[16]

In conclusion, the substitution of a stocking-point system for a direct shipment system affects three important costs in physical distribution: the freight bill, the inventory cost, and the warehouse cost. There is no a priori answer as to which system is preferable. The answer can be found only through a detailed analysis.

FABRICATED PARTS SHIPMENTS TO AN ASSEMBLY PLANT NEAR THE MARKET. A third alternative for the midwestern manufacturer is to establish an assembly plant near the market. The possible merits of this alternative are illustrated in the case of the automobile industry:

[13] Westfall and Boyd, *op. cit.,* pp. 481-88.
[14] For a good illustration of the bigger inventory float implied by multiple stocking points, see Edward W. Smykay, Donald J. Bowersox, and Frank H. Mossman, *Physical Distribution Management* (New York: The Macmillan Company, 1961), pp. 123-26.
[15] See Chapter 10, footnote 46.
[16] See Kuehn and Hamburger, *op. cit.*

For a long time, the automobile industry was concentrated around Detroit and the rest of the country's demand was satisfied by direct shipments to dealers. This resulted in slow delivery, especially to the northeastern and southeastern parts of the country and the West Coast. Furthermore, the shipment charge, whether by rail or rack truck, was high. Customers on the West Coast had to pay substantially higher prices for automobiles and accept longer delivery dates, especially when they did not want to order out of dealer stock.

As the automobile industry passed from the rapid growth stage to one of increasing competitiveness, individual firms adopted one of two solutions to these problems. The use of regional distributional warehouses promised to alleviate the problem of delivery delay. But the first problem—that of higher costs—was not solved by regional warehouses. There were still high freight and inventory costs in shipping Detroit-assembled automobiles to the West Coast, and these costs had to be passed on to the consumers.

The establishment of a branch assembly plant on the West Coast afforded the opportunity to reduce these costs. Parts would be separately shipped in carload quantities to take advantage of substantially lower rates. Furthermore, the inventory in transit represented a lower value because it did not embody the cost of assembly labor or the charge for assembly operations.

Many other industries have found regional branch assembly plants preferable to direct shipment or distributional warehousing. The final decision must rest on an analysis of present and future costs. The major saving a branch assembly plant promises is lower freight charges. There is also the less quantifiable boost to sales which the presence of a regional plant provides through stimulating the increased interest of local salesmen, dealers, and the community at large. Against this must be estimated the increased capital costs and fixed charges of maintaining a branch assembly plant. The earlier discussion of the lease-or-build decision concerning a regional warehouse, as illustrated in Figure 17-5, can be employed in the analysis of the branch assembly plant alternative. The company must consider whether its future sales in the region will be substantial and stable enough to warrant this fixed investment. A fixed investment in an assembly plant is even more risky, besides being more costly, than an investment in a warehouse, because assembly plants are more specialized and therefore more difficult to dispose of. Unless the company has strong confidence in the future pattern of geographical sales, it must be cautious about committing itself to any heavy fixed investment that reduces its flexibility in future physical distribution planning.

ESTABLISHMENT OF A REGIONAL MANUFACTURING PLANT. The midwestern manufacturer's fourth alternative is to establish a regional plant in the East. Establishing a regional manufacturing plant is the ultimate way for a firm to tap a distant market and gain a competitive advantage. For many years, Inland Steel dominated the Greater Chicago market because its plants and main operations were located there. Competitors were able to achieve a respectable share of the market only through expensive sales effort and distributional warehousing. These were still not sufficient to overcome Inland's advantages, and several competitors ultimately decided to locate new plants in the Chicago area.

Yet the decision to build a regional manufacturing plant requires the most detailed factual information and analysis of the local scene. Many

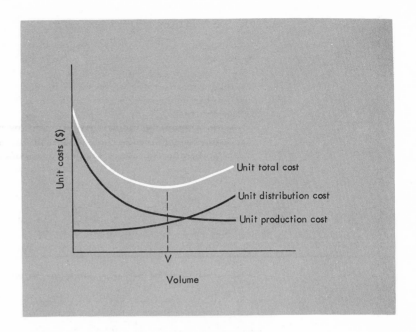

FIGURE 17-6
Unit production and distribution costs for a single plant

factors are involved, including the availability and costs of manpower, energy, land, transportation, and, not the least important, the legal and political environment.[17]

One of the most important factors is the nature of mass production economies in the industry. In industries requiring a relatively heavy fixed investment, a plant has to be quite large in order to achieve cost economies. If unit costs of manufacture decrease continuously with the scale of plant, then one plant could logically supply the entire company volume at minimum *production* costs. However, it would be fallacious to ignore distribution costs, because they tend to be higher at higher volumes. The two considerations are combined in Figure 17-6. Unit production costs decline steadily as increased volume is produced by a single plant, while unit distribution costs tend to rise as the volume requires direct shipment to more distant markets. When the two curves are summed vertically, total costs may in fact rise as a result of using only one plant location. The company should consider a second plant as an alternative to expanding the size of a single plant much past *V*. It is conceivable in this case that two plants, each involving higher unit production costs, may effect a large enough saving in distribution costs to constitute the better arrangement. The main point is that a second plant is not a question of plant efficiency alone, but of distributional efficiency as well.

What we have said about decreasing production-cost industries applies with even greater force to constant- and increasing-cost industries. A rising distribution cost curve imposed upon a constant or rising production cost curve provides even more reason why two or more company plants could offer more total economy, not to mention sales stimulation, than a large single plant.

[17] For an example of a plant location checklist, see Smykay, *op. cit.*, pp. 172-75.

Many of the large companies which do not require extremely large plants to achieve production economies utilize a physical distribution system consisting of many plants and many warehouses. These companies face two questions in regard to the optimality of their physical distribution system. The short-run optimization question is whether the company's factory-to-warehouse shipping pattern minimizes its total freight costs, given its present plant and warehouse locations. We have already seen how linear programming has been used to solve this problem.[18] The long-run optimization question is whether the present number and location of facilities minimize total distribution costs. Here system simulation is a potent technique. A simulation of hypothetical physical distribution changes at General Electric showed how a subsidiary with $50 million sales could save $2.9 million a year through redesigning its market logistics.[19]

NEED FOR FLEXIBILITY. In evaluating alternative systems of physical distribution, the issue often boils down to system economy versus system flexibility. Management must be especially wary when the best-appearing alternative requires heavy, long-term investments in regional plants and/or warehouses. Caution is called for because of the rapid and sudden changes that can occur in the costs or technology of an industry. A good example of this is afforded by the brewery industry.

> Some of the major breweries followed a policy of establishing local branch plants to avoid the high cost of shipping beer long distances. After several firms had made major investments in branch facilities, the technique of producing concentrated beer—similar to the concentrated orange juice process—was perfected, and it apparently became less expensive to produce in one central brewery and transport the product to regional bottling plants. The result was that firms which had not previously decentralized their operations had a significant cost advantage over those that did.

In general, the physical distribution system must be designed not for maximum economy for the present so much as maximum flexibility for the future, even if present costs must be a little higher in order to gain this flexibility. The system must be planned with an awareness of future company product and marketing strategy. The company's plans for entering new product markets, for proliferating additional product styles and models, and for increasing or decreasing the number of distributors all should count in designing the system. The system should also be planned with an awareness of environmental developments, particularly in the technological areas of communications, transportation, and automation. Such innovations as automated warehouses, piggyback freight, electronic hookups between computers in different locations, containerization, and airfreight continue to revolutionize the face of physical distribution.

[18] See Chapter 10, pp. 231-32.
[19] "The Case for 90% Satisfaction." *Business Week,* January 14, 1961.

While marketing management generally does not have full responsibility for inventory policies in most companies, it is deeply involved and generally seeks a strong voice in the making of inventory policy. The marketer's chief concern lies in providing a high level of service for his customers. Inventory policy is viewed by him as an instrument in the demand-creation process. He might, if he could, promise his customers that all their orders would be filled immediately and shipped by the most rapid transportation. He knows that one of the major influences in a customer's choice of suppliers is the probability of getting orders filled quickly and accurately. The customer who can depend upon the supplier to carry a full stock can operate with less of his own inventory, and this is worth dollars to him.

However, it is not realistic from a cost point of view for a company to carry the amount of stock that would virtually guarantee no stockouts. One of the major propositions to emerge from scientific inventory studies is that inventory investment increases at *an increasing rate* as the *customer service standard* approaches 100 per cent. A typical cost relationship is illustrated in Figure 17-7. For example, in order to be able to fill 85 per cent of the total received orders from existing stock, the company has to carry an inventory valued at $400,000. To raise the customer service standard by five percentage points, to 90 per cent, inventory investment must be increased by $100,000. To raise the customer service standard

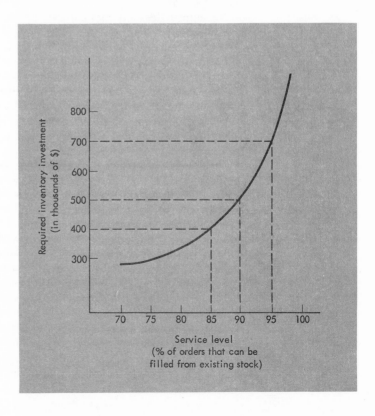

FIGURE 17-7

How the required inventory investment rises with the level of customer service

another five percentage points, to 95 per cent, inventory investment must now be increased by $200,000.

This acceleration of investment does not mean, however, that increases in customer service are never warranted! Obviously, increases in service spell increases in patronage and sales. But how much do sales increase with service? This is the crucial question. The graph only tells us that an increase from 90 to 95 per cent service requires another $200,000 of inventory investment. It does not tell whether sales and profits will increase enough to justify the higher investment. This is an issue requiring careful analysis.

Inventory decisions call for a constant balancing of cost against service considerations. The purpose of this section is to make more explicit the considerations used in inventory decision making so that marketing and nonmarketing personnel can appreciate better their mutual objectives and responsibilities.

TYPES OF INVENTORY DECISIONS

Inventories are carried because *producing* and *using* activities typically take place at different times, in different locations, and at different rates. In the case of agricultural food crops, rate of usage is usually even throughout the year, but harvesting occurs at discrete times. In the case of manufacturing output, factories achieve production economies by producing large runs of items infrequently. The savings in producing large runs generally exceed the cost of storing the goods over the period required for their complete sale.

Inventory decision making can be thought of as a two-step decision process: (1) when to order (order point), and (2) how much to order (order quantity).

WHEN TO ORDER. The basic characteristic of an inventory is that it is drawn down during the period. This calls for a determination of the level at which the remaining stock justifies the placement of a new order. This level is called the order (or reorder) point. An order point of 20 would mean that when the seller's supply of an item falls to 20 units, he should place an order for more stock.

The determination of the order point depends upon the order lead time, the usage rate, and the service standard. The *order lead time* describes how much time elapses on the average between placing the order and receiving the goods. The longer the lead time, the higher the order point. The firm that waits 20 days for delivery obviously has to place its order sooner—use a higher order point—than the firm that waits 10 days.

The *usage rate* describes the average rate per time period at which the inventory is drawn down by customer orders. The higher the usage rate, the higher the order point. The firm selling four units a day has to place its order sooner—use a higher order point—than the firm selling only two units a day.

The *service standard* describes the percentage of orders the company hopes to fill from stock. The higher the service standard, the higher the order point. Suppose, for example, that lead time is exactly 10 days and usage rate is exactly 2 units per day. Then the company could safely adopt

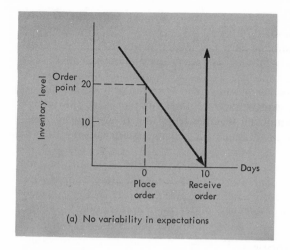

(a) No variability in expectations

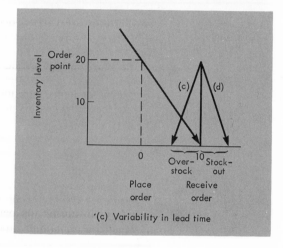

(b) Variability in usage rate

(c) Variability in lead time

FIGURE 17-8
Effect of variability in usage rate or lead time on stockouts

20 as its order point and meet a 100 per cent service standard (order point = lead time × usage rate). This is illustrated in Figure 17-8a. When the company's stock falls to 20, it places an order. In the meantime, its stock falls by 2 units a day. By the tenth day, its stock is depleted, but the situation is saved because of the arrival of new stock.

If there is variability either in the usage rate and/or in the lead time, then a higher order point is necessary to avoid stockouts. The two possibilities are depicted in Figures 17-8b and 17-8c. In Figure 17-8b the usage rate is shown to vary between a higher usage rate than two a day (*a*) and a lower one (*b*). The higher usage rate (*a*) results in stockouts, and the low usage rate (*b*) results in overstock. If the usage rate is equally variable between low and high values, the order point of 20 could result in 50 per cent stockouts. Similarly, Figure 17-8c shows what happens if the usage rate is constant but the lead time is variable. A lead time shorter than average (*c*) results in overstock, and a lead time longer than average (*d*) results in stockout. If the lead time is equally variable between low and

435

high values, the order point of 20 could result in 50 per cent stockouts. The general conclusion is that the greater the variability in the usage rate and/or the lead time, the higher the order point has to be to meet a given service standard. The order point is higher by an amount that is called the *safety stock* (as opposed to the *replenishment stock*). Companies determine the amount of safety stock to carry on the basis of service versus inventory carrying-cost considerations.

Thus the decision when to order amounts to choosing a minimum stock level (order point) which, when reached, signals that a new order should be placed. The order point should be higher, the higher the usage rate, the longer the lead time, and the higher the service rate in the presence of usage rate and/or lead time variability. The order point is fixed on the basis of balancing the risks of stockouts against the costs of overstock.

HOW MUCH TO ORDER. The decision the firm makes on how much to order (its order quantity) directly influences *how often* it has to order. The larger the quantity ordered, the less often an order has to be placed. Placing orders involves costs; maintaining large inventories involves costs. It is through a comparison of these opposing costs that the decision on order quantity can be made.

The costs of placing an order—the *order processing costs*—are somewhat different for the distributor and the manufacturer. The distributor's processing costs consist of whatever materials (stamps, order forms, envelopes, etc.), machine accounting time, and labor are used up every time an order is placed, received, and inspected. Distributors have estimated their order processing costs as low as $1 in some cases and as high as $20-$30 in others. The figure settled upon can make quite a difference in the final determination of optimal order quantity. Some of the variance in the estimates of different firms is real—it is based on actual operating cost differences—and some is artificial—it is based on different accounting methods. Generally speaking, only variable processing costs should be measured. This avoids the problem of highly arbitrary overhead charges, which are usually at the basis of estimating ordering costs as high as $30 an order. If any overhead is included, it should reflect the costs clearly attributable to the level of ordering activity and not to other operations which would go on anyway.

Order processing costs for a manufacturer consist of setup costs and running costs for the item. If setup costs are very low, the manufacturer can produce the item often and the cost per item is pretty constant and equal to the running costs. However, if setup costs are high, the manufacturer can reduce the average cost per unit by producing a long run. In this case, the company would prefer to produce large runs infrequently.

Both the distributor and manufacturer consider their processing costs as one of the two major factors in determining order quantity. Against this cost must be placed the costs of maintaining the order quantity in inventory, called *carrying costs*. The larger the average stock carried, the higher the inventory carrying costs. These carrying costs fall into four major categories:

Storage space charges. Inventories are held in special facilities which require heat, light, and perhaps special services, such as refrigeration or security. These facilities may be rented or owned. In either case, decisions to carry higher levels of inventory will raise the space costs (actual or opportunity costs).

Cost of capital. Inventories represent a form of investment of corporate funds. As a result, the company foregoes the opportunity rate it could make on its money in other uses. This is a very important cost, but one over which there is much disagreement both on concept and measurement.[20] Some companies make a very low charge, slightly above the bank interest rate of 6 per cent, for their cost of capital. Other companies consider their cost of capital to be as high as 30 per cent. Decisions to carry higher inventory levels will, of course, raise the total capital costs.

Taxes and insurance. Inventories are typically insured and also bear tax charges. The variable cost of tax and insurance should enter into the decision on order quantity.

Depreciation and obsolescence. Goods in inventories are subject to a number of risks that can reduce their value; among them are damage, price devaluation, and obsolescence. Although these costs are difficult to measure, the larger the inventory carried, the higher the write-off may have to be.

These costs make up total inventory carrying charges. They have been estimated to be about 25 per cent of the inventory value.[21] This is generally higher than the estimate used by many businessmen, but there is growing recognition that the cost is this high. It means that marketing management in particular must be more persuasive about the sales impact of carrying larger inventories. A company that increased its inventory investment from $400,000 to $500,000 would bear an incremental cost of $25,000 in making this move. The question is whether the resulting higher service standard would increase sales by enough so that the gross profit would exceed $25,000. This is the issue each company must face.

The optimal order quantity can be derived either graphically or mathematically. Figure 17-9 shows how the two opposing costs, processing and carrying costs, behave with different order quantities. The order processing cost per unit is shown to fall with the number of units ordered, because the order costs are spread over more units. Inventory carrying charges per unit are shown to rise with the number of units ordered, because each unit remains longer in inventory. The two cost curves can be summed vertically into a total cost curve. The lowest point on the total cost curve can be projected down on the horizontal axis to find the optimal order quantity $Q*$.

This same order quantity can be derived mathematically. The first task is to express the components of total cost. The following five elements are involved:

Q = order quantity in units
C = unit cost of item
I = percentage of annual carrying cost to unit cost
S = cost to place one order
D = annual demand

[20] See Ezra Solomon, ed., *The Management of Corporate Capital* (New York: Free Press of Glencoe, Inc., 1959).

[21] For sources and a breakdown of this estimate, see J. L. Heskett, Robert M. Ivie, and Nicholas A. Glaskowsky, Jr., *Business Logistics: Management of Physical Supply and Distribution* (New York: The Ronald Press Company, 1964), pp. 13-15.

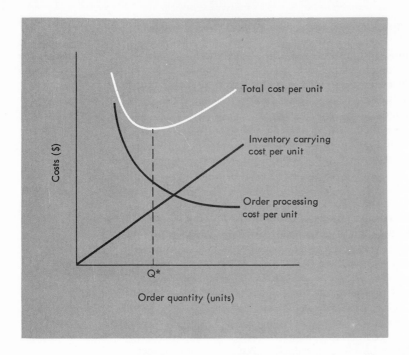

FIGURE 17-9

Determining optimal order quantity (Q*)

From these, we derive the following three variables:

$$\frac{Q}{2} = \text{average quantity on hand}$$

$$\frac{D}{Q} = \text{number of orders per year}$$

$$IC = \text{annual carrying cost per unit}$$

Total cost (T) can be defined as:

T = annual processing costs + annual carrying costs

T = number of orders per year × cost to place one order + average quantity carried (in units) × carrying cost per unit

$$T = \frac{D}{Q} S + \frac{Q}{2} IC$$

Using calculus, the Q which minimizes total cost is: [22]

$$Q^* = \sqrt{\frac{2DS}{IC}}$$

This formula was developed early in the century and is called the economic lot size, or economic order quantity (EOQ) formula. It is widely used in industry, often in modified form to take into account certain real-world complications. For example, the formula assumes a constant ordering cost, a constant cost of carrying an additional unit in inventory, a known demand, and no quantity discounts. When these assumptions are modified, more complicated formulas are necessary.[23]

[22] The first derivative of T is $dT/dQ = -DS/Q^2 + IC/2$. The economic lot size formula emerges by setting the first derivative equal to zero and solving for Q.

[23] See Martin K. Starr and David W. Miller, *Inventory Control: Theory and Practice* (Englewood Cliffs, N.J.: Prentice-Hall, Inc., 1962).

We have explored the main elements in making decisions on order point and order quantity for a single item in inventory. Most firms have to manage inventories for hundreds or even thousands of items. Just keeping the books for such a system is costly. Obviously, some compromises must be made in setting up a practical inventory control system.

Take the question of order point. To implement the previous theory a *perpetual unit control system* is required. The inventory status of all items in the product line has to be updated daily so that it can be determined when an order point is reached. Each day's beginning quantity on hand must be corrected by new stock arrivals and existing stock sales, requiring a considerable amount of posting because of the large number of different items sold and received daily.

The high cost of a perpetual unit control system covering all items has led to a number of compromises. In practice, many firms select only their most important items for perpetual unit control. The fact that relatively few items usually account for the bulk of sales considerably cuts down the cost of inventory control. The level of the other items is checked only periodically. If the company discovers that the stock of an item has fallen below the order point, it then places an order; if the stock is seriously depleted, the company requests rush delivery. Periodic unit review carries more chance of stockout than perpetual unit review, but this danger may not be too serious for noncritical items in the customer supply picture.

Consider also the question of order quantity. One of the key elements in the economic order quantity formula is expected demand (D). A company with hundreds or thousands of items is not in a position to forecast demand carefully for each item. Again, certain compromises are called for. In practice, the company may make careful forecasts for only its most important items. By careful forecasts is meant the use of advanced statistical techniques and their modification by field information and executive judgment as required. Demand for the remaining items may be projected on a largely statistical basis, using classical time series analysis or exponential smoothing.[24]

Over time, companies are likely to make fewer, rather than more, compromises with theoretically desirable systems of inventory control. The present compromises have resulted from the high cost of maintaining through manual means perpetual unit inventory control and complicated forecasting procedures. The major factor changing this is the electronic computer. A growing number of companies are placing their inventory systems on a computer status. The company's inventory of different goods is carried on computer tapes and adjusted daily through taped inputs (taken from punched cards) showing item sales and item arrivals. In conjunction with the record adjustment process, the computer issues a daily report on items that have reached their order points. In another operation, not daily but weekly or monthly, the computer rapidly calculates next-period demand for all (or the most important) items in inventory. In these ways, the computer permits increased inventory control for the same cost. Marketing management derives the benefits along with other management of better inventory information.

[24] See Chapter 5.

Location Decisions

Marketing management has a keen interest in various location decisions facing the firm. Generally speaking, it would like to see the company choose market-oriented locations for its facilities. For plants, this is not pressing, and the marketing department recognizes the economics of locating plants near sources of supply. With regard to warehouse locations, marketing and general management generally agree that market factors should weigh heavily. A major reason for warehouses is to enable faster and cheaper delivery to customers. This does not mean that a warehouse must always be located in a major market. If an eastern firm has good sales in both San Francisco and Los Angeles, it may find it more economical to locate a single warehouse between the two market centers instead of a separate and smaller warehouse in each market. The major point is that the pattern of warehouse locations should be established mainly in reference to the location of the company's markets.

Retail outlets must be located in or very close to major markets. Large organizations, such as supermarkets and department stores, would not dare to locate new outlets far from population centers. Retail outlets have to be established where potential buyers are concentrated, because of the importance of *shopper convenience*. As a general rule, shoppers patronize the closer location of two locations with equal facilities.

The following discussion emphasizes the problem of choosing *retail* locations. Marketing departments tend to have a larger responsibility for retail-location decisions than warehouse-location decisions in companies making both types of decisions. The actual locations chosen for retail outlets also tend to be more critical to their success than the locations chosen for warehouses. Certainly the investment in a retail location can be substantial. A large supermarket chain may invest over $250,000 per outlet, and a large full-line department store may be staking a few million dollars per outlet. Considering the sunk cost and long-term nature of the retail location commitment and also the rapid changes in population and retail merchandising, the retail-location problem stands in the greatest need of better decision making by management.

TYPES OF LOCATION DECISIONS

Location decision making can be thought of as a two-step decision process: (1) choosing a general area, and (2) choosing a specific site.

We can illustrate some of the central issues in retail location by citing the experience of the Rayco Manufacturing Company.[25] Rayco was formed after World War II as a manufacturer of automobile seat covers. Its distribution network consisted of independently financed, franchised dealers who merchandised Rayco products exclusively. By 1955, it had over 150 dealers operating in sixty different cities. Its national retail structure continued to grow, and new lines were taken on, such as convertible tops,

---

[25] The discussion that follows is adapted from "Rayco Manufacturing Company, Inc.: Pinpointing Store Locations by Electronic Computer," Case 3M38, Intercollegiate Case Clearing House, Harvard Graduate School of Business Administration, Boston, by permission of the author, Charles H. Dufton, Northeastern University, Boston.

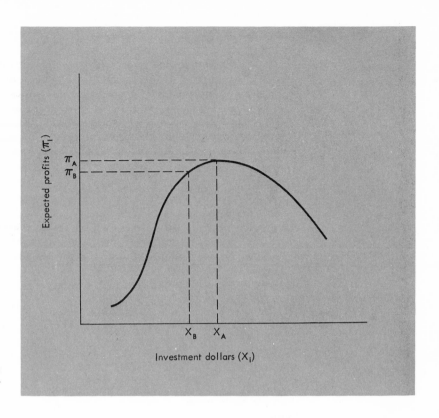

FIGURE 17-10
**Expected profits in area
i for alternative investments of X_i dollars**

automobile replacement parts, and a line of home furnishing fabrics. But
auto seat covers remained its main product.

CHOOSING THE AREA. Rayco's Research Division has the responsibility
of evaluating the profit potential of various areas of the country. The areas
might be cities, standard metropolitan areas, or some other geographical
unit. Suppose a set of *n* areas $(1, 2, 3, \ldots, i, \ldots n)$ is to be evaluated. Let π_i represent the expected profit potential of the *i*th area. Let
X_i be a proposed company dollar investment in developing area *i*. The
expected profit potential will vary with development expenses. That is,
$\pi_i = f(X_i)$. A larger outlet, a better dealer, or a larger promotion budget
would tend to create higher profits, although the rate of profit increase can
be expected to diminish beyond some level of investment. One plausible
relationship is illustrated in Figure 17-10.

It might appear from Figure 17-10 that Rayco should invest X_A dollars
in area *i*, because this sum would maximize the total profits available in
this area. But this would be an erroneous conclusion. Note that the investment increase of $(X_A - X_B)$ produced the relatively small profit increase
of $(\pi_A - \pi_B)$. In other words, the marginal profit on the last few dollars
was relatively small. An allocation of these dollars to another area might
produce higher marginal profits. The best allocation would exist when an

441

additional development dollar would yield the same profit increase in all existing or contemplated areas.[26]

Thus, the area location problem turns out to be simple to solve in principle. In practice, however, everything hinges on being able to estimate expected profits as a function of investment; i.e., $\pi_i = f(X_i)$. Area profits in reality are a complex function of area cost and area demand characteristics. The relevant cost characteristics of an area, such as land costs and advertising rates, are fairly easy to determine. It is the area's demand potential that is usually hard to determine.[27]

Rayco was initially able to identify about 300 variables or forms of variables that might have some logical connection with past or potential sales. However, 300 variables could not be accommodated in the multiple regression analysis because of their high intercorrelation and the availability of only 150 observations (stores). The Research Division examined carefully the logical rationale for each variable and was able to reduce the set to 74. Included among the 74 were such variables as "average January temperature," "per cent of the dwellings which were one-unit detached structures," and an "index for the physical appearance of a store." The reduction of the number of variables to 74 permitted a meaningful fit in terms of the number of observations. An equation was fitted and yielded a multiple coefficient of determination (R^2) of .98. However, several of the variables failed to pass tests of statistical significance, and in the final equation, 37 variables were retained, yielding an R^2 of .92. Presumably, Rayco could now estimate the "market potential" of any new area by inserting its 37 relevant characteristics into the formula.

CHOOSING THE SITE. After determining the areas of good potential, the firm must decide how many outlets to establish and where they should be specifically situated. If San Francisco appears to be a high potential market, Rayco could establish, for about the same investment, one large outlet in a central location or a few smaller outlets in separate parts of the city. If consumers behave as though auto seat covers were shopping or specialty goods, they would be willing to travel longer distances, and this would favor one large, centrally located store. If consumers regarded

---

[26] Suppose the company is able to develop a separate equation for the relationship between expected profit and investment in each area. Given these area expected profit equations and the company's annual development budget (B), the company can identify the best set of areas to invest in as well as the amount to invest in each. The formal solution requires the maximization of the total profit function

$$Z = \sum_{i=1}^{n} \pi_i$$

where

Z = total profit

$\pi_i = f(X_i)$

subject to the budget constraint

$$\sum_{i=1}^{n} X_i < B$$

The solution would have the characteristic that marginal profit would be the same in all areas.

[27] See Chapter 5, pp. 114-21.

Rayco's products as convenience goods, this would favor Rayco's establishing a few smaller outlets.

A store's trading area or reach is affected by a number of other factors besides the type of merchandise. One is the number of different items carried by the store. Baumol and Ide developed an analysis in which they visualized each consumer as calculating his net gain from patronizing a store with N items at a distance, D.[28] They assumed that increases in N more than compensated for increases in D up to a point. Beyond this point, the cost of traveling to the store, and within the store, became dominant. The cost of traveling within a store, which is a function of N, would never reach discouraging proportions in the case of a Rayco outlet but could be a real factor in very large supermarkets and department stores, especially for the shopper who plans to purchase only a few items.

The *utility* expected by a consumer in location i of shopping in outlet j is in reality affected by many variables in addition to N and D. Included are such factors as store image, delivery, credit, service policies, promotion, parking facilities, air conditioning, and so forth. If we assume that utility as a function of these variables could be approximately measured, the choice of the best site and store size from a list of alternatives is solvable in principle.[29] Suppose there are three alternative proposed sites—1, 2, 3—offering utilities 40, 30, and 10, respectively, to a consumer in location i. The probability that this consumer would shop at site 1 is the ratio of the utility of site 1 to the total utility, in this case .50 ($= 40/80$). If there are 1,000 similar consumers clustered at location i, then half of them, or 500, can be expected to patronize proposed site 1. In a more advanced analysis, it would be desirable to distinguish major socioeconomic types of consumers at location i, because there are undoubtedly interactions between consumer type and store type. Socioeconomic characteristics can either be made part of the general utility function, or a separate utility function can be developed for each consumer type.

In practice, firms differ considerably in how analytically they investigate the trade potential of proposed sites. Small firms tend to rely on population census data and on simple traffic counts. Larger firms tend to carry out expensive surveys of consumer shopping habits and to make extensive calculations of expected sales volume. In general, the larger the proposed investment, the greater the justified research outlay to reduce the risk of choosing a poor site.

The expanding firm often develops explicit criteria to guide its search for sites and cut down its search time. Goldblatt's, a million-dollar department store chain centered in Chicago, uses the following principles to narrow down its site choices.[30]

> The store must be designed to do from $3 to $5 million in annual sales volume.
>
> The store must be located in a one-stop shopping center only.
>
> The store must not be located in a major metropolitan center, but rather in secondary areas, such as are found in most suburban shopping centers.

[28] See William J. Baumol and Edward A. Ide, "Variety in Retailing," *Management Science,* October 1956, pp. 93-101.

[29] See David L. Huff, "Defining and Estimating a Trading Area," *Journal of Marketing,* XXVIII (July 1964), 34-38.

[30] See Westfall and Boyd, *op. cit.,* pp. 77-83.

The store must be in an area of population and consumer income growth
  potential, not in an area past its peak.

The store must not be located more than 200 miles from the central Chicago
  store.

Each store unit property must be leased and not bought.

There must be a minimum trading area of 100,000 persons.

While these heuristic principles may lead Goldblatt's to overlook a very
good site, they save the company the expense of considering a great number of potentially poor sites.

In undertaking a detailed *trade analysis* for a proposed site, the firm
first prepares area maps indicating population density and the location of
competitive intercepting facilities. An overlay on this map indicates major
arteries to pinpoint traffic flows. Additional ideas on traffic flow and trading area are obtained by surveying the license plates in the parking lots of
competitive facilities and through inquiries at noncompeting stores as to
customer sources.

The real estate department then determines the availability and cost of
potential sites within the general area. This is done with great secrecy to
avoid causing real estate speculation.

The trade potential of each site is then evaluated. A series of circles is
drawn around each site at varying distances to indicate the primary trading
area, the secondary trading area, and the fringe trading area. The secondary and fringe areas are further away from the new site and closer to
competitive sites; they can be expected to contribute a progressively smaller
amount of per capita sales. Use can be made of intracity versions of Reilly's
Law, which supplies a means for estimating the sales volume drawn by
competing shopping sites as a function of store size and driving time.[31]

[31] Studies were conducted, starting in 1927, by William J. Reilly and subsequently
by Paul D. Converse to measure the retail trade influence of a city. The original
"law" developed by Reilly reads like an adaptation of the law of planetary at-
traction. According to Reilly: "Two cities attract retail trade from any intermediate
city or town in the vicinity of the breaking point approximately in direct proportion
to the population of the two cities and in inverse proportion to the squares of the
distances from these two cities to the intermediate town." Mathematically this can
be expressed as

$$\frac{B_a}{B_b} = \left(\frac{P_a}{P_b}\right)^1 \left(\frac{D_b}{D_a}\right)^2$$

where

B_i = the proportion of retail trade from the
  intermediate town attracted by city i

P_i = the population of city i

D_i = the distance from the intermediate town to city i

$a,\ b$ = the particular cities being compared

Subsequent empirical investigations revealed that the exponents may vary because
of other variables not explicitly included in the equation. Population and distance
are still considered the primary variables, but other variables may warrant different
exponents. Among these second-order variables are lines of transportation and communication; business, social, and amusement attractions of the two cities; psychology of distance prevailing in that part of the country; differences in promotional
intensity; parking facilities, etc. For a good exposition of the various laws of retail
gravitation, see George Schwartz, *Development of Marketing Theory* (Cincinnati:
Southwestern Publishing Company, 1963), pp. 9-34.

The major chains utilize elaborate site location checklists in their evaluation of sites. Richard L. Nelson has published one of the most thorough checklists, a summary of which is reproduced in Figure 17-11. Each listed factor is checked separately for the proposed site and given a rating of excellent, good, fair, or poor. The development of some ratings may require some detailed field work. For example, the development of a rating for parking facilities may require collecting data on parking facilities at various distances from the site, the charge for these facilities, and the typical turnover in these facilities. Each important factor has to be rated, and the result is a profile of the strengths and weaknesses of the proposed sites.

Nelson did not carry this farther, but there exists a significant possibility for a quantitative refinement of his procedure. A quantitative rating scale—ranging from 1 to 4, say, can replace the use of rating adjectives. Then individual weights can be assigned to the various factors based on the subjective judgments of experienced company analysts or a statistical regression analysis of the characteristics of successful existing locations. Letting r_{ij} represent the numerical rating for site i on factor j and w_j the factor's weight or importance, then the value of the ith proposed site (V_i) would be given by

$$V_i = \sum_{j=1}^{n} w_j r_{ij}$$

Some of the data for estimating V may be quite subjective; yet the relative standing of V for the ith site may be a good indicator of its relative desirability.

Each chain organization must experiment separately with such possibilities as the one outlined in order to arrive at a dependable site evaluation formula. The rapidly changing patterns of retailing competition necessitate a continued search for more accurate decision tools. One very large merchandising organization dropped a leading location consultant firm it had used for years when it discovered that the consultant's methods were at the checklist stage. The firm decided to establish its own location research division with specialists in marketing research, sociology, mathematics, and geography. It plans to experiment with operations research procedures such as linear programming and simulation in the hope of finding better site selection procedures.

An improved site selection formula can reduce but never completely eliminate the risks attending the choice. Some factors which may critically affect the trade potential of the site will always be beyond the control of the firm. In evaluating a site at Racine, Wisconsin, Goldblatt's had to assign probabilities to such factors as whether a certain local plant was going to close down, whether a certain main artery would have its pavement improved, and whether the city would locate a bus terminal line at the site.[32] Each of these uncertainties would bear heavily on the success of the site. In addition, there is the ever-present possibility of a competitor's opening a larger and more extravagant outlet near-by. Finally, no site selection formula can protect the outlet against poor management. In fact,

[32] Westfall and Boyd, *op. cit.*

	Rating			
ITEM	E	G	F	P

I. Trading area potential
  A. Public utility connections (residential)
  B. Residential building permits issued
  C. School enrollment
  D. New bank accounts opened
  E. Advertising lineage in local newspapers
  F. Retail sales volume
  G. Sales tax receipts
  H. Employment - specific
  I. Employment - general

II. Accessibility
  A. Public transportation (serving site)
  B. Private transportation (serving site)
  C. Parking facilities
  D. Long-range trends (transportation facilities)

III. Growth potential
  A. Zoning pattern
  B. Zoning changes
  C. Zoning potential
  D. Utilities trend
  E. Vacant land market (land zoned for residential use)
  F. Land use pattern (in areas zoned for other than residential)
  G. Retail-business land use trend
  H. Retail-building trend (building permits issued for new retail business construction)
  I. Retail-improvement trend (permits issued for remodeling, expansion, etc. in existing properties)
  J. Retail-location trend (changes in occupancy of retail business locations)
  K. Income trend for average family unit
  L. Plant and equipment expenditure trend
  M. Payroll trend

IV. Business interception
  A. Location pattern--competitive businesses between site and trade area
  B. Location pattern--competitive businesses between site and trade area (served by and sharing traffic arteries with site)

V. Cumulative-attraction potential
  A. Neighboring business survey

VI. Compatibility
  A. Compatibility factors

VII. Competitive-hazard survey
  A. Competitive pattern--competitors within one mile of site (nonintercepting)

VIII. Site economics
  A. Cost and return analysis
  B. Site efficiency
  C. Natural description
  D. Adjacent amenities (for both vacant land and existing building sites)

FIGURE 17-11

Checklist of factors in site evaluation

Reprinted from Richard L. Nelson, *The Selection of Retail Locations* (New York: F. W. Dodge Corporation, 1958), pp. 349-50. Nelson presents many tables showing the important breakdowns of each factor.

one use of a site evaluation formula is to yield a norm against which to judge the actual performance of the branch's management.

Organizational Responsibility for Physical Distribution

DIVIDED AUTHORITY

By now, it should be abundantly clear that decisions on warehousing, transportation, inventory levels, and locations require a high degree of coordination. Yet in the typical company, physical distribution responsibilities tend to be divided in an ill-coordinated and often arbitrary way among several company departments. Figure 17-12 shows the typical location of various physical distribution activities within the modern company. Not only is control highly fragmented, but worse, each center tends to adopt a very narrow view of the company's physical distribution objective. The *traffic manager* seeks to minimize the freight bill. He prefers less expensive modes of transportation and infrequent and large shipments. The *sales manager* seeks to maximize the level of customer service. He prefers large inventories and premium transportation (unless they are charged to him). The *inventory control manager* seeks to minimize inventory costs. He prefers small inventories because inventory carrying costs tend to be more tangible than stockout costs. Each manager jealously guards his present prerogatives, and often would, if he could, absorb additional responsibilities. The result, in most cases, is system suboptimization.

The major rationale for divided authority is to establish checks and balances to prevent any one functional area from bending the physical distribution system to its own purposes. But this is a dubious gain, given the substantial costs that can be involved when companies fail to coordinate physical distribution decisions.

ORGANIZATIONAL ALTERNATIVES

Companies are increasingly recognizing the potential benefits of developing some coordinating mechanism, and have generally chosen one of two forms. Many companies have set up a permanent committee, composed of men responsible for different physical distribution activities, which meets periodically to work out policies for increasing the efficiency of the over-all distribution system. The committee frequently re-evaluates the present customer service level and develops proposals for any major system changes.

Other companies have chosen to centralize all the physical distribution activities in the hands of a single authority. The thought is that this would lead to more effective coordination and allow the development of physical distribution specialists. The example of the Burroughs Company is particularly illuminating.[33] In August 1961, Burroughs organized the Distribution Services Department to centralize control over its dispersed physical distribution activities. Within two and one-half years following the re-

[33] See L. O. Browne, "Total Distribution in an Age of Computers," *Distribution Age,* July 1964, pp. 33-40.

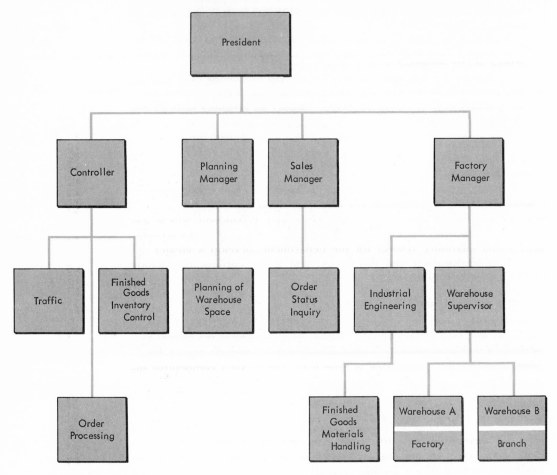

FIGURE 17-12

Typical location of physical distribution responsibilities
From Philip F. Cannon, "How Distribution Management Eliminates the Grey Area Between Manufacturing and Marketing," a speech presented at the American Management Association Conference on Distribution Management at the Hotel Roosevelt, New York City, October 5, 1959.

organization, the company claimed savings of over $2 million annually (on $200 million of sales), plus a higher level of service to field branches and customers. The savings came about in the following ways:

The number of finished machines in inventory has been reduced by over 40% during the past two years. This can be converted into a net annual savings of over $1 million in inventory-carrying costs.

All eight former company regional warehouses in the United States were closed, with net savings in rent and personnel costs in excess of $200,000 each year.

Central distribution of service parts and tools has reduced former space requirements by over 65%, while order-filling efficiency has been increased more than four-fold. The results of these improvements have added more than $300,000 in annual savings.

Transportation savings from pooling of shipments to branches and direct shipments to customers has trimmed over $175,000 from the annual transportation bill.

Reduction in personal property taxes last year exceeded $400,000 on inventories. This savings was due both to the reduction of inventory and the storing of idle inventory in tax-exempt locations.

Savings from a new universal stand to support accounting machines will save another $150,000 annually. This universal stand was engineered under the guidance of Distribution Services to simplify an inventory stocking and distribution problem.[34]

When a company chooses to establish a separate department with responsibility for physical distribution, the major issue is whether the new department should have separate status or be placed within one of the major existing departments. For example, Heinz created a new department of coordinate stature with Marketing and Production which was headed by a Vice-President of Distribution. Heinz hoped that this arrangement would guarantee respect for the department, develop a greater degree of professionalism and objectivity, and avoid partisan domination by Marketing or Production.

On the other hand, Burroughs placed its new Distribution Services Department within the Marketing Department. By this move, Burroughs was expressing the great importance it attached to good customer service relative to the costs of providing it. Wherever marketing is the crucial factor in competitive success, physical distribution is usually placed under the marketing department. This is especially true in such competitive industries as soap, food, and cosmetics, where marketing and physical distribution must be coordinated not only to minimize costs but also to harmonize distribution with frequent advertising campaigns and customer and dealer promotions. One physical distribution executive pointed out: "It is not at all uncommon . . . to receive a request asking that regional warehouse stocks on a product or product group be increased by one or two hundred percent within a 24-hour period." [35]

Those who argue that the physical distribution function should be placed under Production or the Controller are concerned mainly about holding down costs. Furthermore, there is a tendency to think that physical distribution is basically an engineering problem of the type "how to get so many goods from X to Y at the least cost," and therefore belongs in a more engineering-oriented department.

But the location of the department, or even its creation, is a secondary concern. The important thing is the recognition by the company that in the absence of coordination in the planning and operation of its physical distribution activities, it is missing the opportunity for often sizeable cost savings and service improvements. When this fundamental awareness takes place, each company can then make its own determination of what would constitute the most appropriate coordinative mechanism.

[34] *Ibid.*, p. 34.
[35] Ross E. Jones, "Distribution's Role in the Consumer Goods Company," *Traffic World,* July 29, 1961, p. 47.

Summary

Just as the marketing concept is receiving increasing recognition by business firms, a growing number are beginning to heed the physical distribution concept. When traffic managers, inventory managers, and warehouse planners make decisions only with reference to their own framework, they affect each other's costs and demand-creation influences but do not take them into consideration. The physical distribution concept calls for treating all these decisions within a unified total systems framework. Then the important task becomes that of designing physical distribution arrangements which minimize the cost of providing a given level of customer service.

The firm can choose from a number of alternative physical distribution strategies, ranging from direct shipment to field warehousing to local assembly plants to local manufacturing plants. It must develop inventory policies that reconcile the value of a high level of customer service with the need to economize on inventory carrying costs. It must find more accurate ways to evaluate alternative general areas and specific sites for marketing expansion. It must review the whole question of organizational responsibility for physical distribution, particularly how to coordinate the various decisions and where leadership should be located in the organization.

We have deliberately emphasized the planning rather than the operations aspects of physical distribution. Physical distribution is an area where good systems design counts for as much as or more than good operations management. Nevertheless, many of the potential economies come from improved management of the existing system.

Questions and Problems

1. Does it follow that the company offering a high customer service level tends to bear high physical distribution costs in relation to sales?

2. A small midwestern boat company with good sales wants to expand into the eastern part of the country. What physical distribution strategy might it use to bring its boats to the East?

3. What are the two inventory-production policy alternatives facing a seasonal producer?

4. The text mentioned that Rayco approached the problem of finding the characteristics of good locations through multiple regression. (a) Suggest some of the various ways in which the dependent variable, sales, might be defined. (b) How could the research department further reduce the number of independent variables in the market evaluation formula?

chapter 18

Advertising Decisions

In this chapter and the next, we shall discuss decisions on the firm's promotional mix. The firm's product may have excellent styling and quality, it may be priced at the right level, and it may be placed in the right channels. Yet it may fail to sell because it is not promoted to the right people in the right way.

The first section will examine the over-all question of promotional strategy. The following sections will deal with advertising and consider such questions as setting advertising objectives, determining the size of the advertising budget, developing the advertising message, choosing the advertising media, and evaluating advertising effectiveness. Chapter 19 will examine major decisions respecting the other major promotional tool, personal selling. Sales promotion and publicity, two other tools in the promotional mix, will not be treated explicitly, but many of the same principles apply.

Promotional Strategy

In their effort to stimulate sales, companies resort to a variety of activities, such as improving their products, extending their channels, and increasing their services. They also try to stimulate sales *through directing persuasive communications to the buyers. Promotion* is the term used to describe these last activities.

Promotional activities are generally classified into the four subactivities of advertising, personal selling, sales promotion, and publicity. These component activities are defined below:

> *Advertising:* Any paid form of nonpersonal presentation and promotion of ideas, goods, or services by an identified sponsor.
>
> *Personal selling:* Oral presentation in a conversation with one or more prospective purchasers for the purpose of making sales.
>
> *Sales promotion:* Those marketing activities, other than personal selling, advertising and publicity, that stimulate consumer purchasing and dealer effectiveness, such as displays, shows and exhibitions, demonstrations, and various non-recurrent selling efforts not in the ordinary routine.
>
> *Publicity:* Nonpersonal stimulation of demand for a product, service or business unit by planting commercially significant news about it in a pub-

promotion

lished medium or obtaining favorable presentation of it upon radio, television, or stage that is not paid for by the sponsor.[1]

When the firm considers promotion as a whole, it faces two major decisions. The first is how much total effort to invest in promotion; the second is how much relative usage should be made of the different promotional tools.

HOW MUCH FOR PROMOTION?

Since promotion is only one of several ways to stimulate company sales, the company always faces the question of whether promotional funds could not be spent better in new-product development, in lower prices, in more customer services, or in some other way. In fact, these latter alternatives tend to increase directly the real value of the company's offering in the buyer's mind. Buyers, if asked, would probably want the company to cut down on promotion and use the funds to make the offering itself more attractive.

Yet some promotion is essential in order to create customer awareness of the product's existence and characteristics. Furthermore, promotion can create positive psychological associations which can enhance the buyer's satisfaction. It is in this last sense that promotion also may be considered to add to the real value of the company's offering.

The problem of how much for promotion is not difficult in principle. The total promotional budget should be established at a level where the marginal profit from the marginal promotional dollar just equals the marginal profit from using the dollar in the best nonpromotional alternative. The problem is difficult chiefly because of the lack of data on the probable effects of investments in promotion versus other sales stimulants or cost-reduction activities. The ratio of the firm's promotional budget to the total marketing budget is certainly no basis for judging whether the promotional effort is adequate. A relatively high ratio may signify that the firm is trying to compensate for inadequacies in the product, its price, or the service. A relatively low ratio may signify that the product's quality acts in a quasi-promotional capacity. The decision on how much for promotion requires a careful analysis of the individual circumstances surrounding each case.

THE PROMOTIONAL MIX

The total promotional budget itself should be divided among advertising, personal selling, sales promotion, and publicity in a way that gives the same marginal profit on the marginal dollar spent in each of these directions. Again the problem is largely one of measuring the marginal effects of expanding the alternative instruments of promotion.

These marginal effects depend on the company's unique resources, opportunities, and constraints. Quite different promotional mixes may succeed for similar companies. Revlon puts most of its promotional money into advertising while Avon puts most of its into personal selling; both companies enjoy good sales. In the women's apparel industry, the mix ranges

[1] *Marketing Definitions: A Glossary of Marketing Terms,* compiled by the Committee on Definitions of the American Marketing Association, Ralph S. Alexander, Chairman (Chicago: American Marketing Association, 1960).

from a 50-50 split between personal selling and advertising in some cases to an 80-20 split in favor of personal selling.[2]

The promotional mix must be built on an understanding of the comparative costs and capacities of the various promotional elements. Compare the cost of an advertisement and a personal sales call, for example. An advertisement typically may cost the company one-third of a penny per reader-buyer whereas a sales call to the buyer may cost the company $20. The sales call is sixty times more costly. Yet it may also be sixty or more times more effective. The ad may not be noticed; the salesman will be. The ad cannot adapt the message to the particular buyer; the salesman can. The ad cannot go into much detail; the salesman can. The ad cannot close the sale; the salesman can. The ad cannot give the company any feedback; the salesman can.

Yet this is not an argument for exclusive reliance on any one promotional instrument. Various tasks have to be performed in creating sales, and the promotional instruments differ in their effectiveness per dollar in performing these tasks. The selling process calls for creating product awareness, developing customer comprehension of the product offer, producing customer conviction that the offer is good, and instigating the act of purchase. Advertising is probably the most effective instrument per dollar of expenditures for creating awareness. It obviates the need for the salesman to explain who he is and what he is selling. As for developing customer comprehension of the product offer, a combination of advertising and personal selling is probably better than either alone. Personal selling is typically more effective than advertising in producing "conviction," especially if the product is costly and/or technically complex. Personal selling is undoubtedly more effective in triggering the purchase act.

A study for IBM can be cited in this connection. IBM traditionally has considered advertising's role in the sale of its products to be minor compared with personal selling. The company commissioned Seymour Smith Associates to conduct a study of this assumption. After several months of gathering and analyzing data, the consultants concluded that advertising and publicity could be very valuable in creating an awareness of IBM products and a comprehension of some of the benefits offered.[3] This in turn made the salesman's time and effort more effective. The same kind of reasoning, that advertising makes personal selling easier, has been developed by Cyril Freeman into a formal model for apportioning promotional funds between advertising and personal selling on the basis of the selling tasks that each performs more economically.[4]

The optimum promotional mix varies with the nature of the product, its stage in the life cycle, the nature of the buying process, the promotional strategy of competitors, and a host of other factors. Such statements as "advertising is more important in selling consumer goods while personal selling is more important in selling industrial goods" and "advertising is more important for new products while personal selling is more important for mature products" require a number of qualifications to be useful.

[2] Edwin H. Lewis, "Sales Promotion Decisions," *Business News Notes,* No. 18 (Minneapolis: University of Minnesota, November 1954), p. 2.

[3] "Advertising Saves Sales Calls," *Business Week,* December 5, 1959, pp. 69-70.

[4] Cyril Freeman, "How to Evaluate Advertising's Contribution," *Harvard Business Review,* July-August 1962, pp. 137-48.

The instruments of promotion must be coordinated on both the strategic and tactical level if promotional dollars are to be maximally effective. The instruments are under strategic coordination if their broad roles in the selling process are carefully defined and correlated. The instruments are under tactical coordination if in any period they are harmonized in time and space for the accomplishment of specific communication effects and sales goals.

As companies move toward an organizational integration of marketing functions under a single executive—the vice-president of marketing—increased thought will be given to the planning and budgeting of an integrated promotional program rather than the development of separate programs. This may mean putting the four major promotional activities under one officer—a manager of promotion—or simply developing better working procedures among the officers who are responsible for managing the separate promotional activities.[5]

AN INTEGRATED COMMUNICATIONS PROGRAM

Integrated management of promotional activities is desirable not only for effecting better budgeting and timing, but also for achieving more consistency in the firm's marketing communications to the buyers. If the executives in charge of different promotional activities develop their messages independently, there is a good chance that the buyers will receive confused and perhaps conflicting impressions about the company and its products.

It is the responsibility of top management to define the basic communication objectives. Should the company strive for a specific or diffuse image in the mind of the public? If it is to be a specific image, what should be the main constituents? What general impressions should be conveyed by the company advertising, salesmen, and other marketing activities?

The communication objectives must be translated into a specific communications program, based on a careful understanding of the communication process. A model for the marketing communications process is shown in Figure 18-1. The seller, who is the source of the communications, has thoughts which he wishes to direct to the target buyers. These thoughts must be encoded into words and pictures by the seller and/or by encoding surrogates, such as the advertising agency. The encoding results in messages carried through four basic promotional channels. The messages go through a process of decoding by the receivers, i.e., target buyers. The seller tries to pick up feedback from the buyers to check on the fidelity of the messages and their effects on the buyers.[6]

The seller's two problems are to design the best messages possible and to make sure they are received in the intended way by the intended receivers.

---

[5] Textbooks are now appearing which treat the promotional process as a whole, and this is an encouraging trend. See for example Edward L. Brink and William T. Kelley, *The Management of Promotion* (Englewood Cliffs, N.J.: Prentice-Hall, Inc., 1963); or Edgar Crane, *Marketing Communications* (New York: John Wiley & Sons, Inc., 1965).

[6] This is an adaptation of the standard model of the communication process found in communication literature. See, for example, David K. Berlo, *The Process of Communication: An Introduction to Theory and Practice* (New York: Holt, Rinehart & Winston, Inc., 1960), p. 32.

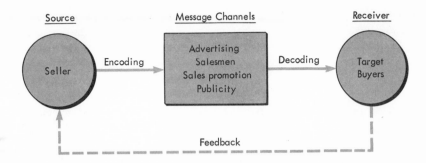

FIGURE 18-1
Model for the marketing communications process

The first requires understanding the target buyer and his needs. The second requires understanding the vulnerable points in the communication process, such as the encoding, message-channels, and decoding. Wilbur Schramm has summarized some of the major conditions for achieving communication effectiveness:

1. The message must be so designed and delivered as to gain the attention of the intended destination.

2. The message must employ signs which refer to experience common to source and destination, so as to "get the meaning across."

3. The message must arouse personality needs in the destination and suggest some ways to meet those needs.

4. The message must suggest a way to meet those needs which is appropriate to the group situation in which the destination finds himself at the time when he is moved to make the desired response.[7]

The study of communication is in its infancy, having been established only recently as an area of separate inquiry. It has attracted the interest and talents of sociologists, psychologists, linguists, physiologists, engineers, and military scientists, among others. As this young science develops, the marketer will want to follow the results in the interest of improving the effectiveness of the firm's communication program.

Advertising Objectives

Advertising is one of the four major activities by which the firm conveys persuasive communications to the target buyers. It consists of *nonpersonal forms of communication conducted through paid media under clear sponsorship.* Advertising, far from being a uniform product, comes in a large variety of forms. It is important to recognize this variety because it shapes the advertising objectives. Here is a list of the different ways in which advertising can be classified.

[7] Wilbur Schramm, "How Communications Work," in Schramm, ed., *The Process and Effects of Mass Communication* (Urbana, Ill.: University of Illinois Press, 1954), p. 13.

By geographical scope
  National
  Regional or local

By content
  Product advertising
  Institutional advertising

By type of appeal
  Factual
  Emotional

By intended effect
  Direct action
  Delayed action

By intended audience
  Consumer
  Industrial
  Trade

By sponsor
  Manufacturer
  Middlemen
  Manufacturer-middlemen (cooperative)
  Private (want ads)

By level of demand influence
  Primary product level
  Selective brand level

PURPOSE OF ADVERTISING

People have sought for many years to define the purpose of advertising. In his *Madison Avenue, U.S.A.,* Martin Mayer sounded a skeptical note by saying: "Only the very brave or the very ignorant . . . can say exactly what advertising does in the market place." It is fairly clear, however, what advertising is *supposed* to do. In ultimate terms, advertising is undertaken to increase company sales and/or profits over what they otherwise would be. Advertising, however, is rarely able to create the sales by itself, for it is not the only force acting on the buyer. At most, it is considered to have done its job by "bringing the buyer to water." But whether he drinks depends upon the product, the price, the packaging, the personal selling, the services, the financing, and other aspects of the marketing process.

More specifically, the purpose of advertising is to make potential buyers respond more favorably to the firm's offering. It seeks to do this by providing information to customers, by trying to modify their desires, and by supplying reasons to prefer the particular company's products.[8]

THE POWER OF ADVERTISING

There is much debate and confusion about the extent of advertising's power to influence buyer behavior. Critics of advertising such as Vance Packard charge that "many of us are being influenced and manipulated, far more than we realize, in the patterns of our everyday lives." [9] Packard believes that the scientific probing into subconscious motives has given advertising agencies unprecedented skill in molding buyer thought processes and purchasing decisions. Others dispute this position. They point to the few messages people really observe out of the thousands they are exposed to. They point to the immunity developed by many Americans to much of the advertising around them. They point to the fact that advertising is only one of several influences on a person's behavior and probably far less important—because it is known to be self-serving—than such influences as peers and personal observation.

It is very difficult really to know how effective advertising is, except in

---

[8] These points are developed in more detail by Alfred R. Oxenfeldt and Carroll Swan, *Management of the Advertising Function* (Belmont, Calif.: Wadsworth Publishing Co., 1964), pp. 7-12.

[9] Vance Packard, *The Hidden Persuaders* (New York: Pocket Books, Inc., 1957), p. 1. For a contrary view, see Raymond A. Bauer, "Limits of Persuasion," *Harvard Business Review,* September-October 1958, pp. 105-10.

the more obvious cases. Direct-action advertising, such as direct mail-order advertising and much of retail advertising, purports to stimulate immediate sales. Its effectiveness is therefore directly measurable. Delayed-action advertising purports to build up favorable attitudes. Therefore it is more difficult to measure its actual impact. There is little doubt that the brand advertising of such companies as Alberto-Culver and Revlon has been a major factor in their success, but one must remember that these companies also offered good products and developed good distribution. Effective advertising alone would not compensate for bad products or other faults in the marketing program. In fact, it can even hasten the demise of a bad product. If the firm's offering is sound, however, advertising can make a significant contribution in the marketing process.

Various lists have been drawn up of the conditions under which advertising is likely to be a significant factor in the marketing process. The contribution of company advertising is likely to be greater:

> When buyer awareness is minimal
> When industry sales are rising rather than remaining stable or declining
> When the product has features normally not observable to the buyer
> When the opportunities for product differentiation are strong
> When primary instead of secondary motives can be tapped

when advertising is most effective.

However, these are general guides rather than specific tools for determining the potential contributions of advertising in the total marketing program. They do not replace an evaluation of what advertising might accomplish in specific situations.

DEFINING ADVERTISING GOALS

The wide diversity of occasions for the use of advertising makes it essential that management develop a clear conception of what it specifically wants to achieve through its over-all advertising effort as well as through particular advertising compaigns down to specific ads. Defining goals is the key requirement for effective advertising planning and the measurement of results.

Yet the failure to define advertising goals is the leading deficiency, according to two recent studies.[10] Different company executives who are asked about the objective(s) of their company's current advertising program usually supply widely different answers. The sales manager may see the advertising as designed to provide his salesmen with talking points. The advertising manager may hope that advertising will increase short-term sales. The company president may think of advertising as building up the company's name and reputation. While all of these purposes may be involved, the lack of an explicit statement of advertising goals, understood and accepted by all the parties, reduces the effectiveness of the company's advertising effort.

Advertising goals should be stated as specifically as possible. The statement "to create brand preference" is much weaker than "to establish 30

[10] See Russell H. Colley, ed., *Defining Advertising Goals* (New York: Association of National Advertisers, 1961); and H. D. Wolfe, J. K. Brown, and G. C. Thompson, *Measuring Advertising Results,* Studies in Business Policy, No. 102 (New York: National Industrial Conference Board, 1962).

per cent preference for brand X among Y million housewives by next year." The more specific the goals, the better they are able to guide the creative team in developing an effective message and copy, the media team in chosing media vehicles, and the research team in evaluating achievement.

What are some of the marketing communication goals which companies may adopt and toward which advertising may contribute? Colley distinguished fifty-two different communication goals which might be used in connection with a single advertisement, a year's campaign for a product, or a company's entire advertising philosophy. Some the possible goals are:

Announce a special reason for "buying now" (price, premium, etc.)
Build familiarity and easy recognition of package or trade mark
Place advertiser in position to select preferred distributors and dealers
Persuade prospect to visit a showroom, ask for a demonstration
Build morale of company sales force
Correct false impressions, misinformation and other obstacles to sales
Implant information or attitude regarding benefits and superior features of brand [11]

WHAT ARE THE MAJOR DECISIONS CALLED FOR IN ADVERTISING?

A clear-cut statement of advertising goals facilitates, although it cannot be expected to resolve, the complex decision problems still remaining in putting together an advertising program. The following major decisions are called for in the realm of advertising:

How much should be spent for over-all company advertising?
What message and mode of presentation should be used?
What media should be used?
How should the advertising be phased during the year?
What are the best methods for knowing what the advertising is accomplishing?

The remainder of this chapter will present major concepts and techniques for dealing more effectively with these problems.

Size of the Advertising Budget

The major recurrent advertising decision facing firms is how much to spend on advertising. This of course should be treated in principle as part of the larger questions of how much to spend on total promotion and what share and tasks should be assigned to advertising within the promotional program. However, there is some value in considering this question separately. Firms have embraced a variety of approaches to determine the advertising budget. The purpose of this section is to examine some of the practices and theories. First, however, it will help to look at the magnitude of advertising expenditure in the United States.

[11] Colley, *op. cit.,* pp. 62-68.

In 1964, the total amount spent on advertising exceeded $14.0 billion —more than was spent by industry for new construction ($13.0 billion) and approximately half of the pretax profits reported by manufacturing concerns ($25.3 billion).[12] Comparative statistics for the postwar period are shown in Table 18-1. One of the interesting things to note is that ad-

TABLE 18-1
**Annual volume of advertising in U.S. by media
(millions of dollars)**

	1950	1955	1960	1964 (prelim.)
Newspaper	$2,076	$3,088	$ 3,703	$ 4,069
Magazines	515	729	941	1,108
Television	171	1,025	1,590	2,236
Radio	605	545	692	830
Direct mail	803	1,299	1,830	2,171
Other	1,540	2,508	3,176	3,567
Grand total	$5,710	$9,194	$11,932	$13,981
Index of advertising expenditure	100	161	209	245
Index of industrial production	100	129	145	176

Source: *Statistical Abstract of the U.S., 1965*, pp. 774, 848.

vertising outlays grew at a more rapid rate than industrial production, indicating the dramatic shift from a production-oriented to a market-oriented economy. It should also be noted that the various media enjoyed different rates of growth, television having shown the greatest increased usage and radio the least.

While almost all firms advertise, the top 125 national advertisers account for as much as one-fifth of all national advertising. Comparative expenditures for the top ten national advertisers are given in Table 18-2.[13]

[12] *Statistical Abstract of the U.S., 1965*, pp. 497, 741, and 848.

[13] Companies vary greatly in their classification of advertising expenses, and this makes direct comparison of different budgets over time or space somewhat hazardous. Some companies use the advertising account as a catchall; it may be charged with expenses for the printing of salesmen's manuals and company stockholder reports, for community chest contributions, for publicity, for point-of-purchase displays, and other miscellaneous items. Some companies list only media billings, while others include the salaries of people in the advertising department and packaging and other costs. It cannot be concluded, therefore, that two companies in the same industry reporting a million-dollar budget for advertising are really spending anywhere near the same amount. A step toward improving this situation has been taken by the editors of *Printers' Ink* in collaboration with several hundred advertisers. They have divided advertising and pseudoadvertising charges into three lists: a white list for charges belonging in the advertising account; a black list for charges that do not belong in the advertising account although frequently put there; and a gray list for borderline charges that sometimes belong in the advertising account and sometimes in others, depending on the circumstances. See "What Charges Belong in the Advertising Account? Guide to Allocation of the Advertising Appropriation," *Printers' Ink*, August 23, 1957, p. 99.

TABLE 18-2

The top ten national advertisers in 1964 *

Rank	Advertiser	Total †	Magazines
1	Procter & Gamble	$160,569,576	$ 8,713,416
2	General Motors Corp.	151,156,442	45,861,192
3	Ford Motor Co.	89,072,943	23,294,410
4	General Foods Corp.	85,147,187	6,798,105
5	Bristol-Myers Co.	81,350,265	14,505,404
6	R. J. Reynolds Tobacco Co.	74,069,462	7,613,967
7	American Home Products	70,775,647	5,790,106
8	Chrysler Corp.	70,642,520	11,608,069
9	Colgate-Palmolive Co.	70,142,663	7,215,470
10	Lever Brothers Co.	67,189,420	7,279,761

* A national advertiser is defined as one who sells outside a single locality.

† This column exceeds the sum of the five others because a number of media are omitted.

Among the most prominent advertisers are automobile companies and soap companies. Procter & Gamble itself accounts for over 1.2 per cent of the nation's advertising bill. Companies in different industries and even within the same industry often have different ideas on the best media mix. Procter & Gamble puts about 92 per cent of its high budget into television, while Colgate-Palmolive and Lever Brothers put about 85 per cent into television. The automobile companies show some confidence in outdoor advertising, while the other companies tend to stay away from this medium.

Companies also have vastly different ideas on the percentage of the sales dollar they should put toward advertising. Drug and cosmetics manufacturers spend an average of 20 cents out of each sales dollar, tobacco companies spend about 6.7 cents, appliance manufacturers spend about 1.4 cents, and oil companies spend about 0.3 cents.[14] The intriguing question is how they arrived at these rates.

COMMON METHODS FOR SETTING THE ADVERTISING BUDGET

Firms use a variety of methods for setting the advertising budget. Four of the more common ones are described below.

"AFFORDABLE" METHOD. Many companies set the advertising budget on the basis of what they think the company can afford, although this is never defined. As told by one advertising executive:

> Why it's simple. First I go upstairs to the controller and ask how much they can afford to give us this year. He says a million and a half. Later, the boss comes to me and asks how much we should spend, and I say "Oh, about a million and a half." Then we have an advertising appropriation.[15]

Setting budgets in this manner is tantamount to saying that the relationship between advertising costs and advertising effects is not understood

[14] *Advertising Age,* August 31, 1964, p. 36.

[15] Quoted in Daniel Seligman, "How Much For Advertising?" *Fortune,* December 1956, p. 123.

TABLE 18-2 (Cont.)
(total expenditures and allocation to five media)

Television	Radio	Newspapers	Outdoor
$148,783,200	$ 729,000	$ 2,046,662	$ —
32,638,960	16,801,000	41,266,990	10,288,136
20,328,740	11,313,000	20,979,915	8,256,070
70,874,800	206,000	6,660,506	98,249
61,519,710	3,386,000	1,465,598	194,711
46,450,000	12,326,000	7,229,619	—
59,422,430	2,771,000	1,388,023	—
24,391,470	13,274,000	18,913,146	1,925,163
59,208,720	1,790,000	1,429,073	—
58,365,220	65,000	1,365,409	7,406

Source: *Advertising Age*, June 28, 1965, pp. 1, 46, 48.

and therefore the company might as well spend what is available after meeting other expenses. Joel Dean suggested that everything above a respectable return on capital could be spent on advertising, "since excess earnings have low utility to management as such, compared with the *possible* contribution of continuous advertising to the eternal life for the firm." [16]

The basic weaknesses of the affordable approach are that it entirely overlooks the firm's current opportunities in the use of advertising, it militates against the long-range planning of advertising investment, and it leads to further opportunism in the dividing of the budget among company products and sales territories.

PERCENTAGE-OF-SALES METHOD. Many companies prefer to set their advertising expenditures at a specified percentage of sales (either current or anticipated) or of the sales price. A railroad company executive said:

> We set our appropriation for each year on December 1 of the preceding year. On that date we add our passenger revenue for the next month, and then take 2% of the total for our advertising appropriation for the new year.[17]

Automobile companies typically budget a fixed percentage for advertising based on the planned price for each car, and oil companies tend to set the appropriation as some fraction of a cent for each gallon of gasoline sold under their own label.

A number of advantages are claimed for this method, in the absence of evidence on the actual productivity of advertising. First, the percentage-of-sales method means that advertising expenditures are likely to vary with what the company can "afford." This pleases the more financial-minded members of top management who feel that expenses of all types should

[16] Joel Dean, *Managerial Economics* (Englewood Cliffs, N.J.: Prentice-Hall, Inc., 1951), p. 368.

[17] Albert Wesley Frey, *How Many Dollars for Advertising* (New York: The Ronald Press Company, 1955), p. 65.

bear a close relation to the movement of corporate income and the business cycle. Second, this method encourages management to think in terms of the relationship between advertising cost, selling price, and profit per unit. Third, the method encourages competitive stability to the extent that competing firms tacitly agree to let advertising follow a close percentage of their sales. In this way, they avoid advertising wars which can be quite costly, especially where industry demand is inelastic with respect to total industry expenditures on advertising.

In spite of these advantages, the percentage-of-sales method has little to justify it on theoretical grounds. It uses circular reasoning in viewing sales as the cause of advertising rather than as the result. It leads to an appropriation set by the availability of funds rather than the opportunities. It discourages experimentation with countercyclical advertising or aggressive spending. The dependence of the advertising budget on year-to-year fluctuations in sales militates against the planning of long-range advertising programs. The method does not provide a logical basis for the choice of a specific percentage, except what has been done in the past, or what competitors are doing, or what the costs will be. And finally it does not encourage the constructive development of advertising appropriations on a product-by-product and territory-by-territory basis, but instead suggests that all allocations be made at the same percentage of sales.

COMPETITIVE-PARITY METHOD. Still other companies prefer to set their budgets specifically to match competitors' outlays; i.e., to maintain competitive parity. This thinking is illustrated by the executive who asked a trade source: "Do you have any figures which other companies in the builders' specialties field have used which would indicate what proportion of gross sales should be given over to advertising?" [18]

Two arguments are advanced for this method. One is that competitors' expenditures represent the collective wisdom of the industry. The other is that maintaining a competitive parity helps to prevent advertising wars.

Neither of these arguments is valid. There are no a priori grounds for believing that competition is using more logical methods for determining outlays. Advertising reputations, resources, opportunities, and objectives are likely to differ so much among companies that their budgets are hardly a guide for another firm to follow. Furthermore, there is no evidence that appropriations based on the pursuit of competitive parity do in fact stabilize industry advertising expenditures.

Knowing what competition is spending on advertising is undoubtedly useful information. But it is one thing to know this and another to follow it blindly. This method suffers from virtually all the criticisms made of the earlier methods.

OBJECTIVE-AND-TASK METHOD. The previous methods called for setting the size of the total advertising budget first. Allocations for products and territories would then be made. But it might be more logical to build up desired advertising appropriations by products and territories until a total is arrived at. This sum would be the desired advertising expenditure level. The procedure employed is the objective-and-task approach.

[18] Frey, *op. cit.*, p. 49.

Each executive is asked to prepare an advertising budget request according to the following three-step procedure: (1) he first defines his advertising objectives as specifically as possible, preferably as numerically stated goals; (2) he then outlines the tasks which must be performed to achieve his objectives; and (3) he then estimates the cost of performing these tasks. The sum of these costs is his appropriation request. The sum of all the appropriation requests is the desired advertising expenditure level.

This method has a certain logic and appeal that accounts for its growing popularity among advertisers. As far back as 1926, it was used by a number of large firms, including Borden's, General Electric, and Fuller Brush.[19] Its popularity grew during World War II because firms were required to justify advertising expenditures for the purposes of taxes and contracts. Postwar surveys by *Printers' Ink*—a long-time advocate of this method—and *Industrial Marketing* document that this method is the most widely used one.[20]

In its simplified form, this method suffers from one major flaw: *it fails to question whether an objective is worth pursuing in terms of the cost*. If, for example, the objective is to increase brand awareness by 20 per cent during the coming year, the required advertising expenditure may be too far out of line with the likely contribution of this objective to profits. The real need is to evaluate objectives in the light of their costs and to choose among the more productive objectives. With this particular modification, the objective-and-task approach reduces to the logically sound method of setting expenditures by reference to estimates of marginal revenues and costs.

THEORETICAL APPROACHES TO SETTING THE ADVERTISING BUDGET

Criticism of the methods currently used by business to determine the advertising appropriation does not suggest that a superior practical method is available. Indeed, the objective-and-task method, in its refined form, represents about as reasonable a procedure as can be feasibly employed at the present time. It is superior to the other methods in that it builds up the total appropriation on the basis of specific advertising objectives, which are evaluated in terms of the cost of attaining them. Yet it pays to consider what would constitute theoretically satisfactory methods in order to appreciate the shortcomings of existing methods and to indicate the major remaining hurdles.

In entering the realm of theory, it will be assumed that the company has accurate information on customer response to advertising and on the possible reactions of competitors to alternative expenditure levels. The reader may think this is the heart of the problem and that the solution is straightforward. Unfortunately, this is not the case. The empirical problems are not the only impediment to improved decision making in advertising; there are some difficult conceptual problems as well.

A major conclusion will be that the appropriate model varies with the advertising situation. The following situations are explored:

[19] Paul Nystrom, ed., *Marketing Handbook* (New York: The Ronald Press Company, 1948), p. 1235.
[20] *Printers' Ink*, December 28, 1946, p. 26; *Industrial Marketing*, January 1956, p. 65.

Direct-action advertising, no competitive reactions

Delayed-action advertising, no competitive reactions

Delayed-action advertising, competitive reactions

Delayed-action advertising with accompanying marketing-mix adjustments, competitive reactions

DIRECT-ACTION ADVERTISING, NO COMPETITIVE REACTIONS. A fairly substantial amount of daily advertising is designed to provoke an immediate buying response rather than a long-term attitudinal change. It is exemplified by retail-sponsored newspaper advertisements, featuring a special sale of dresses starting 9:00 o'clock Monday morning; by manufacturer-sponsored magazine coupon ads, offering a new kitchen gadget or automobile accessory; by direct-mail advertising, offering Christmas cards or magazine subscriptions at special prices; and by private newspaper advertisements, announcing the sale of apartments, dogs, and used musical instruments. In all these cases, the advertiser is not aiming for any brand buildup or cumulative impact. His aim is a sale. Those who respond to the advertisement in the next few days are about all who will ever respond, and the advertisement and its message lose all value in a couple of days. The advertisement amounts to a pure expense to be charged off against the incremental sales it generates.

The advertiser's problem is how much should he spend on these direct promotions. In this situation he generally does not have to worry about competitive reactions. The scale of his effort to stimulate the sales of dresses, kitchen gadgets, and other goods will hardly be noticed by the many other vendors of this merchandise. His incremental sales (ΔS) will diminish the sales of each of the n competing vendors by an average of $\Delta S/n$, an amount that will hardly matter when n is large.

The theoretical solution to this type of problem has already been described in Figure 12-3. Given the shape of the sales/advertising curve, the profit-maximizing advertising outlay can be determined. As for the shape itself, the evidence is mixed.[21] Many analysts hold, however, that the sales/advertising curve is S-shaped. This curve implies initial advertising economies of scale. According to Joel Dean:

> Larger appropriations may make feasible the use of expert services and more economical media. More important than specialization usually are economies of repetition. Each advertising attack starts from ground that was taken in previous forays, and where no single onslaught can overcome the inertia of existing spending patterns, the hammering of repetition often overcomes skepticism by attrition.[22]

Dean has also spelled out the reasons why diminishing returns to advertising can be expected eventually to set in:

> Presumably the most susceptible prospects are picked off first, and progressively stiffer resistance is encountered from layers of prospects who are

[21] For an excellent summary and evaluation of studies bearing on the shape of the sales/advertising curve, see Julian L. Simon, "Are There Economies of Scale in Advertising?" *Journal of Advertising Research,* June 1965, pp. 15-20.

[22] Joel Dean, *op. cit.,* p. 357.

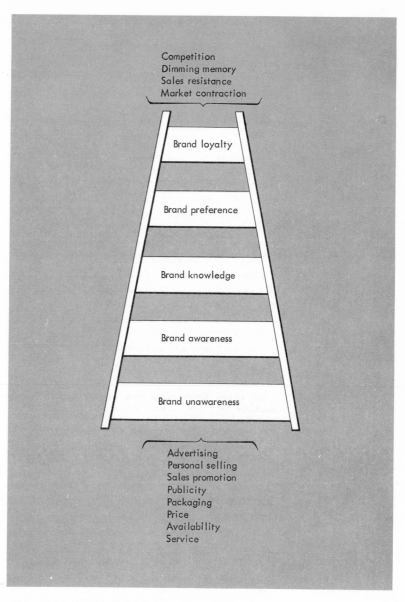

Competition
Dimming memory
Sales resistance
Market contraction

Brand loyalty

Brand preference

Brand knowledge

Brand awareness

Brand unawareness

Advertising
Personal selling
Sales promotion
Publicity
Packaging
Price
Availability
Service

FIGURE 18-2
The brand loyalty ladder

more skeptical, more stodgy about their present spending patterns, or more attached to rival sellers. The rise may also be caused by progressive exhaustion of the most vulnerable geographical areas or the most efficient advertising media. Promotional channels that are ideally adapted to the scale and market of the firm are used first.[23]

DELAYED-ACTION ADVERTISING, NO COMPETITIVE REACTIONS. A substantial amount of advertising is undertaken not in the expectation of provoking quick sales but in the hope of gradually building up a brand

[23] *Ibid.,* p. 358.

preference among consumers. Each individual advertisement is expected to play a small role in a larger scheme of gradually moving prospective buyers up the brand-loyalty ladder pictured in Figure 18-2. The philosophy might read:

> Those who are unaware of the brand name should be made aware; those who know the name should learn the merits; those who know the merits should be persuaded to prefer the brand; and those who prefer the brand should not be permitted to waver.

The ladder tapers at the higher reaches because fewer people are found on each successive rung. The company's objective is to transform the tapering in the other direction.

The figure shows that advertising is but one of several forces available to the company to induce movement up the ladder. In addition, other forces, such as competition and dimming memories, are continuously acting to effect movement down the ladder.

How many dollars should the company spend to improve the attitude of prospective buyers toward the purchase of its product(s)? Several factors need to be considered. First is the *relative ease of moving people through the various states* (called the *sales response rate*). The greater the ease, the lower is the expenditure required to bring about a given increase in profits. Second is the *actual number of prospects in each state*. If all the prospects already have strong brand loyalties, the particular brand would be close to its saturation level. The greater the saturation level, the lower is the required appropriation for profit maximization. Third is the *relative effectiveness of the different promotional tools*. The greater the relative effectiveness of advertising, the greater should be its usage. Fourth is the *rate at which the countervailing forces erode the existing brand franchise in the absence of advertising* (called the *sales decay rate*). The greater the sales decay rate, the greater is the required appropriation for maintaining sales and profits.

These factors have been combined by Vidale and Wolfe into an explicit mathematical model describing sales response to advertising.[24] Their basic equation is:

$$\frac{dS}{dt} = rA \ \frac{M - S}{M} - \lambda S$$

where

S = rate of sales at time t

$\dfrac{dS}{dt}$ = increase in the rate of sales at time t $\quad\Big\}$ variables

A = rate of advertising expenditure at time t

r = sales response constant (defined as the sales generated per advertising dollar when $S = 0$)

M = saturation level of sales $\qquad\qquad\qquad\Big\}$ parameters

λ = sales decay constant (defined as the sales lost when $A = 0$)

24 M. L. Vidale and H. B. Wolfe, "An Operations-Research Study of Sales Response to Advertising," *Operations Research*, June 1957, pp. 370-81.

The right-hand side of the equation shows that the increase in the rate of sales depends on several factors: it will be greater for higher levels of r, A, and $(M - S)/M$, and it will be smaller for higher levels of λ and S. In words, the equation says that the increase in the rate of sales, dS/dt, is equal to the response of sales per dollar of advertising, r, times the number of advertising dollars being spent, A, reduced by the percentage of unsaturated sales, $(M - S)/M$, less the sales being lost through decay, λS.

The main significance of the Vidale-Wolfe model is that it brings together and relates some useful concepts for the analysis of advertising's effect on sales. Less importance should be attached to the specific equational form, since it requires much more testing. It should also be appreciated that the conceptualization takes place at a highly aggregated level. More recent mathematical work on the effect of advertising on sales has incorporated several behavioral refinements.[25]

Because delayed-action advertising is calculated to have carry-over effects,[26] it should be considered as a problem in investment theory rather than a problem in short-run optimization. The company is patiently building up an asset, customer good will, which will yield benefits through time. The analytical tools appropriate for making investment decisions have come to be called *capital budgeting*.[27]

Suppose a company is trying to choose between the four long-range advertising expenditure programs shown in Table 18-3. The company's problem is to decide which investment program would yield the highest rate of return. Program B calls for twice the outlays in program A. Programs C and D call for the same total dollar outlay as in A, although for a different scheduling of the component amounts. In particular, C represents a philosophy of conservatively building up advertising good will. Its main advantage is that if the company finds advertising is not very productive, not so much will have been lost. Program D shows more confidence in the advertising objectives and a desire to establish a large market share as soon as possible. The time pattern in program D makes it more expensive than C because the company parts with a greater amount of dollars in the current period and thereby loses the opportunity to earn interest on these dollars.

The key to the choice among the four programs is their respective rates of returns, but these cannot be determined from an inspection of just the

[25] The work of Alfred A. Kuehn deserves special attention in this connection. Kuehn developed a complicated model where company sales are a function of the percentage of customers with brand loyalty and the rate of decay in this brand loyalty; the percentage of customers not committed to this firm or its main competitor; the size and rate of growth of the total market; the relative influence of product characteristics, price, advertising, and distribution as selling influences; the relative influence of the *interaction* of product characteristics and advertising as a selling influence; and the relative share and effectiveness of this company's advertising expenditure. Using this model to describe company sales for the case of two-firm competition, he went on to derive an optimal advertising decision rule using capital budgeting theory. See Alfred A. Kuehn, "A Model for Budgeting Advertising," in *Mathematical Models and Methods in Marketing*, eds. Frank M. Bass, *et al.* (Homewood, Ill.: Richard D. Irwin, Inc., 1961), pp. 302-53.

[26] See Chapter 12, p. 270.

[27] For a lucid exposition of capital budgeting theory, see Harold Bierman, Jr., and Seymour Smidt, *The Capital Budgeting Decision* (New York: The Macmillan Company, 1960).

TABLE 18-3

**Four alternative advertising investment programs
(in thousand of dollars)**

Year	A	B	C	D
1	$1,000	$2,000	$ 600	$1,400
2	1,000	2,000	800	1,200
3	1,000	2,000	1,000	1,000
4	1,000	2,000	1,200	800
5	1,000	2,000	1,400	600
	$5,000	$10,000	$5,000	$5,000

investment costs. It is necessary to estimate how these expenditures will alter the number of persons on each rung of the brand ladder. Only the highest two rungs spell significant sales for the company. We have to know how long a newly loyal person is likely to remain loyal. We have to know how many present "brand preferers" and "brand loyals" will drop out of the picture. But these estimates are very difficult to make.

The same measurement problems face the company when it considers long-range investments in research laboratories, community good will, and employee fringe benefits. All of these investments must compete for funds on the basis of their prospective yields. Yet the yields are unknown. Until better ways are found to estimate the time-distributed sales impact of delayed-action advertising, the investment approach will provide only general concepts rather than specific guidance for setting the advertising budget.

DELAYED-ACTION ADVERTISING, COMPETITIVE REACTIONS. In the previous discussion, it was assumed implicitly that the firm could choose an advertising expenditure level without worrying about competitive reactions. This is a valid assumption where there are many competitors, none of whom is large; or where it is difficult for companies to know what others are spending for advertising. But in many other situations firms know what others are spending and try to maintain a competitive parity. In these situations, a firm must take competitive reactions into account in determining the optimal advertising appropriation.

Suppose a particular firm has been spending $1 million a year on advertising, and is considering whether to maintain this expenditure rate next year, double it, or triple it. Assume that the rest of the industry has also been spending $1 million a year. Assume that the particular firm now enjoys a 50 per cent share of the market. Table 18-4 has been developed to show the market share consequences of different reactions by competition to this firm's decision. In all three cases it is assumed for simplicity that market shares are proportional to advertising expenditure shares.

Case A shows competition spending $1 million regardless of what the firm does. If the firm spends $3 million, it will account for three-fourths of total industry advertising and achieve a three-fourths share of the market. Case B shows competition ready to increase its appropriation by half of the amount of the firm's increase. Again the firm's share of the market will rise, but not as rapidly. Case C shows competition maintaining

TABLE 18-4

469

*Advertising
Decisions*

**Impact of company advertising on sales given different competitive reactions
(in thousand of dollars)**

		Firm's advertising expenditure (A_1)	Competitors' advertising expenditure (A_2)	Firm's market share (S_1)	Competitors' market share (S_2)
A. No reaction	{	$1,000	$1,000	.50	.50
		2,000	1,000	.67	.33
	{	3,000	1,000	.75	.25
B. Competitors match half the increase	{	$1,000	$1,000	.50	.50
	{	2,000	1,500	.57	.43
	(	3,000	2,000	.60	.40
C. Competitors match the full increase	{	$1,000	$1,000	.50	.50
	{	2,000	2,000	.50	.50
	(	3,000	3,000	.50	.50

a competitive parity in advertising expenditure. The market therefore remains equally divided between the firm and the rest of its competitors.

Given these estimates, should the firm spend $1 million, $2 million, or
$3 million? The reader will quickly realize that the table does not provide
sufficient information for answering this question. For one thing, the
market shares would first have to be translated into profits, if the criterion
is profit maximization. For another thing, it is necessary to determine
which case applies; in other words, probabilities have to be estimated for
the various possible competitive reactions.

Table 18-4 is only a first approximation. Competitive interaction is a
much more dynamic phenomenon. Competitors may adopt a wait-and-see
attitude toward whatever advertising spending level is adopted by the
firm. If the firm's sales increase significantly, competitors may expand their
own expenditures; otherwise they may do nothing. Or competitors may
retaliate in other ways. They may react with a price cut, an expansion
of their sales force, or a sales promotion. Each type of reaction would
have a different effect on market share. Finally, even if competitors did
react by increasing their advertising expenditures, it makes a difference
how they spend the additional funds; that is, whether they develop a new
copy approach, move toward broader media coverage, or adopt some
other strategy. A game-theoretic approach seems almost too simple to
catch the flavor of the uncertainties and issues posed by competition; it
represents only a small beginning in trying to conceptualize the relevant
issues.

DELAYED-ACTION ADVERTISING WITH ACCOMPANYING MARKETING-MIX
ADJUSTMENTS AND COMPETITIVE REACTIONS. Up to now, it has been implicitly assumed that the firm's advertising expenditure decision would
not affect the other elements in its marketing mix. But this is patently
unrealistic. The firm cannot vary its advertising budget without making
corresponding adjustments in the other marketing instruments. It may have
to expand the sales force, change the product price, and make other adjustments.

The great difficulties in estimating the payoffs of alternative advertising budgets now become clear. Each contemplated advertising budget level requires a uniquely adjusted company marketing mix. Competitors react not simply with an adjusted advertising budget but with their own adjusted marketing mix. Therefore, estimates are required of the joint payoffs of many different possible competitive marketing-mix confrontations. Estimates are also required of the probabilities governing the possible strategy reactions by competition. Neither the payoffs nor the probabilities are easy to estimate. The hurdles help to explain why most firms are reconciled to using quite simple rules for setting the advertising appropriation.

Message Design

The effect of advertising on sales is not simply a function of *how much* is spent. Even more important may be *how* it is spent: specifically, what is said, how it is said, where it is said, and how often it is said. Two companies in the same industry may budget the same amount for advertising, offer essentially the same product, and charge the same prices; yet they may enjoy quite different sales, owing in no small way to important differences in their creative advertising strategies.

Most of the *statistical* studies of the effect of advertising on sales or attitude have tended to neglect the creative factor. Creative strategies are thought of as unique, unquantifiable entities. Some analysts rationalize the omission of creative factors in their study of advertising's effect with the argument that all large advertising agencies are equally creative and therefore differences in individual campaigns tend to "wash out." But it is precisely the differences in individual campaigns which advertisers want to note and exploit. The consequence of leaving out the creative factors is that a substantial part of the original movements of market shares remain "unexplained."

A new type of analysis recently reported by the Schwerin Research Corporation claims to have overcome the neglect of the creative factor.[28] A five-year study of 67 different television campaigns led to the development of a multiple regression formula which purportedly "explained" 73 per cent of the fluctuations in market shares. What is most interesting is that one of the three independent variables was a measure of the effectiveness of message content. The Schwerin study's major conclusion is that a campaign's quality is far more important than the number of dollars spent. Whether this is actually so, there is no doubt that differences in creative strategy are a very important factor in advertising success.

"Creative strategy" refers to what the advertiser decides to say (message content) and how he decides to say it (message presentation). The decisions on where he says it and how often are discussed later in this chapter.

[28] See "New Study Tells TV Advertisers How Advertising Builds Sales and Share of Market," *Printers' Ink,* May 8, 1964, pp. 27-38. The Schwerin Company is a well-known research firm providing advertising effectiveness studies for clients, with an emphasis on the pretesting of television commercials.

The advertiser's first task is to decide what image and message he wants to give his product. The number of possibilities for any product is typically large. The advertiser of a detergent can emphasize its power, consistency, gentleness, or sudsiness. The advertiser of a typewriter can emphasize the product's sturdiness, precision, action, or extra features. Through brainstorming or other creative techniques, a great number of possible themes can be generated.

The advertiser will not want to make too many claims for his product. Buyers will neither remember nor believe too many claims. There is a need for message focus if there is to be audience recall and believability. The problem is to find the one or two best themes on which to base the message.

The starting point for developing the theme is the intended audience, for an audience stands at the end of every communication process. The advertiser must define whether and to what extent he is trying to reach influencers or decision makers or buyers or users, if these customer roles differ. He must define basic needs and wants as they relate to the product. He must determine what might be said about the product that will stimulate favorable attitudes or behavior.

Thus the prelude to determining message content is marketing research into the buying process and into buyer motives, attitudes, and behavior. The detergent manufacturer must discover whether the young housewife is concerned more with the gentleness or with the cleaning power of detergents. The typewriter manufacturer must find whether the college student is more concerned with the sturdiness or the action of typewriters.

The buyers' motives and attitudes can be studied in a variety of ways, including questionnaires, psychological tests, and depth interviewing. The object is to determine what motives and attitudes seem most prominent in buyers and what themes are likely to be most effective. Three different examples of research will be described.

ADVERTISING THEMES FOR SOAP. Some years ago, Social Research, Inc., presented the following theme recommendations for the advertising of laundry soaps based on a study of upper-lower- and lower-middle-class housewives in the 24-45 age bracket:

A. Product themes
  1. Don't rely on technical motives.
  2. Make the properties of the product intriguing.
B. Use themes
  1. Do not belabor the familiar in the same old way.
  2. Give a positive promise, present it ingeniously—supported by appeals to other motives.
C. Personal satisfaction themes
  1. Do not show cliché women.
  2. Indicate the product is for real women.
  3. Do not deny the reality of the housewife's problems.
D. Interpersonal satisfaction themes
  1. Do not contribute to feelings of isolation—highly circumscribed focus on the product without reference to others.

2. Broaden the housewife's scope—imply that household performance has a wider meaning.[29]

Franklin B. Evans wanted to see whether these motivational findings about soap actually constituted good advice to advertising planners of soap campaigns. To answer this question, he made a content analysis of 60-odd full-page soap advertisements of nine different brands appearing in *Good Housekeeping* magazine and rated each advertisement on the extent to which it embodied the thematic recommendations of Social Research, Inc. He then correlated the advertisements' ratings on content with their success in creating attention and found a definite and significant positive relationship. Subject to certain qualifications, he concluded:

> From this pilot study it is suggested that there is evidence that the application of motivational research findings can have value for increasing the reader's attention to the advertisements . . . good motivational research may produce new creative ideas for selling products, show people's purchase motives, and aid in creating greater readership of a specific advertising campaign.[30]

ADVERTISING THEMES FOR LIQUOR.   Jean Stoetzel reports a study in which consumers were asked to rank ten different liquors in order of preference but without stating the basis for their preference.[31] The problem was to find a small set of preference factors which would explain a good deal of the observed rankings. A factor analysis [32] of the data revealed that the sweetness versus strength of the liquor was the first consideration leading to different preferences. The implication is that there are two distinct segments of the market for liquor: those who prefer sweet liquors and those who prefer strong liquors. Advertising touting the sweetness of a brand would appeal to some of the consumers and alienate the others. The factor of second greatest importance was cost; a good deal of the preference orderings were correlated with cost. This implied that consumers associated the quality and desirability of a liquor with its cost, and this had obvious implications for the advertising message. The last significant factor was a regional one. Consumer preferences for different liquors showed a homogeneity by region. This implied that it might be desirable to differentiate product offerings and advertising messages by region.

ADVERTISING THEMES FOR APPLES.   A few years ago, the Washington State Apple Commission was trying to decide which of two advertising themes for apples appealed more to housewives. One theme stressed the various *uses* of apples (baked apples, fruit combination salads, other

29 Social Research, Inc., Chicago, Ill., "Study of Motivations Relating to Soaps and Detergents," done for the Chicago *Tribune,* August 1953. Reported in Franklin B. Evans, "Motivation Research and Advertising Readership," *Journal of Business,* April 1957, pp. 141-46. Reprinted by permission of The University of Chicago Press.

30 Evans, *op. cit.,* p. 146.

31 Jean Stoetzel, "A Factor Analysis of the Liquor Preferences of French Consumers," *Journal of Advertising Research,* December 1960, pp. 7-11.

32 Factor analysis is a multivariate technique for finding a small set of basic, mutually independent factors which account for a good deal of the correlations among a large set of variables.

dishes), while the other emphasized the *healthful* qualities of apples (building of strong bodies, dental benefits, etc.). Peter Henderson and his associates set up an elaborate experimental design to find the answer.[33] The experiment involved a total of 72 self-service food stores in six midwestern cities and ran for 16 weeks. Care was exercised to hold constant or take into account the simultaneous effects of price, competitive advantage, in-store conditions, delayed effects of time, and a number of other extraneous variables. An analysis of the final sales results revealed that the apple use theme was significantly more effective in promoting sales than the health theme.

MESSAGE PRESENTATION

In spite of the many possible themes for promoting any product, companies in the same industry often settle on the same theme. Many makers of detergents emphasize the whitening power of their detergent, and many cigarette makers emphasize the quality of their tobacco. The similarity of themes implies that these companies may all be going after the largest segment of the market. Their research has shown the same theme to be the most effective with this segment.

Where this tendency to use the same theme is found, the creative burden is shifted from message content to message presentation. The relative creative quality of the advertising campaign is no longer so much what is said but how it is said.

Advertising agencies are specialists in the translation of themes into effective copy and art work. Within the agency, the creative man is responsible for finding the words, pictures, symbols, and colors that lend potency to the chosen theme. He is backed by technical specialists in color, typography, art, and layout. His first task is to search for presentational angles and ideas. They may come from company symbols, product characteristics, market and motivational research findings, popular culture artifacts, and other objects. There is usually no shortage of presentational ideas. The problem is to find an *inspired* one.

There is an almost infinite number of ways to present a theme to an audience. Consider the following three presentations of the *status theme:*

> The first case involved a printed advertisement for Lord Calvert bearing the arresting caption "Some of my best friends are status seekers." The advertisement showed a distinguished gentleman in formal dress riding a bicycle and smiling at a bottle of Lord Calvert. The advertisement went on to read: "They drive foreign cars, eat in fancy French restaurants, wear custom-made clothes, drink Lord Calvert. They're status seekers, all right. So am I, I guess. I drink Lord Calvert too. . . ."
>
> The second advertisement, also printed, sought to arouse interest in the Conn Organ among the status-seeking middle class. Its caption read: "Are you in the Upper Middle Socio-Economic Level with 2.7 Children? If you answer 'Yes,' . . . you are in very good shape indeed. . . . By this time you have already earned a home, a car (or two), a power mower, and a life membership in the National Geographic. . . ."
>
> The third example involved a manufacturer of premium-priced sausages

[33] See Peter L. Henderson, James F. Hind, and Sidney E. Brown, "Sales Effects of Two Campaign Themes," *Journal of Advertising Research,* December 1961, pp. 2-11.

who wanted to stimulate frankfurter purchases among the middle class. The chosen theme was: "It's smart to serve frankfurters when entertaining." The agency executed this theme in an illustration showing "fashionable and smart looking people serving franks on bright and gay social occasions."

Some of these advertisements reflect a recent transition from a hard sell to a wry sell in advertising copy.[34] But no one has yet proved that humor sells more of a product, or develops a more favorable brand attitude, or even leads to more recall. Nor has anyone proved that believability, another highly touted presentation virtue, makes advertising more effective.[35]

Presentation does not stop with developing an inspired idea for putting across the basic theme. The idea must be embodied in headlines, artwork, and copy. A minor rearrangement or alteration of elements within the advertisement can often change its attention value by several points.[36] The very size of the advertisement makes some unknown difference in its attention-getting value and a known difference in its cost.[37] The use of four-color illustrations instead of black and white increases both selling effectiveness and cost. In an analysis of factors associated with high readership of business advertisements, the two most prominent factors turned out to be pictorial color and size, both of which are mechanical variables rather than content variables in the advertisements.[38]

Creative people should work hand in hand with marketing researchers to produce effective advertisements. Research can provide themes and presentational ideas before the advertisement is prepared and evidence of effectiveness after the advertisement is prepared. Research can often provide do's and don'ts not always obvious to the creative people. This is dramatically illustrated in connection with advertisements prepared for foreign countries. While some national differences are disappearing, the world's markets still present a crazy-quilt pattern of tastes and customs. For example, an American advertiser of soap in Pakistan would be committing suicide to use a "sex appeal" approach. Many American-composed advertisements for the Chilean market make the mistake of showing stereotyped men in big sombreros riding burros. Research indicates that advertising copy directed to Scandinavian countries should appeal to logic rather than fancy, and copy directed to Spain should use big colored illustrations and terse copy.[39]

[34] See *Time*, April 23, 1965, pp. 87-88.

[35] John C. Maloney, "Is Advertising Believability Really Important?" *Journal of Marketing,* XXVII (October 1963), 1-8.

[36] John S. Coulson, "Research Must Predict Ad's Effect," *Advertising Age,* September 30, 1963.

[37] If potential customers noted all advertisements, advertisers would buy the smallest space or time required to carry their message. But people patronize mass media for other reasons than the advertisements. The larger advertisements, therefore, have a better chance to catch attention. They are also more impressive. But how large should advertisements be? The money spent on a few large advertisements could buy many smaller ones. Some published studies indicate that as advertisement size is increased, advertising effectiveness increases but at a declining rate. For a summary of studies, see Simon, *op. cit.,* p. 18.

[38] Dik Warren Twedt, "A Multiple Factor Analysis of Advertising Readership," *Journal of Applied Psychology,* June 1952, pp. 207-15.

[39] These illustrations are found in S. Watson Dunn, *The International Handbook of Advertising* (New York: McGraw-Hill Book Company, 1964).

A very important part of the advertising job is to decide on the best channels or media for carrying the advertising message to the intended audience. The major media categories, and their relative importance, were shown in Table 18-1. The fact that major advertisers have quite different ideas on the most effective combination of media was highlighted in Table 18-2. Here the problem of media choice will be considered more closely. The selection of the major media categories will be examined first and then the selection of specific media vehicles within these categories. The problem of scheduling the advertising will be examined in the following section.

CHOOSING AMONG MAJOR MEDIA CATEGORIES

The extent to which the firm should use television, radio, newspapers, magazines, and other media depends on at least three factors: the target audience's media habits, the media's effectiveness for presenting the product, and the relative costs of the major media categories.

The target audience's media habits provide the first clue to major media selection. Taking an extreme case, a company producing toys for preschoolers—and believing that the children rather than their parents should be reached—would stay away from newspapers, magazines, and radio. The only medium that reaches preschoolers, and reaches them effectively, is television.

The product itself is an important factor in choosing among media. The major media categories have different potentialities for demonstration, visualization, explanation, believability, and color. A product like Polaroid cameras is best advertised through live demonstrations in the television medium. A product like dresses, where color might be important, is best advertised in a color medium like magazines.

The cost of the different media is also important. Television is a very expensive medium whereas newspapers are on the inexpensive side. Yet what is ultimately important is not the absolute cost differences but audience size and composition in relation to these costs. On a per-thousand cost basis, it may be cheaper to reach buyers through television than newspapers.

Within every company and agency are found some executives who strongly favor a particular medium as best for the product and who would like to see all company funds diverted to it. Other executives are found who have no media convictions and favor spreading the funds over all media. Both approaches can be wasteful. It is just as much a mistake to put all the funds in a second-rate medium as to put part of the funds in third- and fourth-rate media. Better allocations will develop as media data and media theory improve.

SELECTING SPECIFIC MEDIA VEHICLES

The first stage of analysis should result in a decision on how much to spend in each media category. The decision may be made, for example, to spend approximately $240,000 out of a $1 million advertising budget on magazines. But which magazines? And how many issues of each should be purchased?

At this point, the media planner generally turns to several shelves of small-print studies on various magazines. A study by Audits and Surveys Company, Inc., provides information on the size and characteristics of the audiences of five magazines.[40] Different volumes put out by Standard Rate and Data provide cost and other information on hundreds of magazines. The prices are given for different ad sizes, color options, ad positions, and quantities of insertions. Most magazines offer quantity discounts varying with the number of purchased insertions for the year.

THE COST-PER-THOUSAND CRITERION. Using this information, media planners try to calculate the *cost per thousand persons* reached by the particular vehicle. If a full-page, four-color advertisement in *Life* costs $50,000 and *Life's* measured readership is 16.7 million persons, then the cost of reaching each 1,000 persons would be $3. The same advertisement in the *Saturday Evening Post* may cost $30,000 but reach only 7.5 million persons, at a cost-per-thousand of $4. The media planner would rank the various magazines according to cost-per-thousand and place advertisements in those magazines with the lowest cost-per-thousand.

The cost-per-thousand criterion, at least in its simple form, has come under increasing attack, and justifiably so. Perhaps its major fault is that it uses the figure for the total readership of the magazine instead of that fraction of the total readership representing potential customers. A million readers of a magazine amounts to a million possible exposures, but its *exposure value* depends on how closely the readers' characteristics match those of the buyer target groups. For a baby lotion advertisement, the exposure value might be one million if all the readers are young mothers and zero if all the readers are old men. The exposure value depends as much on audience composition as on audience size.[41]

The second weakness has to do with the concept of an exposure. It is used in the sense of a potential exposure rather than an actual exposure. An exposure is said to take place to all readers of *Life* when an advertisement is placed in *Life*. In point of fact, only a fraction of *Life's* readers will perceive the advertisement, a smaller fraction will grasp the message, and a still smaller fraction will be impressed positively. The ultimately desirable unit would be the number of target readers who both see and are motivated by the advertisement. But this unit is almost impossible to estimate.

A third weakness of cost-per-thousand is that it neglects qualitative differences which might exist in the editorial image and impact of different magazines. Even if two magazines reach the same number of target buyers, an advertisement may take on more believability, prestige, or other qualities in one magazine than the other.

A fourth weakness of cost-per-thousand is that it tends to be used in an average sense rather than in a marginal sense. If a magazine literally retained its lowest cost-per-thousand standing independently of how much it was used, then logically the entire magazine budget should be spent on it. In reality, the magazine may quickly lose its cost-per-thousand advantage

[40] *The Audiences of Five Magazines* (New York: Newsweek, Inc., 1962).
[41] For a suggested way to adjust audience size for audience composition characteristics, see Philip Kotler, "Toward an Explicit Model for Media Selection," *Journal of Advertising Research,* March 1964, pp. 34-41.

as more advertisements are placed in it. This is because successive-issue ads are seen largely by the same people with possibly diminishing impact in relation to what could be achieved by exposing new readers to the advertisement through new magazines.

COMPUTERIZED MEDIA SELECTION.[42]   Media selection is the one area in advertising where advanced mathematical methods have received publicity for "practical" breakthroughs. *Advertising Age* on October 1, 1962, carried the headline "Y&R, BBD&O Unleash Media Computerization" and later Batten, Barton, Durstine, and Osborn, Inc., sponsored full-page newspaper and magazine advertisements reading "Linear Programming showed one BBD&O Client how to get $1.67 worth of effective advertising for every dollar in his budget."

Other large advertising agencies have taken up the challenge and are experimenting with a number of different models. Often they find that a particular route leads them nowhere. William Moran at Young and Rubicam said his company spent two years trying a linear programming approach and finally gave up, happily, because they found something better.[43]

Three major types of models have been proposed to help in the selection or improvement of media plans. They are linear programming, "high assay," and simulation. They are briefly described below in order to show the diversity of mathematical approaches possible with the same problem.

Linear programming.   The first model, linear programming, seems like a natural format for analyzing the media selection problem. It is applied to problems where several *constraints* need to be satisfied. The constraints in media selection are the size of the advertising budget, the minimum and maximum usages of specific media vehicles and media categories, and the desirable minimum exposure rates to different target buyers. The choice of a "best" plan requires the specification of an *effectiveness criterion.* In media selection, the criterion is the number of effective exposures. Programming is a mathematical method for discovering the media mix that will maximize the number of effective exposures.

Figure 18-3 shows the linear programming statement of the media selection problem, both in abstract form and in example form.[44] The problem is stated as one of trying to find the combination of media which maximizes the number of effective exposures subject to the constraints. In the sample problem, the total advertising budget is $500,000, and at least $250,000 must be spent on medium one. Medium one gives 3,100 (in thousands) effective exposures with each use and costs $15,000. It is

[42] This section is adapted from Philip Kotler, "Computerized Media Selection: Some Notes on the State of the Art," in *Occasional Papers in Advertising* (Babson Park, Mass.: American Academy of Advertising, The Babson Institute, January 1966), pp. 45-52.

[43] William T. Moran, "Practical Media Decisions and the Computer," *Journal of Marketing,* XXVII (July 1963), 26-30.

[44] For additional readings, see James F. Engel and Martin R. Warshaw, "Allocating Advertising Dollars by Linear Programming," *Journal of Advertising Research,* September 1964, pp. 42-48; and Robert D. Buzzell, "Batten, Barton, Durstine & Osborn, Inc.: Use of Linear Programming Methods in the Selection of Advertising Media," chap. 5 in his *Mathematical Models and Marketing Management* (Cambridge, Mass.: Division of Research, Graduate School of Business Administration, Harvard University, 1964), pp. 157-79.

$$\text{Maximize } E = e_1 X_1 + e_2 X_n + \ldots + e_n X_n \left.\right\} \begin{matrix}\text{effectiveness}\\\text{function}\end{matrix}$$

$$\text{Subject to } \quad c_1 X_1 + c_2 X_2 + \ldots + c_n X_n \leq B \left.\right\} \begin{matrix}\text{budget}\\\text{constraint}\end{matrix}$$

$$c_1 X_1 + c_2 X_2 \qquad\qquad \leq B_1 \left.\right\} \begin{matrix}\text{media category}\\\text{usage constraint}\end{matrix}$$

$$X_1 \qquad\qquad\qquad \geq k_{1L}$$
$$X_1 \qquad\qquad\qquad \leq k_{1U}$$
$$X_2 \qquad\qquad \geq k_{2L}$$
$$X_2 \qquad\qquad \leq k_{2U}$$
$$\vdots \qquad \vdots \qquad \vdots$$
$$X_n \geq k_{nL}$$
$$X_n \leq k_{nU}$$

individual medium usage constraints

Sample statement:

$$E = 3,100X_1 + 2,000X_2 + \ldots + 2,400X_n$$

$$15,000X_1 + 4,000X_2 + \ldots + 5,000X_n \leq 500,000$$

$$15,000X_1 \qquad\qquad\qquad\qquad \geq 250,000$$

$$X_1 \qquad\qquad\qquad \geq 0$$
$$X_1 \qquad\qquad\qquad \leq 52$$
$$X_2 \qquad\qquad \geq 1$$
$$X_2 \qquad\qquad \leq 8$$
$$\vdots \qquad \vdots \qquad \vdots$$
$$X_n \geq 6$$
$$X_n \leq 12$$

where:

E = total exposure value (number of rated exposures)

e_i = exposure value of one ad in medium i

X_i = number of ads placed in medium i

c_i = cost of one ad in medium i

B = total advertising budget

B_1 = part of advertising budget

k_{1L} = minimum number of units to purchase of medium i

k_{1U} = maximum number of units to purchase of medium i

FIGURE 18-3
Linear programming model for media selection

possible to buy anywhere between 0 and 52 advertisements in medium one over a year's time. The other values are similarly interpreted. Given these concrete values, a particular mathematical routine is used to find the precise optimum solution to the problem as stated.

The problem as stated, however, contains a number of artificialities arising out of the linear programming formulation. The four most important limitations are:

Linear programming assumes that repeat exposures have a constant marginal effect.

It assumes constant media costs (no discounts).

It cannot handle the problem of audience duplication.

It fails to say anything about when the advertisement should be scheduled.[45]

High assay. The second model, called "high assay" by Young and Rubicam, is based on a sequential rather than simultaneous media selection process. The basic idea is to start with the media available in the first week and select the single best buy. After this selection is made, all

[45] Some of these limitations can be remedied through nonlinear programming.

the remaining media choices are re-evaluated to take into account audience duplication and potential media discounts. Then a second selection is made for the same week if the *achieved* exposure rate for the week is below the *optimal* rate. The latter is a complex function of several marketing and media variables. This continues until the optimal exposure rate for the week is reached, at which point new media choices are considered for the following week. The cycling process is shown in flow diagram form in Figure 18-4.

The sequential procedure used in this model is appealing. In principle, high assay represents an improvement over linear programming because:

It develops a schedule simultaneously with the selection of media.

It handles the audience duplication problem.

It handles the media discount problem.

It incorporates theoretically important variables such as brand switching rates and multiple exposure coefficients.

It is hard to evaluate the model beyond this point because its details have not been made public.

Simulation model.   Both the linear programming model and the high assay model are of the optimizing type. A *simulation model* has been developed by the Simulmatics Corporation which does not profess to find the "best" media plan but rather to estimate the exposure value of any given media plan.[46] The model consists of a sample universe of 2,944 make-believe media users representing a cross section of the American population by sex, age, type of community, employment status, and education. Each individual's media choices are determined probabilistically as a function of his socioeconomic characteristics and location in one of 98 American communities. A particular client media schedule is exposed to all the persons in this hypothetical population, according to Figure 18-5. As the simulation of the year's schedule progresses, the computer tabulates the number and types of people being exposed. Summary graphs and tables are automatically prepared at the end of the hypothetical year's run, and they supply a multidimensional picture of the schedule's probable impact. The advertiser examines these tabulations and decides whether the audience profile and the reach and frequency characteristics of the proposed media schedule are satisfactory.

Simulation complements rather than competes with the two previous models, in that it is not a model for finding the best schedule but rather a means of developing the dynamic reach and/or frequency characteristics over 52 weeks of a given schedule. The major limitations which should be borne in mind when media simulation is considered are:

The method does not include an over-all effectiveness function. Instead it yields a multidimensional picture of impact.

The method lacks a procedure for finding better schedules.

The representativeness of the hypothetical population is always suspect.

[46] See *Simulmatics Media-Mix: Technical Description* (New York: The Simulmatics Corporation, October 1962).

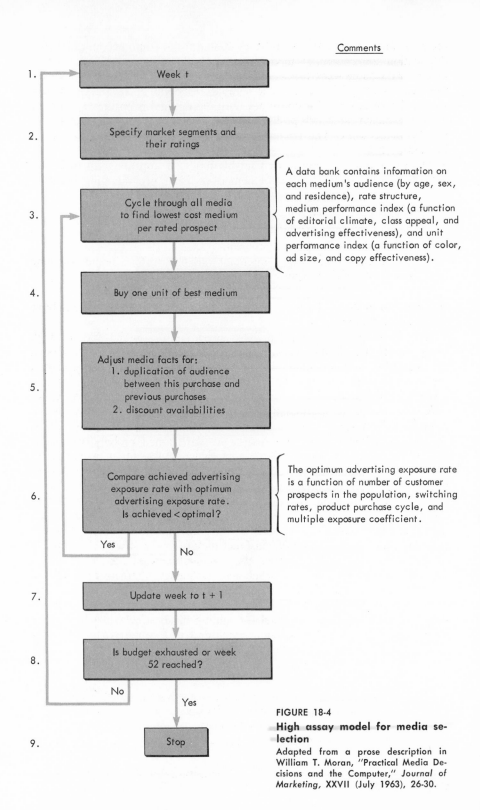

Comments

1. Week t

2. Specify market segments and their ratings

3. Cycle through all media to find lowest cost medium per rated prospect

A data bank contains information on each medium's audience (by age, sex, and residence), rate structure, medium performance index (a function of editorial climate, class appeal, and advertising effectiveness), and unit performance index (a function of color, ad size, and copy effectiveness).

4. Buy one unit of best medium

5. Adjust media facts for:
   1. duplication of audience between this purchase and previous purchases
   2. discount availabilities

6. Compare achieved advertising exposure rate with optimum advertising exposure rate. Is achieved < optimal?

The optimum advertising exposure rate is a function of number of customer prospects in the population, switching rates, product purchase cycle, and multiple exposure coefficient.

Yes   No

7. Update week to t + 1

8. Is budget exhausted or week 52 reached?

No   Yes

9. Stop

FIGURE 18-4

High assay model for media selection

Adapted from a prose description in William T. Moran, "Practical Media Decisions and the Computer," *Journal of Marketing*, XXVII (July 1963), 26-30.

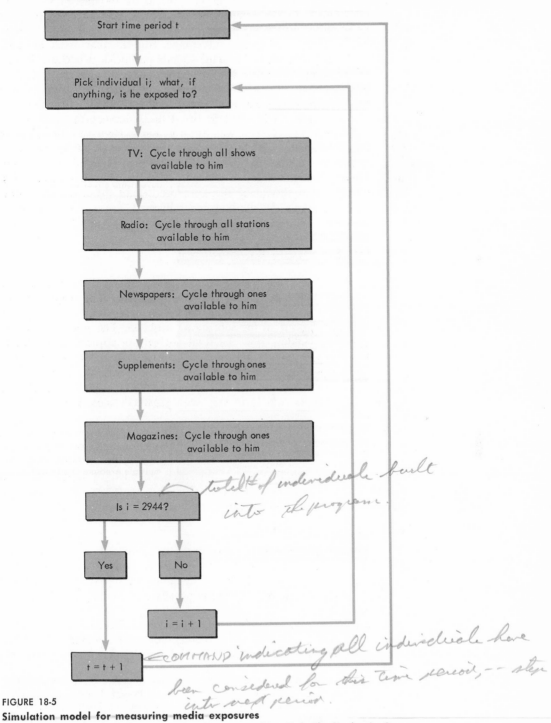

FIGURE 18-5

Simulation model for measuring media exposures

Redrawn from *Simulmatics Media Mix: Technical Description* (New York: The Simulmatics Corporation, October 1962), p. 2.

Computerized media selection models should be thought of as an aid rather than a substitute for executive judgment. The computer can produce or "test" in a matter of hours a media plan that formerly might have taken days or weeks. Speed is its chief advantage. But the plan itself must be regarded only as a starting point. This sounds paradoxical because it may represent the optimum solution to a mathematical programming statement of the media problem. But it must be remembered that the programming statement is somewhat artificial in the weights used and the constraints set up. The media planner will want to bring his judgment to bear on the quality of the plan as a whole as well as on its parts. He may want to revise some of the specifications in the programming statement of the problem. A great advantage of the computer is that new plans can be quickly generated to show the significance of changes made in problem specifications. The final media plan should be the joint product of the machine's ultra-logical mind and man's imagination and judgment.

Timing of Advertising Expenditures

The advertising problem involves much more than just determining the budget, message, and media. The scheduling of the advertising through the year can make a crucial difference in the total impact.[47]

There are two aspects to the scheduling problem. The *macroscheduling* problem involves deciding how the total advertising appropriation should be allocated over the year. If the total advertising appropriation is $1,200,-000, it would generally *not* make sense to spend $100,000 every month, independently of the seasonality of sales. Nor is it necessarily desirable to vary the expenditures exactly in step with seasonal sales. How should it be done?

The *microscheduling* problem involves the best media phasing of, say, a monthly advertising appropriation. If the plan called for thirty radio spot announcements in September, should all thirty be scheduled on one particular day, or should one be sponsored on each of thirty days? In other words, what phasing of the spot announcements would give the best impact? The macroscheduling problem shall be dealt with first.

MACROSCHEDULING PROBLEM

The seasonal scheduling of advertising expenditures is an especially subtle problem where the advertising is expected to have delayed as well as immediate effects. Two quite different approaches have been proposed for helping the decision maker determine seasonal timing for the advertising budget.

Jay Forrester of the Massachusetts Institute of Technology advocates the use of his "industrial dynamics" methodology.[48] He would treat sales/advertising interactions as a *closed-loop, information-feedback system*. He

---

[47] The question of scheduling advertising over the business cycle is not discussed here. A good discussion is found in Roger Blackwell, "Potentials of Contra-Cyclical Advertising," *Business and Government Review*, University of Missouri, September-October 1963, pp. 22-32.

[48] See Jay W. Forrester, "Advertising: A Problem in Industrial Dynamics," *Harvard Business Review*, March-April 1959, pp. 100-110.

visualizes advertising as having a lagged impact on consumer awareness; awareness in turn has a lagged impact on factory sales; and factory sales has a lagged impact on advertising expenditures. He suggests that these time relationships be studied for the individual company and formulated mathematically into a digital computer simulation model. The parameters for this model would be estimated from company operations data supplemented by executive judgment where necessary. Alternative timing strategies would be simulated on the computer in an effort to assess their differential impacts on company sales, costs, and profits. Forrester's main objective is to find a timing pattern for advertising expenditures which minimizes costly fluctuations in production and distribution.

Alfred A. Kuehn of Carnegie Tech has developed a model to explore how advertising should be "timed" for frequently purchased, highly seasonal, low-cost grocery products. He adopted the following product and market assumptions for illustrative purposes:

> The long-run demand for the particular product is stable. The product, however, is subject to a seasonal demand. The timing and magnitude of industry advertising expenditures does not affect the seasonal demand. A company's advertising only influences the company's share of industry demand. Advertising has no effect on retailers. There are two dominant competitors who both develop their timing patterns independently of each other, but optimally. The gross margin from sales is constant throughout the year (no price or cost changes). Other brand merchandising variables, such as product characteristics, retail availability, and competing brand prices, maintain a constant relative appeal to consumers throughout the sales cycle.[49]

Kuehn showed that the appropriate timing pattern depends upon the *degree of advertising carry-over* and the *amount of habitual behavior in customer brand choice*. Carry-over refers to the rate at which the effect of an advertising impulse decays with the passage of time. A carry-over of .75 per month means that the current effect of a past advertising impulse is 75 per cent of its level last month, whereas a carry-over of only .10 per month means that only 10 per cent of last month's effect is carried over. Habitual behavior, the other variable, indicates how much brand holdover there is due to habit, inertia, or brand loyalty, independently of the level of advertising. High habitual purchasing, say .90, means that 90 per cent of the buyers repeat their purchase of the brand regardless of the marketing stimuli.

Kuehn found that in the benchmark case of no advertising carry-over and no habitual purchasing, the decision maker is justified in using a percentage-of-sales rule in budgeting advertising. The optimal timing pattern for advertising expenditures coincides with the expected seasonal pattern of industry sales. But, if there exists any advertising carry-over and/or habitual purchasing, the percentage-of-sales budgeting method is not optimal. In all these cases, it would be better to "time" advertising to lead the sales curve. The peak in advertising expenditures should come before the expected peak in sales, and the trough in advertising expenditures should come before the trough in sales. Lead time should be greater,

---

[49] See Alfred A. Kuehn, "How Advertising Performance Depends on Other Marketing Factors," *Journal of Advertising Research,* March 1962, pp. 2-10.

the higher the carry-over. Furthermore, advertising expenditures should be steadier, the greater the extent of habitual purchasing.

Kuehn's and Forrester's complex models show that the best seasonal allocation of advertising expenditures is not at all obvious. Simple decision rules, such as spreading the appropriation evenly over the year or varying it in a constant proportion to expected sales, can be inefficient and wasteful in many circumstances.

MICROSCHEDULING PROBLEM

Suppose the firm has decided to buy thirty radio spot announcements in the month of September. Which thirty? There is an almost unlimited number of possible schedulings. Among the possible patterns are: one each day at the same time; one each day, always at a different time; two every other day; five every sixth day; ten on September 1, five on September 2, ten on September 29, and five on September 30; all thirty on September 15; and so on.

One way to classify the multitude of possible patterns is shown in Figure 18-6. The left side shows that the sum of advertising messages for the month can be concentrated in a small part of the month ("burst" advertising), dispersed continuously throughout the month, or dispersed intermittently throughout the month. The top side shows that the advertising messages can be beamed with a level frequency, a rising frequency, a falling frequency, or an alternating frequency. The advertiser's problem is to decide which of these twelve general patterns would represent the most effective phasing for the sum of his messages.

The most effective pattern depends upon the advertising communciation objectives in relation to the nature of the product, target customers, distribution channels, and other marketing factors. Some cases are described below.

> A retailer wants to announce the preseason sale of skiing equipment. He recognizes that only certain people will be interested in the message. Furthermore he recognizes that the target buyers only need to hear the message once or twice to know whether they are interested. His objective is to maximize the *reach* of his message, not the *repetition*. He decides to concentrate the messages on the days of the sale at a level rate, but varying the time of day to avoid the same audiences. He uses pattern (1).
>
> A shampoo manufacturer wants to advertise a new brand, and has already filled the channels with an adequate stock. His primary objective is to establish strong brand awareness. He believes that consumer learning and confidence are best built up through continuous and increasing exposure, rather than concentrated exposure to company ads. He likes the idea of building up the frequency because this allows him to re-employ the funds if something changes in the situation and also lets him develop a teasing type of campaign. He uses pattern (6).
>
> A muffler manufacturer-distributor wants to keep his name before the public. Yet he does not want his advertising to be too continuous because only 3 to 5 per cent of the cars on the road need a new muffler at any given time. He has therefore chosen to use intermittent advertising. Furthermore, he recognizes that Fridays are pay days for many potential buyers, and this would influence their interest in replacing a worn-out muffler. So he sponsors a few messages on a midweek day and more messages on Friday. He uses pattern (12).

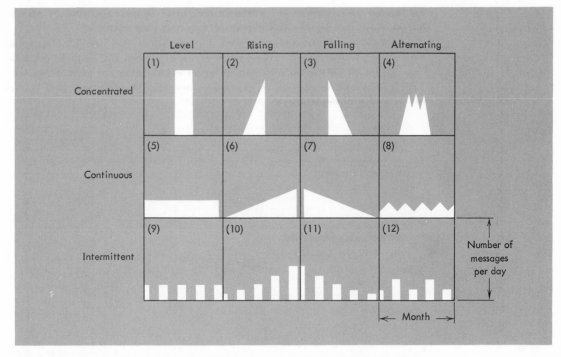

FIGURE 18-6
Classification of advertising time patterns

Often the issue is that of determining how much repetition a particular buyer group should be exposed to if the particular message is to be effective. A low number of repetitions may be a waste, because memorable brand identification can hardly be established. According to Lucas and Britt:

> It can be reasoned that introductory advertisements make too weak an impression to initiate much interest in buying. Succeeding advertisements may sometimes be more effective by building up already established weak impressions to the action level.[50]

A high number of repetitions may also be a waste if they do not bring about any further increase in awareness, message familiarity, or positive brand feelings; the number is positively harmful if they bring about boredom or irritation.

The problem for the manufacturer of a new brand is to succeed in intruding this brand into the consciousness of the prospective buyer as rapidly and memorably as possible. Some authorities feel that the new brand makes a greater dent on the buyer's consciousness if he is exposed to five commercials on one day than to one commercial on each of five successive days. Several psychological studies bear on this point, dating all the way back to the pioneering research of Herman Ebbinghaus of

[50] Darrell B. Lucas and Steuart Henderson Britt, *Measuring Advertising Effectiveness* (New York: McGraw-Hill Book Company, 1963), p. 218.

Berlin before the turn of the century. Ebbinghaus used nonsense syllables and other devices to study the relation between repetition and learning.[51] Among his conclusions were:

> Generally speaking, the greater the number of repetitions, the better the retention.
>
> A residual amount of learning always remains after a long period of time, but forgetting is very rapid in the period of time immediately after learning.
>
> Information learned more quickly is retained better than information learned more slowly.
>
> Repetition beyond the point needed to retain makes possible longer conscious memories.

The second and third points especially would support the case for pulsating the advertising in bursts, where quick and permanent learning is being sought. These findings have generally been supported in subsequent research.

The phasing of the thirty radio spots affects target buyers' awareness, recall, brand attitude, and even believability. Many psychological studies of the effect of the time pattern on these psychological dimensions already exist, and these should be examined whenever possible. However, the phasing of the thirty spots cannot be optimally solved without considering simultaneously the phasing of the other media involved in the campaign. Different media tend to reach overlapping audiences.[52] Therefore, if the media plan is to deliver a specified mix of reach and frequency, all media must be scheduled simultaneously, a problem that is still to be solved satisfactorily.

Measuring Advertising Effectiveness

Good *planning* and *control* of advertising depend critically on measures of advertising effectiveness. Yet the amount of fundamental research on advertising effectiveness is appallingly small. According to Jay Forrester:

> I doubt that there is any other function in industry where management bases so much expenditure on such scanty knowledge. The advertising industry spends 2% or 3% of its gross dollar volume on what it calls "research," and even if this were really true research, the small amount would be surprising. However, I estimate that less than a tenth of this amount would be considered research plus development as these terms are defined in the engineering and product research departments of companies . . . probably no more than ⅕ of 1% of total advertising expenditure is used to achieve an enduring understanding of how to spend the other 99.8%.[53]

[51] Herman Ebbinghaus, *Memory* (New York: Columbia University Press, 1913).

[52] "Seymour Banks did a straightforward analysis of the duplicated readership of multiple magazines and multiple issues. With his method and media sample, four insertions in a single magazine produced only about 1.65 as much unduplicated readership as does a single insertion in that magazine. Placing the ad in several magazines also results in duplicated readership." Quoted from Julian L. Simon, "Are There Economies of Scale in Advertising?" (unpublished first draft, 1963), p. 35.

[53] Forrester, *op. cit.*, p. 102.

As suggested by Forrester, most of the measurement of advertising effectiveness is of an applied nature, dealing with specific advertisements and campaigns. Of the applied part, most of the money is spent by agencies on *pre-testing* the given advertisement or campaign before launching it into national circulation. Relatively less tends to be spent on *post-testing* the effect of given advertisements and campaigns.

The research techniques used to measure advertising effectiveness vary with what the advertiser is trying to accomplish. Robert Lavidge and Gary Steiner proposed how techniques might vary with the particular buyer behavioral state the advertiser is seeking to influence. Their list is shown in Table 18-5.

TABLE 18-5
Advertising and advertising research related to the model

Related behavioral dimensions	Movement toward purchase	Some types of promotion or advertising relevant to various steps	Some research approaches related to steps of greatest applicability
	PURCHASE ↑		
CONATIVE—the realm of motives. Ads stimulate or direct desires.	↑ CONVICTION	Point-of-purchase; retail store ads; deals; "last-chance" offers; price appeals; testimonials	Market or sales tests; split-run tests; intention to purchase; projective techniques
	↑ PREFERENCE		
AFFECTIVE—the realm of emotions. Ads change attitudes and feelings.	↑ LIKING	Competitive ads; argumentative copy; "image" ads; status, glamor appeals	Rank order of preference for brands; rating scales; image measurements, including check lists and semantic differentials; projective techniques
	↑ KNOWLEDGE		
COGNITIVE—the realm of thoughts. Ads provide information and facts.	↑ AWARENESS	Announcements; descriptive copy; classified ads; slogans; jingles; sky writing; teaser campaigns	Information questions; playback analyses; brand awareness surveys; aided recall

Source: Robert J. Lavidge and Gary A. Steiner, "A Model for Predictive Measurements of Advertising Effectiveness," *Journal of Marketing,* XXV (October 1961), 61.

The buyer behavioral change of ultimate interest to the advertiser is the act of purchase. One would therefore expect to find that research on the "sales effect" of advertising predominates. Actually, sales effect research tends to be meager in comparison with "communication effect" research, namely, research to determine the effect of given advertising on buyers' knowledge, feelings, and convictions. Many advertisers feel that the links between sales and advertising are too tenuous, complicated, and long-term to permit measuring the direct impact. They feel instead that the more short-term communication effects of given advertisement should be measured.[54]

COMMUNICATION-EFFECT RESEARCH

This research seeks to discover whether the advertising is achieving the intended communication effects. There are various ways to pre-test or post-test the communication effectiveness of an advertisement or campaign.[55] Perhaps the simplest method is to ask individual potential buyers to describe their reactions to a given advertisement, or parts of the advertisement, such as the copy, typography, or subjects. This is called *opinion research*. A variant of this method is to bring potential buyers into a group and stimulate a discussion of the advertisement. In some agencies, the moderator withdraws from the room in order to avoid affecting the discussion and observes from a control booth equipped with a one-way mirror.

One major limitation of opinion research is that it provides no measurement of the attention-getting value of the advertisement or how long it is remembered. A number of *memory tests* have been developed to get at these later variables. For example, a new advertisement may be shown to a respondent for three seconds and then laid aside. The respondent is then asked to recall whatever he can about the advertisement. At some later period he may be contacted again and asked to recall to the best of his ability elements in the advertisement.

Memory tests are more frequently used to check on advertisements after they have appeared in commercial media. Memory tests break down into two categories, those stressing *recognition* and those stressing *recall*.

The *recognition test,* probably the most widely used of copy tests, consists of a respondent thumbing through a magazine and reporting which advertisements he recognizes from a previous exposure. Various precautions are taken to minimize the respondent's inaccuracies and biases.

The *recall test* is less subject to careless response, in that the subject is not shown any advertisements. In the *unaided* form of the test, he is asked, "What advertisements have you noticed recently?" In the *aided* form of the test he is asked, "Do you remember the ———— advertisement?" High recall is taken as a sign of the advertisement's superior attention-getting power.

In addition to these standard methods, some agencies now use electronic devices to record voluntary and involuntary reactions to various advertisements and parts of advertisements. Several years ago, a pioneer in the field, the Leo Burnett Agency of Chicago, established a creative research workshop, located only 50 yards from copywriters and artists on the same floor.[56] A rough idea for an advertisement can be brought in for testing at 10:00 A.M. and results obtained by 4:00 P.M. the same day. One device is called a "psycho galvanometer" and it is attached to two fingers

[54] "ANA: Probing Ad Effectiveness," *Printers' Ink,* May 8, 1964, pp. 43-44. Eighty per cent of the national advertisers interviewed ranked communications research as very promising or promising, while only 33 per cent ranked operation research-statistical methods in this way.

[55] For an excellent survey of research methods, see Lucas and Britt, *op. cit.*

[56] Emmett Curme, "Burnett Men Get Fast Test Results via Busy Creative Research Workshop," *Advertising Age,* September 10, 1962, pp. 80-81.

of the left hand of respondents. It records changes in blood pressure which may indicate strong and involuntary feelings toward the advertisement. Another device is a tachistoscope, a machine that flashes on an advertisement (or parts of an advertisement) for a variable amount of time until the consumer becomes able to identify the advertisement's basic features. The laboratory also includes an "electronic rating scale," which respondents switch to the right or left depending upon their likes and dislikes. Finally other devices, such as a stereo-dominance rater, size-distance tunnel, and Blurmeter, are used, primarily for the testing of copy on packages. In addition to these electronic devices, the laboratory is equipped with booths, round tables, one-way mirrors, and tape recorders.

Undoubtedly advertising agencies are showing a growing technical ability to measure the communication effects of specific advertising. Nevertheless the marketing manager should be aware of many conceptual and methodological pitfalls in measuring communication effects. In fact, critics of this research, such as Kristian S. Palda and Charles K. Ramond, have recently questioned whether these measures of communication impact are any more reliable than measures of sales impact.[57] The basic problem is that measured changes in awareness and attitude can be the result of many factors other than advertising: word-of-mouth influence, product usage, price changes, and so forth. To attribute buyer attitude changes entirely to advertising may be as much a leap of faith as attributing sales entirely to advertising.[58]

SALES-EFFECT RESEARCH

Communication-effect advertising research undoubtedly helps advertisers improve the quality of message content and presentation, but it reveals very little about how much sales may be affected, if at all. What *sales* conclusion can the advertiser draw in learning that his recent campaign has increased brand awareness by 20 per cent and favorable brand attitudes by 10 per cent? What has the advertiser learned about the productivity of his advertising dollars and therefore how much to spend?

The marketing executive would much prefer to know the direct effect on sales. But the prevailing attitude is well illustrated in the following quotation:

> Generally, it is not considered reasonable to use sales results as a basis of measuring advertising effectiveness, except where advertising is the dominant sales force, where other factors affecting sales remain fairly constant, and where the results of the advertising are quickly reflected in shipments and billings. Where these conditions do not exist, other yardsticks must usually be used.[59]

This may, however, represent too restrictive a view of the circumstances under which the sales effects of advertising may be measurable. It may

[57] Kristian S. Palda, "The Hypothesis of a Hierarchy of Effects: A Partial Evaluation," *Journal of Marketing Research,* February 1966, pp. 13-24; Charles K. Ramond, "Must Advertising Communicate to Sell?" *Harvard Business Review,* September-October 1965, pp. 148-61.

[58] For different positions on the controversy of sales versus communication-effects research, see "Measuring Advertising Effectiveness," *Sales Management,* February 1965, pp. 65-77.

[59] H. D. Wolfe, *et al., op. cit.,* p. 7.

be possible to eliminate certain disturbing factors through experimental design and to allow for other disturbing factors through advanced model building and multivariate statistical analysis.

Much of the unsatisfactory quality of many past studies of the relationship between advertising and sales stems directly from the use of unsatisfactory models and/or data. A common fault is to try to measure current sales as a function of current advertising, as if all advertising were of the "week-end specials" type. This completely overlooks the carry-over effects of advertising. Current sales are better interpreted as a function of the past and current pattern of advertising expenditure.

Another fault is to carry out the investigation as a simple regression instead of a multiple regression. Where historical (nonexperimental) data are being used, it is absolutely essential to incorporate measures of the levels of other independent variables during the period, if the net effect of advertising is to be isolated. Still another fault is that most of the investigations employ a single-equation model, thus ignoring some important feedback relationships between sales and advertising. These relationships could only be expressed in a model consisting of a system of simultaneous equations.

The sales effect of advertising will always be more difficult to measure in certain types of situations than others. Advertising effectiveness is probably easiest to measure in mail-order situations and hardest to measure in mass consumer brand advertising.[60] Effectiveness will also remain more difficult to measure where the data are historical rather than experimental.

Two studies have been moderately successful in isolating the sales effect of mass consumer attitude advertising using historical data. In both cases, however, the number of disturbing variables was few. The first study consisted of a single-equation, multiple-regression study of the effect of advertising on the sales of Lydia Pinkham's Vegetable Compound between 1908 and 1960. Kristian Palda, the investigator, gave the following reasons for choosing this product:

> The firm spent a very high proportion (40-60 per cent) of its sales on advertising. Furthermore, it did not employ many of the customary "parameters" of marketing action: sales force, credit, discounts, frequent changes in package, point of purchase efforts, special offerings, etc. The assumption thus could safely be made that advertising had a measurable effect on Pinkham's sales. The product itself, Lydia Pinkham's Vegetable Compound, had no close substitutes. Competitors' marketing action was not, therefore, a complicating factor to be coped with. By the same token certain allied issues, such as the geographic distribution of Pinkham's marketing effort, could be ignored. During the detailed examination which followed the decision to delve into the Pinkham case, further factors were discovered which added to the simplicity of the ultimate quantitative analysis. On the whole the conclusion was reached that there was remarkable stability (between

[60] Some industrial advertisers claim that it is harder to measure the effectiveness of industrial advertisements than consumer advertisements because there is no equivalent to store audit services; there is no equivalent to consumer panel services; industrial media audience data are poorer; and it is harder to pre-test advertisements on a sample of industrial purchasers. See J. Wesley Rosberg, "Resolved: That Industrial and Consumer Research Require Different Techniques," *Proceedings, 8th Annual Conference of the Advertising Research Foundation* (New York: Advertising Research Foundation, October 2, 1962).

Palda's major objective was to assess the existence, importance, and measurability of the carry-over effects of Pinkham's advertising. As a result of fitting several different equations, he was able to demonstrate that distributed lagged models gave a better fit to the Pinkham data and a better forecast than models which did not incorporate lagged effects. He was able to calculate both the short-term and long-term marginal sales effect of advertising. The marginal advertising dollar seemed to increase sales by only $.50 in the short term, seeming to suggest that Pinkham appropriated too much for advertising. But the long-term marginal sales effect was three times as large; the marginal advertising dollar increased sales by $1.63 in the long term.[62] Palda then went on to calculate the post-tax marginal rate of return on the company's invested advertising dollar. He found it to be in the neighborhood of 37 per cent over the whole period, not an implausible figure for a well-established monopolist.

The other sales effect study involved cigarettes, another consumer product where disturbing influences tend to be minimal.[63] Lester G. Telser reported an elaborate investigation of the relation of sales to advertising for the three largest cigarette brands between 1912 and 1939.[64] In contrast to the simple models used by earlier researchers he employed a Markov probability brand-switching model whose parameters he estimated by least squares techniques. Through manipulations of the model, he was able to estimate the rate of depreciation of advertising capital and the marginal rate of return on the advertising capital. He estimated that cigarette advertising outlays built up a fund of good will that depreciated at a rate varying between 15 and 20 per cent per year. The marginal rate of return on this capital was about 15 per cent for Lucky Strike and about −6.8 per cent for Camel. He interpreted the negative marginal rate of return on Camel's prewar advertising to indicate that consumers were supplied with more Camel advertising than they wanted.

The conclusions reached by Telser and Palda using only historical data were made possible by the simplicity of the product environments, the elegance of their respective models, and the satisfactory quality of the data. In the more normal situation the historical effect of advertising on sales would be highly obscured by other variables and the lack of sufficient data.

Richard E. Quandt has lucidly described the profound statistical hurdles in measuring sales/advertising effectiveness from historical data in the normal case. Quandt explored successively the limitations of cross-sectional

[61] Kristian S. Palda, *The Measurement of Cumulative Advertising Effect* (Englewood Cliffs, N.J.: Prentice-Hall, Inc., 1964), p. 87.

[62] *Ibid.,* p. 80.

[63] "Advertising is undoubtedly the prime mover in the sales of cigarettes. Prices are virtually identical and there is little opportunity for differentiation by other merchandising efforts. The product is quite homogeneous. Seasonal and geographical effects are small. Consumer behavior and loyalties are fairly stable." See Julian L. Simon, "Are There Economies of Scale in Advertising?" (unpublished second draft, 1964), pp. 5-6; and shortened published version, *op. cit.,* pp. 16-17.

[64] Lester G. Telser, "Advertising and Cigarettes," *Journal of Political Economy,* October 1962, pp. 471-99.

models, single-equation time series models, and simultaneous equation time series models. He concluded:

> More than anything, we need to turn back, perhaps to more classical methods of statistics and experimental design. It is possible that the conceptual and practical contamination of data and confounding of models can be avoided by subjecting approximately randomized sets of retail outlets to varying treatments and applying analysis of variance techniques to the results which could then more properly be thought to come from carefully designed experimental situations.[65]

Quandt's advice on the potentiality of experimental design for measuring advertising's effect on sales is independently being recognized by an increasing number of advertising researchers, who have already conducted a number of pioneering advertising experiments with promising results.[66] Altogether, a considerable body of experience and theory on the effects of advertising on sales is building up.[67]

Summary

Promotion, along with product development, pricing, and channel management, is a major marketing task of the firm. Promotion is the company's attempt to stimulate sales through directing persuasive communications to the buyers. The instruments of promotion—advertising, personal selling, sales promotion, and publicity—have separate and overlapping capabilities and require a careful definition of communication goals for their effective coordination.

The size of the advertising budget is commonly determined in a number of ways—according to what can be afforded, or as a regular percentage of the company's sales dollar, or to match competitors' expenditures, or by defining the cost of accomplishing specific communication goals. The theoretically correct level of advertising expenditures depends upon whether the advertising is expected to have immediate or delayed effects and whether competitive responses are a factor. The effectiveness of the advertising dollar will depend upon the development of good message content and inspired presentation. The advertising materials must be placed in the most effective media, a problem which is increasingly being studied through mathematical model-building techniques. The budget must be spent over the business cycle, the seasons, the months and even the days with a careful consideration for delays in impact and the psychology of repetition. A con-

---

[65] Richard E. Quandt, "Estimating Advertising Effectiveness: Some Pitfalls in Econometric Methods," *Journal of Marketing Research,* May 1964, p. 60.

[66] See Chapter 9, pp. 204-5.

[67] For a guide to sales effect research, see Martin Mayer, *The Intelligent Man's Guide to Sales Measures of Advertising* (New York: Advertising Research Foundation, Inc., 1965).

tinuous effort must be made to research the likely communication and sales effects of advertising programs during their development, while they are running, and after they are terminated.

493
Advertising
Decisions

Questions and Problems

1. Consider the following two statements: "The purpose of advertising is to create sales." "The purpose of advertising is to improve the buyers' disposition toward the company's products." Which comes closer to the truth?

2. The advertising manager of a large firm asks the executive committee to approve a $100,000 increase in the advertising budget. He submits that this extra money will probably increase company sales by $500,000 over what they would otherwise be. What other information would you want in order to judge the budget request?

3. A company's advertising expenditures average $5,000 a month. Current sales are $29,000, and the saturation sales level is estimated at $42,000. The sales response constant is $2, and the sales decay constant is 6 per cent per month. Use the Vidale-Wolfe formula to estimate the probable sales increase next month.

4. "My feeling is that the variation in the quality of advertisements is even greater than the variation in quality of media scheduling. Even with intuitive scheduling, the profit increment added by good scheduling is much smaller than the potential profit due to better quality advertising." Do you agree?

5. A canned dog food manufacturer is trying to decide between media A and B. Medium A has 1,000,000 readers and charges $20,000 for a full page ad ($2.00 per 1,000). Medium B has 1,500,000 readers and charges $25,000 for a full page ad ($1.67 per 1,000). Is there any other calculation which might be made before assuming that B is the better medium?

6. Suppose you are the marketing manager for a large firm in an industry where advertising budgets keep rising but where total demand remains relatively unaffected. Everything points to the continuation of costly and increasing advertising warfare for the purpose of shifting market shares. Do you see any solution? Name an industry likely to be in this situation.

chapter 19

Sales-Force Decisions

The previous chapter examined the role of advertising in the promotional mix and the major advertising decisions facing the firm. The other major element in the promotional mix is personal selling. This chapter will consider the major issues in developing an effective selling force, exploring such strategic questions as setting objectives for the sales force, determining the size of the sales force, and designing the sales organization and territories. An examination of tactical-operational procedures in recruiting, selecting, training, assigning, compensating, supervising, and evaluating salesmen will follow.

Sales-Force Objectives

No one set of objectives is appropriate for all sales-force operations. The 1,350,000 salesmen in the American economy operate in a fantastic variety of industries and markets, and are called upon to perform a great variety of tasks. We shall want to review these variations before discussing the determination of specific sales-force objectives.

THE VARIETY OF SELLING JOBS

There are probably more stereotypes about salesmen than any other group. The man in the street is likely to conjure up a picture of Arthur Miller's pitiable Willy Loman or Meredith Willson's ebullient Harold Hill—in either case, a glib, boisterous character always ready with a glad hand and a racy story. The salesman is typically pictured as a guy who loves sociability (in spite of some recent evidence that many salesmen actually dislike it). He is criticized for aggressively foisting goods on people (in spite of the fact that buyers often search out sales representatives).

Actually, the term "salesman" covers a broad range of positions in our economy, within which the differences are often greater than the similarities. Robert N. McMurry offered the following classification of selling positions:

> 1. Positions where the "salesman's" job is predominantly to deliver the product, e.g., milk, bread, fuel oil—His selling responsibilities are secondary. Obviously good service and a pleasant manner will enhance customer acceptance and hence lead to more sales. However, few originate many sales.
>
> 2. Positions where the salesman is predominantly an inside order-taker, e.g., the haberdashery salesman standing behind the counter—Most of his customers have already made up their minds to buy. All he does is serve

them. He may use suggestive selling and upgrade the merchandise they buy, but his opportunities to do more than that are few.

3. Positions where the salesman is also predominantly an order-taker but works in the field, as the packing house, soap, or spice salesman does—In his contacts with chain store personnel, he may even actually be discouraged from applying the hard sell. As with the delivery salesman, good service and a pleasant personality may enhance his personal acceptance, but he too does little creative selling.

4. Positions where the salesman is not expected or permitted to take an order but is called on only to build good will or to educate the actual or potential user—Examples here are the distiller's "missionary man" or the medical "detailer" representing an ethical pharmaceutical house.

5. Positions where the major emphasis is placed on technical knowledge, e.g., the engineering salesman who is primarily a consultant to the "client" companies.

6. Positions which demand the creative sale of tangible products like vacuum cleaners, refrigerators, siding, and encyclopedias—Here the salesman often has a double task: first he must make the prospect dissatisfied with his or her present appliance or situation, then begin to sell his product.

7. Positions requiring the creative sale of intangibles, such as insurance, advertising services, or education—This type of sale is ordinarily more difficult than selling tangibles, of course, because the product is less readily demonstrated and dramatized. (Intangibles are often more difficult for the prospect to comprehend.) [1]

The positions move along a spectrum ranging from the least to the most creative types of selling. The earlier jobs call primarily for maintaining accounts and taking orders while the latter jobs require hunting down prospects and creating new sales. Most of the following discussion deals with the creative type of salesman.

Carl Rieser has predicted the demise of "the old drummer type of salesman" and his replacement by a new breed with a softer touch.[2] The new breed is better schooled, even though less colorful. He is able to absorb a vast amount of information about many products and many customers. He is likely to be a front man with some technical training who is backed by a top-flight team of engineers and market researchers. He counsels his company on new products and his customers on how to use them. He knows how to read the needs of customers and recognizes that they are growing more interested in buying systems and services than single products. He goes after the long-run relationship rather than the quick sale. In the jet age, he is a traveling executive. Even his name has been changed to "field manager" (Ford), or "market specialist" (Wyandotte Chemicals), "sales engineer" (Burroughs), or "medical service representative" (Parke, Davis), to avoid the old stigma. As technology grows more complex and competition more keen, one can expect to see more of this new type of salesman.

A SALESMAN'S DUTIES

The actual act of selling is only one of the many activities and responsibilities a salesman bears. He must also write reports, service customers,

[1] Robert N. McMurry, "The Mystique of Super-Salesmanship," *Harvard Business Review,* March-April 1961, p. 114.

[2] Carl Rieser, "The Salesman Isn't Dead—He's Different," *Fortune,* November 1962, pp. 124-27, 248, 252, 254, 259.

handle complaints, send in leads, and so forth. The actual mix of duties varies with the type of selling job. Each company must define its own concept of the duties of its salesmen at each level. Careful job descriptions help the salesmen know what is expected of them and help the company to develop a better over-all system of compensation and evaluation. An

FIGURE 19-1

Lindstrom Flour Milling Company position description
Reprinted from *Introduction to Sales Management,* 4th ed., by Harry R. Tosdal, pp. 587-88.
Copyright 1957 by McGraw-Hill Book Company. Used by permission.

Title: Retail Salesman   Department: Sales

GENERAL RESPONSIBILITIES:

Under direction of the Branch Office Manager and/or Package Sales Supervisor, contacts retail grocery outlets for the purpose of selling our products, merchandising our products and placing point of purchase advertising materials.

Advises Branch Manager and/or Package Sales Supervisor of competitive activity, new products, etc.; reports daily and weekly to Branch Manager and/or Package Sales Supervisor.

Specific Duties:
(A)   Regular
    1. Call on retail grocery outlets.
    2. Make introductory sales.
    3. Merchandise products in each store.
    4. Effectively place point of purchase material in each store.
    5. Prepare detailed record of each call.
    6. Prepare a daily report form and mail to the office each night.
    7. Prepare a weekly report form and mail to the office each week end.
    8. Prepare a weekly automobile report and mail to the office each week end.
    9. Be responsible for proper maintenance and care of company-owned automobile.
   10. Advise Branch Office Manager and/or Package Sales Supervisor of competitive activity, new products, price changes, business trends in territory.
(B)   Special and Occasional Duties
    1. Attend sales meetings.
    2. Occasionally conduct store sales or demonstrations.
    3. Attend trade association meetings, conventions.
    4. Work in conjunction with other manufacturers' representatives in special promotions.
    5. Travel into other territories to assist in the introduction of new products.

Contacts on the Position:
(A)   Inside Contacts: Branch Office Manager and/or Package Sales Supervisor; occasionally other personnel of the Branch Office.
(B)   Outside Contacts: Retail Grocers and members of various trade associations.

Travel:
Daily travel in company-owned automobile. Extent of travel determined by geographical size of territory.

Supervision:
None

Equipment:
Company-owned automobile

example of a sales job description, in this case for the position of retail salesmen of the Lindstrom Flour Milling Company, is reproduced in Figure 19-1.

DETERMINING OBJECTIVES FOR THE SALES FORCE

Because of the variety of selling jobs and selling duties, each company must carefully define what it expects to accomplish through personal selling activity. A company may not only vary the size of its selling force but may have the option of eliminating it altogether by working through manufacturers' representatives, selling on a mail-order basis, and so forth. If a direct sales force is to be used at all, it is important to define its role in the total marketing program.

The firm's over-all marketing objectives constitute the logical starting point for considering the role of the sales force. These objectives specify the product markets the company wants to cultivate, the company's relative emphasis on immediate versus long-run sales, the relative emphasis on market share versus profits, the level of customer satisfaction sought, and other matters. Each one of these influences the kind, importance, and activities of the sales force. If the company believes in a high level of customer satisfaction, it will utilize a large sales force which makes a generous number of calls on customers and uses a low level of selling pressure. If the company wants rapid growth in total sales, it will want a sales force which spends much of its time pursuing new accounts. Table 19-1 shows one particular choice of product and new-account objectives set by a large company for its sales force.

TABLE 19-1
Division of sales effort in a large company (in per cent)

| | Accounts | | |
	Active	Prospective	Total
Present products	70	15	85
New products	10	5	15
Total	80	20	100

Source: Adapted from William R. Dixon, "Redetermining the Size of the Sales Force: A Case Study," in *Changing Perspectives in Marketing Management,* ed. Martin R. Warshaw (Ann Arbor, Mich.: Bureau of Business Research, Graduate School of Business Administration, The University of Michigan, Michigan Business Reports, No. 37, 1962), p. 58.

Sales-force objectives also come out of decisions on marketing strategy, for marketing strategy indicates how much emphasis will be given to the different promotional instruments, as well as the importance of promotion in the total marketing program. In the food industry, for example, many manufacturers have assigned advertising the primary role in their marketing strategy. Their strategy is to "pull" their brand into the store through the consumer by way of massive consumer advertising. The company salesmen see to it that the retailers carry a sufficient stock, give good shelf exposure, and cooperate in sales promotions. Other firms in the same industry, especially those who have not yet established consumer preference for their brand, often try a strategy of "pushing" the brand into the store by offering the retailer a good margin and other incentives. This strategy calls for salesmen who are more creative at selling, since the retailers are often reluctant and their enthusiasm must be developed. In practice, manufacturers combine the "push" and "pull" strategy although the relative emphasis varies and influences the size and the role of the sales force.

In much industrial selling, especially when the product is technically complex, personal selling is likely to play a more important role than advertising. Advertising is given the job of creating buyer awareness so that the salesman does not walk "cold" into buyers' offices. The actual stimulation and closing of a sale are the task of the salesmen. Industrial marketers generally believe that advertising is more effective in creating awareness while personal selling is more effective in creating preference, per dollar of expenditure.

The company should spell out its personal selling goals as specifically as possible. The checklist of specific advertising goals referred to on pages 457-58 could serve as a checklist of personal selling goals. Once the personal selling goals are defined, they influence the type of salesmen to hire, the kind and length of training, the level of compensation, and the basis of performance evaluation, among other things.

In each planning period, specific objectives should be set for the sales force to provide a basis for planning by the other departments and also a basis for the subsequent evaluation of sales-force performance. Typically, both sales and expense objectives are determined. The company's over-all sales volume objective is translated into specific quotas for the various sales regions, district offices, and individual salesmen. The company's over-all expense budget is also translated into specific budgets for these various levels. These budgets express the fact that the firm has over-all profit objectives as well as sales objectives.

Sales-Force Size

Salesmen are among the most productive assets a company has—and also among the most expensive. Increasing their number is likely to increase sales—and will undoubtedly increase costs. Every company must therefore carefully determine the total number of salesmen to employ.

Sometimes it is fairly obvious that a sales force is too small or too large. Increasing sales and/or customer complaints about the lack of service are preliminary indications that the sales force may be too small. Declining sales and/or less than fully occupied salesmen are preliminary indications that the sales force may be too large. The absence of these indications, however, does not mean that the sales force is at an optimal size. The question is one of the relative changes that would be made in sales and costs by changing the size of the sales force.

A number of different logical approaches have been proposed. The use of modern decision theory to determine sales-force size has already been outlined in Chapter 8. Two other approaches will be reviewed here for the light they shed on other facets of the problem.

In a 1959 article, Walter J. Semlow outlined a solution to the problem of sales-force size which depended upon measuring the sales productivity of salesmen in different size territories.[3] He noted that salesmen in territories rated as having higher sales potential produced more sales but that their sales were less than proportionate to the increase in sales potential. Citing a particular company's case, Semlow found that the sales in a territory with 1 per cent of total national potential were $160,000 and sales in a territory with 5 per cent of total potential were $200,000. In the latter case, there was only $40,000 of sales for every 1 per cent of potential.

Now if the company employed 100 salesmen and wanted them all to work territories of equal potentials, it would create 100 territories, each with 1 per cent of total potential. This means that sales would average $160,000 in each territory, according to the previous analysis. Since there are 100 men, total company sales would be $16 million.

If the company employed only 20 men, it would create 20 territories, each with 5 per cent of the total potential. In this case, sales would average $200,000 in each territory according to the previous analysis. Since there were 20 men, total company sales would be only $4,000,000. Semlow applied the same reasoning to other possible sizes of the sales force. For each size, he was able to conjecture the total sales volume, based on the statistically estimated productivity of salesmen in different size territories.

His final step was to convert each sales volume into operating profit on investment. To do this, he first estimated the operating profit before variable selling cost on each sales volume. Then he deducted the variable selling cost, specifically the number of men times the cost per salesman. This left an estimate of operating profit on that sales volume. Then he estimated the working capital and plant investment required at alternative sales volumes. Finally, he expressed the estimated operating profit as a ratio to the required investment. In his example, the operating profit on investment would be 11.6 per cent with 100 men and only 8.7 per cent with 20 men. Looking at all his figures, the optimal-size sales force called for 65 men, and the estimated rate of return was 22.0 per cent.

Semlow's method depends on having a sufficient number of sales territories in the present operation to allow making a statistical estimate of the sales productivity curve. Furthermore, it assumes the desirability of creating territories of equal sales potential; more shall be said about this later. Finally, it assumes that sales productivity is a function only of territory sales potential, neglecting the variations that might be produced by the mix of accounts in the territory, their geographical dispersion, and other factors.

SALESMAN WORKLOAD APPROACH

A different approach was outlined by Walter J. Talley in 1961.[4] It is based on equalizing the workload of salesmen rather than their territorial

[3] Walter J. Semlow, "How Many Salesmen Do You Need?" *Harvard Business Review,* May-June 1959, pp. 126-32.

[4] Walter J. Talley, "How to Design Sales Territories," *Journal of Marketing,* XXV (January 1961), 7-13.

potential. His method assumes that management already knows, through either experience or experimentation, the economic number of calls to make on accounts of different sizes. In other words, there is an implicit assumption about the productivity of sales call time. His method consists of the following steps:

1. Customers are grouped into size classes according to their annual sales volume.

2. The desirable call frequencies (number of sales calls on an account per year) are established for each class.

3. The number of accounts in each size class are multiplied by the corresponding call frequency to arrive at the total workload for the country, in sales calls per year.

4. The average number of calls a salesman can make per year is determined.

5. The number of salesmen needed is determined by dividing the total annual calls required by the average annual calls made by a salesman.[5]

Talley's method assumes the desirability of developing territories that are equalized in workload. The optimality of the over-all solution depends upon management's accuracy in estimating appropriate call frequencies for different size accounts. Actually, desirable call frequencies depend on other aspects than account size, such as the probable response of the account to additional effort, the costs of servicing, and the gross margin on the product mix purchased by the account.

Still other approaches have been proposed for determining sales-force size, each depending on a special set of assumptions.[6] This is an area which is in need of more theorizing, especially of the kind that will bring advertising and other elements of the marketing mix into simultaneous determination.[7]

[5] Mathematically, Talley's solution is given by

$$N = \frac{\sum_{i=1}^{n} C_i F_i}{P}$$

where

N = desirable number of salesmen
C_i = the number of customers in size class i
F_i = the desirable number of annual calls to make to customers in size class i
P = the annual average number of calls made by a salesman
n = the number of customer size classes

[6] The reader should see S. E. Heymann, "Determining the Optimum Size of the Sales Force," in *Marketing Research in Action* (New York: National Industrial Conference Board Report, Studies in Business Policy, No. 84, 1957), pp. 82-84; and William R. Dixon, "Redetermining the Size of the Sales Force: A Case Study," in *Changing Perspectives in Marketing Management,* ed. Martin R. Warshaw (Ann Arbor, Mich.: Bureau of Business Research, Graduate School of Business Administration, The University of Michigan, Michigan Business Reports, No. 37, 1962), pp. 54-70.

[7] See Cyril Freeman, "How to Evaluate Advertising's Contribution," *Harvard Business Review,* July-August 1962, pp. 137-48.

The effectiveness of a sales force depends a great deal on how it is organized. This section will examine the major alternatives in sales-force structure and the principles of good territorial design.

SALES-FORCE STRUCTURE

A sales force can be organized around company territories, products, customers, or some mixture of the three.

TERRITORIAL-STRUCTURED SALES FORCE. The simplest sales organization is one where each salesman has an exclusive territory in which he represents the company's full line. This sales structure has a number of advantages. First, it results in a very clear definition of the salesman's responsibilities. As the only salesman working the territory, he bears the credit or blame for area sales to the extent that personal selling effort makes a difference. This tends to encourage a high level of effort, especially when management is known to be able to gauge fairly accurately the area's sales potential. Second, his responsibility for a definite territory increases his incentive to cultivate local business and personal ties. These ties tend to improve the quality of both his selling effectiveness and his personal life. Third, salesman travel expenses are likely to be relatively small, since each salesman's travel takes place within the bounds of a small geographical territory.

The territorial form of sales organization works quite well in companies with a relatively homogeneous set of products and customers. But these same companies, as their products or markets become diversified, find this form of sales organization increasingly less effective. At the heart of the problem is the fact that effective sales representation requires that the salesman know his products and his customers. But there is a clear limit to how much knowledge a salesman can acquire about different types of products and customers.

PRODUCT-STRUCTURED SALES FORCE. The importance of salesmen's knowing their products and the desire for product responsibility have led many companies to structure their sales force along product lines. Specialization of the sales force by product is particularly warranted where:

> The company's products are technically complex (such as in the heavy equipment, drugs, or electronics industries)
> The company sells many thousands of products (such as in the grocery or hardware business)
> The company produces completely unrelated lines (such as in highly diversified companies)

The mere existence of many or variegated company products, however, is not always a sufficient argument for specializing the sales force by product. A major drawback may exist if the company's separate product lines are bought by many of the same customers. For example:

> The American Hospital Supply Corporation has four major divisions and several subsidiaries, each with its own sales force. All of these sales forces

call on the same hospitals. It is conceivable that as many as seven different salesmen representing the American Hospital Supply Corporation may call on the same hospital on the same day.[8]

This means that company salesmen travel over the same routes, and each uses up valuable time waiting in the outer office to see the customer's purchasing agents. These extra costs must be weighed against the benefits that may result from the higher level of customer service and the more knowledgeable product representation.

CUSTOMER-STRUCTURED SALES FORCE.   Companies may set up separate sales forces along customer lines. The customers may be differentiated by:

Type of industry. (A large steel strapping firm uses separate sales forces to sell to the railroad industry, the construction industry, and a miscellaneous category.)

Size. (A manufacturer of aluminum products uses separate sales forces to sell to large customers and small ones.)

Channel of distribution. (A food manufacturer uses separate sales forces to sell to the chains, to wholesalers, and to large independents.)

Company. (An automotive parts manufacturer uses separate sales forces to sell to the Ford account, the Chevrolet account, and so forth.)

The most obvious advantage of customer specialization is that each sales force can become more knowledgeable about specific customer needs. At one time General Electric's salesmen specialized in specific products (fan motors, switches, and so forth), but it later switched to specialization in markets, such as the air-conditioning market, because this is how the customer saw the problem of fan motors, switches, etc. A customer-specialized sales force can also sometimes lead to lower total payroll costs. A large pump manufacturer at one time used a single sales force of highly trained sales engineers to sell to both original equipment manufacturers (who needed to deal with technical representatives) and to jobbers (who did not need to deal with technical representatives). Later the company split its sales force and staffed the one selling to jobbers with less highly trained salesmen.

The major disadvantage of customer-structured sales forces arises if the various types of customers are scattered evenly throughout the country. This means an overlapping coverage of territories, which is always more expensive.

COMPLEX SALES-FORCE STRUCTURES.   When a company sells a wide variety of products to many types of customers over a broad geographical area, it often combines several principles of sales-force structure. Salesmen

[8] See Ralph Westfall and Harper C. Boyd, Jr., *Cases in Marketing Management* (Homewood, Ill.: Richard D. Irwin, Inc., 1961), pp. 376-83. This would happen if each salesman made a daily call to each hospital. Actually each salesman called at the same hospital about once in every 10 days. Thus there is a 1/10 chance of a particular salesman calling on a particular day. If all salesmen planned their calls independently of each other, the probability that all seven salesmen would call at a particular hospital on the same day is actually quite low: $(1/10)^7 = 0.0000001$. But the probability that at least one salesman would call on that day is quite substantial: $[1 - (9/10)^7] = 0.52$.

may be specialized by territory-product, territory-customer, product-customer, or ultimately by territory-product-customer. A salesman may then be responsible to one or more line managers and/or one or more staff managers. Multiple lines of supervision should generally be avoided, however.

The structure of a sales force, no matter how effective it may originally be, is always in danger of antiquation in the course of time. A company should reconsider periodically whether its sales force is organized along the most effective lines. In comparing the existing structure to a proposed alternative, the most detailed analysis of the *economic* and *human* factors is required. Even when the economic advantages seem substantial, the human factor should not be treated lightly. If any reorganization is perceived by all or a substantial part of the sales force as reducing its opportunities, all of its alleged economic advantages on paper may never be realized in practice.

TERRITORIAL DESIGN

The great majority of companies assign their salesmen to specific territories whether or not they are further specialized by product or type of customers. The territories are aggregated into larger groupings called *districts,* and in turn these districts may be aggregated into major sales *regions.* Many of the larger companies, for example, utilize an eastern, southern, central, and western regional plan for field operations.

In designing a system of territories, the company generally tries to achieve the following territorial characteristics: the territories are easy to administer; their sales potential is easy to estimate; they keep down total travel time; and they provide a sufficient and equitable workload and sales potential for each salesman. These characteristics are achieved through decisions about the size and shape of territorial units.

TERRITORY SIZE. As we saw earlier, there are two competing philosophies on the proper size of territories. One approach calls for forming territories of *equal sales potential,* and the other calls for forming territories of *equal workload.* Each principle offers advantages at the cost of some real dilemmas.

The logic of creating territories of *equal potential* is to provide each salesman with the same income opportunities and to provide the company with a means of evaluating performance. It is thought that under this principle chronic differences in sales yield by territory reflect differences in the ability or effort of individual salesmen. This awareness, it is concluded, encourages salesmen to work at their top capacity. It is also thought that salesmen regard equal-potential territories as being eminently fair.

Because customer geographical density almost always varies, territories with equal potential typically cover vastly different areas. For example, the potential for the sale of large drill presses is as large in Chicago as it is in a substantial number of the western states (excluding California). A salesman assigned to the Chicago territory can cover the same potential with far less effort than the salesman who sells in the territory spanning the several western states. The Chicago man can spend more time selling and less time traveling than his western counterpart. Although the two territories are equal in potential, they differ greatly in workload.

The problem is that salesmen assigned to the larger and sparser territories are either going to end up with less sales—and income, where commissions are involved—for equal effort or with equal sales only through extraordinary effort. Is there any way around the problem? One possible adjustment is to pay higher compensation to the western salesman, providing him with incentive and insuring that good men will be attracted to larger territories. But this reduces the profits on sales in the larger territories. An alternative adjustment is to acknowledge that territories differ in attractiveness and assign the better men to the better territories. Transfers to the better territories would be awarded on the basis of seniority and demonstrated ability. But this has several disadvantages. The salesmen are taken out of their territories just when they begin to know them well. Their home life is disrupted by the frequent transfers. Transfer expenses, which may be considerable, must be absorbed by the company. And the men who do not get the better territory may be bitter.

The other leading principle for creating territories is to try to equalize the salesmen's workloads. The objective is to permit each salesman to optimize the coverage of his territory. However, this principle generally results in some variation in territory sales potentials. This is not a concern where salesmen are on straight salary. But where salesmen are compensated partly for their sales, territories definitely vary in their attractiveness even though the workloads are approximately equalized. There are the same alternative ways to handle this situation. A lower compensation rate can be paid to salesmen in the territories with the higher sales potential, or the territories with the better potential can go to the men with higher ability and/or seniority.

In practice, many companies develop sales territories which mix the principles of equalizing workload and sales potential. They try to keep territories from becoming too divergent in workloads or potentials. Nevertheless, time itself brings about divergence because territories undergo different rates of growth. Inevitably some territories become more attractive than others. Either the boundaries have to be readjusted, or the pay rates changed, or the better territories given to the better men when vacancies occur.

TERRITORY SHAPE. Territories are formed by combining smaller units, such as counties or states, until they add up to a territory of a given potential or workload. They are put together with reference to the location of natural barriers, the compatibility of adjacent areas, the adequacy of transportation, and so forth. Many companies also try to achieve a certain territory shape because this can influence the cost and ease of coverage and the salesman's satisfaction. Three different common territorial shapes are shown in Figure 19-2.

A *circular-shaped territory* with the salesman headquartered in the center offers two advantages. The circle makes it easier for the salesman to prepare a routing plan that requires a minimum of backtracking. In effect, he travels in a circle, and when finished, he returns to his branch location. Furthermore, he is not very far from any of his accounts when special trips have to be made.

A *clover-leaf pattern* with the salesman headquartered in the center enables the salesman to travel in a series of loops around his territory. If

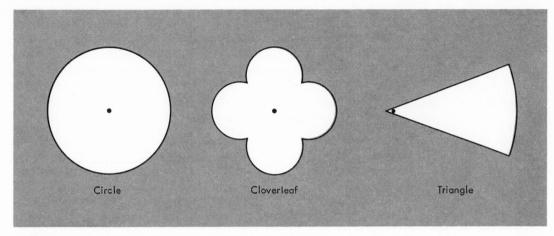

FIGURE 19-2
Alternative shapes for territories

clover leaves are made the right size, the salesman can start out each Monday and finish a clover section by Friday evening and return home. Furthermore, the cost of special trips is low because the accounts are not far away.

A wedge-shaped territory radiating out from a central metropolitan area is often employed when a metropolitan area is too large for one salesman to handle. It also tends to balance rural and urban calls among salesmen. Its major disadvantage is that it places the salesman quite far from some of his accounts. In making special calls on these accounts, his return to headquarters would represent a lot of "deadheading."

Actual routing costs depend on the geographical location of accounts within the territory as well as the territory's shape. It is not generally obvious which routing through a set of points is the most efficient. A hypothetical territory and distribution of accounts is shown in Figure 19-3. The reader can see that there are many conceivable routings through the set of points. Furthermore, there are different standards for what is efficient. Should the salesman seek the routing which minimizes the distance traveled, or the total traveling time, or the total traveling cost? Remember the available roads are not shown, and these roads vary in their posted speed limits and driving conditions. There is usually a choice between using a much shorter route over poor roads or a much longer route over good roads. To the extent that the salesman's time is expensive, he should prefer the costlier but speedier routing.

An increasing number of companies are subjecting the routing problem to mathematical analysis through the use of high-speed computers. By finding solutions to the "traveling salesman problem," they can help their salesmen reduce the cost or time spent in travel.[9]

REVISING EXISTING SALES TERRITORIES. Once territories have been created, they are very difficult to change without upsetting some salesmen and supervisors. Those salesmen who are doing well can be expected to resist territorial reorganization. The company's objective in splitting a

[9] For references, see Chapter 10, footnote 23.

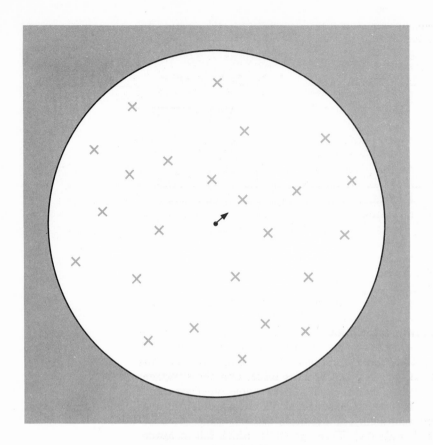

territory may be to improve coverage, but the salesman may interpret the proposal as an attempt by the company to cheat him of sales or make life harder for him. Since his morale and performance are at stake, the company must proceed carefully. A case illustrating the need to proceed cautiously is described below.

In 1958, a large insurance company without any previous operations in an area southeast of Chicago decided to create a new sales district on the basis of fresh estimates of sales potential. The new district was divided into 24 territories, and an energetic district sales manager was appointed. The company expected that by 1960 the area's rate of growth would justify 35 territories, an increase of 11 territories. But by 1960, the district sales manager had only added three new territories. At the same time, the per capita sales of his salesmen were among the highest in all the districts. The manager himself personally sold over one million dollars of insurance each year and earned more than everyone else in the Midwest region except the senior vice president. When he was questioned about his failure to meet the original objective in staff growth, he complained that, rather than having a "cream puff" district, his district was really deteriorating. In a letter to his regional sales director, he stated, "The research department's 1957 analysis is all wrong. There is just not the building boom in our district, and the character of the population is changing in a way which will make future sales more difficult to obtain." As if this statement ended once and for all the question of creating more territories in his district, he went on to request a

506

slice of territory from an adjacent district as the only condition under which he would consider establishing additional sales territories. What action should the home office take?

To give the sales manager the benefit of the doubt, the home office re-examined the potential of this district. Its estimates again confirmed its original position that the district warranted increased market penetration. However, it also concluded that any alienation of the district sales manager would do more harm than good. His loss would be more costly than if he were permitted to operate as he was until his retirement in three years. Consideration was given to the possibility of a compromise arrangement granting him additional area if he would create several new territories.

This case illustrates how territory revision, which is a periodic necessity, must be handled with keen attention to the human factors as well as to the economic factors of good design. Salesmen and district managers must be given confidence that a proposed revision will not injure them personally in the long run, nor if possible, in the short run. Where some injury is unavoidable, the company must carefully weigh the costs of putting through the revision against the costs of postponing it.

Recruiting and Selecting Salesmen

Up to now, we have considered questions of sales-force strategy—the personal selling objectives, the size of the sales force, and the structural and territorial design of the sales force. There is a whole other area connected with the effective day-to-day management of the sales-force operation. Salesmen must be recruited and selected, trained, assigned, compensated, supervised, and evaluated. These are tasks which fall to lower-level sales management—regional sales managers, district sales managers, first-line supervisors. At the same time, the policies guiding these tasks are formulated by the top echelons of marketing management. The distinction between strategy and operations actually blurs in practice.

IMPORTANCE OF CAREFUL SELECTION

At the heart of a successful sales-force operation is the selection of good salesmen. The performance level of an average salesman and that of a top salesman are quite different. A survey of over 500 companies revealed that 27 per cent of the salesmen brought in over 52 per cent of the sales.[10] Beyond the differences in salesman productivity are the great wastes in hiring the wrong men. Of the 16,000 salesmen who were hired by the surveyed companies during 1963, only 68.5 per cent still worked for their company at the end of the year, and only 50 per cent were expected to remain through 1964. The cost of recruiting, training, and supervising an individual salesman for one year was estimated at $8,730. As a result, the surveyed companies were expected to lose around $70 million, or half their investment.

The financial loss due to turnover is only part of the total cost. The new salesman who remains with the company receives a direct income averag-

[10] The survey was conducted by the Sales Executives Club of New York and was reported in *Business Week,* February 1, 1964, p. 52.

ing around half of the direct selling outlay. If he receives $9,000 a year, another $9,000 may go into fringe benefits, expenses for travel and entertainment, supervision, office space, supplies, and secretarial assistance. Consequently the new salesman should be capable of creating sales on which the gross margin at least covers his selling expenses of $18,000. If this margin were 10 per cent for example, he would have to sell at least $180,000 of product to constitute a breakeven resource for his company.

WHAT MAKES A GOOD SALESMAN?

Selecting salesmen would not be so much of a problem if one could be sure what characteristics made up an ideal salesman. If ideal salesmen are outgoing, aggressive, and energetic, it would not be too difficult to check for these characteristics in applicants. But a review of the most successful salesmen in any company is likely to reveal a good number who are introverted, mild-mannered, and far from energetic. The successful group will also include men who are tall and short, articulate and inarticulate, well-groomed and slovenly.

Nevertheless, the search for the magic combination of traits which spell sure-fire sales ability continues unabated. The number of lists that have been drawn up is countless. Most of them recite the same qualities. One observer with broad experience wrote:

> It is my conviction that the possessor of *effective* sales personality is *a habitual "wooer," an individual who has a compulsive need to win and hold the affection of others.* . . . His wooing, however, is not based on a sincere desire for love because, in my opinion, he is convinced at heart that no one will ever love him. Therefore, his wooing is primarily exploitative . . . his relationships tend to be transient, superficial and evanescent.[11]

McMurry went on to list five traits, in addition to the wooing instinct, which made the supersalesman: a high level of energy, abounding self-confidence, a chronic hunger for money, a well-established habit of industry, and a state of mind that regards each objection, resistance, or obstacle as a challenge.[12]

More recently, David Mayer and Herbert M. Greenberg offered one of the shortest lists of traits common to good salesmen.[13] Their seven years of field work led them to conclude that the good salesman has at least two basic qualities:

> *Empathy,* the ability to feel as the customer does
>
> *Ego drive,* a strong personal need to make the sale, not merely for the money to be gained

Using these two traits, they were able to make fairly good predictions of the subsequent performance of applicants for sales positions in three different industries.

It may be true that certain basic traits may make a man a good salesman in any line of selling. From the viewpoint of a particular company,

[11] McMurry, *op. cit.,* p. 117.
[12] *Ibid.,* p. 118.
[13] David Mayer and Herbert M. Greenberg, "What Makes a Good Salesman," *Harvard Business Review,* July-August 1964, pp. 119-25.

however, these basic traits are rarely enough. Each selling job is characterized by a unique set of duties and challenges. One only has to think
about insurance selling, computer selling, and automobile selling to realize
the different educational, intellectual, and personality requirements that
would be sought in the respective salesmen.

How should a company proceed to determine the characteristics its
prospective salesmen should "ideally" possess? A good starting point is
the objectives established by management for the sales-force operation.
Whether the company seeks immediate sales or long-run relationships
with customers would influence the type of salesman sought; whether the
company sees the personal selling effort basically as a servicing or a selling
operation would also be a determining factor.

The particular duties of the job suggest some of the characteristics to
look for in applicants. Is there a lot of paper work? Does the job call for
much travel? Will the salesman confront a high proportion of refusals?
Does the job call for a lot of patience in cultivating potential customers?
These factors suggest corresponding traits to look for in new salesmen.

Many companies believe that crucial traits can be discovered by making
a comparison between their most successful and most unsuccessful salesmen. Of course this begs the question of who are the best salesmen. A poor
salesman in a very good territory may sell more than a good salesman in a
poor territory. In one company, a branch sales manager lost one of his
top producers and felt a great loss, but the new man assigned to the territory soon doubled his predecessor's sales record. One way to get around
the confounding of sales ability and territorial potential is to measure the
ratio of one to the other. The superior salesman can be defined as one
who sells substantially in excess of territorial potential, and the poor salesman is one who sells substantially below it.

Suppose the company compared the characteristics of its top and bottom
salesmen and found the results in Table 19-2. Interpreting the results

TABLE 19-2
**Average ratings (hypothetical) of two groups of salesmen
on various characteristics**

	Successful salesmen	Unsuccessful salesmen
Sales aptitude (median score)	80	77
Aggressiveness (median score)	14	16
Education (mean number of years)	12	10
Appearance (percentage who are well-groomed)	60	60
Grammatical ability (median score)	30	30

literally, it appears that better salesmen have higher sales aptitude, lower
aggressiveness, and more education. The salesman's appearance and
grammatical ability seem irrelevant. If further analysis shows that the apparent differences on the first three traits are statistically significant, management may want to incorporate these traits in their applicant rating
procedures.

After management develops general criteria for new sales personnel, it has the job of stimulating a sufficient number of applicants. The first step is for the company to estimate its future sales manpower needs in the light of turnover characteristics and planned sales growth. One company turned this problem over to operations researchers.

> Northwestern Mutual Life Insurance recently estimated "survival" rates for its agents in various service and age classes. Operations researchers working for this company took these data and analyzed turnover as a Markov process. They developed an elaborate model for simulating the effect of various alternative recruitment patterns on the composition of the future sales force and sales. For a given sales target, they were able to recommend to management the minimum number and types of agents to recruit each year.[14]

The job of recruiting is turned over to the personnel department, which seeks applicants through various means. A large rubber tire company, for example, secured salesmen from three sources:

> About 25 per cent of the new salesmen were recruited from other departments of the company at the suggestion of the department heads, branch managers, or members of the salesforce. . . . Approximately 50 per cent . . . were experienced in sales work with other rubber companies. . . . The remaining 25 per cent were recent college graduates. . . .[15]

More and more companies are turning to the colleges to recruit future sales manpower. Recruitment officers talk not only to business school graduates but also to chemists, medieval history scholars, and whoever else expresses an interest in selling. Yet companies have not found it easy to sell college students on selling. A 1964 survey of 1,000 male students in 123 colleges indicated that only 1 in 17 college men showed an interest in selling.[16] The reluctant ones gave as reasons the fear of insecurity and a dislike of travel and being away from their family. To counter these objections, company recruiters emphasized income opportunities and the fact that one-quarter of the present presidents of large United States companies started out in marketing and sales. These two baits, however, probably worked less well than the recent increases in starting salaries resulting from the keen competition for good sales candidates and their scarcity.

APPLICANT RATING PROCEDURES

Recruitment procedures should lead to the development of more applicants than jobs, and the company's task is to select the better applicants. The selection procedures vary in elaborateness from a single informal interview to highly detailed testing and interviewing, not only of the man

---

[14] Based on an unpublished paper by Joe Midler, formerly with Northwestern Mutual Life Insurance Co., "A Simulation Model of Sales Force Development with Application to Manpower Replacement, Sales Forecasting, and Corporate Growth," 1957.

[15] Harry R. Tosdal, *Introduction to Sales Management,* 2nd ed. (New York: McGraw-Hill Book Company, copyright 1940), pp. 380-381. Used by permission.

[16] "Youth Continues to Snub Selling," *Sales Management,* January 15, 1965, p. 69.

but of his wife as well. Sometimes the effort of a company to find the right man takes on the proportions of a national manhunt:

> A large West Coast company in search of a man started out with 300 leads and narrowed these down to 30 who were interviewed by company-retained psychologists in various American cities. The four with the highest recommendations were flown to the home office in Los Angeles where they were each interviewed for two days. One was finally chosen. The job paid only $13,000!

More typical of the screening procedures of large companies is the one used by the tire company described earlier:

> The branch managers interviewed applicants for sales positions but could hire salesmen only after securing the approval of the sales personnel department in Akron. The sales personnel department recommended that the branch manager have with each prospective salesman at least three interviews which were to be of short duration in order not to give the man time to "sell" himself. The repeated interviews were to give the branch manager an opportunity to judge whether the applicant would "wear well" with the trade. It was further recommended that at least two, and preferably three, members of the executive staff of the branch interview the applicant, each interviewer to make an independent appraisal of the applicant and submit his opinions and recommendations to the sales personnel department on a form. . . .
>
> After the first interview, if the applicant seemed promising, the branch manager gave him an application blank which was used to secure information of a personal nature, educational background, past employers, length of employment, salary and references. The branch manager wrote to all previous employers, to see if the information supplied was correct, and to persons given as references to check on honesty and ability. If the applicant were to be recommended for employment, the completed application from pertinent reference material and the independent appraisals of the branch executives were sent to the sales personnel department in Akron. This department secured a report of an independent investigation, made by the retail credit company, of the man's character, local reputation, credit standing in his community, habits and stability in regard to previous employment. On the basis of this information, the sales personnel department accepted or rejected the recommendations of the branch manager.[17]

An increasing number of companies are giving formal tests to applicants for sales positions. Although test scores are only one information element in a scheme that includes personal characteristics, references, past employment history, and interviewer reactions, they are weighed quite heavily by some companies. This is especially true for companies such as IBM, where the sales job is complicated. Companies such as Procter & Gamble and Gillette also have found psychological tests worthwhile. Gillette claims that the use of tests has resulted in a 42 per cent reduction in turnover and that test scores have correlated well with the subsequent progress of new salesmen in the sales organization. Among the strongest proponents of tests are insurance companies. The abilities needed to sell insurance are fairly measurable, and, according to Franklin Evans, they should have

---

[17] Tosdal, *op. cit.*

more weight than external characteristics such as dress, speech, or any salesman stereotype.[18]

The choice of an appropriate battery of tests is not simple. A multitude of standard tests is available to measure intelligence, interests, sales aptitude, personal adjustment, personality characteristics, and social intelligence. There are also tailor-made tests for special selling situations. These tests vary considerably in reliability and validity. Furthermore, many of them are vulnerable to deliberate distortion by any applicant who so chooses. A man can fake a lower IQ if he thinks this is desirable. He can also spot red-herring questions, such as "Do you prefer golf or reading?" In his *The Organization Man,* William H. Whyte, Jr., laid down the following rules for the erstwhile job applicant who takes company psychological tests: (1) Give the most conventional answer; (2) show that you like things as they are; (3) indicate that you never worry; and (4) deny any taste for books or music.[19]

Since an applicant is not likely to score at the top on every desirable characteristic, management must determine the relative importance of the different characteristics. One applicant may have good experience but may perform only modally on the sales aptitude test; another may have no experience but perform well on the test. Which will be the more productive salesman? Usually company management has intuitive weightings but does not develop any formal weighting scheme. A formal scheme, however, may produce more consistency and over time could be improvable as a predictive instrument. Table 19-3 shows one hypothetical point system which might be developed by a company for deriving an over-all rating of its candidates based on many pieces of information.

Training Salesmen

Not too long ago, many companies sent their salesmen out into the field almost immediately after hiring them. The salesman would be supplied with a pack of samples, order books, and instructions to sell west of the Mississippi. Training programs were considered luxuries. A training program meant large outlays for instructors, materials, and space; the payment of a base salary to a man who is not selling; and lost opportunities because he is not in the field.

Nowadays, a new salesman can expect to spend from a few weeks to many months in the limbo state known as training. In industries such as steel or data processing, the new salesman is not on his own for two years! Companies clearly appear to have reversed their attitude toward training. A number of environmental changes have convinced sales management,

---

[18] Evans found that people tend to buy insurance from people very much like themselves. A salesman is apt to sell mostly to people in his own social class, age group, religion, and nationality. Evans proposed that insurance companies should hire all types of salesmen if they want to achieve broad penetration. The only requirement was that they exhibit the intelligence and kinds of abilities effective in selling insurance. These are measurable to some extent through tests. See Franklin B. Evans, "Selling as a Dyadic Relationship—A New Approach," *The American Behavioral Scientist,* May 1963, pp. 76-79.

[19] William H. Whyte, Jr., *The Organization Man* (New York: Simon and Schuster, Inc., 1956), pp. 405-10.

TABLE 19-3
A point system for rating sales applicants

Factor	Assumption	Rule
Age	Age is an advantage up to 50.	Add one-quarter point for each year of age over 21 up to 50; subtract one-half point for each year over 50.
Marital status	Marriage increases motivation.	Single : 0 Married without child: 3 Married with children: 5 Divorced : 2
Experience	Experience, especially selling experience, is helpful.	One-half point for each year of non-selling business experience up to a maximum of 3; 1 point for each year of field experience up to a maximum of 7.
Interviewer's evaluation	General manner and appearance are important.	Assign from 1 to 5 points on general manner and 1 to 5 points on appearance.
Sales aptitude test	Sales aptitude can be measured to some extent.	One-half point for each point above 100.
Education	College training contributes to success.	One point for each year of college, 2 extra points for an engineer's degree.

even if not the controller, that an extended training period may generate more value than cost. The salesman of today is selling to more cost-conscious and value-conscious buyers. Furthermore, he is selling a host of products, often loosely related, and sometimes technically complex. He is preparing more reports. His company wants him to appear mature, knowledgeable, and experienced although he was recently hired. When all these factors are considered, it is sometimes a wonder that training periods are not longer.

Training the salesman requires decisions on the length and content of the program and the best methods of instruction. From a conceptual point of view, the training period should be extended (or contracted) to the point where the marginal cost of an additional day begins to exceed the marginal value of an additional day. This rule is difficult to use, however, because the marginal value is so hard to assess. A more practical philosophy is that since training time is so expensive, it makes good sense to keep it as short as possible unless there are very good reasons for making it longer.

The question of the optimum length of the training period cannot be separated from the question of training content and methods. Content raises the question of what knowledge and behavioral skills the salesman should have before he can deal effectively with customers. This goes back to management's conception of the role of personal selling in the marketing program. Most companies seek some blend of the following skills and understandings:

The salesman should know his company and identify with it. Most companies devote the first part of the training program to institutional themes. Included are the history and objectives of the company, the organizational setup and lines of authority, the names of the chief officers, the company's financial structure and facilities, and the company's chief products and sales volume. All of this is presented with the idea of developing respect, loyalty, and a sense of opportunity for the individual.

The salesman should know his products. During training the sales trainee is shown how the products are produced and how they function in various uses.

The salesman should know customers' and competitors' characteristics. The salesman should be introduced to the different types of customers, their needs, buying motives, and buying habits. He should also learn about his company's and competitors' policies on credit, shipment, and so forth.

The salesman should learn how to make effective sales presentations. Most companies do not want to leave sales arguments and presentation entirely up to the salesman. Companies explain the major sales arguments for each product, and some go so far as to develop scripts. Part of the training time is used to develop the salesman's personality and provide hints on self-development.[20]

The salesman should be introduced to field procedures and responsibilities. He should know how he is expected to divide his time between active accounts and potential accounts; how he is to use his expense account; how he might route his trips more effectively; and how he is to prepare a multitude of forms and reports.

Given the content objectives, the best instructional methods and aids must be found. New methods of training are continually appearing and must be evaluated for both the speed of learning and the depth of understanding they promise. Among the new methods, role playing has become a standard technique in training salesmen to make more effective sales presentations. Films and film strips have been used effectively to develop product understanding. More recently, programmed learning and teaching machines have been used to speed up the learning of company products and policies. Considering the high cost of training, the company might well want to use experimental design to evaluate the effectiveness of alternative training approaches.

The substantial costs of company training programs raise the question whether a company would be better off to hire experienced men away from other companies. The gain is often illusory, however, because the ex-

[20] Almost a million copies of books on selling are marketed in the United States every year, according to Daniel Seligman. (See "The Latest Secrets of Selling," *Fortune,* June 1956, p. 123.) They bear such provocative titles as *How to Outsell the Born Salesman, The Power of Enthusiastic Selling, How Power Selling Brought Me Success in 6 Hours, Where Do You Go From No,* and *1000 Ways a Salesman Can Increase His Sales.* The reason so much has been written is that so little is known. The books offer different formulas for success. Some emphasize that the salesman should cultivate such virtues as social poise, self-confidence, independence, and ambition. Others emphasize that the salesman should be able to "psychoanalyze" the buyer and know what stimulus to apply. Still other books concentrate on the steps in the persuasion process, such as establishing product need, creating believability, using repetition, etc. Dale Carnegie, whose book *How to Win Friends and Influence People* remains a classic, calls for the adaptable salesman, who becomes whatever the buyer wants him to be.

perienced man is brought in at a higher salary, which sometimes may simply represent a capitalization of the equivalent training costs. From a socioeconomic point of view, there is probably a net loss when an industry practices pirating on a large scale. Some of his specific training and company experience is wasted when a man transfers to another company. Within some industries, companies have entered into tacit agreements not to hire men away from each other.

Assigning Salesmen

The new salesman graduates from training into an assignment in some part of the company's sales organization. Often, at the end of a training program or at a time of high turnover, several men are assigned concurrently to several territories. When the men differ in ability and the territories differ in potential, the assignments must be carefully made. It is not necessarily true that the most able salesman should receive the best territory, the next most able salesman should receive the next best territory, and so on down the line. This neglects the whole question of man-territory interactions, as can be easily illustrated.

Suppose four salesmen are to be assigned to four territories. The sales manager proceeds to make an estimate of what each salesman is likely to sell on the average, irrespective of the territories, and of the average potential of each territory, irrespective of the salesman. Let his estimates be those in Table 19-4. The salesmen and territories are ranked in order

TABLE 19-4
Sales manager's estimates of expected sales by salesman and estimated potential by territory

Salesman	Expected sales	Territory	Estimated potential
A	$83,000	1	$78,750
B	68,500	2	64,250
C	59,750	3	62,000
D	54,000	4	60,250

of expected sales and estimated potential, respectively. The principle of assigning the best salesman to the best territory, the next best salesman to the next best territory, and so on would lead to the assignments A1, B2, C3, and D4.

Now suppose the sales manager made a separate estimate of what he thought each man would sell in each territory, taking into consideration the peculiarities of the men and the territories. His estimates are shown in Table 19-5. This table emphasizes that salesmen can be expected to vary in their effectiveness because the nature of the challenge differs from territory to territory and the abilities they bring vary. It should be noted that there are 24 ($4 \times 3 \times 2 \times 1$) different possible assignments of salesmen to territories. The problem is small enough so that the "best" set of

TABLE 19-5

Sales manager's estimates of annual sales of each salesman for hypothetical assignments to different territories

Salesman	Territory 1	2	3	4	Expected sales
A	$92,000	$95,000	$75,000	$70,000	$83,000
B	90,000	57,000	82,000	45,000	68,500
C	73,000	75,000	40,000	51,000	59,750
D	60,000	30,000	51,000	75,000	54,000
Estimated potential	$78,750	$64,250	$62,000	$60,250	

assignments—the set that maximizes sales—can be easily found by trial and error. The reader should verify that A2, B3, C1, and D4 form the best set of assignments under the given estimates and assumptions, and would yield annual sales of $325,000.

This solution indicates that better salesmen should be assigned the better territories in a rough rather than an exact way. Assignments should reflect man-territory interactions and not just the average ability of salesmen and the average potential of territories.

Compensating Salesmen

The three major requirements for building a top-flight sales force are attracting good men, motivating them, and keeping them. In all three areas company compensation policies can make the crucial difference.

Men applying for sales work are highly interested in a company's compensation plan; for some men, it may be the most important factor. After being hired and trained, their morale as well as the amount and direction of their sales efforts is critically influenced by features of the compensation plan. Finally, unless their income opportunities meet their expectations and remain competitive, the better salesmen may leave the company and destroy a considerable company investment.

It is not easy to formulate a compensation plan that can be trusted to attract, motivate, and keep good salesmen. This is because diverse and often incompatible sets of objectives are sought by salesmen and by management. Prospective salesmen would like a plan which offers the following features:

Income regularity. Since sales are influenced by many factors beyond the salesman's control, he wants to be assured of some regular base income regardless of his sales. This minimum income will help him pay his bills and feed his family in periods of declining sales.

Reward for above-average performance. Most salesmen think they can sell more than the average salesman and want a compensation plan which provides superior income for superior performance.

Fairness. Salesmen want to feel that their pay is about right in relation to their experience and ability, the earnings of co-workers and salesmen working for competitors, and the cost of living.

On the other hand, an ideal compensation plan from management's point of view would emphasize:

Control. Management likes a plan which facilitates their control over how salesmen spend their time.

Economy. Management wants to establish a level of pay which is reasonable in relation to the value of the salesman's effort and the cost and value of company products.

Simplicity. Management prefers a plan which is simple to administer from a payroll point of view, simple to explain to sales supervisors and salesmen, and simple to change as product situations and business conditions alter.

Management is obviously hard pressed to reconcile all these objectives in one plan. Plans with good control features are generally not simple. Management goals, such as economy, conflict with salesmen's goals, such as financial security. In the light of these and other conflicts, it is understandable why compensation plans exhibit a tremendous variety, not only among industries but among companies within the same industry.

In designing a compensation plan, management must seek guidance from the basic objectives established for the personal selling function. What kind of selling effort does it want, what kind of salesman, what kind of duties? The plan must be designed with these things in mind and in light of the compensation levels of competitors, the degree of sales fluctuation in the industry, and so forth. The plan itself will amount to a set of decisions on the level, components, and structure of compensation.

THE LEVEL OF COMPENSATION

Management must determine first the average level of compensation its salesmen should earn. This amount must bear some relation to the "going market price" for the type of sales job and abilities required. If the market price for sales manpower is well defined, as it is in highly competitive markets for homogeneous resources, then the individual firm has little choice but to pay the going rate. To pay less would not bring forth the desired quantity or quality of applicants, and to pay more would be unnecessary. More often, however, the market price for sales manpower is not well defined. For one thing, company plans vary in the importance of fixed and variable salary elements, fringe benefits, and expense allowances. It is difficult to find a linear measure equating these dissimilar elements. And data on the average take-home pay of salesmen working for competitive firms can be misleading because of significant variations in the average seniority and ability levels of the competitors' salesmen. Published comparisons of industry-by-industry salesman compensation levels are infrequent and generally lack sufficient detail.[21]

The theoretical solution to the problem of the optimal compensation level is implicit in the analysis shown earlier in Figure 12-3. Assume a situation where a company is preparing to establish a specialized sales force of 10 men to handle a new product. They will be paid on a straight salary. Higher salary levels would allow the company to recruit better men and

[21] Studies are published by the Dartnell Corporation, the National Industrial Conference Board, and the American Management Association.

lead to higher sales volumes. The sales curve can be assumed to be S-shaped with respect to greater total expenditures on the sales force. From the estimated sales curve would be deducted all costs before the total sales-force expenditures to find gross profits. Then total sales-force expenditures would be deducted from gross profits, allowing a projection to be made of net profits. At the point where net profits are highest, the optimal total sales-force expenditure is found. This figure can be divided by the size of the planned sales force, 10 men in this case, to find the optimal salary level.

THE ELEMENTS OF COMPENSATION

After a firm decides on the average pay level, it must determine the appropriate mixture of the four basic elements of salesmen's compensation —a fixed amount, a variable amount, expenses, and fringe benefits. The fixed amount, which might be salary or a drawing account, is intended to satisfy the salesman's need for some stability of income. The variable amount, which might be commissions, bonus, or profit sharing, is intended to stimulate and reward greater effort. Expense allowances are intended to enable the salesman to undertake selling efforts which are considered necessary or desirable. And, fringe benefits, such as paid vacations, sickness or accident benefits, pensions, life insurance, and the like, are intended to provide security and job satisfaction.

Top sales management must decide which elements should be in the compensation plan and their relative importance. A popular rule seems to favor making about 70 per cent of the salesman's total income fixed and allocating the remaining 30 per cent among the other elements.[22] But the variations around this average are so pronounced that it can hardly serve as a sufficient guide in planning. Depending on the selling situation, different generalizations can be made about the best proportion of fixed to variable income from the company's point of view. For example, fixed compensation should have more emphasis in jobs with a high ratio of non-selling duties to selling duties and in jobs where the selling task is technically complex. Variable compensation should have more emphasis in jobs where sales are cyclical and/or depend on the personal initiative of the salesman.

Fixed and variable compensation taken alone give rise to three basic types of salesman compensation plans—straight salary, straight commission, and some combination of salary and one or more variable elements. Each type of plan has certain strengths and weaknesses which must be considered carefully.

STRAIGHT SALARY. With this plan, the salesman receives a fixed sum at regular intervals in total payment for his services. Generally he also receives an amount to defray part or all of the expenses he has incurred in performing his duties. Once the most popular plan for salesmen, it has been increasingly modified by the addition of incentive elements so that today a minority of firms operate exclusively on this basis.

From management's point of view, a number of advantages are secured under a straight salary plan. The primary one is that management is freer

---

[22] See John C. Aspley and John C. Harkness, *The Sales Manager's Handbook,* 9th rev. ed. (Chicago: The Dartnell Corporation, 1962), pp. 447-48.

to direct and alter salesmen's duties without incurring strong opposition from the men affected. Men on fixed salaries are more ready to go along with requests from management to spend more of their time in activities not associated with immediate sales, such as trying to open new accounts, providing technical services, or filling out longer reports. In addition, straight salary plans are generally less costly to administer and easier to explain. They also simplify the task of projecting the sales payroll for the coming year. Finally, by providing the salesman with security through stability of income, the straight salary plan may lead to a greater evenness in the morale of the salesmen.

The chief weakness of the straight salary plan is that it does not present the salesmen with any direct incentive to do a better than average selling job. This puts a greater supervision burden on management to control, evaluate, and reward the performances of individual salesmen. Other problems posed by straight salary plans are an inflexible selling expense burden during downswings in business; the danger that during upswings salesmen on fixed salaries do not have sufficient incentive to exploit the increased business potential; thorny questions in salary adjustments for ability, rising living costs, length of service; and the probability that the more hard-driving type of salesman is not easy to attract.

Some of these advantages and disadvantages are reversed under straight commission plans.

STRAIGHT COMMISSION PLAN. This plan pays the salesman some fixed or sliding rate related to his sales or profit volume. The salesman may or may not also receive reimbursement for the expenses he incurs in performing his selling function. Although the general trend is away from straight plans, the straight commission plan is still found in many companies and industries, *especially where there is a need for aggressive selling and the salesman's nonselling duties are relatively minor.* Straight commission plans are particularly prominent in the selling of insurance and investment securities, furniture, office equipment, small office machines, clothing, the textile and shoe industries, and drug and hardware wholesaling.

The straight commission plan offers at least three advantages. The most obvious one is that it provides a maximum financial incentive for the salesman to work to capacity.[23] The earnings of individual salesmen are more likely to reflect their true abilities and efforts under this plan. A second advantage is that a straight commission plan leads to selling expenses more closely related to funds either currently available or becoming available through sales revenues. The company avoids the hazards of bearing fixed selling expenses in the face of declining sales revenues. A third advantage is that commission plans enable management to employ *financial* incentives to direct salesmen in their use of selling time. Higher commission rates can be established for those products or accounts which management wants to emphasize.

---

[23] Psychological experiments verify that subjects perform tasks better when they expect a reward and that the level of performance is related to the amount of the promised award. J. W. Atkinson and W. R. Reitman, "Performance as a Function of Motive Strength and Expectancy of Goal Attainment," *Journal of Abnormal and Social Psychology,* November 1956, pp. 361-66.

These advantages of straight commission plans come at a substantial price, however. The foremost difficulty is that management encounters great resistance when it tries to get salesmen to do things that do not generate immediate sales. Salesmen may neglect to follow up leads, fill out reports, or provide sufficient customer service. Their personal financial involvement in getting the sale may lead them to use high-pressure tactics or price discounting which in the long run may damage customer good will and company profits. Second, straight commission plans are generally more costly to administer. The cost arises in auditing salesmen's reports, applying sliding scales, and making more elaborate calculations. Third, straight commission plans provide little security, and could have a deteriorative effect on the morale of salesmen when sales fall through no fault of their own. When this causes worry and hardship for the salesmen, it can take a real toll on their effectiveness.[24]

In developing a commission plan, management has several options regarding the commission base, the nature of commission rates, and the starting point for commissions. The *commission base* may be gross sales volume, net sales after returns, gross margins, or net profits. The *commission rates* may be identical for all sales or differentiated by customers and/or products; they may be constant with sales volume or vary in a progressive or regressive fashion. The *starting point for commissions* may be the first sale or some sales level above a breakeven point.

Most companies base sales commissions on sales volume because of administrative simplicity and because of sales management's traditional interest in promoting volume. But this base is coming under increasing attack by more profit-conscious sales executives. Sales commissions based on sales volumes may not properly relate selling effort to company profitability. The payment of commissions on *gross margin* has been recommended as a better base and one that is practical to administer.[25] It has been shown mathematically that commissions tied to product gross margins would do a superior job of directing the salesmen to act in a way that would maximize the contribution to company profits.[26]

COMBINATION SALARY AND COMMISSION PLANS. The great majority of firms use a combination of salary and commission features in the hope of achieving the advantages of each while avoiding the disadvantages. The combination plan is especially appropriate where sales volume depends upon the salesman's motivation and yet where management wants some control over the amount of nonselling duties performed by the salesman. The plan also means that during downswings the company is not stuck with rigid selling costs but neither does the salesman lose his whole income.

Many companies pay *bonuses* as a supplement or a substitute for commission-type incentives. Bonuses are noncontractual payments for extra

[24] For a comprehensive discussion of the conditions necessary for the successful application of the straight commission plan, see H. R. Tosdal and W. Carson, Jr., *Salesmen's Compensation*, Vol. I (Boston: Harvard University Graduate School of Business Administration, Division of Research, 1953).

[25] See R. L. Day and P. D. Bennett, "Should Salesmen's Compensation Be Geared to Profits?" *Journal of Marketing*, XXVI (October 1962), 6-10.

[26] See John U. Farley, "An Optimal Plan for Salesmen's Compensation," *Journal of Marketing Research*, May 1964, pp. 39-43.

effort or merit or for results beyond normal expectations. They are used to reward salesmen for performing tasks which are desirable but not rewardable through commissions, such as preparing prompt reports, supplying useful selling ideas, protecting the customer's inventory interests, and developing unusual product or market knowledgeability. The main problem with bonuses, however, is that managerial judgment enters into their determination, and this can raise questions of fairness in the minds of individual salesmen.

There is no limit to the variety of incentive-type features which may be added to straight salary plans. The example that follows cites a type of payment called a weekly bonus which combines the features of the pure commission and pure bonus:

> The salesmen were paid a weekly bonus, which was determined by three factors: sales over quota, number of calls, and sales expenses. The bonus was allocated on a point system, with ten points as the maximum. This maximum represented the total bonus that a salesman could earn in his territory; the dollar amount of bonus varied among territories. Of the ten points, eight were allocated to sales over quota, one to number of calls, and one to sales expenses. The degree to which a salesman exceeded his quota determined how many of the eight points would be credited to his bonus. If he did not make his quota, he lost all eight points. Similarly for the number of calls, he received one point. If the salesman made 60 calls (12 calls per day, 5 days a week), he received the full point for number of calls; if he made 59 calls, he received 0.8 point, if 58 calls, 0.6 point, etc. If sales expenses were held to 2 cents per hundred pounds of truck-load freight and 4 cents per hundred pounds of less than truck-load freight shipped from his territory, the salesman got the one point for sales expenses. If expenses were higher, the point credit was reduced proportionately.[27]

This scheme has the plausible purpose of influencing how salesmen spend their time. Whether it succeeds, and whether the administrative complexity does not overwhelm the advantages, remains an open question.

THE STRUCTURE OF COMPENSATION

After determining a desirable level of average salesman pay and the major elements to employ in the compensation plan, company planners must turn to the task of developing a rational pay structure for the various positions in the sales organizations. The simplest sales organization contains sales trainees, junior salesmen, senior salesmen, and sales managers. More complex sales organizations contain separate sales forces differing in ability, type of selling, etc. It is necessary to arrive at some over-all system of compensation which will be regarded as both fair and motivating to the diverse members of the sales force.

Over the years, *job evaluation* techniques have been refined, and they represent a rational management approach to developing a structure of compensation for an organization.[28] Yet sales departments have been generally slower than other company departments to utilize scientific job evaluation procedures. Many sales executives feel that the higher mobility

---

[27] Westfall and Boyd, *op. cit.*, p. 431.
[28] See David W. Hall, *Wage and Salary Administration* (Englewood Cliffs, N.J.: Prentice-Hall, Inc., 1958).

and turnover of sales employees require that their compensation be related more to demand and supply factors in the labor market than to conditions within the firm. But while some attention must be paid to the shifting conditions of demand and supply, to allow a compensation structure to evolve entirely on this basis is to invite chaos. When the payments for different job positions are determined by the circumstances of the moment, great inequities can creep in. It is important that sales departments, as they improve their recruitment, selection, and training capabilities, also turn to scientific job evaluation techniques for pricing the sales job.

Among a number of existing job evaluation systems, one of the best-known and most widely used is the *point system*. It is based on the identification of job factors, such as responsibility, education, creativeness, experience, and other elements deemed to be important. Each factor is assigned a maximum number of points. The points are assigned to each job, representing the amount of each factor required. Finally all jobs are ranked by point values, and ranges of points are set up as compensation classes. Recently linear programming has been used to determine proper factor weights.[29] Sales management should think seriously about these new techniques for rationalizing the pay structure for its sales operation.

Supervising Salesmen

The new salesman is given more than his territory and a salary—he is given supervision. Supervision is the fate of all men who work for someone else. It is the expression of the employer's natural and continuous interest in the activities of his agents. Through supervision, the employer hopes to direct and motivate the salesman to do a better job.

DIRECTING SALESMEN

Companies differ in the extent to which they try to prescribe to their salesmen what they should be doing. Much depends upon the nature of the selling job and the particular salesmen. Salesmen who are paid largely on commission and who are expected to hunt down their own prospects are generally left on their own. Salesmen who are largely salaried and who must cover a definite set of accounts are likely to receive substantial supervision.

The sales manager's major interest is in seeing that the salesmen manage their time in the best manner. Salesmen spend their time in three major activities: traveling, waiting, and selling. In many jobs, they end up spending about one-third of their time in each activity. Their traveling and waiting time is not entirely unproductive, however. They can use this time to plan future activities and report on past activities. The question remains, however, whether salesmen need as much as two-thirds of their working day for planning and reporting. The answer is generally no. Therefore company efforts to assist salesmen in reducing traveling and waiting time are generally desirable.

The company can help in a number of ways. It can clearly define the

---

[29] See Frederick P. Rehmus and Harvey M. Wagner, "Applying Linear Programming to Your Pay Structure," *Business Horizons,* Winter 1963, pp. 89-98.

extent to which salesmen should incur extra costs to reduce traveling time through the use of more expensive modes of transportation. It may be able to help salesmen develop better routing plans, given the calls they make. The company can coach the salesman on how to set up appointments more effectively by phoning ahead, suggesting luncheon engagements, and so forth.

These efforts can be described as engineering greater salesman efficiency "in the small." While they can be a source of substantial savings, their significance pales in comparison to the more central issue of making the right calls in the first place. In this connection there are two problems. One is knowing how much call time to give to different types of current accounts. The other is knowing how to find the best new prospects for business.

DEVELOPING CALL NORMS. Many companies develop a detailed classification of accounts and recommend a *call norm* for each type of account. The call norms may be expressed in terms of the *number of calls* a salesman should make per year and/or the length of each call. A small example can be given to illustrate the logic of call norms. Call norms are established on the principle that profits vary with the amount of call investment in each type of account. Suppose the relation between profits and the number of calls on different accounts is that shown in Table 19-6.

TABLE 19-6
Profits and call frequency

	Sales calls per year		
	3	6 *	9
Net cash profit			
Account type A	50	150	150
Account type B	100	100	100
Account type C	150	150	300

* Previous call frequency, all three types of accounts.

If the salesmen made six calls a year to each account, this policy would result in profits of $400 ($150 + $100 + $150) for the three accounts. But more total profits could be achieved by making 6, 3, and 9 calls respectively on the three accounts, the profits being $550 ($150 + $100 + $300).

Everything depends of course on a correct assessment of sales response to the number of calls. Typically management uses its informed judgment. However, at least two descriptions of attempts to derive the sales response function empirically have been published, one relying on a multiple regression performed on past sales data and the other relying on a planned experiment to generate data.

The first investigation was made by the Operations Research Group at Case Institute for the General Electric Company.[30] Customer accounts

[30] Clark Waid, Donald F. Clark, and Russell L. Ackoff, "Allocation of Sales Effort in the Lamp Division of the General Electric Company," *Operations Research,* December 1956, pp. 629-47.

were sorted into classes on the basis of similar characteristics. The accounts in each class were sorted again into subclasses on the basis of the call time spent with the account. Then the average dollar volume was computed for each subclass. Finally a curve was drawn through the scatter of points to show the relationship between average dollar volume and sales call time.

The scatter for each class of account lay in a basically positive direction, but was too diffused to permit the fitting of a statistically significant curve. The operations researchers tried other approaches, but these did not help. They concluded that the lack of a clear relationship could be explained by one of three hypotheses:

> Uniform sales response curves do not exist within groups of accounts.
>
> Sales response curves exist, but are difficult to find because of imperfections in the classification of accounts and the basic data.
>
> Sales response curves exist, but the data in this case reveal the upper plateaus of the curves.

The consultants rejected the first hypothesis because it would remove the major justification for call norms and went against intuition. They rejected the second hypothesis because experienced salesmen reported that they thought the classification of accounts was quite discriminating. This left the third hypothesis, which they tentatively accepted but could not prove. It implied that salesmen typically spent more time with accounts than was necessary. On the basis of this hypothesis, they recommended that the number of calls be cut back. They strongly felt that some diversion of calls from present accounts to new accounts was warranted and would result in a substantial net increase in business.

A major reason the Case group had trouble finding a meaningful relationship between call time and sales response is that they worked with uncontrolled historical data rather than experimentally produced data. In a different paper, John F. Magee described an experiment where salesmen were asked to vary their call pattern in a particular way to determine what effect this would have on sales.[31] The experiment called first for sorting accounts into major classes. Each account class was then randomly split into three sets. The respective salesmen were asked, for a specified period of time, to spend less than five hours a month with accounts in the first set, five to nine hours a month with the second set, and more than nine hours a month with the third set. The final results of these differential efforts are summarized in Table 19-7. The results seem to demonstrate that call time does have an effect on sales volume. The best call norm in this particular situation appears to be five to nine hours a month for at least three months. This cannot be definitely concluded, however, until the percentage differences are tested for significance, and the expected revenues and costs of different levels of sales effort are brought into the calculation.

[31] See John F. Magee, "Determining the Optimum Allocation of Expenditures for Promotional Effort with Operations Research Methods," in *The Frontiers of Marketing Thought and Science,* Frank M. Bass, ed. (Chicago: American Marketing Association, 1958), pp. 140-56. See also Arthur A. Brown, Frank T. Hulswit, and John D. Kettelle, "A Study of Sales Operations," *Operations Research,* June 1956, pp. 296-308.

TABLE 19-7
Conversion to customers vs. selling effort

Level of effort	Per cent converted within		
	1 month	2 months	3 months
Under 5 hours/month	0	0	8
5-9 hours/month	10	31	53
Over 9 hours/month	25	40	40

Source: John F. Magee, "Determining the Optimum Allocation of Expenditures for Promotional Effort with Operations Research Methods," in *The Frontiers of Marketing Thought and Science,* Frank M. Bass, ed. (Chicago: American Marketing Association, 1958), p. 144.

The effect of call time on sales nevertheless remains difficult to pin down because of data problems and ambiguities in the very concept of the curve. The effect depends on the attitude of the buyer toward increased calls, the effectiveness of the salesman, the call time put in by competitors, and so forth. Furthermore, call time has a delayed rather than an immediate effect on sales. Even after three or four sales calls, the buyer may not place an order until he is sure and a need arises.[32]

The position taken here is that call norms are desirable, but as guidelines rather than requirements.[33] Management formulates them to suggest not what is right in a particular situation but rather what an economic and desirable investment of time is for particular types of accounts by average salesmen, over the long run.[34]

GUIDES FOR NEW ACCOUNTS. We have been discussing how much time salesmen should give to various customers, without drawing much distinction between present customers and prospects. Yet the distinction is an important one. Spector Freight System, for example, established the following guidelines for its salesmen:

> You should use a call division of 75 per cent active and 25 per cent prospective. Therefore, each day you would have nine active accounts and three prospects.
> After you have made 3 calls on a prospective account with no production results, the account should be reviewed by the terminal manager or the district sales manager and yourself.[35]

There are a number of reasons why many companies try to set up a minimum requirement for the canvassing of new accounts. If left alone, many salesmen tend to spend most of their time in the offices of present customers. Present customers are better-known quantities. The salesmen can depend upon them for some business whereas a prospect may never deliver any business or deliver it only after many months of effort. Unless

[32] "3 or 4 Pre-Sale Calls?" *Industrial Marketing,* July 1961, pp. 25-28.
[33] See "A Useful Policy Guide," *Industrial Marketing,* January 1962, pp. 96-98.
[34] The story is often told about a salesman who thought he literally had to make 12 prospect calls a day. At 4:45 P.M. he was still talking with the eleventh prospect, who was getting increasingly interested in the company's products. "Tell me more, young man," said the prospect. "I'm sorry, sir," replied the salesman. "There are only 15 minutes left, and I must leave to make my last call."
[35] Westfall and Boyd, *op. cit.,* p. 427.

the salesman receives a bonus for new accounts, he assumes the risks during the courting period. Some companies try to open new accounts by using salaried missionary salesmen exclusively.

In addition to the problem of how much time salesmen should spend in cultivating prospects, there is the problem of which prospects to cultivate. This problem is especially acute in situations where there are more prospects than time available for developing them. Somehow they must be ranked, and salesmen should concentrate on the prospects at the top of the list. One useful basis for ranking is the *expected rate of return on a call investment to that prospect.* Specifically, consider the following formula:

$$R_i = \frac{P_i V_i - C_i}{C_i}$$

where

R_i = the expected rate of return for a call investment of C_i to the ith prospect

P_i = the probability that the ith prospect will become a customer with a call investment of C_i

V_i = the discounted value of the ith prospect's business (in profit dollars)

C_i = the expected cost of converting the ith prospect into a customer

The product, $P_i V_i$, represents the expected discounted value of the ith prospect's business. From this must be subtracted the expected cost of getting his business, or C_i. The net expected value of this business, $P_i V_i - C_i$, is then expressed as a ratio to the expected cost of the conversion. This ratio represents the expected rate of return in cultivating this prospect. It follows that a prospect with an R of 20 per cent would be more desirable to pursue than a prospect with an R of 10 per cent.

A possible shortcoming of this measure is that two prospects may have the same R and yet may not seem equally worth pursuing. For example, would it be better to go after a prospect worth $5,000 with an .8 probability of conversion or a prospect worth $20,000 with a .2 probability of conversion, assuming the same call investment was involved? Individual salesmen are not likely to be indifferent toward these two prospects. If salesmen are asked to choose between them, the majority would probably prefer to pursue the surer prospect. If the surer prospects would receive too much attention, the formula would have to be modified.

MOTIVATING SALESMEN

Management must not only set guidelines for the salesmen but must also stimulate them to perform at their maximum ability. A small percentage of salesmen in any sales force can be expected to do their best without any special stimulation from management. To them, selling is the most fascinating job in the world. These men are ambitious, and they are self-starters. But the majority of salesmen on nearly every sales force require personal encouragement and special incentives to work at their best level. This is especially true for creative door-to-door or office-to-office selling for the following reasons:

The nature of the job. The selling job is unavoidably one of frequent frustration. The salesman works alone; his hours are irregular; he does not lead a normal family life; he confronts aggressive competing salesmen; he is in an inferior status relative to the buyer; he sometimes does not have the authority to do what is necessary to win an account.

Human nature. Most men operate below capacity in the absence of special incentive. They won't "kill themselves" unless there is some gain seen in financial terms or social recognition.

Personal problems. The salesman, like everyone else, is occasionally preoccupied with personal problems, such as sickness in the family, marital discord, or debt.

Management can affect the morale and performance of the salesmen by establishing a good general climate and providing specific motivations.

General climate refers to the character of the opportunities and working conditions as perceived by the salesmen. A poor general climate is signaled by conditions of low morale and high turnover. The underlying factors may be poor pay, disagreeable supervision, or unreasonable performance requirements. When these factors operate, the low morale is not likely to be cured by special incentives. When the general work climate is poor, it is important to discover what or who is at fault. The answer(s) will indicate what remedies to apply.

Management can employ a number of *specific motivational techniques* to spur salesmen to a high level of sales effort. We discussed elsewhere the use of incentive pay features and the establishment of quotas. Personal encouragement is a third method. The responsibility falls primarily to the salesman's immediate supervisor. The supervisor keeps in touch with the salesman through periodic correspondence, personal visits in the field, and evaluation sessions in the home office. A good sales manager is the salesman's boss, companion, coach, and confessor. Periodic sales meetings are another device for stimulating sales-force enthusiasm. For salesmen, they provide a social occasion, a break from routine, a chance to meet and talk with "company brass," a chance to air feelings and to identify with a larger group. Companies also sponsor sales contests when they want to spur salesmen to make a special selling effort above what would be reasonably expected. Planning these contests has developed into a real science, and requires experienced administration if the company wants to get good results.

In addition to positive motivations, a judicious amount of management pressure may be required to stimulate maximum effort from individual salesmen. Management's ultimate weapon, of course, is the power to terminate a man's job. But management can rely on a set of more mundane pressures to motivate its men. The salesman should feel pressure when his performance is below quota, when other salesmen are outperforming him, when his supervisor interrogates him, and so forth.[36] An effective system of motivation works on the following principle:

[36] Bonini has combined these factors into an index of pressure on the salesman. See Charles P. Bonini, *Simulation of Information and Decision Systems in the Firm* (Englewood Cliffs, N.J.: Prentice-Hall, Inc., 1963), p. 55.

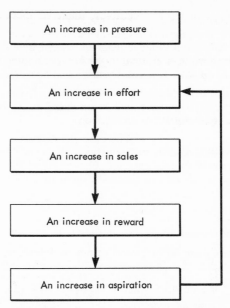

What is the relative effectiveness of different types of incentives on salesmen? This topic has not been researched experimentally. One of the few studies is a survey of the opinions of sales executives conducted a number of years ago. The sales executives were asked: "Which of the following methods will do the most to stimulate your *average* salesman to *better* his usual or normal performance?" Their assigned rankings were converted into ratings with the results shown in Table 19-8.

TABLE 19-8
Effectiveness of incentives to stimulate average salesmen to better their usual performance *

Factor	Rating
Basic compensation plan	100
Sales contests	58
Bonus payments	55
Friendly, informal supervisors	44
Scientific planning of quotas and territories	34
Honor awards and letters of commendation	23
Sales conventions	18
Profit sharing plan	17
Fringe benefits—retirement, hospitalization, etc.	14
Vacations with pay	11
Suggestion systems	2
Complaint procedures	1

* The ratings were derived in the following manner. Executives were asked to select the five most important incentives from the list and to rank them one to five. The answers were weighted by assigning values from five down to one point for the five rankings. The highest total rating went to basic compensation plans, and all other ratings were expressed as a percentage of this figure.

Source: Albert Haring and Robert H. Myers, "Special Incentives for Salesmen," *Journal of Marketing*, XVIII (October 1953), 159.

In the opinion of sales executives, financial incentives assume the first three positions of importance. They are followed by a succession of more social incentives. Thus in the minds of sales executives, dollar motivation is of prime importance, but must be complemented by social sources of motivation.

Evaluating Salesmen

In the preceding pages, we described the *feedforward* aspects of supervision—the efforts of management to communicate to the salesmen what they should be doing and to motivate them to do it. But good feedforward requires good feedback. And good feedback means getting regular information from and about salesmen to evaluate their performance.

SOURCES OF INFORMATION

Management gains information about its salesmen through a number of channels. Probably the most important source of information is the salesmen's periodic reports. Additional information comes through personal observation, customers' letters and complaints, and through other salesmen's conversations.

A distinction can be drawn between salesmen reports which represent *plans for future activities* and those which represent *write-ups of completed activities*. The best example of the former is the *salesman's work plan,* which most salesmen are required to submit for a specified future period, usually a week or a month in advance. The plan describes the calls he will make and the routing he will use. This report serves the purposes of encouraging the salesman to plan and schedule his activities, informing management of the salesman's whereabouts, and providing a basis for comparing his plans with his accomplishments. The salesman can be evaluated for his ability to "plan his work and work his plan." Occasionally, management contacts the salesman after receiving his plan and suggests improvements.

Companies moving toward annual marketing planning in depth are beginning to require their salesmen to draft an annual *territory marketing plan* in which they outline their program for developing new accounts and increasing business from existing accounts. The formats vary considerably, some asking merely for ideas on territory development and others asking for detailed estimates. This type of report reflects the conception of the salesman as an entrepreneur and as the manager of his territory. The plans are studied by the immediate supervisor and become the bases for rendering constructive suggestions to salesmen and developing branch sales objectives and estimates for higher-level management.

Several forms are used by salesmen to write up their completed activities and accomplishments. Perhaps the best-known is the *call report* (or progress report) on which the salesman records pertinent aspects of his dealings with a customer, including competitive brands used, best time for calling, degree and types of resistance, and future account promise. Call reports serve the objectives of keeping management informed of the salesman's activities, indicating the status of the customer's account, and providing information which might be useful in subsequent calls.

Salesmen also report their *expenses* incurred in the performance of selling duties, for which they are partly or wholly reimbursed. The objective from management's standpoint is primarily to exercise control over the type and amount of expenses and secondarily to have the requisite expense data for income tax purposes. It is also hoped that the salesmen will exercise more care in incurring expenses by having to report them in some detail.

Additional types of reports which some companies require from their salesmen are:

> *A report on new business secured or potential new business.* This alerts management to new accounts and new prospects for which it can formulate special marketing plans in the form of direct mail, team solicitation, etc. It is also used to evaluate the extent and effectiveness of the salesman's prospecting work.
>
> *A report on lost business.* This report enables the company to keep abreast of competitive efforts, needed product or service improvements, and, not the least important, to evaluate the effectiveness of the individual salesman.
>
> *A periodic report on local business and economic conditions.* This report aids the development of territory norms and sales programs, although it must be recognized that salesmen sometimes distort the local picture to rationalize their own performance.

The reports which companies require their salesmen to submit contain a wealth of information (and no small amount of misinformation). Salesmen, however, frequently complain that they have to devote too much time to writing when they should be selling and that their reports are not read. Management must guard against these criticisms by thinking carefully through the intended uses of the information. The forms should be brief and easy to fill out, and a premium should be put on accuracy.

FORMAL EVALUATION OF PERFORMANCE

The salesmen's reports along with other reports from the field and the manager's personal observations supply the raw materials for evaluating sales performance. In one sense, evaluation is always taking place between the sales manager and his men. The sales manager forms impressions of John Smith's performance and ability every time he receives his field reports or sees him. But we shall use "evaluation" to describe a periodic and formal management appraisal of the strengths and weaknesses of individual salesmen.

Formal evaluation procedures lead to at least three benefits. First, they lead management to develop specific and uniform standards for judging salesman performance. Second, they lead management to draw together all its information and impressions about individual salesmen and make more systematic, point-by-point evaluations. Third, they tend to have a constructive effect on the performance of salesmen. The constructive effect comes about because the salesmen know that they will have to sit down one fine morning with their supervisor and explain certain facets of their routing or call decisions or their failure to secure or maintain certain accounts, and the like.

The actual content of the evaluation must be determined by each firm.

A salesman's performance during the year has so many aspects and bases for comparison that it is difficult to know where to begin. Performance could mean his sales, the gross profit on his sales, his percentage of quota achieved, his number of calls, the number of new accounts, and so on. His current performance might be compared with that of other company salesmen, his own past record, or his potential opportunities in the territory. His performance may be broken down and analyzed by product, by customer type, by county. The cost of gathering and evaluating all this information for each individual salesman would be prohibitive. Here, as in other problems of information, firms must decide which information best satisfies their objectives while keeping down costs.

SALESMAN-TO-SALESMAN COMPARISONS. One type of evaluation frequently made is to compare a salesman's current performance with that of other company salesmen. Such comparisons, however, can be misleading. Relative sales performances are meaningful only if there are no variations from territory to territory in the market potential, workload, degree of competition, company promotional effort, and so forth. Furthermore, sales are not the best denominator of achievement. Management should be more interested in how much each salesman contributed to net profits. And this cannot be known until the salesman's sales mix and his sales expenses are examined. A possible ranking criterion would be the *salesman's actual contribution to company net profits as a ratio to his territory's potential contribution to company net profits.* A ratio of 1.00 would mean that the salesman did the best job possible in his territory. A ratio of .50 would mean that a salesman earned only 50 per cent of what a perfect salesman could have earned in that territory. The lower a salesman's ratio, the more supervision and counseling he needs.

CURRENT-TO-PAST SALES COMPARISON. A second common type of evaluation is to compare a salesman's current performance to his own past performance. This should provide a more direct record of his progress. An example of a possible format is shown in Table 19-9.

Many things can be learned by the sales manager from the information in this table. (The reader is encouraged to examine the data before reading on.) One of the first things to note is that Smith's total sales increased every year (line 3). This does not necessarily mean that Smith is doing a better job. The product breakdown shows that he has been able to push further the sales of product B than product A (lines 1 and 2). According to his quotas for the two products (lines 4 and 5), his success in increasing sales of product B may be at the expense of product A. According to gross profits (lines 6 and 7), the company earns about twice as much on A as B. The picture begins to emerge that John Smith may be pushing the higher-volume, lower-margin product at the expense of the more profitable product. In fact, although he increased total sales by $1,100 between 1963 and 1964 (line 3), the gross profits on his total sales actually decreased by $580 (line 8).

Sales expense (line 9) shows a steady increase, although total expense as a percentage of total sales seems to be under control (line 10). The upward trend in Smith's total dollar expense does not seem to be explained by any increase in the number of calls (line 11) although it may

TABLE 19-9

Form for evaluating salesman's progress

	TERRITORY	Midland		
	SALESMAN	John Smith		
	1961	1962	1963	1964
1. Net sales product A	$251,300	$253,200	$270,000	$263,100
2. " product B	$423,200	$439,200	$553,900	$561,900
3. " total	$674,500	$692,400	$823,900	$825,000
4. Per cent of quota product A	95.6	92.0	88.0	84.7
5. " product B	120.4	122.3	134.9	130.8
6. Gross profits product A	$ 50,260	$ 50,640	$ 54,000	$ 52,620
7. " product B	$ 42,320	$ 43,920	$ 55,390	$ 56,190
8. " total	$ 92,580	$ 94,560	$109,390	$108,810
9. Sales expense	$251,300	$ 11,100	$ 11,600	$ 13,200
10. Sales expense to total sales (%)	1.5	1.6	1.4	1.6
11. Number of calls	1,675	1,700	1,680	1,660
12. Cost per call	$ 6.09	$ 6.53	$ 6.90	$ 7.95
13. Average number of customers	320	324	328	334
14. Number of new customers	13	14	15	20
15. Number of lost customers	8	10	11	14
16. Average sales per customer	$ 2,108	$ 2,137	$ 2,512	$ 2,470
17. Average gross profit per customer	$ 289	$ 292	$ 334	$ 326

be related in part to his success in acquiring new customers (line 14). However, there is a possibility that in prospecting for new customers, he is neglecting present customers, as indicated by an upward trend in the annual number of lost customers (line 15).

The last two lines show the level and trend in Smith's sales per customer and the gross profits on his sales per customer. These figures become more meaningful when they are compared to over-all company averages. For example, if John Smith's average gross profit per customer is lower than the company's average, he may be concentrating on the wrong customers or may not be spending enough time with each customer. Looking back at his annual number of calls (line 11), it may be that Smith is making fewer annual calls than the average salesman. If distances in his territory are not much different, this may mean he is not putting in a full workday, he is poor at planning his routing or minimizing his waiting, or he spends too much time with certain accounts.

This only represents a surface reading of the possible meanings latent in the data in Table 19-9. Considering that the table covers only one salesman, four years, two products, and seventeen variables, an executive can appreciate the desirability of carefully thinking through what information is required.

SALES-TO-TERRITORY-POTENTIAL COMPARISONS. Most companies also examine the salesman's performance against expectations for his territory.

To illustrate this type of evaluation, consider the procedures of a very large distributor of medical supplies. The company's marketing research department supplies each district sales manager with information on each county's percentage of physicians, hospitals, drugstores, and population as a percentage of the district's totals. Illustrative indicators of potential are shown for two counties, Prairie and Central, in columns 1-4, of Table 19-10. Prairie is the smaller county in terms of potential, averaging about

TABLE 19-10
Comparison of salesman's input and output in relation to potential (in per cent)

TERRITORY   Midland

SALESMAN   John Smith

| County | Indicators of potential | | | | Average potential | Salesman's input and output | |
	Physicians	Hospitals	Drugstores	Pop.		Time spent	Sales
	(1)	(2)	(3)	(4)	(5)	(6)	(7)
Prairie	6	7	3	4	5	2	3
Central	21	19	22	18	20	30	25
:	.	.	.	.	.	.	.
.	.	.	.	.	.	.	.
.	.	.	.	.	.	.	.
Total	100	100	100	100	100	100	100

5 per cent of the total potential in Smith's territory (see column 5). Central, on the other hand, averages about 20 per cent of the total potential of Smith's territory.

The next question is how much time did Smith spend in each of these counties and how much did he sell. The district sales manager looks for the answers in columns 6 and 7 respectively. In Prairie, it appears that Smith spent proportionately less time than the size of the county warranted, and this may explain why his sales seem proportionately lower than the county's potential warranted. The situation is reversed for Central where Smith spent proportionately more time and sales were also higher. Note, however, that although Smith spent 30 per cent of his time in Central, he only drew 25 per cent of his sales from this county. The sales manager may want to ask Smith why he did not spend a little more time in Prairie. Smith may offer such reasons as:

> Prairie may be a relatively costly county to service. It may be a large rural county far from Smith's home office with accounts scattered widely.
> Smith may have relied relatively more on the telephone in selling to accounts in Prairie, and this time is not reflected in column 6.
> Smith may be concentrating on the drug stores in Prairie whose potential is only 3 per cent, which is what Smith is selling in Prairie.
> Smith may be putting in proportionately more time in Central than the

potential seems to warrant because Central may contain some key distributors whose influence radiates beyond Central.

The fact that Smith may be able to explain his allocation pattern does not negate the usefulness of such queries. Smith's awareness that the supervisor will make these comparisons should lead Smith to plan his calls and routing more carefully.

QUALITATIVE APPRAISAL OF SALESMEN.   The appraisal usually includes an evaluation of the salesman's knowledge, personality, and motivation. He can be rated on the extent of his knowledge of his company, products, customers, competitors, territory, and responsibilities. Personality characteristics can also be rated, such as his general manner, appearance, speech, and temperament. The supervisor can also consider any problems in motivation or compliance. Since there is an almost endless number of qualitative factors which might be included, each company must decide what would be most useful to know. It also should communicate these criteria to the salesmen so that they are aware of how their performance is judged.

The appraisal of each salesman serves a number of useful purposes. It is the basis of a meeting with the salesman to discuss possible areas of performance improvement. It becomes part of the historical record of the salesman's progress in various area. It also may serve as the basis for determining the salesman's bonus for the year. In general, the performance review is not an attempt to pass sentence on the salesman, but to help him to help himself.

Summary

The great majority of companies utilize salesmen, and many assign them the pivotal role in the creation of sales. Because salesmen are capable of performing a wide variety of tasks, each company faces the challenge of deciding exactly what it expects to accomplish through direct selling. The objectives set for the sales force influence the strategies and tactical decisions arising in the management of an effective sales operation.

At the strategic level, the company must decide on the size of its sales force and how it should be organized. In principle, the sales force should be expanded up to the point where an additional salesman would impose more cost on the company than he generates in the way of a gross margin on sales. In practice, sales-force size decisions are made on estimates of salesman productivity in different territories or feasible territory workloads. The effectiveness of the sales force will depend upon whether it is organized along territorial, product, or customer lines and whether sales territories are designed thoughtfully in terms of size and shape.

Salesmen must be continuously recruited and selected on the

basis of scientific procedures to hold down the high costs of hiring the wrong men. Salesman training programs are growing more elaborate and require careful thought and planning to justify their costs. Salesmen who emerge from the training program must be assigned to territories in a way that recognizes their varying productivity in different possible assignments. Compensation is probably the most important single element in their motivation, and should somehow provide a measure of both incentive and security to be maximally effective. The average salesman needs supervision and continuous encouragement because he must make a large number of decisions and is subject to many frustrations. Periodically his performance must be formally evaluated not for the sake of criticism but to help him to help himself do a better job.

Questions and Problems

1. A district sales manager voiced the following complaint at a sales meeting. "The average salesman costs our company $20,000 in compensation and expenses. Why can't we buy a few less $20,000 full-page advertisements in *Life* magazine and use the money to hire more men? Surely one man working a full year can sell more product than a one-page ad in one issue of *Life*." Evaluate this argument.

2. The text described some of the characteristics which might be looked for in salesmen. What characteristics should be looked for in selecting district sales managers? What about the top sales manager?

3. (a) Show diagrammatically, in terms of distances traveled, why a product-structured sales force involves more total travel distance than an unspecialized sales force.

   (b) Show diagrammatically why a customer-structured sales force involves more total travel distance than an unspecialized sales force.

4. The sales manager of a large company would like to determine how many sales calls per month his men should make to average-size accounts. Describe how an experiment might be set up to answer the question.

5. A sales manager is trying to figure out the most that should be spent to win a particular account. This account would produce sales of $10,000 a year, and the company is likely to retain it for at least four years. The company's profit margin on sales is 15 per cent. The company wants its various investments to earn 8 per cent. What is the most that the company should spend to win this account?

6. Suppose a salesman in a particular industry can make an average of 1,600 calls a year. If he has been writing $420,000 worth of business a year, how many calls can the salesman afford to make to a $10,000-a-year account without diluting his total business written during the year?

7. Describe several types of selling situations where a straight salary plan seems appropriate.

chapter 20

Marketing Decisions and the Law

Hardly a major marketing decision is unaffected in some way by law and public policy. Decisions on product, price, marketing channels, sales force, and advertising are all tinged with legal considerations. This final chapter of Part III will discuss the rationale of legal regulation in marketing, the historical development of business and marketing legislation, and the manner in which each of the major marketing decisions is affected by the law.

The Rationale for Legislation
Regulating Business

The American economic system is based on the principles of private enterprise and free competition. These principles were given their first clear enunciation in the late eighteenth century. They represented a reaction to the prevailing philosophy of heavy governmental control and protectionism on all economic fronts. In his *Wealth of Nations,* Adam Smith argued that economic welfare would be maximized if every firm enjoyed maximum freedom to pursue its economic interests. Smith attacked governmental intervention in the form of bounties, discriminatory taxes, cartel protections, wage regulation, and other measures which established special privileged groups or hindered free competition. He argued that the role of government should be limited to defense, public works, and foreign relations. He felt that under free competition, the powerful motive of self-interest would lead everyone to make a maximum contribution to the common good. Each would be rewarded according to his contribution. He labored to establish that the pursuit of profit was unselfish and that there would be natural harmony and social progress in the actions of free men.

This doctrine of the benefits of free competition has since undergone many refinements. Marshall C. Howard expressed the contemporary rationale succinctly in the following words:

> The producer-seller must satisfy the customers' wants. To do this he must know the customers' wants and be able to satisfy them as well as or better than business rivals can. Competition can be in terms of price, quality, nature of the product or service, or conditions of sale. The successful producer-seller is the one who has been most skillful in researching the buyers' wants, in procuring the resources to satisfy those wants, and in promoting sales. Other things being equal, this is accomplished by offering the best-quality goods at the lowest prices and on the most convenient terms of sale

and delivery. Competition forces the business rivals to provide the best for the least. The efficient firms will be profitable and survive; the inefficient will not.[1]

There would be no need for law if all firms would play the competitive game according to these rules. The fact is, however, that there is considerable temptation for firms to engage in a variety of practices which violate the spirit or letter of this system and thus subvert its benefits. These practices fall into the two broad categories of *monopoly actions* and *deceptive actions.*

Monopoly actions have the effect of substantially lessening competition. The firm may pursue monopoly actions alone or in concert with others. Examples of singular monopoly action are predatory acts designed to destroy competitors, buying up competitors, and excluding new competitors by tying up sources of supply. Examples of concerted monopoly actions are industry price fixing, dividing up the market, and cornering the market. To the extent the firm succeeds in lessening competition, it enjoys a greater control over total output and prices. The presumption is that it will use its economic power to restrict output and increase prices to enhance its profits. But these actions are contrary to public interest.

Deceptive actions create company sales by implying things about its products or services which are untrue or highly overstated or which falsify or disparage competitors' products or services. Examples would be false advertising, bait advertising, misrepresented quality, and false labeling. Such practices are unfair and harmful both to consumers who end up with less than they expected and to competitors who have lost the sale. If not curbed, they tend to destroy bona fide competitors and cause the remaining ones to adopt the same practices as a matter of survival.

Because monopoly actions and deceptive actions are contrary to the interest of customers and other business firms, many laws have been passed in this country with the ostensible aim of preserving competition. When businessmen become angry because their freedom is restricted by this or that law, they should recognize the contribution which the totality of laws makes in preserving their freedom against predatory or deceptive actions of others. Probably the chief complaint of businessmen is directed at the vagueness of the typical piece of legislation, where the effect is to leave the firm uncertain whether a contemplated action is legal or illegal. But some vagueness is unavoidable, and may in fact be desirable for at least three reasons.

First, there is often a fine line between different actions which may appear to harm competitors or consumers. A firm may grow into a monopoly position not because of unfair practices, but because of superior efficiency. Is this firm to be restrained because it takes advantage of its superior efficiency to outperform other firms? Implicit in the notion of competition is possible harm to less progressive competitors. Or consider the fine line between actions which puff up the benefits of a product to a customer (these are typical of advertising) and actions which distort these benefits to the point of deception. The vagueness in the legislation

[1] Marshall C. Howard, *Legal Aspects of Marketing* (New York: McGraw-Hill Book Company, 1964), pp. 1-2. This section is indebted to Howard's discussion. Used by permission.

reflects the difficulty of spelling out in fine detail the differences between these things.

Second, the vagueness contributes more flexibility to the law. More is left to judicial interpretation, and the judges are freer to recognize new definitions of public interest.

Third, the vagueness has the effect of keeping businessmen alert and thinking twice about the ethical and public interest aspects of their actions. If the laws were specific, some businessmen might invent unethical practices not proscribed by law. The vagueness of the law means that new forms of dubious competitive action may be brought under existing laws through judicial reinterpretation. The over-all effect is to create more conservatism in the actions firms might take affecting their competitors or customers.

Historical Development of Business and Marketing Legislation

There is a vast amount of American law affecting business competition and marketing decision making—much more than any marketing executive can be expected to know. On the federal level, there are at least eight major acts and amendments and dozens of minor acts. There are scores of federal court decisions, which represent significant turning points in the interpretation of these acts. Each of the fifty states has its own special legislation and court interpretations. In addition to statutory law, there is a vast body of common law which spells out improper practices in the conduct of business. Hundreds of government agencies oversee competition, ranging from such well-known bodies as the Antitrust Division of the Department of Justice and the Federal Trade Commission, all the way down to city and state commissions, which license businesses, and Better Business Bureaus, which keep a check on deceptive practices. Each year that passes adds new acts, new powers, new interpretations. Knowing the laws is a full-time job, and even legal specialists can never be sure of the answers. Nevertheless, legal specialists must be turned to for advice at every step of the way. The only purpose in describing the historical development of legislation affecting competition is to make the marketing executive conscious of the basis for the legal questions that may be raised as he prepares to take new marketing actions. With this consciousness, he would know enough to consult legal experts for the answers.

The best way to begin is by looking at the major milestones in federal legislation affecting competition. Eight acts are listed in Table 20-1. An attempt will be made to show why each act was passed, how its interpretation evolved, and what weaknesses still remained.

SHERMAN ANTITRUST ACT (1890)

The post-Civil War period witnessed a growth in cartels, pools, and trusts and led to the fear of rigged outputs and increased prices. Public and business opposition to the "robber barons" grew strong enough by 1890 to lead to the passage of this act, which was the first to establish a statutory public policy toward the restraint of trade and monopoly in interstate and foreign commerce. Prior to it, monopoly actions could only be opposed on

TABLE 20-1
Milestone legislation affecting marketing

Sherman Antitrust Act (1890)

Prohibited (a) "monopolies or attempts to monopolize" and (b) "contracts, combinations, or conspiracies in restraint of trade."

Pure Food and Drug Act (1906)

Forbade the manufacture, sale, or transport of adulterated or fraudulently labeled foods and drugs in interstate commerce. (Supplanted by the Food, Drug, and Cosmetic Act, 1938; amended by Food Additives Act, 1958).

Meat Inspection Act (1906)

Provided for the enforcement of sanitary regulations in packing establishments, and for federal inspection of all companies selling meats in interstate commerce.

Federal Trade Commission Act (1914)

Established the commission, a body of specialists with broad powers to investigate and to issue cease and desist orders to enforce Section 5, which declared that "unfair methods of competition in commerce are unlawful." (Amended by Wheeler-Lea Act, 1938, which added the phrase "and unfair or deceptive acts or practices.")

Clayton Act (1914)

Supplemented the Sherman Act by prohibiting certain specific practices (certain types of price discrimination, tying clauses and exclusive dealing, intercorporate stockholdings, and interlocking directorates) "where the effect . . . may be to substantially lessen competition or tend to create a monopoly in any line of commerce." Provided that violating corporate officials could be held individually responsible; exempted labor and agricultural organizations from its provisions.

Robinson-Patman Act (1936)

Amended the Clayton Act. Added the phrase "to injure, destroy, or prevent competition." Defined price discrimination as unlawful (subject to certain defenses) and provided the FTC with the right to establish limits on quantity discounts, to forbid brokerage allowances except to independent brokers, and to prohibit promotional allowances or the furnishing of services or facilities except where made available to all "on proportionately equal terms."

Miller-Tydings Act (1937)

Amended the Sherman Act to exempt interstate fair-trade (price fixing) agreements from antitrust prosecution. (The McGuire Act, 1952, reinstated the legality of the nonsigner clause.)

Antimerger Act (1950)

Amended Section 7 of the Clayton Act by broadening the power to prevent intercorporate acquisitions where the acquisition may have a substantially adverse effect on competition.

the basis of the common law, which was far from clear-cut, or under various state antimonopoly laws, which were enforced only laxly.

Although the act defined the intent of Congress to prevent monopolies and restraints of trade, it was vague, and the early courts rendered unsympathetic interpretations. The act did not have much effect on the growth of trusts until Theodore Roosevelt became President. He took up the cause of more vigorous enforcement and won a series of positive decisions, the most notable ones being against Northern Securities (1904), Standard Oil Company (1911), and American Tobacco Company (1911). In the *Standard Oil* case, the Supreme Court introduced the "rule of reason," which suggested that the plaintiff's act must constitute an unreasonable restraint of trade to be unlawful.[2] This meant that each case had to be judged individually against the rule of reason. This and other

[2] Standard Oil Company of New Jersey v. United States, 221 U.S. 1 (1911).

weaknesses in the Sherman Act made it clear that stronger legislation was needed to preserve competition.

PURE FOOD AND DRUG ACT AND MEAT-INSPECTION ACT (1906)

For years some food and drug manufacturers and meat packers had been selling dangerous drugs and adulterated foods to the public. These practices were exposed by Harvey W. Wiley, the Chief Chemist of the Agricultural Department, and by Upton Sinclair in his novel *The Jungle*. Public indignation finally led Theodore Roosevelt to press for legislation and the Congress enacted two new acts in 1906. They were the first major federal acts to protect consumers against deceptive or harmful practices. The Pure Food and Drug Act made the misbranding or adulteration of foods and drugs unlawful and empowered Wiley's Bureau of Chemistry to make tests and recommend prosecutions. Cosmetics and therapeutic devices were added in the 1938 revision. The Meat-Inspection Act empowered the federal government to inspect and certify processed meat.

FEDERAL TRADE COMMISSION ACT (1914)

By the time Woodrow Wilson came into power, it was clear that the Sherman Act under the "rule of reason" interpretation was not strong enough to combat the power of the trusts. It was felt that a commission of specialists should be established to handle the more economic and technical issues in antitrust to guide the courts. This commission was established by the passage of the Federal Trade Commission Act in 1914. It was given the power to investigate and issue cease and desist orders. The act declared "unfair methods of competition" to be illegal, this giving slightly more latitude for prosecution. In particular, the act was designed to help catch in their incipiency practices which might lead eventually to monopoly. The commission was expected to work out its own meaning of unfair methods of competition. However, the courts continued to act unsympathetically. The commission turned to efforts to have industry develop trade practice codes which would protect individual firms' and consumers' interests. The Trade Practice Conferences were only partially successful, many persons opposing them on the grounds that they would amount to giving government sanction to restrictive or collusive industry practices.

Some of the early FTC efforts were also directed to exposing false advertising and branding, but in 1931 a court held that the FTC's power was limited to exposing "injury to competition," not to consumers.[3] This limitation was finally remedied in 1938 by the Wheeler-Lea Act, which added to "unfair methods of competition" the phrase "and unfair or deceptive acts or practices." Today, the FTC regulates a broad variety of business practices which may tend to hurt other businesses or consumers.

CLAYTON ACT (1914)

In addition to creating the FTC, Congress strengthened the Sherman Act by passing the Clayton Act. The Clayton Act broadened the latitude of antitrust prosecution by defining practices as unlawful "where the effect . . . may be to substantially lessen competition or tend to create a monopoly." In other words, the government no longer had to produce proof

---

[3] Federal Trade Commission v. Raladam Co., 283 U.S. 643 (1931).

of actual monopoly or conspiracy. Four practices were singled out in particular so that the law would be more specific. They were certain types of price discrimination (Section 2), tying and exclusive agreements (Section 3), intercorporate stockholdings (Section 7), and interlocking directorates (Section 8). These practices were not illegal per se, but only if they substantially lessened competition. The enforcement agencies were still left with the task of working out guides for "competition" and the term "substantially lessen."

ROBINSON-PATMAN ACT (1936)

The advent of the Depression put great pressure on prices and stimulated the growth of chain organizations which could pass on lower prices to consumers. These chain organizations enjoyed certain operating economies and also managed in many instances to obtain special prices or brokerage concessions from suppliers. For example, the Great Atlantic and Pacific Tea Company would get price concessions from food manufacturers by implying that it might take its business elsewhere or do its own manufacturing. It also collected brokerage fees through a wholly owned subsidiary, gaining a further price edge. Small groceries found it hard to compete with A&P, and many went under. Yet it was difficult to prove that the practices of the A&P tended to lessen competition *substantially*. This, and similar activities of other chains, struck many as imperiling the future of small businesses and led to considerable lobbying for new legislation. Finally, in 1936, the Robinson-Patman Act was passed, with its primary mission to save small business by regulating price discrimination.

The Robinson-Patman Act held:

> It shall be unlawful . . . to discriminate in price between different purchasers of commodities of like grade and quality . . . where the effect of such discrimination may be substantially to lessen competition or tend to create a monopoly, *or to injure, destroy, or prevent competition* . . . provided. . . . [Italics added.]

There are two important points to notice about this wording. First, the phrase "to injure, destroy, or prevent competition" was added for the first time. A company action no longer had to be shown to lessen competition substantially to be unlawful; it might be unlawful if it *injured* competition. The FTC and many of the courts have interpreted "injury to competition" to mean "injury to competitors." It is easier to point to specific competitors who are injured than to prove a general injury to competition.

But this interpretation opens up a hornet's nest of problems. Almost every competitive action is designed to enhance the company's position at the expense of the competitors' positions. Companies which innovate or which advertise better, for example, injure competitors all the time. The major criticism of the Robinson-Patman Act is that it has been interpreted in ways that have protected inefficient firms against creative competition. Instead of promoting competition, the act protects many firms against the effects of bona fide competition.

The second point is that price discrimination is not prohibited per se. The act specifies several circumstances under which price differentials are permitted, the major one being where the differentials reflect different costs in dealing with the buyers.[4] This defense has made it necessary for every management contemplating the use of differential prices to work up a careful set of cost data in the event the differentials are challenged. Even then, there are different ways to measure cost, and this may still lead to a court challenge. Some other defenses against the charge of unlawful price discrimination are that the action did not involve interstate commerce, that the action did not tend to lessen competition, that the action met (but did not exceed) the lower price of a competitor, or that the action represented distress sales under court order.

Besides price differentials, the Robinson-Patman Act regulated against discrimination through advertising allowances, brokerage fees, or special services or facilities. All of these have to be made available to all on "proportionately equal terms"; otherwise they could amount to disguised ways to give preferential treatment to some firms and thus injure their competitors. The phrase "proportionately equal terms" is obviously vague. Does it mean giving the same advertising allowance to large and small stores, in which case the small ones would seem to gain a disproportionate benefit; or does it mean giving an allowance in proportion to sales, in which case the small stores would hardly get enough to be able to achieve any promotional impact?

The over-all effect of the Robinson-Patman Act is to create an extreme amount of caution among businessmen in the use of prices, allowances, and so forth, which might appear discriminatory. One result is that businessmen are more interested in cost pricing than demand pricing.[5] Another result is that active price competition is to some extent discouraged in favor of other planes of competition, such as promotion and service.[6]

MILLER-TYDINGS RESALE PRICE MAINTENANCE ACT (1937)

During the Depression of the 1930's, some retailers tried to stimulate the sales of trade-marked items by cutting their prices below manufacturers' suggested prices. Other retailers were opposed, and asked manufacturers to see to it that uniform resale prices were maintained. But this would amount to vertical price fixing, and its status under state and federal antitrust laws was unclear. In 1931 California passed an act permitting manufacturers or wholesalers to set retail prices through requiring retailers to sign contracts agreeing to price. Since this did not bind nonsigning retailers, and hence was not particularly effective, California passed a nonsigner's clause in 1933 binding all retailers in the state if one retailer signed the contract. This was a victory for the small retailers in California and led to widespread lobbying in other states. Eventually, 45 states passed these laws.

Nevertheless, the doubt still lingered whether the state laws protecting price fixing were supportable under federal antitrust law. To make this

---

[4] Even when the company can prove a substantial cost difference exists, it may not be able to set prices which fully reflect the differentials when this would be too injurious of competition. See *Business Week*, January 12, 1957, p. 121, and April 26, 1958, p. 57.

[5] See Chapter 15, pp. 361-64.

[6] One of the best studies of the law on price discrimination is Frederick M. Rowe, *Price Discrimination under the Robinson-Patman Act* (Boston: Little, Brown & Co., 1962).

clear, Congress passed the Miller-Tydings Act in 1937, allowing manufacturers in interstate commerce to make these contracts in states which had resale price maintenance laws, thus exempting these contracts from federal antitrust legislation. However, the contracts did not have legal status in states which had not passed resale price maintenance laws.

The Miller-Tydings Act did not, however, specifically recognize the nonsigner's clause. This was tested before the Supreme Court in 1951, and the court ruled that the Miller-Tydings Act did not envision or support the nonsigner's clause.[7] Nonsigners quickly began to cut prices, creating a dilemma for those who signed contracts. Congress clarified its intent the next year by passing the McGuire Act (1952), which reinstated the legality of the nonsigner's clause. Thus, all dealers in a fair-trade state had to agree to price maintenance as long as one dealer did.

Resale price maintenance (or fair trade, as it is called by its supporters) has been used most prominently in the sale of drug and cosmetic items, books, phonograph records, electrical appliances, fountain pens, and photographic equipment. Many manufacturers who used resale price maintenance contracts did it reluctantly, under pressure, particularly from their drug customers. But as the manufacturers' sales moved increasingly into nondrug outlets, many manufacturers abandoned the contracts. They found them difficult to police (the burden is on them), costly to take to court, and likely to offend the more vigorous channel members. Fair Trade was dealt a severe blow in 1958 when the Supreme Court ruled that the Masters Mail Order Company of Washington, D.C., did not have to adhere to General Electric's fair-trade prices because Masters took title to the goods in a nonfair-trade state.[8] At this point, General Electric, which had earnestly fair-traded its small appliances, gave up, and other manufacturers soon followed suit. Since then, several states have repealed their resale price maintenance legislation, and until recently it appeared that fair trade was a dying cause. However, a new push appeared in the early 1960's in the form of the controversial Quality Stabilization Bill.[9] This bill would allow manufacturers of trade-marked, brand-name goods to establish minimum resale prices and to enforce them against any price cutter, regardless of state laws on the subject. Thus, fair-trade legislation is far from dead. Each marketing executive will want to consider carefully the implications of fair trade as a managerial tool. It has implications for retail prices, channel design, channel member loyalties, and policing effort. From a social point of view, it has broad implications for consumer welfare and the nature of competition.[10]

ANTIMERGER ACT (1950)

In 1950, Congress passed the Celler-Kefauver amendment to Section 7 of the Clayton Act. The new law, known as the Antimerger Act, was designed to remedy loopholes in the existing legislation regarding corporate growth through merger and acquisition. The Clayton Act, as interpreted

---

7 Schwegmann Brothers v. Calvert Distillers Corporation, 341 U.S. 384 (1951).

8 General Electric Co. v. Masters Mail Order Company, 78 S.Ct. 32 (1958).

9 "Fair Trade Comeback," *Business Week,* July 11, 1959, p. 63.

10 See E. R. Corey, "Fair Trade Pricing: A Reappraisal," *Harvard Business Review,* September-October 1952, pp. 47-62; Jerome C. Darnell, "The Impact of Quality Stabilization," *Journal of Marketing Research,* August 1965, pp. 274-82.

by the courts, prevented intercorporate acquisition of stock, but not of assets, where the effect was to lessen competition substantially. Furthermore, the Clayton Act was viewed as applying mainly to horizontal mergers, and vertical mergers went unregulated. Many critics believed that the continuing number of mergers was the leading factor in increasing the size of businesses and the amount of concentration in American industry.[11] They insisted new legislation was needed.

The Antimerger Act widened Section 7 of the Clayton Act to apply to both stock and assets acquisitions, and where the effect was substantially to lessen competition in "any line of commerce in *any section of the country.*" The italicized phrase broadened the capability of the government to act where it discerned an incipient threat to competition, even though it was local. Yet it is only in the last few years that the government has really stepped up its antimerger activity. In the thirteen-year period 1951-1963, the average number of cases per year brought about by the Department of Justice and the Federal Trade Commission was ten, but in 1964 alone, twenty-one new cases were started.[12] Furthermore, the Supreme Court handed down only two decisions between 1950-1963, and four decisions in 1964 alone.[13] These cases considered acquisitions with horizontal, vertical, and conglomerate aspects, and the Supreme Court ruled clearly against the mergers in five of the six cases.

The effect of the Antimerger Act and its increasingly vigorous enforcement is that large companies find it increasingly difficult to acquire other large, or even medium-sized, companies in their own or closely related markets. Large companies wishing to expand will find horizontal mergers and vertical integration less open to them; they will have to expand into highly unrelated lines. For example, Ekco Products Company was ordered by the FTC to divest itself of a recently acquired meat-handling equipment company and to refrain from acquiring the whole or any part of any manufacturer of meat-handling equipment for the next 20 years without FTC approval.[14] Thus, the act should have the effect of increasing the diversification of company product lines. This puts a new set of conditions and constraints on the planning of long-run corporate growth.[15]

OTHER LAWS

A host of other federal laws affect business compeition. Many of them regulate practices found in specific industries. Their content is often sug-

[11] One estimate held that 80 corporations owed between one-third and one-fourth of their 1948 size to past acquisitions and mergers. J. Fred Weston, *The Role of Mergers in the Growth of Large Firms* (Berkeley: University of California Press, 1953).

[12] See Betty Bock, *Mergers and Markets, An Economic Analysis of the 1964 Supreme Court Merger Decisions,* 4th ed., Studies in Business Economics, No. 87 (New York: National Industrial Conference Board, Inc., 1965), p. 11.

[13] *Ibid.,* p. 3. The cases were Brown Shoe Co. v. U.S., 370 U.S. 326 (1962); U.S. v. Philadelphia National Bank, 374 U.S. 321 (1963); U.S. v. El Paso Natural Gas Co., 376 U.S. 651 (1964); U.S. v. Aluminum Co. of America, 377 U.S. 271 (1964); U.S. v. Continental Can Co., 378 U.S. 441 (1964); and U.S. v. Penn-Olin Chemical Co., 378 U.S. 158 (1964).

[14] "Legal Developments in Marketing," *Journal of Marketing,* XXIX (January 1965), 75.

[15] See Jesse W. Markham, "Antitrust Trends and New Constraints," *Harvard Business Review,* May-June 1963, pp. 84-92.

gested by their names: Federal Communication Act (1934), Motor Carrier Act (1935), Wool Products Labeling Act (1939), Landham Trademark Act (1946), Flammable Fabric Act (1953), Auto Dealers' Act (1956), and Automobile Information Disclosure Act (1958). Every year Congress considers several new bills which would introduce further controls on monopoly acts or deceptive practices. In 1959, for example, Congress considered but did not pass a bill to require companies in highly oligopolized industries to go through federal hearings before every price boost, a bill to allow auto makers to prevent dealers from selling outside their territories, a bill to require manufacturers to grant wholesalers a bigger discount than they give to large retail chains, and a bill to protect independent retailers from price competition by a manufacturer who does retailing of his own.[16]

Marketing executives have to contend not only with many federal laws, but also with an almost endless number of state and local laws to regulate competition within the state. (Federal laws apply only to business involving interstate commerce.) There are State Unfair Practices Acts regulating minimum prices, state fair-trade laws, local laws regulating Sunday and evening selling, laws requiring licenses for certain businesses, laws preventing the out-of-state importation of certain commodities, laws against door-to-door selling, and so forth. Virtually all states have their own statutory provisions against restraint of trade and against deceptive practices. By and large, however, most state and local laws are aimed at, or have been used to limit competition. They reflect the disproportionate influence of small wholesalers, retailers, and local associations on the state legislatures.

Major Marketing Decisions Affected by the Law

In reviewing the history of United States legislation affecting competition, the marketing decisions affected are implicit in each case. In this section, these areas will be stated more explicitly. The purpose is to draw together the major legal questions that might be raised in each category of marketing decision so that the marketing executive senses the possible legal constraints on his decision making. A summary of these legal questions is shown in Figure 20-1.[17]

COMPETITIVE RELATIONS DECISIONS

The firm must proceed cautiously with respect to the use of different competitive instruments that might expand its size or its share of market. This includes attempts to grow through acquisition or merger, to develop cooperative relations with competitors, or to adopt certain hard tactics against competitors.

EXPANSION.   In the case of acquisitions, the law holds it is not a ques-

[16] "Fair Trade Comeback," *op. cit.*
[17] This classification of marketing decision areas affected by law is adapted from Edward W. Cundiff and Richard R. Still, *Basic Marketing: Concepts, Environment and Decisions* (Englewood Cliffs, N.J.: Prentice-Hall, Inc., 1964), pp. 216-36.

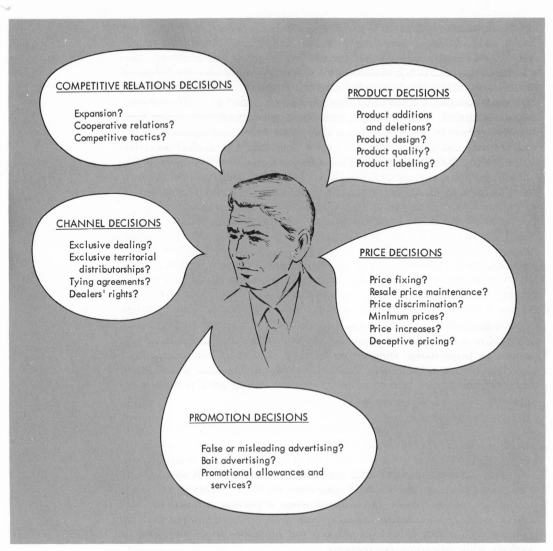

FIGURE 20-1

Major marketing decision areas that may be called into question under the law

tion of the good or bad intentions of the acquiring firm, but only of the effects of the acquisition on competition. The courts have rejected such defenses as competitive intent, growth needs, declining position of acquiring company, lack of competition, rapid expansion of an industry, ease of entry, and so forth. If there is a reasonable probability that the acquisition will substantially lessen competition "in any line of commerce in any section of the country," then the acquisition may be prevented by the government. The case hinges on how the relevant market is defined and how the acquisition will affect competition in this market. Regarding the first point, Lever Brothers' 1957 acquisition of Monsanto Chemical's "All," a low-sudsing, heavy-duty detergent, was prosecuted by the FTC on the charge that it increased Lever Brothers' market share of the "heavy-duty detergent market" from 16.5 to 21.1 per cent between 1950 and 1960. But a district court dropped the charge by ruling that the relevant market was "low-sudsing heavy-duty detergents," in which Lever Brothers' share was nil at the time of the acquisition.[18] In Continental Can's acquisition of Hazel-Atlas Glass, the Supreme Court had to decide whether metal cans and glass containers constituted two markets or one.[19] If they constituted different markets, then the acquisition could not substantially lessen competition. However, the Court ruled that there was active competition between metal and glass containers (in baby foods, soft drinks, beer, and so forth) and therefore instead of Continental Can's diversifying by adding a glass container to its metal can line, it was increasing its dominance in the "metal and glass container" market. Once the Court defined the market in this way, it found that Continental Can accounted for 22 per cent of the combined shipments of metal and glass containers and Hazel-Atlas accounted for three per cent. The Court felt that the acquisition would raise Continental Can's share of this market to a dangerous level. In general, after the relevant market is determined, the courts try to appraise how the acquisition would affect market share, company size, and further acquisitions.

COOPERATIVE RELATIONS.   The law also bears down hard on any signs of collusive relations between presumably competing companies. Such joint actions as price fixing, splitting up markets, excluding new competitors, agreeing on various customers, and so forth, would constitute a conspiracy. Price agreements are held to be illegal per se; that is, no defenses are acceptable. This applies to obvious violations such as rigged bids or the use of common basing points in quoting price, and even such apparently minor actions as exchanging price lists for information purposes, or parallel pricing action.[20] A sensational case involved the sentencing of 44 major executives in the electrical equipment industry (General Electric, Westinghouse, and many other companies) after the Justice Department was able to show that price rigging in this industry had gone on for 25 years.[21] The TVA had tipped off the Justice Department when it became aroused in 1959 over a succession of almost identical bids. The evidence showed that top electrical equipment executives worked out common prices and split up markets while attending conventions.

COMPETITIVE TACTICS.   The law will also condemn a firm which uses hard or predatory tactics against its competitors. This includes cutting off a competitor's source of supply, disparaging a competitor's products or ability, or threatening or using actual intimidation. The FTC brought U.S. Industries to court on the charge that the salesmen of its distributors were disparaging competitors' products.[22] The FTC issued a cease and

[18] U.S. v. Lever Brothers Company and Monsanto Chemical Company 216 F. Supp. 887 (1963).

[19] U.S. v. Continental Can Co., 378 U.S. 441 (1964).

[20] The doctrine of conscious parallel action in pricing is discussed by Michael Conant, "Consciously Parallel Action in Restraint of Trade," *Minnesota Law Review,* XXXVIII (1953-1954), pp. 797-825.

[21] "The Great Conspiracy," *Time,* February 17, 1961, pp. 84-85.

[22] Commerce Clearing House, *Trade Regulation Reporter* (1954), Par. 25, 148, and 25, 363.

desist order to the Washington Crab Association to stop coercing fishermen to join the association and to limit their catching of crabs.

PRODUCT DECISIONS

Marketing management must take cognizance of the law in making decisions respecting product additions and deletions, product design, product quality, and labeling.

PRODUCT ADDITIONS AND DELETIONS. The firm's product mix changes through the process of adding new products and dropping old ones. Decisions to add products, particularly through acquisitions, may be prevented under the Antimerger Act if the effect threatens to lessen competition. Decisions to drop old products must be made with an awareness that the firm has legal obligations, written or implied, to its suppliers, dealers, and customers who have a stake in the discontinued product.

PRODUCT DESIGN. The firm must design its new products in the context of the complicated U.S. patent laws. The patent laws are both a constraint and an opportunity for any firm. They are a constraint in the sense that the innovating firm is prevented from designing a product which is "illegally similar" to another company's established product. This may be quite difficult to determine, the definition of "similar" resting on whether consumers consider the design or outward appearance to be the same. After a patent is granted, the patent laws represent an opportunity, because the firm's new product is protected against "illegally similar" products for three and a half, seven, or fourteen years, depending on the patentable period. The firm may license manufacturing rights to others in return for a royalty, but is under no legal compulsion to do so. The role of patents as an opportunity and a constraint in product decisions also applies to trade-marks and copyrights. All three legal areas must be competently considered in all new product introductions. At the same time, not all company designs are protectable, especially those which are transient. Style piracy is quite common in the women's apparel industry because the patents are rarely secured before the season is over.

PRODUCT QUALITY AND LABELING. Manufacturers of foods, drugs, cosmetics, and certain fibers must comply with specific laws in establishing product quality and labeling. The Pure Food and Drug Act and its later revisions forbid any product adulteration or misbranding. Food canners have to take cognizance of the grades established for many canned foods. Under the Food Additives Amendment (1958), a firm proposing to use a new additive must pretest it and satisfy the Food and Drug Administration that the chemical amounts are safe under the conditions of intended use. Labels must identify the manufacturer or distributor, the package contents and quality, and contain warnings if the product is dangerous or habit-forming. The Flammable Fabric Act requires that flammable fabrics be labeled as such. The Textile Fiber Products Identification Act requires that fabrics be labeled to show the names and percentage of each major fiber, and the country of origin if imported. In addition to these and other specific federal laws, states and localities are active, especially in regulating the quality of dairy products. The quality and labeling laws are primarily designed to protect consumers. Although manufacturers may regard many of them as a nuisance, this is a small price to pay when it is recognized that the laws also protect them against unscrupulous competition.

PRICE DECISIONS

Pricing is one of the major marketing decision areas where a knowledge of the law is essential. Management must avoid price fixing (except for resale price maintenance), price discrimination, charging less than the minimum legal price, raising prices unduly, or advertising deceptive prices.

PRICE FIXING. Pricing agreements among competitors, called horizontal price fixing, were discussed earlier and were shown to be generally prosecutable under the Sherman and Clayton Acts. The courts have even ruled that a company cannot fix the prices charged by its subsidiaries, where they may be in competition.[23] The only exceptions occur where the price agreements are carried out under the supervision of a government agency, as is the case in many local milk industry agreements, in the regulated transportation industries, and in fruit and vegetable cooperatives.

RESALE PRICE MAINTENANCE. Price agreements among firms at different stages of production and distribution, called vertical price agreements, are not illegal under state Resale Price Maintenance Acts and the enabling federal Miller-Tydings Act. A manufacturer can legally require dealers who carry his product to charge a specified retail price in fair-trade states.[24] This applies to dealers who have signed an agreement with the manufacturer, except in states with the nonsigner clause where it applies to all dealers. This legislation reflects the power of small retailers, because vertical price fixing clearly constitutes a restraint on trade and substantially lessens competition. At least four states have declared their resale price maintenance acts to be unconstitutional. In general, manufacturers who have chosen to apply fair trade have had to bear the expense of policing and have often found the courts to rule in favor of the defendant because of some extenuating circumstance or other.

PRICE DISCRIMINATION. Probably the regulations against price discrimination under the Robinson-Patman Act cause more corporate legal work and headaches than any other federal law. Back in 1954, one expert suggested that "if the Robinson-Patman lightning is no more likely to strike than 20 times a year, it is a little difficult to see why a lot of money should be spent on a detailed accounting system which is good only for Robinson-Patman Act purposes." [25] This gamble would no longer make sense today. The number of Robinson-Patman cases now averages over 200 per year. Marketing management must be careful in developing its price differentials for different classes of customers and conditions of sale (as well as any

[23] Commerce Clearing House, *Trade Regulation Reporter* (1952), Vol. III, Par. 11, 203 and 11, 660.
[24] Sellers cannot refuse to sell to noncooperating dealers in nonfair-trade states. See U.S. v. *Parke, Davis & Co.,* 362 U.S. 29 (1960).
[25] Herbert F. Taggart, *Conference on Sales Management,* Michigan Business Papers, No. 28 (Ann Arbor, Mich.: School of Business Administration, The University of Michigan, March 12, 1954), p. 30. Quoted in Markham, *op. cit.,* p. 84.

differentials in advertising allowances, facilities, services, and so forth).
Price differentials are justified to some extent where the products are not
of like grade and quality, particularly in the buyers' minds. Otherwise, these
differentials must be based on cost differences, although the arbitrariness
of overhead cost allocations always leaves a cloud of uncertainty hanging
over this defense. Usually it is easiest to justify discounts based on the
size of orders (noncumulative quantity discounts) because of the obvious
savings in the cost of manufacturing, selling, or delivering of larger orders.
But these quantity discounts must be the same for buyers at the same stage
of distribution. Discounts based on the amount purchased over a specified
period (cumulative quantity discounts), while not specifically outlawed,
are harder to justify under the cost savings argument. The costs would
vary depending upon whether the buyer purchased small amounts frequently or large amounts infrequently. Discounts which vary with the customer stage in the distribution process (functional discounts) are not prohibited as such, but may come under FTC scrutiny if the discount differences could injure competition. Thus wholesalers typically receive larger
discounts than retailers, but this may be subject to legal action if the wholesalers also compete with the retailers in selling directly to the customer.
If wholesalers do not compete with retailers, then functional discounts can
be defended not necessarily on the grounds of cost differences, but on the
grounds that competition is not injured. Marketing management may also
employ price differentials where the purpose is to "meet competition" in
"good faith," providing the firm is trying to meet competitors at its own
level of competition and that the price discrimination is temporary, localized, and defensive rather than offensive. The Supreme Court ruled in
the *Sun Oil* case that Sun Oil could not aid its dealers to meet the prices
established by independent gasoline operators, because they were at a
different level of competition.[26]

MINIMUM PRICES.   Wholesalers and retailers face laws in over half the
states requiring a minimum percentage markup over their cost of merchandise plus transportation. Called Unfair Trade Practices Acts, they are designed to protect smaller merchants from larger merchants who might
otherwise sell certain items at or below cost for a while to attract customers. Without this protection, larger competitors could ruin their smaller
competitors. The average markups required in these states are 2 per cent
at wholesale and 6 per cent at retail. At these low levels, they are mainly
relevant to the most rapid turnover items in supermarkets, such as dairy
items. Otherwise, they make very little difference to the pricing of most
items. Furthermore, the injured merchants, rather than public agencies,
are responsible for bringing complaints to court, and so enforcement tends
to be weak.

PRICE INCREASES.   In contrast to price floors, there is no peace-time
legislation (since the days of war control) which places price ceilings
on sellers' goods. The seller is generally free to increase the price of his
goods to any level, the only hurdle being economic. The major exception
occurs in the case of public-regulated utilities. Since they have monopoly

---

[26] Federal Trade Commission v. Sun Oil Co., 83 S.Ct. 383 (1963).

power in their respective areas, their price schedules are regulated and approved in the public's interest. More recently, the executive branch of the government has used its influence to discourage major industry price increases because of inflationary concerns. The most dramatic example occurred in April, 1962, when President Kennedy moved sternly without the sanction of law to pressure the leading steel companies to rescind their price increases.[27] Later President Johnson emphasized his sympathy with this policy by promising he would "keep a close watch on price and wage developments, with the aid of an early warning system which is being set up." [28] Management in major industries, therefore, should not be surprised if their freedom to raise prices is constrained in the future by voluntary or legal price formulas.

DECEPTIVE PRICING. After management decides on its prices, it must avoid stating them in a way that may be considered deceptive. The Wheeler-Lea Act (1938) gave the FTC clear power to regulate "unfair or deceptive acts or practices." Deceptive pricing is a more common problem in the sale of consumer goods than business goods, because consumers typically possess less information and buying acumen. The heyday of deceptive pricing occurred in the late 1950's when listed prices bore little relation to selling prices. Consumers were hungry for bargains, and sellers satisfied this hunger by advertising hot sales reductions from artificially high list prices. In 1958, the Automobile Information Disclosure Act was passed, requiring auto manufacturers to affix on the windshield of each new automobile a statement giving the manufacturer's suggested retail price, the prices of optional equipment, and the dealer's transportation charges. In the same year, the FTC issued its *Guides Against Deceptive Pricing,* admonishing sellers not to claim a price reduction unless it is a saving from the usual retail price, not to advertise "factory" or "wholesale" prices unless this is true, not to advertise comparable value prices on imperfect goods, and so forth. New guides were issued in the summer of 1964 reflecting a slight loosening of these standards, through the introduction of such phrases as "reasonably certain," for example. Another area that has received increased attention is the "truth in lending" campaign of Senator Paul Douglas to require lenders to provide uniform and explicit statements of installment credit costs to would-be borrowers.

PROMOTION DECISIONS

The seller must develop his promotion program so that it does not invite charges of deception or of discrimination. Advertising is more vulnerable to legal action than personal selling, because it leaves a clearer record of itself. Nevertheless, actions have been brought against salesmen when the evidence indicated conscious deception of their customers.

FALSE AND MISLEADING ADVERTISING. Marketing executives have to worry most about false and misleading advertising. They can avoid the former by refraining from deliberate misrepresentation. There are cases, of course, which are not always clear-cut. Thus the Continental Wax

[27] *Business Week,* April 14, 1962, p. 51.
[28] Quoted in Arthur F. Burns, "Wages and Prices by Formula?" *Harvard Business Review,* March-April 1965, p. 62.

Corporation was ordered by the FTC to refrain from describing its product as a "Six Month Floor Wax," although under certain conditions (not typical ones) the wax's quality held up that long.[29] In other cases, companies have been asked to desist from advertising their products as comparable to leading brands when by all counts they were not. Misleading rather than false advertising is the major headache for sellers. The FTC under the Wheeler-Lea Act can issue a temporary restraining order against any advertisement which seems to have the capacity to deceive, even though no one may be deceived. The problem is one of distinguishing between puffery in advertising, which is normal, and distortion. The seller must avoid using words which imply his product is something other than it is, such as "Havana" cigars when they are not made of Cuban tobacco or "handmade" linens when they are produced in a factory. The advertiser must avoid making claims which cannot be demonstrated, such as that face creams restore youth or that drugs cure common colds. He must avoid hinting that the product is approved by some reputable organization or individuals when such approval is actually highly qualified, as when an aspirin manufacturer implied its brand had American Medical Association endorsement.[30] He must avoid making product guarantees that are misleading, such as "life-time guarantees" where it is the life of the product rather than the buyer.[31] Labels and packages must not appear deceptively large in size, nor be less than fully filled, nor be wrongly described as "giant" or "economy" size. Visual advertisements must not use mock-ups and undisclosed props where they may lead the viewer into believing that he has witnessed a demonstration of a claim.[32] These are some of the many legal questions which might arise in connection with the seller's promotion program.

BAIT ADVERTISING. Bait advertising, where the seller attracts buyers' interest on false pretenses, comes under FTC surveillance, and is also specifically prohibited in many states. The seller offers or advertises an exceptionally good buy and then finds some excuse for not selling the advertised item but selling something else. He may refuse to sell the product, disparage its features, demonstrate a defective one, or impose unreasonable delivery dates or service terms. Having baited the buyer, he tries to sell a substitute product which is more profitable to him.

PROMOTIONAL ALLOWANCES AND SERVICES. In planning his promotional program, the seller must be sure to make promotional allowances

[29] *Journal of Marketing,* XXVII (October 1963), 81.

[30] In its advertising, Bayer's Aspirin quoted favorable comments about its brand from an article by three government-supported physicians in the *Journal of the American Medical Association.* While the quote was correct, the FTC felt that Sterling Drug, Inc., the makers of Bayer Aspirin, was misleading the public into thinking that its brand had AMA endorsement. The lower courts did not uphold the FTC's charges. See *Journal of Marketing,* XXVII (October 1963), 84-85.

[31] See *Guides Against Deceptive Advertising in Guarantees,* FTC, January 12, 1961.

[32] The Supreme Court ruled in 1965 against a Rapid Shave commercial (Colgate-Palmolive Co.) which supposedly showed Rapid Shave would help in the shaving of sandpaper. The advertising agency used a sand-covered plastic when filming the commercial, claiming sandpaper would not photograph properly. *Time,* April 16, 1965, p. 86.

and services available to all cusomers on proportionately equal terms, according to Sections 2(d) and 2(e) of the Robinson-Patman Act. However, as mentioned earlier, it is difficult to establish what constitutes proportionately equal terms where small and large customers are involved. Issues arise, for example, as to what small stores should be given as a good substitute service for a store demonstrator in large stores, or for city-wide newspaper advertising by large stores. The FTC has issued guides to help sellers interpret the law in this area.

CHANNEL DECISIONS

By and large, the manufacturer is free under the law to develop whatever channel arrangements suit him. In fact, much of the force of the law affecting channels is to make sure he is not foreclosed from using channels as the result of the exclusionary tactics of others. But this places him under obligation to proceed cautiously in his own possible use of exclusionary tactics. Most of the law is concerned with the mutual rights and duties of the manufacturer and channel members once they have formed a relationship. We have already described the legislation affecting price discrimination, resale price maintenance, and vertical acquisitions. Here the law on exclusive dealing, exclusive territorial distributorships, tying contracts, and dealers' rights will be examined.

EXCLUSIVE DEALING.   Many manufacturers and wholesalers like to develop exclusive channels for their products. The policy is called "exclusive distribution" when the seller enfranchises only certain outlets to carry his products. It is called "exclusive dealing" when the seller requires these outlets to agree to handle only his products, or conversely, not to handle competitors' products.

Both parties tend to draw benefits from exclusive dealing, the seller enjoying a more dependable and enthusiastic set of outlets without having to invest capital in them, and the distributors gaining a steady source of supply and seller support. However, the result of exclusive dealing is that other manufacturers are excluded from selling to these dealers. This has brought exclusive dealing contracts under the purview of the Clayton Act, although such contracts are not made illegal per se. According to Section 3 of the Clayton Act, they are illegal only if their result is substantially to lessen competition or tend to create a monopoly. In most of the oil industry cases tried under this law, courts have ruled against contracts where the major oil companies required their retail service stations to handle exclusively their supplies of tires, batteries, and accessories.[33] The courts have argued that such contracts were illegal in this industry because, as a widespread practice, it tended to close retail service stations to other suppliers, thereby lessening competition. These contracts have also been ruled against in industries marked by a dominant seller, because the effect is to close a majority of outlets to other suppliers.[34] On the other hand, exclusive dealing contracts have been allowed when they are practiced by small

[33] Standard Oil Co. of California, *et al.* v. U.S., 337 U.S. 293, 314 (1949); U.S. v. Sun Oil Co., 176 F.Supp. 715 (1959).
[34] Standard Fashion Co. v. Magrane-Houston Co., 268 U.S. 346 (1922).

sellers and do not threaten substantially to lessen competition in the industry.[35]

EXCLUSIVE TERRITORIAL DISTRIBUTORSHIPS.   Exclusive dealing often includes territorial agreements as well as exclusive source agreements. The seller may agree not to sell to other distributors in the area, and/or the buyer may agree to confine sales to his own territory. The first practice is fairly normal under franchise systems, being regarded as a way to promote increased dealer enthusiasm and dealer investment in the area. The seller is under no legal compulsion to establish more outlets than he wishes. The second practice, where the manufacturer tries to restrain each dealer to sell only in his own formal territory, has become a major legal issue. This comes close to dividing up the market, even though in this case it is the market for a brand (vertical market division) rather than a product (horizontal market division). Horizontal market division is illegal per se. In the *White Motor* case the courts considered for the first time whether vertical market division is also illegal per se.[36] The Supreme Court decided to remand the case to the district court for a further hearing, because the issue of whether territorial restrictions on intrabrand competition decreased or increased interbrand competition did not get a full hearing. The courts have also considered whether General Motors is violating the Sherman Act by actively discouraging its dealers from selling through discount houses.[37] GM insists that its franchised dealers are already in active competition, whereas the Antitrust Division argues that GM is trying to lessen the competition (and public benefits) that come from discount selling. To date, it is uncertain whether territorial restrictions imposed by manufacturers on their distributors will be declared illegal per se or made subject to the rule of reason.

TYING AGREEMENTS.   Manufacturers with a brand in strong demand occasionally sell it to dealers on condition they take some or all of the rest of the line. In the latter case, this practice is called "full line forcing." Such tying arrangements are not illegal per se, but they do run afoul of Section 3 of the Clayton Act if they tend to lessen competition substantially. Buyers are prevented from exercising their free choice among competing suppliers of these other goods. Furthermore, the mere fact that the seller might induce this agreement may imply something about his monopoly power with respect to the tying product. Tying contracts have usually been held illegal where the seller sold through a substantial number of outlets, and therefore could foreclose a substantial part of the market to other suppliers.[38]

DEALERS' RIGHTS.   Sellers are largely free to select their dealers, but their right to terminate dealerships is somewhat qualified. In general, sellers can drop dealers "for cause." But they cannot drop dealers, for example,

---

[35] See Leonard J. Konopa, "Exclusive Dealing Arrangements in Marketing," *Business Topics,* Summer 1964, pp. 63-72.

[36] White Motor Co. v. U.S., 83 S.Ct. 696 (1963).

[37] "Is the Franchise System Legal?" *Business Week,* April 3, 1965, pp. 66-68.

[38] See International Business Machines Corp. v. U.S., 298 U.S. 131 (1936); Automatic Canteen Co. of America v. FTC, 194 F.2d 433, 437 (1952).

if the latter refuse to cooperate in a dubious legal arrangement, such as exclusive dealing or tying arrangements. The acuteness of this problem in the automobile industry led to the passage of the Automobile Dealers Franchise Act in 1956, which established the rights of automobile dealers to secure a judicial determination whenever they feel a manufacturer has not acted toward them in good faith. This act did much to redress the balance of power between manufacturers and dealers in favor of the latter, and may be a portent of further legislation on the subject of channel member rights.

Summary

There are a formidable number of federal, state, and local laws designed to regulate competition in the interest of providing maximal protection to business and consumers. Many of these laws seek to preserve competition because of the classic benefits it brings; others are set up to protect consumers against deceptive practices.

Marketing executives must understand the major laws and their purpose because they act as a major constraint on marketing decision making. The law affects company decisions that might have a competitive implication, such as expansion, interfirm cooperation, or aggressive tactics. Decisions on adding or dropping products, or on product design, quality, or labeling all are subject to legal considerations. The law requires that company pricing decisions be made independently and in a way that does not discriminate among dealers, injure competition, or deceive the public. Management must be careful not to promote its products in a way that can be interpreted as false, misleading, or baiting. The whole effort to set up effective channels is circumscribed by laws bearing on exclusive dealing, exclusive territories, tying agreements, and dealers' rights. The marketing executive must watch the law and indeed the whole range of government actions in the areas of taxation, monetary policy, antipoverty actions, and the like. They all create new and evolving constraints and opportunities for marketing decision making.

Questions and Problems

1. Would you support or not support each of the following new legislative proposals (give your reasoning): (a) a bill to require companies in concentrated industries to go through federal hearings before each price boost; (b) a bill to allow auto makers to prevent dealers from selling outside their territories; (c) a bill to require manufacturers to grant wholesalers a bigger discount than they give to large retail chains; (d) a bill to protect independent retailers from price competition by a manufacturer who does retailing of his own.

2. When Thurman Arnold headed the Attorney General's office during the New Deal, he had a definite policy of trying to keep business-men on their toes through a loose interpretation of the antitrust laws. More contemporary antitrust thinking holds that the laws and interpretation of what is right and wrong should be made more precise so that business will not be in the dark about the legality of a contemplated move. What is your position on this?

3. Executives who participate in illegal price-fixing agreements often feel they are doing what is necessary to stabilize sales and jobs in the industry. Would it be better if industry price-fixing agreements were legally recognized, as is the case in many European countries? Or should such agree-ments continue to be treated as illegal per se and the executives made per-sonally subject to jail sentences and fines?

4. In 1955, Du Pont was the defendant before the Supreme Court in a suit charging monopolization of cellophane manufacture and sale. Al-though Du Pont's share of cellophane sales was 68 per cent, its lawyers held that the relevant market was "transparent flexible packaging materials," which included such materials as glassene, cellulose, pliofilm, polyethylene, and saran. In this market, Du Pont contended that its share was only 17.9 per cent. How would you define the relevant market?

5. If you were a tobacco company executive, what position would you take on government proposals to (a) limit the amount that cigarette companies can spend on advertising; (b) prohibit brand endorsements by athletes and celebrities; (c) forego advertising in college publications? How do you see your ethical responsibilities if you were privately convinced cigarettes were harmful to health?

4

No matter how well a company plans its marketing program, unexpected developments in the environment will undoubtedly occur and call for appropriate revisions in marketing strategy and tactics. Thus, the company's planning will be completely effective only if it is supplemented by controls to insure that the goals are being pursued at all times with the best possible program.

Chapter 21, "Marketing Control," examines the requisites for control in marketing and the vital role played by continuous marketing intelligence. Chapter 22, "Sales and Cost Analysis," describe the specific tools by which marketing management appraises the effectiveness of day-to-day operations. Finally, Chapter 23, "The Marketing Audit," examines a more sweeping tool for periodically appraising not just the marketing operations but the over-all objectives and strategy of the firm in pursuit of its goals.

Controlling the Marketing Effort

557

chapter 21

Marketing Control

The best laid plans of men are subject to the caprices of other men and the surprises of nature. Therefore, it is not sufficient merely to develop plans. Plans are not self-fulfilling. Provision must be made to monitor the results of company efforts and to make adjustments when they seem warranted. Planning must be matched by control.

This chapter applies major control concepts and techniques to the area of marketing. The first section explores the nature and importance of control in business. The second examines the six types of control problems arising from the marketing subsystem. The third describes four major elements common to all control processes. The final section considers the development of marketing information systems for better control.

The Nature and Importance of Control

Because control is a familiar idea, it tends to be taken for granted. The purpose of this section is to develop an explicit conception of what is meant by control, to explain the factors which complicate the problem of control in business, and to describe the most important advances in control technology and theory of relevance to marketing.

THE MEANING OF CONTROL

Control takes on meaning in the context of a conscious agent who desires to achieve certain results. The results desired by the agent go under the name of *objectives* or *standards*. The objectives must be achieved within a certain range, or else the agent is dissatisfied. The agent plans and observes the actual results and compares them to the desired results. If there is too much deviation, he undertakes certain activities to close the gap. Control is *the process of taking steps to bring actual results and desired results closer together*.

Thus, control is predicated on the following conditions:

The agent is able to observe the actual results.

Not all results are acceptable to him.

He has devices available for influencing the disparity between actual and desired results.

The meaning of control is clarified by contrasting it to two other processes: *analysis* and *planning. Analysis* is undertaken by an agent to understand where he is, why he is there, and what his opportunities are. *Planning* is undertaken by an agent to specify a direction in which he would like to go and a means of getting there. However, the setting of goals and the laying of plans do not insure the achievement of the desired results. The environment is never perfectly predictable because of natural complexity, random disturbances, and evolutionary change. In order to secure desired results, analysis and planning must be supplemented by procedures for dealing with the unexpected. The body of such procedures constitutes control.

THE GROWING IMPORTANCE OF CONTROL

Two trends in the economy make the problem of control increasingly challenging with the passage of time. The first is that *enterprises are becoming larger*. Size alone complicates the problem of control. Consider this in terms of a hypothetical one-man enterprise, say a self-employed craftsman. This owner-operator buys materials, transforms them into products, and sells them on a market. His control problems are few. He has no subordinates to control. Since his inventories are likely to be small and readily observable, they do not give rise to many control problems. Since he is likely to face many small competitors and customers, his influence over them is likely to be negligible. His major control problem is to check the materials and final products for quality.

What happens as his enterprise grows? When sales reach a certain level, the owner-operator finds it desirable to add a few employees. He may hire an apprentice to help in production, a salesman to help him find more customers, an office worker to help him keep better financial records and take care of correspondence. As sales increase still further, he hires still more employees. He begins to hire middlemen for control; i.e., managers. Instead of watching the activities of many individual employees, he exercises control indirectly through managers.

He may also begin to differentiate the product, offering more style and variety. Instead of monitoring only one product, he must watch the performance of several products. The expansion of the product line requires more complicated systems of sales forecasting, production scheduling, inventory control, materials purchasing, and cash flow management.

As sales continue to increase, the entrepreneur may find it desirable to open plants and branch offices in other locations. The company eventually becomes a far-flung network of productive, financial, personnel, and marketing activities, yet one which in principle receives its basic signals from a central office located in a single city. These basic signals are predicated on information feedback to the central office. Top management has little direct contact with the many salesmen on the road, the many employees in the plants, the stocks of materials in the warehouses, or the state of company equipment and facilities. All it receives is information—and very summary information at that. And on the basis of this information, and through the intermediation of various subsystems, it exercises its control. Thus, the trend toward bigness complicates the problem of control.

A second trend of great importance increases the problem of control. It is that *the environment faced by the typical enterprise is changing more rapidly than ever before*. The era is marked by a constant outpouring of new products and brands, by radical innovations in technology, and by new techniques in management. Competitors grow larger and tend to spend more in the fast-paced race for the customers' dollar. Governmental influence grows more pronounced in such areas as mergers, taxes, interest rates, and oligopoly pricing. The Cold War skirmishes continue to create instability in the environment and make it harder to plan. To the extent that accurate planning becomes more difficult, management has to shift its emphasis to control; that is, to reliance on monitoring devices and program flexibility.

PROGRESS IN CONTROL TECHNIQUES

The trends toward enterprise growth and environmental instability have increased management's interest in more advanced control systems. Their growing interest is being matched by new developments in control technology and theory.

The three most important developments in control technology are high-speed electronic computers, new information-retrieval systems, and improved electronic means of communication. Electronic computers represent the most profound of these technological breakthroughs. Computers have increased the speed at which current field information can be aggregated and summarized for management review; increased the ability of management to solve complex mathematical models of company problems; and served as an instrument for direct control of automated production and some warehousing operations. The development of information-retrieval systems, in some cases allied to computers and in some cases utilizing different equipment, has also extended management's control capabilities by making stored information available on a speedier and more comprehensive basis. Electronic communication innovations, such as television hookups between company offices, new picture sending and copying equipment, and new telephonic equipment, also are extending management's ability to control company operations.

Of comparable importance to these developments in control technology has been the continuing refinement of *control theory,* to the development of which many academic disciplines have contributed. *Physical systems engineers* have approached control from the point of view of designing safety devices (governors, brakes, etc.) and feedback control devices (thermostats, gauges, etc.) to regulate the behavior of physical equipment and systems. Servomechanism theory is their major contribution.[1] *Mathematical statisticians* have developed various probability models for describing environments that are less than perfectly predictable and various decision models for optimizing control in such environments.[2] *Industrial statisticians* have worked out useful concepts and procedures for quality control which can be generalized to other areas of management control.[3]

[1] See, for example, Gordon S. Brown and Donald P. Campbell, *Principles of Servomechanisms* (New York: John Wiley & Sons, Inc., 1948). For an application of servomechanism theory to industrial systems, see Jay W. Forrester, *Industrial Dynamics* (Cambridge, Mass.: M.I.T. Press, 1961).

[2] See William Feller, *An Introduction to Probability Theory and Its Applications,* Vol. 1, 2nd ed. (New York: John Wiley & Sons, Inc., 1950); and J. Halcombe Laning, Jr., and Richard H. Batton, *Random Processes in Automatic Control* (New York: McGraw-Hill Book Company, 1956).

[3] Dudley J. Cowden, *Statistical Methods in Quality Control* (Englewood Cliffs, N.J.: Prentice-Hall, Inc., 1957).

Industrial engineers have developed control models for the sequencing and scheduling of industrial processes and projects.[4] *Economists* have developed extensive theory for improving control over economic fluctuations and growth.[5] They have also applied price theory to the problem of achieving efficiency in intracorporate transfers of resources.[6] *Behavioral scientists* have developed many concepts in connection with the control of social problems, the motivation of individual and group behavior, and the molding of social thought.[7] And the problems of man-machine control systems have been given a rich formulation in the writings on *cybernetics* of Norbert Wiener and those who followed him.[8]

All told, there has been no lack of interest in problems of control by scientists in various disciplines. Before turning to the underlying theory of control systems, let us consider the major problem areas in marketing control.

The Major Problems of Control in Marketing

As one of the major action subsystems found within a business firm, marketing consists of a collection of individuals, facilities, and activities whose purpose is to promote and facilitate the movement of company products to the market place and market information to the company. Six facets of the marketing subsystem give rise to issues of control. They are discussed in the following paragraphs.

TOP MANAGEMENT CONTROL OVER THE MARKETING SUBSYSTEM

The first control problem arises because the outputs of the marketing subsystem intimately affect the outputs of the company's other subsystems, such as production, finance, and personnel. This defines the first problem in marketing control; i.e., how can top management secure better control over the operation of the company's marketing subsystem? Five major control devices can be defined.

[4] Evan D. Scheele, William L. Westerman, and Robert J. Wimmert, *Principles and Design of Production Control Systems* (Englewood Cliffs, N.J.: Prentice-Hall, Inc., 1960).

[5] Among the many references, see John Maynard Keynes, *The General Theory of Employment, Interest, and Money* (New York: Harcourt, Brace & Company, 1935); Milton Friedman, "A Monetary and Fiscal Framework for Economic Stability," *American Economic Review,* June 1948, pp. 245-64; and Arnold Tustin, *The Mechanism of Economic Systems* (London: William Heinemann, Ltd., 1953).

[6] See Myron J. Gordon, "The Use of Administered Price Systems to Control Large Organizations," and Jack Hirschleifer, "Internal Pricing and Decentralized Decisions," both in *Management Controls: New Directions in Basic Research,* Charles P. Bonini, Robert K. Jaedicke, and Harvey M. Wagner, eds. (New York: McGraw-Hill Book Company, 1963).

[7] See Warren G. Bennis, Kenneth D. Benne, and Robert Chin, eds., *The Planning of Change: Readings in the Applied Behavioral Sciences* (New York: Holt, Rinehart and Winston, Inc., 1961).

[8] See Norbert Wiener, *Cybernetics* (New York: John Wiley & Sons, Inc., 1948) and *The Human Use of Human Beings* (New York: Houghton Mifflin Company, 1950). For the relevance of cybernetics to management control, see Stafford Beer, *Cybernetics and Management* (New York: John Wiley & Sons, Inc., 1959).

is top management's main control link with the activities of the department. This man, variously called the sales manager, the marketing director, and more recently the vice-president of marketing, is being given greater responsibility over time for defining and implementing actions in all spheres of marketing. The general trend is toward consolidating in his hands control of field selling, advertising, customer servicing, forecasting, and physical distribution. It is, therefore, important from a corporate control point of view to define the extent and limits of his powers. An increasing number of companies have prepared formal descriptions for the position of vice-president of marketing, detailing his specific powers, responsibilities and relationships.[9]

SALES TARGETS.   Top management will want to establish specific sales targets for the short run and intermediate run. These targets arise out of the corporate planning process in which the chief marketing officer is an important participant. The sales targets represent his and general management's view of what the company is capable of achieving.

MARKETING BUDGETS.   Top management must also work out with the chief marketing officer a budget that is adequate for him to achieve the company's sales targets. This budget becomes an important tool in evaluating the performance of this officer. The question is not only whether the sales targets are achieved, but whether they are achieved within the budgeted expenses, which is the true measure of their profit impact.

MARKETING AUDITS.   Top management will also want to conduct marketing audits periodically to determine whether the department is working with maximum efficiency and effectiveness. It may be worthwhile occasionally to hire an outside consulting firm to take a hard look at various strategic features of the marketing subsystem, such as the channel structure, the physical distribution system, the process of allocating advertising money, or the organization of the field sales force.

PROFIT CENTER.   In principle, the ideal way for management to control the marketing department is to treat it as a separate profit center. This means conceiving of the marketing department as an independent middleman which purchases the products of the manufacturing department and in turn sells them to the market. The profit on the marketing operation would be the difference between company sales and marketing department costs. Its costs include the transfer price on the stocks taken over from manufacturing and the costs of selling, storing, and shipping these stocks. The profitability of the department would be considered the ratio of profit to investment in the department. The chief marketing officer would be evaluated on the basis of the annual rate of return he produces. Thus he would have a strong incentive not only to achieve good sales volume (the traditionally dominant goal of marketing management) but to achieve it with good cost control.

[9] For an example, see Ken K., Doscher, "The Vice President for Marketing: What Kind of Man Must He Be?", *The Marketing Job* (New York: American Management Association, 1961), pp. 27-31.

The second control problem arises because the outputs of the other subsystems intimately affect the marketing subsystem's outputs. Here the problem is how the chief marketing officer can gain more influence over interdependent corporate activities, such as production, inventory control, traffic, and purchasing.

The marketing concept has been a weapon in the struggle for more control over other company activities affecting marketing. This has led to no small amount of interorganizational conflict.[10] The remedy would appear to lie not in substantially increased authority for the marketing department so much as in the development of better communication and interorganizational understandings about what is the interest of the company as a whole.

MARKETING'S CONTROL OVER OUTSIDE AGENTS

A third control problem arises when the marketing subsystem deals with various external agents, such as manufacturers' representatives, wholesalers, shipping and warehousing firms, and advertising agencies. How can the chief marketing officer and his staff achieve better control over the performance of agents who act as links to the market place?

The producer's control over the performance of various agencies depends upon the degree of independence of each agency and the nature of the relationship. The producer can bring relatively strong influence to bear on franchised middlemen and upon advertising agencies and weaker influence to bear on independent wholesalers and large chains. The producer achieves maximum control by buying out an agency, and the next degree of control where its business represents a substantial share of the agent's business. Whatever the degree of control, it is desirable that the producer's and agent's mutual rights and responsibilities be formally spelled out.

MARKETING'S CONTROL OVER MARKETING EMPLOYEES

The fourth control problem arises in connection with marketing personnel, such as salesmen, product managers, advertising specialists, and marketing researchers. How can the chief marketing officer achieve better control over the performance of individuals and groups under his authority?

Marketing departments range in size from one-man operations to thousands of employees in some of the larger organizations. The control problem increases with the size of the marketing organization. In the larger organizations, the chief marketing officer exercises his control through such officers as the sales manager, advertising manager, marketing research manager, and product managers and through such instruments as budgets, bonuses, and performance reviews.

MARKETING'S CONTROL OVER PROGRAM EFFECTIVENESS

The fifth control problem arises out of the fact that the company's performance in the market place often differs from expectations because of unanticipated moves by competitors, government, and the buyers themselves. The problem is how marketing strategy can be quickly reformulated to meet new conditions in the market place.

[10] See Chapter 6, pp. 138-39.

Flexibility is the first important attribute of any marketing operation. The chief marketing officer must be able to redeploy his sales force, alter the advertising program, and change the terms of sales to meet new conditions. Management must also know the right changes to make and be able to make them quickly. Of particular importance are the quality of the information system and the extent to which contingency plans are formulated. The extent to which these should be undertaken requires balancing the costs of better control against the penalties for being without them.

MARKETING'S CONTROL OVER SPECIAL PROJECTS

The sixth control problem arises in connection with special projects undertaken by the marketing organization, such as the development of a new product, a major advertising campaign, or the invasion of a new territory. The problem is how to keep these projects on schedule and within budgeted expense.

Among the important control tools in this area are critical path scheduling, budgets, and program effectiveness research. Since these tools are described elsewhere (Chapter 7, pp. 163-69, and Chapters 22 and 23), only their mention is necessary here.

The Control Process

In all control problems arising in connection with the marketing subsystem, there is an agent who wishes to secure certain results from an environment that is less than perfectly predictable and/or through means that are less than perfectly effective. His problem is one of setting up control systems appropriate to the type and complexity of the control problems.

All control systems possess the four common elements illustrated in Figure 21-1. The first element consists of the definition of goals and standards by the agent (Goals). The second consists of the development of a program for achieving these goals (Program). The third element consists of the measurement of actual results (Information). And the fourth element consists of making adjustments either in the goals, program, or both, if the goals are not being achieved (Corrective action). Although simple in outline, this model of the control process has many ramifications.

GOALS

Good control requires the establishment of clear and specific goals for the system whose behavior is to be regulated. These goals should be understood and accepted by those within the system. Generally it is desirable to couch them numerically where this is feasible. Numerical standards facilitate the problem of evaluating results. The magnitude of deviation as well as the direction of deviation can be measured. Numerically defined standards are easier to communicate to the performing agent. They may also tend to incite agents to greater effort.

How high should goals be set? The issue here is how agents are likely to react to the level at which the goal is set. Consider sales quotas, for example. Some sales managers are of the opinion that quotas should be

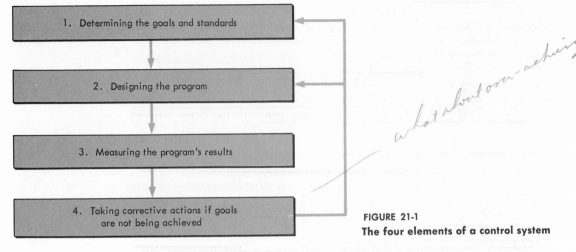

1. Determining the goals and standards

2. Designing the program

3. Measuring the program's results

4. Taking corrective actions if goals are not being achieved

what about over-achieving

FIGURE 21-1
The four elements of a control system

set realistically in terms of normally attainable levels ("loose but attainable standards"), while others are of the opinion that quotas should be set on the high side to spur extra efforts ("tight standards"). To this Heckert has observed:

> Actual experience with sales quotas, as with all standards, will reveal that sales representatives react to them somewhat differently, particularly at first. Some are stimulated to their highest efficiency, others are discouraged. Some sales executives place considerable emphasis upon this human element in setting their quotas. In general, however, good men will in the long run respond favorably to intelligently devised quotas, particularly when compensation is fairly adjusted to performance.[11]

Is this a definition of a good man?

Among the factors affecting the individual agent's reaction are his level of aspiration, his sense of what other salesmen will do, and the company's sanctions for underachievement.[12]

How much deviation should be tolerated? When numerical standards are set, it is not expected that they will be achieved perfectly. The controlling agent usually establishes a range of tolerable deviation (or tolerances) within which normal performance should lie.[13] The range should not be so broad as to excuse all degrees of performance nor so narrow as to cause investigation and/or corrective action to be applied too frequently. Important issues are whether the tolerances (in addition to the standards) should be communicated explicitly to the performing agent and, if so, how the information would affect the agent's effort. This raises behavioral issues similar to those considered earlier. Specifically, how will the performing agent react when he knows that the standard need not be

[11] J. B. Heckert, *Business Budgeting and Control* (New York: The Ronald Press Company, 1946), p. 138.

[12] An interesting experimental investigation of the effect of high versus low goals upon performance is reported by Andrew C. Stedry, *Budget Control and Cost Behavior* (Englewood Cliffs, N.J.: Prentice-Hall, Inc., 1960).

[13] The reader should be careful to distinguish between setting the standard high or low and allowing the tolerances about the standard to be large or small. There are four possible cases.

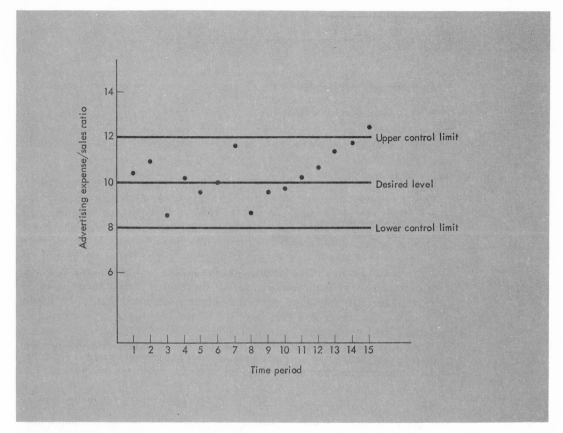

FIGURE 21-2
The standard control chart model

met very closely or when he knows that the standard must be met very closely to avoid an investigation? There are no general answers; each control problem requires its own solution.

The idea of normal tolerance around a standard is basic to statistical control procedures. The basic instrument is the statistical control chart illustrated in Figure 21-2. The chart is a means of observing successive levels of a particular performance indicator in relation to desired and normal levels. Suppose a company wishes to control the advertising expense/sales ratio. Suppose advertising is normally set at 10 per cent of sales, but may fluctuate between 8 and 12 per cent because of random factors. In fact, suppose the range 8-12 per cent represents normal variation of the advertising expense/sales ratio in 99 out of 100 cases.[14] As long as the sales process is "in control," *virtually* all the future ratios are expected to be between 8 and 12 per cent on the basis of chance.

What happens when the advertising expense/sales ratio lies outside

[14] The normal range used in statistical quality control is three standard deviations. For a lucid explanation of the theory and computations, see Chapter 6 in Edward H. Bowman and Robert B. Fetter, *Analysis for Production Management,* rev. ed. (Homewood, Ill.: Richard D. Irwin, Inc., 1961), pp. 155-94.

of these control limits? This happened in Figure 21-2 on the fifteenth observation of the process. One of two opposing hypotheses can explain this occurrence:

> *Hypothesis A:* The company still has good control over sales, and this represents one of those rare chance events. (Remember, one out of 100 times the ratio can exceed the control limits by chance. Furthermore, it can happen on any trial.)
>
> *Hypothesis B:* The company has lost control over sales as a result of some assignable cause, such as a new competitor or a new distribution channel.

If hypothesis A is accepted, no investigation is made to determine whether the environment has changed. The risk in doing this is that some real change has occurred and the company will fall behind. If hypothesis B is accepted, the environment would be investigated at the risk that the investigation will uncover nothing and be a waste of time and effort.

This control model can be modified in a number of ways to make it more useful in particular circumstances. In the first place, the behavior of successive observations even within the control limits should also be watched for patterns which seem difficult to explain by chance. In Figure 21-2, it should be noted that the level of the performance indicator rose steadily from period nine onward. The probability of encountering a pattern of six successive increases in what should be a random and independent process is only one out of 64.[15] This unusual pattern should have led to an investigation sometime before the fifteenth sample.

In the second place, for some processes the controlling agent may feel that only a performance outside of one of the control limits (either the upper or the lower) will require an investigation. If the performance indicator is *market share,* for example, only a performance outside of the lower control limit may be investigated, because, it is felt, a significant slip in market share requires action, whereas a significant increase in market share is a gratuitous development. This is a tricky business, however, for a highly favorable development may point just as strongly to the occurrence of a new factor(s) in the situation, one which may repay investigation and revised programs. Some control philosophies even say that samples of performances within control should also be investigated occasionally to make sure the results are normal for the right reasons. Generally, however, the philosophy is one of "management by exception."

PROGRAM

The setting of goals and standards for the performing agent must be followed by the development of a *program* for their achievement. A program is a detailed plan on how resources should be used over a specified time period for the achievement of the goals. As we saw earlier, a marketing program has at least four components:

A level of total marketing effort

[15] There is a chance of ½ that any succeeding observation will be higher and the same chance that it will be lower (excluding the possibility that two successive values are identical). Therefore the probability of finding six successively higher values is given by $(½)^6 = 1/64$.

An allocation of the effort to different products, customers, and territories

A phasing of the marketing effort over time

Each component interacts with every other component, thus requiring a mutual and simultaneous determination of the program. A program is said to change when a change occurs in one or more of the components.

It is very difficult to formulate a perfect program for a given state of the environment; and since the typical environment changes, even a perfect program would have to be revised periodically. When actual performance deviates significantly from desired performance, a review of the adequacy of the program or some of its components is desirable.

INFORMATION

Actual performance is gauged from various types of information gathered by the company. In spite of the crucial role of information in the control process, only recently has management begun to think systematically about information economics, design, and management.[16] Such information-manipulative company operations as accounting and marketing research highlight the heavy costs of collecting, processing, storing, and transmitting information. The great cost makes it desirable to assess carefully the information needs of various executives. Specifically, it should be established who needs what information, when, where, and in what form. The challenge is to design a company information system where the value of the information is maximized for a given expenditure or the cost is minimized to achieve a given mix of information.

Information is needed on actual performance to check against desired performance. The comparisons may be made *continuously* (daily field reports) or *intermittently* (quarterly profit reports). Where many performance indicators are involved, much time may be required just to make the comparisons. For example, an expense budget for a sales territory usually involves dozens of items. After the period is over, all of these items must be compared for unusual budgetary variances. It would help to automate these comparisons where possible.

Under a computerized accounting system, comparisons of actual performances against standards can be made part of the regular output. In some cases, it may even be possible to incorporate a mechanism that will give an automatic signal on the occasion of a significant discrepancy, thus averting the need for continuous human attention. The computer might print out only the names of salesmen who are not currently meeting their quotas.

CORRECTIVE ACTIONS

The final step in the control process calls for taking corrective actions when actual performance deviates too much from desired performance. Control is the last step in the control process.

In this connection, a distinction is made between *open- and closed-loop* control systems. Both are illustrated in Figure 21-3. In both systems, the executive develops the initial input (the standards and marketing program),

[16] See Adrian M. McDonough, *Information Economics and Management Systems* (New York: McGraw-Hill Book Company, 1963).

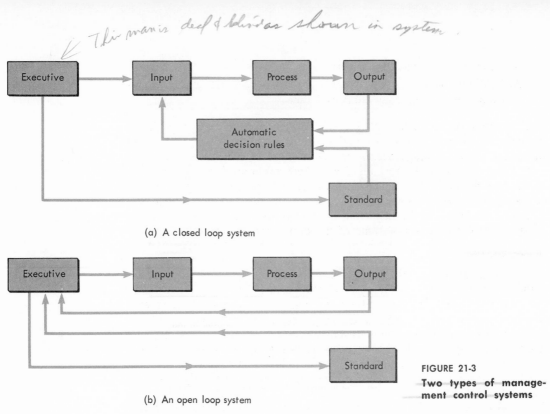

This man is deaf & blind as shown in system.

(a) A closed loop system

(b) An open loop system

FIGURE 21-3

Two types of management control systems

the inputs pass through a process (the market), and the process yields certain outputs (sales and profits), which are compared against the standards. In the *closed-loop system,* the comparisons are made through decision rules and devices capable of automatically revising the inputs if necessary to bring about more conformance between the outputs and standards. In the *open-loop system,* the executive makes the comparison between outputs and standards and uses his discretion concerning whether any action is required and, if so, what kind.

CLOSED-LOOP SYSTEMS. Where both systems are equally feasible, the closed-loop model undoubtedly represents the more elegant solution. It economizes on human effort, and can be depended upon to act with more swiftness and consistency. It has found many applications in physical engineering areas, such as refinery operations and missile launchings. An everyday example of a closed-loop system is found in the thermostatic control of home temperature. The objective of the system is to maintain the temperature at a certain level. This means that the furnace must be switched on and off during the day. It must be switched on when the room temperature drops below a certain point, and it must be switched off again when the room temperature rises above a certain point. If the homeowner were to make these adjustments himself (an open-loop system), he would be kept quite busy. Instead, this function is carried out by a thermostat which switches the furnace on and off as the room temperature approaches the lower and upper control points, respectively.

The application of pure feedback principles in management control systems is more limited but nevertheless is found. Consider the typical company's reactions to a sharp drop in sales. Almost regardless of the

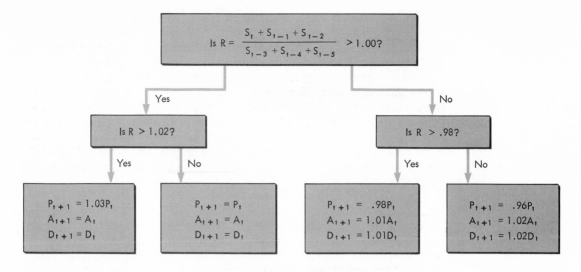

$$\text{Is } R = \frac{S_t + S_{t-1} + S_{t-2}}{S_{t-3} + S_{t-4} + S_{t-5}} > 1.00?$$

Yes   No

Is R > 1.02?   Is R > .98?

Yes   No   Yes   No

$P_{t+1} = 1.03P_t$ $P_{t+1} = P_t$ $P_{t+1} = .98P_t$ $P_{t+1} = .96P_t$
$A_{t+1} = A_t$ $A_{t+1} = A_t$ $A_{t+1} = 1.01A_t$ $A_{t+1} = 1.02A_t$
$D_{t+1} = D_t$ $D_{t+1} = D_t$ $D_{t+1} = 1.01D_t$ $D_{t+1} = 1.02D_t$

where R = Ratio of seasonally adjusted sales in last
                  three periods to previous three periods
        S_t = Sales, this period
        P_t = Price, this period
        A_t = Advertising expenditures, this period
        D_t = Distribution expenditures, this period

FIGURE 21-4

A logical flow diagram for revising the marketing mix in response to a change in sales

Adapted from Philip Kotler, "Competitive Strategies for New Product Marketing over the Life Cycle," *Management Science*, December 1965, p. B-112.

cause, this event triggers off a series of company actions designed to restore sales or profits. One of the first moves is to cut down peripheral expenditures.[17] At about the same time, pressures are increased on various employees, especially salesmen. Subsequently, the company undertakes to re-evaluate its basic marketing program and targets.

The evaluation of the marketing program is likely to lead the company to reduce its prices and increase its promotional expenditures to counteract the decline in sales. In principle, the marketing responses could be prescribed by a set of decision rules. A specific, hypothetical, automatic control strategy is illustrated in Figure 21-4. The triggering event is the ratio of recent sales to past sales, R. If recent sales have increased by more than 2 per cent over past company sales (after seasonal adjustment), the product's price is increased by 3 per cent to take advantage of this development while marketing expenditures are maintained at their previous level. If the increase is between zero and 2 per cent, the marketing variables are

[17] The determination of which expenditures are peripheral is not easy to make. Usually community programs are cut down first, followed by a budget reduction for most of the staff functions, including marketing research and executive training. Some executives will also want to cut down expenditures on advertising and personal selling. This is a difficult decision to make because while they represent expenses, they also have a sales-creating impact, which is precisely what the company needs.

571

all kept at their previous levels. If there is a sales decline between zero and 2 per cent, price is cut by 2 per cent, and marketing expenditures are increased by 1 per cent. If sales decline by more than 2 per cent, price is cut by 4 per cent and marketing expenditures are increased by 2 per cent.

However, pure automatic feedback controls are sparingly used in marketing, for two reasons. The first is that performance deviations can arise from a multitude of different causes. A drop in sales (as opposed to room temperature) may be caused by a company price increase, a competitor's new promotion program, a decline in business activity, or other factors. Each cause may warrant a different corrective action. Until management can develop complex interpretive rules and decision rules, most marketing control systems will remain of the open-loop variety.

The second reason is that standards may be as much at fault as performance. When a sales district underachieves its quota, the trouble may lie in a poor performance, or it may lie in an unrealistically high quota. Both hypotheses warrant investigation. The investigation may lead to a revision of the inputs, the standards, both, or neither. (See Figure 21-1.) It would be difficult to develop a feedback control system to make these judgments.

SPEED VERSUS PRECISION OF RESPONSE. In some ways, the issue between automatic control and discretionary control in the realm of management systems is one of *speed* versus *precision* of response. Automatic systems can detect faults and correct them with more dispatch than is typical of discretionary management systems. This can be appreciated by recognizing that all management action systems are subject to at least four types of time delays, illustrated in Figure 21-5. The first delay occurs between the

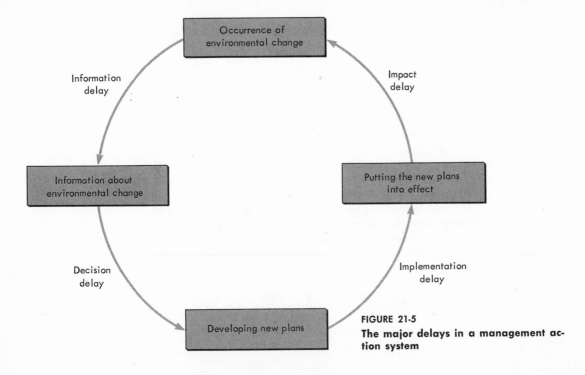

FIGURE 21-5
The major delays in a management action system

development of significant changes in the environment and their apprehension in the form of information (information delay). The second delay occurs between the apprehension of these changes and the development of new plans (decision delay). The third delay occurs between the development of new plans and their execution (implementation delay). The fourth delay occurs between the implementation of the new plans and their creation of tangible effects in the environment (impact delay).

In order to increase a control system's speed of response, efforts must be made to reduce each type of delay. Nothing can be done about the impact delay because a program's effect is distributed over time. The information delay can be reduced through improved data collection, processing, and routing. The decision delay can be reduced through developing clear decisions rules which lead from performance variances into revised programs without the need for committee meetings or prolonged executive deliberation. The implementation delay can be shortened by introducing more efficient procedures.

A good action taken too late may do more harm than no action at all. For example, a firm selling below capacity may decide to increase advertising. The fact that sales have turned up already may not be known because of an information delay. The natural and the artificial stimulants may combine to overtax the firm's productive facilities and raise costs.

The virtue of automatic control is that it promises to reduce the decision and implementation delays and the bad consequences of these delays. However, speed of response is gained at the possible price of an imprecise response. No matter how complex the decision rules are, they are no substitute for a specific analysis of the concrete situation, its causes, and the desirable remedies. Decision rules will produce a quick response, but one that may be inferior to alternative courses of action as grasped by management judgment. Some of the decision delay noted in real decision-making situations is an expression of the need for time to understand fully what had occurred in the environment and to prepare an appropriate response. In designing a control system, therefore, management finds itself on the horns of a dilemma between the danger of a belated response under discretionary control systems and the danger of an imprecise response under automatic control systems.

The Information Process

The previous section indicated that information is one of the four major components of the control process. In spite of this, until recently, management has not given systematic attention to the information function.

Executives are almost completely at the mercy of their information. At least six types of complaints about the information system can be heard in many organizations.

> *Too much information of the wrong kind.* Executives often are deluged with information, but find much of it irrelevant for decision-making purposes.
> *Too little information of the right kind.* Executives often need specific facts which should be present somewhere in the company but are not.

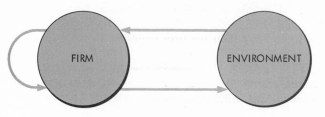

1. Marketing intelligence
(Inward information flow)

2. Internal marketing information (Internal information flow)

FIRM   ENVIRONMENT

3. Marketing communications
(Outward information flow)

FIGURE 21-6
Three important marketing information flows

Information is too decentralized. Executives often need specific facts which are present somewhere in the company, but the location is difficult to determine.

Information is suppressed. Executives often do not receive information that would reflect unfavorably on others in the company.

Information comes late. Executives often receive important information which should have reached them sooner.

Information is unverified. Executives often receive information with no idea of its validity and no one to turn to for confirmation.

Complaints such as these have led a few companies to try out new concepts and techniques for the management of information. One such company is Du Pont:

> Du Pont is moving toward marketing information centers. . . . Basically, it means storing in a computer a great deal of information about specific markets, your position and your competitor's in those markets, the vehicles which cover the markets, etc. When the time comes to make a move, all this information is at your fingertips, so you're working on facts, not hunches.[18]

Another company, the advertising agency of Benton & Bowles, has established a director of information management with a staff of over 100. Companies such as General Electric, Mead Paper, Monsanto, and Westinghouse are making concerted efforts to develop total information systems.

Every company is enmeshed in the three marketing information flows illustrated in Figure 21-6. The first, or *marketing intelligence flow,* is the flow of information from the marketing environment to relay points within the firm. (A relay point is any person or center in the firm who receives messages and is capable of relaying them, such as a salesman, or marketing research personnel.) The second, or *internal information flow,* is the flow of information among relay points within the firm. The third, or *marketing communications flow,* is the flow of information from the firm outward to the environment. Since marketing communications are discussed elsewhere in the book, nothing more will be said about them here.[19]

[18] "An Interview with Malcolm McNiven," *Sales Management,* April 19, 1963, p. 42.
[19] See Chapters 18 and 19.

The flow of information known as marketing intelligence consists of salient facts about institutions and developments in the environment affecting the company's opportunities and performance. Figure 21-7 shows the eight major institutions in the environment which the firm monitors for marketing intelligence.

Marketing intelligence is used broadly. It embraces raw data, summary statistics, qualitative inferences, expert and lay opinions, impressions and even rumors. Examples of marketing intelligence would be:

Figures showing that a certain important customer is beginning to divert some of his purchases to competitors

Rumors that a competitor is developing a substantially improved product

A survey indicating that many customers are dissatisfied with the service provided by the manufacturer's representative.

Each item constitutes marketing intelligence since it has potential action implications for one or more marketing executives in the firm. The first bit of information, about a wavering customer, is useful intelligence to a district sales manager. (However, it would be of trivial interest to the new-

FIGURE 21-7
Major sources of marketing intelligence

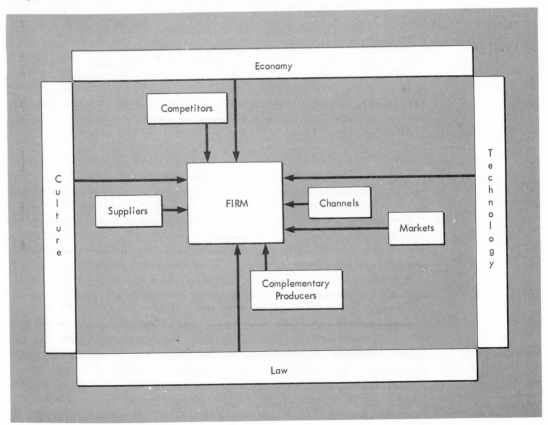

product manager.) The second bit of information, about a competitor's development of a new product, would be useful to the new-product manager. The third bit of information, about customer dissatisfaction with the manufacturer's representative, would be useful to the trade relations manager.

The idea of marketing intelligence comes from the military. The high-level military decision maker is usually far removed from the battlefield and therefore totally dependent upon second-hand information in directing the battle. He requires continuous data on the current position of his troops, the occurrence and outcomes of skirmishes, and the plans of the enemy. He needs hunches and rumors, as well as hard facts, reported to him.

The marketing executive is in an analogous situation. He fights for terrain (markets) with allies (channels) against an enemy (competitors) for a prize (sales). Because he is remote from the immediate battle scenes, he requires continuous information on the positions and effectiveness of his salesmen, on the resistance they are encountering, and on the activities of competitors. He needs current and accurate facts and also some sense of the talk and gossip of the market place.

The ease with which marketing information is obtained varies markedly. Information about broad characteristics of the market, such as the number of buyers or their geographical dispersion, is the easiest to obtain. The information is overt, and can often be drawn routinely from secondary sources such as government and trade associations. Information about present and potential customer preferences and attitudes is a little more difficult to obtain. Although overt, it generally does not exist in published form. Since it may have to be gathered as primary information, its value must be considered carefully in relation to its cost. The most difficult information to collect is related to the marketing expenditures and plans of competitors. The information is covert and tightly controlled for security reasons. The firm that wants it must develop an industrial espionage unit within the marketing intelligence unit. This, however, raises fundamental issues of business ethics.

THE INTERNAL INFORMATION FLOW

A crucial point about marketing intelligence is that its usefulness depends upon its reaching the right executive. The information must not only flow to the firm but also through it.

The internal information flow itself is made up of downward, upward, and horizontal flows. The *downward flow* consists of communications from higher company officials to subordinates. The *upward flow* consists of requisitioned as well as unsolicited information moving from lower to higher levels in the organization. The *horizontal flow* consists of information passing among company employees who occupy approximately the same levels.

In the typical company, these internal flows are left to take place in a natural, unmediated way. It is assumed that employees generally will know where to find needed information within the company and that they will receive vital intelligence from others in the company as a matter of course. But are these assumptions justified about the free flow of internal information in an unmanaged communication system?

In one of the few experimental studies of this question, the investigator's findings were negative.[20] Gerald Albaum set out to trace the transmission of important market information from original relay points to company decision centers in a large decentralized company. With management's co-operation, he arranged with company customers to pass on six fabricated pieces of important market information to company salesmen. Albaum wanted to discover how far, how fast, and how accurately this information would travel within the company.

Of the six pieces of market information, only two ever traveled beyond the salesman (the original company relay point)! For one reason or another, the majority of the salesmen did not pass on their intelligence to anyone else in the company. Of the two that reached decision centers, one arrived in three days, but was seriously distorted; the other arrived in about ten days in fairly accurate form. Only one piece of information out of six arrived accurately although its usefulness might have been diminished by its tardiness. Albaum concluded that there was not a free and dependable flow of unsolicited information within this company.

As mentioned earlier, an increasing number of companies are looking into the possible benefits of setting up an organization unit charged with managing the company's various marketing information flows. This unit would have four major responsibilities.

> *Search.* The unit would go inside and outside of the firm in search of both requested information and gratuitous information.
>
> *Filtering.* The unit would try to validate the information, reduce it to its essentials, and prepare it in suitable form.
>
> *Dissemination.* The unit would undertake to pass on unsolicited information to those in the company who might use it.
>
> *Storage.* The unit would codify and store the information for easy retrieval.

Albaum suggested that such a unit might innovate new techniques for information collection and dispersal. One would be the use of *search reports;* the unit might regularly send out forms to employees asking them to report any new intelligence they may have received and in some cases to supply specific information. Another would be the use of *news reports;* the unit regularly would prepare tailor-made summaries of new intelligence for specific officials.

There is general agreement that the information unit should be a head-quarters staff service and should work through a number of specialized information centers located at various points in the company. William T. Kelley has proposed:

> The Vice President, Intelligence Services, has six departments reporting to him: marketing research, economic research, market data, administrative data, internal information, and reports. The library could be made a separate department (the seventh), or could be put under market data. . . . In addition, a Special Projects Department might be added. This would undertake special research involving covert sources of information, both internal and external.[21]

[20] Gerald S. Albaum, "Horizontal Information Flow: An Exploratory Study," *Journal of the Academy of Management,* March 1964, pp. 21-33.

[21] William T. Kelley, "Marketing Intelligence for Top Management," *Journal of Marketing,* XXIX (October 1965), 21.

There is much that is exciting in the new concepts of information management. Substantial innovation can be expected in the coming years.

Summary

"Control" refers to those efforts by management to keep its program relevant to current market opportunities so that the company's objectives are achieved. As companies grow larger in size and as the environment becomes more difficult to predict, the problem of providing good controls becomes more acute.

Control in the marketing area arises at six different levels. First, top management must exercise control over the marketing system. The remaining five levels deal with the exercise of control by the chief marketing officer over other company subsystems, outside agents, marketing department employees, the marketing program, and special projects.

All management control systems consist of four elements. The first is the determination of goals and standards; the second, the formulation of a program; the third, the measurement of actual performance; and the fourth, the undertaking of corrective action when required.

Information is a vital ingredient in the control process. Information flowing to the company from the environment is called marketing intelligence; information flowing within the company is called internal information. A good company information system produces information which is relevant, accurate, and readily available. A growing number of companies are creating marketing information centers responsible for the search, filtering, dissemination, and storage of information.

Questions and Problems

1. List as many control devices used in marketing as you can think of.

2. Name some marketing performance variables which you think can be usefully tracked on statistical control charts. Do you think all exceptional deviations from the normal should be investigated?

3. The idea of treating the marketing department as a profit center raises several difficult problems. Name them and suggest possible solutions.

4. Develop a diagram to show how tardy corrective action may make a situation worse than if no action had been taken at all. (Hint: put time on the x axis and output on the y axis.)

5. Information can be classified in many ways. Define each of the following types of information, and give a marketing example of each: (a) Quantitative and qualitative; (b) hard facts and soft facts; (c) multipurpose and limited purpose; (d) overt and covert; (e) raw and derived; (f) primary and secondary; (g) routine and sporadic; (h) company and environmental; and (i) internal and external.

6. Are "marketing research" and "marketing intelligence" two names for the same function, or is one more comprehensive than the other? Define the two terms, and discuss their relationship.

chapter 22

Sales and Cost Analysis

In other parts of the book we have discussed the kinds of information necessary for determining market opportunities and developing marketing plans. After a specific plan is put into effect, continuous information is necessary to appraise the ongoing marketing effort. Are management's basic assumptions about the economy, customers, and competitors being met? Are various company policies having the calculated impact? Are various employees performing according to company expectations? Have any new elements entered the picture to warrant a revision of marketing strategy?

At a basic level, these questions require continuous marketing intelligence about sales and costs. When sales and cost information is recast from raw form into various derived indicators, it provides useful clues regarding areas of weakness and strength in the marketing program. Supplementary information can then be drawn in to aid in discovering the causal forces at work.

The first section of this chapter discusses the uses of sales analysis; the second, cost analysis.

Sales Analysis

Most marketing managers regard current sales as the best single indicator of current marketing performance. They watch orders coming in from the field with bated breath, much as the stock trader watches the ticker tape. When sales come in at the expected rate, they are relieved. When sales show unexpected strength, they are delighted. When sales show unexpected weakness, they are despondent. Probably no other type of information stirs as much emotion among marketing personnel as sales.

Sales information indeed is a vital indicator of current performance. But it is easy to err in the use of sales information. It is a mistake to pay attention only to gross sales movements or to fail to analyze sales information in conjunction with sales standards, competitors' sales, and marketing costs. Sometimes there is error in the other direction, in devoting too much time to sales analysis, although this tends to be the exception rather than the rule. Each management must define for itself the most useful level and types of sales analysis.

THE BASIC SALES TRANSACTION

Sales information is reported in a great and often confusing variety of ways. At the end of the month a marketing executive may examine:

Dollar sales in territory Y

The number of units of a particular model of product X sold through channel Z

The company's market share on the East Coast

Seasonally adjusted total dollar sales

These varied forms of sales information represent different ways to summarize the company's sales transactions. A sales transaction is the basic and original piece of sales information. A sales transaction is *the order of (1) a particular customer for (2) a particular quantity of (3) a particular company product from (4) a particular sales representative on (5) a particular date (6) under particular terms*. These six elements characterize every sales transaction.

At one extreme we can visualize the marketing executive examining every sales transaction that occurs. This gives him a complete and continuous sense of who is buying what in what quantities and when. Undoubtedly certain transactions suggest things to investigate regarding the quality or adequacy of sales effort. But at what price! This marketing executive spends all of his time in sales analysis. He finds many small faults. He may miss the larger ones. He does not have time for anything else.

At the other extreme is the marketing executive who watches only total company sales. This figure represents the ultimate aggregation of individual sales with all indications of customer, sales representative, product, and quantities removed. This executive manages to sense the over-all movement of sales. If sales move in the expected way, he is satisfied that he has good control. He has also saved himself a great deal of time and effort.

Neither executive is making the best use of sales information. One is wasting his time on minutiae, and the other is probably overlooking areas of sales deficiency. The art of sales analysis lies in using information that is aggregated somewhere between the levels of the basic sales transaction and the grand total.

Each company must decide separately which elements of the basic sales transaction merit the most attention. When the company has a complete record of the sales transaction, it can break down sales by customer, sales representative, product, quantity, terms, or date.[1] Some of the major possibilities are discussed below.

CUSTOMER. If the company sells only to a few customers, the marketing executive will want continuous information on purchases by individual buyers. He especially wants to detect early any evidence that a key customer may be diverting his business to another seller. Any unexplained fall in sales to that customer would justify investigating the cause(s) and taking

[1] The producer's sales to dealers are usually marked by a complete record of the transaction in the form of a sales invoice. However, sales to ultimate buyers are often not expressed in complete sales documents available to the producer. This is true of cash sales. It is also true where the dealers' records are incomplete or unavailable. If the producer wants information about the characteristics of sales transactions to ultimate customers, he may have to subscribe to a store audit service or consumer panel service or conduct his own surveys.

corrective action, if necessary. The executive will also want a periodic sales report on the percentage of sales accounted for by each customer. This, along with cost and other information, will help him determine how much he is making or losing on each customer.

If the company sells to many customers, the marketing executive still may want a periodic report of sales to the key customers. He may also want sales reports that summarize customer sales by *types of customer* and/or by *customer geographical locations*.

SALES REPRESENTATIVE. Sales information broken down by sales representative can help the marketing executive discern strong and weak men in its organization.[2] Further useful breakdowns are by sales regions and sales districts. If the company uses different methods of selling, such as mail order, telephone solicitation, and personal sales calls, the marketing executive may also want periodic reports classified by method.

PRODUCTS. Sales information is also useful when sorted by product and/or some product dimension, such as model or package size. In a multi-product organization, it is easy for the faltering of certain products or product versions to go unnoticed unless sales information is periodically reported by specific product breakdowns.

MISCELLANEOUS BREAKDOWNS. Sales information can also be broken down by quantity, by terms of sale, and by date. The executive then is able to watch for shifts in the size of orders, in the terms of sale, or in the importance of certain days or weeks. Each management must determine what sales reports are the most important to have for control purposes. For example, a company that manufactures photographic supplies regularly prepares the following ten sales reports:

Monthly Report of Sales by Products. Total dollar sales broken down between sales of nineteen products, percentages of total shown for each product; also cumulative dollar sales and percentage of total for each product for the year to date; percentage breakdown of total sales among products shown for the previous year for purposes of comparison.

Monthly Report of Sales by Products in Physical Units. Same information presented as above, but in physical units rather than in value terms.

Monthly Sales to House Accounts. Dollar sales to wholesalers, chain stores, mail-order houses, government (direct), service accounts (Army and Navy), and other accounts handled directly from the home office; percentage of total sales made to each type of account; cumulative sales to date for the year, both in dollar figures and in percentages for each type of account.

Daily Record of Sales, Production, and Inventories in Physical Units by Products.

Monthly Reports on Sales and Commissions of Each Salesman. Net sales during past month, sales year to date; commissions earned, commissions year to date; extra commission (for introduction and sale of new products); extra commission as a percentage of the salesman's total sales.

Monthly Comparison between Actual Sales and Projected Sales by Products in Physical Units. Sales data, and percentages over or under

[2] See Chapter 19, pp. 530-34.

projected sales (projections are made monthly and are used largely for production and inventory control).

Monthly Dollar Sales by Zones. Actual sales, other than to house accounts, broken down on a percentage basis between ninety-eight zones and by products in each zone.

Quarterly Report on Sales to Key Accounts in Total and by Products. (Like many concerns, this company makes a large proportion of its total sales to a relatively small number of key accounts; therefore, if difficulties are being encountered in any particular zone or in any particular product, an analysis of sales to key accounts may isolate the difficulty and suggest the solution.)

Occasional Study of Sales by Sizes of Account. (A frequency distribution is made of accounts by sales in dollars for a given period. Then computations are made to determine what proportions of total sales are made to various proportions of total accounts.)

Occasional Reports on the Proportions of Total Sales Made to Different Types of Buyers. (Management wishes to be informed of the increasing or decreasing importance of different types of retail stores and house accounts as outlets for the company's products.) [3]

At one time, this number of sales reports would have been prohibitively costly to prepare. Each would have required going through all the invoices, manually sorting and recording the information, and using desk calculators to arrive at the total. In addition to the high clerical costs, the reports would have taken a long time to prepare, reducing their value as a basis for quick action. Thus, there were good reasons for marketing executives' seeming neglect in the past to make sufficient use of current sales information. All this, however, is changed by the development of electronic data processing.[4]

SUPPLEMENTARY INFORMATION TO AID IN SALES ANALYSIS

The main function of the various sales reports is to alert the marketing executive to questions he should raise about current marketing effort. The sales information is rarely sufficient to provide the answers to the questions. For this, he must check actual company sales movements against other types of information, particularly sales standards, competitors' sales, and marketing costs.

SALES STANDARDS. Actual sales are not very meaningful unless they are examined in relation to expected sales. A sales increase of 20 per cent is not very impressive if sales should have increased by 40 per cent. A salesman accounting for 5 per cent of total company sales is not very effective if his territory should have yielded 10 per cent of total company sales. Actual sales become useful only when they are examined in conjunction with standards developed in the planning phase of the marketing operation.

This is illustrated in the following example:

A sales manager examined his company's sales by region and noted that Pacific Coast sales were about 2 per cent below the quota. To probe this

[3] D. Maynard Phelps and J. Howard Westing, *Marketing Management*, rev. ed. (Homewood, Ill.: Richard D. Irwin, Inc., 1960), pp. 821-22.

[4] See Chapter 10, p. 242.

further, the sales manager examined district sales figures. He discovered that the Portland sales district within the Pacific Coast region was responsible for most of the underachievement. He then examined the individual sales of the four salesmen in the Portland district. This examination revealed that the top salesman, Smith, had filled only 69 per cent of his quota for the period. The sales manager was not through yet. He found that Smith was underachieving mainly with his large accounts rather than his small ones. Just to check a final hunch, the sales manager compared Smith's sales by product and found that he was meeting or doing better on all his product quotas except portable phonographs. A further check revealed that most of the company's salesmen in the Pacific Coast region were having trouble selling portable phonographs, although the national sales of portable phonographs were satisfactory. This pointed to the real problem, one that was concealed in the aggregate sales figures. Apparently a competitor had been using the Pacific Coast region and particularly Smith's district to promote its existing phonograph with better pricing, advertising, and trade terms.[5]

This case illustrates a number of principles:

Sales information is aggregated initially in order to give the marketing executive a broad view of sales developments. However, if this information is left in a highly aggregated form, many of the sales undercurrents go undetected.

Broad breakdowns of the sales information provide the initial clues to areas of sales weakness. This comes about by comparing actual sales to sales standards. But the true character of the weaknesses may not be revealed in broad breakdowns. If the sales manager takes them at their face value, he may take the wrong corrective actions.

The true character of the weakness may require sleuthing through successively finer breakdowns of the sales information. (If the sleuthing had stopped with the breakdown by salesmen, the mistaken conclusion might have been drawn that Smith was loafing.)

The underachievement of a sales standard may sometimes be due to faulty standards rather than faulty performance. The sales manager occasionally has to review the reasonableness of the standard before judging the performance.

COMPETITORS' SALES. Many managements look for the true measure of their success not in absolute sales performance but in their sales performance relative to competitors. The key statistic in this connection is their *market share*.

There are at least two reasons for management's interest in market share measurement for appraising performance.[6] In the first place, it suggests whether changes in company sales were due to uncontrollable outside forces or weaknesses in the company's marketing program. If a company's sales fall but its market share remains constant, this implies that the whole industry was affected by similar environmental forces. In the second place, the market share standard implies a comparison of the company's performance with the average performance of the other companies in the

[5] Adapted from E. Jerome McCarthy, *Basic Marketing, A Managerial Approach,* rev. ed. (Homewood, Ill.: Richard D. Irwin, 1964), pp. 133-36.

[6] See Alfred R. Oxenfeldt, "How to Use Market-Share Measurement," *Harvard Business Review,* January-February 1959, pp. 59-68.

industry rather than with the performance of the best companies. If management could not maintain its share of the market, the implication is that the company's marketing mix or its execution is seriously at fault.

Market share measurement is a useful tool because these two assumptions have some validity. But several qualifications should be kept in mind to avoid drawing the wrong conclusions from market share measurements:

The assumption that outside forces affect all companies in the same way is often not true. The Surgeon General's report on the harmful consequences of cigarette smoking caused total cigarette sales to falter but not equally for all companies. The companies that had established a reputation for a better filter were hit less hard.

The assumption that a company's performance should be judged against the average performance of all companies also is not always valid. A company with greater than average opportunities should register a growing market share. If its market share remains constant, this may imply deficient rather than average management.

If a new firm enters the industry, then every existing firm's market share may fall (again, not necessarily equally). Here is a case where a fall in the company's market share does not mean that the company is performing below the average of the industry.

Sometimes the decline in a company's market share is the result of a deliberate policy to improve profits. Management, for example, may drop unprofitable customers or products, with resulting decline in market share.

Market shares fluctuate for many reasons. For example, the market share in a particular period can be affected by whether a large sale is made on the last day of the period or at the beginning of the following period. A current shift in market share does not always have a significant marketing implication.

Market share analysis, like sales analysis, increases in value when the data are disaggregated along various dimensions. If the data are available, the company might watch the progress of its market share by product line, customer type, region, or other breakdowns.

International Harvester's truck sales in the Los Angeles metropolitan area registered an absolute increase between 1952 and 1953. An analysis of their market share, however, showed a steady decline. Apparently total truck sales in Los Angeles were growing faster than Harvester's sales. This led the company to consider whether it was handicapped by too few sales branches in the Los Angeles area relative to its competitors.[7]

A company would also want to note the market share trends of individual competitors. It will want to know which companies are gaining and losing customers and from what other companies these gains and losses are coming. It will want especially to note the trend in the market share of its closest rival. If the rival's share is growing relatively faster, then the company will want to re-examine its basic marketing strategy.

[7] See Ralph Westfall and Harper W. Boyd, Jr., *Cases in Marketing Management* (Homewood, Ill.: Richard D. Irwin, Inc., 1961), pp. 214-21.

The effectiveness of a marketing program cannot be evaluated solely in terms of the sales it generates. Many times, however, this is precisely what is done. Top management keeps watching the volume of sales and rewards marketing executives accordingly. Marketing executives take this cue and concentrate on building up sales volume. They press hard for additional budgets to build up sales volume. They resist suggestions to drop weaker products or customers. As long as marketing is viewed as the sales-building center, marketing executives may be tempted to relegate cost control to a secondary level of importance.

THE NEED FOR MORE COST CONTROL

However, weak cost control by marketing executives runs counter to their own best interests in the long run. In the first place, properly detailed cost information may reveal opportunities for shifting the fixed marketing funds to better sales-generating uses. Cost information can aid in the detection of weak products, customers, and territories and thereby stimulate earlier corrective action.

In the second place, accurate cost information is necessary in order to make correct decisions on prices. If the marketing executive thinks that costs are higher than they really are, he may overprice certain products to the possible detriment of sales.

In the third place, other officers of the company resist placing too much money in the hands of marketing executives who do not show a proper respect for costs. It is bad enough that some officers view advertising and some other marketing expenses as wasteful. The best antidote to organizational hostility is for the marketing executive to show a keen concern for cost. This should not be just for "show." The marketing executive should be active in outlining cost-cutting proposals and in preparing profit rationales to back requests for new appropriations.

All told, the marketing executive is more effective to the extent that he joins cost analysis to sales analysis in the planning and control of the marketing effort.

NATURE OF MARKETING COSTS

A company incurs all kinds of costs in the conduct of its business. Typical examples are material costs, factory wages, rent, freight, advertising, and general management salaries. These costs reflect different types of exertions by the company. Some of the costs are incurred to obtain the productive inputs and produce the products—these may be called *production costs*. Some of the costs are incurred to stimulate orders for the products—these may be called *promotional costs*. Still other costs are incurred to maintain and move the products—these may be called *physical distribution costs*. The promotional and physical distribution costs together constitute *marketing costs*.

This way of looking at costs still leaves some ambiguities. For example, is packaging a production cost, a promotional cost, or a physical distribution cost? Is airfreight a solely physical distribution cost or partly promotional? What about the salaries of top management, especially if most of their time is spent in stimulating sales?

The main reason for trying to tag different costs is to determine whose responsibility they are. Marketing costs should be the responsibility of marketing management.

For a number of reasons, marketing costs are more difficult to measure and control than production costs.

> *There are more bases over which to allocate marketing costs.* Production costs are assigned to products and processes; marketing costs can be allocated to such bases or marketing entities as products, customers, territories, size of orders, channels of distribution, and salesmen.
>
> *The allocation of marketing costs is more arbitrary.* Production costs like material and labor can be assigned to tangible products. But the basic product of marketing effort is the sales order. It is harder to identify the specific costs that create different orders.
>
> *The consequences of decisions to alter marketing costs are more difficult to estimate.* The effect of adding another machine in the factory is easier to estimate than the effect of increasing advertising expenditures. The effect on physical output of dropping a worker is easier to estimate than the effect on sales of dropping a salesman.

For these reasons, production cost accounting, with its emphasis on the setting of standards and the measurement of variances, cannot be applied without modification in appraising the cost of marketing activities. In fact, distribution cost accounting is not addressed to the development of standards so much as the costing of different marketing activities.[8] The main legacy from production cost accounting consists of a body of useful cost concepts.

THE METHODOLOGY OF DISTRIBUTION COST ANALYSIS

Distribution cost analysis is a tool for aiding the marketing executive to determine whether any current marketing activities should be eliminated, added, or altered in scale. Distribution cost analysis pinpoints the costs of conducting the activity. When these costs are considered along with the value of the activity, the marketing executive can make better decisions on marketing activity levels.

The starting point for distribution cost analysis is the company's profit and loss statement. A simplified profit and loss statement is shown in Table 22-1. Profits are arrived at by subtracting cost of goods sold and other expenses from sales. The marketing executive's interest would be in developing analogous profit statements by functional marketing breakdowns, such as products, customers, or territories. In order to do this, the "natural" expense designations (such as salaries, rent, supplies) would have to be reclassified into "functional" expense designations. To show how this is done, the following example is used:

The marketing vice-president of a lawn mower firm wishes to determine

---

[8] The basic texts on distribution cost accounting are J. Brooks Heckert and Robert B. Miner, *Distribution Costs*, 2nd ed. (New York: The Ronald Press Company, 1953); and Donald R. Longman and Michael Schiff, *Practical Distribution Cost Analysis* (Homewood, Ill.: Richard D. Irwin, Inc., 1955).

TABLE 22-1

587

Sales and
Cost Analysis

A simplified profit and loss statement

Sales		$60,000
Cost of goods sold		39,000
Gross margin		$21,000
Expenses		
Salaries	$9,300	
Rent	3,000	
Supplies	3,500	
		15,800
Net profit		$ 5,200

the costs and profits of selling through three different types of retail channels, namely, hardware stores, garden supply shops, and department stores.
The company produces only one model of lawn mower. Its profit and loss
statement is the one shown in Table 22-1.

STEP 1: IDENTIFYING THE FUNCTIONAL EXPENSES.   Let us assume that
the expenses listed in Table 22-1 are incurred to carry out the activities of
selling the product, advertising the product, packing and delivering the
product, and billing and collecting. The first task is to show how much of
each natural expense was incurred in each of these activities.

Suppose, for example, that most of the salaries went to salesmen and the
rest went to an advertising manager, packing and delivery help, and an
office accountant. Let the breakdown of the $9,300 be $5,100, $1,200,
$1,400, and $1,600, respectively. Table 22-2 shows allocation of the salary
expense to these four activities.

TABLE 22-2
Mapping natural expenses into functional expenses

Natural accounts		Selling	Advertising	Packing and delivery	Billing and collecting
Salaries	$9,300	$5,100	$1,200	$1,400	$1,600
Rent	3,000	—	400	2,000	600
Supplies	3,500	400	1,500	1,400	200
	$15,800	$5,500	$3,100	$4,800	$2,400

Table 22-2 also shows the rent account of $3,000 as allocated to the
four activities. Since the salesmen work away from the office, none of the
building's rent expense is assigned to the selling activity. Most of the floor
space and rental of equipment arises in connection with packing and
delivery. A small portion of the floor space is taken up by the activities
of the advertising manager and the office accountant.

Finally, the natural account item for supplies lumps together promotional materials, packing materials, fuel purchases for delivery, and home

office stationery. The $3,500 in this account should be reassigned to the functional uses made of the supplies. The result of this and the previous breakdowns is that the total expenses of $15,800 are reclassified from a natural basis into a functional activity basis.

STEP 2: ASSIGNING THE FUNCTIONAL EXPENSES TO THE MARKETING ENTITIES. The problem is now to determine how much of each activity has gone into serving each type of channel. Consider the selling effort, for example. The selling effort devoted to serving each channel is approximated by the number of sales hours or sales calls spent with each channel. Suppose sales-call information is used as shown in the first column of Table 22-3. Altogether 275 sales calls were made during the period. Since the total selling expense amounted to $5,500 (see Table 22-2), then the selling expense per call averaged $20.

TABLE 22-3
Bases for allocating functional expenses to channels

Channel type	Selling No. of sales calls in period	Advertising No. of advertise- ments	Packing and delivery No. of orders placed in period	Billing and collecting No. of orders placed in period
Hardware	200	50	50	50
Garden supply	65	20	21	21
Department stores	10	30	9	9
	275	100	80	80
Functional expense = No. of units	$5,500 / 275	$3,100 / 100	$4,800 / 80	$2,400 / 80
=	$20	$31	$60	$30

As for advertising expense, Table 22-3 shows that this has been allocated on the basis of the number of advertisements that were addressed to the different trade channels. Since there were 100 advertisements altogether, the advertising expense of $3,100 means that the average advertisement cost $31.

The basis chosen for allocating the packing and delivery expense was the number of orders placed by each type of channel; this same basis also was used for allocating the expense of billing and collections.

STEP 3: PREPARING A PROFIT AND LOSS STATEMENT FOR EACH MAR-KETING ENTITY. It is now possible to prepare a separate profit and loss statement for each type of channel. The results are shown in Table 22-4. Since hardware stores accounted for one-half of total sales ($30,000 out of $60,000), this channel is charged with half of the cost of goods sold ($19,500 out of $39,000).[9] This leaves a gross margin from hardware

[9] This assumes that the same mix of goods is sold to the various channels. Otherwise, a finer determination of the cost of goods sold by channel would have to be made.

TABLE 22-4

589
Sales and
Cost Analysis

Profit and loss statements for channels

	Hardware	Garden supply	Dept. stores	Whole company
Sales	$30,000	$10,000	$20,000	$60,000
Cost of goods sold	19,500	6,500	13,000	39,000
Gross margin	$10,500	$ 3,500	$ 7,000	$21,000
Expenses				
Selling ($20 per call)	$ 4,000	$ 1,300	$ 200	$ 5,500
Advertising ($31 per advertisement)	1,550	620	930	3,100
Packing and delivery ($60 per order)	3,000	1,260	540	4,800
Billing ($30 per order)	1,500	630	270	2,400
Total expenses	$10,050	$ 3,810	$ 1,940	$15,800
Net Profit (or loss)	$ 450	$ (310)	$ 5,060	$ 5,200

stores of $10,500. From this must be deducted the proportions of the functional expenses that hardware stores consumed. According to Table 22-3, hardware stores received 200 out of 275 total sales calls. At an imputed value of $20 a call, hardware stores have to be charged with $4,000 of the selling expense. Table 22-3 also shows that hardware stores were the target of 50 advertisements. At $31 an advertisement, the hardware stores are charged with $1,550 of the advertising activity. The same reasoning applies in computing the share of the other functional expenses to charge to hardware stores. The result is that hardware stores gave rise to $10,050 of the total expenses. Subtracting this from the gross margin, the profit from the activities of selling to hardware stores is small ($450).

The same analysis is repeated for the other channels. It turns out that the company is losing money in selling through garden supply shops and makes virtually all of its profits from sales to department stores.

This is an important finding for future policy if management had no inkling of it. If management had sensed this all along, the distribution cost analysis would provide a dollar measure of the profit differences in selling through the different channels.

The same type of cost analysis can be conducted to determine the profitability of marketing entities other than channels, such as product lines, territories, and order sizes. The marketing executive will want some of these cost studies (for example, by product and territory) to be made periodically and others (possibly the cost of handling small orders) to be made only for special decision purposes. One of the big factors in the number and frequency of such reports is their cost. They are more difficult and costly to prepare than the typical sales reports for sales analysis. They require the keeping of detailed information and often special fact gathering. However, with the increased use of high-speed data-processing equipment for accounting purposes, the burden of preparing distribution cost reports on a regular basis has been considerably reduced.

GENERAL CONSIDERATIONS AFFECTING THE USE
OF DISTRIBUTION COST ANALYSIS

As is true of all information tools, distribution cost analysis is capable of leading or misleading the marketing executive, depending upon the degree to which he understands its processes and limitations. He should have two understandings in particular concerning its proper use. The first is that the assignments of costs involve some arbitrariness; therefore, the resulting profitability measures are subject to some margin of error. The second is that the proper corrective action is still a matter of marketing judgment.

THE QUESTION OF ACCURACY. The hypothetical example showed that some arbitrariness occurs in the choice of bases for allocating the functional expenses to the marketing entities being evaluated. Thus the "number of sales calls" was used to allocate selling expenses when in principle "number of sales man-hours" would have been a more accurate indicator of cost. The former base was used because it generally involves less record keeping and computation. (The salesmen only have to list their calls and not the hours spent with each account.) Such approximations may not involve the loss of too much accuracy, but the marketing executive should be cognizant of this judgmental element in determining distribution costs.[10]

Far more serious may be another judgmental element affecting the computation of distribution costs. This is the matter of whether to allocate *full costs* or only *direct and traceable costs*. The example sidestepped this problem by assuming only simple costs which seemed to fit in with marketing activities. But it cannot be avoided in an actual analysis of distribution costs. Three classes of costs have to be distinguished.

Direct costs. These are costs which can be assigned directly to the marketing entities that give rise to them. For example, sales commissions are a direct cost in a cost analysis of sales territories, salesmen, or customers. Advertising expenditures are a direct cost in a cost analysis of products to the extent that each advertisement promotes only one company product. Other costs that are direct for some purposes are salesmen salaries, supplies, and traveling expenses.

Traceable common costs. These are costs which can be assigned only indirectly, but on a plausible basis, to the marketing entities. In the example, rent was analyzed in this way. The company's floor space reflected the need to carry on three different marketing activities, and it was possible to estimate how much floor space supported each activity. In principle, if any of these activities were eliminated, smaller premises would be used or the space would be rented to another user. So, although rent is a common cost of the enterprise and fixed in the short run, it can be traced plausibly to the activities it supports.

Nontraceable common costs. These are costs whose allocation to the respective marketing entities is necessarily arbitrary. Consider "corporate image" expenditures. How can these expenditures be allocated to products? It would be arbitrary to allocate them equally among all products since all products do not benefit equally from corporate image making. It would be arbitrary to allocate them proportionately to the sales of the various products since relative product sales reflect many factors besides corporate image making. Other typical examples of common costs that are difficult

[10] For a list of common bases of allocation, see Charles H. Sevin, *How Manufacturers Reduce Their Distribution Costs,* Economic Series No. 72, U.S. Department of Commerce (Washington, D.C.: Government Printing Office, 1948), p. 31.

to assign are management salaries, taxes, interest, and other types of overhead.

There is no controversy concerning the inclusion of direct costs in the distribution cost analysis; direct costs in fact form the heart of the analysis of profitability. There is a small amount of controversy concerning the inclusion of traceable common costs. Traceable common costs lump together costs which would change with the scale of the marketing activity and costs which probably would not change in the near future. If the lawn mower manufacturer drops garden supply shops, he is likely to continue to pay the same rent, for contractual reasons or through inertia. If this is so, his profits would not rise immediately by the amount of the present loss in selling to garden supply shops ($310). The profit figures are more meaningful in the long run when fixed traceable costs can be liquidated.

The major controversy concerns whether the nontraceable common costs should be allocated to the marketing entities. This is called the *full cost approach,* and its advocates defend it on the grounds that all costs ultimately must be imputed in order to determine true profitability. But this argument tends to confuse the use of accounting for financial reporting with the use of accounting to provide a quantitative basis for decision making and profit planning. Full costing has three major weaknesses:

> The relative profitability of different marketing entities can shift quite radically by substituting one highly arbitrary way to allocate nontraceable common costs for another. This tends to weaken confidence in the tool.
>
> The arbitrariness leads to argument and demoralization, especially by those who feel that their performance or interest is being judged adversely as a result.
>
> The inclusion of nontraceable common costs may weaken efforts at real cost control. Operating management is most effective in controlling direct costs and traceable common costs. Arbitrary assignments of nontraceable common costs may lead them to spend their time fighting the arbitrary allocations or to feel discouraged in their cost responsibility altogether.

THE QUESTION OF CORRECTIVE ACTIONS. Table 22-4 indicated that virtually all the company's profits came from selling through department stores, that selling through hardware stores involved a slight profit, and selling through garden supply shops involved a slight loss. Let us assume that marketing management has confidence in the accuracy of these estimates. The real question from a control point of view is what management should do about it.

The results of a distribution cost analysis do not constitute an adequate informational basis for deciding on corrective action. It would be naïve to conclude that garden supply shops (and possibly hardware stores) should be dropped as channels in order to concentrate on department stores. Information would be needed first on such questions as:

> To what extent do buyers buy on the basis of the type of retail outlet versus the brand? Would they seek out the brand in those channels that are not eliminated?
>
> What are the future market trends with respect to the importance of these three channels?

Have marketing efforts and policies directed at the three channels been optimal?

On the basis of this and other information, marketing management will want to define, develop, and evaluate the major alternatives open to them. The alternatives include:

Establish a special charge for handling smaller orders to encourage larger orders. This move is based on the assumption that small orders are the ultimate cause of the relative unprofitability of dealing with garden supply shops and hardware stores.

Give more aid to garden supply shops and hardware stores. This is based on the assumption that the managers of these stores could increase their sales with more coaching or promotional materials. Here the producer decides to bear larger costs in the short run in order to generate disproportionately greater sales in the long run.

Reduce the number of sales calls and the amount of advertising going to garden supply shops and hardware stores. This is based on the assumption that some of these costs can be saved without reducing proportionately the level of sales to these channels. It seeks to improve profitability through cost reduction rather than sales expansion and is the converse of the preceding alternative.

Do nothing. This is based on the assumption that current marketing efforts are optimal and that either future marketing trends point to an imminent improvement in the profitability of the weaker channels or dropping any type of channel would reduce rather than improve profits because of repercussions on production costs or on demand.

Don't abandon any channel as a whole but only the weakest retail units in each channel. This is based on the assumption that a more detailed cost study would reveal many profitable garden shops and hardware stores whose profits are concealed by the poor performance of other stores in these categories.

To evaluate these alternatives, each would have to be spelled out in greater detail. How much of a special charge would be made for handling small orders? How many additional dollars would be spent to stimulate sales of marginal channels? How weak would a weak retail outlet have to be to be dropped?

In general, distribution cost analysis provides information on the relative profitability of different channels, products, territories, or other marketing entities. It does not imply that the best course of action is to drop the unprofitable marketing entities, nor does it actually measure the likely profit improvement if these marginal marketing entities were dropped. The cost studies represent a very important initial information input, but not the only one, in the evaluation of marketing activities.

Summary

We have examined the use and interpretation of sales and cost information for the control of company marketing effort. The elements of the basic sales transaction—customer, sales representative, products, quantities, dates, terms—become the basis for developing useful sales reports which signal areas of strength and weakness in the current marketing program. These reports, which are increasingly easy to prepare through the use of high-speed computers, must be carefully interpreted against supplementary information such as sales standards and trends in competitors' sales.

Cost analysis can be joined to sales analysis through the concept of distribution cost analysis to determine the actual profitability of different marketing entities, such as the company's channels, products, or territories. The results of a distribution cost analysis, however, contain some amount of error, owing to problems of allocating common costs accurately, and do not alone indicate the desirable corrective action without other types of information and analysis.

Questions and Problems

1. Suppose a company's market share falls for a couple of periods. The marketing vice-president, however, refuses to take any action, calling it a "random walk." What does he mean? Is he justified?

2. Market share analysis requires data on total industry sales and/or competitors' sales. Are these data generally easy to obtain? How can the company collect the needed information?

3. Company XYZ produces five products, and its salesmen represent the full product line on each sales call. In order to determine the profit contribution of each product, salesmen costs (salary, commission, and expenses) have to be allocated among the five products. How should this be done?

4. A large manufacturer of industrial equipment has a salesman assigned to each major industrial city. Regional sales managers supervise the salesmen in several cities. The chief marketing officer wants to evaluate the profit contribution of the different cities. How might each of the following costs be allocated to the cities? (a) billing; (b) district sales manager's expenses; (c) national magazine advertising; (d) marketing research.

5. A company conducts a distribution cost study to determine the minimum size order for breaking even. After finding this size, should the company refuse to accept orders below this size? What issues and alternatives should be considered?

chapter 23

The Marketing Audit

This final chapter will consider the marketing audit as something apart from and more comprehensive than the other control efforts of the firm. Its examination here provides an opportunity for reviewing the major ingredients in effective contemporary marketing as they have been presented in this book.

The first section examines the nature and special characteristics of marketing audits. The second describes the character and components of a system-level marketing audit. The third describes the character and components of an activity-level marketing audit. The final section examines procedural aspects of conducting marketing audits, such as who should conduct them and how often.

The Nature of Marketing Audits

Webster defines an audit as: "a formal or official examination and verification of an account; a methodical examination and review." This is clearly the idea behind the accounting audit, which is probably the most familiar type of audit in business. The accounting audit is an examination of the firm's financial reporting for the purpose of verifying its adequacy and accuracy. The audit is carried on by one group of outsiders (certified public accountants) for the protection mainly of other outsiders (creditors, stockholders, and the public). It might also be added that the accounting audit is carried out according to a regular timetable, is widely recognized as an indispensable adjunct to financial control, and is composed of a highly standardized set of procedures.

Other types of business audits share some but not all of these features. The purpose of an *inventory audit* for example is to verify that the company has on hand the stock it is supposed to have. The audit is warranted because of the possibilities of errors in record keeping and theft or damage to goods in inventory. Companies also undertake *personnel audits,* but here the purpose is not to verify something but rather to establish the quality and sufficiency of the company's personnel. The personnel audit is undertaken to help in planning future manpower.

When it comes to the *marketing audit,* there is really no clear and agreed upon usage. The term is sometimes used to describe the independent investigation by an outside consultant of the problems facing a company in trouble when the trouble is traced to the marketing area. The term is also used to describe the reappraisal of a particular company marketing activity, such as field sales, for the purpose of seeing whether any changes should be made. More recently, the term has been used to describe an audit with the regularity and the technical procedures of the accounting audit but more sweeping in scope. Still other conceptions of the marketing audit can be found, emphasizing one feature or another found in some other type of business audit.

TWO TYPES OF MARKETING AUDITS

Some of the confusion in usage can be clarified by distinguishing between two distinct levels or types of marketing audit, the horizontal and the vertical. Richard D. Crisp drew the following distinction between them:

> The *horizontal* audit examines all of the elements that go into the marketing whole, with particular emphasis upon the relative importance of these elements and the "mix" between them. It is often referred to as a "marketing mix" audit. The *vertical* audit singles out certain functional elements of the marketing operation and subjects them to thorough, searching study and evaluation.[1]

The horizontal audit (which we shall also call a system-level audit) is an attempt to develop a total evaluation of the company's marketing effort. Interest centers not so much on particular marketing activities but rather on their relationships with one another. However, some attempt is made to identify activities that need closer examination. Such activities then become the subject of vertical audits (which we shall also call activity-level audits). The vertical audit is a microscopic counterpart of the horizontal audit, but the two are sufficiently different to justify treating them separately.

THE BASIC NATURE OF MARKETING AUDITS

How does an audit differ from various other company efforts to solve problems or improve operations? Is the audit simply a general term to describe "taking the time out to look at how an operation is being conducted," or is it a specific framework for evaluation? Here the audit will be presented as a specific framework for evaluation.

Very few company activities are ever managed with such skill and wisdom that there is no room for improvement. The better executives are constantly seeking improvements. With them, analysis, planning, and control are not managerial functions to be applied periodically but rather matters of daily effort. The problem that arises, however, is that these executives are so close to their activities that they cannot always recognize whether the activities are being performed in the best way possible. What is lacking is a fresh point of view, an independent evaluation of the quality of the effort. This is important even when there is not the slightest doubt about the individual executive's competence. It is even more important when there are doubts. Thus the primary purpose of an audit is to develop *an independent judgment* of the quality and direction of the effort.

In accounting, the standards against which work is to be judged are quite clear. Because they are clear, the accounting audit strives primarily

---

[1] Richard D. Crisp, "Auditing the Functional Elements of a Marketing Operation," in *Analyzing and Improving Marketing Performance,* Report No. 32 (New York: American Management Association, 1959), pp. 16-17.

to verify that the standards are being met. It represents largely an effort at policing rather than at policy evaluation. The marketing audit has a much broader purpose than the accounting audit. It is not limited to checking whether the executives are complying with the standards, for in marketing, the standards themselves are open to question. The marketing audit in its most advanced form is an evaluation not only of the daily activities but also of the framework within which they take place. In an area as dynamic as marketing, the company's basic marketing premises must be examined periodically in order to be sure of their current appropriateness.

It is useful to think of the marketing audit as covering the company's marketing objectives, program, implementation, and organization. These components apply both to the horizontal and to the vertical audit. Structurally the audit consists of three steps: a determination of how things are being done; an appraisal of what is found; and recommendations as to what should be done. The marketing audit, can be defined as follows:

> A *marketing audit* is an independent examination of the entire marketing effort of a company, or some specific marketing activity, covering objectives, program, implementation, and organization, for the triple purpose of determining what is being done, appraising what is being done, and recommending what should be done in the future.

This conception of marketing auditing is shown in Figure 23-1.

The System-Level Marketing Audit

THE OLD CONCEPTION

Historically, marketing audits were undertaken primarily by companies that had reached a desperate position either because of deteriorating markets or ineffectual marketing policies. For example, the Elgin Watch Company [2] and the Arno Company [3] were ripe for marketing audits, since conditions in each company had reached a point where a fresh appraisal was needed. Usually such audits were performed by outside consultants and were directed toward solving the immediate problem.

Such audits proved helpful in many cases, but they were not as deep or as broad as desirable for at least two reasons.[4] First, such audits are colored by the need to find an immediate solution. There is a tendency to concentrate only on the most grossly inadequate current phases of the marketing program instead of trying to develop basic and comprehensive reforms. In the second place, because companies are usually short of funds during times of crisis, the marketing audit is likely to be conducted with far less money than is required to do a proper job.

THE NEW CONCEPTION

A growing number of marketing scholars and practitioners are advocating a more comprehensive concept of the marketing audit, one that im-

---

[2] See Chapter 1, p. 4.

[3] See Chapter 7, pp. 155-59.

[4] Abe Shuchman, "The Marketing Audit: Its Nature, Purposes, and Problems," in *Analyzing and Improving Marketing Performance,* pp. 16-17. Shuchman's essay is an excellent statement of the new marketing audit concept, and much of this section relies on it.

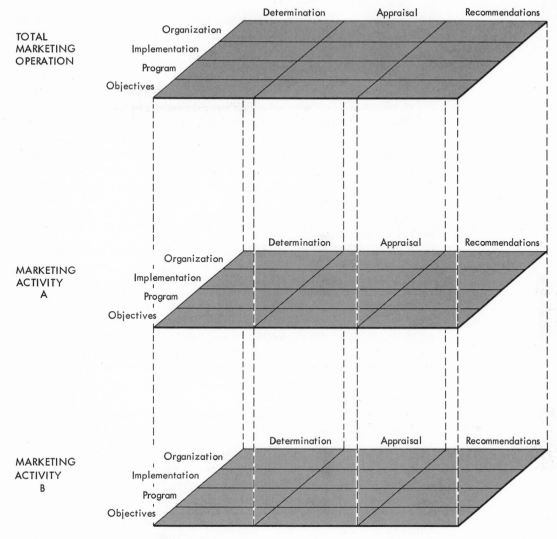

FIGURE 23-1
The concept of marketing audits

poses greater demands upon the firm but promises greater rewards. They
call for an audit of the company's entire marketing operation which is:

 Periodic rather than used only during a crisis
 Concerned with evaluating the basic framework for marketing action as
 well as the performance within the framework
 Interested in appraising all the elements of the marketing operation and not
 just the most problem-ridden ones

PERIODIC.   The use of marketing audits only on the occasion of company difficulties takes too narrow a view of their purpose and potential.

597

The implication is that at other times the company's marketing program is substantially unimprovable. But to this Shuchman says:

> The marketing audit is a tool that can be of tremendous value not only to the less successful, crisis-ridden company but also to the highly successful and profitable industry leader. No marketing operation is ever so good that it cannot be improved. Even the best can be made better. In fact, even the best *must* be better, for few if any marketing operations can remain successful over the years by maintaining the status quo.[5]

The desirability of audits for successful operations as well as troubled ones is based on two valid concerns. The first is the tendency of success to breed complacency and laxity in a company, or what Cyert and March call "organizational slack." [6] The second is the fact that the marketing environment is highly dynamic and changing, underscoring the desirability of periodic reappraisal. Shuchman sees the marketing audit in the successful company as providing "a kind of insurance against subversion by success." [7] Through it, the successful company can maintain a critical view of outside developments and inside operations, so important to its continued success.

Once it is accepted that marketing audits can benefit successful as well as troubled companies, it follows that they should be scheduled fairly regularly. In fact, the marketing audit should be made a regular part of the process of periodically revising the long-range corporate plan. The marketing audit is virtually equivalent to the first two steps of the planning process: diagnosis and prognosis. Through it, the company takes stock of its situation, and this in turn becomes the basis for laying new plans. By tying the marketing audit to the company long-range planning process, it becomes a regularly programmed appraisal.

BASIC. A distinction can be drawn between the use of a marketing audit to evaluate control at the *operational* level and at the *strategic* level. Control is effective at the operational level when the marketing performance comes close to meeting the marketing objectives. Thus in one conception, the marketing audit is viewed as an instrument for analyzing whether the company is achieving its marketing objectives, and if not, what the causes are for the deviation. Another conception of the marketing audit is that it must appraise the objectives themselves; that is, are the objectives appropriate to the company's resources and opportunities? This is an appraisal of the company's marketing at the strategic level. The new conception of the system-level marketing audit calls for a basic appraisal of the company marketing effort at both the strategic and operational levels.

COMPREHENSIVE. System-level audits often collapse into activity-level audits because one or two company activities seem to be at the center of a company's difficulties. Thus in a company like Arno,[8] the low morale and high turnover of the sales force could preoccupy the auditor's attention

---

[5] *Ibid.,* p. 14.
[6] Richard M. Cyert and James G. March, *A Behavioral Theory of the Firm* (Englewood Cliffs, N.J.: Prentice-Hall, Inc., 1963), pp. 36-38.
[7] Shuchman, *op. cit.,* p. 17.
[8] Chapter 7, pp. 155-59.

and the result would be a less than comprehensive appraisal of the total marketing operation. The new concept calls for all the marketing activities to be examined. It also calls for particular attention to the mix of marketing activities. The new type of marketing audit is a reaction to the idea that it is sufficient to improve the separate parts of the marketing program one at a time in order to reach an optimally effective total program. It is a recognition that all the marketing instruments are substitutable and interactive and that their relative emphasis must be reviewed from time to time.

COMPONENTS

A marketing audit should cover the company's marketing objectives, program, implementation, and organization.

OBJECTIVES. The first step in a system-level marketing audit is to get a clear statement of the company's marketing objectives. This is often a harder task than appraising the marketing objectives. Many companies have never bothered to make them explicit or to make them more specific than "to achieve a high sales volume" or "to make a high profit on sales." The auditor is likely to find different executives with different views of the company's marketing objectives. In such situations, one of the main benefits of the audit is its exposure of the lack of clear, specific, and widely held objectives and the confusion this creates in the realm of operating policy.

Following the determination of specific company objectives is the task of appraising how well they tap the firm's opportunities and resources. Objectives can grow obsolete because of the continuous changes occurring in the company's marketing environment. J. C. Penney Co. had to reappraise its policy of selling only soft goods; General Electric had to reappraise its policy of selling only through a costly network of franchised dealers; and U. S. Steel had to reappraise its assumption that there was little room for innovation in steel products. Whether or not these reappraisals were spurred by marketing audits, one of the primary functions of the marketing audit is to provoke management to consider such questions.

In auditing the company's marketing objectives, the auditor especially wants to consider whether they reflect a sufficient degree of market orientation. Statements such as "We want to produce the best screwdriver" or "We want to achieve the highest sales volume" are too reminiscent of the old concept of marketing. The auditor can make an important contribution by impressing management with the desirability, under most circumstances, of reorienting corporate marketing objectives to customers' needs rather than company products, and to creating want satisfactions rather than sales volume per se. The auditor must get company management to start thinking about its product in generic rather than specific terms, so that it will perceive its operations in a broader context of opportunities. He makes a further contribution by leading management to examine more closely the distinct segments of its market and to re-evaluate the relative desirability of undifferentiated versus differentiated versus concentrated marketing. The audit is helpful if it provokes the firm's management to clarify its market targets.

PROGRAM. After determining and appraising the company's current objectives, the auditor should turn to the company's program for achieving these objectives. At this stage the auditor is not interested in how efficiently the program is implemented but rather in the program's structure. The program itself consists of a set of decisions and policies on the level, allocation, and mix of the total marketing effort.

The auditor first wants to examine the *level* of resources the company is channeling into marketing effort and its adequacy in light of the firm's objectives. This is, of course, an extremely difficult question, one that management is perpetually deliberating and debating. The appropriate level of market effort often is a matter of marketing philosophy rather than cold logic. Thus, executives at Alberto-Culver express the following view about the proper level of effort:

> We have found an astounding fact: the more we invest in advertising, the less our advertising-to-sales ratio becomes . . . once we get a brand off the ground, its ability to grow and return profits to the company accelerates at a much greater rate than the increased advertising expenditure.[9]

Yet many other managements would expect diminishing returns to total marketing expenditure to set in much sooner. In general, all the auditor can do is offer management another opinion on the subject, but one backed up by as many facts and as much logic as he can muster.

The auditor also wants to examine how the total budget is *allocated* by management to various target segments of the market. Again it is a very difficult task to appraise whether this allocation maximizes the total possible response of the market, given this budget. The auditor can only point to particular territories, products, or customer segments which in his opinion would benefit from increased, reduced, or terminated effort.

One of the most important contributions an auditor can make is to appraise critically whether there is a proper *mix* or balance among the company's marketing activities. The company's current apportioning of funds often reflects the unusual persuasiveness of a particular functional-area executive or some earlier historical rationale that is no longer well-founded. A mix tends to persist because of the desire for stability, the usual lack of positive proof that the mix is obsolete, the usual executive inertia, and executive preoccupation with daily operating problems. But the dynamic and continuous changes in the economy warrant periodic reappraisals of the mix. One marketer recently argued that the more progressive industrial-goods firms have been modifying their mix to resemble the mix of consumer firms: proportionately more advertising, proportionately less reliance on personal selling, proportionately more use of distributors, and proportionately more research and development.[10] Admittedly it is hard to know when to shift dollars from personal selling to advertising or from price reductions to improved product styling. The auditor, however, has the responsibility of raising these questions and producing his best recommendations in light of the evidence.

[9] John S. Lynch, "Turmoil in Toiletries—the Rise of Alberto-Culver," *Food Business,* November 1962, p. 19.

[10] Fred C. Alexander, "Is Industrial Marketing Ready to 'Go Consumer'?" *Industrial Marketing,* December 1964, pp. 74-77.

IMPLEMENTATION.   After examining the program designed by the firm to achieve its objectives, the auditor must examine the tactical means and procedures employed to carry out the program. A company may have designed the perfect program, and yet achieve disappointing results because of poor program execution.

The implementation of a program requires many lower-level decisions, which may be called *tactics*. That these tactical decisions are by no means inconsequential to the success of a program can be made clear by examining the following partial list of them:

Choice of salesmen compensation scheme
Criteria used in hiring salesmen
Choice of advertising media
Choice of an advertising agency
Choice among different modes of transportation
Decision on number and location of field warehouses
Decision on schedule of trade discounts with volume purchased
Choice of a manufacturers' representative

The auditor wants to examine the more important tactical decisions. He wants to know what alternatives were available, why the particular choice was made, and what the consequences seem to be.

Procedures describe the ways in which actions of various kinds actually take place in the company. They answer the questions of who does what, when, and how. Every company is the locus of countless procedures regulating the flow of men, machines, materials, and information. Some of these procedures are formally established and recognized (standard operating procedures), and others are informal and not officially recognized. Among the procedures affecting the effectiveness of marketing action are those used for:

Developing current sales and cost information
Routing sales opportunity and sales control information through the firm
Handling and expediting customer orders
Determining the current status of inventory
Gathering competitive intelligence
Handling and acting on new-product and sales ideas
Forecasting sales
Preparing marketing plans
Training new salesmen

The auditor wants to examine the more critical procedures to see whether they are the best available. For example, the success of many marketing projects depends upon their being completed on time; yet many companies use scheduling procedures predating such powerful techniques as PERT. Here is an area where the auditor could point out a superior procedure. Or the auditor may recommend that a company develop more comprehensive and frequent sales reports through putting the entire sales analysis on a computer.

ORGANIZATION.   Related to implementation and yet separate from it is the whole matter of organization, encompassing such issues as the formal lines of authority and responsibility, the informal power and status relations, the principal bases for allocating marketing tasks, the adequacy of the personnel as a group, and the adequacy of individuals in key jobs. The auditor wants to consider such questions as the following in appraising the marketing organization:

Has the company centralized the marketing operations under one responsible head and given him authority commensurate with his responsibility?

Does the chief marketing officer have enough voice over adjacent matters such as inventory levels, speed of customer shipments, and new-product development?

Is the marketing organization structured in the most effective way (function-structured, product-structured, regionally structured, customer-structured)?

Is the marketing research operation of sufficient size to meet the information needs of the company, and is it staffed by the most competent personnel?

Are the company's sundry physical distribution activities fairly well integrated?

Are any of the marketing subfunctions in need of an internal reorganization?

Are the marketing subfunctions of marketing research, marketing intelligence, and marketing planning combined in the best organizational way?

Is there enough coordination or liaison among officers responsible for the communications mix; i.e., sales, advertising, and promotion executives?

Is a committee or department organization more appropriate in this company for carrying out new-product planning and marketing planning?

Does the company need a product manager concept; if it has one, do the product managers have enough authority to carry out their responsibilities?

Are the facilities for communication between key marketing officials as good as they could be?

Is the marketing organization too line heavy or too staff heavy?

Are the key executives adequate for their tasks?

On the basis of his appraisal of the marketing organization, the auditor will recommend what he visualizes as desirable changes. He is aware, of course, that such proposals, especially radical ones, are likely to be received quite coolly, because of a general wish to avoid disrupting job relationships and expectations. His function is to bring the best arguments forward, and it is up to management to decide whether it wants to move in that direction.

The Activity-Level Marketing Audit

The description of the system-level marketing audit makes clear that it is a very sizable task, one requiring many months of digging, reflecting, and testing of conclusions. Even then, it is largely macroscopic, an evaluation of relationships in the large. There is no time to go into depth or make a microscopic probe of the internal sufficiency of the various parts or activities of the marketing organization, except perhaps one or two critical areas that require special attention. In general, the system-level marketing audit stops with pointing out which areas need detailed auditing; it does not perform these audits. The company must undertake a separate audit to come up with recommendations for improving the activity in question.

Actually activity-level marketing audits are fairly common, whether or not the company conducts a system-level marketing audit. They may be conducted when something seems wrong with selling effort, advertising, channels, pricing, or physical distribution. The coverage of the activity-level marketing audit is the same as that of the system-level marketing audit (see Figure 23-1). The auditor first determines and appraises management's *objectives* with respect to the particular activity. He asks whether they are carefully chosen in terms of the firm's market targets, opportunities, and resources. Next he considers whether a satisfactory *program* has been designed for achieving the activity's objectives. This involves examining whether the activity's total budget is adequate, whether the budget is effectively allocated, and whether the particular mix of sub-activities is well balanced. Then he examines the department's *implementation* of the program, specifically the choice of tactics and procedures. He may discover that the department has made some poor tactical decisions or lacks effective procedures for handling information or other flows. Finally, he examines departmental *organization,* noting in particular the division of tasks, the distribution of authority and responsibility, the level of intra- and interdepartment coordination, and the caliber of the men who fill the positions. Thus, the framework used to make the system-level audit is also useful for auditing any specific marketing activity.

Implementing a Marketing Audit

A marketing audit is a serious, time-consuming, and expensive undertaking. Whether it pays for itself depends to a large extent upon who conducts it and its timing.

SELECTING THE AUDITORS

The term "auditor" has been used, but it has not been clarified whether he is a single person or several people and whether he is an insider or an outsider. The reason for this is that a variety of auditing arrangements are possible and their relative desirability varies with the situation. At least six conceptually different auditing arrangements can be distinguished.[11]

SELF-AUDIT. Some companies ask the executive who is directly in charge of an activity to appraise its strengths and weaknesses. The sup-

[11] Some of these approaches are briefly discussed by Alfred R. Oxenfeldt, "The Marketing Audit as a Total Evaluation Program," in *Analyzing and Improving Marketing Performance,* Report No. 32 (New York: American Management Association, 1959), pp. 35-36; and by Crisp, in his article already cited from the same report, pp. 42-44.

posed advantages of the approach are twofold. The executive is intimately familiar with the operation; and it is the least expensive method of auditing. However the limitations of this method are so substantial that one hesitates to call this a bona fide method of auditing. It misses the whole point about needing an independent appraisal. The executive self-auditor almost inevitably suppresses any shortcomings in his operation and tries to highlight his accomplishments. It is an approach likely to lead only to minor suggestions. While the executive may benefit from recognizing certain improvements that are possible, the report is not likely to be very informative. As pointed out by Crisp: "What it boils down to is a redirection of executives' attention to the tasks which they are paid to do as well as they can—and which they are presumably doing as well as they can." [12]

"AUDIT-FROM-ACROSS." Sometimes a company assigns persons in a related activity on the same functional level to prepare an audit of the neighboring activity. For example, the sales manager may be asked to prepare a critical report of the advertising operation. Such an auditor brings familiarity to the task, and it is expected that he would point out any difficulties in the performance or cooperation of the neighboring department. But this is another case where genuine objectivity is intrinsically lacking. The auditor may either whitewash the other department's operation because of personal relations or be excessively critical of it for the sake of promoting his own department. In addition there is no evidence that another department is knowledgeable enough about what constitutes a good operation in the other area. This approach also falls short of the standard for a bona fide audit.

"AUDIT-FROM-ABOVE." This approach calls for activities to be audited by superiors. For example, the advertising and other marketing departments might be audited by the vice-president of marketing and his staff. However, it is not easy to distinguish such an audit from the continuous responsibility that a chief officer has for surveillance of all the activities under him. Furthermore, such audits are lacking in an independent point of view, and nothing radically new can be expected to come from them.

COMPANY AUDITING OFFICE. This approach calls for establishing a particular office with the responsibility for conducting all company marketing audits. This office may be located within marketing research, or the planning department or be specially established. Among the advantages are that the company auditor would be familiar with the company's total situation and yet be sufficiently detached so that he could conduct a fairly independent appraisal; it would lead to the benefits that come with specialization in this activity, that of more skilled and professional appraisals. The major disadvantage, at least compared to an outside auditor, is that the auditor's major experience is limited to one company and furthermore that he is not independent enough to be truly critical.

COMPANY TASK-FORCE AUDIT. This approach calls for company marketing operations to be audited by a team of company executives with varied

12 Crisp, *op. cit.,* p. 43.

backgrounds and experience. Presumably such a task force can make a more balanced and critical appraisal, and its views are likely to be respected more. This approach is more likely to stimulate consideration of major marketing policy problems and expose misgivings other department heads have about the department's effectiveness. However, it should be recognized that using a company task force is an expensive approach to auditing. It means using up a lot of their time which might be better spent in improving their own operations. Small companies, in particular, are unlikely to have sufficient executive talent to spare for a task force. Also, the approach, in common with previous ones, lacks the advantages of an outside point of view.

OUTSIDE AUDIT.   This approach calls for the marketing audit to be conducted by an outside individual or agency. Although this typically means a professional consulting organization, it may be done by the company's advertising agency or by individuals who are expert in the area. Crisp points out three advantages which are gained by hiring an outside consultant to conduct the marketing audit:

> The first of these factors is the consultant's *broad experience* in many different kinds of companies and many different industries, which makes it possible for the company to learn and profit from the experience of other companies, thus avoiding the anguish and financial costs of duplicating their mistakes. The second factor is the *objectivity* which is a major part of a qualified consultant's stock in trade, and indeed the very reason for his being. The third factor is *time:* Only someone who is not concerned with time-consuming day-to-day operating details can give major marketing problems the concentrated attention required to execute a marketing audit.[13]

The major disadvantage is that as an outsider, the consultant has a great deal to learn about the inside situation of the company before he can make a responsible appraisal. In other words, he must spend a lot of time in determination before he can appraise or recommend. This defect is remedied, however, where the company enters into a long-term relationship with a consulting organization. The consultants become increasingly familiar with the company's operations over time; yet they remain sufficiently detached to render an independent point of view. They can audit the company's operations on a more or less continuous basis—doing the job on one activity and then moving on to another activity. Their effectiveness can be further enhanced if they work with an inside company task force which provides information, studies the auditor's reports, and carries out the more urgent recommendations.

Thus there are several distinct ways to get an audit conducted. The two major dimensions along which they differ are "probable informativeness" and "cost." The probable informativeness of an audit depends upon such things as the auditor's objectivity, his ability to understand the company's total situation, his breadth of experience, and his skill at analysis. The cost depends upon the executive level of participation and amount of time involved. In general, the more expensive auditing approaches are likely to be more informative. The choice must ultimately rest on what the

13 *Ibid.,* p. 44.

company can afford on the one hand and how seriously good auditing is needed on the other.

SCHEDULING THE AUDIT

It is desirable to conduct marketing audits on a periodic basis rather than only on occasions of company crisis. First, no company's marketing operations are so perfect that they cannot be made better, and second, continuous environmental change warrants a periodic reappraisal of the operations. For these reasons, a system-level marketing audit should be scheduled annually if change is extremely rapid, or once every two or three years if change is less rapid. If the company does formal long-range planning, then the marketing audit should be made an integral part of the planning process.

It is usually helpful to carry out the audit according to a definite timetable and to meet the deadline if at all possible. If the audit drags on too long, the information may become dated by the time the recommendations are ready to be made. Advance appointments should be made with the company personnel from whom information is needed. It is also important that the auditor not appear threatening to company executives from whom he solicits information. They must recognize that the auditor's main role is one of recommending ways to improve the operations rather than one of judging the competence of the executives. The auditor ultimately has to offer some appraisal of personnel, but this should not be considered the main purpose of the audit.

Activity-level audits need not be scheduled on a periodic basis. The periodic system-level audit will reveal the marketing activities that may benefit from more thoroughgoing appraisals. Whenever it appears that an activity is in bad need of surveillance or reform, steps should be taken to schedule its audit as soon as possible. It would be desirable that the audit itself be conducted by someone who is a specialist in the functional area and who has wide experience with many companies.

Summary

Those who are responsible for an activity can be expected to engage in continuous analysis, planning, and control. But they are so close to the activity that they may not recognize the need for changes. The idea of an audit is basically that of calling someone else in to take an independent look at the effectiveness with which an activity is being managed. The auditor is to determine what is being done, appraise what is being done, and recommend what should be done in the future.

We have distinguished between the system-level marketing audit and the activity-level marketing audit. Both levels cover the same ground—objectives, program, implementation, and organization. The auditor seeks to discover whether the objectives are clear, specific, and market-oriented. With respect to the program, the auditor seeks to evaluate company decisions on the level, allocation, and mix of current marketing effort. On implementation, he seeks to appraise some of the key lower-level, or tactical decisions and also the procedures used in the marketing operation to develop and route information and other important flows. Finally, the auditor seeks to evaluate the adequacy of the organizational framework for marketing action and the effectiveness of personnel.

The company can have the audit performed in a variety of ways. The paramount considerations are the auditor's objectivity, familiarity with the company's situation, skill, and breadth of experience; against these must be measured the cost of the auditing methods and how seriously the company needs a good audit. Once the auditor is selected, the audit should be conducted according to a timetable so that the information does not become too dated. Maximum effort should be made to assure the executives that the audit is primarily an attempt to find ways of improving marketing effectiveness and not to evaluate individual competences.

Questions and Problems

1. This chapter suggested that a marketing audit could be thought of as covering the company's marketing objectives, program, implementation, and organization. Can you suggest any alternative frameworks for auditing?

2. You are the founder of a firm which conducts marketing audits. You receive a call from the president of General Motors. He asks you to do a system-level marketing audit of his company, and you accept the assignment. Where would you begin? What areas would you tackle? How large a staff would you use? How long would it take? What would you hope to accomplish?

3. Do you foresee a professional marketing auditing association which licenses practitioners, on the model of professional certified public accountants? Why or why not? Do you think it is a good idea?

4. Suggest areas where marketing auditors might recommend studies or innovations to reduce marketing costs.

5. What are the main problems an outside marketing auditor is likely to encounter on a first-time assignment in a company?

INDEXES

Name Index

Subject Index